SOCIAL ETHICS

Morality and Social Policy

FIFTH EDITION

Thomas A. Mappes

Frostburg State University

Jane S. Zembaty

University of Dayton

The McGraw-Hill Companies, Inc.
New York   St. Louis   San Francisco   Auckland   Bogotá
Caracas   Lisbon   London   Madrid   Mexico City   Milan
Montreal   New Delhi   San Juan   Singapore
Sydney   Tokyo   Toronto

McGraw-Hill

A Division of The McGraw·Hill Companies

SOCIAL ETHICS
Morality and Social Policy

This book is printed on acid-free paper.

4 5 6 7 8 9 0 FGR FGR 9 0

ISBN 0-07-040143-8

This book was set in Times Roman by ComCom, Inc.
The editors were Bill McLane and Larry Goldberg;
the production supervisor was Denise L. Puryear.
The cover was designed by Joan Greenfield.
Quebecor Printing/Fairfield was printer and binder.

Library of Congress Cataloging-in-Publication Data

Mappes, Thomas A.
    Social ethics: morality and social policy / Thomas A. Mappes,
Jane S. Zembaty.—5th ed.
        p.   cm
    Includes bibliographical references.
    ISBN 0-07-040143-8
    1. Social Ethics. 2. United States—Social policy. 3. United
States—Moral conditions. I. Zembaty, Jane S. II. Title.
HM216.M27   1997
170—dc20   96-7924

About the Authors

Thomas A. Mappes, professor of philosophy at Frostburg State University, is the coeditor of *Biomedical Ethics* (McGraw-Hill, 4th ed., 1996). He is the author of several articles, including (with Jane S. Zembaty) "Patient Choices, Family Interests, and Physician Obligations." In 1985, the Frostburg State University Foundation presented him with the Faculty Achievement Award for Teaching.

Jane S. Zembaty, professor of philosophy at the University of Dayton, specializes in classical Greek philosophy and social ethics. She coedited the first three editions of *Biomedical Ethics,* and her published work includes articles on Greek philosophy, such as "Plato's *Republic* and Greek Morality on Lying" and "Aristotle on Lying."

Contents

CHAPTER 10   ANIMALS   **432**

CHAPTER 11   THE ENVIRONMENT   **476**

Preface

Is the death penalty a morally acceptable type of punishment? Is the interest of human beings in eating meat sufficient to justify the way in which we raise and slaughter animals? Do more affluent individuals and countries have a moral obligation to eliminate starvation and malnutrition among the needy? Is society justified in enacting laws that limit individual liberty in sexual matters? What obligations, if any, does society have to undo some of the self-perpetuating inequalities caused by past racial and sexual discrimination?

The way we answer such moral questions and the social policies we adopt in keeping with our answers will directly affect our lives. It is not surprising, therefore, that discussions of these and other contemporary moral issues often involve rhetorical arguments whose intent is to elicit highly emotional, unreflective responses. This book is designed to provide material that will encourage a reflective and critical examination of some contemporary moral problems. To achieve this end, we have developed chapters that bring the central issues into clear focus, while allowing the supporting arguments for widely diverse positions to be presented by those who embrace them.

In this fifth edition, we have introduced one entirely new chapter, "Sexism, Racism, and Oppression." We have also restructured several chapters to include new topics. Articles on hate speech have been added to the chapter on censorship, articles on physician-assisted suicide have been added to the euthanasia chapter, and the chapter on world hunger now includes material on global justice.

We are confident that *teachability* will continue to be the most salient characteristic of *Social Ethics*. All of the editorial features employed in earlier editions to enhance teachability have been retained in the fifth. An introduction to each chapter both sets the ethical issues and scans the various positions together with their supporting argumentation. Every selection is prefaced by a headnote that provides both biographical data on the author and a short statement of some of the key points or arguments to be found in the selection. Every selection is followed by questions whose purpose is to elicit further critical analysis and discussion. Finally, each chapter concludes with a short annotated bibliography designed to guide the reader in further research.

We have tried to provide readings that are free of unnecessary technical jargon and yet introduce serious moral argumentation. Further, in order to emphasize the connection of contemporary moral problems with matters of social policy, we have liberally incorporated relevant legal opinions. We have taken substantial editorial license by deleting almost all the numerous citations that usually attend legal writing in order to render the legal opinions maximally readable to the nonlegal eye. Those interested in further legal research can check the appropriate credit lines for the necessary bibliographical data to locate the cases in their original form. We should also note that, where appropriate, both in legal cases and in other readings, we have renumbered footnotes.

We would be remiss not to express our indebtedness to all those whose work is reprinted in these pages. We are also indebted to Joy Kroeger-Mappes, Frostburg State University, and Marilyn Fischer, University of Dayton, for their helpful critical comments, and to the following reviewers who provided us with very useful reactions and suggestions: Herbert H. Meyer, Merrimack College; Elias Baumgarten, University of Michigan; Nelson Potter, University of Nebraska; Scott Rae, Biola University; Frank Fleckenstein, Frostburg State University; William Wilcox, California Polytechnic State University; Jordan Curnutt, St. Cloud State University; Fred J. Blomgren, Monroe Community College; Joan McGregor, Arizona State University; Bonnie Steinbock, SUNY at Albany; Jim Stone, University of New Orleans; Leonard Geller, Tompkins-Cortland Community College; Howard M. Ducharme, University of Akron; Barbara Tucker, Trident Technical College; Melanie Armstrong, College of St. Mary; Mario Morelli, Western Illinois University; Charles Krecz, University of Texas at Austin; S. Jack Odell, University of Maryland; Thomas F. Wall, Emmanuel College; Williard F. Williamson, William Rainey Harper College; C. Stephen Layman, Seattle Pacific University; William R. Brown, Southwest Missouri State University; Robert S. Trotter, William Jewell College; Ann E. Lange, Bentley College; Donald Blakeley, California State University; David Reiter, Calvin College. Finally, we must express our thanks to Sara Chant for her exemplary work as a research assistant, to Shelley Drees for her help with manuscript preparation, and to Fergus Laughland for his assistance in proofreading, and we continue to be grateful to the reference librarians at both the University of Dayton and Frostburg State University.

Thomas A. Mappes
Jane S. Zembaty

CHAPTER 1

Abortion

The primary concern in this chapter is the ethical (moral) acceptability of abortion. Some attention is also given to the social policy aspects of abortion, especially in conjunction with developments in the United States Supreme Court.

ABORTION: THE ETHICAL ISSUE

Discussions of the ethical acceptability of abortion often take for granted (1) an awareness of the various kinds of reasons that may be given for having an abortion and (2) an acquaintance with the biological development of a human fetus.

1 Reasons for Abortion

Why would a woman have an abortion? The following catalog, not meant to provide an exhaustive survey, is sufficient to indicate that there is a wide range of potential reasons.

(a) In certain extreme cases, if the fetus is allowed to develop normally and come to term, the pregnant woman herself will die.

(b) In other cases it is not the woman's life but her health, physical or mental, that will be severely endangered if the pregnancy is allowed to continue.

(c) There are also cases in which the pregnancy will probably, or surely, produce a severely impaired child.

(d) There are others in which the pregnancy is the result of rape or incest.[1]

(e) There are instances in which the pregnant woman is unmarried, and there will be the social stigma of illegitimacy.

(f) There are other instances in which having a child, or having another child, will be an unbearable financial burden.

---

[1]The expression *therapeutic abortion* suggests abortion for medical reasons. Accordingly, abortions corresponding to reasons (a), (b), and (c) are usually said to be therapeutic. More problematically, abortions corresponding to reason (d) have often been identified as therapeutic. Perhaps it is presumed that pregnancies resulting from rape or incest are traumatic, thus a threat to mental health. Alternatively, perhaps calling such an abortion "therapeutic" is just a way of indicating that it is thought to be justifiable.

1

(g) Certainly common, and perhaps most common of all, are those instances in which having a child will interfere with the happiness of the woman, the joint happiness of the parents, or even the joint happiness of a family unit that already includes children. Regarding this final category, there are almost endless possibilities. The woman may desire a professional career. A couple may be content and happy together and feel their relationship would be damaged by the intrusion of a child. Parents may have older children and not feel up to raising another child, and so forth.

2   The Biological Development of a Human Fetus

During the course of a human pregnancy, in the nine-month period from conception to birth, the product of conception undergoes a continual process of change and development. *Conception* takes place when a male germ cell (the spermatozoon) combines with a female germ cell (the ovum), resulting in a single cell (the single-cell zygote), which embodies the full genetic code, twenty-three pairs of chromosomes. The single-cell zygote soon begins a process of cellular division. The resultant multicell zygote, while continuing to grow and beginning to take shape, proceeds to move through the fallopian tube and then to undergo gradual *implantation* at the uterine wall. The developing entity is formally designated a zygote up until the time that implantation is complete, almost two weeks after conception. Thereafter, until the end of the eighth week, the developing entity is formally designated an embryo. It is in this embryonic period that organ systems and other human characteristics begin to undergo noticeable development; in particular, brain waves can be detected at the end of the sixth week. From the end of the eighth week until birth, the developing entity is formally designated a *fetus*. (The term "fetus," however, is commonly used as a general term to designate the developing entity, whatever its stage of development.) Two other points in the development of the fetus are especially noteworthy as relevant to discussions of abortion, but these points are usually identified by reference to gestational age as calculated not from conception but from the first day of the woman's last menstrual period. Accordingly, somewhere between the twelfth and the sixteenth week there usually occurs *quickening,* the point at which the woman begins to feel the movements of the fetus. And somewhere in the neighborhood of the twenty-fourth week, *viability* becomes a realistic possibility. Viability is the point at which the fetus is capable of surviving outside the womb.

With the facts of fetal development in view, it may be helpful to indicate the various medical techniques of abortion. Early (first trimester) abortions were at one time performed by *dilatation and curettage* (D&C) but are now commonly performed by *uterine aspiration,* also called "suction curettage." (The use of chemical methods for the termination of early pregnancies is discussed later in this introduction.) D&C involves the stretching (dilatation) of the cervix and the scraping (curettage) of the inner walls of the uterus. In uterine aspiration, the fetus is sucked out of the uterus by means of a tube connected to a suction pump. Later abortions require procedures such as *dilatation and evacuation* (D&E), *induction techniques,* or *hysterotomy.* In D&E, which is the abortion procedure commonly used in the early stages of the second trimester, a forceps is used to dismember the fetus within the uterus; the fetal remains are then withdrawn through the cervix. In one commonly employed induction technique, a saline solution injected into the amniotic cavity induces labor, thereby expelling the fetus. Another important induction technique employs prostaglandins (hormonelike substances) to induce labor. Hysterotomy—in essence a miniature cesarean section—is a major surgical procedure and is not commonly employed in the United States.

A brief discussion of fetal development together with a cursory survey of various reasons for abortion has prepared the way for a formulation of the ethical issue of abortion in its broadest terms. *Up to what point of fetal development, if any, and for what reasons, if any, is abortion ethically acceptable?* Some hold that abortion is *never* ethically acceptable, or at most that it is acceptable only when necessary to save the life of the pregnant woman. This view is frequently termed the *conservative* view on abortion. Others hold that abortion is *always* ethically acceptable—at any point of fetal development and for any of the standard reasons. This view is frequently termed the *liberal* view on abortion. Still others are anxious to defend perspectives that are termed *moderate* views, holding that abortion is ethically acceptable up to a certain point of fetal development *and/or* holding that some reasons provide a sufficient justification for abortion whereas others do not.

THE CONSERVATIVE VIEW AND THE LIBERAL VIEW

The *moral status* of the fetus has been a pivotal issue in discussions of the ethical acceptability of abortion. To say that the fetus has *full moral status* is to say that it is entitled to the same degree of moral consideration as more fully developed human beings, such as the writer and the reader of these words. In particular, assigning full moral status to the fetus entails that the fetus has a right to life that must be taken as seriously as the right to life of any other human being. On the other hand, to say that the fetus has *no (significant) moral status* is to say that it has no rights worth talking about. In particular, it does not possess a significant right to life. Conservatives typically claim that the fetus has full moral status, and liberals typically claim that the fetus has no significant moral status. (Some moderates argue that the fetus has a subsidiary or *partial moral status.*) Since the fetus has no significant moral status, the liberal is prone to argue, it has no more right to life than a piece of tissue such as an appendix, and an abortion is no more morally objectionable than an appendectomy. Since the fetus has full moral status, the conservative is prone to argue, its right to life must be respected with the utmost seriousness and an abortion, except perhaps to save the life of a pregnant woman, is as morally objectionable as any other murder.

Discussions of the moral status of the fetus often refer directly to the biological development of the fetus and pose the question: At what point in the continuous development of the fetus does a human life exist? In the context of such discussions, *human* implies full moral status, *nonhuman* implies no (significant) moral status, and any notion of partial moral status is systematically excluded. To distinguish the human from the nonhuman, to "draw the line," and to do so in a nonarbitrary way, is the central matter of concern. The *conservative* on abortion typically holds that the line must be drawn at conception. Usually the conservative argues that conception is the only point at which the line can be nonarbitrarily drawn. Against attempts to draw the line at points such as implantation, quickening, viability, or birth, considerations of continuity in the development of the fetus are pressed. The conservative argues that a line cannot be securely drawn anywhere along the path of fetal development. It is said that the line will inescapably slide back to the point of conception in order to find objective support—by reference to the fact that the full genetic code is present subsequent to conception, whereas it is not present prior to conception.

With regard to drawing the line, the *liberal* typically contends that the fetus remains nonhuman even in its most advanced stages of development. The liberal, of course, does not mean to deny that a fetus is biologically a human fetus. Rather the claim is that the fetus is not human in any morally significant sense, that is, the fetus has no (significant) moral status. This point is often made in terms of the concept of personhood. Mary Anne Warren, who defends the liberal view on abortion in one of this chapter's selections, argues that the fetus is not a person. She also contends that the fetus bears so little resemblance to a person that it cannot be said to have a significant right to life. Indeed, as Warren analyzes the concept of personhood, even a newborn baby is not a person. This conclusion, as might be expected, prompts Warren to a consideration of the moral justifiability of infanticide, an issue closely related to the problem of abortion.

Although the conservative view on abortion is most commonly predicated on the straightforward contention that the fetus is a person from conception, there are at least two other lines of argument that have been advanced in its defense. One conservative, advancing what might be labeled "the presumption argument," writes:

> In being willing to kill the embryo, we accept responsibility for killing what we must admit *may* be a person. There is some reason to believe it is—namely the *fact* that it is a living, human individual and the inconclusiveness of arguments that try to exclude it from the protected circle of personhood.
>
> *To be willing to kill what for all we know could be a person is to be willing to kill it if it is a person.* And since we cannot absolutely settle if it is a person except by a metaphysical postulate, for all practical purposes we must hold that to be willing to kill the embryo is to be willing to kill a person.[2]

In accordance with this line of argument, although it may not be possible to show conclusively that the fetus is a person from conception, we must presume that it is. Another line of argument that has been advanced by some conservatives emphasizes the potential rather than the actual personhood of the fetus. Even if the fetus is not a person, it is said, there can be no doubt that it is a potential person. Accordingly, by virtue of its potential personhood, the fetus must be accorded a right to life. Warren, in response to this line of argument, argues that the potential personhood of the fetus provides no basis for the claim that it has a significant right to life.

---

[2]Germain Grisez, *Abortion: The Myths, the Realities, and the Arguments* (New York: Corpus Books, 1970), p. 306.

In one of the readings in this chapter, Don Marquis argues for a very conserva-tive view on abortion, although he does not argue for what is commonly referred to as "the" conservative view on abortion. Whereas the standard conservative is com-mitted to a "sanctity-of-life" viewpoint, according to which the lives of all biologi-cally human beings (assuming their moral innocence) are considered immune from attack, Marquis bases his opposition to abortion on a distinctive theory about the wrongness of killing. Although Marquis claims that there is a strong moral pre-sumption against abortion, and although he clearly believes that the vast majority of abortions are seriously immoral, he is not committed to the standard conservative contention that the only possible exception is the case in which abortion is neces-sary to save the life of the pregnant woman.

MODERATE VIEWS

The conservative and liberal views, as explicated, constitute two extreme poles on the spectrum of ethical views on abortion. Each of the extreme views is marked by a formal simplicity. The conservative proclaims abortion to be immoral, irrespec-tive of the stage of fetal development and irrespective of alleged justifying reasons. The one exception, admitted by some conservatives, is the case in which abortion is necessary to save the life of the pregnant woman. The liberal proclaims abortion to be morally acceptable, irrespective of the stage of fetal development.[3] Moreover, there is no need to draw distinctions between those reasons that are sufficient to justify abortion and those that are not. No justification is needed. The moderate, in vivid contrast to both the conservative and the liberal, is unwilling either to condemn or condone abortion in sweeping terms. Some abortions are morally justifiable; some are morally objectionable. In some moderate views, the stage of fetal development is a relevant factor in assessing the moral acceptability of abortion. In other moder-ate views, the alleged justifying reason is a relevant factor in assessing the moral ac-ceptability of abortion. In still other moderate views, both the stage of fetal devel-opment and the alleged justifying reason are relevant factors in assessing the moral acceptability of abortion.

Moderate views have been developed in accordance with the following clearly identifiable strategies.

1 Moderation of the Conservative View

One strategy for generating a moderate view presumes the typical conservative con-tention that the fetus is a person (i.e., has full moral status) from conception. What

---

[3]In considering the liberal contention that abortions are morally acceptable irrespective of the stage of fetal development, we should take note of an ambiguity in the concept of abortion. Does *abortion* refer merely to the termination of a pregnancy in the sense of detaching the fetus from the pregnant woman, or does *abortion* entail the death of the fetus as well? Whereas the abortion of a *previable* fetus entails its death, the "abortion" of a *viable* fetus, by means of hysterotomy (a miniature cesarean sec-tion), does not entail the death of the fetus and would seem to be tantamount to the birth of a baby. With regard to the "abortion" of a *viable* fetus, liberals can defend the woman's right to detach the fetus from her body without contending that the woman has the right to insist on the death of the child.

is denied, however, is that we must conclude to the moral impermissibility of abortion in *all* or nearly all cases. In one of this chapter's readings, Jane English attempts to moderate the conservative view in just this way. She argues that certain abortion cases may be assimilated to cases of self-defense. Thus, for English, even if it is presumed that the fetus is a person from conception, abortion is morally justified in a significant range of cases.

2 Moderation of the Liberal View

A second strategy for generating a moderate view presumes the liberal contention that the fetus has no (significant) moral status, even in the latest stages of pregnancy. What is denied, however, is that we must conclude to the moral permissibility of abortion in *all* cases. It might be said, in accordance with this line of thought, that abortion, even though it does not violate the rights of the fetus (which is presumed to have no rights), remains ethically problematic to the extent that negative social consequences flow from its practice. Such an argument seems especially forceful in the later stages of pregnancy, when the fetus increasingly resembles a newborn infant. It is argued that very late abortions have a brutalizing effect on those involved and, in various ways, lead to the breakdown of attitudes associated with respect for human life. English, in an effort to moderate the liberal view, advances an argument of this general type. Even if the fetus is not a person, she holds, it is gradually becoming increasingly personlike. Appealing to the need for "coherence of attitudes," she argues that abortion demands more weighty justifying reasons in the later stages of pregnancy than it does in the earlier stages.

3 Moderation in "Drawing the Line"

A third strategy for generating a moderate view, in fact a whole range of moderate views, is associated with "drawing-the-line" discussions. Whereas the conservative typically draws the line between human (full moral status) and nonhuman (negligible moral status) at conception and the liberal typically draws that same line at birth (or sometime thereafter), a moderate view may be generated by drawing the line somewhere between these two extremes. For example, one might draw the line at implantation, at the point where brain activity begins, at quickening, at viability, and so forth.[4] Whereas drawing the line at implantation would tend to generate a rather "conservative" moderate view, drawing the line at viability would tend to generate a rather "liberal" moderate view. Wherever the line is drawn, it is the burden of any such moderate view to show that the point specified is a nonarbitrary one. Once such a point has been specified, it might be argued that abortion is ethically acceptable

---

[4]L. W. Sumner argues that the line should be drawn at the point at which the fetus becomes sentient, that is, capable of feeling pleasure and pain. "It is likely that a fetus is unable to feel pleasure or pain at the beginning of the second trimester and likely that it is able to do so at the end of that trimester. If this is so, then the threshold of sentience, and thus also the threshold of moral standing, occurs sometime during the second trimester." L. W. Sumner, "Abortion," in Donald VanDeVeer and Tom Regan, eds., *Health Care Ethics: An Introduction* (Philadelphia: Temple University Press, 1987), p. 179.

before that point and ethically unacceptable after that point. Of course, further stipulations may be added in accordance with strategies (1) and (2) above.

4   Moderation in the Assignment of Moral Status

A fourth strategy for generating a moderate view is dependent upon assigning the fetus some sort of *partial moral status*. Although this approach is not reflected in the readings in this chapter,[5] it seems to have some measure of intuitive plausibility. It would seem, however, that anyone who defends a moderate view based on the concept of partial moral status must first of all face the problem of explicating the nature of such partial moral status. Second, and closely related, there is a problem of showing how the interests of those with partial moral status are to be weighed against the interests of those with full moral status.

FEMINISM AND ABORTION

The views of Warren, English, and Marquis represent different positions (liberal, moderate, conservative) on the morality of abortion, as that issue has typically been constructed in the philosophical mainstream. In another of this chapter's selections, Susan Sherwin reacts against mainstream analyses in general and presents a distinctively *feminist* approach to abortion. Since feminist perspectives will also be introduced in several other chapters of this book, there is good reason at this point to introduce the concepts of feminism in general and feminist ethics in particular.

Although feminism is a school of thought (and a political movement) whose complexities defy any easy explication, it is probably fair to say that the following set of beliefs are common among feminists: (1) traditional society is patriarchal, that is, male-dominated; (2) the institutions of contemporary society continue to advantage men at the expense of women; and (3) traditional values and thought patterns typically express a male point of view, often submerging or distorting the experience of women. A feminist also typically believes that this state of affairs is fundamentally unfair, that women must be liberated from it, and that society must be extensively restructured (reformed, revolutionized), although there is a wide range of opinion within feminism about what exactly needs to be done.

When ethical analysis proceeds from a feminist point of view, there is a commitment to take seriously the moral experience of women and a consistent effort to eliminate any traces of male bias in ethical thinking. Among other things, taking seriously the moral experience of women involves insistence on the importance of *relationships* and the responsibilities to which relationships give rise. In accordance with the moral experience of women, feminists tend to view human beings as fundamentally connected and interdependent rather than radically independent individuals, as more traditional (male) paradigms might suggest. Feminist ethics is also deeply committed to the overriding moral importance of ending oppression in gen-

---

[5]Daniel Callahan embraces this approach in *Abortion: Law, Choice and Morality* (New York: Macmillan, 1970), chap. 14, pp. 493–501.

eral and the oppression of women in particular. (The concept of oppression is thoroughly examined in Chapter 6.) In feminist ethics, when a particular institution or social practice is being morally evaluated, it is always important to determine if that institution or practice has any systematic connection with the oppression of women.

Sherwin's discussion of abortion clearly reflects some of the characteristic concerns and emphases of feminist ethics. She constructs personhood as a social concept: "personhood is a relational concept that must be defined in terms of interactions and relationships with others." Her account of fetal value is responsive to the fundamental fact that a fetus exists only by virtue of its relationship to a pregnant woman, and she insists that abortion decisions must be viewed within the overall context of women's lives. As might be expected, Sherwin ultimately argues that pregnant women must be free to make abortion decisions. Indeed, in her view, political opposition to abortion is a reflection of patriarchy and is systematically connected with other forms of patriarchal oppression.

ABORTION AND SOCIAL POLICY

In the United States, the Supreme Court's decision in *Roe v. Wade* (1973) has been the focal point of the social policy debate over abortion. This case had the effect, for all practical purposes, of legalizing "abortion on request." The Court held that it was unconstitutional for a state to have laws prohibiting the abortion of a previable fetus. According to the *Roe* Court, a woman has a constitutionally guaranteed right to terminate a pregnancy (prior to viability), although a state, for reasons related to maternal health, may restrict the manner and circumstances in which abortions are performed subsequent to the end of the first trimester. The reasoning underlying the Court's holding in *Roe* can be found in the majority opinion reprinted in this chapter.

Since the action of the Court in *Roe* had the practical effect of establishing a woman's legal right to choose whether or not to abort, it was enthusiastically received by "right-to-choose" forces. On the other hand, "right-to-life" forces, committed to the conservative view on the morality of abortion, vehemently denounced the Court for "legalizing murder." In response to *Roe,* right-to-life forces adopted a number of political strategies, several of which are discussed here.

Right-to-life forces originally worked for the enactment of a constitutional amendment directly overruling *Roe.* The proposed "human life amendment"—declaring the personhood of the fetus—was calculated to achieve the legal prohibition of abortion, allowing an exception only for abortions necessary to save the life of a pregnant woman. Right-to-life support also emerged for the idea of a constitutional amendment allowing Congress and/or each state to decide whether to restrict abortion. (If this sort of amendment were enacted, it would undoubtedly have the effect of prohibiting abortion or at least severely restricting it in a number of states.) Right-to-choose forces reacted in strong opposition to these proposed constitutional amendments. In their view, any effort to achieve the legal prohibition of abortion represents an illicit attempt by one group (conservatives on abortion) to impose their moral views on those who have different views.

In 1980 right-to-life forces were notably successful in working toward a more limited political aim, the cutoff of Medicaid funding for abortion. Medicaid is a social program designed to provide public funds to pay for the medical care of impoverished people. At issue in *Harris v. McRae,* decided by the Supreme Court in 1980, was the constitutionality of the so-called Hyde amendment, legislation that had passed Congress with vigorous right-to-life support. The Hyde amendment, in the version considered by the Court, restricted federal Medicaid funding to (1) cases in which the pregnant woman's life is endangered and (2) cases of rape and incest. The Court, in a five-to-four decision, upheld the constitutionality of the Hyde amendment. According to the Court, a woman's right to an abortion does not entail *the right to have society fund the abortion.* However, if there is no constitutional obstacle to the cutoff of Medicaid funding for abortion, it must still be asked whether society's refusal to fund the abortions of poor women is an ethically sound social policy. Considerations of social justice are often pressed by those who argue that it is not.

With the decision of the Supreme Court in *Webster v. Reproductive Health Services* (1989), right-to-life forces celebrated a dramatic victory. Two crucial provisions of a Missouri statute were upheld. One provision bans the use of *public* facilities and *public* employees in the performance of abortions. Another requires physicians to perform tests to determine the viability of any fetus believed to be 20 weeks or older. From the perspective of right-to-life forces, the Court's holding in *Webster* represented the first benefits of a long-term strategy to undermine *Roe v. Wade* by controlling (through the political process) the appointment of new Supreme Court justices. More important than the actual holding of the case was the fact that the Court had apparently indicated its willingness to abandon *Roe.* In *Planned Parenthood of Southeastern Pennsylvania v. Casey, Governor of Pennsylvania* (1992), however, the Court once again reflected ongoing changes in its membership and reaffirmed the "essential holding" of *Roe.* The controlling opinion in *Casey,* written by Justices Sandra Day O'Connor, Anthony M. Kennedy, and David H. Souter, is reprinted in this chapter.

The recent emergence of RU 486 (mifepristone), a drug developed in France, has further complicated the social policy debate over abortion in the United States. RU 486 can be taken as an "abortion pill" and effectively functions to terminate early pregnancies.[6] Initial research in France indicated that the drug, when used within forty-nine days of a missed menstrual period, is 96 percent effective in inducing menses and thereby terminating pregnancy. Although minor side effects (e.g., heavier than normal bleeding, nausea, and fatigue) have sometimes been observed, there are no apparent long-term negative effects. Worries about safety aside, RU 486 has been warmly endorsed by right-to-choose forces. If the drug becomes legally available in the United States, women would have access to a very private, nonsurgical form of abortion. Of course, right-to-life forces are bitterly opposed to the legal avail-

---

[6]Another drug, methotrexate, is being discussed as the basis of a chemical method for the termination of early pregnancies. Methotrexate is presently used as an anticancer medication because it functions to stop malignant cell division; it also functions to stop fetal cell division.

ability of RU 486. They refer to the drug as a "human pesticide" and denounce its employment as "chemical warfare on the unborn."

Thomas A. Mappes

On the Moral and Legal Status of Abortion

Mary Anne Warren

Mary Anne Warren is associate professor of philosophy at San Francisco State University. Among her published articles are "The Moral Significance of Birth," "Secondary Sexism and Quota Hiring," and "Is Androgyny the Answer to Sexual Stereotyping?" She is also the author of *The Nature of Woman: An Encyclopedia and Guide to the Literature* (1980) and *Gendercide: The Implications of Sex Selection* (1985).

Warren, defending the liberal view on abortion, promptly distinguishes two senses of the term "human": (1) One is *human in the genetic sense* when one is a member of the biological species *Homo sapiens.* (2) One is *human in the moral sense* when one is a full-fledged member of the moral community. Warren attacks the presupposition underlying the standard conservative argument against abortion—that the fetus is human in the moral sense. She contends that the moral community, the set of beings with full and equal moral rights, consists of all and only people (persons). (Thus she takes the concept of personhood to be equivalent to the concept of humanity in the moral sense.) After analyzing the concept of a person, she concludes that a fetus is so unlike a person as to have no significant right to life. Nor, she argues, does the fetus's *potential* for being a person provide us any basis for ascribing to it any significant right to life. It follows, she contends, that a woman's right to obtain an abortion is absolute. Abortion is morally justified at any stage of fetal development. It also follows, she contends, that no legislation against abortion can be justified on the grounds of protecting the rights of the fetus. In a concluding postscript, Warren briefly assesses the moral justifiability of infanticide.

The question which we must answer in order to produce a satisfactory solution to the problem of the moral status of abortion is this: How are we to define the moral community, the set of beings with full and equal moral rights, such that we can decide whether a human fetus is a member of this community or not? What sort of entity, exactly, has the inalienable rights to life, liberty, and the pursuit of happiness? Jefferson attributed these rights to all *men,* and it may or may not be fair to suggest that he intended to attribute them *only* to men. Perhaps he ought to have attributed

Reprinted with the permission of the author and the publisher from *The Monist,* vol. 57, no. 1 (January 1973). "Postscript on Infanticide" reprinted with permission of the author from Richard Wasserstrom, ed., *Today's Moral Problems* (New York: Macmillan, 1975).

them to all human beings. If so, then we arrive, first, at [John] Noonan's problem of defining what makes a being human, and, second, at the equally vital question which Noonan does not consider, namely, What reason is there for identifying the moral community with the set of all human beings, in whatever way we have chosen to define that term?

1 ON THE DEFINITION OF "HUMAN"

One reason why this vital second question is so frequently overlooked in the debate over the moral status of abortion is that the term "human" has two distinct, but not often distinguished, senses. This fact results in a slide of meaning, which serves to conceal the fallaciousness of the traditional argument that since (1) it is wrong to kill innocent human beings, and (2) fetuses are innocent human beings, then (3) it is wrong to kill fetuses. For if "human" is used in the same sense in both (1) and (2) then, whichever of the two senses is meant, one of these premises is question-begging. And if it is used in two different senses then of course the conclusion doesn't follow.

Thus, (1) is a self-evident moral truth,[1] and avoids begging the question about abortion, only if "human being" is used to mean something like "a full-fledged member of the moral community." (It may or may not also be meant to refer exclusively to members of the species *Homo sapiens.*) We may call this the *moral* sense of "human." It is not to be confused with what we will call the *genetic* sense, i.e., the sense in which *any* member of the species is a human being, and no member of any other species could be. If (1) is acceptable only if the moral sense is intended, (2) is non-question-begging only if what is intended is the genetic sense.

In "Deciding Who Is Human," Noonan argues for the classification of fetuses with human beings by pointing to the presence of the full genetic code, and the potential capacity for rational thought.[2] It is clear that what he needs to show, for his version of the traditional argument to be valid, is that fetuses are human in the moral sense, the sense in which it is analytically true that all human beings have full moral rights. But, in the absence of any argument showing that whatever is genetically human is also morally human, and he gives none, nothing more than genetic humanity can be demonstrated by the presence of the human genetic code. And, as we will see, the *potential* capacity for rational thought can at most show that an entity has the potential for *becoming* human in the moral sense.

2 DEFINING THE MORAL COMMUNITY

Can it be established that genetic humanity is sufficient for moral humanity? I think that there are very good reasons for not defining the moral community in this way. I would like to suggest an alternative way of defining the moral community, which I will argue for only to the extent of explaining why it is, or should be, self-evident. The suggestion is simply that the moral community consists of all and only *people,* rather than all and only human beings;[3] and probably the best way of demonstrating its self-evidence is by considering the concept of personhood, to see what sorts of entity are and are not persons, and what the decision that a being is or is not a person implies about its moral rights.

What characteristics entitle an entity to be considered a person? This is obviously not the place to attempt a complete analysis of the concept of personhood, but we do not need such a fully adequate analysis just to determine whether and why a fetus is or isn't a person. All we need is a rough and approximate list of the most basic criteria of personhood, and some idea of which, or how many, of these an entity must satisfy in order to properly be considered a person.

In searching for such criteria, it is useful to look beyond the set of people with whom we are acquainted, and ask how we would decide whether a totally alien being was a person or not. (For we have no right to assume that genetic humanity is necessary for personhood.) Imagine a space traveler who lands on an unknown planet and encounters a race of beings utterly unlike any he has ever seen or heard of. If he wants to be sure of behaving morally toward these beings, he has to somehow decide whether they are people, and hence have full moral rights, or whether they are the sort of thing which he need not feel guilty about treating as, for example, a source of food.

How should he go about making this decision? If he has some anthropological background, he might look for such things as religion, art, and the manufacturing of tools, weapons, or shelters, since these factors have been used to distinguish our human from our prehuman ancestors, in what seems to be closer to the moral than the genetic sense of "human." And no doubt he would be right to consider the presence of such factors as good evidence that the alien beings were people, and morally human. It would, however, be overly anthropocentric of him to take the absence of these things as adequate evidence that they were not, since we can imagine people who have progressed beyond, or evolved without ever developing, these cultural characteristics.

I suggest that the traits which are most central to the concept of personhood, or humanity in the moral sense, are, very roughly, the following:

1 consciousness (of objects and events external and/or internal to the being), and in particular the capacity to feel pain;

2 reasoning (the *developed* capacity to solve new and relatively complex problems);

3 self-motivated activity (activity which is relatively independent of either genetic or direct external control);

4 the capacity to communicate, by whatever means, messages of an indefinite variety of types, that is, not just with an indefinite number of possible contents, but on indefinitely many possible topics;

5 the presence of self-concepts, and self-awareness, either individual or racial, or both.

Admittedly, there are apt to be a great many problems involved in formulating precise definitions of these criteria, let alone in developing universally valid behavioral criteria for deciding when they apply. But I will assume that both we and our explorer know approximately what (1)–(5) mean, and that he is also able to determine whether or not they apply. How, then, should he use his findings to decide whether or not the alien beings are people? We needn't suppose that an entity must have *all* of these attributes to be properly considered a person; (1) and (2) alone may well be sufficient for personhood, and quite probably (1)–(3) are sufficient. Neither do we need to insist that any one of these criteria is *necessary* for personhood, although once again (1) and (2) look like fairly good candidates for necessary conditions, as does (3), if "activity" is construed so as to include the activity of reasoning.

All we need to claim, to demonstrate that a fetus is not a person, is that any being which satisfies *none* of (1)–(5) is certainly not a person. I consider this claim to be so obvious that I think anyone who denied it, and claimed that a being which satisfied none of (1)–(5) was a person all the same, would thereby demonstrate that he had no notion at all of what a person is—perhaps because he had confused the concept of a person with that of genetic humanity. If the opponents of abortion were to deny the appropriateness of these five criteria, I do not know what further arguments would convince them. We would probably have to admit that our conceptual schemes were indeed irreconcilably different, and that our dispute could not be settled objectively.

I do not expect this to happen, however, since I think that the concept of a person is one which is very nearly universal (to people), and that it is common to both proabortionists and antiabortionists, even though neither group has fully realized the relevance of this concept to the resolution of their dispute. Furthermore, I think that on reflection even the antiabortionists ought to agree not only that (1)–(5) are central to the concept of personhood, but also that it is a part of this concept that all and only people have full moral rights. The concept of a person is in part a moral concept; once we have admitted that x is a person we have recognized, even if we have not agreed to respect, x's right to be treated as a member of the moral community. It is true that the claim that x is a human being is more commonly voiced as part of an appeal to treat x decently than is the claim that x is a person, but this is either because "human being" is here used in the sense which implies personhood, or because the genetic and moral senses of "human" have been confused.

Now if (1)–(5) are indeed the primary criteria of personhood, then it is clear that genetic humanity is neither necessary nor sufficient for establishing that an entity is a person. Some human beings are not people, and there may well be people who are not human beings. A man or woman whose consciousness has been permanently obliterated but who remains alive is a human being which is no longer a person; defective human beings, with no appreciable mental capacity, are not and presumably never will be people; and a fetus is a human being which is not yet a person, and which therefore cannot coherently be said to have full moral rights. Citizens of the next century should be prepared to recognize highly advanced, self-aware robots or computers, should such be developed, and intelligent inhabitants of other worlds, should such be found, as people in the fullest sense, and to respect their moral rights. But to ascribe full moral rights to an entity which is not a person is as absurd as to ascribe moral obligations and responsibilities to such an entity.

3   FETAL DEVELOPMENT AND THE RIGHT TO LIFE

Two problems arise in the application of these suggestions for the definition of the moral community to the determination of the precise moral status of a human fetus. Given that the paradigm example of a person is a normal adult human being, then (1) How like this paradigm, in particular how far advanced since conception, does a human being need to be before it begins to have a right to life by virtue, not of being fully a person as of yet, but of being *like* a person? and (2) To what extent, if any, does the fact that a fetus has the *potential* for becoming a person endow it with some of the same rights? Each of these questions requires some comment.

In answering the first question, we need not attempt a detailed consideration of the moral rights of organisms which are not developed enough, aware enough, intelligent enough, etc., to be considered people, but which resemble people in some respects. It does seem reasonable to suggest that the more like a person, in the relevant respects, a being is, the stronger is the case for regarding it as having a right to life, and indeed the stronger its right to life is. Thus we ought to take seriously the suggestion that, insofar as "the human individual develops biologically in a continuous fashion . . . the rights of a human person might develop in the same way."[4] But we must keep in mind that the attributes which are relevant in determining whether or not an entity is enough like a person to be regarded as having some of the same moral rights are no different from those which are relevant to determining whether or not it is fully a person—i.e., are no different from (1)–(5)—and that being genetically human, or having recognizably human facial and other physical features, or detectable brain activity, or the capacity to survive outside the uterus, are simply not among these relevant attributes.

Thus it is clear that even though a seven- or eight-month fetus has features which make it apt to arouse in us almost the same powerful protective instinct as is commonly aroused by a small infant, nevertheless it is not significantly more personlike than is a very small embryo. It is *somewhat* more personlike; it can apparently feel and respond to pain, and it may even have a rudimentary form of consciousness, insofar as its brain is quite active. Nevertheless, it seems safe to say that it is not fully conscious, in the way that an infant of a few months is, and that it cannot reason, or communicate messages of indefinitely many sorts, does not engage in self-motivated activity, and has no self-awareness. Thus, in the *relevant* respects, a fetus, even a fully developed one, is considerably less personlike than is the average mature mammal, indeed the average fish. And I think that a rational person must conclude that if the right to life of a fetus is to be based upon its resemblance to a person, then it cannot be said to have any more right to life than, let us say, a newborn guppy (which also seems to be capable of feeling pain), and that a right of that magnitude could never override a woman's right to obtain an abortion, at any stage of her pregnancy.

There may, of course, be other arguments in favor of placing legal limits upon the stage of pregnancy in which an abortion may be performed. Given the relative safety of the new techniques of artificially inducing labor during the third trimester, the danger to the woman's life or health is no longer such an argument. Neither is the fact that people tend to respond to the thought of abortion in the later stages of pregnancy with emotional repulsion, since mere emotional responses cannot take the place of moral reasoning in determining what ought to be permitted. Nor, finally, is the frequently heard argument that legalizing abortion, especially late in the pregnancy, may erode the level of respect for human life, leading, perhaps, to an increase in unjustified euthanasia and other crimes. For this threat, if it is a threat, can be better met by educating people to the kinds of moral distinctions which we are making here than by limiting access to abortion (which limitation may, in its disregard for the rights of women, be just as damaging to the level of respect for human rights).

Thus, since the fact that even a fully developed fetus is not personlike enough to have any significant right to life on the basis of its personlikeness shows that no legal restrictions upon the stage of pregnancy in which an abortion may be performed can be justified on the grounds that we should protect the rights of the older fetus, and since there is no other apparent justification for such restrictions, we may conclude that they are entirely unjustified. Whether or not it would be *indecent* (whatever that means) for a woman in her seventh month to obtain an abortion just to avoid having to postpone a trip to Europe, it would not, in itself, be *immoral,* and therefore it ought to be permitted.

4   POTENTIAL PERSONHOOD AND THE RIGHT TO LIFE

We have seen that a fetus does not resemble a person in any way which can support the claim that it has even some of the same rights. But what about its *potential,* the fact that if nurtured and allowed to develop naturally it will very probably become a person? Doesn't that alone give it at least some right to life? It is hard to deny that the fact that an entity is a potential person is a strong prima facie reason for not destroying it; but we need not conclude from this that a potential person has a right to life, by virtue of that potential. It may be that our feeling that it is better, other things being equal, not to destroy a potential person is better explained by the fact that potential people are still (felt to be) an invaluable resource, not to be lightly squandered. Surely, if every speck of dust were a potential person, we would be much less apt to conclude that every potential person has a right to become actual.

Still, we do not need to insist that a potential person has no right to life whatever. There may well be something immoral, and not just imprudent, about wantonly destroying potential people, when doing so isn't necessary to protect anyone's rights. But even if a potential person does have some prima facie right to life, such a right could not possibly outweigh the right of a woman to obtain an abortion, since the rights of any actual person invariably outweigh those of any potential person, whenever the two conflict. Since this may not be immediately obvious in the case of a human fetus, let us look at another case.

Suppose that our space explorer falls into the hands of an alien culture, whose scientists decide to create a few hundred thousand or more human beings, by breaking his body into its component cells, and using these to create fully developed human beings, with, of course, his genetic code. We may imagine that each of these newly created men will have all of the original man's abilities, skills, knowledge, and so on, and also have an individual self-concept, in short that each of them will be a bona fide (though hardly unique) person. Imagine that the whole project will take only seconds, and that its chances of success are extremely high, and that our explorer knows all of this, and also knows that these people will be treated fairly. I maintain that in such a situation he would have every right to escape if he could, and thus to deprive all of these potential people of their potential lives; for his right to life outweighs all of theirs together, in spite of the fact that they are all genetically human, all innocent, and all have a very high probability of becoming people very soon, if only he refrains from acting.

Indeed, I think he would have a right to escape even if it were not his life which the alien scientists planned to take, but only a year of his freedom, or, indeed, only a day. Nor would he be obligated to stay if he had gotten captured (thus bringing all these people-potentials into existence) because of his own carelessness, or even if he had done so deliberately, knowing the consequences. Regardless of how he got captured, he is not morally obligated to remain in captivity for *any* period of time for the sake of permitting any number of potential people to come into actuality, so great is the margin by which one actual person's right to liberty outweighs whatever right to life even a hundred thousand potential people have. And it seems reasonable to conclude that the rights of a woman will outweigh by a similar margin whatever right to life a fetus may have by virtue of its potential personhood.

Thus, neither a fetus's resemblance to a person, nor its potential for becoming a person provides any basis whatever for the claim that it has any significant right to life. Consequently, a woman's right to protect her health, happiness, freedom, and even her life,[5] by terminating an unwanted pregnancy, will always override whatever right to life it may be appropriate to ascribe to a fetus, even a fully developed one. And thus, in the absence of any overwhelming social need for every possible child, the laws which restrict the right to obtain an abortion, or limit the period of pregnancy during which an abortion may be performed, are a wholly unjustified violation of a woman's most basic moral and constitutional rights.[6]

POSTSCRIPT ON INFANTICIDE

Since the publication of this article, many people have written to point out that my argument appears to justify not only abortion, but infanticide as well. For a newborn infant is not significantly more personlike than an advanced fetus, and consequently it would seem that if the destruction of the latter is permissible so too must be that of the former. Inasmuch as most people, regardless of how they feel about the morality of abortion, consider infanticide a form of murder, this might appear to represent a serious flaw in my argument.

Now, if I am right in holding that it is only people who have a full-fledged right to life, and who can be murdered, and if the criteria of personhood are as I have described them, then it obviously follows that killing a newborn infant isn't murder. It does *not* follow, however, that infanticide is permissible, for two reasons. In the first place, it would be wrong, at least in this country and in this period of history, and other things being equal, to kill a newborn infant, because even if its parents do not want it and would not suffer from its destruction, there are other people who would like to have it, and would, in all probability, be deprived of a great deal of pleasure by its destruction. Thus, infanticide is wrong for reasons analogous to those which make it wrong to wantonly destroy natural resources, or great works of art.

Secondly, most people, at least in this country, value infants and would much prefer that they be preserved, even if foster parents are not immediately available. Most of us would rather be taxed to support orphanages than allow unwanted infants to be destroyed. So long as there are people who want an infant preserved, and who are willing and able to provide the means of caring for it, under reasonably humane conditions, it is *ceteris paribus*, wrong to destroy it.

But, it might be replied, if this argument shows that infanticide is wrong, at least at this time and in this country, doesn't it also show that abortion is wrong? After all, many people value fetuses, are disturbed by their destruction, and would much prefer that they be preserved, even at some cost to themselves. Furthermore, as a potential source of pleasure to some foster family, a fetus is just as valuable as an infant. There is, however, a crucial difference between the two cases: so long as the fetus is unborn, its preservation, contrary to the wishes of the pregnant woman, violates her rights to freedom, happiness, and self-determination. Her rights override the rights of those who would like the fetus preserved, just as if someone's life or limb is threatened by a wild animal, his right to protect himself by destroying the animal overrides the rights of those who would prefer that the animal not be harmed.

The minute the infant is born, however, its preservation no longer violates any of its mother's rights, even if she wants it destroyed, because she is free to put it up for adoption. Consequently, while the moment of birth does not mark any sharp discontinuity in the degree to which an infant possesses the right to life, it does mark the end of its mother's right to determine its fate. Indeed, if abortion could be performed without killing the fetus, she would never possess the right to have the fetus destroyed, for the same reasons that she has no right to have an infant destroyed.

On the other hand, it follows from my argument that when an unwanted or defective infant is born into a society which cannot afford and/or is not willing to care for it, then its destruction is permissible. This conclusion will, no doubt, strike many people as heartless and immoral; but remember that the very existence of people who feel this way, and who are willing and able to provide care for unwanted infants, is reason enough to conclude that they should be preserved.

NOTES

1 Of course, the principle that it is (always) wrong to kill innocent human beings is in need of many other modifications, e.g., that it may be permissible to do so to save a greater number of other innocent human beings, but we may safely ignore these complications here.

2 John Noonan, "Deciding Who Is Human," *Natural Law Forum,* 13 (1968), 135.

3 From here on, we will use "human" to mean genetically human, since the moral sense seems closely connected to, and perhaps derived from, the assumption that genetic humanity is sufficient for membership in the moral community.

4 Thomas L. Hayes, "A Biological View," *Commonweal,* 85 (March 17, 1967), 677–78;

quoted by Daniel Callahan, in *Abortion: Law, Choice and Morality* (London: Macmillan & Co., 1970).

5 That is, insofar as the death rate, for the woman, is higher for childbirth than for early abortion.

6 My thanks to the following people, who were kind enough to read and criticize an earlier version of this paper: Herbert Gold, Gene Glass, Anne Lauterbach, Judith Thomson, Mary Mothersill, and Timothy Binkley.

QUESTIONS

1 Would you endorse Warren's analysis of the concept of personhood?
2 Does the fetus, even if it is not an *actual* person, have a serious right to life on the grounds that it is a *potential* person?
3 Is a newborn infant a person? In any case, are there any circumstances in which infanticide would be morally permissible?

Abortion and the Concept of a Person

Jane English

Jane English (1947–1978) was a philosopher whose life came to a tragic end, at the age of thirty-one, in a mountain-climbing accident on the Matterhorn. She had taught at the University of North Carolina, Chapel Hill, and had published such articles as "Justice between Generations" and "Sex Equality in Sports." She was also the editor of *Sex Equality* (1977) and the coeditor of *Feminism and Philosophy* (1977).

English begins by arguing that one of the central issues in the abortion debate, whether a fetus is a person, cannot be decisively resolved. However, she contends, whether we presume that the fetus is or is not a person, we must arrive at a moderate stance on the problem of abortion. In an effort to moderate the *conservative* view, English argues that it is unwarranted to conclude, from the presumption that the fetus is a person, that abortion is always morally impermissible. Reasoning on the basis of a self-defense model, she finds abortion morally permissible in many cases. In an effort to moderate the *liberal* view, English argues that it is unwarranted to conclude, from the presumption that the fetus is not a person, that abortion is always morally permissible. Even if the fetus is not a person, she argues, the similarity between a fetus and a baby is sufficient to make abortion problematic in the later stages of pregnancy.

The abortion debate rages on. Yet the two most popular positions seem to be clearly mistaken. Conservatives maintain that a human life begins at conception and that

Reprinted with permission of the publisher from the *Canadian Journal of Philosophy,* vol. 5, no. 2 (October 1975), pp. 233–243.

therefore abortion must be wrong because it is murder. But not all killings of humans are murders. Most notably, self defense may justify even the killing of an innocent person.

Liberals, on the other hand, are just as mistaken in their argument that since a fetus does not become a person until birth, a woman may do whatever she pleases in and to her own body. First, you cannot do as you please with your own body if it affects other people adversely.[1] Second, if a fetus is not a person, that does not imply that you can do to it anything you wish. Animals, for example, are not persons, yet to kill or torture them for no reason at all is wrong.

At the center of the storm has been the issue of just when it is between ovulation and adulthood that a person appears on the scene. Conservatives draw the line at conception, liberals at birth. In this paper I first examine our concept of a person and conclude that no single criterion can capture the concept of a person and no sharp line can be drawn. Next I argue that if a fetus is a person, abortion is still justifiable in many cases; and if a fetus is not a person, killing it is still wrong in many cases. To a large extent, these two solutions are in agreement. I conclude that our concept of a person cannot and need not bear the weight that the abortion controversy has thrust upon it.

I

The several factions in the abortion argument have drawn battle lines around various proposed criteria for determining what is and what is not a person. For example, Mary Anne Warren[2] lists five features (capacities for reasoning, self-awareness, complex communication, etc.) as her criteria for personhood and argues for the permissibility of abortion because a fetus falls outside this concept. Baruch Brody[3] uses brain waves. Michael Tooley[4] picks having-a-concept-of-self as his criterion and concludes that infanticide and abortion are justifiable, while the killing of adult animals is not. On the other side, Paul Ramsey[5] claims a certain gene structure is the defining characteristic. John Noonan[6] prefers conceived-of-humans and presents counterexamples to various other candidate criteria. For instance, he argues against viability as the criterion because the newborn and infirm would then be non-persons, since they cannot live without the aid of others. He rejects any criterion that calls upon the sorts of sentiments a being can evoke in adults on the grounds that this would allow us to exclude other races as non-persons if we could just view them sufficiently unsentimentally.

These approaches are typical: foes of abortion propose sufficient conditions for personhood which fetuses satisfy, while friends of abortion counter with necessary conditions for personhood which fetuses lack. But these both presuppose that the concept of a person can be captured in a strait jacket of necessary and/or sufficient conditions.[7] Rather, "person" is a cluster of features, of which rationality, having a self concept and being conceived of humans are only part.

What is typical of persons? Within our concept of a person we include, first, certain biological factors: descended from humans, having a certain genetic makeup, having a head, hands, arms, eyes, capable of locomotion, breathing, eating, sleeping. There are psychological factors: sentience, perception, having a concept of self and of one's own interests and desires, the ability to use tools, the ability to use language or symbol systems, the ability to joke, to be angry, to doubt. There are rationality factors: the ability to reason and draw conclusions, the ability to generalize and to learn from past experience, the ability to sacrifice present interests for greater gains in the future. There are social factors: the ability to work in groups and respond to peer pressures, the ability to recognize and consider as valuable the interests of others, seeing oneself as one among "other minds," the ability to sympathize, encourage, love, the ability to evoke from others the responses of sympathy, encouragement, love, the ability to work with others for mutual advantage. Then there are legal factors: being subject to the law and protected by it, having the ability to sue and enter contracts, being counted in the census, having a name and citizenship, the ability to own property, inherit, and so forth.

Now the point is not that this list is incomplete, or that you can find counterinstances to each of its points. People typically exhibit rationality, for instance, but someone who was irrational would not thereby fail to qualify as a person. On the other hand, something could exhibit the majority of these features and still fail to be a person, as an advanced robot might. There is no single core of necessary and sufficient features which we can draw upon with the assurance that they constitute what really makes a person; there are only features that are more or less typical.

This is not to say that no necessary or sufficient conditions can be given. Being alive is a necessary condition for being a person, and being a U.S. Senator is sufficient. But rather than falling inside a sufficient condition or outside a necessary one, a fetus lies in the penumbra region where our concept of a person is not so simple. For this reason I think a conclusive answer to the question whether a fetus is a person is unattainable.

Here we might note a family of simple fallacies that proceed by stating a necessary condition for personhood and showing that a fetus has that characteristic. This is a form of the fallacy of affirming the consequent. For example, some have mistakenly reasoned from the premise that a fetus is human (after all, it is a human fetus rather than, say, a canine fetus), to the conclusion that it is *a* human. Adding an equivocation on "being," we get the fallacious argument that since a fetus is something both living and human, it is a human being.

Nonetheless, it does seem clear that a fetus has very few of the above family of characteristics, whereas a newborn baby exhibits a much larger proportion of them—and a two-year-old has even more. Note that one traditional anti-abortion argument has centered on pointing out the many ways in which a fetus resembles a baby. They emphasize its development ("It already has ten fingers. . . .") without mentioning its dissimilarities to adults (it still has gills and a tail). They also try to evoke the sort of sympathy on our part that we only feel toward other persons ("Never to laugh . . . or feel the sunshine?"). This all seems to be a relevant way to argue, since its purpose is to persuade us that a fetus satisfies so many of the important features on the list that it ought to be treated as a person. Also note that a fetus near the time of birth satisfies many more of these factors than a fetus in the early months of development. This could provide reason for making distinctions among the different stages of pregnancy, as the U.S. Supreme Court has done.[8]

Historically, the time at which a person has been said to come into existence has varied widely. Muslims date personhood from fourteen days after conception. Some medievals followed Aristotle in placing ensoulment at forty days after conception for a male fetus and eighty days for a female fetus.[9] In European common law since the Seventeenth Century, abortion was considered the killing of a person only after quickening, the time when a pregnant woman first feels the fetus move on its own. Nor is this variety of opinions surprising. Biologically, a human being develops gradually. We shouldn't expect there to be any specific time or sharp dividing point when a person appears on the scene.

For these reasons I believe our concept of a person is not sharp or decisive enough to bear the weight of a solution to the abortion controversy. To use it to solve that problem is to clarify *obscurum per obscurius*.

II

Next let us consider what follows if a fetus is a person after all. Judith Jarvis Thomson's landmark article, "A Defense of Abortion,"[10] correctly points out that some additional argumentation is needed at this point in the conservative argument to bridge the gap between the premise that a fetus is an innocent person and the conclusion that killing it is always wrong. To arrive at this conclusion, we would need the additional premise that killing an innocent person is always wrong. But killing an innocent person is sometimes permissible, most notably in self defense. Some examples may help draw out our intuitions or ordinary judgments about self defense.

Suppose a mad scientist, for instance, hypnotized innocent people to jump out of the bushes and attack innocent passers-by with knives. If you are so attacked, we agree you have a right to kill the attacker in self defense, if killing him is the only way to protect your life or to save yourself from serious injury. It does not seem to matter here that the attacker is not malicious but himself an innocent pawn, for your killing of him is not done in a spirit of retribution but only in self defense.

How severe an injury may you inflict in self defense? In part this depends upon the severity of the injury to be avoided: you may not shoot someone merely to avoid having your clothes torn. This might lead one to the mistaken conclusion that the defense may only equal the threatened injury in severity; that to avoid death you may kill, but to avoid a black eye you may only inflict a black eye or the equivalent. Rather, our laws and customs seem to say that you may create an injury somewhat, but not enormously, greater than the injury to be avoided. To fend off an attack whose outcome would be as serious as rape, a severe beating or the loss of a finger, you may shoot; to avoid having your clothes torn, you may blacken an eye.

Aside from this, the injury you may inflict should only be the minimum necessary to deter or incapacitate the attacker. Even if you know he intends to kill you, you are not justified in shooting him if you could equally well save yourself by the simple expedient of running away. Self defense is for the purpose of avoiding harms rather than equalizing harms.

Some cases of pregnancy present a parallel situation. Though the fetus is itself innocent, it may pose a threat to the pregnant woman's well-being, life prospects or health, mental or physical. If the pregnancy presents a slight threat to her interests, it seems self defense cannot justify abortion. But if the threat is on a par with a serious beating or the loss of a finger, she may kill the fetus that poses such a threat, even if it is an innocent person. If a lesser harm to the fetus could have the same defensive effect, killing it would not be justified. It is unfortunate that the only way to free the woman from the pregnancy entails the death of the fetus (except in very late stages of pregnancy). Thus a self defense model supports Thomson's point that the woman has a right only to be freed from the fetus, not a right to demand its death.[11]

The self defense model is most helpful when we take the pregnant woman's point of view. In the pre-Thomson literature, abortion is often framed as a question for a third party: do you, a doctor, have a right to choose between the life of the woman and that of the fetus? Some have claimed that if you were a passer-by who witnessed a struggle between the innocent hypnotized attacker and his equally innocent victim, you would have no reason to kill either in defense of the other. They have concluded that the self defense model implies that a woman may attempt to abort herself, but that a doctor should not assist her. I think the position of the third party is somewhat more complex. We do feel some inclination to intervene on behalf of the victim rather than the attacker, other things equal. But if both parties are innocent, other factors come into consideration. You would rush to the aid of your husband whether he was attacker or attackee. If a hypnotized famous violinist were attacking a skid row bum, we would try to save the individual who is of more value to society. These considerations would tend to support abortion in some cases.

But suppose you are a frail senior citizen who wishes to avoid being knifed by one of these innocent hypnotics, so you have hired a bodyguard to accompany you. If you are attacked, it is clear we believe that the bodyguard, acting as your agent, has a right to kill the attacker to save you from a serious beating. Your rights of self defense are transferred to your agent. I suggest that we should similarly view the doctor as the pregnant woman's agent in carrying out a defense she is physically incapable of accomplishing herself.

Thanks to modern technology, the cases are rare in which pregnancy poses as clear a threat to a woman's bodily health as an attacker brandishing a switchblade. How does self defense fare when more subtle, complex and long-range harms are involved?

To consider a somewhat fanciful example, suppose you are a highly trained surgeon when you are kidnapped by the hypnotic attacker. He says he does not intend to harm you but to take you back to the mad scientist who, it turns out, plans to hypnotize you to have a permanent mental block against all your knowledge of medicine. This would automatically destroy your career which would in turn have a serious adverse impact on your family, your personal relationships and your happiness. It seems to me that if the only way you can avoid this outcome is to shoot the innocent attacker, you are justified in so doing. You are defending yourself from a drastic injury to your life prospects. I think it is no exaggeration to claim that unwanted pregnancies (most obviously among teenagers) often have such adverse life-long consequences as the surgeon's loss of livelihood.

Several parallels arise between various views on abortion and the self defense model. Let's suppose further that these hypnotized attackers only operate at night, so that it is well known that they can be avoided completely by the considerable inconvenience of never leaving your house after dark. One view is that since you could stay home at night, therefore if you go out and are selected by one of these hypnotized people, you have no right to defend yourself. This parallels the view that abstinence is the only acceptable way to avoid pregnancy. Others might hold that you ought to take along some defense such as Mace which will deter the hypnotized person without killing him, but that if this defense fails, you are obliged to submit to the resulting injury, no matter how severe it is. This parallels the view that contraception is all right but abortion is always wrong, even in cases of contraceptive failure.

A third view is that you may kill the hypnotized person only if he will actually kill you, but not if he will only injure you. This is like the position that abortion is permissible only if it is required to save a woman's life. Finally we have the view that it is all right to kill the attacker, even if only to avoid a very slight inconvenience to yourself and even if you knowingly walked down the very street where all these incidents have been taking place without taking along any Mace or protective escort. If we assume that a fetus is a person, this is the analogue of the view that abortion is always justifiable, "on demand."

The self defense model allows us to see an important difference that exists between abortion and infanticide, even if a fetus is a person from conception. Many have argued that the only way to justify abortion without justifying infanticide would be to find some characteristic of personhood that is acquired at birth. Michael Tooley, for one, claims infanticide is justifiable because the really significant characteristics of person are acquired some time after birth. But all such approaches look to characteristics of the developing human and ignore the relation between the fetus and the woman. What if, after birth, the presence of an infant or the need to support it posed a grave threat to the woman's sanity or life prospects? She could escape this threat by the simple expedient of running away. So a solution that does not entail the death of the infant is available. Before birth, such solutions are not available because of the biological dependence of the fetus on the woman. Birth is the crucial point not because of any characteristics the fetus gains, but because after birth the woman can defend herself by a means less drastic than killing the infant. Hence self defense can be used to justify abortion without necessarily thereby justifying infanticide.

III

On the other hand, supposing a fetus is not after all a person, would abortion always be morally permissible? Some opponents of abortion seem worried that if a fetus is not a full-fledged person, then we are justified in treating it in any way at all. However, this does not follow. Non-persons do get some consideration in our moral code, though of course they do not have the same rights as persons have (and in general they do not have moral responsibilities), and though their interests may be overridden by the interests of persons. Still, we cannot just treat them in any way at all.

Treatment of animals is a case in point. It is wrong to torture dogs for fun or to kill wild birds for no reason at all. It is wrong Period, even though dogs and birds do not have the same rights persons do. However, few people think it is wrong to use dogs as experimental animals, causing them considerable suffering in some cases, provided that the resulting research will probably bring discoveries of great benefit to people. And most of us think it all right to kill birds for food or to protect our crops. People's rights are different from the consideration we give to animals, then, for it is wrong to experiment on people, even if others might later benefit a great deal as a result of their suffering. You might volunteer to be a subject, but this would be supererogatory; you certainly have a right to refuse to be a medical guinea pig.

But how do we decide what you may or may not do to non-persons? This is a difficult problem, one for which I believe no adequate account exists. You do not want to say, for instance, that torturing dogs is all right whenever the sum of its effects on people is good—when it doesn't warp the sensibilities of the torturer so much that he mistreats people. If that were the case, it would be all right to torture dogs if you did it in private, or if the torturer lived on a desert island or died soon afterward, so that his actions had no effect on people. This is an inadequate account, because whatever moral consideration animals get, it has to be indefeasible, too. It will have to be a general proscription of certain actions, not merely a weighing of the impact on people on a case-by-case basis.

Rather, we need to distinguish two levels on which consequences of actions can be taken into account in moral reasoning. The traditional objections to Utilitarianism focus on the fact that it operates solely on the first level, taking all the consequences into account in particular cases only. Thus Utilitarianism is open to "desert island" and "lifeboat" counterexamples because these cases are rigged to make the consequences of actions severely limited.

Rawls' theory could be described as a teleological sort of theory, but with teleology operating on a higher level.[12] In choosing the principles to regulate society from the original position, his hypothetical choosers make their decision on the basis of the total consequences of various systems. Furthermore, they are constrained to choose a general set of rules which people can readily learn and apply. An ethical theory must operate by generating a set of sympathies and attitudes toward others which reinforces the functioning of that set of moral principles. Our prohibition against killing people operates by means of certain moral sentiments including sympathy, compassion and guilt. But if these attitudes are to form a coherent set, they carry us further: we tend to perform supererogatory actions, and we tend to feel similar compassion toward person-like non-persons.

It is crucial that psychological facts play a role here. Our psychological constitution makes it the case that for our ethical theory to work, it must prohibit certain treatment of non-persons which are significantly person-like. If our moral rules allowed people to treat some person-like non-persons in ways we do not want people to be treated, this would undermine the system of sympathies and attitudes that makes the ethical system work. For this reason, we would choose in the original position to make mistreatment of some sorts of animals wrong in general (not just wrong in the cases with public impact), even though animals are not themselves parties in the original position. Thus it makes sense that it is those animals whose appearance and behavior are most like those of people that get the most consideration in our moral scheme.

It is because of "coherence of attitudes," I think, that the similarity of a fetus to a baby is very significant. A fetus one week before birth is so much like a newborn baby in our psychological space that we cannot allow any cavalier treatment of the former while expecting full sympathy and nurturative support for the latter. Thus, I think that anti-abortion forces are indeed giving their strongest arguments when they point to the similarities between a fetus and a baby, and when they try to evoke our emotional attachment to and sympathy for the fetus. An early horror story from New York about nurses who were expected to alternate between caring for six-week premature infants and disposing of viable 24-week aborted fetuses is just that—a horror story. These beings are so much alike that no one can be asked to draw a distinction and treat them so very differently.

Remember, however, that in the early weeks after conception, a fetus is very much unlike a person. It is hard to develop these feelings for a set of genes which doesn't yet have a head, hands, beating heart, response to touch or the ability to move by itself. Thus it seems to me that the alleged "slippery slope" between conception and birth is not so very slippery. In the early stages of pregnancy, abortion can hardly be compared to murder for psychological reasons, but in the latest stages it is psychologically akin to murder.

Another source of similarity is the bodily continuity between fetus and adult. Bodies play a surprisingly central role in our attitudes toward persons. One has only to think of the philosophical literature on how far physical identity suffices for personal identity or Wittgenstein's remark that the best picture of the human soul is the human body. Even after death, when all agree the body is no longer a person, we still observe elaborate customs of respect for the human body; like people who torture dogs, necrophiliacs are not to be trusted with people.[13] So it is appropriate that we show respect to a fetus as the body continuous with the body of a person. This is a degree of resemblance to persons that animals cannot rival.

Michael Tooley also utilizes a parallel with animals. He claims that it is always permissible to drown newborn kittens and draws conclusions about infanticide.[14] But it is only permissible to drown kittens when their survival would cause some hardship. Perhaps it would be a burden to feed and house six more cats or to find other homes for them. The alternative of letting them starve produces even more suffering than the drowning. Since the kittens get their rights second-hand, so to speak, *via* the need for coherence in our attitudes, their interests are often overridden by the interests of full-fledged persons. But if their survival would be no inconvenience to people at all, then it is wrong to drown them, *contra* Tooley.

Tooley's conclusions about abortion are wrong for the same reason. Even if a fetus is not a person, abortion is not always permissible, because of the resemblance of a fetus to a person. I agree with Thomson that it would be wrong for a woman who is seven months pregnant to have an abortion just to avoid having to postpone a trip to Europe. In the early months of pregnancy when the fetus hardly resembles a baby at all, then, abortion is permissible whenever it is in the interests of the pregnant woman or her family. The reasons would only need to outweigh the pain and inconvenience of the abortion itself. In the middle months, when the fetus comes to resemble a person, abortion would be justifiable only when the continuation of the pregnancy or the birth of the child would cause harms—physical, psychological, economic or social—to the woman. In the late months of pregnancy, even on our current assumption that a fetus is not a person, abortion seems to be wrong except to save a woman from significant injury or death.

The Supreme Court has recognized similar gradations in the alleged slippery slope stretching between conception and birth. To this point, the present paper has been a discussion of the moral status of abortion only, not its legal status. In view of the great physical, financial and sometimes psychological costs of abortion, perhaps the legal arrangement most compatible with the proposed moral solution would be the absence of restrictions, that is, so-called abortion "on demand."

So I conclude, first, that application of our concept of a person will not suffice to settle the abortion issue. After all, the biological development of a human being is gradual. Second, whether a fetus is a person or not, abortion is justifiable early in pregnancy to avoid modest harms and seldom justifiable late in pregnancy except to avoid significant injury or death.[15]

NOTES

1 We also have paternalistic laws which keep us from harming our own bodies even when no one else is affected. Ironically, antiabortion laws were originally designed to protect pregnant women from a dangerous but tempting procedure.
2 Mary Anne Warren, "On the Moral and Legal Status of Abortion," *The Monist* 57 (1973), p. 55.
3 Baruch Brody, "Fetal Humanity and the Theory of Essentialism," in Robert Baker and Frederick Elliston, eds., *Philosophy and Sex* (Buffalo, N.Y., 1975).
4 Michael Tooley, "Abortion and Infanticide," *Philosophy and Public Affairs* 2 (1971).
5 Paul Ramsey, "The Morality of Abortion," in James Rachels, ed., *Moral Problems* (New York, 1971).
6 John Noonan, "Abortion and the Catholic Church: A Summary History," *Natural Law Forum* 12 (1967), pp. 125–131.
7 Wittgenstein has argued against the possibility of so capturing the concept of a game, *Philosophical Investigations* (New York, 1958), §66–71.
8 Not because the fetus is partly a person and so has some of the rights of persons, but rather because of the rights of person-like non-persons. This I discuss in part III below.
9 Aristotle himself was concerned, however, with the different question of when the soul takes form. For historical data, see Jimmye Kimmey, "How the Abortion Laws Happened," *Ms.* 1 (April, 1973), pp. 48ff, and John Noonan, *loc. cit.*
10 J. J. Thomson, "A Defense of Abortion," *Philosophy and Public Affairs* 1 (1971).
11 *Ibid.,* p. 52.
12 John Rawls, *A Theory of Justice* (Cambridge, Mass., 1971), §3–4.
13 On the other hand, if they can be trusted with people, then our moral customs are mistaken. It all depends on the facts of psychology.
14 *Op. cit.,* pp. 40, 60–61.
15 I am deeply indebted to Larry Crocker and Arthur Kuflik for their constructive comments.

QUESTIONS

1 Is English successful in her effort to moderate both the conservative view and the liberal view on abortion?

2 Is the following a justifiable criticism? In moderating the conservative view, English winds up with a rather "conservative" moderate view, whereas in moderating the liberal view, she winds up with a rather "liberal" moderate view. Therefore, she is not successful in showing that the problem of abortion can be effectively resolved without first establishing whether or not the fetus is a person.

Why Abortion Is Immoral

Don Marquis

Don Marquis is professor of philosophy at the University of Kansas. He specializes in applied ethics and medical ethics. His published articles include "Four Versions of Double Effect," "An Argument that All Prerandomized Clinical Trials Are Unethical," and "Harming the Dead."

Marquis argues that abortion, with rare exceptions, is seriously immoral. He bases this conclusion on a theory that he presents and defends about the wrongness of killing. In his view, killing another adult human being is wrong precisely because the victim is deprived of all the value—"activities, projects, experiences, and enjoyments"—of his or her future. Since abortion deprives a typical fetus of a "future like ours," he contends, the moral presumption against abortion is as strong as the presumption against killing another adult human being.

The view that abortion is, with rare exceptions, seriously immoral has received little support in the recent philosophical literature. No doubt most philosophers affiliated with secular institutions of higher education believe that the anti-abortion position is either a symptom of irrational religious dogma or a conclusion generated by seriously confused philosophical argument. The purpose of this essay is to undermine this general belief. This essay sets out an argument that purports to show, as well as any argument in ethics can show, that abortion is, except possibly in rare cases, seriously immoral, that it is in the same moral category as killing an innocent adult human being.

This argument is based on a major assumption: If fetuses are in the same category as adult human beings with respect to the moral value of their lives, then the *presumption* that any particular abortion is immoral is exceedingly strong. Such a presumption could be overridden only by considerations more compelling than a woman's right to privacy. The defense of this assumption is beyond the scope of this essay.[1]

Furthermore, this essay will neglect a discussion of whether there are any such compelling considerations and what they are. Plainly there are strong candidates:

Reprinted, as slightly modified by the author, with permission of the author and the publisher from the *Journal of Philosophy*, vol. 86 (April 1989).

abortion before implantation, abortion when the life of a woman is threatened by a pregnancy or abortion after rape. The casuistry of these hard cases will not be explored in this essay. The purpose of this essay is to develop a general argument for the claim that, subject to the assumption above, the overwhelming majority of deliberate abortions are seriously immoral. . . .

. . . A necessary condition of resolving the abortion controversy is a . . . theoretical account of the wrongness of killing. After all, if we merely believe, but do not understand, why killing adult human beings such as ourselves is wrong, how could we conceivably show that abortion is either immoral or permissible? . . .

In order to develop such an account, we can start from the following unproblematic assumption concerning our own case: it is wrong to kill *us*. Why is it wrong? Some answers can be easily eliminated. It might be said that what makes killing us wrong is that a killing brutalizes the one who kills. But the brutalization consists of being inured to the performance of an act that is hideously immoral; hence, the brutalization does not explain the immorality. It might be said that what makes killing us wrong is the great loss others would experience due to our absence. Although such hubris is understandable, such an explanation does not account for the wrongness of killing hermits, or those whose lives are relatively independent and whose friends find it easy to make new friends.

A more obvious answer is better. What primarily makes killing wrong is neither its effect on the murderer nor its effect on the victim's friends and relatives, but its effect on the victim. The loss of one's life is one of the greatest losses one can suffer. The loss of one's life deprives one of all the experiences, activities, projects, and enjoyments that would otherwise have constituted one's future. Therefore, killing someone is wrong, primarily because the killing inflicts (one of) the greatest possible losses on the victim. To describe this as the loss of life can be misleading, however. The change in my biological state does not by itself make killing me wrong. The effect of the loss of my biological life is the loss to me of all those activities, projects, experiences, and enjoyments which would otherwise have constituted my future personal life. These activities, projects, experiences, and enjoyments are either valuable for their own sakes or are means to something else that is valuable for its own sake. Some parts of my future are not valued by me now, but will come to be valued by me as I grow older and as my values and capacities change. When I am killed, I am deprived both of what I now value which would have been part of my future personal life, but also what I would come to value. Therefore, when I die, I am deprived of all of the value of my future. Inflicting this loss on me is ultimately what makes killing me wrong. This being the case, it would seem that what makes killing *any* adult human being prima facie seriously wrong is the loss of his or her future.[2]

How should this rudimentary theory of the wrongness of killing be evaluated? It cannot be faulted for deriving an 'ought' from an 'is', for it does not. The analysis assumes that killing me (or you, reader) is prima facie seriously wrong. The point of the analysis is to establish which natural property ultimately explains the wrongness of the killing, given that it is wrong. A natural property will ultimately explain the wrongness of killing, only if (1) the explanation fits with our intuitions about the matter and (2) there is no other natural property that provides the basis for a better explanation of the wrongness of killing. This analysis rests on the intuition that what makes killing a particular human or animal wrong is what it does to that particular human or animal. What makes killing wrong is some natural effect or other of the killing. Some would deny this. For instance, a divine-command theorist in ethics would deny it. Surely this denial is, however, one of those features of divine-command theory which renders it so implausible.

The claim that what makes killing wrong is the loss of the victim's future is directly supported by two considerations. In the first place, this theory explains why we regard killing as one of the worst of crimes. Killing is especially wrong, because it deprives the victim of more than perhaps any other crime. In the second place, people with AIDS or cancer who know they are dying believe, of course, that dying is a very bad thing for them. They believe that the loss of a future to them that they would otherwise have experienced is what makes their premature death a very bad thing for them. A better theory of the wrongness of killing would require a different natural property associated with killing which better fits with the attitudes of the dying. What could it be?

The view that what makes killing wrong is the loss to the victim of the value of the victim's future gains additional support when some of its implications are examined. In the first place, it is incompatible with the view that it is wrong to kill only beings who are biologically human. It is possible that there exists a different species from another planet whose members have a future like ours. Since having a future like that is what makes killing someone wrong, this theory entails that it would be wrong to kill members of such a species. Hence, this theory is opposed to the claim that only life that is biologically human has great moral worth, a claim which many anti-abortionists have seemed to adopt. This opposition, which this theory has in common with personhood theories, seems to be a merit of the theory.

In the second place, the claim that the loss of one's future is the wrong-making feature of one's being killed entails the possibility that the futures of some actual nonhuman mammals on our own planet are sufficiently like ours that it is seriously wrong to kill them also. Whether some animals do have the same right to life as human beings depends on adding to the account of the wrongness of killing some additional account of just what it is about my future or the futures of other adult human beings which makes it wrong to kill us. No such additional account will be offered in this essay. Undoubtedly, the provision of such an account would be a very difficult matter. Undoubtedly, any such account would be quite controversial. Hence, it surely should not reflect badly on this sketch of an elementary theory of the wrongness of killing that it is indeterminate with respect to some very difficult issues regarding animal rights.

In the third place, the claim that the loss of one's future is the wrong-making feature of one's being killed does not entail, as sanctity of human life theories do, that active euthanasia is wrong. Persons who are severely and incurably ill, who face a future of pain and despair, and who wish to die will not have suffered a loss if they are killed. It is, strictly speaking, the value of a human's future which makes killing wrong in this theory. This being so, killing does not necessarily wrong some persons who are sick and dying. Of course, there may be other reasons for a prohibition of active euthanasia, but that is another matter. Sanctity-of-human-life theories seem to hold that active euthanasia is seriously wrong even in an individual case where there seems to be good reason for it independently of public policy considerations. This consequence is most implausible, and it is a plus for the claim that the loss of a future of value is what makes killing wrong that it does not share this consequence.

In the fourth place, the account of the wrongness of killing defended in this essay does straightforwardly entail that it is prima facie seriously wrong to kill children and infants, for we do presume that they have futures of value. Since we do believe that it is wrong to kill defenseless little babies, it is important that a theory of the wrongness of killing easily account for this. Personhood theories of the wrongness of killing, on the other hand, cannot straightforwardly account for the wrongness of killing infants and young children. Hence, such theories must add special ad hoc accounts of the wrongness of killing the young. The plausibility of such ad hoc theories seems to be a function of how desperately one wants such theories to work. The claim that the primary wrong-making feature of a killing is the loss to the victim of the value of its future accounts for the wrongness of killing young children and infants directly; it makes the wrongness of such acts as obvious as we actually think it is. This is a further merit of this theory. Accordingly, it seems that this value of a future-like-ours theory of the wrongness of killing shares strengths of both sanctity-of-life and personhood accounts while avoiding weaknesses of both. In addition, it meshes with a central intuition concerning what makes killing wrong.

The claim that the primary wrong-making feature of a killing is the loss to the victim of the value of its future has obvious consequences for the ethics of abortion. The future of a standard fetus includes a set of experiences, projects, activities, and such which are identical with the futures of adult human beings and are identical with the futures of young children. Since the reason that is sufficient to explain why it is wrong to kill human beings after the time of birth is a reason that also applies to fetuses, it follows that abortion is prima facie seriously morally wrong.

This argument does not rely on the invalid inference that, since it is wrong to kill persons, it is wrong to kill potential persons also. The category that is morally central to this analysis is the category of having a valuable future like ours; it is not the category of personhood. The argument to the conclusion that abortion is prima facie seriously morally wrong proceeded independently of the notion of person or potential person or any equivalent. Someone may wish to start with this analysis in terms of the value of a human future, conclude that abortion is, except perhaps in rare circumstances, seriously morally wrong, infer that fetuses have the right to life, and then call fetuses "persons" as a result of their having the right to life. Clearly, in this case, the category of person is being used to state the *conclusion* of the analysis rather than to generate the *argument* of the analysis.

The structure of this anti-abortion argument can be both illuminated and defended by comparing it to what appears to be the best argument for the wrongness of the wanton infliction of pain on animals. This latter argument is based on the assumption that it is prima facie wrong to inflict pain on me (or you, reader). What is the natural property associated with the infliction of pain which makes such infliction wrong? The obvious answer seems to be that the infliction of pain causes suffering and that suffering is a misfortune. The suffering caused by the infliction of pain is what makes the wanton infliction of pain on me wrong. The wanton infliction of pain on other adult humans causes suffering. The wanton infliction of pain on animals causes suffering. Since causing suffering is what makes the wanton infliction of pain wrong and since the wanton infliction of pain on animals causes suffering, it follows that the wanton infliction of pain on animals is wrong.

This argument for the wrongness of the wanton infliction of pain on animals shares a number of structural features with the argument for the serious prima facie wrongness of abortion. Both arguments start with an obvious assumption concerning what it is wrong to do to me (or you, reader). Both then look for the characteristic or the consequence of the wrong action which makes the action wrong. Both recognize that the wrong-making feature of these immoral actions is a property of actions sometimes directed at individuals other than postnatal human beings. If the structure of the argument for the wrongness of the wanton infliction of pain on animals is sound, then the structure of the argument for the prima facie serious wrongness of abortion is also sound, for the structure of the two arguments is the same. The structure common to both is the key to the explanation of how the wrongness of abortion can be demonstrated without recourse to the category of person. In neither argument is that category crucial. . . .

Of course, this value of a future-like-ours argument, if sound, shows only that abortion is prima facie wrong, not that it is wrong in any and all circumstances. Since the loss of the future to a standard fetus, if killed, is, however, at least as great a loss as the loss of the future to a standard adult human being who is killed, abortion, like ordinary killing, could be justified only by the most compelling reasons. The loss of one's life is almost the greatest misfortune that can happen to one. Presumably abortion could be justified in some circumstances, only if the loss consequent on failing to abort would be at least as great. Accordingly, morally permissible abortions will be rare indeed unless, perhaps, they occur so early in pregnancy that a fetus is not yet definitely an individual. Hence, this argument should be taken as showing that abortion is presumptively very seriously wrong, where the presumption is very strong— as strong as the presumption that killing another adult human being is wrong. . . .

In this essay, it has been argued that the correct ethic of the wrongness of killing can be extended to fetal life and used to show that there is a strong presumption that any abortion is morally impermissible. If the ethic of killing adopted here entails, however, that contraception is also seriously immoral, then there would appear to be a difficulty with the analysis of this essay.

But this analysis does not entail that contraception is wrong. Of course, contraception prevents the actualization of a possible future of value. Hence, it follows from the claim that futures of value should be maximized that contraception is prima facie immoral. This obligation to maximize does not exist, however; furthermore, nothing in the ethics of killing in this paper entails that it does. The ethics of killing in this essay would entail that contraception is wrong only if something were denied a human future of value by contraception. Nothing at all is denied such a future by contraception, however.

Candidates for a subject of harm by contraception fall into four categories: (1) some sperm or other, (2) some ovum or other, (3) a sperm and an ovum separately, and (4) a sperm and an ovum together. Assigning the harm to some sperm is utterly arbitrary, for no reason can be given for making a sperm the subject of harm rather than an ovum. Assigning the harm to some ovum is utterly arbitrary, for no reason can be given for making an ovum the subject of harm rather than a sperm. One might attempt to avoid these problems by insisting that contraception deprives both the sperm and the ovum separately of a valuable future like ours. On this alternative, too many futures are lost. Contraception was supposed to be wrong, because it deprived us of one future of value, not two. One might attempt to avoid this problem by holding that contraception deprives the combination of sperm and ovum of a valuable future like ours. But here the definite article misleads. At the time of contraception, there are hundreds of millions of sperm, one (released) ovum and millions of possible combinations of all of these. There is no actual combination at all. Is the subject of the loss to be a merely possible combination? Which one? This alternative does not yield an actual subject of harm either. Accordingly, the immorality of contraception is not entailed by the loss of a future-like-ours argument simply because there is no nonarbitrarily identifiable subject of the loss in the case of contraception. . . .

The purpose of this essay has been to set out an argument for the serious presumptive wrongness of abortion subject to the assumption that the moral permissibility of abortion stands or falls on the moral status of the fetus. Since a fetus possesses a property, the possession of which in adult human beings is sufficient to make killing an adult human being wrong, abortion is wrong. This way of dealing with the problem of abortion seems superior to other approaches to the ethics of abortion, because it rests on an ethics of killing which is close to self-evident, because the crucial morally relevant property clearly applies to fetuses, and because the argument avoids the usual equivocations on 'human life', 'human being', or 'person'. The argument rests neither on religious claims nor on Papal dogma. It is not subject to the objection of "speciesism." Its soundness is compatible with the moral permissibility of euthanasia and contraception. It deals with our intuitions concerning young children.

Finally, this analysis can be viewed as resolving a standard problem—indeed, *the* standard problem—concerning the ethics of abortion. Clearly, it is wrong to kill adult human beings. Clearly, it is not wrong to end the life of some arbitrarily chosen single human cell. Fetuses seem to be like arbitrarily chosen human cells in some respects and like adult humans in other respects. The problem of the ethics of abortion is the problem of determining the fetal property that settles this moral controversy. The thesis of this essay is that the problem of the ethics of abortion, so understood, is solvable.

NOTES

1 Judith Jarvis Thomson has rejected this assumption in a famous essay, "A Defense of Abortion," *Philosophy and Public Affairs* 1, #1 (1971), 47–66.

2 I have been most influenced on this matter by Jonathan Glover, *Causing Death and Saving Lives* (New York: Penguin, 1977), ch. 3; and Robert Young, "What Is So Wrong with Killing People?" *Philosophy,* LIV, 210 (1979): 515–528.

QUESTIONS

1 If the wrongness of killing derives from the fact that the victim is deprived of the value of his or her future, does it follow that it is less wrong to kill someone fifty years old than it is to kill someone twenty years old? If so, does this implication suggest that there is some deficiency in Marquis's theory about the wrongness of killing?
2 Does Marquis provide a satisfactory response to the possible objection that his theory about the wrongness of killing implies that contraception is morally wrong?
3 If Marquis's basic approach is accepted, which abortions could still be considered morally justified?

Majority Opinion in *Roe v. Wade*

Justice Harry A. Blackmun

Harry A. Blackmun, a graduate of Harvard Law School, was associate justice of the United States Supreme Court from 1970 to 1994. After some fifteen years in private practice he became legal counsel to the Mayo Clinic (1950–1959). Justice Blackmun also served as United States circuit judge (1959–1970) before his appointment to the Supreme Court.

In this case, a pregnant single woman, suing under the fictitious name of Jane Roe, challenged the constitutionality of the existing Texas criminal abortion law. According to the Texas Penal Code, the performance of an abortion, except to save the life of the pregnant woman, constituted a crime that was punishable by a prison sentence of two to five years. At the time this case was finally resolved by the Supreme Court, abortion legislation varied widely from state to state. Some states, principally New York, had already legalized abortion on demand. Most other states, however, had legalized various forms of therapeutic abortion but had retained some measure of restrictive abortion legislation.

Justice Blackmun, writing an opinion concurred in by six other justices, argues that a woman's decision to terminate a pregnancy is encompassed by a *right to privacy*—but only up to a certain point in the development of the fetus. As the right to privacy is not an absolute right, it must yield at some point to the state's legitimate interests. Justice Blackmun contends that the state has a legitimate interest in protecting the health of the pregnant woman and that this interest becomes compelling at approximately the end of the first trimester in the development of the fetus. He also contends that the state has a legitimate interest in protecting potential life and that this interest becomes compelling at the point of viability.

United States Supreme Court. 410 U.S. 113 (1973).

It is . . . apparent that at common law, at the time of the adoption of our Constitution, and throughout the major portion of the 19th century, abortion was viewed with less disfavor than under most American statutes currently in effect. Phrasing it another way, a woman enjoyed a substantially broader right to terminate a pregnancy than she does in most States today. At least with respect to the early stage of pregnancy, and very possibly without such a limitation, the opportunity to make this choice was present in this country well into the 19th century. Even later, the law continued for some time to treat less punitively an abortion procured in early pregnancy. . . .

Three reasons have been advanced to explain historically the enactment of criminal abortion laws in the 19th century and to justify their continued existence.

It has been argued occasionally that these laws were the product of a Victorian social concern to discourage illicit sexual conduct. Texas, however, does not advance this justification in the present case, and it appears that no court or commentator has taken the argument seriously. . . .

A second reason is concerned with abortion as a medical procedure. When most criminal abortion laws were first enacted, the procedure was a hazardous one for the woman. This was particularly true prior to the development of antisepsis. Antiseptic techniques, of course, were based on discoveries by Lister, Pasteur, and others first announced in 1867, but were not generally accepted and employed until about the turn of the century. Abortion mortality was high. Even after 1900, and perhaps until as late as the development of antibiotics in the 1940's, standard modern techniques such as dilatation and curettage were not nearly so safe as they are today. Thus it has been argued that a State's real concern in enacting a criminal abortion law was to protect the pregnant woman, that is, to restrain her from submitting to a procedure that placed her life in serious jeopardy.

Modern medical techniques have altered this situation. Appellants and various *amici* refer to medical data indicating that abortion in early pregnancy, that is, prior to the end of first trimester, although not without its risk, is now relatively safe. Mortality rates for women undergoing early abortions, where the procedure is legal, appear to be as low as or lower than the rates for normal childbirth. Consequently, any interest of the State in protecting the woman from an inherently hazardous procedure, except when it would be equally dangerous for her to forgo it, has largely disappeared. Of course, important state interests in the area of health and medical standards do remain. The State has a legitimate interest in seeing to it that abortion, like any other medical procedure, is performed under circumstances that insure maximum safety for the patient. This interest obviously extends at least to the performing physician and his staff, to the facilities involved, to the availability of after-care, and to adequate provision for any complication or emergency that might arise. The prevalence of high mortality rates at illegal "abortion mills" strengthens, rather than weakens, the State's interest in regulating the conditions under which abortions are performed. Moreover, the risk to the woman increases as her pregnancy continues. Thus the State retains a definite interest in protecting the woman's own health and safety when an abortion is performed at a late stage of pregnancy.

The third reason is the State's interest—some phrase it in terms of duty—in protecting prenatal life. Some of the argument for this justification rests on the theory that a new human life is present from the moment of conception. The State's interest and general obligation to protect life then extends, it is argued, to prenatal life. Only when the life of the pregnant mother herself is at stake, balanced against the life she carries within her, should the interest of the embryo or fetus not prevail. Logically, of course, a legitimate state interest in this area need not stand or fall on acceptance of the belief that life begins at conception or at some other point prior to live birth. In assessing the State's interest, recognition may be given to the less rigid claim that as long as at least *potential* life is involved, the State may assert interests beyond the protection of the pregnant woman alone.

Parties challenging state abortion laws have sharply disputed in some courts the contention that a purpose of these laws, when enacted, was to protect prenatal life. Pointing to the absence of legislative history to support the contention, they claim that most state laws were designed solely to protect the woman. Because medical advances have lessened this concern, at least with respect to abortion in early pregnancy, they argue that with respect to such abortions the laws can no longer be justified by any state interest. There is some scholarly support for this view of original purpose. The few state courts called upon to interpret their laws in the late 19th and early 20th centuries did focus on the State's interest in protecting the woman's health rather than in preserving the embryo and fetus. . . .

The Constitution does not explicitly mention any right of privacy. In a line of decisions, however, going back perhaps as far as *Union Pacific R. Co. v. Botsford* (1891), the Court has recognized that a right of personal privacy, or a guarantee of certain areas or zones of privacy, does exist under the Constitution. In varying contexts the Court or individual Justices have indeed found at least the roots of that right in the First Amendment, . . . in the Fourth and Fifth Amendments . . . in the penumbras of the Bill of Rights . . . in the Ninth Amendment . . . or in the concept of liberty guaranteed by the first section of the Fourteenth Amendment. . . . These decisions make it clear that only personal rights that can be deemed "fundamental" or "implicit in the concept of ordered liberty," . . . are included in this guarantee of personal privacy. They also make it clear that the right has some extension to activities relating to marriage, . . . procreation, . . . contraception, . . . family relationships, . . . and child rearing and education. . . .

This right of privacy, whether it be founded in the Fourteenth Amendment's concept of personal liberty and restrictions upon state action, as we feel it is, or, as the District Court determined, in the Ninth Amendment's reservation of rights to the people, is broad enough to encompass a woman's decision whether or not to terminate her pregnancy. . . .

. . . [A]ppellants and some *amici* argue that the woman's right is absolute and that she is entitled to terminate her pregnancy at whatever time, in whatever way, and for whatever reason she alone chooses. With this we do not agree. Appellants' arguments that Texas either has no valid interest at all in regulating the abortion decision, or no interest strong enough to support any limitation upon the woman's sole determination, is unpersuasive. The Court's decisions recognizing a right of privacy also acknowledge that some state regulation in areas protected by that right is appropriate.

As noted above, a state may properly assert important interests in safe-guarding health, in maintaining medical standards, and in protecting potential life. At some point in pregnancy, these respective interests become sufficiently compelling to sustain regulation of the factors that govern the abortion decision. The privacy right involved, therefore, cannot be said to be absolute. . . .

We therefore conclude that the right of personal privacy includes the abortion decision, but that this right is not unqualified and must be considered against important state interests in regulation.

We note that those federal and state courts that have recently considered abortion law challenges have reached the same conclusion. . . .

Although the results are divided, most of these courts have agreed that the right of privacy, however based, is broad enough to cover the abortion decision; that the right, nonetheless, is not absolute and is subject to some limitations; and that at some point the state interests as to protection of health, medical standards, and prenatal life, become dominant. We agree with this approach. . . .

The appellee and certain *amici* argue that the fetus is a "person" within the language and meaning of the Fourteenth Amendment. In support of this they outline at length and in detail the well-known facts of fetal development. If this suggestion of personhood is established, the appellant's case, of course, collapses, for the fetus' right to life is then guaranteed specifically by the Amendment. The appellant conceded as much on reargument. On the other hand, the appellee conceded on reargument that no case could be cited that holds that a fetus is a person within the meaning of the Fourteenth Amendment. . . .

All this, together with our observation, *supra,* that throughout the major portion of the 19th century prevailing legal abortion practices were far freer than they are today, persuades us that the word "person," as used in the Fourteenth Amendment, does not include the unborn. . . . Indeed, our decision in *United States v. Vuitch* (1971) inferentially is to the same effect, for we there would not have indulged in statutory interpretation favorable to abortion in specified circumstances if the necessary consequence was the termination of life entitled to Fourteenth Amendment protection.

. . . As we have intimated above, it is reasonable and appropriate for a State to decide that at some point in time another interest, that of health of the mother or that of potential human life, becomes significantly involved. The woman's privacy is no longer sole and any right of privacy she possesses must be measured accordingly.

Texas urges that, apart from the Fourteenth Amendment, life begins at conception and is present throughout pregnancy, and that, therefore, the State has a compelling interest in protecting that life from and after conception. We need not resolve the difficult question of when life begins. When those trained in the respective disciplines of medicine, philosophy, and theology are unable to arrive at any consensus, the judiciary, at this point in the development of man's knowledge, is not in a position to speculate as to the answer.

It should be sufficient to note briefly the wide divergence of thinking on this most sensitive and difficult question. There has always been strong support for the view that life does not begin until live birth. This was the belief of the Stoics. It appears to be the predominant, though not the unanimous, attitude of the Jewish faith. It may be taken to represent also the position of a large segment of the Protestant community, insofar as that can be ascertained; organized groups that have taken a formal position on the abortion issue have generally regarded abortion as a matter for the conscience of the individual and her family. As we have noted, the common law found greater significance in quickening. Physicians and their scientific colleagues have regarded that event with less interest and have tended to focus either upon conception or upon live birth or upon the interim point at which the fetus becomes "viable," that is, potentially able to live outside the mother's womb, albeit with artificial aid. Viability is usually placed at about seven months (28 weeks) but may occur earlier, even at 24 weeks. . . .

In areas other than criminal abortion the law has been reluctant to endorse any theory that life, as we recognize it, begins before live birth or to accord legal rights to the unborn except in narrowly defined situations and except when the rights are contingent upon live birth. . . . In short, the unborn have never been recognized in the law as persons in the whole sense.

In view of all this, we do not agree that, by adopting one theory of life, Texas may override the rights of the pregnant woman that are at stake. We repeat, however, that the State does have an important and legitimate interest in preserving and protecting the health of the pregnant woman, whether she be a resident of the State or a nonresident who seeks medical consultation and treatment there, and that it has still *another* important and legitimate interest in protecting the potentiality of human life. These interests are separate and distinct. Each grows in substantiality as the woman approaches term and, at a point during pregnancy, each becomes "compelling."

With respect to the State's important and legitimate interest in the health of the mother, the "compelling" point, in the light of present medical knowledge, is at approximately the end of the first trimester. This is so because of the now established medical fact . . . that until the end of the first trimester mortality in abortion is less than mortality in normal childbirth. It follows that, from and after this point, a State may regulate the abortion procedure to the extent that the regulation reasonably relates to the preservation and protection of maternal health. Examples of permissible state regulation in this area are requirements as to the qualifications of the person who is to perform the abortion; as to the licensure of that person; as to the facility in which the procedure is to be performed, that is, whether it must be a hospital or may be a clinic or some other place of less-than-hospital status; as to the licensing of the facility; and the like.

This means, on the other hand, that, for the period of pregnancy prior to this "compelling" point, the attending physician, in consultation with his patient, is free to determine, without regulation by the State, that in his medical judgment the patient's pregnancy should be terminated. If that decision is reached, the judgment may be effectuated by an abortion free of interference by the State.

With respect to the State's important and legitimate interest in potential life, the "compelling" point is at viability. This is so because the fetus then presumably has the capability of meaningful life outside the mother's womb. State regulation protective of fetal life after viability thus has both logical and biological justifications. If the State is interested in protecting fetal life after viability, it may go so far as to proscribe abortion during that period except when it is necessary to preserve the life or health of the mother. . . .

To summarize and repeat:

1 A state criminal abortion statute of the current Texas type, that excepts from criminality only a *life saving* procedure on behalf of the mother, without regard to pregnancy stage and without recognition of the other interests involved, is violative of the Due Process Clause of the Fourteenth Amendment.

(a) For the stage prior to approximately the end of the first trimester, the abortion decision and its effectuation must be left to the medical judgment of the pregnant woman's attending physician.

(b) For the stage subsequent to approximately the end of the first trimester, the State, in promoting its interest in the health of the mother, may, if it chooses, regulate the abortion procedure in ways that are reasonably related to maternal health.

(c) For the stage subsequent to viability the State, in promoting its interest in the potentiality of human life, may, if it chooses, regulate, and even proscribe, abortion except where it is necessary, in appropriate medical judgment, for the preservation of the life or health of the mother.

2 The State may define the term "physician," as it has been employed [here], to mean only a physician currently licensed by the State, and may proscribe any abortion by a person who is not a physician as so defined.

. . . The decision leaves the State free to place increasing restrictions on abortion as the period of pregnancy lengthens, so long as those restrictions are tailored to the recognized state interests. The decision vindicates the right of the physician to administer medical treatment according to his professional judgment up to the points where important state interests provide compelling justifications for intervention. Up to those points the abortion decision in all its aspects is inherently, and primarily, a medical decision, and basic responsibility for it must rest with the physician. If an individual practitioner abuses the privilege of exercising proper medical judgment, the usual remedies, judicial and intraprofessional, are available. . . .

QUESTIONS

1 Justice Blackmun contends that the state's legitimate interest in protecting the health of the mother becomes *compelling* at the end of the first trimester. Does the Court's choice of this particular point as "compelling" have any substantial justification, or is the choice fundamentally arbitrary?

2 Justice Blackmun contends that the state's legitimate interest in protecting potential life becomes *compelling* at the point of viability. Does the Court's choice of this particular point as "compelling" have any substantial justification, or is the choice fundamentally arbitrary?

3 Justice Blackmun *explicitly* disavows entering into philosophical speculation on the problem of the beginning of human life. To what extent could it be said that he *implicitly* takes a philosophical position on this problem?

Opinion in *Planned Parenthood of Southeastern Pennsylvania v. Casey, Governor of Pennsylvania*

Justices
Sandra Day O'Connor,
Anthony M. Kennedy,
and David H. Souter

Sandra Day O'Connor, Anthony M. Kennedy, and David H. Souter are associate justices of the United States Supreme Court. Justice O'Connor was serving on the Arizona Court of Appeals when, in 1981, she became the first woman ever appointed to the Supreme Court. She had earlier served as Arizona assistant attorney general (1965–1969) and Arizona state senator (1969–1975). Justice Kennedy was appointed to the Court in 1988. He had previously spent a number of years in private practice and also served as judge, United States Court of Appeals, Ninth Circuit (1976–1988). Justice Souter received his appointment to the Court in 1990. He had earlier served as attorney general of New Hampshire (1976–1978), associate justice of the New Hampshire Superior Court (1978–1983), and associate justice of the New Hampshire Supreme Court (1983–1990).

At issue in this case is the constitutionality of the various provisions of the Pennsylvania Abortion Control Act. Of principal concern are (1) the informed consent provision, which includes a specification of a twenty-four-hour waiting period, (2) the spousal notification provision, and (3) the parental consent provision. In announcing the judgment of a Court deeply divided on the fundamental issues, Justices O'Connor, Kennedy, and Souter reaffirm the "essential holding" of *Roe v. Wade* while at the same time rejecting the trimester framework so closely identified with that landmark ruling. Committed instead to an "undue burden analysis," the three justices conclude that the informed consent and parental consent provisions are constitutional but the spousal notification provision is not.

I

Liberty finds no refuge in a jurisprudence of doubt. Yet 19 years after our holding that the Constitution protects a woman's right to terminate her pregnancy in its early stages, *Roe* v. *Wade* (1973), that definition of liberty is still questioned. Joining the respondents as *amicus curiae,* the United States, as it has done in five other cases in the last decade, again asks us to overrule *Roe.*

At issue . . . are five provisions of the Pennsylvania Abortion Control Act of 1982 as amended in 1988 and 1989. . . . The Act requires that a woman seeking an abortion give her informed consent prior to the abortion procedure, and specifies that she be provided with certain information at least 24 hours before the abortion is performed. §3205. For a minor to obtain an abortion, the Act requires the informed consent of one of her parents, but provides for a judicial bypass option if the minor does not wish to or cannot obtain a parent's consent. §3206. Another provision of the Act

United States Supreme Court. 112 S.Ct. 2791 (1992).

requires that, unless certain exceptions apply, a married woman seeking an abortion must sign a statement indicating that she has notified her husband of her intended abortion. §3209. The Act exempts compliance with these three requirements in the event of a "medical emergency," which is defined in §3203 of the Act. In addition to the above provisions regulating the performance of abortions, the Act imposes certain reporting requirements on facilities that provide abortion services.

Before any of these provisions took effect, the petitioners, who are five abortion clinics and one physician representing himself as well as a class of physicians who provide abortion services, brought this suit seeking declaratory and injunctive relief. Each provision was challenged as unconstitutional on its face. The District Court entered a preliminary injunction against the enforcement of the regulations, and, after a 3-day bench trial, held all the provisions at issue here unconstitutional, entering a permanent injunction against Pennsylvania's enforcement of them. The Court of Appeals for the Third Circuit affirmed in part and reversed in part, upholding all of the regulations except for the husband notification requirement. . . .

. . . [W]e find it imperative to review once more the principles that define the rights of the woman and the legitimate authority of the State respecting the termination of pregnancies by abortion procedures.

After considering the fundamental constitutional questions resolved by *Roe,* principles of institutional integrity, and the rule of *stare decisis,* we are led to conclude this: the essential holding of *Roe* v. *Wade* should be retained and once again reaffirmed.

It must be stated at the outset and with clarity that *Roe*'s essential holding, the holding we reaffirm, has three parts. First is a recognition of the right of the woman to choose to have an abortion before viability and to obtain it without undue interference from the State. Before viability, the State's interests are not strong enough to support a prohibition of abortion or the imposition of a substantial obstacle to the woman's effective right to elect the procedure. Second is a confirmation of the State's power to restrict abortions after fetal viability, if the law contains exceptions for pregnancies which endanger a woman's life or health. And third is the principle that the State has legitimate interests from the outset of the pregnancy in protecting the health of the woman and the life of the fetus that may become a child. These principles do not contradict one another; and we adhere to each.

II

Constitutional protection of the woman's decision to terminate her pregnancy derives from the Due Process Clause of the Fourteenth Amendment. It declares that no State shall "deprive any person of life, liberty, or property, without due process of law." The controlling word in the case before us is "liberty." . . .

. . . It is a promise of the Constitution that there is a realm of personal liberty which the government may not enter. We have vindicated this principle before. Marriage is mentioned nowhere in the Bill of Rights and interracial marriage was illegal in most States in the 19th century, but the Court was no doubt correct in finding it to be an aspect of liberty protected against state interference by the substantive component of the Due Process Clause. . . .

Neither the Bill of Rights nor the specific practices of States at the time of the adoption of the Fourteenth Amendment marks the outer limits of the substantive sphere of liberty which the Fourteenth Amendment protects. . . . It is settled now, as it was when the Court heard arguments in *Roe* v. *Wade,* that the Constitution places limits on a State's right to interfere with a person's most basic decisions about family and parenthood, as well as bodily integrity.

The inescapable fact is that adjudication of substantive due process claims may call upon the Court in interpreting the Constitution to exercise that same capacity which by tradition courts always have exercised: reasoned judgment. . . .

III

. . . No evolution of legal principle has left *Roe*'s doctrinal footings weaker than they were in 1973. No development of constitutional law since the case was decided has implicitly or explicitly left *Roe* behind as a mere survivor of obsolete constitutional thinking. . . .

We have seen how time has overtaken some of *Roe*'s factual assumptions: advances in maternal health care allow for abortions safe to the mother later in pregnancy than was true in 1973, and advances in neonatal care have advanced viability to a point somewhat earlier. But these facts go only to the scheme of time limits on the realization of competing interests, and the divergences from the factual premises of 1973 have no bearing on the validity of *Roe*'s central holding, that viability marks the earliest point at which the State's interest in fetal life is constitutionally adequate to justify a legislative ban on nontherapeutic abortions. The soundness or unsoundness of that constitutional judgment in no sense turns on whether viability occurs at approximately 28 weeks, as was usual at the time of *Roe,* at 23 to 24 weeks, as it sometimes does today, or at some moment even slightly earlier in pregnancy, as it may if fetal respiratory capacity can somehow be enhanced in the future. Whenever it may occur, the attainment of viability may continue to serve as the critical fact, just as it has done since *Roe* was decided; which is to say that no change in *Roe*'s factual underpinning has left its central holding obsolete, and none supports an argument for overruling it. . . .

The Court's duty in the present case is clear. In 1973, it confronted the already-divisive issue of governmental power to limit personal choice to undergo abortion, for which it provided a new resolution based on the due process guaranteed by the Fourteenth Amendment. Whether or not a new social consensus is developing on that issue, its divisiveness is no less today than in 1973, and pressure to overrule the decision, like pressure to retain it, has grown only more intense. A decision to overrule *Roe*'s essential holding under the existing circumstances would address error, if error there was, at the cost of both profound and unnecessary damage to the Court's legitimacy, and to the Nation's commitment to the rule of law. It is therefore imperative to adhere to the essence of *Roe*'s original decision, and we do so today.

IV

From what we have said so far it follows that it is a constitutional liberty of the woman to have some freedom to terminate her pregnancy. . . .

. . . Liberty must not be extinguished for want of a line that is clear. And it falls to us to give some real substance to the woman's liberty to determine whether to carry her pregnancy to full term.

We conclude the line should be drawn at viability, so that before that time the woman has a right to choose to terminate her pregnancy. We adhere to this principle for two reasons. First . . . is the doctrine of *stare decisis.* Any judicial act of line-drawing may seem somewhat arbitrary, but *Roe* was a reasoned statement, elaborated with great care. We have twice reaffirmed it in the face of great opposition. . . .

The second reason is that the concept of viability, as we noted in *Roe,* is the time at which there is a realistic possibility of maintaining and nourishing a life outside the womb, so that the independent existence of the second life can in reason and all fairness be the object of state protection that now overrides the rights of the woman. . . . We must justify the lines we draw. And there is no line other than viability which is more workable. To be sure, as we have said, there may be some medical developments that affect the precise point of viability, but this is an imprecision within tolerable limits given that the medical community and all those who must apply its discoveries will continue to explore the matter. The viability line also has, as a practical matter, an element of fairness. In some broad sense it might be said that a woman who fails to act before viability has consented to the State's intervention on behalf of the developing child.

The woman's right to terminate her pregnancy before viability is the most central principle of *Roe* v. *Wade.* It is a rule of law and a component of liberty we cannot renounce. . . .

Yet it must be remembered that *Roe* v. *Wade* speaks with clarity in establishing not only the woman's liberty but also the State's "important and legitimate interest in potential life." That portion of the decision in *Roe* has been given too little acknowledgement and implementation by the Court in its subsequent cases. . . .

Roe established a trimester framework to govern abortion regulations. Under this elaborate but rigid construct, almost no regulation at all is permitted during the first trimester of pregnancy; regulations designed to protect the woman's health, but not to further the State's interest in potential life, are permitted during the second trimester; and during the third trimester, when the fetus is viable, prohibitions are permitted provided the life or health of the mother is not at stake. Most of our cases since *Roe* have involved the application of rules derived from the trimester framework.

The trimester framework no doubt was erected to ensure that the woman's right to choose not become so subordinate to the State's interest in promoting fetal life that her choice exists in theory but not in fact. We do not agree, however, that the trimester approach is necessary to accomplish this objective. . . .

Though the woman has a right to choose to terminate or continue her pregnancy before viability, it does not at all follow that the State is prohibited from taking steps to ensure that this choice is thoughtful and informed. Even in the earliest stages of pregnancy, the State may enact rules and regulations designed to encourage her to know that there are philosophic and social arguments of great weight that can be brought to bear in favor of continuing the pregnancy to full term and that there are procedures and institutions to allow adoption of unwanted children as well as a certain degree of state assistance if the mother chooses to raise the child herself. . . .

. . . Numerous forms of state regulation might have the incidental effect of increasing the cost or decreasing the availability of medical care, whether for abortion or any other medical procedure. The fact that a law which serves a valid purpose, one not designed to strike at the right itself, has the incidental effect of making it more difficult or more expensive to procure an abortion cannot be enough to invalidate it. Only where state regulation imposes an undue burden on a woman's ability to make this decision does the power of the State reach into the heart of the liberty protected by the Due Process Clause. . . .

. . . Before viability, *Roe* and subsequent cases treat all governmental attempts to influence a woman's decision on behalf of the potential life within her as unwarranted. This treatment is, in our judgment, incompatible with the recognition that there is a substantial state interest in potential life throughout pregnancy.

The very notion that the State has a substantial interest in potential life leads to the conclusion that not all regulations must be deemed unwarranted. Not all burdens on the right to decide whether to terminate a pregnancy will be undue. In our view, the undue burden standard is the appropriate means of reconciling the State's interest with the woman's constitutionally protected liberty. . . .

. . . We give this summary:

(a) To protect the central right recognized by *Roe* v. *Wade* while at the same time accommodating the State's profound interest in potential life, we will employ the undue burden analysis as explained in this opinion. An undue burden exists, and therefore a provision of law is invalid, if its purpose or effect is to place a substantial obstacle in the path of a woman seeking an abortion before the fetus attains viability.

(b) We reject the rigid trimester framework of *Roe* v. *Wade.* To promote the State's profound interest in potential life, throughout pregnancy the State may take measures to ensure that the woman's choice is informed, and measures designed to advance this interest will not be invalidated as long as their purpose is to persuade the woman to choose childbirth over abortion. These measures must not be an undue burden on the right.

(c) As with any medical procedure, the State may enact regulations to further the health or safety of a woman seeking an abortion. Unnecessary health regulations that have the purpose or effect of presenting a substantial obstacle to a woman seeking an abortion impose an undue burden on the right.

(d) Our adoption of the undue burden analysis does not disturb the central holding of *Roe* v. *Wade,* and we reaffirm that holding. Regardless of whether exceptions are made for particular circumstances, a State may not prohibit any woman from making the ultimate decision to terminate her pregnancy before viability.

(e) We also reaffirm *Roe*'s holding that "subsequent to viability, the State in promoting its interest in the potentiality of human life may, if it chooses, regulate, and even proscribe, abortion except where it is necessary, in appropriate medical judgment, for the preservation of the life or health of the mother."

These principles control our assessment of the Pennsylvania statute, and we now turn to the issue of the validity of its challenged provisions.

V

The Court of Appeals applied what it believed to be the undue burden standard and upheld each of the provisions except for the husband notification requirement. We agree generally with this conclusion, but refine the undue burden analysis in accordance with the principles articulated above. We now consider the separate statutory sections at issue.

[A]

We [now] consider the informed consent requirement. §3205. Except in a medical emergency, the statute requires that at least 24 hours before performing an abortion a physician inform the woman of the nature of the procedure, the health risks of the abortion and of childbirth, and the "probable gestational age of the unborn child." The physician or a qualified nonphysician must inform the woman of the availability of printed materials published by the State describing the fetus and providing information about medical assistance for childbirth, information about child support from the father, and a list of agencies which provide adoption and other services as alternatives to abortion. An abortion may not be performed unless the woman certifies in writing that she has been informed of the availability of these printed materials and has been provided them if she chooses to view them.

Our prior decisions establish that as with any medical procedure, the State may require a woman to give her written informed consent to an abortion. . . .

In *Akron* v. *Akron Center for Reproductive Health, Inc.* (1983) *(Akron I),* we invalidated an ordinance which required that a woman seeking an abortion be provided by her physician with specific information "designed to influence the woman's informed choice between abortion or childbirth." As we later described the *Akron I* holding in *Thornburgh* v. *American College of Obstetricians and Gynecologists* (1986), there were two purported flaws in the Akron ordinance: the information was designed to dissuade the woman from having an abortion and the ordinance imposed "a rigid requirement that a specific body of information be given in all cases, irrespective of the particular needs of the patient. . . ."

. . . It cannot be questioned that psychological well-being is a facet of health. Nor can it be doubted that most women considering an abortion would deem the impact on the fetus relevant, if not dispositive, to the decision. In attempting to ensure that a woman apprehend the full consequences of her decision, the State furthers the legitimate purpose of reducing the risk that a woman may elect an abortion, only to discover later, with devastating psychological consequences, that her decision was not fully informed. If the information the State requires to be made available to the woman is truthful and not misleading, the requirement may be permissible.

We also see no reason why the State may not require doctors to inform a woman seeking an abortion of the availability of materials relating to the consequences to the fetus, even when those consequences have no direct relation to her health. An example illustrates the point. We would think it constitutional for the State to require that in order for there to be informed consent to a kidney transplant operation the recipient must be supplied with information about risks to the donor as well as risks to himself or herself. A requirement that the physician make available information similar to that mandated by the statute here was described in *Thornburgh* as "an outright attempt to wedge the Commonwealth's message discouraging abortion into the privacy of the informed-consent dialogue between the woman and her physician." We conclude, however, that informed choice need not be defined in such narrow terms that all considerations of the effect on the fetus are made irrelevant. As we have made clear, we depart from the holdings of *Akron I* and *Thornburgh* to the extent that we permit a State to further its legitimate goal of protecting the life of the unborn by enacting legislation aimed at ensuring a decision that is mature and informed, even when in so doing the State expresses a preference for childbirth over abortion. In short, requiring that the woman be informed of the availability of information relating to fetal development and the assistance available should she decide to carry the pregnancy to full term is a reasonable measure to insure an informed choice, one which might cause the woman to choose childbirth over abortion. This requirement cannot be considered a substantial obstacle to obtaining an abortion, and, it follows, there is no undue burden. . . .

The Pennsylvania statute also requires us to reconsider the holding in *Akron I* that the State may not require that a physician, as opposed to a qualified assistant, provide information relevant to a woman's informed consent. Since there is no evidence on this record that requiring a doctor to give the information as provided by the statute would amount in practical terms to a substantial obstacle to a woman seeking an abortion, we conclude that it is not an undue burden. . . .

Our analysis of Pennsylvania's 24-hour waiting period between the provision of the information deemed necessary to informed consent and the performance of an abortion under the undue burden standard requires us to reconsider the premise behind the decision in *Akron I* invalidating a parallel requirement. In *Akron I* we said: "Nor are we convinced that the State's legitimate concern that the woman's decision be informed is reasonably served by requiring a 24-hour delay as a matter of course." We consider that conclusion to be wrong. The idea that important decisions will be more informed and deliberate if they follow some period of reflection does not strike us as unreasonable, particularly where the statute directs that important information become part of the background of the decision. The statute, as construed by the Court of Appeals, permits avoidance of the waiting period in the event of a medical emergency and the record evidence shows that in the vast majority of cases, a 24-hour delay does not create any appreciable health risk. In theory, at least, the waiting period is a reasonable measure to implement the State's interest in protecting the life of the unborn, a measure that does not amount to an undue burden.

Whether the mandatory 24-hour waiting period is nonetheless invalid because in practice it is a substantial obstacle to a woman's choice to terminate her pregnancy is a closer question. The findings of fact by the District Court indicate that because of the distances many women must travel to reach an abortion provider, the practical effect will often be a delay of much more than a day because the waiting period requires that a woman seeking an abortion make at least two visits to the doctor. The District Court also found that in many instances this will increase the exposure of women seeking abortions to "the harassment and hostility of anti-abortion protestors demonstrating outside a clinic." As a result, the District Court found that for those women who have the fewest financial resources, those who must travel long distances, and those who have difficulty explaining their whereabouts to husbands, employers, or others, the 24-hour waiting period will be "particularly burdensome."

These findings are troubling in some respects, but they do not demonstrate that the waiting period constitutes an undue burden. . . .

[B]

Section 3209 of Pennsylvania's abortion law provides, except in cases of medical emergency, that no physician shall perform an abortion on a married woman without receiving a signed statement from the woman that she has notified her spouse that she is about to undergo an abortion. The woman has the option of providing an alternative signed statement certifying that her husband is not the man who impregnated her; that her husband could not be located; that the pregnancy is the result of spousal sexual assault which she has reported; or that the woman believes that notifying her husband will cause him or someone else to inflict bodily injury upon her. A physician who performs an abortion on a married woman without receiving the appropriate signed statement will have his or her license revoked, and is liable to the husband for damages. . . .

. . . In well-functioning marriages, spouses discuss important intimate decisions such as whether to bear a child. But there are millions of women in this country who are the victims of regular physical and psychological abuse at the hands of their husbands. Should these women become pregnant, they may have very good reasons for not wishing to inform their husbands of their decision to obtain an abortion. Many may have justifiable fears of physical abuse, but may be no less fearful of the consequences of reporting prior abuse to the Commonwealth of Pennsylvania. Many may have a reasonable fear that notifying their husbands will provoke further instances of child abuse; these women are not exempt from §3209's notification requirement. Many may fear devastating forms of psychological abuse from their husbands, including verbal harassment, threats of future violence, the destruction of possessions, physical confinement to the home, the withdrawal of financial support, or the disclosure of the abortion to family and friends. These methods of psychological abuse may act as even more of a deterrent to notification than the possibility of physical violence, but women who are the victims of the abuse are not exempt from §3209's notification requirement. And many women who are pregnant as a result of sexual assaults by their husbands will be unable to avail themselves of the exception for spousal sexual assault, because the exception requires that the woman have notified law enforcement authorities within 90 days of the assault, and her husband will be notified of her report once an investigation begins. If anything in this field is certain, it is that victims of spousal sexual assault are extremely reluctant to report the abuse to the government; hence, a great many spousal rape victims will not be exempt from the notification requirement imposed by §3209.

The spousal notification requirement is thus likely to prevent a significant number of women from obtaining an abortion. It does not merely make abortions a little more difficult or expensive to obtain; for many women, it will impose a substantial obstacle. We must not blind ourselves to the fact that the significant number of women who fear for their safety and the safety of their children are likely to be deterred from procuring an abortion as surely as if the Commonwealth had outlawed abortion in all cases. . . .

[C]

We next consider the parental consent provision. Except in a medical emergency, an unemancipated young woman under 18 may not obtain an abortion unless she and one of her parents (or guardian) provides informed consent as defined above. If neither a parent nor a guardian provides consent, a court may authorize the performance of an abortion upon a determination that the young woman is mature and capable of giving informed consent and has in fact given her informed consent, or that an abortion would be in her best interests.

We have been over most of this ground before. Our cases establish, and we reaffirm today, that a State may require a minor seeking an abortion to obtain the consent of a parent or guardian, provided that there is an adequate judicial bypass procedure. Under these precedents, in our view, the one-parent consent requirement and judicial bypass procedure are constitutional. . . .

QUESTIONS

1 Justices O'Connor, Kennedy, and Souter endorse the "essential holding" of *Roe v. Wade* yet renounce its trimester framework. To what extent does their analysis represent a significant departure from the holding of the Court in *Roe?*
2 In your view, does a twenty-four-hour waiting period place a "substantial obstacle" in the path of a woman seeking an abortion?
3 Justices O'Connor, Kennedy, and Souter present an analysis of the spousal notification provision of the Pennsylvania Abortion Control Act. Is their analysis essentially correct?

Abortion: A Feminist Perspective

Susan Sherwin

Susan Sherwin is professor of philosophy at Dalhousie University, Halifax, Nova Scotia. She is coeditor of *Moral Problems in Medicine* (1976; 2d ed., 1983) and the author of *No Longer Patient: Feminist Ethics and Health Care* (1992), from which this selection is reprinted. Her published articles include "Feminist and Medical Ethics: Two Different Approaches to Contextual Ethics."

Sherwin defends the right of pregnant women to make abortion decisions by constructing a feminist account of the moral status of the fetus. It is wrongheaded, she argues, to think of a fetus existing as an independent being; the very existence of the fetus is uniquely dependent on a pregnant woman. In Sherwin's view, fetal value is relational, not absolute. The value of a particular fetus is determined by the pregnant woman, in accordance with the particular circumstances of her life. Sherwin also provides a feminist analysis of political opposition to abortion.

A FEMINIST VIEW OF THE FETUS

Because the public debate has been set up as a competition between the rights of women and those of fetuses, feminists have often felt pushed to reject claims of fetal value, in order to protect women's needs. As Kathryn Addelson (1987) has argued, however, viewing abortion in this way "rips it out of the context of women's lives." Other accounts of fetal value are more plausible and less oppressive to women.

On a feminist account fetal development is examined in the context in which it occurs, within women's bodies, rather than in the isolation of imagined abstraction. Fetuses develop in specific pregnancies that occur in the lives of particular women. They are not individuals housed in generic female wombs or full persons at risk only because they are small and subject to the whims of women. Their very existence is relationally defined, reflecting their development within particular women's bodies; that relationship gives those women reason to be concerned about them. Many feminists argue against a perspective that regards the fetus as an independent being and suggest that a more accurate and valuable understanding of pregnancy would involve regarding the pregnant woman "as a biological and social unit" (Rothman 1986, 25).

On this view, fetuses are morally significant, but their status is relational rather than absolute. Unlike other human beings, fetuses do not have any independent existence; their existence is uniquely tied to the support of a specific other. Most nonfeminist accounts have ignored the relational dimension of fetal development and have presumed that the moral status of fetuses could be resolved solely in terms of abstract, metaphysical criteria of personhood as applied to the fetus alone (Tooley 1972; Warren 1973). Throughout much of the nonfeminist literature, commentators argue that some set of properties (such as genetic heritage, moral agency, self-consciousness, language use, or self-determination) will entitle all who possess it to be granted the moral status of persons. They seek some feature by which we can neatly divide the world into moral persons (who are to be valued and protected) and others (who are not entitled to the same group privileges).

This vision, however, misinterprets what is involved in personhood and what is especially valued about persons. Personhood is a social category, not an isolated state. Persons are members of a community, and they should be valued in their concrete, discrete, and different states as specific individuals, not merely as conceptually undifferentiated entities. To be a morally significant category, personhood must involve personality as well as biological integrity.[1] It is not sufficient to consider persons simply as Kantian atoms of rationality, because persons are embodied, conscious beings with particular social histories. Annette Baier has developed a concept of persons as "second persons," which helps explain the sort of social dimension that seems fundamental to any moral notion of personhood:

> A person, perhaps, is best seen as one who was long enough dependent upon other persons to acquire the essential arts of personhood. Persons essentially are *second* persons, who grow up with other persons. . . . The fact that a person has a life *history,* and that a people collectively have a history depends upon the humbler fact that each person has a childhood in which a cultural heritage is transmitted, ready for adolescent rejection and adult discriminating selection and contribution. Persons come after and before other persons (Baier 1985, 84–5).

Persons, in other words, are members of a social community that shapes and values them, and personhood is a relational concept that must be defined in terms of interactions and relationships with others.[2]

Because humans are fundamentally relational beings, it is important to remember that fetuses are characteristically limited in the "relationships" in which they can "participate"; within those relationships, they can make only the most restricted "contributions."[3] After birth human beings are capable of a much wider range of roles in relationships with a broad variety of partners; that very diversity of possibility and experience leads us to focus on the abstraction of the individual as a constant through all these different relationships. Until birth, however, no such variety is possible, so the fetus must be understood as part of a complex entity that includes the woman who currently sustains the fetus and who will, most likely, be principally responsible for it for many years to come.

A fetus is a unique sort of human entity, then, for it cannot form relationships freely with others, and others cannot readily form relationships with it. A fetus has a primary and particularly intimate sort of "relationship" with the woman in whose womb it develops; connections with any other persons are necessarily indirect and must be mediated through the pregnant woman. The relationship that exists between a woman and her fetus is clearly asymmetrical, because she is the only party to it who is capable of even considering whether the interaction should continue; further, the fetus is wholly dependent on the woman who sustains it, whereas she is quite capable of surviving without it.

Most feminist views of what is valuable about persons reflect the social nature of individual existence. No human, especially no fetus, can exist apart from relationships; efforts to speak of the fetus itself, as if it were not inseparable from the woman in whom it develops, are distorting and dishonest. Fetuses have a unique physical status—within and dependent on particular women. That gives them also a unique social status. However much some might prefer it to be otherwise, no one other than the pregnant woman in question can do anything to support or harm a fetus without doing something to the woman who nurtures it. Because of this inexorable biological reality, the responsibility and privilege of determining a fetus's specific social status and value must rest with the woman carrying it.

Many pregnancies occur to women who place a very high value on the lives of the particular fetuses they carry and choose to see their pregnancies through to term, despite the possible risks and costs involved; it would be wrong of anyone to force such a woman to terminate her pregnancy. Other women, or some of these same women at other times, value other things more highly (for example, their freedom, their health, or previous responsibilities that conflict with those generated by the pregnancies), and so they choose not to continue their pregnancies. The value that women ascribe to individual fetuses varies dramatically from case to case and may well change over the course of any particular pregnancy. The fact that fetal lives can neither be sustained nor destroyed without affecting the women who support them implies that whatever value others may attach to fetuses generally or to specific fetuses individually should not be allowed to outweigh the ranking that is assigned to them by the pregnant women themselves.

No absolute value attaches to fetuses apart from their relational status, which is determined in the context of their particular development. This is not the same, however, as saying that they have no value at all or that they have merely instrumental value, as some liberals suggest. The value that women place on their own fetuses is the sort of value that attaches to an emerging human relationship.

Nevertheless, fetuses are not persons, because they have not developed sufficiently in their capacity for social relationships to be persons in any morally significant sense (that is, they are not yet second persons). In this way they differ from newborns, who immediately begin to develop into persons by virtue of their place as subjects in human relationships; newborns are capable of some forms of communication and response. The moral status of fetuses is determined by the nature of their primary relationship and the value that is created there. Therefore, feminist accounts of abortion emphasize the importance of protecting women's rights to continue or to terminate pregnancies as each sees fit.

THE POLITICS OF ABORTION

Feminist accounts explore the connections between particular social policies and the general patterns of power relationships in our society. With respect to abortion in this framework, Mary Daly observes that "one hundred percent of the bishops who oppose the repeal of antiabortion laws are men and one hundred percent of the people who have abortions are women. . . . To be comprehended accurately, they [arguments against abortion] must be seen within the context of sexually hierarchical society" (Daly 1973, 106).

Antiabortion activists appeal to arguments about the unconditional value of human life. When we examine their rhetoric more closely, however, we find other ways of interpreting their agenda. In addition to their campaign to criminalize abortion, most abortion opponents condemn all forms of sexual relations outside of heterosexual marriage, and they tend to support patriarchal patterns of dominance within such marriages. Many are distressed that liberal abortion policies support permissive sexuality by allowing women to "get away with" sex outside of marriage. They perceive that ready access to abortion supports women's independence from men.[4]

Although nonfeminist participants in the abortion debates often discount the significance of its broader political dimensions, both feminists and antifeminists consider them crucial. The intensity of the antiabortion movement correlates closely with the increasing strength of feminism in achieving greater equality for women. The original American campaign against abortion can be traced to the middle of the nineteenth century, that is, to the time of the first significant feminist movement in the United States (Luker 1984). Today abortion is widely perceived as supportive of increased freedom and power for women. The campaign against abortion intensified in the 1970s, which was a period of renewed interest in feminism. As Rosalind Petchesky observes, the campaign rested on some powerful symbols: "To feminists and antifeminists alike, it came to represent the image of the 'emancipated woman' in her contemporary identity, focused on her education and work more than on marriage or childbearing; sexually active outside marriage and outside the disciplinary boundaries of the parental family; independently supporting herself and her children; and consciously espousing feminist ideas" (Petchesky 1985, 241). Clearly, much more than the lives of fetuses is at stake in the power struggle over abortion.

When we place abortion in the larger political context, we see that most of the groups active in the struggle to prohibit abortion also support other conservative measures to maintain the forms of dominance that characterize patriarchy (and often class and racial oppression as well). The movement against abortion is led by the Catholic church and other conservative religious institutions, which explicitly endorse not only fetal rights but also male dominance in the home and the church. Most opponents of abortion also oppose virtually all forms of birth control and all forms of sexuality other than monogamous, reproductive sex; usually, they also resist having women assume positions of authority in the dominant public institutions (Luker 1984). Typically, antiabortion activists support conservative economic measures that protect the interests of the privileged classes of society and ignore the needs of the oppressed and disadvantaged (Petchesky 1985). Although they stress their commitment to preserving life, many systematically work to dismantle key social programs that provide life necessities to the underclass. Moreover, some current campaigns against abortion retain elements of the racism that dominated the North American abortion literature in the early years of the twentieth century, wherein abortion was opposed on the grounds that it amounted to racial suicide on the part of whites.[5]

In the eyes of its principal opponents, then, abortion is not an isolated practice; their opposition to abortion is central to a set of social values that runs counter to feminism's objectives. Hence antiabortion activists generally do not offer alternatives to abortion that support feminist interests in overturning the patterns of oppression that confront women. Most deny that there are any legitimate grounds for abortion, short of the need to save a woman's life—and some are not even persuaded by this criterion (Nicholson 1977). They believe that any pregnancy can and should be endured. If the mother is unable or unwilling to care for the child after birth, then they assume that adoption can be easily arranged.

It is doubtful, however, that adoptions are possible for every child whose mother cannot care for it. The world abounds with homeless orphans; even in the industrialized West, where there is a waiting list for adoption of healthy (white) babies, suitable homes cannot always be found for troubled adolescents; inner-city, AIDS babies, or many of the multiply handicapped children whose parents may have tried to care for them but whose marriages broke under the strain.

Furthermore, even if an infant were born healthy and could be readily adopted, we must recognize that surrendering one's child for adoption is an extremely difficult act for most women. The bond that commonly forms between women and their fetuses over the full term of pregnancy is intimate and often intense; many women find that it is not easily broken after birth. Psychologically, for many women adoption is a far more difficult response to unwanted pregnancies than abortion. Therefore, it is misleading to describe pregnancy as merely a nine-month commitment; for most women, seeing a pregnancy through to term involves a lifetime of responsibility and involvement with the resulting child and, in the overwhelming majority of cases, disproportionate burden on the woman through the child-rearing years. An ethics that cares about women would recognize that abortion is often the only acceptable recourse for them.

NOTES

1 This apt phrasing is taken from Petchesky (1985), 342.

2 E.g., Held (1987) argues that personhood is a social status, created by the work of mothering persons.

3 Fetuses are almost wholly individuated by the women who bear them. The fetal "contributions" to the relationship are defined by the projections and interpretations of the pregnant woman in the latter stages of pregnancy, if she chooses to perceive fetal movements in purposeful ways (e.g., "it likes classical music, spicy food, exercise").

4 See Luker (1984), esp. chaps. 6 and 7, and Petchesky (1985), esp. chaps. 7 and 8, for documentation of these associations in the U.S. antiabortion movement and Collins (1985), esp. chap. 4, and McLaren and McLaren (1986) for evidence of similar trends in the Canadian struggle.

5 See McLaren and McLaren (1986) and Petchesky (1985).

REFERENCES

Addelson, Kathryn Pyne. 1987. "Moral Passages." In *Women and Moral Theory,* ed. Eva Feder Kittay and Diana T. Meyers. Totowa, N.J.: Rowman & Littlefield.

Baier, Annette C. 1985. *Postures of the Mind: Essays on Mind and Morals.* Minneapolis: University of Minnesota Press.

Collins, Anne. 1985. *The Big Evasion: Abortion, the Issue That Won't Go Away.* Toronto: Lester & Orpen Dennys.

Daly, Mary. 1973. *Beyond God the Father: Toward a Philosophy of Women's Liberation.* Boston: Beacon Press.

Held, Virginia. 1987. "Feminism and Moral Theory." In *Women and Moral Theory. See* Addelson 1987.

Luker, Kristin. 1984. *Abortion and the Politics of Motherhood.* Berkeley: University of California Press.

McLaren, Angus, and Arlene Tigar McLaren. 1986. *The Bedroom and the State: The Changing Practices and Politics of Contraception and Abortion in Canada, 1880–1980.* Toronto: McClelland & Stewart.

Nicholson, Susan T. 1977. "The Roman Catholic Doctrine of Therapeutic Abortion." In *Feminism and Philosophy,* ed. Mary Vetterling-Braggin, Frederick A. Elliston, and Jane English. Totowa, N.J.: Littlefield, Adams & Co.

Petchesky, Rosalind Pollack. 1985. *Abortion and Woman's Choice: The State, Sexuality, and Reproductive Freedom.* Boston: Northeastern University Press.

Rothman, Barbara Katz. 1986. "Commentary: When a Pregnant Woman Endangers Her Fetus." *Hastings Center Report* 16(1): 25.

Tooley, Michael. 1972. "Abortion and Infanticide." *Philosophy and Public Affairs* 2(1): 37–65.

Warren, Mary Anne. 1973. "On the Moral and Legal Status of Abortion." *The Monist* 57: 43–61.

QUESTIONS

1 Do you agree with Sherwin's account of fetal value?

2 Does Sherwin provide an accurate analysis of political opposition to abortion?

SUGGESTED ADDITIONAL READINGS FOR CHAPTER 1

BOLTON, MARTHA BRANDT: "Responsible Women and Abortion Decisions." In Onora O'Neill and William Ruddick, eds., *Having Children: Philosophical and Legal Reflections on Parenthood.* New York: Oxford University Press, 1979, pp. 40–51. In defending a moderate view on the morality of abortion, Bolton emphasizes the importance of contextual features in the life of a pregnant woman. She argues that the decision to bear a child must "fit" into a woman's life and make sense in terms of her responsibilities to her family and to the larger society.

BRODY, BARUCH: "On the Humanity of the Foetus." In Robert L. Perkins, ed., *Abortion: Pro and Con.* Cambridge, Mass.: Schenkman, 1974, pp. 69–90. Brody critically examines various proposals for "drawing the line" on the humanity of the fetus, ultimately suggesting that the most defensible view would draw the line at the point where fetal brain activity begins.

ENGELHARDT, H. TRISTRAM, JR.: "The Ontology of Abortion." *Ethics,* vol. 84, April 1974, pp. 217–234. Engelhardt focuses attention on the issue of "whether or to what extent the fetus is a person." He argues that, strictly speaking, a human person is not present until the later stages of infancy. However, he finds the point of viability significant in that, with viability, an infant can play the social role of "child" and thus be treated "as if it were a person."

FEINBERG, JOEL, ed.: *The Problem of Abortion,* 2d ed. Belmont, Calif.: Wadsworth, 1984. This excellent anthology features a wide range of articles on the moral justifiability of abortion.

LANGERAK, EDWARD A.: "Abortion: Listening to the Middle." *Hastings Center Report,* vol. 9, October 1979, pp. 24–28. Langerak suggests a theoretical framework for a moderate view that incorporates two "widely shared beliefs": (1) that there is something about the fetus *itself* that makes abortion morally problematic and (2) that late abortions are significantly more problematic than early abortions.

NOONAN, JOHN T., JR.: "An Almost Absolute Value in History." In John T. Noonan, Jr., ed., *The Morality of Abortion: Legal and Historical Perspectives.* Cambridge, Mass.: Harvard University Press, 1970, pp. 51–59. In this well-known statement of the conservative view on the morality of abortion, Noonan argues that conception is the only objectively based and nonarbitrary point at which to "draw the line" between the nonhuman and the human.

POJMAN, LOUIS P., and FRANCIS J. BECKWITH, eds.: *The Abortion Controversy: A Reader.* Boston: Jones and Bartlett, 1994. The articles in this long anthology are organized under eight headings, including "Evaluations of *Roe v. Wade,*" "Personhood Arguments on Abortion," and "Feminist Arguments on Abortion."

ROSS, STEVEN L.: "Abortion and the Death of the Fetus." *Philosophy and Public Affairs,* vol. 11, Summer 1982, pp. 232–245. Ross draws a distinction between abortion as the termination of pregnancy and abortion as the termination of the life of the fetus. He proceeds to defend abortion in the latter sense, insisting that it is justifiable for a woman to desire not only the termination of pregnancy but also the death of the fetus.

STONE, JIM: "Why Potentiality Matters." *Canadian Journal of Philosophy,* vol. 17, December 1987, pp. 815–830. Stone argues that a fetal right to life can be effectively grounded in the fact that a fetus is *potentially* an adult human being.

THOMSON, JUDITH JARVIS: "A Defense of Abortion." *Philosophy and Public Affairs,* vol. 1, Fall 1971, pp. 47–66. In this widely discussed article, Thomson attempts to "moderate the conservative view." For the sake of argument, she grants the premise that the fetus (from conception) is a person. Still, she argues, abortion is morally justified in a significant range of cases.

TOOLEY, MICHAEL: *Abortion and Infanticide.* New York: Oxford University Press, 1983. In this long book, Tooley defends the liberal view on the morality of abortion. He insists that the question of the morality of abortion cannot be satisfactorily resolved "in isolation from the questions of the morality of infanticide and of the killing of nonhuman animals."

CHAPTER 2

Euthanasia and Physician-Assisted Suicide

The mercy killing of patients by physicians, whether called "active euthanasia" (as it is here) or simply "euthanasia," is a topic of long-standing controversy. Can active euthanasia—especially in response to the request of a competent patient—be morally justified? Should it be legalized? Parallel questions can be raised about physician-assisted suicide, a closely related topic that has generated intense discussion in the 1990s. This chapter is designed to deal with ethical and social policy questions about active euthanasia and physician-assisted suicide.

EUTHANASIA: SOME IMPORTANT DISTINCTIONS

There is both a narrow and a broad sense of *euthanasia,* and the difference between the two is best understood by reference to the categories of killing and allowing to die, although the distinction between killing and allowing to die is itself a controversial one. Understood in the narrow sense, the category of euthanasia is limited to mercy *killing.* Thus, if a physician administers a lethal dose of a drug to a terminally ill patient (on grounds of mercy), this act is a paradigm of euthanasia. On the other hand, if a physician *allows a patient to die* (e.g., by withholding or withdrawing a respirator), this does not count as euthanasia. Although the narrow sense of euthanasia is becoming increasingly common, many writers still use the word in the broad sense. Understood in the broad sense, the category of euthanasia encompasses both killing and allowing to die (on grounds of mercy). Those who employ the broad sense of euthanasia typically distinguish between *active* euthanasia (i.e., killing) and *passive* euthanasia (i.e., allowing to die).

One other distinction is of central importance in discussions of euthanasia. *Voluntary* euthanasia proceeds in response to the (informed) request of a competent patient. *Nonvoluntary* euthanasia involves an individual who is incompetent to give consent. The possibility of nonvoluntary euthanasia might arise with regard to adults who have for any number of reasons (e.g., Alzheimer's disease) lost their decision-making capacity, and it might arise with regard to newborn infants, children, and severely retarded adults. Both voluntary and nonvoluntary euthanasia may be further distinguished from *involuntary* euthanasia, which entails acting *against the will* or, at any rate, without the permission of a competent person. (Some writers use the phrase "involuntary euthanasia" to mean what has been identified here as "nonvoluntary euthanasia.")

If the voluntary/nonvoluntary distinction is combined with the active/passive distinction, four types of euthanasia can be distinguished: (1) voluntary active euthanasia, (2) nonvoluntary active euthanasia, (3) voluntary passive euthanasia, and (4) nonvoluntary passive euthanasia. Contemporary debate, however, focuses on the moral legitimacy of active euthanasia, especially voluntary active euthanasia. The moral legitimacy of passive euthanasia, whether voluntary or nonvoluntary, is relatively uncontroversial. The idea that it can be morally appropriate to withhold or withdraw life-sustaining treatment is firmly established, at least in the United States. This is not to say, of course, that there are no issues related to the specific conditions that must be satisfied in order for the withholding or withdrawing of life-sustaining treatment to be morally appropriate. In particular, there are areas of controversy related to withholding or withdrawing life-sustaining treatment from incompetent patients in various categories (e.g., severely impaired newborn infants).

ADVANCE DIRECTIVES

Depending on a patient's particular circumstances, life-sustaining treatment can take a variety of forms—for example, mechanical respiration, cardiopulmonary resuscitation, kidney dialysis, surgery, antibiotics, and artificial nutrition and hydration. The ordinary presumption is that a competent adult has both a moral and a legal right to refuse any medical treatment, including life-sustaining treatment. However, the rigors of incurable illness and the dying process frequently deprive previously competent patients of their decision-making capacity. How can a person best ensure that his or her personal wishes with regard to life-sustaining treatment (in various possible circumstances) will be honored even if decision-making capacity is lost? Although communication of one's attitudes and preferences to one's physician, family, and friends surely provides some measure of protection, it is frequently asserted that the most effective protection comes through the formation of *advance directives*.

There are two basic types of advance directives, and each has legal status in a large majority (if not all) of the states. In executing an *instructional* directive, a person specifies instructions about his or her care in the event that decision-making capacity is lost. Such a directive, especially when it deals specifically with a person's wishes regarding life-sustaining treatment in various possible circumstances, is commonly called a "living will." In executing a *proxy* directive, a person specifies a surrogate decision maker to make health care decisions for him or her in the event that decision-making capacity is lost. The legal mechanism for executing a proxy directive is called a "durable power of attorney" for health care. Since purging ambiguities from even the most explicit written directives is difficult, as is foreseeing all the contingencies that might give rise to a need for treatment decisions, many commentators recommend the execution of a durable power of attorney for health care even if a person has already executed a living will.

THE MORALITY OF ACTIVE EUTHANASIA

James Rachels argues in this chapter for the moral legitimacy of active euthanasia. One of his central claims is that there is no morally significant distinction between killing and allowing to die. Daniel Callahan, by way of contrast, defends the coherence and moral importance of the distinction between killing and allowing to die. Callahan is opposed to active euthanasia and argues that killing patients is incompatible with the role of the physician in society. In his view, the power of the physician is appropriately used to cure or comfort but must never be used to kill. Dan W. Brock, in turn, rejects the idea that active euthanasia is incompatible with the fundamental professional responsibilities of a physician. Further, in stating a case for the moral legitimacy of voluntary active euthanasia, Brock appeals to the centrality of two fundamental values—individual autonomy (self-determination) and individual well-being.

Those, like Rachels, who argue for the moral legitimacy of active euthanasia usually emphasize considerations of humaneness. When the intent of argument (as in the case of Brock) is to provide a defense of *voluntary* active euthanasia, the humanitarian appeal is typically conjoined with an appeal to the primacy of individual autonomy. Thus the overall case for the moral legitimacy of voluntary active euthanasia incorporates two basic arguments: (1) It is cruel and inhumane to refuse the plea of a terminally ill person for his or her life to be mercifully ended in order to avoid future suffering and/or indignity. (2) Individual choice should be respected to the extent that it does not result in harm to others; since no one is harmed by terminally ill patients' undergoing active euthanasia, a decision to have one's life ended in this fashion should be respected.

Those who argue against the moral legitimacy of active euthanasia typically rest their case on one or all of the following claims: (1) Killing an innocent person is intrinsically wrong. (2) Killing is incompatible with the professional responsibilities of the physician. (3) Any systematic acceptance of active euthanasia would lead to detrimental social consequences (e.g., via a lessening of respect for human life.) This third line of argument is the one that is typically most emphasized in discussions concerning the legalization of active euthanasia.

ACTIVE EUTHANASIA AND SOCIAL POLICY

Should active euthanasia be legalized? If so, in what form or forms and with what safeguards? Although active euthanasia is presently illegal in all fifty states, proposals for its legalization have been recurrently advanced. Most commonly, it is the legalization of *voluntary* active euthanasia that has been proposed.

There are some who consider active euthanasia in any form intrinsically immoral (sometimes on overtly religious grounds) and for this reason are opposed to the legalization of voluntary active euthanasia. Others are opposed to legalization because of their conviction that physicians in particular should not kill. Still others, such as Stephen G. Potts in this chapter, do not necessarily object to individual acts of voluntary active euthanasia, but still stand opposed to any social policy that would permit its practice. The concern is with the adverse social consequences of legalization. It is said, for example, that the risk of abuse is too great, that legalization would create a disincentive for the availability of supportive services for the dying, and that public trust and confidence in physicians would be undermined. Another consequentialist concern is embodied in the frequently made "slippery slope" argument: the legalization of *voluntary* active euthanasia would lead us down a slippery slope to the legalization of *nonvoluntary* (and perhaps *involuntary*) euthanasia. Those who support the legalization of voluntary active euthanasia recognize that some bad consequences may result from legalization. However, they typically seek to establish that potential dangers are either overstated or can be minimized with appropriate safeguards.

Consider, for a moment, some of the issues that might arise in specifying limits for a practice of voluntary active euthanasia. Would we want to restrict the practice to patients who are terminally ill (according to some definition), to patients who are experiencing unbearable suffering (according to some definition), or to patients who are *both* terminally ill and experiencing unbearable suffering? Would we want to insist that a patient be competent at the time he or she undergoes active euthanasia, or would we want to allow for the possibility of active euthanasia in accordance with an advance directive?

Voluntary active euthanasia is a well-established practice in The Netherlands (often referred to simply as "Holland"). One of the interesting aspects of the Dutch system is the fact that there is a requirement that active euthanasia be available only if the patient is experiencing unbearable (and unrelievable) suffering, but there is no requirement that the patient be terminally ill. Another interesting feature of the system as it actually operates is the apparent acceptance of an advance directive principle. That is, active euthanasia is sometimes provided for patients who have become incompetent but who had clearly expressed their wishes while competent.[1] In one of this chapter's readings, Margaret P. Battin provides a discussion of the Dutch practice of voluntary active euthanasia. Although she believes that the practice is morally appropriate in relation to existing social conditions in Holland, she cites many important differences between the United States and Holland and ultimately concludes that "the United States is in many respects an untrustworthy candidate for practicing active euthanasia." In Battin's view, the United States is better suited for the practice of physician-assisted suicide.

PHYSICIAN-ASSISTED SUICIDE AND SOCIAL POLICY

Underlying a consideration of physician-assisted suicide are philosophical questions about suicide itself, questions that cannot be fully addressed in this chap-

---

[1]Norman L. Cantor, "Review Essay: *Regulating Death,*" *Criminal Justice Ethics,* vol. 12, Winter/Spring 1993, p. 73.

ter.[2] Suicide, according to a more-or-less standard definition, is the intentional termination of one's own life. Under what conditions, if at all, is suicide morally acceptable? Classical literature on the morality of suicide provides a number of sources who issue a strong moral condemnation of suicide. The traditional arguments against suicide are both religiously based and philosophical in character. Saint Thomas Aquinas (1225–1274), for example, argues that suicide is to be condemned not only because it violates our duty to God but also because it violates the natural law, and, moreover, because it injures the community. A contrasting point of view has a more contemporary ring but is not without support in the classical literature: suicide is morally acceptable to the extent that it does no substantial damage to the interests of other individuals.

Closely associated with the issue of the morality of suicide is the issue of the rationality of suicide. Clearly, many suicides are irrational, the product of disordered thinking. But it is sometimes asserted that a suicidal intention is necessarily irrational, thus a symptom of mental illness and incompetence. In other words, it is impossible for a competent adult to have a suicidal intention. Although this point seems to be built into some psychiatric theories, it is considered by many philosophers to be an implausible contention. Consider in particular the case of a terminally ill patient experiencing intense suffering with no realistic prospect of relief. If it is correct to say that such a person is better off dead, then it is hard to deny that suicide could be a rational choice. Of course, none of this is meant to deny the distorting effects that depression can exercise over human judgment.

Physician-assisted suicide usually involves a physician in one or both of the following activities: (1) providing *information* to a patient about how to commit suicide in an effective manner; (2) providing the *means* necessary for an effective suicide (most commonly, by writing a prescription for a lethal amount of medication). Other possible modes of physician assistance include providing moral support for the patient's decision, "supervising" the actual suicide, and helping the patient carry out the necessary physical actions. For example, a very frail patient might need a certain amount of physical assistance just to take pills.

In both physician-assisted suicide and voluntary active euthanasia, a physician plays an active role in bringing about the death of a patient. However, at face value, there is a notable difference between the two. In voluntary active euthanasia, it is the physician who ultimately kills the patient. In physician-assisted suicide, it is the patient who ultimately kills himself or herself, albeit with the assistance of the physician. It is a controversial issue whether this difference in terms of ultimate causal agency can serve as a basis for the claim that there is a morally significant difference between physician-assisted suicide and voluntary active euthanasia.

Should the practice of physician-assisted suicide be permitted in our society? Although many of the arguments advanced against the legalization of voluntary active

---

[2]For one avenue into the philosophical literature on suicide, see M. Pabst Battin and David J. Mayo, eds., *Suicide: The Philosophical Issues* (New York: St. Martin's Press, 1980). This valuable collection of articles includes material on the concept of suicide, the morality of suicide, and the rationality of suicide.

euthanasia can also be advanced against the legalization of physician-assisted suicide, there may be good reason to believe that there is far less risk of abuse involved in the legalization of physician-assisted suicide. This point of view is embraced by David T. Watts and Timothy Howell in one of this chapter's readings. These two physicians recommend the legalization of physician-assisted suicide, although they do not favor allowing a physician to "supervise" or directly aid a patient in committing suicide. They would restrict physicians to providing information about suicide and writing prescriptions for a lethal amount of medication. According to another point of view, since terminally ill patients are already free to refuse hydration and nutrition, and thereby bring about death, there is no compelling need to legalize either voluntary active euthanasia or physician-assisted suicide.[3]

One concrete model for the legalization of physician-assisted suicide has emerged in Oregon. In November 1994, voters in Oregon approved by a margin of 52 to 48 percent a ballot initiative—Measure 16—under the heading of The Oregon Death with Dignity Act. Measure 16 was designed to permit physicians in Oregon to prescribe lethal drugs for terminally ill adult patients who want to end their own lives. In order for a patient to be eligible for such assistance, the attending physician must determine that the patient has a terminal illness and is expected to die within six months, and a consulting physician must confirm the diagnosis and prognosis. The following requirements are also stipulated: (1) The patient must make an initial oral request, reiterate the oral request after fifteen days have passed, and also submit a written request, supported by two witnesses. (2) Before writing the prescription, the attending physician must wait at least fifteen days after the patient's initial request and at least forty-eight hours after the written request. (3) The attending physician must fully inform the patient with regard to diagnosis and prognosis, as well as feasible alternatives—including comfort care, hospice care, and pain control. (4) Both the attending physician and the consulting physician must certify that the patient is "capable" (i.e., has decision-making capacity), is acting voluntarily, and has made an informed choice. (5) If either physician believes that the patient's judgment might be impaired (e.g., by depression), the patient must be referred for counseling. Measure 16 also provides that the attending physician and others may be present when the patient takes the lethal dose.

Constitutional questions about physician-assisted suicide arise from two different directions. Oregon's voter-approved Measure 16 did not go into effect as originally scheduled because its constitutionality was challenged in federal court. Indeed, in August 1995 a United States District Court ruled that the measure was unconstitutional, citing concerns about inadequate safeguards. On the other hand, many states presently have statutes that ban assisted suicide, and these statutes have sometimes been challenged on constitutional grounds. In one important case, *Compassion in Dying v. State of Washington,* a three-judge panel of the United States Court of Appeals, Ninth Circuit, ruled that a statute prohibiting "promoting a suicide attempt"

[3]See, for example, James L. Bernat, Bernard Gert, and R. Peter Mogielnicki, "Patient Refusal of Hydration and Nutrition: An Alternative to Physician-Assisted Suicide or Voluntary Active Euthanasia," *Archives of Internal Medicine,* vol. 153, December 27, 1993, pp. 2723–2728.

was constitutional. The majority opinion of this three-judge panel is reprinted in this chapter. Subsequently, however, the case was reheard by the entire Court of Appeals, and the statute at issue was declared unconstitutional.

Thomas A. Mappes

Active and Passive Euthanasia

James Rachels

James Rachels is professor of philosophy at the University of Alabama at Birmingham. Specializing in ethics, he is the author of *The Elements of Moral Philosophy* (1986; 2d ed., 1993), *The End of Life: Euthanasia and Morality* (1986), and *Created from Animals: The Moral Implications of Darwinism* (1990).

In this classic article, Rachels identifies the "conventional doctrine" on the morality of euthanasia as the doctrine that allows passive euthanasia but does not allow active euthanasia. He then argues that the conventional doctrine may be challenged for four reasons. First, active euthanasia is in many cases more humane than passive euthanasia. Second, the conventional doctrine leads to decisions concerning life and death on irrelevant grounds. Third, the doctrine rests on a distinction between killing and letting die that itself has no moral importance. Fourth, the most common argument in favor of the doctrine is invalid.

The distinction between active and passive euthanasia is thought to be crucial for medical ethics. The idea is that it is permissible, at least in some cases, to withhold treatment and allow a patient to die, but it is never permissible to take any direct action designed to kill the patient. This doctrine seems to be accepted by most doctors, and it is endorsed in a statement adopted by the House of Delegates of the American Medical Association on December 4, 1973:

> The intentional termination of the life of one human being by another—mercy killing— is contrary to that for which the medical profession stands and is contrary to the policy of the American Medical Association.
>
> The cessation of the employment of extraordinary means to prolong the life of the body when there is irrefutable evidence that biological death is imminent is the decision of the patient and/or his immediate family. The advice and judgment of the physician should be freely available to the patient and/or his immediate family.

However, a strong case can be made against this doctrine. In what follows, I will set out some of the relevant arguments, and urge doctors to reconsider their views on this matter.

Reprinted with permission from *The New England Journal of Medicine*, vol. 292, no. 2 (January 9, 1975), pp. 78–80.

To begin with a familiar type of situation, a patient who is dying of incurable cancer of the throat is in terrible pain, which can no longer be satisfactorily alleviated. He is certain to die within a few days, even if present treatment is continued, but he does not want to go on living for those days since the pain is unbearable. So he asks the doctor for an end to it, and his family joins in the request.

Suppose the doctor agrees to withhold treatment, as the conventional doctrine says he may. The justification for his doing so is that the patient is in terrible agony, and since he is going to die anyway, it would be wrong to prolong his suffering needlessly. But now notice this. If one simply withholds treatment, it may take the patient longer to die, and so he may suffer more than he would if more direct action were taken and a lethal injection given. This fact provides strong reason for thinking that, once the initial decision not to prolong his agony has been made, active euthanasia is actually preferable to passive euthanasia, rather than the reverse. To say otherwise is to endorse the option that leads to more suffering rather than less, and is contrary to the humanitarian impulse that prompts the decision not to prolong his life in the first place.

Part of my point is that the process of being "allowed to die" can be relatively slow and painful, whereas being given a lethal injection is relatively quick and painless. Let me give a different sort of example. In the United States about one in 600 babies is born with Down's syndrome. Most of these babies are otherwise healthy—that is, with only the usual pediatric care, they will proceed to an otherwise normal infancy. Some, however, are born with congenital defects such as intestinal obstructions that require operations if they are to live. Sometimes, the parents and the doctor will decide not to operate, and let the infant die. Anthony Shaw describes what happens then:

> . . . When surgery is denied [the doctor] must try to keep the infant from suffering while natural forces sap the baby's life away. As a surgeon whose natural inclination is to use the scalpel to fight off death, standing by and watching a salvageable baby die is the most emotionally exhausting experience I know. It is easy at a conference, in a theoretical discussion, to decide that such infants should be allowed to die. It is altogether different to stand by in the nursery and watch as dehydration and infection wither a tiny being over hours and days. This is a terrible ordeal for me and the hospital staff—much more so than for the parents who never set foot in the nursery.[1]

I can understand why some people are opposed to all euthanasia, and insist that such infants must be allowed to live. I think I can also understand why other people favor destroying these babies quickly and painlessly. But why should anyone favor letting "dehydration and infection wither a tiny being over hours and days?" The doctrine that says that a baby may be allowed to dehydrate and wither, but may not be given an injection that would end its life without suffering, seems so patently cruel as to require no further refutation. The strong language is not intended to offend, but only to put the point in the clearest possible way.

My second argument is that the conventional doctrine leads to decisions concerning life and death made on irrelevant grounds.

Consider again the case of the infants with Down's syndrome who need operations for congenital defects unrelated to the syndrome to live. Sometimes, there is no operation, and the baby dies, but when there is no such defect, the baby lives on. Now, an operation such as that to remove an intestinal obstruction is not prohibitively difficult. The reason why such operations are not performed in these cases is, clearly, that the child has Down's syndrome and the parents and doctor judge that because of that fact it is better for the child to die.

But notice that this situation is absurd, no matter what view one takes of the lives and potentials of such babies. If the life of such an infant is worth preserving, what does it matter if it needs a simple operation? Or, if one thinks it better that such a baby should not live on, what difference does it make that it happens to have an unobstructed intestinal tract? In either case, the matter of life and death is being decided on irrelevant grounds. It is the Down's syndrome, and not the intestines, that is the issue. The matter should be decided, if at all, on that basis, and not be allowed to depend on the essentially irrelevant question of whether the intestinal tract is blocked.

What makes this situation possible, of course, is the idea that when there is an intestinal blockage, one can "let the baby die," but when there is no such defect there is nothing that can be done, for one must not "kill" it. The fact that this idea leads to such results as deciding life or death on irrelevant grounds is another good reason why the doctrine should be rejected.

One reason why so many people think that there is an important moral difference between active and passive euthanasia is that they think killing someone is morally worse than letting someone die. But is it? Is killing, in itself, worse than letting die? To investigate this issue, two cases may be considered that are exactly alike except that one involves killing whereas the other involves letting someone die. Then, it can be asked whether this difference makes any difference to the moral assessments. It is important that the cases be exactly alike, except for this one difference, since otherwise one cannot be confident that it is this difference and not some other that accounts for any variation in the assessments of the two cases. So, let us consider this pair of cases:

In the first, Smith stands to gain a large inheritance if anything should happen to his six-year-old cousin. One evening while the child is taking his bath, Smith sneaks into the bathroom and drowns the child, and then arranges things so that it will look like an accident.

In the second, Jones also stands to gain if anything should happen to his six-year-old cousin. Like Smith, Jones sneaks in planning to drown the child in his bath. However, just as he enters the bathroom Jones sees the child slip and hit his head, and fall face down in the water. Jones is delighted; he stands by, ready to push the child's head back under if it is necessary, but it is not necessary. With only a little thrashing about the child drowns all by himself, "accidentally," as Jones watches and does nothing.

Now Smith killed the child, whereas Jones "merely" let the child die. That is the only difference between them. Did either man behave better, from a moral point of view? If the difference between killing and letting die were in itself a morally important matter, one should say that Jones's behavior was less reprehensible than

Smith's. But does one really want to say that? I think not. In the first place, both men acted from the same motive, personal gain, and both had exactly the same end in view when they acted. It may be inferred from Smith's conduct that he is a bad man, although that judgment may be withdrawn or modified if certain further facts are learned about him—for example, that he is mentally deranged. But would not the very same thing be inferred about Jones from his conduct? And would not the same further considerations also be relevant to any modification of this judgment? Moreover, suppose Jones pleaded, in his own defense, "After all, I didn't do anything except just stand there and watch the child drown. I didn't kill him; I only let him die." Again, if letting die were in itself less bad than killing, this defense should have at least some weight. But it does not. Such a "defense" can only be regarded as a grotesque perversion of moral reasoning. Morally speaking, it is no defense at all.

Now, it may be pointed out, quite properly, that the cases of euthanasia with which doctors are concerned are not like this at all. They do not involve personal gain or the destruction of normally healthy children. Doctors are concerned only with cases in which the patient's life is of no further use to him, or in which the patient's life has become or will soon become a terrible burden. However, the point is the same in these cases: the bare difference between killing and letting die does not, in itself, make a moral difference. If a doctor lets a patient die, for humane reasons, he is in the same moral position as if he had given the patient a lethal injection for humane reasons. If his decision was wrong—if, for example, the patient's illness was in fact curable—the decision would be equally regrettable no matter which method was used to carry it out. And if the doctor's decision was the right one, the method used is not in itself important.

The AMA policy statement isolates the crucial issue very well; the crucial issue is "the intentional termination of the life of one human being by another." But after identifying this issue, and forbidding "mercy killing," the statement goes on to deny that the cessation of treatment is the intentional termination of a life. This is where the mistake comes in, for what is the cessation of treatment, in these circumstances, if it is not "the intentional termination of the life of one human being by another?" Of course, it is exactly that, and if it were not, there would be no point to it.

Many people will find this judgment hard to accept. One reason, I think, is that it is very easy to conflate the question of whether killing is, in itself, worse than letting die, with the very different question of whether most actual cases of killing are more reprehensible than most actual cases of letting die. Most actual cases of killing are clearly terrible (think, for example, of all the murders reported in the newspapers), and one hears of such cases every day. On the other hand, one hardly ever hears of a case of letting die, except for the actions of doctors who are motivated by humanitarian reasons. So one learns to think of killing in a much worse light than of letting die. But this does not mean that there is something about killing that makes it in itself worse than letting die, for it is not the bare difference between killing and letting die that makes the difference in these cases. Rather, the other factors—the murderer's motive of personal gain, for example, contrasted with the doctor's humanitarian motivation—account for different reactions to the different cases.

I have argued that killing is not in itself any worse than letting die; if my contention is right, it follows that active euthanasia is not any worse than passive euthanasia. What arguments can be given on the other side? The most common, I believe, is the following:

"The important difference between active and passive euthanasia is that, in passive euthanasia, the doctor does not do anything to bring about the patient's death. The doctor does nothing, and the patient dies of whatever ills already afflict him. In active euthanasia, however, the doctor does something to bring about the patient's death: he kills him. The doctor who gives the patient with cancer a lethal injection has himself caused his patient's death; whereas if he merely ceases treatment, the cancer is the cause of the death."

A number of points need to be made here. The first is that it is not exactly correct to say that in passive euthanasia the doctor does nothing, for he does do one thing that is very important: he lets the patient die. "Letting someone die" is certainly different, in some respects, from other types of action—mainly in that it is a kind of action that one may perform by way of not performing certain other actions. For example, one may let a patient die by way of not giving medication, just as one may insult someone by way of not shaking his hand. But for any purpose of moral assessment, it is a type of action nonetheless. The decision to let a patient die is subject to moral appraisal in the same way that a decision to kill him would be subject to moral appraisal: it may be assessed as wise or unwise, compassionate or sadistic, right or wrong. If a doctor deliberately let a patient die who was suffering from a routinely curable illness, the doctor would certainly be to blame for what he had done, just as he would be to blame if he had needlessly killed the patient. Charges against him would then be appropriate. If so, it would be no defense at all for him to insist that he didn't "do anything." He would have done something very serious indeed, for he let his patient die.

Fixing the cause of death may be very important from a legal point of view, for it may determine whether criminal charges are brought against the doctor. But I do not think that this notion can be used to show a moral difference between active and passive euthanasia. The reason why it is considered bad to be the cause of someone's death is that death is regarded as a great evil—and so it is. However, if it has been decided that euthanasia—even passive euthanasia—is desirable in a given case, it has also been decided that in this instance death is no greater an evil than the patient's continued existence. And if this is true, the usual reason for not wanting to be the cause of someone's death simply does not apply.

Finally, doctors may think that all of this is only of academic interest—the sort of thing that philosophers may worry about but that has no practical bearing on their own work. After all, doctors must be concerned about the legal consequences of what they do, and active euthanasia is clearly forbidden by the law. But even so, doctors should also be concerned with the fact that the law is forcing upon them a moral doctrine that may well be indefensible, and has a considerable effect on their practices. Of course, most doctors are not now in the position of being coerced in this matter, for they do not regard themselves as merely going along with what the law requires. Rather, in statements such as the AMA policy statement that I have quoted, they are endorsing this doctrine as a central point of medical ethics. In that statement, active euthanasia is condemned not merely as illegal but as "contrary to that for which the medical profession stands," whereas passive euthanasia is approved. However, the preceding considerations suggest that there is really no moral difference between the two, considered in themselves (there may be important moral differences in some cases in their *consequences,* but, as I pointed out, these differences may make active euthanasia, and not passive euthanasia, the morally preferable option). So, whereas doctors may have to discriminate between active and passive euthanasia to satisfy the law, they should not do any more than that. In particular, they should not give the distinction any added authority and weight by writing it into official statements of medical ethics.

NOTE

1 A. Shaw: "Doctor, Do We Have a Choice?" *The New York Times Magazine,* Jan. 30, 1972, p. 54.

QUESTIONS

1 Can the conventional doctrine on active and passive euthanasia be defended against Rachels's arguments?

2 Rachels seems to argue for the moral legitimacy of active euthanasia in general, not the moral legitimacy of *voluntary* active euthanasia in particular. Is nonvoluntary active euthanasia ever morally justified?

3 Can you imagine medical circumstances in which you would be better off dead? If so, would you welcome the possibility of active euthanasia, or only passive euthanasia? Do your religious beliefs play any role in your thinking on this issue?

Killing and Allowing to Die

Daniel Callahan

Daniel Callahan cofounded The Hastings Center in 1969, retired as its president in 1996, and presently serves on its staff. His numerous publications reflect an enduring concern with issues in biomedical ethics. He is, for example, the author of *Setting Limits: Medical Goals in an Aging Society* (1987), *What Kind of Life: The Limits of Medical Progress* (1990), and *The Troubled Dream of Life: Living with Mortality* (1993).

Callahan maintains that there is a valid distinction between killing and allowing to die, and he defends the distinction by reference to three overlapping perspectives—metaphysical, moral, and medical. In terms of a metaphysical perspective, Callahan emphasizes that the external world is distinct from the self

Reprinted with permission of the author and the publisher from *Hastings Center Report,* vol. 19 (January/February 1989), Special Supplement, pp. 5–6. © The Hastings Center.

and has its own causal dynamism. In terms of a moral perspective, he emphasizes the difference between *physical causality* and *moral culpability*. In conjunction with a medical perspective, he insists that killing patients is incompatible with the role of the physician in society.

. . . No valid distinction, many now argue, can be made between killing and allowing to die, or between an act of commission and one of omission. The standard distinction being challenged rests on the commonplace observation that lives can come to an end as the result of: (a) the direct action of another who becomes the cause of death (as in shooting a person), and (b) the result of impersonal forces where no human agent has acted (death by lightning, or by disease). The purpose of the distinction has been to separate those deaths caused by human action, and those caused by nonhuman events. It is, as a distinction, meant to say something about human beings and their relationship to the world. It is a way of articulating the difference between those actions for which human beings can be held rightly responsible, or blamed, and those of which they are innocent. At issue is the difference between physical causality, the realm of impersonal events, and moral culpability, the realm of human responsibility.

The challenges encompass two points. The first is that people can become equally dead by our omissions as well as our commissions. We can refrain from saving them when it is possible to do so, and they will be just as dead as if we shot them. It is our decision itself that is the reason for their death, not necessarily how we effectuate that decision. That fact establishes the basis of the second point: if we *intend* their death, it can be brought about as well by omitted acts as by those we commit. The crucial moral point is not how they die, but our intention about their death. We can, then, be responsible for the death of another by intending that they die and accomplish that end by standing aside and allowing them to die.

Despite these criticisms—resting upon ambiguities that can readily be acknowledged—the distinction between killing and allowing to die remains, I contend, perfectly valid. It not only has a logical validity but, no less importantly, a social validity whose place must be central in moral judgments. As a way of putting the distinction into perspective, I want to suggest that it is best understood as expressing three different, though overlapping, perspectives on nature and human action. I will call them the metaphysical, the moral, and the medical perspectives.

Metaphysical   The first and most fundamental premise of the distinction between killing and allowing to die is that there is a sharp difference between the self and the external world. Unlike the childish fantasy that the world is nothing more than a projection of the self, or the neurotic person's fear that he or she is responsible for everything that goes wrong, the distinction is meant to uphold a simple notion: there is a world external to the self that has its own, and independent, causal dynamism. The mistake behind a conflation of killing and allowing to die is to assume that the self has become master of everything within and outside of the self. It is as if the conceit that modern man might ultimately control nature has been internalized: that, if the self might be able to influence nature by its actions, then the self and nature must be one.

Of course that is a fantasy. The fact that we can intervene in nature, and cure or control many diseases, does not erase the difference between the self and the external world. It is as "out there" as ever, even if more under our sway. That sway, however great, is always limited. We can cure disease, but not always the chronic illness that comes with the cure. We can forestall death with modern medicine, but death always wins in the long run because of the innate limitations of the body, inherently and stubbornly beyond final human control. And we can distinguish between a diseased body and an aging body, but in the end if we wait long enough they always become one and the same body. To attempt to deny the distinction between killing and allowing to die is, then, mistakenly to impute more power to human action than it actually has and to accept the conceit that nature has now fallen wholly within the realm of human control. Not so.

Moral   At the center of the distinction between killing and allowing to die is the difference between physical causality and moral culpability. To bring the life of another to an end by an injection kills the other directly; our action is the physical cause of the death. To allow someone to die from a disease we cannot cure (and that we did not cause) is to permit the disease to act as the cause of death. The notion of physical causality in both cases rests on the difference between human agency and the action of external nature. The ambiguity arises precisely because we can be morally culpable for killing someone (if we have no moral right to do so, as we would in self-defense) and no less culpable for allowing someone to die (if we have both the possibility and the obligation of keeping that person alive). Thus there are cases where, morally speaking, it makes no difference whether we killed or allowed to die; we are equally responsible. In those instances, the lines of physical causality and moral culpability happen to cross. Yet the fact that they can cross in some cases in no way shows that they are always, or even usually, one and the same. We can normally find the difference in all but the most obscure cases. We should not, then, use the ambiguity of such cases to do away altogether with the distinction between killing and allowing to die. The ambiguity may obscure, but does not erase, the line between the two.

There is one group of ambiguous cases that is especially troublesome. Even if we grant the ordinary validity between killing and allowing to die, what about those cases that combine (a) an illness that renders a patient unable to carry out an ordinary biological function (to breathe or eat on his own, for example), and (b) our turning off a respirator or removing an artificial feeding tube? On the level of physical causality, have we killed the patient or allowed him to die? In one sense, it is our action that shortens his life, and yet in another sense his underlying disease brings his life to an end. I believe it reasonable to say that, since his life was being sustained by artificial means (respirator or feeding tube) made necessary because of the fact that he had an incapacitating disease, his disease is the ultimate reality behind his death. But for its reality, there would be no need for artificial sustenance in the first place and no moral issue at all. To lose sight of the paramount reality of the disease is to lose sight of the difference between our selves and the outer world.

I quickly add, and underscore, a moral point: the person who, without good moral reason, turns off a respirator or pulls a feeding tube, can be morally culpable; that the patient has been allowed to die of his underlying condition does not morally excuse him. The moral question is whether we are obliged to continue treating a life that is being artifically sustained. To cease treatment may or may not be morally acceptable; but it should be understood, in either case, that the physical cause of death was the underlying disease.

Medical An important social purpose of the distinction between killing and allowing to die has been that of protecting the historical role of the physician as one who tries to cure or comfort patients rather than to kill patients. Physicians have been given special knowledge about the body, knowledge that can be used to kill or to cure. They are also given great privileges in making use of that knowledge. It is thus all the more important that physicians' social role and power be, and be seen to be, a limited power. It may be used only to cure or comfort, never to kill. They have not been given, nor should they be given, the power to use their knowledge and skills to bring life to an end. It would open the way for powerful misuse and, no less importantly, represent an intrinsic violation of what it has meant to be a physician.

Yet if it is possible for physicians to misuse their knowledge and power to kill people directly, are they thereby required to use that same knowledge always to keep people alive, always to resist a disease that can itself kill the patient? The traditional answer has been: not necessarily. For the physician's ultimate obligation is to the welfare of the patient, and excessive treatment can be as detrimental to that welfare as inadequate treatment. Put another way, the obligation to resist the lethal power of disease is limited—it ceases when the patient is unwilling to have it resisted, or where the resistance no longer serves the patient's welfare. Behind this moral premise is the recognition that disease (of some kind) ultimately triumphs and that death is both inevitable sooner or later and not, in any case, always the greatest human evil. To demand of the physician that he always struggle against disease, as if it was in his power always to conquer it, would be to fall into the same metaphysical trap mentioned above: that of assuming that no distinction can be drawn between natural and human agency.

A final word. I suggested [in an earlier discussion] that the most potent motive for active euthanasia and assisted suicide stems from a dread of the power of medicine. That power then seems to take on a drive of its own regardless of the welfare or wishes of patients. No one can easily say no—not physicians, not patients, not families. My guess is that happens because too many have already come to believe that it is their choice, and their choice alone, which brings about death; and they do not want to exercise that kind of authority. The solution is not to erase the distinction between killing and allowing to die, but to underscore its validity and importance. We can bring disease as a cause of death back into the care of the dying.

QUESTIONS

1 Is there a valid distinction between killing and allowing to die?
2 Do you agree with Callahan that the power of the physician must be used "only to cure or comfort, never to kill"?

Voluntary Active Euthanasia

Dan W. Brock

Dan W. Brock is professor of philosophy and biomedical ethics at Brown University, where he is also director of the Center for Biomedical Ethics. Many of his articles are collected in *Life and Death: Philosophical Essays in Biomedical Ethics* (1993) and he is the coauthor of *Deciding for Others: The Ethics of Surrogate Decision Making* (1989).

In this excerpt from a much longer article, Brock argues that two fundamental ethical values support the ethical permissibility of voluntary active euthanasia. These values are individual self-determination (autonomy) and individual well-being, the same two values that support the consensus view that patients have a right to make decisions about life-sustaining treatment. Brock also argues that allowing physicians to perform euthanasia is not incompatible with the "moral center" of medicine.

. . . The central ethical argument for [voluntary active] euthanasia is familiar. It is that the very same two fundamental ethical values supporting the consensus on patient's rights to decide about life-sustaining treatment also support the ethical permissibility of euthanasia. These values are individual self-determination or autonomy and individual well-being. By self-determination as it bears on euthanasia, I mean people's interest in making important decisions about their lives for themselves according to their own values or conceptions of a good life, and in being left free to act on those decisions. Self-determination is valuable because it permits people to form and live in accordance with their own conception of a good life, at least within the bounds of justice and consistent with others doing so as well. In exercising self-determination people take responsibility for their lives and for the kinds of persons they become. A central aspect of human dignity lies in people's capacity to direct their lives in this way. The value of exercising self-determination presupposes some minimum of decision-making capacities or competence, which thus limits the scope of euthanasia supported by self-determination; it cannot justifiably be administered, for example, in cases of serious dementia or treatable clinical depression.

Does the value of individual self-determination extend to the time and manner of one's death? Most people are very concerned about the nature of the last stage of their lives. This reflects not just a fear of experiencing substantial suffering when dying, but also a desire to retain dignity and control during this last period of life. Death is today increasingly preceded by a long period of significant physical and mental decline, due in part to the technological interventions of modern medicine. Many people adjust to these disabilities and find meaning and value in new activities and ways. Others find the impairments and burdens in the last stage of their lives at some point sufficiently great to make life no longer worth living. For many patients near death, maintaining the quality of one's life, avoiding great suffering,

Reprinted with permission of the author and the publisher from *Hastings Center Report,* vol. 22 (March/April 1992), pp. 16, 20. © The Hastings Center.

maintaining one's dignity, and insuring that others remember us as we wish them to become of paramount importance and outweigh merely extending one's life. But there is no single, objectively correct answer for everyone as to when, if at all, one's life becomes all things considered a burden and unwanted. If self-determination is a fundamental value, then the great variability among people on this question makes it especially important that individuals control the manner, circumstances, and timing of their dying and death.

The other main value that supports euthanasia is individual well-being. It might seem that individual well-being conflicts with a person's self-determination when the person requests euthanasia. Life itself is commonly taken to be a central good for persons, often valued for its own sake, as well as necessary for pursuit of all other goods within a life. But when a competent patient decides to forgo all further life-sustaining treatment then the patient, either explicitly or implicitly, commonly decides that the best life possible for him or her with treatment is of sufficiently poor quality that it is worse than no further life at all. Life is no longer considered a benefit by the patient, but has now become a burden. The same judgment underlies a request for euthanasia: continued life is seen by the patient as no longer a benefit, but now a burden. Especially in the often severely compromised and debilitated states of many critically ill or dying patients, there is no objective standard, but only the competent patient's judgment of whether continued life is no longer a benefit.

Of course, sometimes there are conditions, such as clinical depression, that call into question whether the patient has made a competent choice, either to forgo life-sustaining treatment or to seek euthanasia, and then the patient's choice need not be evidence that continued life is no longer a benefit for him or her. Just as with decisions about treatment, a determination of incompetence can warrant not honoring the patient's choice; in the case of treatment, we then transfer decisional authority to a surrogate, though in the case of voluntary active euthanasia a determination that the patient is incompetent means that choice is not possible.

The value or right of self-determination does not entitle patients to compel physicians to act contrary to their own moral or professional values. Physicians are moral and professional agents whose own self-determination or integrity should be respected as well. If performing euthanasia became legally permissible, but conflicted with a particular physician's reasonable understanding of his or her moral or professional responsibilities, the care of a patient who requested euthanasia should be transferred to another. . . .

. . . Permitting physicians to perform euthanasia, it is said, would be incompatible with their fundamental moral and professional commitment as healers to care for patients and to protect life. Moreover, if euthanasia by physicians became common, patients would come to fear that a medication was intended not to treat or care, but instead to kill, and would thus lose trust in their physicians. This position was forcefully stated in a paper by Willard Gaylin and his colleagues:

> The very soul of medicine is on trial. . . . This issue touches medicine at its moral center; if this moral center collapses, if physicians become killers or are even licensed to kill, the profession—and, therewith, each physician—will never again be worthy of trust and respect as healer and comforter and protector of life in all its frailty.

These authors go on to make clear that, while they oppose permitting anyone to perform euthanasia, their special concern is with physicians doing so:

> We call on fellow physicians to say that they will not deliberately kill. We must also say to each of our fellow physicians that we will not tolerate killing of patients and that we shall take disciplinary action against doctors who kill. And we must say to the broader community that if it insists on tolerating or legalizing active euthanasia, it will have to find nonphysicians to do its killing.[1]

If permitting physicians to kill would undermine the very "moral center" of medicine, then almost certainly physicians should not be permitted to perform euthanasia. But how persuasive is this claim? Patients should not fear, as a consequence of permitting *voluntary* active euthanasia, that their physicians will substitute a lethal injection for what patients want and believe is part of their care. If active euthanasia is restricted to cases in which it is truly voluntary, then no patient should fear getting it unless she or he has voluntarily requested it. (The fear that we might in time also come to accept nonvoluntary, or even involuntary, active euthanasia is a slippery slope worry I address [in a later section].) Patients' trust of their physicians could be increased, not eroded, by knowledge that physicians will provide aid in dying when patients seek it.

Might Gaylin and his colleagues nevertheless be correct in their claim that the moral center of medicine would collapse if physicians were to become killers? This question raises what at the deepest level should be the guiding aims of medicine, a question that obviously cannot be fully explored here. But I do want to say enough to indicate the direction that I believe an appropriate response to this challenge should take. In spelling out above what I called the positive argument for voluntary active euthanasia, I suggested that two principal values—respecting patients' self-determination and promoting their well-being—underlie the consensus that competent patients, or the surrogates of incompetent patients, are entitled to refuse any life-sustaining treatment and to choose from among available alternative treatments. It is the commitment to these two values in guiding physicians' actions as healers, comforters, and protectors of their patients' lives that should be at the "moral center" of medicine, and these two values support physicians' administering euthanasia when their patients make competent requests for it.

What should not be at that moral center is a commitment to preserving patients' lives as such, without regard to whether those patients want their lives preserved or judge their preservation a benefit to them. . . .

REFERENCE

1 Willard Gaylin, Leon R. Kass, Edmund D. Pellegrino, and Mark Siegler, "Doctors Must Not Kill," *JAMA* 259 (1988): 2139–40.

QUESTIONS

1 Are considerations of self-determination and individual well-being sufficient to establish the moral legitimacy of voluntary active euthanasia?

2 Is the provision of voluntary active euthanasia by physicians "incompatible with their fundamental moral and professional commitment as healers"? If voluntary active euthanasia were legalized, would patients lose trust in physicians?

Objections to the Institutionalisation of Euthanasia

Stephen G. Potts

Stephen G. Potts, a British physician, is research fellow, Royal Edinburgh Hospital. His contributions to the literature of bioethics include "Headaches in Britain over Brain Death Criteria" and "The QALY and Why It Should Be Revisited."

Potts argues against any scheme that would institutionalize—that is, legalize— (voluntary active) euthanasia. He identifies and briefly discusses a wide range of risks posed by legalization, and he insists that the burden of proof falls on the proponents of legalization. Potts endorses the "right to die" but insists that this right does not entail the right to receive assistance in suicide or the right to be killed.

[I am opposed] to any attempt to institutionalise euthanasia . . . because the risks of such institutionalisation are so grave as to outweigh the very real suffering of those who might benefit from it.

RISKS OF INSTITUTIONALISATION

Among the potential effects of a legalised practice of euthanasia are the following:

1   Reduced Pressure to Improve Curative or Symptomatic Treatment   If euthanasia had been legal forty years ago, it is quite possible that there would be no hospice movement today. The improvement in terminal care is a direct result of attempts made to minimise suffering. If that suffering had been extinguished by extinguishing the patients who bore it, then we may never have known the advances in the control of pain, nausea, breathlessness and other terminal symptoms that the last twenty years have seen.

Some diseases that were terminal a few decades ago are now routinely cured by newly developed treatments. Earlier acceptance of euthanasia might well have undercut the urgency of the research efforts which led to the discovery of those treatments. If we accept euthanasia now, we may well delay by decades the discovery of effective treatments for those diseases that are now terminal.

Reprinted with permission of the publisher from Stephen G. Potts, "Looking for the Exit Door: Killing and Caring in Modern Medicine," *Houston Law Review,* vol. 25 (1988), pp. 504–509, 510–511.

2   Abandonment of Hope   Every doctor can tell stories of patients expected to die within days who surprise everyone with their extraordinary recoveries. Every doctor has experienced the wonderful embarrassment of being proven wrong in their pessimistic prognosis. To make euthanasia a legitimate option as soon as the prognosis is pessimistic enough is to reduce the probability of such extraordinary recoveries from low to zero.

3   Increased Fear of Hospitals and Doctors   Despite all the efforts at health education, it seems there will always be a transference of the patient's fear of illness from the illness to the doctors and hospitals who treat it. This fear is still very real and leads to large numbers of late presentations of illnesses that might have been cured if only the patients had sought help earlier. To institutionalise euthanasia, however carefully, would undoubtedly magnify all the latent fear of doctors and hospitals harbored by the public. The inevitable result would be a rise in late presentations and, therefore, preventable deaths.

4   Difficulties of Oversight and Regulation   [Proposals to legalise euthanasia typically] list sets of precautions designed to prevent abuses. They acknowledge that such abuses are a possibility. I am far from convinced that the precautions are sufficient to prevent either those abuses that have been foreseen or those that may arise after passage of the law. The history of legal "loopholes" is not a cheering one: Abuses might arise when the patient is wealthy and an inheritance is at stake, when the doctor has made mistakes in diagnosis and treatment and hopes to avoid detection, when insurance coverage for treatment costs is about to expire, and in a host of other circumstances.

5   Pressure on the Patient   [Proposals to legalise euthanasia typically] seek to limit the influence of the patient's family on the decision, again acknowledging the risks posed by such influence. Families have all kinds of subtle ways, conscious and unconscious, of putting pressure on a patient to request euthanasia and relieve them of the financial and social burden of care. Many patients already feel guilty for imposing burdens on those who care for them, even when the families are happy to bear that burden. To provide an avenue for the discharge of that guilt in a request for euthanasia is to risk putting to death a great many patients who do not wish to die.

6   Conflict with Aims of Medicine   The pro-euthanasia movement cheerfully hands the dirty work of the actual killing to the doctors who, by and large, neither seek nor welcome the responsibility. There is little examination of the psychological stresses imposed on those whose training and professional outlook are geared to the saving of lives by asking them to start taking lives on a regular basis. Euthanasia advocates seem very confident that doctors can be relied on to make the enormous efforts sometimes necessary to save some lives, while at the same time assenting to requests to take other lives. Such confidence reflects, perhaps, a high opinion of doctors' psychic robustness, but it is a confidence seriously undermined by the shocking rates of depression, suicide, alcoholism, drug addiction, and marital discord consistently recorded among this group.

7   Dangers of Societal Acceptance   It must never be forgotten that doctors, nurses, and hospital administrators have personal lives, homes, and families, or that they are something more than just doctors, nurses, or hospital administrators. They are *citizens* and a significant part of the society around them. I am very worried about what the institutionalisation of euthanasia will do to society, in general, and, particularly how much it will further erode our attachment to the sixth commandment. ["Thou shalt not kill."] How will we regard murderers? What will we say to the terrorist who justifies killing as a means to his political end when we ourselves justify killing as a means to a humanitarian end? I do not know and I daresay the euthanasia advocates do not either, but I worry about it and they appear not to. They need to justify their complacency.

8   The Slippery Slope   How long after acceptance of voluntary euthanasia will we hear the calls for nonvoluntary euthanasia? There are thousands of comatose or demented patients sustained by little more than good nursing care. They are an enormous financial and social burden. How soon will the advocates of euthanasia be arguing that we should "assist them in dying"—for, after all, they won't mind, will they?

How soon after *that* will we hear the calls for involuntary euthanasia, the disposal of the burdensome, the unproductive, the polluters of the gene pool? We must never forget the way the Nazi euthanasia programme made this progression in a few short years. "Oh, but they were barbarians," you say, and so they were, but not at the outset.

If developments in terminal care can be represented by a progression from the CURE mode of medical care to the CARE mode, enacting voluntary euthanasia legislation would permit a further progression to the KILL mode. The slippery slope argument represents the fear that, if this step is taken, then it will be difficult to avoid a further progression to the CULL mode, as illustrated:

CURE   The central aim of medicine
CARE   The central aim of terminal care once patients are beyond cure
KILL   The aim of the proponents of euthanasia for those patients beyond cure and not helped by care
CULL   The feared result of weakening the prohibition on euthanasia

I do not know how easy these moves will be to resist once voluntary euthanasia is accepted, but I have seen little evidence that the modern euthanasia advocates care about resisting them or even worry that they might be possible.

9   Costs and Benefits   Perhaps the most disturbing risk of all is posed by the growing concern over medical costs. Euthanasia is, after all, a very cheap service. The cost of a dose of barbiturates and curare and the few hours in a hospital bed that it takes them to act is minute compared to the massive bills incurred by many patients in the last weeks and months of their lives. Already in Britain, there is a serious underprovision of expensive therapies like renal dialysis and intensive care, with the result that many otherwise preventable deaths occur. Legalising euthanasia would save substantial financial resources which could be diverted to more "useful" treatments. These economic concerns already exert pressure to accept euthanasia, and, if accepted, they will inevitably tend to enlarge the category of patients for whom euthanasia is permitted.

Each of these objections could, and should, be expanded and pressed harder. I do not propose to do so now, for it is sufficient for my purposes to list them as *risks,* not inevitabilities. Several elements go into our judgment of the severity of a risk: the *probability* that the harm in question will arise (the odds), the *severity* of the harm in question (the stakes), and the ease with which the harm in question can be corrected (the *reversibility*). The institutionalisation of euthanasia is such a radical departure from anything that has gone before in Western society that we simply cannot judge the probability of any or all of the listed consequences. Nor can we rule any of them out. There must, however, be agreement that the severity of each of the harms listed is enough to give serious cause for concern, and the severity of all the harms together is enough to horrify. Furthermore, many of the potential harms seem likely to prove very difficult, if not impossible, to reverse by reinstituting a ban on euthanasia.

WEIGHING THE RISKS

For all these reasons, the burden of proof *must* lie with those who would have us gamble by legalising euthanasia. They should demonstrate beyond reasonable doubt that the dangers listed will not arise, just as chemical companies proposing to introduce a new drug are required to demonstrate that it is safe as well as beneficial. Thus far, the proponents of euthanasia have relied exclusively on the compassion they arouse with tales of torment mercifully cut short by death, and have made little or no attempt to shoulder the burden of proving that legalising euthanasia is safe. Until they make such an attempt and carry it off successfully, their proposed legislation must be rejected outright.

THE RIGHT TO DIE AND THE DUTY TO KILL

The nature of my arguments should have made it clear by now that I object, not so much to individual acts of euthanasia, but to institutionalising it as a practice. All the pro-euthanasia arguments turn on the individual case of the patient in pain, suffering at the center of an intolerable existence. They exert powerful calls on our compassion, and appeal to our pity, therefore, we assent too readily when it is claimed that such patients have a *"right to die"* as an escape from torment. So long as the right to die means no more than the right to refuse life-prolonging treatment and the right to rational suicide, I agree. The advocates of euthanasia want to go much further than this though. They want to extend the right to die to encompass the right to receive assistance in suicide and, beyond that, the right to be killed. Here, the focus shifts from the patient to the agent, and from the killed to the killer; but, the argument begins to break down because our compassion does not extend this far.

If it is true that there is a right to be assisted in suicide or a right to be killed, then it follows that someone, somewhere, has a *duty* to provide the assistance or to do the killing. When we look at the proposed legislation, it is very clear upon whom the advocates of euthanasia would place this duty: the doctor. It would be the doctor's job to provide the pills and the doctor's job to give the lethal injection. The regulation of euthanasia is meant to prevent anyone, other than the doctor, from doing it. Such regulation would ensure that the doctor does it with the proper precautions and consultations, and would give the doctor security from legal sanctions for doing it. The emotive appeal of euthanasia is undeniably powerful, but it lasts only so long as we can avoid thinking about who has to do the killing, and where, and when, and how. Proposals to institutionalise euthanasia force us to think hard about these things, and the chill that their contemplation generates is deep enough to freeze any proponent's ardor. . . .

[One final objection to the institutionalisation of euthanasia] relates to another set out above (#5. Pressure on the patient). The objection turns on the concern that many requests for euthanasia will not be truly voluntary because of pressure on the patient or the patient's fear of becoming a burden. There is a significant risk that legalising voluntary euthanasia out of respect for the *right* to die will generate many requests for euthanasia out of a perceived *duty* to die. . . .

QUESTIONS

1 Does Potts provide a compelling case against the legalization of voluntary active euthanasia?

2 Should voluntary active euthanasia be legalized? If so, what procedures and safeguards should be introduced to govern the practice?

Euthanasia: The Way We Do It, The Way They Do It

Margaret P. Battin

Margaret P. Battin is professor of philosophy at the University of Utah. She is the author of *Ethical Issues in Suicide* (1982; 1995) and *Ethics in the Sanctuary: Examining the Practices of Organized Religion* (1990). Many of her published articles are collected in *The Least Worst Death: Essays in Bioethics on the End of Life* (1994).

Battin identifies three cultural models for dealing with dying. In the United States, there is an exclusive emphasis placed on the withholding or withdrawing of life-sustaining treatment. In the Netherlands (Holland), voluntary active euthanasia is an available option. In Germany, active euthanasia is prohibited,

Reprinted, in a version slightly updated by the author, by permission of Elsevier Science Inc. from the *Journal of Pain and Symptom Management*, vol. 6, no. 5, pp. 298–305. Copyright 1991 by the U.S. Cancer Pain Relief Committee.

and physicians themselves are expected not to assist in a patient's suicide, but assisted suicide outside of a medical setting is an option that is legally available. Battin discusses various objections and problems associated with each of these cultural models. In the end, she argues, none of these models is well suited for the United States at this point in time. Taking into account the specific characteristics of contemporary life in the United States, she ultimately recommends the practice of permitting physician-assisted suicide.

Because we tend to be rather myopic in our discussions of death and dying, especially about the issues of active euthanasia and assisted suicide, it is valuable to place the question of how we go about dying in an international context. We do not always see that our own cultural norms may be quite different from those of other nations, and that our background assumptions and actual practices differ dramatically. Thus, I would like to examine the perspectives on end-of-life dilemmas in three countries, Holland, (West) Germany,* and the USA.

Holland, Germany, and the United States are all advanced industrial democracies. They all have sophisticated medical establishments and life expectancies over 70 years of age; their populations are all characterized by an increasing proportion of older persons. They are all in what has been called the fourth stage of the epidemiologic transition[1]—that stage of societal development in which it is no longer the case that most people die of acute parasitic or infectious diseases. In this stage, most people do not die of diseases with rapid, unpredictable onsets and sharp fatality curves; rather, the majority of the population—as much as perhaps 70%–80%—dies of degenerative diseases, especially delayed degenerative diseases, that are characterized by late, slow onset and extended decline. Most people in highly industrialized countries die from cancer, atherosclerosis, heart disease (by no means always suddenly fatal), chronic obstructive pulmonary disease, liver, kidney or other organ disease, or degenerative neurological disorders. Thus, all three of these countries are alike in facing a common problem: how to deal with the characteristic new ways in which we die.

DEALING WITH DYING IN THE UNITED STATES

In the United States, we have come to recognize that the maximal extension of life-prolonging treatment in these late-life degenerative conditions is often inappropriate. Although we could keep the machines and tubes—the respirators, intravenous lines, feeding tubes—hooked up for extended periods, we recognize that this is inhumane, pointless, and financially impossible. Instead, as a society we have developed a number of mechanisms for dealing with these hopeless situations, all of which involve withholding or withdrawing various forms of treatment.

Some mechanisms for withholding or withdrawing treatment are exercised by the patient who is confronted by such a situation or who anticipates it; these include refusal of treatment, the patient-executed DNR order, the Living Will, and the Durable Power of Attorney. Others are mechanisms for decision by second parties about a patient who is no longer competent or never was competent. The latter are reflected in a long series of court cases, including *Quinlan, Saikewicz, Spring, Eichner, Barber, Bartling, Conroy, Brophy,* the trio *Farrell, Peter* and *Jobes,* and *Cruzan.* These are cases that attempt to delineate the precise circumstances under which it is appropriate to withhold or withdraw various forms of therapy, including respiratory support, chemotherapy, antibiotics in intercurrent infections, and artificial nutrition and hydration. Thus, during the past 15 years or so, roughly since *Quinlan* (1976), we have developed an impressive body of case law and state statute that protects, permits, and facilitates our characteristic American strategy of dealing with end-of-life situations. These cases provide a framework for withholding or withdrawing treatment when we believe there is no medical or moral point in going on. This is sometimes termed *passive euthanasia;* more often, it is simply called *allowing to die,* and is ubiquitous in the United States.

For example, a recent study by Miles and Gomez indicates that some 85% of deaths in the United States occur in health-care institutions, including hospitals, nursing homes, and other facilities, and of these, about 70% involve electively withholding some form of life-sustaining treatment.[2] A 1989 study cited in the *Journal of the American Medical Association* claims that 85%–90% of critical care professionals state that they are withholding and withdrawing life-sustaining treatments from patients who are "deemed to have irreversible disease and are terminally ill."[3] Still another study identified some 115 patients in two intensive-care units from whom care was withheld or withdrawn; 110 were already incompetent by the time the decision to limit care was made. The 89 who died while still in the intensive-care unit accounted for 45% of all deaths there.[4] It is estimated that 1.3 million American deaths a year follow decisions to withhold life support;[5] this is a majority of the just over 2 million American deaths per year. Withholding and withdrawing treatment is the way we in the USA go about dealing with dying, and indeed "allowing to die" is the only legally protected alternative to maximal treatment recognized in the United States. We do not legally permit ourselves to actively cause death.

DEALING WITH DYING IN HOLLAND

In the Netherlands, voluntary active euthanasia is also an available response to end-of-life situations. Although active euthanasia remains prohibited by statutory law, it is protected by a series of lower and supreme court decisions and is widely regarded as legal, or, more precisely, *gedoeken,* legally "tolerated." These court decisions have the effect of protecting the physician who performs euthanasia from prosecution, provided the physician meets a rigorous set of guidelines.

These guidelines, variously stated, contain five central provisions:

1 that the patient's request be voluntary;
2 that the patient be undergoing intolerable suffering;
3 that all alternatives acceptable to the patient for relieving the suffering have been tried;
4 that the patient has full information;

5 that the physician has consulted with a second physician whose judgment can be expected to be independent.

Of these criteria, it is the first which is central: euthanasia may be performed only at the voluntary request of the patient. This criterion is also understood to require that the patient's request be a stable, enduring, reflective one—not the product of a transitory impulse. Every attempt is to be made to rule out depression, psychopathology, pressures from family members, unrealistic fears, and other factors compromising voluntariness. In general, pain is not the basis for euthanasia, since pain can, in most cases, be effectively treated; "intolerable suffering," understood to mean suffering that is in the patient's (rather than the physician's) view intolerable, may also include fear of or unwillingness to endure *entluisterung,* or that gradual effacement and loss of personal identity that characterizes the end stages of many terminal illnesses. It is also required that euthanasia be performed only by a physician; it may not be performed by a nurse, family member, or other party.

Until 1990, the physician who performed euthanasia was supposed to report it to the police or the Ministry of Justice, which would then decide if the case should be prosecuted. Not surprisingly, self-reports were comparatively few: just 454 in that year. With changes in the law, a physician now reports directly to the medical examiner, not the police, and the rate of reporting has been climbing. Although speculation concerning the actual number of cases had been rampant, ranging anywhere from 2,000 to 20,000 cases a year, a major empirical study published in 1991, the Remmelink Commission report, revealed that there are in fact around 2,300 cases of euthanasia per year (about 1.8% of the total annual mortality) and another 400 cases of physician-assisted suicide (0.3% of the annual mortality).[6] There are also about 1,000 cases (0.8% of the annual mortality) of what the Dutch call "life-terminating acts without explicit request," or LAWER, of which about 600 involved competent or incompetent patients who had previously made informal requests ("Doctor, please don't let me suffer too long") and about 400 involved patients, all incompetent, in severe suffering and very close to death.[7] Although a substantial proportion of patients, about 25,000 a year, seek their doctors' reassurance of assistance if their suffering becomes unbearable, only 9,000 explicit requests for euthanasia are made annually, and of these, fewer than one-third are honored. Euthanasia is performed in about 1:25 of deaths that occur at home, about 1:75 hospital deaths, and about 1:800 nursing home deaths.[8]

More than half (54%) of Dutch physicians report that they have performed euthanasia; 34% say they would be prepared to do so if the occasion arose; and 12% say they have not and would never do so. If euthanasia deaths were distributed equally (which they are not) among the Netherlands' 30,000 physicians, this would mean that only 1 in every 12 or 13 physicians would perform a case of euthanasia in a given year, or that a given physician would perform euthanasia once or at most twice in a decade of practice. But although euthanasia is comparatively rare, it is nevertheless a conspicuous alternative to terminal illness well known to both physicians and the general public. Surveys of public opinion have shown growing public support for a liberal euthanasia policy (increasing from 40% in 1966 to a high of 81%

in 1988), and while there is a vocal minority opposed to the practice, including some physicians, both the majority of the population in the Netherlands and the majority of Dutch physicians support it.

In Holland, many hospitals now have protocols for the performance of euthanasia; these serve to ensure that the court-established guidelines have been met. However, most euthanasia is practiced in the patient's home, typically by the *huisarts* or general practitioner who is the patient's long-term family physician. Euthanasia is usually performed after aggressive hospital treatment has failed to arrest the patient's terminal illness; the patient has come home to die, and the family physician is prepared to ease this passing. Whether practiced at home or in the hospital, euthanasia often takes place in the presence of the family members, perhaps the visiting nurse, and often, the patient's pastor or priest, with the doctor in continuous attendance. Many doctors say that performing euthanasia is never easy, but that it is something they believe a doctor ought to do for his or her patient, when nothing else can help.

Thus, in Holland a patient facing the end of life has an option not openly practiced in the United States: to ask the physician to bring his or her life to an end. Although not everyone does so—indeed, over 97% of people who die in a given year do not—it is a choice widely understood as available.

FACING DEATH IN GERMANY

In part because of its very painful history of Nazism, Germany appears to believe that doctors should have no role in causing death. Although societal generalizations are always risky, it is fair to say that there is vigorous and nearly universal opposition in Germany to the notion of active euthanasia. Euthanasia is viewed as always wrong, and the Germans view the Dutch as stepping out on a dangerously slippery slope.

However, although under German law killing on request, including active euthanasia, is illegal, German law has not prohibited assistance in suicide since the time of Frederick the Great (1751)—provided the person committing suicide is determined to do so, and is both competent and in control of his or her actions. Taking advantage of this situation, there has developed a private organization, the *Deutsche Gesellschaft für Humanes Sterben* (DGHS), or German Society for Humane Dying, which has openly provided support to its very extensive membership in choosing suicide as an alternative to terminal illness.[9] Although in the wake of a recent scandal concerning its former president and under the threat of more restrictive federal legislation the DGHS's activities are currently being redirected towards promoting living wills and other advance directives, the DGHS has for many years provided information about suicide, assisted its members in gaining access to the means for suicide, and, if requested, has provided *Sterbebegleitung* or "accompaniment in dying" for the person about to commit suicide, sending someone to be with the person who takes a fatal dose, especially if that person is alone or does not have a family supportive of such a choice. These practices all take place outside the medical system.

Furthermore, these practices are supported by a feature of German language that makes it possible to conceptualize them in more benign ways: while English, French, Spanish, and many other languages have just a single primary word for suicide, German has four: *Selbstmord, Selbstötung, Suizid,* and *Freitod,* of which the latter has comparatively positive, even somewhat heroic connotations. Thus Germans can think about the deliberate termination of their lives in a linguistic way not easily available to speakers of other languages, and the DGHS has consistently used *Freitod* rather than the language's other, more negative terms to describe the practice with which it provides assistance. No reliable figures are available about the number of suicides with which this organization has assisted, but it is fair to say, both because of the existence of this organization and the different conceptual horizons of German-speakers, that the option of self-produced death outside the medical system is more clearly open in Germany than it has been in the Netherlands or the United States.

OBJECTIONS TO THE THREE MODELS OF DYING

In response to the dilemmas raised by the new circumstances of death, in which the majority of the population in each of the advanced industrial nations dies of degenerative diseases after an extended period of terminal deterioration, different countries develop different practices. The United States legally permits only withholding and withdrawal of treatment, though of course active euthanasia and assisted suicide do occur. Holland also permits voluntary active euthanasia, and although Germany rejects euthanasia, it tolerates assisted suicide. But there are serious moral objections to be made to each of these practices, objections to be considered before resolving the issue of which practice our own culture ought to adopt.

Objections to the German Practice

German law does not prohibit assisting suicide, but postwar German culture discourages physicians from taking any active role in death. This gives rise to distinctive moral problems. For one thing, it appears that there is little professional help or review provided for patients' choices about suicide; because the patient makes this choice essentially outside the medical establishment, medical professionals are not in a position to detect or treat impaired judgment on the part of the patient, especially judgment impaired by depression. Similarly, if the patient must commit suicide assisted only by persons outside the medical profession, there are risks that the patient's diagnosis and prognosis are inadequately confirmed, that the means chosen for suicide will be unreliable or inappropriately used, that the means used for suicide will fall into the hands of other persons, and that the patient will fail to recognize or be able to resist intrafamilial pressures and manipulation. The DGHS policy for providing assistance has required that the patient be terminally ill and have been a member of the DGHS for at least 1 year in order to make use of its services, the latter requirement intended to provide evidence of the stability of such a choice, but these minimal requirements are hardly sufficient to answer the charge that suicide decisions, which are made for medical reasons but must be made without medical help, may be rendered under less than ideally informed and voluntary conditions.

Objections to the Dutch Practice

The Dutch practice of physician-performed active voluntary euthanasia also raises a number of ethical issues, many of which have been discussed vigorously both in the Dutch press and in commentary on the Dutch practices from abroad. For one thing, it is sometimes said that the availability of physician-performed euthanasia creates a disincentive for providing good terminal care. I have seen no evidence that this is the case; on the contrary, Peter Admiraal, the anesthesiologist who is perhaps Holland's most vocal proponent of voluntary active euthanasia, insists that pain should rarely or never be the occasion for euthanasia, as pain (in contrast to suffering) is comparatively easily treated.[10] Instead, it is a refusal to endure the final stages of deterioration, both mental and physical, that motivates requests.

It is also sometimes said that active euthanasia violates the Hippocratic Oath. Indeed, it is true that the original Greek version of the Oath prohibits the physician from giving a deadly drug, even when asked for it; but the original version also prohibits performing surgery and taking fees for teaching medicine, neither of which prohibitions has survived into contemporary medical practice. Dutch physicians often say that they see performing euthanasia—where it is genuinely requested by the patient and nothing else can be done to relieve the patient's condition—as part of their duty to the patient, not as a violation of it.

The Dutch are also often said to be at risk of starting down the slippery slope, that is, that the practice of voluntary active euthanasia for patients who meet the criteria will erode into practicing less-than-voluntary euthanasia on patients whose problems are not irremediable, and perhaps by gradual degrees develop into terminating the lives of people who are elderly, chronically ill, handicapped, mentally retarded, or otherwise regarded as undesirable. This risk is often expressed in vivid claims of widespread fear and wholesale slaughter, claims that are repeated in the Right-to-Life press in both Holland and the USA; however, these claims are simply not true. However, it is true that the Dutch are now beginning to agonize over the problems of the incompetent patient, the mentally ill patient, the newborn with serious deficits, and other patients who cannot make voluntary choices, though with some exceptions these are largely understood as issues about withholding or withdrawing treatment, not about direct termination.[11]

What is not often understood is that this new and acutely painful area of reflection for the Dutch—withholding and withdrawing treatment from incompetent patients—has already led in the United States to the development of a vast, highly developed body of law: namely, that series of cases just cited, beginning with *Quinlan* and culminating in *Cruzan.* Americans have been discussing these issues for a long time, and have developed a broad set of practices that are regarded as routine in withholding and withdrawing treatment. The Dutch see Americans as much further out on the slippery slope than they are, because Americans have already become accustomed to second-party choices about other people. Issues involving second-party choices are painful to the Dutch in a way they are not to us precisely because *voluntariness* is so central in the Dutch understanding of choices about dying. Concomitantly, the Dutch see the Americans' squeamishness about first-party choices—

voluntary euthanasia, assisted suicide—as evidence that we are not genuinely committed to recognizing *voluntary* choice after all. For this reason, many Dutch commentators believe that the Americans are at a much greater risk of sliding down the slippery slope into involuntary killing than they are. I fear, I must add, that they are right about this.

Objections to the American Practice

There may be moral problems raised by the German and the Dutch practices, but there are also moral problems raised by the American practice of relying on withholding and withdrawal of treatment in end-of-life situations. The German, Dutch, and American practices all occur within similar conditions—in industrialized nations with highly developed medical systems, where a majority of the population dies of illnesses exhibiting characteristically extended downhill courses—but the issues raised by our own response to this situation may be even more disturbing than those of the Dutch or the Germans. We often assume that our approach is "safer" because it involves only letting someone die, not killing him or her; but it too raises very troubling questions.

The first of these issues is a function of the fact that withdrawing and especially withholding treatment are typically less conspicuous, less pronounced, less evident kinds of actions than direct killing, even though they can equally well lead to death. Decisions about nontreatment have an invisibility that decisions about directly causing death do not have, even though they may have the same result, and hence there is a much wider range of occasions in which such decisions can be made. One can decline to treat a patient in many different ways, at many different times—by not providing oxygen, by not instituting dialysis, by not correcting electrolyte imbalances, and so on—all of which will cause the patient's death; open medical killing also brings about death, but is a much more overt, conspicuous procedure. Consequently, letting die also invites many fewer protections. In contrast to the earlier slippery slope argument which sees killing as riskier than letting die, the slippery slope argument warns that because our culture relies primarily on decisions about nontreatment, grave decisions about living or dying are not as open to scrutiny as they are under more direct life-terminating practices, and hence, are more open to abuse.

Second, and closely related, reliance on withholding and withdrawal of treatment invites rationing in an extremely strong way, in part because of the comparative invisibility of these decisions. When a health-care provider does not offer a specific sort of care, it is not always possible to discern the motivation; the line between believing that it would not provide benefit to the patient and that it would not provide benefit worth the investment of resources in the patient can be very thin. This is a particular problem where health-care financing is highly decentralized, as in the United States, and where rationing decisions without benefit of principle are not always available for easy review.

Third, relying on withholding and withdrawal of treatment can often be cruel. It requires that the patient who is dying from one of the diseases that exhibits a characteristic extended, downhill course (as the majority of patients in Holland, Germany, and the US do) must in effect wait to die until the absence of a certain treatment will cause death. For instance, the cancer patient who forgoes chemotherapy or surgery does not simply die from this choice; he or she continues to endure the downhill course of the cancer until the tumor finally destroys some crucial bodily function or organ. The patient with amyotrophic lateral sclerosis who decides in advance to decline respiratory support does not die at the time this choice is made, but continues to endure increasing paralysis until breathing is impaired and suffocation occurs. We often try to ameliorate these situations by administering pain medication or symptom control at the same time we are withholding treatment, but these are all ways of disguising the fact that we are letting the disease kill the patient rather than directly bringing about death. But the ways diseases kill people are far more cruel than the ways physicians kill patients when performing euthanasia or assisting in suicide.

THE PROBLEM: A CHOICE OF CULTURES

Thus we see three similar cultures and countries and three similar sets of circumstances, but three quite different basic practices in approaching death. All three of these practices generate moral problems; none of them, nor any others we might devise, is free of moral difficulty. But the question that faces us is this: which of these practices is best?

It is not possible to answer this question in a less-than-ideal world without some attention to the specific characteristics and deficiencies of the society in question. In asking which of these practices is best, we must ask which is best *for us.* That we currently employ one set of these practices rather than others does not prove that it is best for us; the question is, would practices developed in other cultures or those not yet widespread in any be better for our own culture than that which has developed here? Thus, it is necessary to consider the differences between our own society and these European cultures that have real bearing on which model of approach to dying we ought to adopt.

First, notice that different cultures exhibit different degrees of closeness between physicians and patients—different patterns of contact and involvement. The German physician is sometimes said to be more distant and more authoritarian than the American physician; on the other hand, the Dutch physician is sometimes said to be closer to his or her patients than either the American or the German is. In Holland, basic primary care is provided by the *huisarts,* the general practitioner or family physician, who typically lives in the neighborhood, makes house calls frequently, and maintains an office in his or her own home. The *huisarts* is usually the physician for the other members of the patient's family, and will remain the family's physician throughout his or her practice. Thus, the patient for whom euthanasia becomes an issue—say, the terminal cancer patient who has been hospitalized in the past but who has returned home to die—will be cared for by the trusted family physician on a regular basis. Indeed, for a patient in severe distress, the physician, supported by the visiting nurse, may make house calls as often as once a day, twice a day, or more (after all, it is right in the neighborhood), and is in continuous contact with the family. In contrast, the traditional American institution of the family doctor who makes house calls is rapidly becoming a thing of the past, and whereas some patients who die at home have access to hospice services and house calls from their long-term physician, many have no such long-term care and receive most of it from staff at a clinic or housestaff rotating through the services of a hospital. The degree of continuing contact the patient can have with a familiar, trusted physician clearly influences the nature of his or her dying, and also plays a role in whether physician-performed active euthanasia, assisted suicide, and/or withholding and withdrawing treatment is appropriate.

Second, the United States has a much more volatile legal climate than either Holland or Germany; our medical system is increasingly litigious, much more so than that of any other country in the world. Fears of malpractice action or criminal prosecution color much of what physicians do in managing the dying of their patients. We also tend to evolve public policy through court decisions, and to assume that the existence of a policy puts an end to any moral issue. A delicate legal and moral balance over the issue of euthanasia, as is the case in Holland, would not be possible here.

Third, we in the United States have a very different financial climate in which to do our dying. Both Holland and Germany, as well as every other industrialized nation except South Africa, have systems of national health insurance or national health care. Thus the patient is not directly responsible for the costs of treatment, and consequently the patient's choices about terminal care and/or euthanasia need not take personal financial considerations into account. Even for the patient who does have health insurance in the United States, many kinds of services are not covered, whereas the national health care or health insurance programs of many other countries variously provide many sorts of relevant services, including at-home physician care, home nursing care, home respite care, care in a nursing-home or other long-term facility, dietician care, rehabilitation care, physical therapy, psychological counseling, and so on. The patient in the United States needs to attend to the financial aspects of dying in a way that patients in many other countries do not, and in this country both the patient's choices and the recommendations of the physician are very often shaped by financial considerations.

There are many other differences between the USA on the one hand and Holland and Germany, with their different models of dying, on the other. There are differences in degrees of paternalism in the medical establishment and in racism, sexism, and ageism in the general culture, as well as awareness of a problematic historical past, especially Nazism. All of these and the previous factors influence the appropriateness or inappropriateness of practices such as active euthanasia and assisted suicide. For instance, Holland's tradition of close physician/patient contact, its absence of malpractice-motivated medicine, and its provision of comprehensive health insurance, together with its comparative lack of racism and ageism and its experience in resistance to Nazism, suggest that this culture is able to permit the practice of voluntary active euthanasia, performed by physicians, without risking abuse. On the other hand, it is sometimes said that Germany still does not trust its physicians, remembering the example of Nazi experimentation, and given a comparatively authoritarian medical climate in which the contact between physician and patient is quite distanced, the population could not be comfortable with the practice of active euthanasia. There, only a wholly patient-controlled response to terminal situations, as in non-physician-assisted suicide, is a reasonable and prudent practice.

But what about the United States? This is a country where 1) sustained contact with a personal physician is decreasing, 2) the risk of malpractice action is increasing, 3) much medical care is not insured, 4) many medical decisions are financial as well, 5) racism is on the rise, and 6) the public is naive about direct contact with Nazism or similar totalitarian movements. Thus, the United States is in many respects an untrustworthy candidate for practicing active euthanasia. Given the pressures on individuals in an often atomized society, encouraging solo suicide, assisted if at all only by nonprofessionals, might well be open to considerable abuse too.

However, there is one additional difference between the United States and both Holland and Germany that may seem relevant here. At first, it appears to be a trivial, superficial difference—the apparent fact that we Americans are the biggest consumers of "pop psychology" in the world. While of course things are changing and our cultural tastes are widely exported, the fact remains that the ordinary American's cultural diet contains more in the way of do-it-yourself amateur psychology and self-analysis than anyone else's. This long tradition of pop psychology and self-analysis may put us in a better position for certain kinds of end-of-life practices than many other cultures—despite whatever other deficiencies we have, just because we live in a culture that encourages us to inspect our own motives, anticipate the impact of our actions on others, and scrutinize our own relationships with others, including our physicians. What, then, is appropriate for our own cultural situation? Physician-performed euthanasia, though not in itself morally wrong, is morally jeopardized where the legal, time allotment, and especially financial pressures on both patients and physicians are severe; thus, it is morally problematic in our culture in a way that it is not in Holland. Solo suicide outside the institution of medicine (as in Germany) is problematic in a culture (like the United States) that is increasingly alienated, offers deteriorating and uneven social services, is increasingly racist, and in other ways imposes unusual pressures on individuals. Reliance only on withholding and withdrawing treatment (as in the United States) can be, as we've seen, cruel, and its comparative invisibility invites erosion under cost containment and other pressures. These are the three principal alternatives we've considered; but none of them seems wholly suited to our actual situation for dealing with the new fact that most of us die of extended-decline, deteriorative diseases. However, permitting physicians to supply patients with the means for ending their own lives still grants physicians some control over the circumstances in which this can happen—only, for example, when the prognosis is genuinely grim and the alternatives for symptom control are poor— but leaves the fundamental decision about whether to use these means to the patient alone. It is up to the patient then, and his or her advisors, including family, clergy, physician, other health-care providers, and a raft of pop-psychology books, to be clear about whether he or she really wants to use these means or not. Thus, the physician is involved, but not directly; and it is the patient's choice, but the patient is not alone in making it. We live in a quite imperfect world, but, of the alternatives for facing death—which we all eventually must—I think that the practice of permitting physician-assisted suicide is the one most nearly suited to the current state of our own somewhat flawed society. This is a model not yet central in any of the three countries examined here—Holland, Germany, or the United States—but it is the one I think suits us best.

NOTE

* As the medical care system in the German Democratic Republic (East Germany) was structurally different and was faced with many unique problems, especially in terms of shortages in high-tech equipment, I will only be referring to what was known as the Federal Republic of (West) Germany up until 1990.

REFERENCES

1 Olshansky SJ, Ault AB. The fourth stage of the epidemiological transition: the age of delayed degenerative diseases. Milbank Memorial Fund Quarterly/Health and Society 1986;64:355–391.
2 Miles S, Gomez C. Protocols for elective use of life-sustaining treatment. New York: Springer-Verlag, 1988.
3 Sprung CL. Changing attitudes and practices in foregoing life-sustaining treatments. JAMA 1990;263:2213.
4 Smedira NG et al. Withholding and withdrawal of life support from the critically ill. N Engl J Med 1990;322:309–315.
5 New York Times, July 23, 1990, p. A13.
6 van der Maas PJ, van Delden JJM, and Pijnenborg L. Euthanasia and other medical decisions concerning the end of life: an investigation performed upon request of the Commission of Inquiry into the Medical Practice Concerning Euthanasia. Published in full in English as a special issue of Health Policy 1992; 22 (nos. 1 and 2), and, with Looman CWN, in summary in The Lancet 1991;338:669–74.
7 The LAWER cases are examined in Pijnenborg L, van der Maas PJ, van Delden JJM, and Looman CWN. Life-terminating acts without explicit request of patient. The Lancet 1993;341:1196–1199. This study finds just two cases, both from the early 1980s, in which a competent patient was euthanized without that patient's knowledge.
8 Dillmann RJM, van der Wal G, and van Delden JJM. Euthanasia in the Netherlands: the state of affairs. Manuscript in progress, Royal Dutch Medical Association, Utrecht.
9 Battin MP. Assisted suicide: can we learn from Germany? The Hastings Center Report, March–April 1992;41–51. Reprinted in Battin MP. The least worst death. New York: Oxford University Press, 1994:254–270.
10 Admiraal P. Euthanasia in a general hospital. Address to the Eighth World Congress of the International Federation of Right-To-Die Societies, Maastricht, Holland, June 8, 1990.
11 ten Have H. Coma: controversy and consensus. Newsletter of the European Society for Philosophy of Medicine and Health Care. May 1990;8:19–20.

QUESTIONS

1 Battin argues that "the United States is in many respects an untrustworthy candidate for practicing active euthanasia." Do you agree?
2 How serious are the problems associated with the American model of dealing with dying? What model would be best for the United States at this point in time?

Assisted Suicide Is Not Voluntary Active Euthanasia

David T. Watts and Timothy Howell

David T. Watts is associate professor of medicine at the University of Wisconsin, Madison. Timothy Howell is professor of psychiatry and family medicine at the University of Wisconsin, Madison. Watts and Howell are frequent collaborators; their other coauthored articles include "Geriatricians' Attitudes Toward Assisting Suicide of Dementia Patients" and "Dangerous Behavior in a Demented Patient: Preserving Autonomy in a Patient with Diminished Competence."

Watts and Howell argue that it is important to distinguish between voluntary active euthanasia and physician-assisted suicide and also to distinguish among three types of assisted suicide: (1) providing information, (2) providing the means (typically, by writing a prescription for a lethal amount of medication), and (3) supervising or directly aiding. Although they believe that the legalization of voluntary active euthanasia would have severe adverse consequences, and thus endorse many of the standard arguments against voluntary active euthanasia, they find these same arguments to be substantially weaker when directed against assisted suicide. In their view, physician-assisted suicide should be legalized. However, they argue that physicians should be limited to indirect participation in a patient's suicide, that is, the provision of information or means; physicians should not be permitted to supervise or directly aid a patient in committing suicide.

. . . [Ongoing] developments highlight some of the confusion emerging from discussions of voluntary active euthanasia (V.A.E.) and assisted suicide. A significant source of confusion has been the tendency to join these concepts or even to consider them synonymous. For example, the AGS Position Statement on V.A.E. and a recent article by Teno and Lynn in the *Journal of the American Geriatrics Society* both reject easing restrictions on V.A.E. and assisted suicide while making arguments *only* against euthanasia.[1, 2] The National Hospice Organization also opposes euthanasia and assisted suicide, but it, too, appears to blur the distinction between them in stating that "euthanasia encompasses . . . in some settings, physician-assisted suicide".[3] Others appear to use the terms euthanasia and assisted suicide synonymously in arguing against both.

In contrast, the AMA Ethics and Health Policy Counsel argues against physician-assisted suicide and distinguishes this from euthanasia.[4] The AMA Council on Ethical and Judicial Affairs also acknowledges there is "an ethically relevant distinction between euthanasia and assisted suicide that makes assisted suicide a more attractive option." Yet it then goes on to assert that "the ethical concerns about

Reprinted with permission of the publisher from *Journal of the American Geriatrics Society,* vol. 40 (October 1992), pp. 1043–1046.

physician-assisted suicide are similar to those of euthanasia since both are essentially interventions intended to cause death."[5]

In order to weigh and appreciate the merits of the different arguments for and against V.A.E. and physician-assisted suicide, it is critical that appropriate distinctions be made. For example, we believe the arguments made in the references cited above and by others[6, 7] against euthanasia are telling. However, we find that these same arguments are substantially weaker when used against assisted suicide. And while we agree with the AMA Council on Ethical and Judicial Affairs that an ethically relevant distinction exists between euthanasia and assisted suicide, we think it is important to distinguish further between different forms of assisted suicide. Only by doing so can we begin to sort out some of the apparent confusion in attitudes toward these issues. We caution our readers that the literature on this topic, while growing, remains preliminary, with little empirical research yet completed. Our arguments, however, are philosophical in nature and do not ultimately stand or fall on empirical data.

DEFINITIONS

Voluntary active euthanasia: Administration of medications or other interventions intended to cause death at a patient's request.

Assisted suicide: Provision of information, means, or direct assistance by which a patient may take his or her own life. Assisted suicide involves several possible levels of assistance: *providing information,* for example, may mean providing toxicological information or describing techniques by which someone may commit suicide; *providing the means* can involve written prescriptions for lethal amounts of medication; *supervising or directly aiding* includes inserting an intravenous line and instructing on starting a lethal infusion.

These levels of assistance have very different implications. Providing only information or means allows individuals to retain the greatest degree of control in choosing the time and mode of their deaths. Physician participation is only indirect. This type of limited assistance is exemplified by the widely reported case of Dr. Timothy Quill, who prescribed a lethal quantity of barbiturates at the request of one of his patients who had leukemia.[8] By contrast, supervising or directly aiding is the type of physician involvement characterizing the case of Dr. Jack Kevorkian and Janet Adkins. Adkins was a 54-year-old woman with a diagnosis of Alzheimer-type dementia who sought Kevorkian's assistance in ending her life. Dr. Kevorkian inserted an intravenous catheter and instructed Mrs. Adkins on activating a lethal infusion of potassium following barbiturate sedation, a process personally monitored by Kevorkian. This form of assisted suicide carries significant potential for physician influence or control of the process, and from it there is only a relatively short step to physician initiation (ie, active euthanasia). We therefore reject physician-supervised suicide for the arguments commonly made against V.A.E., namely, that legalization would have serious adverse consequences, including potential abuse of vulnerable persons, mistrust of physicians, and diminished availability of supportive services for the dying.[2, 3, 5–7] We find each of these arguments, however, insufficient when applied to more limited forms of physician-assisted suicide (ie, providing information or means).

WILL ASSISTED SUICIDE LEAD TO ABUSE OF VULNERABLE PERSONS?

A major concern is that some patients will request euthanasia or assisted suicide out of convenience to others.[2,4] It is certainly possible that a patient's desire to avoid being a burden could lead to such a request. With euthanasia, there is danger that a patient's request might find too ready acceptance. With assisted suicide, however, the ultimate decision, and the ultimate action, are the patient's, not the physician's. This places an important check and balance on physician initiation or patient acquiescence in euthanasia. As the AMA Council on Ethical and Judicial Affairs acknowledges, a greater level of patient autonomy is afforded by physician-assisted suicide than by euthanasia.[5]

Culturally or socially mediated requests for assisted suicide would remain a significant concern. Patients might also request aid in suicide out of fear, pain, ambivalence, or depression. The requirement that patients commit the ultimate act themselves cannot alone provide a sufficient safeguard. It would be incumbent on physicians to determine, insofar as possible, that requests for assisted suicide were not unduly influenced and that reversible conditions were optimally treated. As to how physicians might respond to such requests, data from the Netherlands indicate that about 75% of euthanasia requests in that country are refused.[9] It is our impression that most requests for assisted suicide, therefore, appear to represent opportunities for improved symptom control. We believe most serious requests would likely come from patients experiencing distressing symptoms of terminal illness.[10] By opening the door for counseling or treatment of reversible conditions, requests for assisted suicide might actually lead to averting some suicides which would have otherwise occurred.

Another concern regarding euthanasia is that it could come to be accepted without valid consent and that such a practice would more likely affect the frail and impoverished. The Remmelink Commission's investigation of euthanasia in the Netherlands appeared to justify such concerns in estimating that Dutch physicians may have performed 1,000 acts of involuntary euthanasia involving incompetent individuals.[11] But while euthanasia opens up the possibility of invalid consent, with assisted suicide consent is integral to the process. Because the choice of action clearly rests with the individual, there is substantially less likelihood for the abuse of assisted suicide as a societal vehicle for cost containment. And there is little basis for assuming that requests for assisted suicide would come primarily from frail and impoverished persons. Prolonged debilitation inherent in many illnesses is familiar to an increasing number of patients, family members, and health professionals. Such illnesses represent a greater financial threat to the middle- and upper-middle class, since the poor and disenfranchised have less to spend down to indigency. Thus, we suspect requests for assisted suicide might actually be more common from the educated, affluent, and outspoken.

Patients diagnosed with terminal or debilitating conditions are often vulnerable. We agree that such patients might request assisted suicide out of fear of pain, suffering, or isolation, and that too ready acceptance of such requests could be disastrous. Yet, we believe that patients' interests can be safeguarded by requirements for persistent, competent requests as well as thorough assessments for conditions, such as clinical depression, which could be reversed, treated, or ameliorated. Foley recently outlined an approach to the suicidal cancer patient.[12] We share her view that many such patients' requests to terminate life are altered by the availability of expert, continuing hospice services. We concur with Foley and others in calling for the wider availability of such services,[1,2] so that requests for assisted suicide arising from pain, depression, or other distressing symptoms can be reduced to a minimum.

WOULD ASSISTED SUICIDE UNDERMINE TRUST BETWEEN PATIENTS AND PHYSICIANS?

The cardinal distinction between V.A.E. and assisted suicide is that V.A.E. is killing by physicians, while suicide is self-killing. Prohibiting both euthanasia and physician-supervised suicide (ie, with direct physician involvement) should diminish worries that patients might have about physicians wrongly administering lethal medicine. At present, physician-patient trust is compromised by widespread concern that physicians try too hard to keep dying patients alive. The very strength of the physician-patient relationship has been cited as a justification for physician involvement in assisted suicide.[13]

A number of ethicists have expressed concern that both euthanasia and assisted suicide, if legalized, would have a negative impact on the way society perceives the role of physicians.[2,4,6,7] Limited forms of assisted suicide, however, have been viewed more positively.[14] Public and professional attitudes appear to be evolving on this issue. A 1990 Gallup poll found that 66% of respondents believed someone in great pain, with "no hope of improvement," had the moral right to commit suicide; in 1975 the figure was 41%.[15] A panel of distinguished physicians has stated that it is not immoral for a physician to assist in the rational suicide of a terminally ill person.[16] The recent publication of a book on techniques of committing or assisting suicide evoked wide interest and significant support for the right of people to take control of their dying.[17] For a significant segment of society, physician involvement in assisted suicide may be welcomed, not feared. Furthermore, while relatively few might be likely to seek assistance with suicide if stricken with a debilitating illness, a substantial number might take solace knowing they could request such assistance.

There is another argument raised against V.A.E. that we believe also falters when used to object to assisted suicide. It has been maintained that prohibiting euthanasia forces physicians to focus on the humane care of dying patients, including meticulous attention to their symptoms.[2,10] This argument implies that physicians find it easier to relieve the suffering of dying patients by ending their lives rather than attempting the difficult task of palliating their symptoms. But for some patients, the suffering may not be amenable to even the most expert palliation. Even in such instances, some argue that limited forms of assisted suicide should be prohibited on the grounds that not to forbid them would open the door for more generalized, less stringent applications of assisted suicide.

To us, this "slippery slope" argument seems to imply that the moral integrity of the medical profession must be maintained, even if at the cost of prolonged, unnecessary suffering by at least some dying patients. We believe such a posture is itself inhumane and not acceptable. It contradicts a fundamental principle that is an essential ingredient of physician-patient trust: that patient comfort should be a primary goal of the physician in the face of incurable illness. Furthermore, by allowing limited physician involvement in assisted suicide, physicians can respect both the principle of caring that guides them and the patients for whom caring alone is insufficient. We concede that there is another alternative: terminally ill patients who cannot avoid pain while awake may be given continuous anesthetic levels of medication.[2] But this is exactly the sort of dying process we believe many in our society want to avoid.

WILL ASSISTED SUICIDE AND EUTHANASIA WEAKEN SOCIETAL RESOLVE TO INCREASE RESOURCES ALLOCATED TO CARE OF THE DYING?

This argument assumes that V.A.E. and assisted suicide would both be widely practiced, and that their very availability would decrease tangible concern for those not choosing euthanasia or suicide. However, euthanasia is rarely requested even by terminal cancer patients.[2] In the Netherlands, euthanasia accounts for less than 2% of all deaths.[9] These data suggest that even if assisted suicide were available to those with intractable pain or distressing terminal conditions, it would likely be an option chosen by relatively few. With assisted suicide limited to relatively few cases, this argument collapses. For with only a few requesting assisted suicide, the vast number of patients with debilitating illnesses would be undiminished, and their numbers should remain sufficient to motivate societal concern for their needs. Furthermore, to withhold assisted suicide from the few making serious, valid requests would be to subordinate needlessly the interests of these few to those of the many. Compounding their tragedy would be the fact that these individuals could not even benefit from any increase in therapeutic resources prompted by their suffering, insofar as their conditions are, by definition, not able to be ameliorated.

CONCLUSION

We have argued that assisted suicide and voluntary active euthanasia are different and that each has differing implications for medical practice and society. Further discussion should consider the merits and disadvantages of each, a process enhanced by contrasting them. We have further argued that different forms of assisted suicide can be distinguished both clinically and philosophically. Although some may argue that all forms of assisted suicide are fundamentally the same, we believe the differences can be contrasted as starkly as a written prescription and a suicide machine.

We do not advocate ready acceptance of requests for suicide, nor do we wish to romanticize the concept of rational suicide.[18] In some situations, however, where severe debilitating illness cannot be reversed, suicide may represent a rational choice. If this is the case, then physician assistance could make the process more humane. Along with other geriatricians, we often face dilemmas involving the management of chronic illnesses in late life. We believe we can best serve our patients, and preserve their trust, by respecting their desire for autonomy, dignity, and quality, not only of life, but of dying.

REFERENCES

1 AGS Public Policy Committee. Voluntary active euthanasia. J Am Geriatr Soc 1991;39:826.

2 Teno J, Lynn J. Voluntary active euthanasia: The individual case and public policy. J Am Geriatr Soc 1991;39:827–830.

3 National Hospice Organization. Statement of the National Hospice Organization Opposing the Legalization of Euthanasia and Assisted Suicide. Arlington, VA: National Hospice Organization, 1991.

4 Orentlicher D. Physician participation in assisted suicide. JAMA 1989;262:1844–1845.

5 AMA. Report of the Council on Ethical and Judicial Affairs: Decisions Near the End of Life. Chicago, IL: American Medical Association, 1991.

6 Singer PA. Should doctors kill patients? Can Med Assoc J 1988;138:1000–1001.

7 Singer PA, Siegler M. Euthanasia—a critique. N Engl J Med 1990;322:1881–1883.

8 Quill TE. Death and dignity: A case of individualized decision making. N Engl J Med 1991;324:691–694.

9 Van der Maas PJ, Van Delden JJM, Pijnenborg L, Looman CWN. Euthanasia and other medical decisions concerning the end of life. Lancet 1991;338:669–74.

10 Palmore EB. Arguments for assisted suicide (letter). Gerontologist 1991;31:854.

11 Karel R. Undertreatment of pain, depression needs to be addressed before euthanasia made legal in U.S. Psychiatric News, December 20, 1991, pp 5, 13, 23.

12 Foley KM. The relationship of pain and symptom management to patient requests for physician-assisted suicide. J Pain Symptom Manag 1991;6:289–297.

13 Jecker NS. Giving death a hand. When the dying and the doctor stand in a special relationship. J Am Geriatr Soc 1991;39:831–835.

14 American College of Physicians. ACP to DA, Grand Jury: Dr. Quill acted "humanely." ACP Observer, September, 1991, p. 5.

15 Ames K, Wilson L, Sawhill R et al. Last rights. Newsweek August 26, 1991, pp 40–41.

16 Wanzer SH, Federman DD, Adelstein SJ et al. The physician's responsibility toward hopelessly ill patients: A second look. N Engl J Med 1989;320:844–849.

17 Humphry D. Final Exit: The Practicalities of Self-Deliverance and Assisted Suicide for the Dying. Eugene, OR: The Hemlock Society, (distributed by Carol Publishing, Secaucus, NJ), 1991.

18 Conwell Y, Caine ED. Rational suicide and the right to die: Reality and myth. N Engl J Med 1991;325:1100–1103.

QUESTIONS

1 Would the social consequences of legalizing physician-assisted suicide be less problematic than the social consequences of legalizing voluntary active euthanasia?

2 Should physician-assisted suicide be legalized? If so, should physicians be permitted to supervise or directly aid a patient in committing suicide, or should they be limited to providing information and means?

Majority Opinion in *Compassion in Dying v. State of Washington*

Judge John T. Noonan, Jr.

John T. Noonan, Jr., is judge, United States Court of Appeals, Ninth Circuit. Formerly professor of law at the University of California, Berkeley, he is the author of books such as *Contraception: A History of Its Treatment by the Catholic Theologians and Canonists* (1965) and
Persons and Masks of the Law (1976).

At issue in this case is the constitutionality of a Washington State statute
prohibiting "promoting a suicide attempt." The United States District Court for
the Western District of Washington concluded that the statute was
unconstitutional, but this ruling was reversed by a three-judge panel of the United
States Court of Appeals, Ninth Circuit. The decision of the three-judge panel was
by a two-to-one majority, and Judge Noonan wrote the majority opinion. (In a
subsequent development, this case was reheard by the entire Court of Appeals,
and the statute at issue was declared unconstitutional.)

   Judge Noonan rejects the reasoning of the District Court. He argues that the
Washington statute neither deprives the plaintiffs of a liberty protected by the
Fourteenth Amendment nor denies them the equal protection of the law. Judge
Noonan organizes his overall argument into seven sections. Of particular
interest are his articulation of the various state interests underlying the
Washington statute and his affirmation of a constitutionally significant
distinction between physician-assisted suicide and the refusal of life-sustaining
medical treatment.

The state of Washington (Washington) appeals the decision of the District Court holding unconstitutional Washington's statute on promoting a suicide attempt. Finding
no basis for concluding that the statute violates the Constitution, we reverse the District Court.

THE STATUTE

The challenged statute reads as follows: Promoting a suicide attempt (1) A person
is guilty of promoting a suicide attempt when he knowingly causes or aids another
person to attempt suicide. (2) Promoting a suicide is a Class C felony. Wash. Rev.
Code 9A.36.060.

United States Court of Appeals, Ninth Circuit. 49 F.3d 586 (1995).

THE PLAINTIFFS

Compassion in Dying is a nonprofit incorporated in the state of Washington. Its avowed purpose is to assist persons described by it as "competent" and "terminally ill" to hasten their deaths by providing them information, counseling and emotional support but not by administering fatal medication.

Three individuals were plaintiffs in their own right. Their identities are cloaked by an order permitting them to litigate under pseudonyms. They are now deceased. Jane Roe was a 69-year-old physician suffering from cancer; she had been bedridden for seven months at the time the suit was brought and died before judgment was entered by the District Court. John Doe was a 44-year-old artist, who was partially blind at the time of suit and was also suffering from AIDS; he had been advised that his disease was incurable; he died prior to judgment. James Poe was a 69-year-old patient suffering from chronic obstructive pulmonary disease; he was connected to an oxygen tank at all times. He died after judgment but prior to the hearing of this appeal.

Four physicians also joined the suit, asserting their own rights and those of their patients. Harold Glucksberg has specialized in the care of cancer since 1985 and is a clinical assistant professor at the University of Washington School of Medicine. According to his sworn declaration, he "occasionally" encounters patients whom he believes he should assist in terminating their lives, but does not because of the statute; he refers to two such patients, both deceased.

Abigail Halpern is the medical director of Uptown Family Practice in Seattle and serves as a clinical faculty member at the University of Washington School of Medicine. In her practice, according to her sworn declaration, she "occasionally" treats patients dying of cancer or AIDS, whose death she believes she should hasten, but does not because of the statute; she refers to one such patient, now deceased.

Thomas A. Preston is chief of cardiology at Pacific Medical Center in Seattle and professor of Medicine at the University of Washington School of Medicine. According to his sworn declaration, he "occasionally" treats patients whose death he believes he should hasten, but does not on account of the statute; he refers to one such patient, now deceased.

Peter Shalit is in private practice in Seattle and the medical director of the Seattle Gay Clinic; he is a clinical instructor at the University of Washington School of Medicine. According to his sworn declaration, he "occasionally" treats patients whose death he believes he should hasten, but does not on account of the statute; he refers to one such patient, now deceased.

PROCEEDINGS

. . . The District Court reached its conclusion as to unconstitutionality on two grounds. First, the court held that the statute violated the liberty guaranteed by the 14th Amendment against deprivation by a state. The court reached this conclusion by noting "a long line of cases" protecting "personal decisions relating to marriage, procreation, contraception, family relationships, child rearing and education." The court quoted as the explanation of this line the statement made in *Planned Parenthood vs. Casey* (1992):

> These matters, including the most intimate and personal choices a person may make in a lifetime, choices central to personal dignity and autonomy, are central to the liberty protected by the 14th Amendment. At the heart of the liberty is the right to define one's own concept of existence, of meaning, of the universe and of the mystery of human life. Beliefs about these matters could not define the attributes of personhood were they formed under compulsion of the state.

The District Court analogized the "terminally ill person's choice to commit suicide" to the choice of abortion protected by *Casey*, stating: "This court finds the reasoning in *Casey* highly instructive and almost prescriptive." Like the abortion decision, the court found the decision by a terminally ill person to end his or her life to be one of the most intimate and personal that could be made in a lifetime and a choice central to personal autonomy and dignity.

The District Court also found *Cruzan vs. Director, Missouri Dept. of Health* (1990) to be "instructive." It quoted that case's reference to "the recognition of a general liberty interest in refusing medical treatment," and the assumption for purposes of the decision in *Cruzan* "that the U.S. Constitution would grant a competent person a constitutionally protected right to refuse lifesaving hydration and nutrition." The District Court stated that it did not believe that a distinction of constitutional significance could be drawn "between refusing life-sustaining medical treatment and physician-assisted suicide by an uncoerced, mentally competent, terminally ill adult." Combining its exegesis of *Casey* and *Cruzan,* the District Court reached its conclusion that there was a constitutional right to physician-assisted suicide.

The District Court then reviewed the statute to determine whether, on its face, it imposed an "undue burden" on a personal right of the *Casey* kind. See *Casey* (concluding that a statute regulating abortion was invalid on its face because "in a large fraction of the cases" in which the statute would operate it would "operate as a substantial obstacle to a woman's choice to undergo an abortion" and therefore placed "an undue burden"). The District Court declared that there was "no question" that the "total ban" on physician-assisted suicide for the terminally ill was "an undue burden" on the constitutional right that the District Court had discovered. Consequently, the statute was invalid.

Second, the District Court held that the statute violated the equal protection clause of the 14th Amendment, requiring that all similarly situated persons be treated alike. Washington law, enacted in 1992, provides: "Any adult person may execute a directive directing the withholding or withdrawal of life-sustaining treatment in a terminal condition or permanent unconscious condition." Wash. Rev. Code 70.122.030. Any physician who participates in good faith "in the withholding or withdrawal of life-sustaining treatment" in accordance with such a directive is immune from civil or criminal or professional liability. Id. 70.122.051. The District Court could see no constitutional distinction between the terminally ill able to direct the withdrawal or withholding of life support and the terminally ill seeking medical aid to end their lives. Accordingly, it found an unequal application of the laws.

Washington appeals.

ANALYSIS

The conclusion of the District Court that the statute deprived the plaintiffs of a liberty protected by the 14th Amendment and denied them the equal protection of the laws cannot be sustained.

First. The language taken from *Casey,* on which the District Court pitched its principal argument, should not be removed from the context in which it was uttered. Any reader of judicial opinions knows they often attempt a generality of expression and a sententiousness of phrase that extend far beyond the problem addressed. It is commonly accounted an error to lift sentences or even paragraphs out of one context and insert the abstracted thought into a wholly different context. To take three sentences out of an opinion over 30 pages in length dealing with the highly charged subject of abortion and to find these sentences "almost prescriptive" in ruling on a statute proscribing the promotion of suicide is to make an enormous leap, to do violence to the context and to ignore the differences between the regulation of reproduction and the prevention of the promotion of killing a patient at his or her request.

The inappropriateness of the language of *Casey* in the situation of assisted suicide is confirmed by considering what this language, as applied by the District Court, implies. The decision to choose death, according to the District Court's use of *Casey*'s terms, involves "personal dignity and autonomy" and "the right to define one's own concept of existence, of meaning, of the universe and of the mystery of human life." The District Court attempted to tie these concepts to the decision of a person terminally ill. But there is no way of doing so. The category created is inherently unstable. The depressed 21-year-old, the romantically devastated 28-year-old, the alcoholic 40-year-old who choose suicide are also expressing their views of existence, meaning, the universe and life; they are also asserting their personal liberty. If at the heart of the liberty protected by the 14th Amendment is this uncurtailable ability to believe and to act on one's deepest beliefs about life, the right to suicide and the right to assistance in suicide are the prerogative of at least every sane adult. The attempt to restrict such rights to the terminally ill is illusory. If such liberty exists in this context, as *Casey* asserted in the context of reproductive rights, every man and woman in the United States must enjoy it. The conclusion is a *reductio ad absurdum.*

Second. While *Casey* was not about suicide at all, *Cruzan* was about the termination of life. The District Court found itself unable to distinguish between a patient refusing life support and a patient seeking medical help to bring about death and therefore interpreted *Cruzan*'s limited acknowledgment of a right to refuse treatment as tantamount to an acceptance of a terminally ill patient's right to aid in self-killing. The District Court ignored the far more relevant part of the opinion in *Cruzan* that "there can be no gainsaying" a state's interest "in the protection and preservation of human life" and, as evidence of that legitimate concern, the fact that "the majority of states in this country have laws imposing criminal penalties on one who assists another to commit suicide." Whatever difficulty the District Court experienced in distinguishing one situation from the other, it was not experienced by the majority in *Cruzan.*

Third. Unsupported by the gloss on *liberty* written by *Casey,* a gloss on a gloss, inasmuch as *Casey* developed an interpretation of *liberty* first elaborated in *Eisenstadt vs. Baird* (1972), and implicitly controverted by *Cruzan,* the decision of the District Court lacks foundation in recent precedent. It also lacks foundation in the traditions of our nation. In the 205 years of our existence no constitutional right to aid in killing oneself has ever been asserted and upheld by a court of final jurisdiction. Unless the federal judiciary is to be a floating constitutional convention, a federal court should not invent a constitutional right unknown to the past and antithetical to the defense of human life that has been a chief responsibility of our constitutional government.

Fourth. The District Court extrapolated from *Casey* to hold the statute invalid on its face. That extrapolation, like the quotation from *Casey,* was an unwarranted extension of abortion jurisprudence, often unique, to a very different field. The normal rule—the rule that governs here—is that a facial challenge to a statute "must establish that no set of circumstances exists under which the act would be valid." The District Court indeed conceded that there were circumstances in which the statute could operate constitutionally, for example to deter suicide by teen-agers or to prevent fraud upon the elderly. The District Court did not even attempt the calculation carried out in *Casey* to show that in "a large fraction of the cases" the statute would operate unconstitutionally. From the declarations before it, the District Court had at most the opinion of several physicians that they "occasionally" met persons whom the statute affected detrimentally and their recitation of five case histories. There was no effort made to compare this number with the number of persons whose lives were guarded by the statute. The facial invalidation of the statute was wholly unwarranted.

Fifth. The District Court declared the statute unconstitutional on its face without adequate consideration of Washington's interests that, individually and convergently, outweigh any alleged liberty of suicide. The most comprehensive study of our subject by a governmental body is *When Death Is Sought. Assisted Suicide and Euthanasia in the Medical Context* (1994). The study was conducted by the New York State Task Force, a commission appointed by Governor Cuomo in 1985, which filed its report in May 1994. The task force was composed of 24 members representing a broad spectrum of ethical and religious views and ethical, health, legal and medical competencies. Its membership disagreed on the morality of suicide. Unanimously the members agreed against recommending a change in New York law to permit assisted suicide. Washington's interest in preventing such suicides is as strong as the interests that moved this diverse commission to its unanimous conclusion.

A Michigan commission, set up in 1992, by majority vote in June 1994 recommended legislative change in the Michigan law against assisted suicide and set out a proposed new statute as a legislative option; the commission did not challenge the constitutionality of the existing Michigan legislation. Michigan Commission on Death and Dying, *Final Report* (1994).

Neither the New York nor the Michigan reports were available to the District Court. We take them into account on this appeal as we take into account the legal and medical articles cited by the parties and amici as representative professional judgments in this area of law. In the light of all these materials, Washington's interests are at least these:

1 The interest in not having physicians in the role of killers of their patients. "Physician-assisted suicide is fundamentally incompatible with the physician's role as healer," declares the American Medical Association's Code of Medical Ethics (1994). From the Hippocratic oath with its promise "to do no harm," to the AMA's code, the ethics of the medical profession have proscribed killing. Washington has an interest in preserving the integrity of the physician's practice as understood by physicians.

Not only would the self-understanding of physicians be affected by removal of the state's support for their professional stance; the physician's constant search for ways to combat disease would be affected if killing were as acceptable an option for the physician as curing. The physician's commitment to curing is the medical profession's commitment to medical progress. Medically assisted suicide as an acceptable alternative is a blind alley; Washington has a stake in barring it.

2 The interest in not subjecting the elderly and even the not-elderly but infirm to psychological pressure to consent to their own deaths. For all medical treatments, physicians decide which patients are the candidates. If assisted suicide was acceptable professional practice, physicians would make a judgment as to who was a good candidate for it. Physician neutrality and patient autonomy, independent of their physician's advice, are largely myths. Most patients do what their doctors recommend. As an eminent commission concluded, "Once the physician suggests suicide or euthanasia, some patients will feel that they have few if any alternatives but to accept the recommendation." New York State Task Force, *When Death Is Sought,* 122. Washington has an interest in preventing such persuasion.

3 The interest in protecting the poor and minorities from exploitation. The poor and minorities would be especially open to manipulation in a regime of assisted suicide for two reasons: Pain is a significant factor in creating a desire for assisted suicide, and the poor and minorities are notoriously less provided for in the alleviation of pain. Id. at 100. The desire to reduce the cost of public assistance by quickly terminating a prolonged illness cannot be ignored: "The cost of treatment is viewed as relevant to decisions at the bedside." Id. at 129. Convergently, the reduction of untreated (although treatable) pain and economic logic would make the poorest the primest candidates for physician-assisted and physician-recommended suicide.

4 The interest in protecting all of the handicapped from societal indifference and antipathy. Among the many briefs we have received from amici curiae there is one on behalf of numerous residents of nursing homes and long-term care facilities. The vulnerability of such persons to physician-assisted suicide is foreshadowed in the discriminatory way that a seriously disabled person's expression of a desire to die is interpreted. When the nondisabled say they want to die, they are labeled as suicidal; if they are disabled, it is treated as "natural" or "reasonable." In the climate of our achievement-oriented society, "simply offering the option of 'self-deliverance' shifts a burden of proof so that helpless patients must ask themselves why they are not availing themselves of it." Richard Doerflinger, "Assisted Suicide: Pro-choice or Anti-

Life?" 19 Hastings Center Report 16, 17 (1989). An insidious bias against the handicapped—again coupled with a cost-saving mentality—makes them especially in need of Washington's statutory protection.

5 An interest in preventing abuse similar to what has occurred in the Netherlands where, since 1984, legal guidelines have tacitly allowed assisted suicide or euthanasia in response to a repeated request from a suffering, competent patient. In 1990, approximately 1.8 percent of all deaths resulted from this practice. At least an additional 0.8 percent of all deaths, and arguably more, come from direct measures taken to end the person's life without a contemporaneous request to end it. New York State Task Force, *When Death Is Sought,* 133–134.

Sixth. The scope of the District Court's judgment is, perhaps necessarily, indefinite. The judgment of the District Court was entered in favor of Jane Roe and John Doe although they were dead. This unheard-of judgment was a nullity. The judgment in favor of James Poe lapsed with his death pending appeal. The judgment in favor of Drs. Glucksberg, Halperin, Preston and Shalit was "insofar as they raise claims on behalf of their terminally ill patients." No such patients were identified by these doctors except patients who were already deceased. Presumably, then, the judgment was [on] behalf of terminally ill patients that these doctors might encounter in the future. The term *terminally ill* was not defined by the court. No class was certified by the court. There is a good deal of uncertainty on whose behalf the judgment was entered.

It was suggested in argument that a definition of the terminally ill could be supplied from the Washington statute on the refusal of life-sustaining treatment which does define *terminal condition.* Wash. Rev. Code 70.122.020(9). There are three difficulties: *terminal condition* and *terminally ill* are different terms; the examples given by the plaintiffs show considerable variation in whom they considered [the] terminally ill to be; there is wide disagreement in definition of the terminally ill among the states. See New York State Task Force, *When Death Is Sought,* 23–35. Life itself is a terminal condition, unless *terminal condition* is otherwise defined by a specific statute. A terminal illness can vary from a sickness causing death in days or weeks to cancer, which Dr. Glucksberg notes is "very slow" in its deadly impact, to a heart condition, which Dr. Preston notes can be relieved by a transplant, to AIDS, which Dr. Shalit declares is fatal once contracted. One can only guess which definition of the terminally ill would satisfy the constitutional criteria of the District Court. Consequently, an amorphous class of beneficiaries has been created in this non-class action; and the District Court has mandated Washington to reform its law against the promotion of suicide to safeguard the constitutional rights of persons whom the District Court has not identified.

Seventh. At the heart of the District Court's decision appears to be its refusal to distinguish between actions taking life and actions by which life is not supported or ceases to be supported. This refusal undergirds the District Court's reading of *Cruzan* as well as its holding that the statute violates equal protection. The distinction, being drawn by the legislature not on the basis of race, gender or religion or membership in any protected class and not infringing any fundamental constitutional right, must be upheld unless the plaintiffs can show "that the legislature's actions were irra-tional." The plaintiffs have not sustained this burden.

Against the broad background of moral experience that everyone acquires, the law of torts and the law of criminal offenses against the person have developed. "At com-mon law, even the touching of one person by another without consent and without legal justification was a battery." The physician's medical expertness is not a license to inflict medical procedures against your will. Protected by the law of torts, you can have or reject such medical treatment as you see fit. You can be left alone if you want. Privacy in the primordial sense in which it entered constitutional parlance—"the right to be let alone"—is yours.

Tort law and criminal law have never recognized a right to let others enslave you, mutilate you or kill you. When you assert a claim that another—and especially an-other licensed by the state—should help you bring about your death, you ask for more than being let alone; you ask that the state, in protecting its own interest, not prevent its licensee from killing. The difference is not of degree but of kind. You no longer seek the ending of unwanted medical attention. You seek the right to have a second person collaborate in your death. To protect all the interests enumerated under Fifth above, the statute rightly and reasonably draws the line.

Compassion, according to the reflections of Prince Myshkin, is "the most impor-tant, perhaps the sole law of human existence." Feodor Dostoevsky, *The Idiot,* 292 (Alan Myers, trans.) (1991). In the vernacular, compassion is trumps. No one can read the accounts of the sufferings of the deceased plaintiffs supplied by their dec-larations or the accounts of the sufferings of their patients supplied by the physicians without being moved by them. No one would inflict such sufferings on another or want them inflicted on himself; and since the horrors recounted are those that could attend the end of life, anyone who reads of them must be aware that they could be attendant on his own death. The desire to have a good and kind way of forestalling them is understandably evident in the declarations of the plaintiffs and in the deci-sion of the District Court.

Compassion is a proper, desirable, even necessary component of judicial charac-ter; but compassion is not the most important, certainly not the sole law of human existence. Unrestrained by other virtues, as *The Idiot* illustrates, it leads to catastro-phe. Justice, prudence and fortitude are necessary too. Compassion cannot be the compass of a federal judge. That compass is the Constitution of the United States. Where, as here in the case of Washington, the statute of a state comports with that compass, the validity of the statute must be upheld.

For all the foregoing reasons, the judgment appealed from is reversed.

QUESTIONS

1 Judge Noonan concludes that the Washington State statute prohibiting "promoting a sui-cide attempt" is not unconstitutional. In your view, does this statute constitute sound so-cial policy or should it be revised to allow physicians to assist in the suicide of a patient?
2 Would you endorse Judge Noonan's analysis of the various state interests underlying the Washington statute?

SUGGESTED ADDITIONAL READINGS FOR CHAPTER 2

DOWNING, A. B., ed.: *Euthanasia and the Right to Death: The Case for Voluntary Euthanasia.* New York: Humanities Press; London: Peter Owen, 1969. Two articles are especially notable in this collection. In "The Principle of Euthanasia," Antony Flew constructs "a general moral case for the establishment of a legal right" to voluntary (active) euthanasia. In a well-known article, "Euthanasia Legislation: Some Non-Religious Objections," Yale Kamisar argues against the legalization of voluntary (active) euthanasia.

GOMEZ, CARLOS F.: *Regulating Death: Euthanasia and the Case of the Netherlands.* New York: Free Press, 1991. Gomez describes and criticizes the practice of (active) euthanasia in the Netherlands. He argues that the Dutch system is plagued with inadequate controls.

Hastings Center Report, vol. 22, March–April 1992. This issue provides a collection of articles under the heading "Dying Well? A Colloquy on Euthanasia and Assisted Suicide." Several of the articles deal specifically with the practice of (active) euthanasia in the Netherlands. Also, Dan W. Brock offers an extensive defense of voluntary active euthanasia, which Daniel Callahan opposes in "When Self-Determination Runs Amok."

Journal of Pain and Symptom Management, vol. 6, July 1991. This special issue provides a diverse collection of articles on physician-assisted suicide and (active) euthanasia.

MILLER, FRANKLIN G., et al.: "Regulating Physician-Assisted Death." *New England Journal of Medicine,* vol. 331, July 14, 1994, pp. 119–123. A group of six authors, well-known in bioethics, argues for the legalization of "physician-assisted death," that is, both physician-assisted suicide and voluntary active euthanasia, in accordance with a detailed proposal for regulation of the practice.

THE NEW YORK STATE TASK FORCE ON LIFE AND THE LAW: *When Death Is Sought: Assisted Suicide and Euthanasia in the Medical Context.* Albany: Health Education Services, 1994. Providing an extensive analysis of clinical, legal, and ethical considerations, the task force unanimously recommends that the laws prohibiting assisted suicide and (active) euthanasia in New York not be changed.

PELLEGRINO, EDMUND D.: "Doctors Must Not Kill." *The Journal of Clinical Ethics,* vol. 3, Summer 1992, pp. 95–102. Pellegrino contends that (1) the moral arguments in favor of (active) euthanasia are flawed, (2) killing by physicians would seriously distort the healing relationship, and (3) the social consequences of allowing such killing would be very detrimental.

QUILL, TIMOTHY E.: "Death and Dignity: A Case of Individualized Decision Making." *New England Journal of Medicine,* vol. 324, March 7, 1991, pp. 691–694. Quill presents a brief account of a case in which he assisted in the suicide of one of his patients. The case is often referred to as "the case of Diane."

STEINBOCK, BONNIE, ed.: *Killing and Letting Die.* Englewood Cliffs, N.J.: Prentice-Hall, 1980. This anthology provides a wealth of material on the killing/letting die distinction.

WEIR, ROBERT F.: "The Morality of Physician-Assisted Suicide." *Law, Medicine & Health Care,* vol. 20, Spring–Summer 1992, pp. 116–126. Weir surveys the ethical arguments for and against physician-assisted suicide. He believes that the practice is justified under certain conditions.

CHAPTER 3

The Death Penalty

Strong convictions are firmly entrenched on both sides of the death penalty controversy. From one side, we hear in forceful tones that "murderers deserve to die." We are also told that no lesser punishment than the death penalty will suffice to deter potential murderers. From the other side of the controversy, in tones of equal conviction, we are told that the death penalty is a cruel and barbarous practice, effectively serving no purpose that could not be equally well served by a more humane punishment. "How long," it is asked, "must we indulge this uncivilized and pointless lust for revenge?" In the face of such strongly held but opposed views, each of us is invited to confront an important ethical issue, the morality of the death penalty. Before approaching the death penalty in its ethical dimensions, however, it will be helpful to briefly discuss its constitutional dimensions. Many of the considerations raised in discussions of the constitutionality of the death penalty parallel those raised in discussions of its morality.

THE CONSTITUTIONALITY OF THE DEATH PENALTY

The Eighth Amendment to the Constitution of the United States explicitly prohibits the infliction of *cruel and unusual* punishment. If the death penalty is a cruel and unusual punishment, it is unconstitutional. But is it cruel and unusual? In a landmark case, *Furman v. Georgia* (1972), the Supreme Court ruled that the death penalty was unconstitutional *as then administered.* The Court did not comprehensively rule, however, that the death penalty was unconstitutional *by its very nature.* Indeed, subsequent developments in the Court have made clear that the death penalty is not unconstitutional—as long as it is administered in accordance with certain procedural requirements.

The decision reached in *Furman* was by a mere five-to-four majority. There was a basic divergence of viewpoint among those who voted with the majority. Both Justice Marshall and Justice Brennan argued straightforwardly that the death penalty is a cruel and unusual punishment *by its very nature.* From this perspective it would not matter how much the procedures of its administration might be modified. It would still remain a cruel and unusual punishment. Among the reasons advanced to support this contention, two are especially noteworthy: (1) The death penalty is excessive in the sense of being unnecessary; lesser penalties are capable of serving the desired legislative purpose. (2) The death penalty is abhorrent to currently existing moral values.

The other three justices (Douglas, White, and Stewart) who voted with the majority did not commit themselves to the position that the death penalty is unconstitutional *by its very nature.* Leaving this underlying issue unresolved, they simply advanced the more guarded contention that the death penalty was unconstitutional *as then administered.* In their view, the death penalty was unconstitutional primarily because it was being administered in an arbitrary and capricious manner. The essence of their argument can be reconstructed in the following way. The death penalty is typically imposed at the discretion of a jury (or sometimes a judge). The absence of explicit standards to govern the decision between life and death allows a wide range of unchecked prejudice to operate freely under the heading of *discretion.* For example, discretion seems to render blacks more prone than whites to the death penalty. Such standardless discretion violates not only the Eighth Amendment but also the Fourteenth Amendment, which guarantees "due process of law."

As matters developed in the wake of *Furman,* it was the Court's objection to *standardless discretion* that provided an opening for the many individual states still anxious to retain the death penalty as a viable component of their legal systems. These states were faced with the challenge of devising procedures for imposing the death penalty that would not be open to the charge of standardless discretion. Two such approaches gained prominence. (1) Some states (e.g., North Carolina) moved to dissolve the objection of standardless discretion by simply making the death penalty *mandatory* for certain crimes. (2) Other states (e.g., Georgia) took an equally obvious approach. It consisted in the effort to establish standards that would provide guidance for the jury (or the judge) in deciding between life and death.

Subsequent developments have made clear that the second approach is constitutionally acceptable whereas the first is not. In *Woodson v. North Carolina* (1976), the Court rule (though by a mere five-to-four majority) that mandatory death sentences are unconstitutional. In *Gregg v. Georgia* (1976), however, the Court ruled (with only Justice Marshall and Justice Brennan dissenting) that the death penalty is not unconstitutional when imposed at the discretion of a jury for the *crime of murder,*[1] so long as appropriate safeguards are provided against any arbitrary or capricious imposition. Most important, there must be explicit standards established for the guidance of jury deliberations. The attitude of the Court in this regard is made clear by Justices Stewart, Powell, and Stevens in their opinion in *Gregg,* which appears in this chapter. Also appearing in this chapter is the dissenting opinion of Justice Marshall.

---

[1]In *Gregg,* the Supreme Court considered only the constitutionality of imposing the death penalty for the *crime of murder.* In *Coker v. Georgia* (1977), 433 U.S. 584, the Court subsequently considered the constitutionality of imposing the death penalty for the *crime of rape.* Holding death to be a "grossly disproportionate" punishment for the crime of rape, the Court declared such an employment of the death penalty unconstitutional.

THE ETHICAL ISSUE

In any discussion of the morality of the death penalty, it is important to remember that the death penalty is a kind of punishment. Indeed, it is normally thought to be the most serious kind of punishment, hence it is called *capital* punishment. Most philosophers agree that punishment in general (as contrasted with capital punishment in particular) is a morally justified social practice. For one thing, however uneasy we might feel about inflicting harm on another person, it is hard to visualize a complex society managing to survive without an established legal system of punishment. However, to say that most philosophers agree that punishment is a morally justified social practice is not to say that there are no dissenters from this view. Some argue that it is possible to structure society in ways that would not necessitate commitment to a legal system of punishment as we know it. One possibility suggested is that undesirable social behavior could be adequately kept in check by therapeutic treatment rather than by traditional kinds of punishment. Such a system would seem to have the advantage of being more humane, but surely it is implausible to believe that present therapeutic techniques are anywhere near adequate to the task. Perhaps future advances in the behavioral sciences will render such an alternative more viable. If so, it may one day be plausible to argue that the whole practice of (nontherapeutic) punishment must be rejected on moral grounds. Still, for now, there is widespread agreement on the moral defensibility of punishment as an overall social practice. What stands out as an open and hotly debated ethical issue is whether or not the death penalty, as a distinctive kind of punishment, ought to continue to play a role in our legal system of punishment.

Those in favor of retaining the death penalty are commonly called *retentionists*. Retentionists differ among themselves regarding the kinds of cases in which they find it appropriate to employ the death penalty. They also differ among themselves regarding the supporting arguments they find acceptable. But anyone who supports the retention of the death penalty—for employment in whatever kinds of cases and for whatever reason—is by definition a retentionist. Those in favor of abolishing the death penalty are commonly called *abolitionists*. Abolitionists, by definition, refuse to support any employment of the death penalty. Like the retentionists, however, they differ among themselves concerning the supporting arguments they find acceptable.

There is one extreme, and not widely embraced, abolitionist line of thought. It is based on the belief that the sanctity of human life demands absolute nonviolence. On this view, killing of any kind, for whatever reason, is always and everywhere morally wrong. No one has the right to take a human life, not in self-defense, not in war, not in any circumstance. Thus, since the death penalty obviously involves a kind of killing, it is a morally unacceptable form of punishment and must be abolished. This general view, which is associated with the Quakers and other pacifists, has struck most moral philosophers as implausible. Can we really think that killing, when it is the only course that will save oneself from an unprovoked violent assault, is morally wrong? Can we really think that it would be morally wrong to kill a terrorist if that were the *only* possible way of stopping him or her from exploding a bomb in the midst of a kindergarten class? The defender of absolute nonviolence is sometimes inclined to argue at this point that violence will only breed violence. There may indeed be much truth in this claim. Still, most people do not believe that such a claim provides adequate support for the contention that *all* killing is morally wrong, and if some killing is morally acceptable, perhaps the death penalty is as well. What arguments can be made on its behalf?

RETENTIONIST ARGUMENTS

Broadly speaking, arguments for the retention of the death penalty usually emphasize either (1) considerations of *justice* or (2) considerations of *social utility.* Those who emphasize considerations of justice typically develop their case along the following line: When the moral order is upset by the commission of some offense, it is only right that the disorder be rectified by punishment that is equal to or proportional to the offense. This view is reflected in remarks such as "The scales of justice demand retribution" and "The offender must pay for the crime." Along this line, the philosopher Immanuel Kant (1724–1804) is famous for his unequivocal defense of the *lex talionis*—the law (or principle) of retaliation, often expressed as "an eye for an eye." According to this principle, punishment is to be inflicted in a measure that will equalize the offense. And when the offense is murder, *only* capital punishment is sufficient to equalize it.

In one of this chapter's readings, Igor Primoratz argues for retention of the death penalty on retributive grounds. Stephen Nathanson, an abolitionist, provides a contrasting point of view. Nathanson argues that no adequate retributive rationale can be provided for the death penalty.

Although the demand for retribution continues to play a prominent role in the overall case for the death penalty, many retentionists (and obviously abolitionists as well) have come to feel quite uneasy with the notion of imposing the death penalty "because the wrongdoer *deserves* it." Perhaps this uneasiness can be traced, at least in part, to our growing awareness of the way in which social conditions, such as ghetto living, seem to spawn criminal activity. If so, then it seems that we have arrived at a point of intersection with a venerable—and vexing—philosophical problem, the problem of "freedom and determinism." Pure retributive thinking seems to presuppose a radical sense of human freedom and its correlate, a radical sense of personal responsibility and accountability for one's actions. This is undoubtedly why retentionists who espouse a retributive rationale often insist that the death penalty does not constitute a denial of the wrongdoer's dignity and worth as a human being. On the contrary, they say, the death penalty reaffirms the dignity and worth of a convicted murderer—by holding the person strictly responsible for the crime that has been committed and giving the person what he or she deserves. Of course, if someone is uneasy with the radical sense of human freedom that seems to underlie pure retributive thinking, that person will surely be uneasy with the retributive rationale for retention of the death penalty. So let us turn our attention to the utilitarian side of the retentionist coin.

Since considerations of social utility are commonly advanced in defense of the practice of punishment in general, it is not surprising to find that they are also commonly advanced in defense of retaining the death penalty. Utilitarianism, as a distinct school of moral philosophy, locates the primary justification of punishment in its social utility. Utilitarians acknowledge that punishment consists in the infliction of evil on another person, but they hold that such evil is far outweighed by the future benefits that will accrue to society. Imprisonment, for example, might lead to such socially desirable effects as (1) *rehabilitation* of the criminal, (2) *incapacitation,* whereby we achieve temporary or permanent protection from the imprisoned criminal, and (3) *deterrence* of other potential criminals. When utilitarian considerations are recruited in support of the retention of the *death* penalty, it is clear that rehabilitation of the criminal can play no part in the case. But retentionists do frequently promote considerations of incapacitation and deterrence.

Retentionists who appeal to considerations of incapacitation typically argue that the death penalty is the only effective way to protect society from a certain subset of convicted murderers—namely, those who are at once *violence-prone and irreformable.* (Notice that an important difficulty here would be finding effective criteria for the identification of those already convicted murderers who are truly violence-prone and irreformable.) Life imprisonment, it is said, cannot assure society of the needed protection, because even if "life imprisonment" were really life imprisonment—that is, even if a sentence of life imprisonment excluded the possibility of parole—violence-prone and irreformable inmates would still pose an imminent threat to prison guards and fellow inmates. Furthermore, escape is always possible. Thus, the death penalty is the only truly effective way of achieving societal protection against the continuing threat posed by some convicted murderers.

According to many retentionists, however, the fundamental justification for retaining the death penalty lies in the fact that the death penalty is a *uniquely effective deterrent.* But is this central factual claim true? Is the death penalty a more substantial deterrent than life imprisonment or even long-term imprisonment? At this point, a natural move is to look to the findings of the social sciences, but most scholars familiar with the social science literature on this issue would say that the available evidence is conflicting and ultimately inconclusive. If it is true that empirical studies have failed to resolve the central factual question, what else can be said about the deterrence rationale for the death penalty?

Many retentionists, willing to acknowledge that scientific findings are inconclusive, argue that we must simply rely on common sense. Since people typically fear death much more than they fear life imprisonment, it just stands to reason, they say, that the death penalty is superior to life imprisonment as a deterrent. Although the threat of life imprisonment or even long-term imprisonment may well be sufficient to deter many would-be murderers, the threat of execution would deter an even greater number. Thus the death penalty ought to be retained in our system of criminal justice because it is a more substantial deterrent than is life imprisonment.

The commonsense argument for the death penalty as a uniquely effective deterrent might be countered with the following claim: It does not follow from the mere fact that one punishment is more severe than another that the former will be a more substantial deterrent than the latter. Indeed, it might be the case that anyone *capable of being deterred* from murder by the threat of the death penalty would be equally well deterred by the threat of life imprisonment. In one of this chapter's readings, Jonathan Glover takes issue with the commonsense argument for the death penalty as a uniquely effective deterrent.

There is one other important argument made by retentionists dedicated to the deterrence rationale. This argument, advanced by Ernest van den Haag in this chapter, takes uncertainty—our uncertainty whether or not the death penalty is a uniquely effective deterrent—as its point of departure. If we retain the death penalty, the argument goes, we run the risk of needlessly eradicating the lives of convicted murderers; perhaps the death penalty is *not* a uniquely effective deterrent. On the other hand, if we abolish the death penalty, we run the risk of innocent people becoming future murder victims; perhaps the death penalty *is* a uniquely effective deterrent. Faced with such uncertainty, the argument concludes, it is our moral obligation to retain the death penalty. Whichever way we go, there is a risk to be run, but it is better from a moral point of view to risk the lives of the guilty than to risk the lives of the innocent.

A critic might respond to van den Haag's argument as follows. In claiming that retention risks the lives of the guilty, whereas abolition risks the lives of the innocent, the argument overlooks the possibility that retention of the death penalty has what is sometimes called a "counter-deterrent effect." The idea here is that state-sponsored killing in the form of execution has a brutalizing effect on society, that it actually functions to weaken inhibitions on the part of the populace against killing. Thus, in the long run, there might well be more murders in a retentionist society than there would be in an abolitionist society. So it is not correct to say that retention of the death penalty risks only guilty lives; relative to the possibility that the death penalty has a counter-deterrent effect, retention also places innocent lives at risk.

THE CASE FOR ABOLITION

What can be said of the abolitionist case against the death penalty? Most abolitionists do not care to argue the extreme position, already discussed, of absolute nonviolence, yet they typically do want to commit themselves seriously to the "sanctity of human life." They emphasize the inherent worth and dignity of each individual and insist that the taking of a human life, while perhaps sometimes morally permissible, is a very serious matter and not to be permitted in the absence of weighty overriding reasons. At face value, they argue, the death penalty is cruel and inhumane; and since retentionists have failed to advance substantial reasons in its defense, it must be judged a morally unacceptable practice. Against retentionist arguments based on retribution as a demand of justice, abolitionists frequently argue that the "demand of justice" is nothing but a mask for a barbarous vengeance. Against retentionist arguments based on considerations of social utility, abolitionists simply argue that other more humane punishments will serve equally well. We do not need the death penalty to incapacitate convicted murderers because life imprisonment can provide us with a sufficient measure of societal protection. Also, since there is no reason to believe that the death penalty is a more effective deterrent than long-term imprisonment, retention cannot be justified on the basis of considerations of deterrence.

In addition to advancing arguments that directly counter retentionist claims, abolitionists typically incorporate two further arguments into their overall case against the death penalty. The first of these arguments can be stated as follows: It is impossible to guarantee that mistakes will not be made in the administration of punishment, but this factor is especially important in the case of the death penalty, because only *capital* punishment is irrevocable. Thus only the death penalty eradicates the possibility of compensating an innocent person who has been wrongly punished. A second abolitionist argument focuses attention on patterns of discrimination in the administration of the death penalty. In our society, it is said, blacks are more likely to receive the death penalty than whites, and the poor and uneducated are more likely to receive the death penalty than the affluent and educated. A retentionist counter to each of these abolitionist arguments is provided by Primoratz.

In the final reading of this chapter, Richard C. Dieter argues for abolition of the death penalty. In his view, retention makes no social sense in the United States; the practical burdens resulting from continued employment of the death penalty are simply too great.

Thomas A. Mappes

Opinion in *Gregg v. Georgia*

**Justices
Potter Stewart,
Lewis F. Powell, Jr.,
and John Paul Stevens**

Potter Stewart (1915–1985) and Lewis F. Powell, Jr., served as associate justices of the United States Supreme Court. John Paul Stevens continues to serve as associate justice of the Court. Justice Stewart, a graduate of Yale University Law School, spent some years in private practice, served as judge of the United States Court of Appeals, Sixth Circuit (1954–1958), and served on the Supreme Court from 1958 to 1981. Justice Powell, LL.B (Washington and Lee), LL.M (Harvard), practiced law in Richmond, Virginia, for nearly forty years prior to his appointment in 1971 to the Supreme Court. He retired from the Court in 1987. Justice Stevens, a graduate of Northwestern University School of Law, spent a number of years in private practice, served as judge of the United States Court of Appeals, Seventh Circuit (1970–1975), and was appointed to the Supreme Court in 1975.

The state of Georgia reacted to the Court's decision in *Furman v. Georgia* (1972) by drafting a death penalty statute calculated to avoid the Court's objection to standardless discretion. Georgia's approach, in contrast to the approach of those states that made the death penalty mandatory for certain crimes, embodied an effort to specify standards that would guide a jury (or a judge) in deciding between the death penalty and life imprisonment. In this case, with only Justice

United States Supreme Court. 428 U.S. 153 (1976).

Marshall and Justice Brennan dissenting, the Court upheld the constitutionality of imposing the death penalty for the crime of murder under the law of Georgia.

Justices Stewart, Powell, and Stevens initially consider the contention that the death penalty for the crime of murder is, under all circumstances, cruel and unusual punishment, thus unconstitutional. On their analysis, a punishment is cruel and unusual if it fails to accord with "evolving standards of decency." Moreover, even if a punishment does accord with contemporary values, it must still be judged cruel and unusual if it fails to accord with the "dignity of man," the "basic concept underlying the Eighth Amendment." They take this second stipulation to rule out "excessive" punishment, identified as (1) that which involves the unnecessary and wanton infliction of pain or (2) that which is grossly out of proportion to the severity of the crime. In light of these considerations, Justices Stewart, Powell, and Stevens argue that the imposition of the death penalty for the crime of murder does not invariably violate the Constitution. They contend that legislative developments since *Furman* have made clear that the death penalty is acceptable to contemporary society. Moreover, they contend, the death penalty is not invariably excessive: (1) It may properly be considered necessary to achieve two principal social purposes— retribution and deterrence. (2) When the death penalty is imposed for the crime of murder, it may properly be considered not disproportionate to the severity of the crime.

Turning their attention to the death sentence imposed under the law of Georgia in this case, Justices Stewart, Powell, and Stevens maintain that a carefully drafted statute, ensuring "that the sentencing authority is given adequate information and guidance," makes it possible to avoid imposing the death penalty in an arbitrary or capricious manner. The revised Georgia statutory system under which Gregg was sentenced to death, they conclude, does not violate the Constitution.

The issue in this case is whether the imposition of the sentence of death for the crime of murder under the law of Georgia violates the Eighth and Fourteenth Amendments.

I

The petitioner, Troy Gregg, was charged with committing armed robbery and murder. In accordance with Georgia procedure in capital cases, the trial was in two stages, a guilt stage and a sentencing stage. . . .

. . . The jury found the petitioner guilty of two counts of armed robbery and two counts of murder.

At the penalty stage, which took place before the same jury, . . . the trial judge instructed the jury that it could recommend either a death sentence or a life prison sentence on each count. . . . The jury returned verdicts of death on each count.

The Supreme Court of Georgia affirmed the convictions and the imposition of the death sentences for murder. . . . The death sentences imposed for armed robbery, however, were vacated on the grounds that the death penalty had rarely been imposed in Georgia for that offense. . . .

II

. . . The Georgia statute, as amended after our decision in *Furman v. Georgia* (1972), retains the death penalty for six categories of crime: murder, kidnaping for ransom or where the victim is harmed, armed robbery, rape, treason, and aircraft hijacking. . . .

III

We address initially the basic contention that the punishment of death for the crime of murder is, under all circumstances, "cruel and unusual" in violation of the Eighth and Fourteenth Amendments of the Constitution. In Part IV of this opinion, we will consider the sentence of death imposed under the Georgia statutes at issue in this case.

The Court on a number of occasions has both assumed and asserted the constitutionality of capital punishment. In several cases that assumption provided a necessary foundation for the decision, as the Court was asked to decide whether a particular method of carrying out a capital sentence would be allowed to stand under the Eighth Amendment. But until *Furman v. Georgia* (1972), the Court never confronted squarely the fundamental claim that the punishment of death always, regardless of the enormity of the offense or the procedure followed in imposing the sentence, is cruel and unusual punishment in violation of the Constitution. Although this issue was presented and addressed in *Furman,* it was not resolved by the Court. Four Justices would have held that capital punishment is not unconstitutional *per se;* two justices would have reached the opposite conclusion; and three Justices, while agreeing that the statutes then before the Court were invalid as applied, left open the question whether such punishment may ever be imposed. We now hold that the punishment of death does not invariably violate the Constitution.

A

The history of the prohibition of "cruel and unusual" punishment already has been reviewed at length. The phrase first appeared in the English Bill of Rights of 1689, which was drafted by Parliament at the accession of William and Mary. The English version appears to have been directed against punishments unauthorized by statute and beyond the jurisdiction of the sentencing court, as well as those disproportionate to the offense involved. The American draftsmen, who adopted the English phrasing in drafting the Eighth Amendment, were primarily concerned, however, with proscribing "tortures" and other "barbarous" methods of punishment.

In the earliest cases raising Eighth Amendment claims, the Court focused on particular methods of execution to determine whether they were too cruel to pass constitutional muster. The constitutionality of the sentence of death itself was not at issue, and the criterion used to evaluate the mode of execution was its similarity to "torture" and other "barbarous" methods. . . .

But the Court has not confined the prohibition embodied in the Eighth Amendment to "barbarous" methods that were generally outlawed in the 18th century. Instead, the Amendment has been interpreted in a flexible and dynamic manner. The Court early recognized that a "principle to be vital must be capable of wider application than the mischief which gave it birth." Thus the Clause forbidding "cruel and unusual" punishments "is not fastened to the obsolete but may acquire meaning as public opinion becomes enlightened by a humane justice." . . .

It is clear from the foregoing precedents that the Eighth Amendment has not been regarded as a static concept. As Mr. Chief Justice Warren said, in an oftquoted phrase, "[t]he Amendment must draw its meaning from the evolving standards of decency that mark the progress of a maturing society." Thus, an assessment of contemporary values concerning the infliction of a challenged sanction is relevant to the application of the Eighth Amendment. As we develop below more fully, this assessment does not call for a subjective judgment. It requires, rather, that we look to objective indicia that reflect the public attitude toward a given sanction.

But our cases also make clear that public perceptions of standards of decency with respect to criminal sanctions are not conclusive. A penalty also must accord with "the dignity of man," which is the "basic concept underlying the Eighth Amendment." This means, at least, that the punishment not be "excessive." When a form of punishment in the abstract (in this case, whether capital punishment may ever be imposed as a sanction for murder) rather than in the particular (the propriety of death as a penalty to be applied to a specific defendant for a specific crime) is under consideration, the inquiry into "excessiveness" has two aspects. First, the punishment must not involve the unnecessary and wanton infliction of pain. Second, the punishment must not be grossly out of proportion to the severity of the crime.

B

Of course, the requirements of the Eighth Amendment must be applied with an awareness of the limited role to be played by the courts. This does not mean that judges have no role to play, for the Eighth Amendment is a restraint upon the exercise of legislative power. . . .

But, while we have an obligation to insure that constitutional bounds are not overreached, we may not act as judges as we might as legislators. . . .

Therefore, in assessing a punishment selected by a democratically elected legislature against the constitutional measure, we presume its validity. We may not require the legislature to select the least severe penalty possible so long as the penalty selected is not cruelly inhumane or disproportionate to the crime involved. And a heavy burden rests on those who would attack the judgment of the representatives of the people.

This is true in part because the constitutional test is intertwined with an assessment of contemporary standards and the legislative judgment weighs heavily in ascertaining such standards. "[I]n a democratic society legislatures, not courts, are constituted to respond to the will and consequently the moral values of the people."

The deference we owe to the decisions of the state legislatures under our federal system is enhanced where the specification of punishments is concerned, for "these are peculiarly questions of legislative policy." Caution is necessary lest this Court become, "under the aegis of the Cruel and Unusual Punishment Clause, the ultimate arbiter of the standards of criminal responsibility . . . throughout the country." A decision that a given punishment is impermissible under the Eighth Amendment cannot be reversed short of a constitutional amendment. The ability of the people to express their preference through the normal democratic processes, as well as through ballot referenda, is shut off. Revisions cannot be made in the light of further experience.

C

In the discussion to this point we have sought to identify the principles and considerations that guide a court in addressing an Eighth Amendment claim. We now consider specifically whether the sentence of death for the crime of murder is a *per se* violation of the Eighth and Fourteenth Amendments to the Constitution. We note first that history and precedent strongly support a negative answer to this question.

The imposition of the death penalty for the crime of murder has a long history of acceptance both in the United States and in England. . . .

It is apparent from the text of the Constitution itself that the existence of capital punishment was accepted by the Framers. At the time the Eighth Amendment was ratified, capital punishment was a common sanction in every State. Indeed, the First Congress of the United States enacted legislation providing death as the penalty for specified crimes. . . .

For nearly two centuries, this Court, repeatedly and often expressly, has recognized that capital punishment is not invalid *per se*. . . .

Four years ago, the petitioners in *Furman* and its companion cases predicated their argument primarily upon the asserted proposition that standards of decency had evolved to the point where capital punishment no longer could be tolerated. The petitioners in those cases said, in effect, that the evolutionary process had come to an end, and that standards of decency required that the Eighth Amendment be construed finally as prohibiting capital punishment for any crime regardless of its depravity and impact on society. This view was accepted by two Justices. Three other Justices were unwilling to go so far; focusing on the procedures by which convicted defendants were selected for the death penalty rather than on the actual punishment inflicted, they joined in the conclusion that the statutes before the Court were constitutionally invalid.

The petitioners in the capital cases before the Court today renew the "standards of decency" argument, but developments during the four years since *Furman* have undercut substantially the assumptions upon which their argument rested. Despite the continuing debate, dating back to the 19th century, over the morality and utility of capital punishment, it is now evident that a large proportion of American society continues to regard it as an appropriate and necessary criminal sanction.

The most marked indication of society's endorsement of the death penalty for murder is the legislative response to *Furman*. The legislatures of at least 35 States have enacted new statutes that provide for the death penalty for at least some crimes that result in the death of another person. And the Congress of the United States, in 1974, enacted a statute providing the death penalty for aircraft piracy that results in death. These recently adopted statutes have attempted to address the concerns expressed by the Court in *Furman* primarily (i) by specifying the factors to be weighed and the procedures to be followed in deciding when to impose a capital sentence, or (ii) by making the death penalty mandatory for specified crimes. But all of the post-*Furman* statutes make clear that capital punishment itself has not been rejected by the elected representatives of the people. . . .

The jury also is a significant and reliable objective index of contemporary values because it is so directly involved. The Court has said that "one of the most important functions any jury can perform in making . . . a selection [between life imprisonment and death for a defendant convicted in a capital case] is to maintain a link between contemporary community values and the penal system." It may be true that evolving standards have influenced juries in recent decades to be more discriminating in imposing the sentence of death. But the relative infrequency of jury verdicts imposing the death sentence does not indicate rejection of capital punishment *per se.* Rather, the reluctance of juries in many cases to impose the sentence may well reflect the humane feeling that this most irrevocable of sanctions should be reserved for a small number of extreme cases. Indeed, the actions of juries in many States since *Furman* are fully compatible with the legislative judgments, reflected in the new statutes, as to the continued utility and necessity of capital punishment in appropriate cases. At the close of 1974 at least 254 persons had been sentenced to death since *Furman,* and by the end of March 1976, more than 460 persons were subject to death sentences.

As we have seen, however, the Eighth Amendment demands more than that a challenged punishment be acceptable to contemporary society. The Court also must ask whether it comports with the basic concept of human dignity at the core of the Amendment. Although we cannot "invalidate a category of penalties because we deem less severe penalties adequate to serve the ends of penology," the sanction imposed cannot be so totally without penological justification that it results in the gratuitous infliction of suffering.

The death penalty is said to serve two principal social purposes: retribution and deterrence of capital crimes by prospective offenders.[1]

In part, capital punishment is an expression of society's moral outrage at particularly offensive conduct. This function may be unappealing to many, but it is essential in an ordered society that asks its citizens to rely on legal processes rather than self-help to vindicate their wrongs.

> The instinct of retribution is part of the nature of man, and channeling that instinct in the administration of criminal justice serves an important purpose in promoting the stability of a society governed by law. When people begin to believe that organized society is unwilling or unable to impose upon criminal offenders the punishment they "deserve," then there are sown the seeds of anarchy—of self-help, vigilante justice, and lynch law. *Furman v. Georgia* (Stewart, J., concurring).

"Retribution is no longer the dominant objective of the criminal law," but neither is it a forbidden objective nor one inconsistent with our respect for the dignity of men.

Indeed, the decision that capital punishment may be the appropriate sanction in extreme cases is an expression of the community's belief that certain crimes are themselves so grievous an affront to humanity that the only adequate response may be the penalty of death.

Statistical attempts to evaluate the worth of the death penalty as a deterrent to crimes by potential offenders have occasioned a great deal of debate. The results simply have been inconclusive. . . .

Although some of the studies suggest that the death penalty may not function as a significantly greater deterrent than lesser penalties, there is no convincing empirical evidence either supporting or refuting this view. We may nevertheless assume safely that there are murderers, such as those who act in passion, for whom the threat of death has little or no deterrent effect. But for many others, the death penalty undoubtedly is a significant deterrent. There are carefully contemplated murders, such as murder for hire, where the possible penalty of death may well enter into the cold calculus that precedes the decision to act. And there are some categories of murder, such as murder by a life prisoner, where other sanctions may not be adequate.

The value of capital punishment as a deterrent of crime is a complex factual issue the resolution of which properly rests with the legislatures, which can evaluate the results of statistical studies in terms of their own local conditions and with a flexibility of approach that is not available to the courts. Indeed, many of the post-*Furman* statutes reflect just such a responsible effort to define those crimes and those criminals for which capital punishment is most probably an effective deterrent.

In sum, we cannot say that the judgment of the Georgia Legislature that capital punishment may be necessary in some cases is clearly wrong. Considerations of federalism, as well as respect for the ability of a legislature to evaluate, in terms of its particular State, the moral consensus concerning the death penalty and its social utility as a sanction, require us to conclude, in the absence of more convincing evidence, that the infliction of death as a punishment for murder is not without justification and thus is not unconstitutionally severe.

Finally, we must consider whether the punishment of death is disproportionate in relation to the crime for which it is imposed. There is no question that death as a punishment is unique in its severity and irrevocability. When a defendant's life is at stake, the Court has been particularly sensitive to insure that every safeguard is observed. But we are concerned here only with the imposition of capital punishment for the crime of murder, and when a life has been taken deliberately by the offender,[2] we cannot say that the punishment is invariably disproportionate to the crime. It is an extreme sanction, suitable to the most extreme of crimes.

We hold that the death penalty is not a form of punishment that may never be imposed, regardless of the circumstances of the offense, regardless of the character of the offender, and regardless of the procedure followed in reaching the decision to impose it.

IV

We now consider whether Georgia may impose the death penalty on the petitioner in this case.

A

While *Furman* did not hold that the infliction of the death penalty *per se* violates the Constitution's ban on cruel and unusual punishments, it did recognize that the penalty of death is different in kind from any other punishment imposed under our system of criminal justice. Because of the uniqueness of the death penalty, *Furman* held that it could not be imposed under sentencing procedures that created a substantial risk that it would be inflicted in an arbitrary and capricious manner. . . .

Furman mandates that where discretion is afforded a sentencing body on a matter so grave as the determination of whether a human life should be taken or spared, that discretion must be suitably directed and limited so as to minimize the risk of wholly arbitrary and capricious action.

It is certainly not a novel proposition that discretion in the area of sentencing be exercised in an informed manner. We have long recognized that "[f]or the determination of sentences, justice generally requires . . . that there be taken into account the circumstances of the offense together with the character and propensities of the offender." . . .

Jury sentencing has been considered desirable in capital cases in order "to maintain a link between contemporary community values and the penal system—a link without which the determination of punishment could hardly reflect 'the evolving standards of decency that mark the progress of a maturing society.' " But it creates special problems. Much of the information that is relevant to the sentencing decision may have no relevance to the question of guilt, or may even be extremely prejudicial to a fair determination of that question. This problem, however, is scarcely insurmountable. Those who have studied the question suggest that a bifurcated procedure—one in which the question of sentence is not considered until the determination of guilt has been made—is the best answer. . . . When a human life is at stake and when the jury must have information prejudicial to the question of guilt but relevant to the question of penalty in order to impose a rational sentence, a bifurcated system is more likely to ensure elimination of the constitutional deficiencies identified in *Furman.*

But the provision of relevant information under fair procedural rules is not alone sufficient to guarantee that the information will be properly used in the imposition of punishment, especially if sentencing is performed by a jury. Since the members of a jury will have had little, if any, previous experience in sentencing, they are unlikely to be skilled in dealing with the information they are given. To the extent that this problem is inherent in jury sentencing, it may not be totally correctable. It seems clear, however, that the problem will be alleviated if the jury is given guidance regarding the factors about the crime and the defendant that the State, representing organized society, deems particularly relevant to the sentencing decision. . . .

While some have suggested that standards to guide a capital jury's sentencing deliberations are impossible to formulate, the fact is that such standards have been developed. When the drafters of the Model Penal Code faced this problem, they concluded "that it is within the realm of possibility to point to the main circumstances of aggravation and of mitigation that should be weighed *and weighed against each other* when they are presented in a concrete case.[3] While such standards are by necessity somewhat general, they do provide guidance to the sentencing authority and thereby reduce the likelihood that it will impose a sentence that fairly can be called capricious or arbitrary. Where the sentencing authority is required to specify the factors it relied upon in reaching its decision, the further safeguard of meaningful appellate review is available to ensure that death sentences are not imposed capriciously or in a freakish manner.

In summary, the concerns expressed in *Furman* that the penalty of death not be imposed in an arbitrary or capricious manner can be met by a carefully drafted statute that ensures that the sentencing authority is given adequate information and guidance. As a general proposition these concerns are best met by a system that provides for a bifurcated proceeding at which the sentencing authority is apprised of the information relevant to the imposition of sentence and provided with standards to guide its use of the information.

We do not intend to suggest that only the above-described procedures would be permissible under *Furman* or that any sentencing system constructed along these general lines would inevitably satisfy the concerns of *Furman,* for each distinct system must be examined on an individual basis. Rather, we have embarked upon this general exposition to make clear that it is possible to construct capital-sentencing systems capable of meeting *Furman's* constitutional concerns.

B

We now turn to consideration of the constitutionality of Georgia's capital-sentencing procedures. In the wake of *Furman,* Georgia amended its capital punishment statute, but chose not to narrow the scope of its murder provisions. Thus, now as before *Furman,* in Georgia "[a] person commits murder when he unlawfully and with malice aforethought, either express or implied, causes the death of another human being." All persons convicted of murder "shall be punished by death or by imprisonment for life."

Georgia did act, however, to narrow the class of murderers subject to capital punishment by specifying 10 statutory aggravating circumstances, one of which must be found by the jury to exist beyond a reasonable doubt before a death sentence can ever be imposed. In addition, the jury is authorized to consider any other appropriate aggravating or mitigating circumstances. The jury is not required to find any mitigating circumstance in order to make a recommendation of mercy that is binding on the trial court, but it must find a *statutory* aggravating circumstance before recommending a sentence of death.

These procedures require the jury to consider the circumstances of the crime and the criminal before it recommends sentence. No longer can a Georgia jury do as Furman's jury did: reach a finding of the defendant's guilt and then, without guidance or direction, decide whether he should live or die. Instead, the jury's attention is directed to the specific circumstances of the crime: Was it committed in the course of another capital felony? Was it committed for money? Was it committed upon a peace officer or judicial officer? Was it committed in a particularly heinous way or in a manner that endangered the lives of many persons? In addition, the jury's attention is focused on the characteristics of the person who committed the crime: Does he have a record of prior convictions for capital offenses? Are there any special facts about this defendant that mitigate against imposing capital punishment (*e.g.,* his youth, the extent of his cooperation with the police, his emotional state at the time of the crime). As a result, while some jury discretion still exists, "the discretion to be exercised is controlled by clear and objective standards so as to produce non-discriminatory application."

As an important additional safeguard against arbitrariness and caprice, the Georgia statutory scheme provides for automatic appeal of all death sentences to the State's Supreme Court. That court is required by statute to review each sentence of death and determine whether it was imposed under the influence of passion or prejudice, whether the evidence supports the jury's finding of a statutory aggravating circumstance, and whether the sentence is disproportionate compared to those sentences imposed in similar cases.

In short, Georgia's new sentencing procedures require as a prerequisite to the imposition of the death penalty, specific jury findings as to the circumstances of the crime or the character of the defendant. Moreover, to guard further against a situation comparable to that presented in *Furman,* the Supreme Court of Georgia compares each death sentence with the sentences imposed on similarly situated defendants to ensure that the sentence of death in a particular case is not disproportionate. On their face these procedures seem to satisfy the concerns of *Furman.* No longer should there be "no meaningful basis for distinguishing the few cases in which [the death penalty] is imposed from the many cases in which it is not." . . .

V

The basic concern of *Furman* centered on those defendants who were being condemned to death capriciously and arbitrarily. Under the procedures before the Court in that case, sentencing authorities were not directed to give attention to the nature or circumstances of the crime committed or to the character or record of the defendant. Left unguided, juries imposed the death sentence in a way that could only be called freakish. The new Georgia sentencing procedures, by contrast, focus the jury's attention on the particularized nature of the crime and the particularized characteristics of the individual defendant. While the jury is permitted to consider any aggravating or mitigating circumstances, it must find and identify at least one statutory aggravating factor before it may impose a penalty of death. In this way the jury's discretion is channeled. No longer can a jury wantonly and freakishly impose the death sentence; it is always circumscribed by the legislative guidelines. In addition, the review function of the Supreme Court of Georgia affords additional assurance that the concerns that prompted our decision in *Furman* are not present to any significant degree in the Georgia procedure applied here.

For the reasons expressed in this opinion, we hold that the statutory system under which Gregg was sentenced to death does not violate the Constitution. Accordingly, the judgment of the Georgia Supreme Court is affirmed.

NOTES

1 Another purpose that has been discussed is the incapacitation of dangerous criminals and the consequent prevention of crimes that they may otherwise commit in the future.

2 We do not address here the question whether the taking of the criminal's life is a proportionate sanction where no victim has been deprived of life—for example, when capital punishment is imposed for rape, kidnaping, or armed robbery that does not result in the death of any human being.

3 The Model Penal Code proposes the following standards: "(3) Aggravating Circumstances.

"(a) The murder was committed by a convict under sentence of imprisonment.

"(b) The defendant was previously convicted of another murder or of a felony involving the use or threat of violence to the person.

"(c) At the time the murder was committed the defendant also committed another murder.

"(d) The defendant knowingly created a great risk of death to many persons.

"(e) The murder was committed while the defendant was engaged or was an accomplice in the commission of, or an attempt to commit, or flight after committing or attempting to commit robbery, rape or deviate sexual intercourse by force or threat of force, arson, burglary or kidnapping.

"(f) The murder was committed for the purpose of avoiding or preventing a lawful arrest or effecting an escape from lawful custody.

"(g) The murder was committed for pecuniary gain.

"(h) The murder was especially heinous, atrocious or cruel, manifesting exceptional depravity.

"(4) Mitigating Circumstances.

"(a) The defendant has no significant history of prior criminal activity.

"(b) The murder was committed while the defendant was under the influence of extreme mental or emotional disturbance.

"(c) The victim was a participant in the defendant's homicidal conduct or consented to the homicidal act.

"(d) The murder was committed under circumstances which the defendant believed to provide a moral justification or extenuation for his conduct.

"(e) The defendant was an accomplice in a murder committed by another person and his participation in the homicidal act was relatively minor.

"(f) The defendant acted under duress or under the domination of another person.

"(g) At the time of the murder, the capacity of the defendant to appreciate the criminality [wrongfulness] of his conduct or to conform his conduct to the requirements of law was impaired as a result of mental disease or defect or intoxication.

"(h) The youth of the defendant at the time of the crime." ALI Model Penal Code § 210.6 (Proposed Official Draft 1962).

QUESTIONS

1 With regard to the imposition of the death penalty for the crime of murder, Justices Stewart, Powell, and Stevens write, "we cannot say that the punishment is invariably disproportionate to the crime." The Georgia statute under which Gregg was sentenced, however, retained the death penalty not only for the crime of murder but also for "kidnaping for ransom or where the victim is harmed, armed robbery, rape, treason, and aircraft hijacking." In your view, is the death penalty a disproportionate punishment for such crimes?

2 In note 3, we find a set of proposed model standards for the guidance of a jury in deciding

whether a murderer warrants the death penalty or some lesser penalty, typically life imprisonment. Is the proposed set of aggravating circumstances (those whose presence should
incline a jury toward the death penalty) defensible and complete? Is the proposed set of mitigating circumstances (those whose presence should incline a jury away from the death
penalty) defensible and complete?

Dissenting Opinion in *Gregg v. Georgia*

Justice Thurgood Marshall

Thurgood Marshall (1908–1993), the first black ever appointed to the United States Supreme
Court, served as associate justice from 1967 to 1993. Much of his distinguished private career was given over to providing legal counsel for groups dedicated to the advancement of
civil rights. Justice Marshall also served as United States circuit judge (1961–1965) and
United States solicitor general (1965–1967).

Justice Marshall reaffirms the conclusion he had reached in *Furman v. Georgia*
(1972): The death penalty is unconstitutional for two individually sufficient
reasons. (1) It is excessive. (2) The American people, if fully informed, would
consider it morally unacceptable. He insists that his conclusion in *Furman* has not
been undercut by subsequent developments. Despite the fact that legislative
activity since *Furman* would seem to indicate that the American people do not
consider the death penalty morally unacceptable, Justice Marshall continues to
maintain that the citizenry, *if fully informed,* would consider it morally
unacceptable. At any rate, he maintains, the death penalty is unconstitutional
because it is excessive, i.e., unnecessary to accomplish a legitimate legislative
purpose. Neither deterrence nor retribution, the principal purposes asserted by
Justices Stewart, Powell, and Stevens, can sustain the death penalty as
nonexcessive in Justice Marshall's view. Since the available evidence does not
show the death penalty to be a more effective deterrent than life imprisonment, he
contends, the death penalty is not necessary to promote the goal of deterrence.
Moreover, the death penalty is unnecessary to "further any legitimate notion of
retribution." According to Justice Marshall, the notion that a murderer "deserves"
death constitutes a denial of the wrongdoer's dignity and worth and thus is
fundamentally at odds with the Eighth Amendment.

In *Furman v. Georgia* (1972) (concurring opinion), I set forth at some length my
views on the basic issue presented to the Court in [this case]. The death penalty, I
concluded, is a cruel and unusual punishment prohibited by the Eighth and Fourteenth
Amendments. That continues to be my view.

I have no intention of retracing the "long and tedious journey" that led to my conclusion in *Furman.* My sole purposes here are to consider the suggestion that my con-

United States Supreme Court. 428 U.S. 153 (1976).

clusion in *Furman* has been undercut by developments since then, and briefly to evaluate the basis for my Brethren's holding that the extinction of life is a permissible
form of punishment under the Cruel and Unusual Punishments Clause.

In *Furman* I concluded that the death penalty is constitutionally invalid for two
reasons. First, the death penalty is excessive. And second, the American people, fully
informed as to the purposes of the death penalty and its liabilities, would in my view
reject it as morally unacceptable.

Since the decision in *Furman,* the legislatures of 35 States have enacted new
statutes authorizing the imposition of the death sentence for certain crimes, and
Congress has enacted a law providing the death penalty for air piracy resulting in
death. I would be less than candid if I did not acknowledge that these developments
have a significant bearing on a realistic assessment of the moral acceptability of the
death penalty to the American people. But if the constitutionality of the death penalty
turns, as I have urged, on the opinion of an *informed* citizenry, then even the enactment of new death statutes cannot be viewed as conclusive. In *Furman,* I observed
that the American people are largely unaware of the information critical to a judgment on the morality of the death penalty, and concluded that if they were better informed they would consider it shocking, unjust, and unacceptable. A recent study,
conducted after the enactment of the post-*Furman* statutes, has confirmed that the
American people know little about the death penalty, and that the opinions of an informed public would differ significantly from those of a public unaware of the consequences and effects of the death penalty.

Even assuming, however, that the post-*Furman* enactment of statutes authorizing
the death penalty renders the prediction of the views of an informed citizenry an uncertain basis for a constitutional decision, the enactment of those statutes has no bearing whatsoever on the conclusion that the death penalty is unconstitutional because
it is excessive. An excessive penalty is invalid under the Cruel and Unusual Punishments Clause "even though popular sentiment may favor" it. The inquiry here,
then, is simply whether the death penalty is necessary to accomplish the legitimate
legislative purposes in punishment, or whether a less severe penalty—life imprisonment—would do as well.

The two purposes that sustain the death penalty as nonexcessive in the Court's
view are general deterrence and retribution. In *Furman,* I canvassed the relevant data
on the deterrent effect of capital punishment. The state of knowledge at that point,
after literally centuries of debate, was summarized as follows by a United Nations
Committee:

> It is generally agreed between the retentionists and abolitionists, whatever their opinions
> about the validity of comparative studies of deterrence, that the data which now exist show
> no correlation between the existence of capital punishment and lower rates of capital
> crime.

The available evidence, I concluded in *Furman,* was convincing that "capital punishment is not necessary as a deterrent to crime in our society." ...

... The evidence I reviewed in *Furman* remains convincing, in my view, that "capital punishment is not necessary as a deterrent to crime in our society." The justification for the death penalty must be found elsewhere.

The other principal purpose said to be served by the death penalty is retribution. The notion that retribution can serve as a moral justification for the sanction of death finds credence in the opinion of my Brothers STEWART, POWELL, and STEVENS. . . . It is this notion that I find to be the most disturbing aspect of today's unfortunate [decision].

The concept of retribution is a multifaceted one, and any discussion of its role in the criminal law must be undertaken with caution. On one level, it can be said that the notion of retribution or reprobation is the basis of our insistence that only those who have broken the law be punished, and in this sense the notion is quite obviously central to a just system of criminal sanctions. But our recognition that retribution plays a crucial role in determining who may be punished by no means requires approval of retribution as a general justification for punishment. It is the question whether retribution can provide a moral justification for punishment—in particular, capital punishment—that we must consider.

My Brothers STEWART, POWELL, and STEVENS offer the following explanation of the retributive justification for capital punishment:

> The instinct for retribution is part of the nature of man, and channeling that instinct in the administration of criminal justice serves an important purpose in promoting the stability of a society governed by law. When people begin to believe that organized society is unwilling or unable to impose upon criminal offenders the punishment they "deserve," then there are sown the seeds of anarchy—of self-help, vigilante justice, and lynch law.

This statement is wholly inadequate to justify the death penalty. As my Brother BRENNAN stated in *Furman,* "[t]here is no evidence whatever that utilization of imprisonment rather than death encourages private blood feuds and other disorders." It simply defies belief to suggest that the death penalty is necessary to prevent the American people from taking the law into their own hands.

In a related vein, it may be suggested that the expression of moral outrage through the imposition of the death penalty serves to reinforce basic moral values—that it marks some crimes as particularly offensive and therefore to be avoided. The argument is akin to a deterrence argument, but differs in that it contemplates the individual's shrinking from antisocial conduct, not because he fears punishment, but because he has been told in the strongest possible way that the conduct is wrong. This contention, like the previous one, provides no support for the death penalty. It is inconceivable that any individual concerned about conforming his conduct to what society says is "right" would fail to realize that murder is "wrong" if the penalty were simply life imprisonment.

The foregoing contentions—that society's expression of moral outrage through the imposition of the death penalty pre-empts the citizenry from taking the law into its own hands and reinforces moral values—are not retributive in the purest sense. They are essentially utilitarian in that they portray the death penalty as valuable because of its beneficial results. These justifications for the death penalty are inadequate because the penalty is, quite clearly I think, not necessary to the accomplishment of those results.

There remains for consideration, however, what might be termed the purely retributive justification for the death penalty—that the death penalty is appropriate, not because of its beneficial effect on society, but because the taking of the murderer's life is itself morally good. Some of the language of the opinion of my Brothers STEWART, POWELL, and STEVENS . . . appears positively to embrace this notion of retribution for its own sake as a justification for capital punishment. They state:

> [T]he decision that capital punishment may be the appropriate sanction in extreme cases is an expression of the community's belief that certain crimes are themselves so grievous an affront to humanity that the only adequate response may be the penalty of death.

They then quote with approval from Lord Justice Denning's remarks before the British Royal Commission on Capital Punishment:

> The truth is that some crimes are so outrageous that society insists on adequate punishment, because the wrong-doer deserves it, irrespective of whether it is a deterrent or not.

Of course, it may be that these statements are intended as no more than observations as to the popular demands that it is thought must be responded to in order to prevent anarchy. But the implication of the statements appears to me to be quite different— namely, that society's judgment that the murderer "deserves" death must be respected not simply because the preservation of order requires it, but because it is appropriate that society make the judgment and carry it out. It is this latter notion, in particular, that I consider to be fundamentally at odds with the Eighth Amendment. The mere fact that the community demands the murderer's life in return for the evil he has done cannot sustain the death penalty, for as JUSTICES STEWART, POWELL, and STEVENS remind us, "the Eighth Amendment demands more than that a challenged punishment be acceptable to contemporary society." To be sustained under the Eighth Amendment, the death penalty must "compor[t] with the basic concept of human dignity at the core of the Amendment;" the objective in imposing it must be "[consistent] with our respect for the dignity of [other] men." Under these standards, the taking of life "because the wrongdoer deserves it" surely must fail, for such a punishment has as its very basis the total denial of the wrongdoer's dignity and worth.

The death penalty, unnecessary to promote the goal of deterrence or to further any legitimate notion of retribution, is an excessive penalty forbidden by the Eighth and Fourteenth Amendments. I respectfully dissent from the Court's judgment upholding the [sentence] of death imposed upon the [petitioner in this case].

QUESTIONS

1 Is Justice Marshall correct in claiming that the American people, *if fully informed* about the death penalty, would consider it morally unacceptable?
2 Is the death penalty, as Justice Marshall claims, "unnecessary to promote the goal of deterrence or to further any legitimate notion of retribution"?

A Life for a Life

Igor Primoratz

Igor Primoratz is senior lecturer in philosophy at the Hebrew University of Jerusalem. His many published articles on the topic of punishment include "Punishment and Utilitarianism" and "Punishment as Language." He is the author of *Justifying Legal Punishment* (1989), from which this selection is excerpted.

Primoratz endorses a retributive rationale for the retention of the death penalty and defends this rationale against commonly made abolitionist arguments. He rejects the idea that the death penalty violates a murderer's right to life and insists that there is no contradiction involved in a system of criminal law that prohibits murder and yet allows the state to administer the death penalty. He also defends the retributive rationale against arguments claiming to show that the death penalty is in reality a disproportionate penalty for the crime of murder. Finally, Primoratz argues that neither the possibility of executing an innocent person nor the discriminatory application of the death penalty can provide a credible basis for abolition.

. . . According to the retributive theory, consequences of punishment, however important from the practical point of view, are irrelevant when it comes to its justification; *the* moral consideration is its justice. Punishment is morally justified insofar as it is meted out as retribution for the offense committed. When someone has committed an offense, he deserves to be punished: it is just, and consequently justified, that he be punished. The offense is the sole ground of the state's right and duty to punish. It is also the measure of legitimate punishment: the two ought to be proportionate. So the issue of capital punishment within the retributive approach comes down to the question, Is this punishment ever proportionate retribution for the offense committed, and thus deserved, just, and justified?

The classic representatives of retributivism believed that it was, and that it was the only proportionate and hence appropriate punishment, if the offense was *murder*—that is, criminal homicide perpetrated voluntarily and intentionally or in wanton disregard of human life. In other cases, the demand for proportionality between offense and punishment can be satisfied by fines or prison terms;[1] the crime of murder, however, is an exception in this respect, and calls for the literal interpretation of the *lex talionis*. The uniqueness of this crime has to do with the uniqueness of the value which has been deliberately or recklessly destroyed. We come across this idea as early as the original formulation of the retributive view—the biblical teaching on punishment: "You shall accept no ransom for the life of a murderer who is guilty of death; but he shall be put to death."[2] The rationale of this command—one that clearly distinguishes the biblical conception of the criminal law from contemporaneous

From Igor Primoratz, *Justifying Legal Punishment* (1989), pp. 158–159, 161–166. Reprinted with the permission of Humanities Press International, Atlantic Highlands, NJ.

criminal law systems in the Middle East—is that man was not only created *by* God, like every other creature, but also, alone among all the creatures, *in the image of God:*

> That man was made in the image of God . . . is expressive of the peculiar and supreme worth of man. Of all creatures, Genesis 1 relates, he alone possesses this attribute, bringing him into closer relation to God than all the rest and conferring upon him the highest value. . . . This view of the uniqueness and supremacy of human life . . . places life beyond the reach of other values. The idea that life may be measured in terms of money or other property . . . is excluded. Compensation of any kind is ruled out. The guilt of the murderer is infinite because the murdered life is invaluable; the kinsmen of the slain man are not competent to say when he has been paid for. An absolute wrong has been committed, a sin against God which is not subject to human discussion. . . . Because human life is invaluable, to take it entails the death penalty.[3]

This view that the value of human life is not commensurable with other values, and that consequently there is only one truly equivalent punishment for murder, namely death, does not necessarily presuppose a theistic outlook. It can be claimed that, simply because we have to be alive if we are to experience and realize any other value at all, there is nothing equivalent to the murderous destruction of a human life except the destruction of the life of the murderer. Any other retribution, no matter how severe, would still be less than what is proportionate, deserved, and just. As long as the murderer is alive, no matter how bad the conditions of his life may be, there are always at least *some* values he can experience and realize. This provides a plausible interpretation of what the classical representatives of retributivism as a philosophical theory of punishment, such as Kant and Hegel, had to say on the subject.[4]

It seems to me that this is essentially correct. With respect to the larger question of the justification of punishment in general, it is the retributive theory that gives the right answer. Accordingly, capital punishment ought to be retained where it obtains, and reintroduced in those jurisdictions that have abolished it, although we have no reason to believe that, as a means of deterrence, it is any better than a very long prison term. It ought to be retained, or reintroduced, for one simple reason: that justice be done in cases of murder, that murderers be punished according to their deserts.

There are a number of arguments that have been advanced against this rationale of capital punishment. . . .

[One] abolitionist argument . . . simply says that capital punishment is illegitimate because it violates the right to life, which is a fundamental, absolute, sacred right belonging to each and every human being, and therefore ought to be respected even in a murderer.[5]

If any rights are fundamental, the right to life is certainly one of them; but to claim that it is absolute, inviolable under any circumstances and for any reason, is a different matter. If an abolitionist wants to argue his case by asserting an absolute right to life, she will also have to deny moral legitimacy to taking human life in war, revolution, and self-defense. This kind of pacifism is a consistent but farfetched and hence implausible position.

I do not believe that the right to life (nor, for that matter, any other right) is absolute. I have no general theory of rights to fall back upon here; instead, let me pose a question. Would we take seriously the claim to an absolute, sacred, inviolable right to life—coming from the mouth of a *confessed murderer?* I submit that we would not, for the obvious reason that it is being put forward by the person who confessedly denied another human being this very right. But if the murderer cannot plausibly claim such a right for himself, neither can *anyone else* do that in his behalf. This suggests that there is an element of reciprocity in our general rights, such as the right to life or property. I can convincingly claim these rights only so long as I acknowledge and respect the same rights of others. If I violate the rights of others, I thereby lose the same rights. If I am a murderer, I have no *right* to live.

Some opponents of capital punishment claim that a criminal law system which includes this punishment is contradictory, in that it prohibits murder and at the same time provides for its perpetration: "It is one and the same legal regulation which prohibits the individual from murdering, while allowing the state to murder. . . . This is obviously a terrible irony, an abnormal and immoral logic, against which everything in us revolts."[6]

This seems to be one of the more popular arguments against the death penalty, but it is not a good one. If it were valid, it would prove too much. Exactly the same might be claimed of other kinds of punishment: of prison terms, that they are "contradictory" to the legal protection of liberty; of fines, that they are "contradictory" to the legal protection of property. Fortunately enough, it is not valid, for it begs the question at issue. In order to be able to talk of the state as "murdering" the person it executes, and to claim that there is "an abnormal and immoral logic" at work here, which thrives on a "contradiction," one has to use the word "murder" in the very same sense—that is, in the usual sense, which implies the idea of the *wrongful* taking the life of another—both when speaking of what the murderer has done to the victim and of what the state is doing to him by way of punishment. But this is precisely the question at issue: whether capital punishment *is* "murder," whether it is wrongful or morally justified and right.

The next two arguments attack the retributive rationale of capital punishment by questioning the claim that it is only this punishment that satisfies the demand for proportion between offense and punishment in the case of murder. The first points out that any two human lives are different in many important respects, such as age, health, physical and mental capability, so that it does not make much sense to consider them equally valuable. What if the murdered person was very old, practically at the very end of her natural life, while the murderer is young, with most of his life still ahead of him, for instance? Or if the victim was gravely and incurably ill, and thus doomed to live her life in suffering and hopelessness, without being able to experience almost anything that makes a human life worth living, while the murderer is in every respect capable of experiencing and enjoying things life has to offer? Or the other way round? Would not the death penalty in such cases amount either to taking a more valuable life as a punishment for destroying a less valuable one, or *vice versa?* Would it not be either too much, or too little, and in both cases disproportionate, and thus unjust and wrong, from the standpoint of the retributive theory itself?[7]

Any plausibility this argument might appear to have is the result of a conflation of differences between, and value of, human lives. No doubt, any two human lives are *different* in innumerable ways, but this does not entail that they are not *equally valuable.* I have no worked-out general theory of equality to refer to here, but I do not think that one is necessary in order to do away with this argument. The modern humanistic and democratic tradition in ethical, social, and political thought is based on the idea that all human beings are equal. This finds its legal expression in the principle of equality of people under the law. If we are not willing to give up this principle, we have to stick to the assumption that, all differences notwithstanding, any two human lives, *qua* human lives, are equally valuable. If, on the other hand, we allow that, on the basis of such criteria as age, health, or mental or physical ability, it can be claimed that the life of one person is more or less valuable than the life of another, and we admit such claims in the sphere of law, including criminal law, we shall thereby give up the principle of equality of people under the law. In all consistency, we shall not be able to demand that property, physical and personal integrity, and all other rights and interests of individuals be given equal consideration in courts of law either—that is, we shall have to accept systematic discrimination between individuals on the basis of the same criteria across the whole field. I do not think anyone would seriously contemplate an overhaul of the whole legal system along these lines.

The second argument having to do with the issue of proportionality between murder and capital punishment draws our attention to the fact that the law normally provides for a certain period of time to elapse between the passing of a death sentence and its execution. It is a period of several weeks or months; in some cases it extends to years. This period is bound to be one of constant mental anguish for the condemned. And thus, all things considered, what is inflicted on him is disproportionately hard and hence unjust. It would be proportionate and just only in the case of "a criminal who had warned his victim of the date at which he would inflict a horrible death on him and who, from that moment onward, had confined him at his mercy for months."[8]

The first thing to note about this argument is that it does not support a full-fledged abolitionist stand; if it were valid, it would not show that capital punishment is *never* proportionate and just, but only that it is *very rarely* so. Consequently, the conclusion would not be that it ought to be abolished outright, but only that it ought to be restricted to those cases that would satisfy the condition cited above. Such cases do happen, although, to be sure, not very often; the murder of Aldo Moro, for instance, was of this kind. But this is not the main point. The main point is that the argument actually does not hit at capital punishment itself, although it is presented with that aim in view. It hits at something else: a particular way of carrying out this punishment, which is widely adopted in our time. Some hundred years ago and more, in the Wild West, they frequently hanged the man convicted to die almost immediately after pronouncing the sentence. I am not arguing here that we should follow this example today; I mention this piece of historical fact only in order to show that the interval between sentencing someone to death and carrying out the sentence is not a *part* of capital punishment itself. However unpalatable we might find those Wild

West hangings, whatever objections we might want to voice against the speed with which they followed the sentencing, surely we shall not deny them the *description* of "executions." So the implication of the argument is not that we ought to do away with capital punishment altogether, nor that we ought to restrict it to those cases of murder where the murderer had warned the victim weeks or months in advance of what he was going to do to her, but that we ought to reexamine the procedure of carrying out this kind of punishment. We ought to weigh the reasons for having this interval between the sentencing and executing, against the moral and human significance of the repercussions such an interval inevitably carries with it.

These reasons, in part, have to do with the possibility of miscarriages of justice and the need to rectify them. Thus we come to the argument against capital punishment which, historically, has been the most effective of all: many advances of the abolitionist movement have been connected with discoveries of cases of judicial errors. Judges and jurors are only human, and consequently some of their beliefs and decisions are bound to be mistaken. Some of their mistakes can be corrected upon discovery; but precisely those with most disastrous repercussions—those which result in innocent people being executed—can never be rectified. In all other cases of mistaken sentencing we can revoke the punishment, either completely or in part, or at least extend compensation. In addition, by exonerating the accused we give moral satisfaction. None of this is possible after an innocent person has been executed; capital punishment is essentially different from all other penalties by being completely irrevocable and irreparable.[9] Therefore, it ought to be abolished.

A part of my reply to this argument goes along the same lines as what I had to say on the previous one. It is not so far-reaching as abolitionists assume; for it would be quite implausible, even fanciful, to claim that there have *never* been cases of murder which left no room whatever for reasonable doubt as to the guilt and full responsibility of the accused. Such cases may not be more frequent than those others, but they do happen. Why not retain the death penalty at least for them?

Actually, this argument, just as the preceding one, does not speak out against capital punishment itself, but against the existing procedures for trying capital cases. Miscarriages of justice result in innocent people being sentenced to death and executed, even in the criminal-law systems in which greatest care is taken to ensure that it never comes to that. But this does not stem from the intrinsic nature of the institution of capital punishment; it results from deficiencies, limitations, and imperfections of the criminal law procedures in which this punishment is meted out. Errors of justice do not demonstrate the need to do away with capital punishment; they simply make it incumbent on us to do everything possible to improve even further procedures of meting it out.

To be sure, this conclusion will not find favor with a diehard abolitionist. "I shall ask for the abolition of Capital Punishment until I have the infallibility of human judgement demonstrated to me," that is, as long as there is even the slightest possibility that innocent people may be executed because of judicial errors, Lafayette said in his day.[10] Many an opponent of this kind of punishment will say the same today. The demand to do away with capital punishment altogether, so as to eliminate even the smallest chance of that ever happening—the chance which, admittedly, would remain even after everything humanly possible has been done to perfect the procedure, although then it would be very slight indeed—is actually a demand to give a privileged position to murderers as against all other offenders, big and small. For if we acted on this demand, we would bring about a situation in which proportionate penalties would be meted out for all offenses, *except* for murder. Murderers would not be receiving the only punishment truly proportionate to their crimes, the punishment of death, but some other, lighter, and thus disproportionate penalty. All other offenders would be punished according to their deserts; only murderers would be receiving less than *they* deserve. In all other cases justice would be done in full; only in cases of the gravest of offenses, the crime of murder, justice would not be carried out in full measure. It is a great and tragic miscarriage of justice when an innocent person is mistakenly sentenced to death and executed, but systematically giving murderers advantage over all other offenders would also be a grave injustice. Is the fact that, as long as capital punishment is retained, there is a possibility that over a number of years, or even decades, an injustice of the first kind may be committed, unintentionally and unconsciously, reason enough to abolish it altogether, and thus end up with a system of punishments in which injustices of the second kind are perpetrated daily, consciously, and inevitably?[11]

There is still another abolitionist argument that actually does not hit out against capital punishment itself, but against something else. Figures are sometimes quoted which show that this punishment is much more often meted out to the uneducated and poor than to the educated, rich, and influential people; in the United States, much more often to blacks than to whites. These figures are adduced as a proof of the inherent injustice of this kind of punishment. On account of them, it is claimed that capital punishment is not a way of doing justice by meting out deserved punishment to murderers, but rather a means of social discrimination and perpetuation of social injustice.

I shall not question these findings, which are quite convincing, and anyway, there is no need to do that in order to defend the institution of capital punishment. For there seems to be a certain amount of discrimination and injustice not only in sentencing people to death and executing them, but also in meting out other penalties. The social structure of the death rows in American prisons, for instance, does not seem to be basically different from the general social structure of American penitentiaries. If this argument were valid, it would call not only for abolition of the penalty of death, but for doing away with other penalties as well. But it is not valid; as Burton Leiser has pointed out,

> . . . this is not an argument, either against the death penalty or against any other form of punishment. It is an argument against the unjust and inequitable distribution of penalties. If the trials of wealthy men are less likely to result in convictions than those of poor men, then something must be done to reform the procedure in criminal courts. If those who have money and standing in the community are less likely to be charged with serious offenses than their less affluent fellow citizens, then there should be a major overhaul of the entire system of criminal justice. . . . But the maldistribution of penalties is no argument against any particular form of penalty.[12]

NOTES

1 Cf. I. Primoratz, *Justifying Legal Punishment* (Atlantic Highlands, N.J.: Humanities Press, 1989), pp. 85–94.
2 Numbers 35.31 (R.S.V.).
3 M. Greenberg, "Some Postulates of Biblical Criminal Law," in J. Goldin (ed.), *The Jewish Expression* (New York: Bantam, 1970), pp. 25–26. (Post-biblical Jewish law evolved toward the virtual abolition of the death penalty, but that is of no concern here.)
4 "There is no *parallel* between death and even the most miserable life, so that there is no equality of crime and retribution [in the case of murder] unless the perpetrator is judicially put to death" (I. Kant, "The Metaphysics of Morals," *Kant's Political Writings,* ed. H. Reiss, trans. H. B. Nisbet [Cambridge: Cambridge University Press, 1970], p. 156). "Since life is the full compass of a man's existence, the punishment [for murder] cannot simply consist in a 'value', for none is great enough, but can consist only in taking away a second life" (G. W. F. Hegel, *Philosophy of Right,* trans. T. M. Knox [Oxford: Oxford University Press, 1965], p. 247).
5 For an example of this view, see L. N. Tolstoy, *Smertnaya kazn i hristianstvo* (Berlin: I. P. Ladizhnikov, n.d.), pp. 40–41.
6 S. V. Vulović, *Problem smrtne kazne* (Belgrade: Geca Kon, 1925), pp. 23–24.
7 Cf. W. Blackstone, *Commentaries on the Laws of England,* 4th ed., ed. J. DeWitt Andrews (Chicago: Callaghan & Co., 1899), p. 1224.
8 A. Camus, "Reflections on the Guillotine," *Resistance, Rebellion and Death,* trans. J. O'Brien (London: Hamish Hamilton, 1961), p. 143.
9 For an interesting critical discussion of this point, see M. Davis, "Is the Death Penalty Irrevocable?," *Social Theory and Practice* 10 (1984).
10 Quoted in E. R. Calvert, *Capital Punishment in the Twentieth Century* (London: G. P. Putnam's Sons, 1927), p. 132.
11 For a criticism of this argument, see L. Sebba, "On Capital Punishment—A Comment," *Israel Law Review* 17 (1982), pp. 392–395.
12 B. M. Leiser, *Liberty, Justice and Morals: Contemporary Value Conflicts* (New York: Macmillan, 1973), p. 225.

QUESTIONS

1 Would you endorse a retributive rationale for the retention of the death penalty? If so, would you say that *all* murderers deserve to die or just *some?* If just some deserve to die, which ones?
2 If blacks are more likely to receive the death penalty than whites, if the poor and uneducated are more likely to receive the death penalty than the affluent and educated, do these facts constitute a compelling argument for abolition of the death penalty?

An Eye for an Eye?

Stephen Nathanson

Stephen Nathanson is professor of philosophy at Northeastern University. He is the author of *The Ideal of Rationality* (1985), *An Eye for an Eye? The Morality of Punishing by Death* (1987), *Should We Consent to Be Governed? A Short Introduction to Political Philosophy* (1992), and *Patriotism, Morality, and Peace* (1993).

Nathanson, an abolitionist, distinguishes between *equality* retributivism and *proportional* retributivism and argues that neither of these retributive approaches can provide a justification for the death penalty. In his view: (1) Equality retributivism—committed to the principle that punishment should be equal to the crime ("an eye for an eye")—fails because it does not provide a systematically satisfactory criterion for determining appropriate punishment. (2) Proportional retributivism—committed to the principle that punishment should be proportional to the crime—fails because it does not require that murderers be executed. Nathanson also argues that a societal decision to abolish the death penalty would convey two important symbolic messages. First, we would thereby express our respect for the dignity of all human beings, even those guilty of murder. Second, in restraining the expression of our anger against murderers, we would reinforce the conviction that only defensive violence is justifiable.

Suppose we . . . try to determine what people deserve from a strictly moral point of view. How shall we proceed?

The most usual suggestion is that we look at a person's actions because what someone deserves would appear to depend on what he or she does. A person's actions, it seems, provide not only a basis for a moral appraisal of the person but also a guide to how he should be treated. According to the *lex talionis* or principle of "an eye for an eye," we ought to treat people as they have treated others. What people deserve as recipients of rewards or punishments is determined by what they do as agents.

This is a powerful and attractive view, one that appears to be backed not only by moral common sense but also by tradition and philosophical thought. The most famous statement of philosophical support for this view comes from Immanuel Kant, who linked it directly with an argument for the death penalty. Discussing the problem of punishment, Kant writes,

> What kind and what degree of punishment does legal justice adopt as its principle and standard? None other than the principle of equality . . . the principle of not treating one side more favorably than the other. Accordingly, any undeserved evil that you inflict on someone else among the people is one that you do to yourself. If you vilify, you vilify yourself; if you steal from him, you steal from yourself; if you kill him, you kill yourself. Only the law of retribution *(jus talionis)* can determine exactly the kind and degree of punishment.[1]

Kant's view is attractive for a number of reasons. First, it accords with our belief that what a person deserves is related to what he does. Second, it appeals to a moral standard and does not seem to rely on any particular legal or political institutions. Third, it seems to provides a measure of appropriate punishment that can be used as a guide to creating laws and instituting punishments. It tells us that the punishment is to be identical with the crime. Whatever the criminal did to the victim is to be done in turn to the criminal.

In spite of the attractions of Kant's view, it is deeply flawed. When we see why, it will be clear that the whole "eye for an eye" perspective must be rejected.

PROBLEMS WITH THE EQUAL PUNISHMENT PRINCIPLE

. . . [Kant's view] does not provide an adequate criterion for determining appropriate levels of punishment.

. . . We can see this, first, by noting that for certain crimes, Kant's view recommends punishments that are not morally acceptable. Applied strictly, it would require that we rape rapists, torture torturers, and burn arsonists whose acts have led to deaths. In general, where a particular crime involves barbaric and inhuman treatment, Kant's principle tells us to act barbarically and inhumanly in return. So, in some cases, the principle generates unacceptable answers to the question of what constitutes appropriate punishment.

This is not its only defect. In many other cases, the principle tells us nothing at all about how to punish. While Kant thought it obvious how to apply his principle in the case of murder, his principle cannot serve as a general rule because it does not tell us how to punish many crimes. Using the Kantian version or the more common "eye for an eye" standard, what would we decide to do to embezzlers, spies, drunken drivers, airline hijackers, drug users, prostitutes, air polluters, or persons who practice medicine without a license? If one reflects on this question, it becomes clear that there is simply no answer to it. We could not in fact design a system of punishment simply on the basis of the "eye for an eye" principle.

In order to justify using the "eye for an eye" principle to answer our question about murder and the death penalty, we would first have to show that it worked for a whole range of cases, giving acceptable answers to questions about amounts of punishment. Then, having established it as a satisfactory general principle, we could apply it to the case of murder. It turns out, however, that when we try to apply the principle generally, we find that it either gives wrong answers or no answers at all. Indeed, I suspect that the principle of "an eye for an eye" is no longer even a principle. Instead, it is simply a metaphorical disguise for expressing belief in the death penalty. People who cite it do not take it seriously. They do not believe in a kidnapping for a kidnapping, a theft for a theft, and so on. Perhaps "an eye for an eye" once was a genuine principle, but now it is merely a slogan. Therefore, it gives us no guidance in deciding whether murderers deserve to die.

In reply to these objections, one might defend the principle by saying that it does not require that punishments be strictly identical with crimes. Rather, it requires only that a punishment produce an amount of suffering in the criminal which is equal to the amount suffered by the victim. Thus, we don't have to hijack airplanes belonging to airline hijackers, spy on spies, etc. We simply have to reproduce in them the harm done to others.

Unfortunately, this reply really does not solve the problem. It provides no answer to the first objection, since it would still require us to behave barbarically in our treatment of those who are guilty of barbaric crimes. Even if we do not reproduce their actions exactly, any action which caused equal suffering would itself be barbaric. Second, in trying to produce equal amounts of suffering, we run into many problems. Just how much suffering is produced by an airline hijacker or a spy? And how do we apply this principle to prostitutes or drug users, who may not produce any suffering at all? We have rough ideas about how serious various crimes are, but this may not correlate with any clear sense of just how much harm is done.

Furthermore, the same problem arises in determining how much suffering a particular punishment would produce for a particular criminal. People vary in their tolerance of pain and in the amount of unhappiness that a fine or a jail sentence would cause them. Recluses will be less disturbed by banishment than extroverts. Nature lovers will suffer more in prison than people who are indifferent to natural beauty. A literal application of the principle would require that we tailor punishments to individual sensitivities, yet this is at best impractical. To a large extent, the legal system must work with standardized and rather crude estimates of the negative impact that punishments have on people.

The move from calling for a punishment that is identical to the crime to favoring one that is equal in the harm done is no help to us or to the defense of the principle. "An eye for an eye" tells us neither what people deserve nor how we should treat them when they have done wrong.

PROPORTIONAL RETRIBUTIVISM

The view we have been considering can be called "equality retributivism," since it proposes that we repay criminals with punishments equal to their crimes. In the light of problems like those I have cited, some people have proposed a variation on this view, calling not for equal punishments but rather for punishments which are *proportional* to the crime. In defending such a view as a guide for setting criminal punishments, Andrew von Hirsch writes:

> If one asks how severely a wrongdoer deserves to be punished, a familiar principle comes to mind: Severity of punishment should be commensurate with the seriousness of the wrong. Only grave wrongs merit severe penalties; minor misdeeds deserve lenient punishments. Disproportionate penalties are undeserved—severe sanctions for minor wrongs or vice versa. This principle has variously been called a principle of "proportionality" or "just deserts"; we prefer to call it commensurate deserts.[2]

Like Kant, von Hirsch makes the punishment which a person deserves depend on that person's actions, but he departs from Kant in substituting proportionality for equality as the criterion for setting the amount of punishment.

In implementing a punishment system based on the proportionality view, one would first make a list of crimes, ranking them in order of seriousness. At one end would be quite trivial offenses like parking meter violations, while very serious crimes such as murder would occupy the other. In between, other crimes would be ranked according to their relative gravity. Then a corresponding scale of punishments would be constructed, and the two would be correlated. Punishments would be proportionate to crimes so long as we could say that the more serious the crime was, the higher on the punishment scale was the punishment administered.

This system does not have the defects of equality retributivism. It does not require that we treat those guilty of barbaric crimes barbarically. This is because we can set the upper limit of the punishment scale so as to exclude truly barbaric punishments. Second, unlike the equality principle, the proportionality view is genuinely general, providing a way of handling all crimes. Finally, it does justice to our ordinary belief that certain punishments are unjust because they are too severe or too lenient for the crime committed.

The proportionality principle does, I think, play a legitimate role in our thinking about punishments. Nonetheless, it is no help to death penalty advocates, because it does not require that murderers be executed. All that it requires is that if murder is the most serious crime, then murder should be punished by the most severe punishment on the scale. The principle does not tell us what this punishment should be, however, and it is quite compatible with the view that the most severe punishment should be a long prison term.

This failure of the theory to provide a basis for supporting the death penalty reveals an important gap in proportional retributivism. It shows that while the theory is general in scope, it does not yield any *specific* recommendations regarding punishment. It tells us, for example, that armed robbery should be punished more severely than embezzling and less severely than murder, but it does not tell us how much to punish any of these. This weakness is, in effect, conceded by von Hirsch, who admits that if we want to implement the "commensurate deserts" principle, we must supplement it with information about what level of punishment is needed to deter crimes.[3] In a later discussion of how to "anchor" the punishment system, he deals with this problem in more depth, but the factors he cites as relevant to making specific judgments (such as available prison space) have nothing to do with what people deserve. He also seems to suggest that a range of punishments may be appropriate for a particular crime. This runs counter to the death penalty supporter's sense that death alone is appropriate for some murderers.[4]

Neither of these retributive views, then, provides support for the death penalty. The equality principle fails because it is not in general true that the appropriate punishment for a crime is to do to the criminal what he has done to others. In some cases this is immoral, while in others it is impossible. The proportionality principle may be correct, but by itself it cannot determine specific punishments for specific crimes. Because of its flexibility and open-endedness, it is compatible with a great range of different punishments for murder.[5] . . .

THE SYMBOLISM OF ABOLISHING THE DEATH PENALTY

What is the symbolic message that we would convey by deciding to renounce the death penalty and to abolish its use?

I think that there are two primary messages. The first is the most frequently emphasized and is usually expressed in terms of the sanctity of human life, although I think we could better express it in terms of respect for human dignity. One way we express our respect for the dignity of human beings is by abstaining from depriving them of their lives, even if they have done terrible deeds. In defense of human well-being, we may punish people for their crimes, but we ought not to deprive them of everything, which is what the death penalty does.

If we take the life of a criminal, we convey the idea that by his deeds he has made himself worthless and totally without human value. I do not believe that we are in a position to affirm that of anyone. We may hate such a person and feel the deepest anger against him, but when he no longer poses a threat to anyone, we ought not to take his life.

But, one might ask, hasn't the murderer forfeited whatever rights he might have had to our respect? Hasn't he, by his deeds, given up any rights that he had to decent treatment? Aren't we morally free to kill him if we wish?

These questions express important doubts about the obligation to accord any respect to those who have acted so deplorably, but I do not think that they prove that any such forfeiture has occurred. Certainly, when people murder or commit other crimes, they do forfeit some of the rights that are possessed by the law-abiding. They lose a certain right to be left alone. It becomes permissible to bring them to trial and, if they are convicted, to impose an appropriate—even a dreadful—punishment on them.

Nonetheless, they do not forfeit all their rights. It does not follow from the vileness of their actions that we can do anything whatsoever to them. This is part of the moral meaning of the constitutional ban on cruel and unusual punishments. No matter how terrible a person's deeds, we may not punish him in a cruel and unusual way. We may not torture him, for example. His right not to be tortured has not been forfeited. Why do these limits hold? Because this person remains a human being, and we think that there is something in him that we must continue to respect in spite of his terrible acts.

One way of seeing why those who murder still deserve some consideration and respect is by reflecting again on the idea of what it is to *deserve* something. In most contexts, we think that what people deserve depends on what they have done, intended, or tried to do. It depends on features that are qualities of individuals. The best person for the job deserves to be hired. The person who worked especially hard deserves our gratitude. We can call the concept that applies in these cases *personal* desert.

There is another kind of desert, however, that belongs to people by virtue of their humanity itself and does not depend on their individual efforts or achievements. I will call this impersonal kind of desert *human* desert. We appeal to this concept when we think that everyone deserves a certain level of treatment no matter what their individual qualities are. When the signers of the Declaration of Independence affirmed that people had inalienable rights to "life, liberty, and the pursuit of happiness," they were appealing to such an idea. These rights do not have to be earned by people. They are possessed "naturally," and everyone is bound to respect them.

According to the view that I am defending, people do not lose all of their rights when they commit terrible crimes. They still deserve some level of decent treatment simply because they remain living, functioning human beings. This level of moral desert need not be earned, and it cannot be forfeited. This view may sound controversial, but in fact everyone who believes that cruel and unusual punishment should be forbidden implicitly agrees with it. That is, they agree that even after someone has committed a terrible crime, we do not have the right to do anything whatsoever to him.

What I am suggesting is that by renouncing the use of death as a punishment, we express and reaffirm our belief in the inalienable, unforfeitable core of human dignity.

Why is this a worthwhile message to convey? It is worth conveying because this belief is both important and precarious. Throughout history, people have found innumerable reasons to degrade the humanity of one another. They have found qualities in others that they hated or feared, and even when they were not threatened by these people, they have sought to harm them, deprive them of their liberty, or take their lives from them. They have often felt that they had good reasons to do these things, and they have invoked divine commands, racial purity, and state security to support their deeds.

These actions and attitudes are not relics of the past. They remain an awful feature of the contemporary world. By renouncing the death penalty, we show our determination to accord at least minimal respect even to those whom we believe to be personally vile or morally vicious. This is, perhaps, why we speak of the *sanctity* of human life rather than its value or worth. That which is sacred remains, in some sense, untouchable, and its value is not dependent on its worth or usefulness to us. Kant expressed this ideal of respect in the famous second version of the Categorical Imperative: "So act as to treat humanity, whether in thine own person or in that of any other, in every case as an end withal, never as a means only." . . .

[THE SECOND SYMBOLIC MESSAGE]

. . . When the state has a murderer in its power and could execute him but does not, this conveys the idea that even though this person has done wrong and even though we may be angry, outraged, and indignant with him, we will nonetheless control ourselves in a way that he did not. We will not kill him, even though we could do so and even though we are angry and indignant. We will exercise restraint, sanctioning killing only when it serves a protective function.

Why should we do this? Partly out of a respect for human dignity. But also because we want the state to set an example of proper behavior. We do not want to encourage people to resort to violence to settle conflicts when there are other ways available. We want to avoid the cycle of violence that can come from retaliation and counter-retaliation. Violence is a contagion that arouses hatred and anger, and if unchecked, it simply leads to still more violence. The state can convey the message that the contagion must be stopped, and the most effective principle for stopping it is the idea that only defensive violence is justifiable. Since the death penalty is not an instance of defensive violence, it ought to be renounced.

We show our respect for life best by restraining ourselves and allowing murderers to live, rather than by following a policy of a life for a life. Respect for life and restraint of violence are aspects of the same ideal. The renunciation of the death penalty would symbolize our support of that ideal.

NOTES

1 Kant, *Metaphysical Elements of Justice,* translated by John Ladd (Indianapolis: Bobbs-Merrill, 1965), 101.
2 *Doing Justice* (New York: Hill & Wang, 1976), 66; reprinted in *Sentencing,* edited by H. Gross and A. von Hirsch (Oxford University Press, 1981), 243. For a more recent discussion and further defense by von Hirsch, see his *Past or Future Crimes* (New Brunswick, N.J.: Rutgers University Press, 1985).
3 Von Hirsch, *Doing Justice,* 93–94. My criticisms of proportional retributivism are not novel. For helpful discussions of the view, see Hugo Bedau, "Concessions to Retribution in Punishment," in *Justice and Punishment,* edited by J. Cederblom and W. Blizek (Cambridge, Mass.: Ballinger, 1977), and M. Golding, *Philosophy of Law* (Englewood Cliffs, N.J.: Prentice Hall, 1975), 98–99.
4 See von Hirsch, *Past or Future Crimes,* ch. 8.
5 For more positive assessments of these theories, see Jeffrey Reiman, "Justice, Civilization, and the Death Penalty," *Philosophy and Public Affairs* 14 (1985):115–48; and Michael Davis, "How to Make the Punishment Fit the Crime," *Ethics* 93 (1983).

QUESTIONS

1 To what extent, if at all, should the principle of "an eye for an eye" be incorporated into our system of criminal justice?
2 Can a retributive rationale for retention of the death penalty be defended against the objections presented by Nathanson?
3 Does Nathanson's appeal to "the symbolism of abolishing the death penalty" provide a compelling argument for abolition? Could a retentionist develop a compelling argument based on the symbolism of *retaining* the death penalty?

Deterrence and Murder

Jonathan Glover

Jonathan Glover is fellow and tutor in philosophy at New College, Oxford. He is the author of *Causing Death and Saving Lives* (1977), *What Sort of People Should There Be?* (1984), and *I: The Philosophy and Psychology of Personal Identity* (1988). He is also the editor of *Utilitarianism and Its Critics* (1990).

Rejecting the deterrence rationale for the death penalty, Glover concentrates especially on the commonsense (or "intuitive") argument for the death penalty as a uniquely effective deterrent. He denies that the death penalty can be known to be a better deterrent than long-term or even life imprisonment simply because criminals typically prefer life imprisonment to execution. He also emphasizes that the threat of the death penalty does not present itself to a would-be murderer as the certainty of immediate death; most murderers do not get the death penalty, and even when the death penalty is imposed, there is a significant time lag between the murder and the execution. Glover also provides a brief critical commentary on "the best-bet argument," which is essentially the argument advanced by van den Haag in the next selection.

The arguments over whether capital punishment deters murder more effectively than less drastic methods are of two kinds: statistical and intuitive. The statistical arguments are based on various kinds of comparisons of murder rates. Rates are compared before and after abolition in a country, and, where possible, further comparisons are made with rates after reintroduction of capital punishment. Rates are compared in neighbouring countries, or neighbouring states of the U.S.A., with and without the death penalty. I am not a statistician and have no special competence to discuss the issue, but will merely purvey the received opinion of those who have looked into the matter. Those who have studied the figures are agreed that there is no striking correlation between the absence of capital punishment and any alteration in the curve of the murder rate. Having agreed on this point, they then fall into two schools. On one view, we can conclude that capital punishment is not a greater deterrent to murder than the prison sentences that are substituted for it. On the other, more cautious, view, we can only conclude that we do not know that capital punishment is a deterrent. I shall not attempt to choose between these interpretations. For, given that capital punishment is justified only where there is good evidence that it is a substantial deterrent, either interpretation fails to support the case for it.

If the statistical evidence were conclusive that capital punishment did not deter more than milder punishments, this would leave no room for any further discussion. But, since the statistical evidence may be inconclusive, many people feel there is room left for intuitive arguments. Some of these deserve examination. The intuitive case was forcefully stated in 1864 by Sir James Fitzjames Stephen:[1]

> No other punishment deters men so effectually from committing crimes as the punishment of death. This is one of those propositions which it is difficult to prove, simply because they are in themselves more obvious than any proof can make them. It is possible to display ingenuity in arguing against it, but that is all. The whole experience of mankind is in the other direction. The threat of instant death is the one to which resort has always been made when there was an absolute necessity for producing some result . . . No one goes to certain inevitable death except by compulsion. Put the matter the other way. Was there ever yet a criminal who, when sentenced to death and brought out to die, would refuse the offer of a commutation of his sentence for the severest secondary punishment? Surely not. Why is this? It can only be because. 'All that a man has will he give for his life.' In any secondary punishment, however terrible, there is hope; but death is death; its terrors cannot be described more forcibly.

These claims turn out when scrutinized to be much more speculative and doubt-ful than they at first sight appear.

The first doubt arises when Stephen talks of 'certain inevitable death'. The Royal Commission, in their *Report,* after quoting the passage from Stephen above, quote figures to show that, in the fifty years from 1900 to 1949, there was in England and Wales one execution for every twelve murders known to the police. In Scotland in the same period there was less than one execution for every twenty-five murders known to the police. Supporters of Stephen's view could supplement their case by advocating more death sentences and fewer reprieves, or by optimistic speculations about better police detection or greater willingness of juries to convict. But the re-ality of capital punishment as it was in these countries, unmodified by such recom-mendations and speculations, was not one where the potential murderer faced cer-tain, inevitable death. This may incline us to modify Stephen's estimate of its deterrent effect, unless we buttress his view with the further speculation that a fair number of potential murderers falsely believed that what they would face was cer-tain, inevitable death.

The second doubt concerns Stephen's talk of 'the threat of instant death'. The re-ality again does not quite fit this. By the time the police conclude their investigation, the case is brought to trial, and verdict and sentence are followed by appeal, petition for reprieve and then execution, many months have probably elapsed, and when this time factor is added to the low probability of the murderers being executed, the pic-ture looks very different. For we often have a time bias, being less affected by threats of future catastrophes than by threats of instant ones. The certainty of immediate death is one thing; it is another thing merely to increase one's chances of death in the fu-ture. Unless this were so, no one would smoke or take on such high-risk jobs as div-ing in the North Sea.

There is another doubt when Stephen very plausibly says that virtually all crim-inals would prefer life imprisonment to execution. The difficulty is over whether this entitles us to conclude that it is therefore a more effective deterrent. For there is the possibility that, compared with the long term of imprisonment that is the alternative, capital punishment is what may appropriately be called an 'overkill'. It may be that, for those who will be deterred by threat of punishment, a long prison sentence is suf-ficient deterrent. I am not suggesting that this is so, but simply that it is an open ques-tion whether a worse alternative here generates any additional deterrent effect. The answer is *not* intuitively obvious.

Stephen's case rests on the speculative psychological assumptions that capital pun-ishment is not an overkill compared with a prison sentence; and that its additional deterrent effect is not obliterated by time bias, nor by the low probability of execu-tion, nor by a combination of these factors. Or else it must be assumed that, where the additional deterrent effect would be obliterated by the low probability of death, either on its own or in combination with time bias, the potential murderer thinks the probability is higher than it is. Some of these assumptions may be true, but, when they are brought out into the open, it is by no means obvious that the required com-bination of them can be relied upon.

Supporters of the death penalty also sometimes use what David A. Conway, in his valuable discussion of this issue, calls 'the best-bet argument'.[2] On this view, since there is no certainty whether or not capital punishment reduces the number of murders, either decision about it involves gambling with lives. It is suggested that it is better to gamble with the lives of murderers than with the lives of their innocent potential victims. This presupposes the attitude, rejected here, that a murder is a greater evil than the execution of a murderer. But, since this attitude probably has overwhelmingly widespread support, it is worth noting that, even if it is accepted, the best-bet argument is unconvincing. This is because, as Conway has pointed out, it overlooks the fact that we are not choosing between the chance of a murderer dying and the chance of a victim dying. In leaving the death penalty, we are opting for the certainty of the murderer dying which we hope will give us a chance of a potential victim being saved. This would look like a good bet only if we thought an execution substantially preferable to a murder and either the statistical evidence or the intuitive arguments made the effectiveness of the death penalty as a deterrent look reasonably likely.

Since the statistical studies do not give any clear indication that capital punishment makes any difference to the number of murders committed, the only chance of its supporters discharging the heavy burden of justification would be if the intuitive arguments were extremely powerful. We might then feel justified in supposing that other factors distorted the murder rate, masking the substantial deterrent effect of capital punishment. The intuitive arguments, presented as the merest platitudes, turn out to be speculative and unobvious. I conclude that the case for capital punishment as a substantial deterrent fails.

NOTES

1 James Fitzjames Stephen: Capital Punishments, *Fraser's Magazine,* 1864.
2 David A. Conway: 'Capital Punishment and Deterrence', *Philosophy and Public Affairs,* 1974.

QUESTIONS

1 Is it reasonable to assume that the death penalty is a more effective deterrent than long-term or even life imprisonment?
2 Is the life of a convicted murderer worth as much as the life of a potential murder victim?

Deterrence and Uncertainty

Ernest van den Haag

Ernest van den Haag, now retired, was a practicing psychoanalyst. He also served as professor of jurisprudence and public policy at Fordham University. He is the author of such works as *Political Violence and Civil Disobedience* (1972) and *Punishing Criminals: Concerning a Very Old and Painful Question* (1975).

The retentionist argument advanced by van den Haag is based on our uncertainty concerning the deterrent effect of the death penalty (whether or not it is a uniquely effective deterrent). According to his analysis, if we retain the death penalty, we run the risk of needlessly eradicating the lives of convicted murderers; perhaps the death penalty is *not* a uniquely effective deterrent. On the other hand, if we abolish the death penalty, we run the risk of innocent people becoming future murder victims; perhaps the death penalty *is* a uniquely effective deterrent. Faced with such uncertainty, van den Haag maintains, it is our moral obligation to retain the death penalty. "We have no right to risk additional future victims of murder for the sake of sparing convicted murderers."

. . . If we do not know whether the death penalty will deter others [in a uniquely effective way], we are confronted with two uncertainties. If we impose the death penalty, and achieve no deterrent effect thereby, the life of a convicted murderer has been expended in vain (from a deterrent viewpoint). There is a net loss. If we impose the death sentence and thereby deter some future murderers, we spared the lives of some future victims (the prospective murderers gain too; they are spared punishment because they were deterred). In this case, the death penalty has led to a net gain, unless the life of a convicted murderer is valued more highly than that of the unknown victim, or victims (and the non-imprisonment of the deterred non-murderer).

The calculation can be turned around, of course. The absence of the death penalty may harm no one and therefore produce a gain—the life of the convicted murderer. Or it may kill future victims of murderers who could have been deterred, and thus produce a loss—their life.

To be sure, we must risk something certain—the death (or life) of the convicted man, for something uncertain—the death (or life) of the victims of murderers who may be deterred. This is in the nature of uncertainty—when we invest, or gamble, we risk the money we have for an uncertain gain. Many human actions, most commitments—including marriage and crime—share this characteristic with the deterrent purpose of any penalization, and with its rehabilitative purpose (and even with the protective).

More proof is demanded for the deterrent effect of the death penalty than is demanded for the deterrent effect of other penalties. This is not justified by the absence

Reprinted with permission of the publisher from the *Journal of Criminal Law, Criminology and Police Science,* vol. 60, no. 2 (1969).

of other utilitarian purposes such as protection and rehabilitation; they involve no less uncertainty than deterrence.[1]

Irrevocability may support a demand for some reason to expect more deterrence than revocable penalties might produce, but not a demand for more proof of deterrence, as has been pointed out above. The reason for expecting more deterrence lies in the greater severity, the terrifying effect inherent in finality. Since it seems more important to spare victims than to spare murderers, the burden of proving that the greater severity inherent in irrevocability adds nothing to deterrence lies on those who oppose capital punishment. Proponents of the death penalty need show only that there is no more uncertainty about it than about greater severity in general.

The demand that the death penalty be proved more deterrent than alternatives can not be satisfied any more than the demand that six years in prison be proved to be more deterrent than three. But the uncertainty which confronts us favors the death penalty as long as by imposing it we might save future victims of murder. This effect is as plausible as the general idea that penalties have deterrent effects which increase with their severity. Though we have no proof of the positive deterrence of the penalty, we also have no proof of zero, or negative effectiveness. I believe we have no right to risk additional future victims of murder for the sake of sparing convicted murderers; on the contrary, our moral obligation is to risk the possible ineffectiveness of executions. However rationalized, the opposite view appears to be motivated by the simple fact that executions are more subjected to social control than murder. However, this applies to all penalties and does not argue for the abolition of any.

NOTES

1 Rehabilitation or protection are of minor importance in our actual penal system (though not in our theory). We confine many people who do not need rehabilitation and against whom we do not need protection (e.g., the exasperated husband who killed his wife); we release many unrehabilitated offenders against whom protection is needed. Certainly rehabilitation and protection are not, and deterrence is, the main actual function of legal punishment, if we disregard nonutilitarian purposes.

QUESTIONS

1 If we are unsure whether or not the death penalty is a uniquely effective deterrent, does our uncertainty favor retention, abolition, or neither?
2 Would you endorse either of the following claims? (a) We should abolish the death penalty unless retentionists can prove that it is a uniquely effective deterrent. (b) We should retain the death penalty unless abolitionists can prove that it is not a uniquely effective deterrent.

The Practical Burdens of Capital Punishment

Richard C. Dieter

Richard C. Dieter is executive director of the Death Penalty Information Center, Washington, D.C. His published articles include "Ethical Choices for Attorneys Whose Clients Elect Execution."

Dieter argues against the death penalty by emphasizing the practical burdens associated with its continued employment. He introduces evidence that the death penalty is applied in a racially discriminatory manner, and he argues that its continued employment functions to exacerbate racial tensions in American society and to undermine respect for the law. He also argues that death penalty cases will always be very expensive and very time consuming. In Dieter's view, the high financial costs of the death penalty should convince us to abolish it; the money could be used much more effectively in other programs designed to reduce crime and bring about a safer society.

. . . Assuming that the death penalty is ethically acceptable, and even constitutional in theory, are there, nevertheless, practical burdens which capital punishment places on society? Whether one supports the death penalty or not, are its negative effects outweighing the personal satisfaction which some may get from using it?

RACISM AND RESPECT FOR THE LAW

Many strongly believe that the death penalty is applied in a racially discriminatory manner. Apart from the question of whether that accusation is on the mark, the *perception* that minorities are being treated unjustly when it comes to capital punishment has profound implications for our society and the respect for law.

There is certainly considerable evidence that the death penalty is discriminatory. For example, the U.S. General Accounting Office in 1990 found "a pattern of evidence indicating racial disparities in the charging, sentencing, and imposition of the death penalty after the *Furman* decision."[1] Presently, about half the people on death row are from minority groups that represent only about twenty percent of the country's population. About forty percent of those who have been executed since the death penalty was allowed to resume in 1976 have been African-Americans, even though they constitute only twelve percent of the population.[2]

It could well be that forty percent of death row is made up of African-Americans because African-Americans commit forty percent of the murders in this country. Even if that were true, however, it just points to deeper problems in the fabric of our society. When we choose to inflict society's worst punishment on blacks at a

From Richard C. Dieter, "Secondary Smoke Surrounds the Capital Punishment Debate," *Criminal Justice Ethics,* vol. 13, Winter/Spring 1994, pp. 2, 82–84. Reprinted by permission of The Institute for Criminal Justice Ethics, 899 Tenth Avenue, New York, NY, 10019.

rate three and a half times their proportion in the population, resentment is inevitable. . . .

. . . In a national poll of jurors, *The National Law Journal* found that over sixty-seven percent of black jurors agreed that blacks are unfairly given the death penalty more often than whites.[3] A death penalty which has such a grossly disproportionate impact on one racial minority creates a festering sore which our nation can ill afford. The riots which erupted in Los Angeles following the first Rodney King trial are a telling reminder of the danger in perceived wrongs.

The issue of race and the death penalty is compounded when one looks at the race of the victims in capital cases. Then it appears that not only is the death penalty targeted more often toward black defendants, it is used almost exclusively when the *victim is white.* Eighty-five percent of the victims in cases resulting in execution since 1976 have been white even though whites constitute only about fifty percent of murder victims overall.[4] Thus, both the perception and the reality converge on the conclusion that if you kill a white person in this country, you're far more likely to receive the death penalty than if you kill a black person. To put it another way, the criminal justice system appears to place a higher premium on white lives than on black lives.

Statistical studies have not been able to account for this large discrepancy. Nor can they explain why there has only been one death sentence carried out on a white defendant when the victim was black while sixty-three black defendants have been executed for the murder of whites.[5] In any case, statistical theories do little to dispel the perception that the death penalty in America is a striking symbol that black lives are worth less than white lives. In short, the death penalty exacerbates the racial tension which already exists and causes an underlying disrespect for the law.

This perception is reinforced by the political lines drawn when legislation is proposed to remedy racial discrimination. For years, civil rights leaders in Congress have been trying to pass the Racial Justice Act to combat systemic racism in the administration of the death penalty. Invariably, it is opposed by those who have attempted to thwart other civil rights legislation with claims of quotas and threats of filibusters.

The most ironic attack on the Racial Justice Act was the claim that if passed, it would do away with the death penalty. Probably the exact opposite is true: that is, without the Racial Justice Act the death penalty's days may well be numbered. If death penalty laws have a racially disparate impact on blacks, and legislatures are not willing to do anything to remedy the situation, then the courts are more likely to stop the punishment all together.

THE PRACTICAL IMPLICATIONS OF INNOCENCE

For many people, the danger that the death penalty could result in a mistaken execution is enough to make them oppose it on philosophical grounds. But the question of innocence raises practical considerations as well. Death penalty cases will always take longer and cost more than other criminal cases because the consequences of a mistake are so disastrous.

The typical capital case takes eight years from conviction to execution.[6] The facile solution to this dilemma is to just eliminate or greatly curtail death penalty appeals. This, however, is not realistic. Despite decisions by the Supreme Court drastically limiting appeals, and despite numerous Congressional attempts to address this problem, the length of time prior to an execution has not gotten shorter in the last five years.[7]

The reasons for long appeals are numerous. For one thing, Americans are ambivalent when it comes to actually carrying out executions. Another reason is that insufficient attention is paid to the "main event," the trial. Frequently, inexperienced and inadequately paid attorneys are appointed to death penalty cases. Their trial mistakes then have to be litigated for years. For example, Federico Macias was released from death row last year when a federal court found that he had been ineffectively represented at trial. The trial counsel had missed strong evidence which could have proved Macias' innocence. In overturning the conviction, the court said: "The state paid defense counsel $11.84 per hour. Unfortunately, the justice system got only what it paid for."[8]

Forty percent of the death penalty cases considered by federal courts have resulted in a finding of constitutional error in either the conviction or sentencing stages and the cases have had to be sent back to the state courts.[9] Re-trials and re-sentencings are common. All of this adds to the expense and length of time in capital cases.

Moreover, the errors in capital cases are not mere "legal technicalities." Since 1970, the courts have released at least 50 death row inmates with strong evidence of their innocence, including five people last year.[10] It took an average of six and a half years between their convictions and their release. Some came within hours of being executed.

Justice Scalia recently vented his frustration at death penalty appeals when the Supreme Court decided that juries must be told that a defendant would receive a sentence of life without possibility of parole if not given the death penalty. He complained: "The heavily outnumbered opponents of capital punishment have successfully opened yet another front in their guerrilla war to make this unquestionably constitutional sentence a practical impossibility."[11]

Scalia managed to recognize one truth about death penalty cases which should figure into the calculations of anyone evaluating their practical costs: whenever a defendant's life is on the line, good attorneys, civil liberties groups, and other committed individuals are going to fight that person's execution with every ounce of strength they have. Even if forced to work for little or nothing, many attorneys will file every plausible motion and appeal every adverse decision. And judges will often listen, many will take their time with these cases, and will render careful decisions which may err on the side of caution. The possibility that an innocent person could be executed means that the death penalty will always be very expensive, very time consuming, and very frustrating for those who believe in swift and sure punishments.

THE FINANCIAL COSTS

. . . [T]he death penalty is just becoming too expensive even for those who endorse it. The high costs of the death penalty are related to the danger of executing the innocent, but they go further because of our Constitutional guarantees of due process.

The Supreme Court has long maintained that "death is different."[12] The implication of this ruling is that those facing society's ultimate punishment must be afforded enhanced legal protections. Death penalty cases cost more to investigate, more pretrial experts are necessary, jurors must be individually polled on their death penalty views, defendants will choose jury trials which will take longer than other trials, and the sentencing phase will be a separate jury trial, often taking longer than the guilt phase. After the sentencing, a long and complicated appeals process will begin, incurring considerable expense for prosecution and defense.

The best available study on the costs of the death penalty was done at Duke University and released last year.[13] The researchers, who had access to prosecution, defense, and judicial costs, concluded that the state was paying at least $2 million *more per execution* than if no death penalty was sought and the inmate sentenced to life imprisonment.[14] With almost three thousand people awaiting execution on the death rows of this country, this represents an enormous financial burden on the justice system. And the studies on the deterrent effect of all this expenditure indicate no measurable gain in society's safety.[15]

The practical implication of this huge financial outlay on relatively few cases is that money spent on one program is not available for other programs which may be more effective. The ultimate goal of the death penalty, even when it is used for recrimination, is still a safer society. Two million dollars spent to achieve one execution could add forty more police employed in a community policing program, or it could tighten up and improve parole and probation systems so that the wrong people are not released, or it could be used for any number of educational or community-based programs designed to reduce crime.

The state's money is only available for so many programs. Those programs which prove effective in making society safer deserve support. Those programs which are extremely litigious and cost intensive and affect only a few individuals should probably be abandoned. . . .

VOICES OF DISSATISFACTION

. . . Some of the most profound criticism of the death penalty has come from two Supreme Court Justices who had upheld capital punishment during their long tenures on the Court. Former Justice Lewis Powell recently said that his votes in support of the death penalty were a mistake and that he would now vote against it in every case.[16] And Justice Harry Blackmun announced from the bench that he would "no longer . . . tinker with the machinery of death. . . . I feel morally and intellectually obligated," he said, "to concede that the death penalty experiment has failed."[17]

Blackmun and Powell were both appointed to the Court by Richard Nixon. Both dissented when the Supreme Court halted the death penalty in 1972 and both voted to uphold the restored death penalty in 1976. Now both have concluded that the death penalty is so flawed in its application, apart from any theory, that it violates our constitution.

This mounting discomfort with the [practical burdens] of capital punishment is confirmed by prosecutors who decline to seek the death penalty because it is too expensive, by victims' family members who refuse to ask for executions because of the years of uncertainty leading, at best, to another death, and by law enforcement officers who see better ways to spend the limited crime prevention dollar. Perhaps an extremely limited death penalty will linger on. . . . But the days of a broad use of capital punishment against thousands of defendants as exists today is insupportable because of the burdens it imposes on society.

NOTES

1 U.S. GENERAL ACCOUNTING OFFICE, DEATH PENALTY SENTENCING: RESEARCH INDICATES PATTERN OF RACIAL DISPARITIES 5 (1990).
2 NAACP LEGAL DEFENSE & EDUCATIONAL FUND, INC., DEATH ROW, U.S.A. 1,5 (Spring 1994); WORLD ALMANAC AND BOOK OF FACTS 549, 554 (1991). (1990 U.S. population 84.1% white by race; 12.4% black by race; hispanics make up 8%.)
3 *Racial Divide Affects Black, White Panelists,* NAT'L L.J., Feb. 22, 1993, at S9.
4 *See* NAACP LEGAL DEFENSE & EDUCATIONAL FUND, INC., *supra* note 2, at 5 (figures updated Aug. 1, 1994, by the Death Penalty Information Center); LaFraniere, *FBI Finds Major Increase in Juvenile Violence in Past Decade,* Wash. Post, Aug. 30, 1992, at A13 (half of U.S. murder victims are black).
5 *See* NAACP LEGAL DEFENSE & EDUCATIONAL FUND, INC., *supra* note 2, at 6-10 (one additional interracial capital case was added since that survey).
6 BUREAU OF JUSTICE STATISTICS, CAPITAL PUNISHMENT 1992, at 9, table 12 (1993) (average since 1984).
7 *Id.*
8 Martinez-Macias v. Collins, 979 F.2d 1067 (5th Cir. 1992). The state subsequently failed even to get an indictment against Macias and he was released.
9 Memorandum to Sen. Joseph Biden, Chair, Senate Judiciary Com., from James S. Liebman, Professor of Law, Columbia Univ. School of Law 4 (July 15, 1991) (Rate of Reversible Constitutional Error in State Capital Convictions and Sentences that Underwent Federal Habeas Corpus Review Between 1976–1991, Revised).
10 *See* SUBCOMMITTEE ON CIVIL AND CONSTITUTIONAL RIGHTS, COMMITTEE ON THE JUDICIARY, INNOCENCE AND THE DEATH PENALTY: ASSESSING THE DANGER OF MISTAKEN EXECUTIONS, 103rd Congress, 1st Sess. (Oct. 21, 1993) (staff report). . . .
11 Simmons v. South Carolina, No. 92-9059, slip op., at 8 (U.S. June 17, 1994) (Scalia, J., dissenting).
12 *See, e.g.,* Gardner v. Florida, 430 U.S. 349, 357 (1977).
13 P. COOK & D. SLAWSON, THE COSTS OF PROCESSING MURDER CASES IN NORTH CAROLINA (1993).
14 *Id.* at 1.
15 *See* H. BEDAU, THE CASE AGAINST THE DEATH PENALTY 3-7 (1992) (no credible evidence of a deterrent effect).
16 *See* Von Drehle, *Retired Justice Changes Stand on Death Penalty,* Wash. Post, June 10, 1994, at A1.
17 Callins v. Collins, No. 93-7054, slip op., at 4 (U.S. Feb. 22, 1994) (Blackmun, J., dissenting).

QUESTIONS

1 Are the practical burdens of the death penalty sufficient to establish the conclusion that retention of the death penalty is unsound social policy in the United States?
2 Do economic considerations support abolition or retention of the death penalty?

SUGGESTED ADDITIONAL READINGS FOR CHAPTER 3

BAIRD, ROBERT M., and STUART E. ROSENBAUM, eds.: *Punishment and the Death Penalty: The Current Debate.* Amherst, N.Y.: Prometheus, 1995. Part One of this anthology provides a set of articles on the justification of punishment. Part Two provides a wide range of articles on the death penalty.

BEDAU, HUGO ADAM: "Capital Punishment." In Tom Regan, ed., *Matters of Life and Death,* 3d ed. New York: McGraw-Hill, 1993, pp. 160–194. Bedau, a prominent abolitionist, presents an expansive discussion of the morality of the death penalty. Part V of this long article is dedicated to a critical analysis and rejection of the view that considerations of retributive justice can provide an adequate justification for retention.

BERNS, WALTER: *For Capital Punishment.* New York: Basic, 1979. In this book, which provides a wide-ranging discussion of issues relevant to the death penalty controversy, Berns insists that capital punishment can be effectively defended on retributive grounds.

BLACK, CHARLES L., JR.: *Capital Punishment: The Inevitability of Caprice and Mistake,* 2d ed. New York: Norton, 1981. Black argues for abolition on the grounds that it is virtually impossible to eliminate arbitrariness and mistake from the numerous decisions that lead to the imposition of the death penalty.

DAVIS, MICHAEL: "Death, Deterrence, and the Method of Common Sense." *Social Theory and Practice,* vol. 7, Summer 1981, pp. 146–177. Davis argues that common sense is sufficient to establish the claim that death is the most effective deterrent. For other reasons, however, he is unwilling to endorse retention of the death penalty.

GOLDBERG, STEVEN: "On Capital Punishment." *Ethics,* vol. 85, October 1974, pp. 67–74. Goldberg, ultimately sympathetic to retention of the death penalty, focuses on the difficulties involved in the factual question of whether or not the death penalty is a uniquely effective deterrent.

NATHANSON, STEPHEN: *An Eye for an Eye? The Morality of Punishing by Death.* Totawa, N.J.: Rowman & Littlefield, 1987. Nathanson touches on all aspects of the death penalty controversy and constructs an overall case for abolition.

REIMAN, JEFFREY H.: "Justice, Civilization, and the Death Penalty: Answering van den Haag." *Philosophy and Public Affairs,* vol. 14, Spring 1985, pp. 115–148. Reiman argues that "abolition of the death penalty is part of the civilizing mission of modern states." In his view, although it is just to execute murders, it is not unjust to forgo execution and punish murderers with long-term imprisonment. Counterarguments by Ernest van den Haag can be found in the same issue—"Refuting Reiman and Nathanson" (pp. 165–176).

SORELL, TOM: "Aggravated Murder and Capital Punishment." *Journal of Applied Philosophy,* vol. 10, 1993, pp. 201–213. Sorell appeals to both John Stuart Mill and Immanuel Kant in constructing a "hybrid argument" that "provides at least the basis for a sound defense of execution for the most serious murders."

VAN DEN HAAG, ERNEST and JOHN P. CONRAD: *The Death Penalty: A Debate.* New York: Plenum, 1983. Van den Haag (a retentionist) and Conrad (an abolitionist) touch on all aspects of the death penalty controversy as they develop their respective cases and critically respond to each other's arguments.

WALLER, BRUCE N.: "From Hemlock to Lethal Injection: The Case for Self-Execution." *International Journal of Applied Philosophy,* vol. 4, Fall 1989, pp. 53–58. Waller argues that prisoners condemned to death should be allowed the alternative of killing themselves. He considers self-execution desirable because (1) it would cause less suffering and (2) it would show greater respect for the humanity of the prisoner.

CHAPTER 4

Sexual Morality

Individuals are sometimes described as having "loose morals" when their *sexual* behavior is out of line with what is considered morally appropriate. But assessments of morally appropriate sexual behavior vary enormously. Conventionalists consider sex morally appropriate only within the bounds of marriage. Some conventionalists even insist that there are substantial moral restrictions on sex *within marriage;* they are committed to the principle that sexual activity may not take place in a way that cuts off the possibility of procreation. More liberal thinkers espouse various degrees of permissiveness. Some would allow a full and open promiscuity; some would not. Some would allow homosexual acts; some would not. In this chapter, various views on the topic of sexual morality are investigated.

CONVENTIONAL SEXUAL MORALITY

According to conventional sexual morality, sex is morally legitimate only within the bounds of marriage; nonmarital sex is immoral. The category of *nonmarital sex* is applicable to any sexual relation other than that between marriage partners. Thus it includes sexual relations between single people as well as adulterous sexual relations. Both religious and nonreligious arguments are advanced in support of conventional sexual morality, but our concern here is with the nonreligious arguments that are advanced in its defense.

One common defense of the traditional convention that sex is permissible only within the bounds of marriage is based on considerations of *social utility*. It takes the following form: A stable family life is absolutely essential for the proper raising of children and the consequent welfare of society as a whole. But the limitation of sex to marriage is a necessary condition of forming and maintaining stable family units. The availability of sex within marriage will reinforce the loving relationship between husband and wife, the *exclusive* availability of sex within marriage will lead most people to get married and to stay married, and the unavailability of extramarital sex will keep the marriage strong. Therefore, the convention that sex is permissible only within the bounds of marriage is solidly based on considerations of social utility.

This argument is criticized in various ways. Sometimes it is argued that stable family units are not really so essential. More commonly, it is argued that the availability of nonmarital sex does not really undercut family life. Whereas adultery might very well undermine a marital relationship, it is argued, premarital sex often prepares one for marriage. At any rate, it is pointed out, people continue to marry even after they have had somewhat free access to sexual relations.

Another prominent defense of conventional sexual morality is intimately bound up with *natural law theory,* an approach to ethics that is historically associated with the medieval philosopher and theologian Thomas Aquinas (1225–1274). The fundamental principle of natural law theory may be expressed in rather rough form as follows: Actions are morally appropriate insofar as they accord with our nature and end as human beings and morally inappropriate insofar as they fail to accord with our nature and end as human beings. With regard to sexual morality, Aquinas argues as follows:

> . . . the emission of semen ought to be so ordered that it will result in both the production of the proper offspring and in the upbringing of this offspring.
>
> It is evident from this that every emission of semen, in such a way that generation cannot follow, is contrary to the good for man. And if this be done deliberately, it must be a sin. Now, I am speaking of a way from which, *in itself,* generation could not result; such would be any emission of semen apart from the natural union of male and female. For which reason, sins of this type are called *contrary to nature.* . . .
>
> Likewise, it must also be contrary to the good for man if the semen be emitted under conditions such that generation could result but the proper upbringing would be prevented. . . .
>
> Now, it is abundantly evident that the female in the human species is not at all able to take care of the upbringing of offspring by herself, since the needs of human life demand many things which cannot be provided by one person alone. Therefore, it is appropriate to human nature that a man remain together with a woman after the generative act, and not leave her immediately to have such relations with another woman, as is the practice with fornicators. . . .
>
> Now we call this society *matrimony.* Therefore, matrimony is natural for man, and promiscuous performance of the sexual act, outside matrimony, is contrary to man's good. For this reason, it must be a sin.[1]

According to Aquinas, procreation is the natural purpose or end of sexual activity. Accordingly, sexual activity is morally legitimate only when it accords with this fundamental aspect of human nature. Since sex is for the purpose of procreation, and since the proper upbringing of children can occur only within the framework of marriage, nonmarital sex violates the natural law; it is thereby immoral. In this way, then, Aquinas constructs a defense of conventional sexual morality.

Notice, however, that Aquinas is also committed to substantial restrictions on marital sex itself. Since procreation is the natural purpose or end of sexual activity, he contends, any sexual act that cuts off the possibility of procreation is "contrary to

---

[1]Thomas Aquinas, *On the Truth of the Catholic Faith,* Book Three, "Providence," Part II, trans. Vernon J. Bourke (New York: Doubleday, 1956).

nature." It follows that such practices as oral intercourse, anal intercourse, mutual masturbation, and the use of artificial birth control are illicit, even within marriage. Of course, Aquinas also condemns masturbation and homosexual intercourse as "contrary to nature."

One common criticism of Aquinas's point of view on sexual morality centers on his insistence that sexual activity must not frustrate its natural purpose—procreation. Granted, it is said, procreation is in a biological sense the *natural* purpose of sex. Still, the argument goes, it is not clear that sexual activity cannot legitimately serve other important human purposes. Why cannot sex legitimately function as a means for the expression of love? Why, for that matter, cannot sex legitimately function simply as a source of intense (recreational) pleasure?

In contemporary times, Aquinas's point of view on sexual morality is essentially incorporated in the formal teaching of the Roman Catholic Church. In the 1968 papal encyclical *Humanae Vitae,* artificial birth control is once again identified as immoral, a violation of the natural law: "Each and every marriage act must remain open to the transmission of life."[2] In a subsequent Vatican document, entitled "Declaration on Some Questions of Sexual Ethics," the natural law framework of Aquinas is equally apparent.[3] "The deliberate use of the sexual faculties outside of normal conjugal relations essentially contradicts its finality." "Homosexual acts are disordered by their very nature." "Masturbation is an intrinsically and seriously disordered act."[4]

In one of this chapter's readings, Vincent C. Punzo provides a somewhat distinctive defense of conventional sexual morality. At the core of his argument is the idea of existential integrity. In Punzo's view, existential integrity is compromised whenever sexual intercourse is detached from the framework of commitment that is constitutive of marriage.

THE LIBERAL VIEW

In vivid contrast to conventional sexual morality is an approach that will be referred to here as the *liberal* view of sexual morality. Liberals reject as unfounded the conventionalist claim that nonmarital sex is immoral. They also reject the related claim (made by some conventionalists) that sex is immoral if it cuts off the possibility of procreation. Nor are liberals willing to accept the claim (defended by some non-conventionalists) that *sex without love* is immoral. Yet liberals insist that there are important moral restrictions on sexual activity. In the liberal view, sexual activity (like any other type of human activity) is morally objectionable to the extent that it is incompatible with a justified moral rule or principle. Accordingly, it is argued, the way to construct a defensible account of sexual morality is simply to work out the implications of relevant moral rules or principles in the area of sexual behavior.

---

[2]Pope Paul VI, *Humanae Vitae* (1968), section 11. This encyclical is widely reprinted. See, for example, Robert Baker and Frederick Elliston, eds., *Philosophy and Sex,* new rev. ed. (Buffalo, N.Y.: Prometheus, 1975), pp. 167–184.

[3]This document was issued by the Sacred Congregation for the Doctrine of the Faith and approved by Pope Paul VI. *The Pope Speaks,* vol. 21, no. 1 (1976), pp. 60–73.

[4]Ibid., pp. 67, 66, 67.

In this vein, since it is widely acknowledged that the infliction of personal harm is morally objectionable, *some* sexual activity may be identified as immoral simply because it involves one person inflicting harm on another. For example, the seduction of a minor who does not even know "what it's all about" is morally objectionable on the grounds that the minor will almost inevitably be psychologically harmed. Rape, of course, is a moral outrage, in no small part because it typically involves the infliction of both physical and psychological harm. Its immorality, however, can also be established by reference to another widely acknowledged (when properly understood) moral principle, roughly the principle that it is wrong for one person to "use" another person.

Since the domain of sexual interaction seems to offer ample opportunity for "using" another person, the concept of using is worthy of special attention in this context. In one of this chapter's selections, Thomas A. Mappes attempts to clarify what he calls the morally significant sense of "using another person." His ultimate aim is to determine the conditions under which someone would be guilty of *sexually* using another person, and the essence of his view is that the sexual using of another person takes place whenever there is a violation of the requirement of *voluntary informed consent* (to sexual interaction). Mappes especially emphasizes both *deception* and *coercion* as mechanisms for the sexual using of another person.

Is nonmarital sex immoral? Is sex that cuts off the possibility of procreation immoral? Is sex without love immoral? According to the liberal, *no* sexual activity is immoral unless some well-established moral rule or principle is transgressed. Does one's sexual activity involve the infliction of harm on another? Does it involve the using of another? Does it involve promise breaking, another commonly recognized ground of moral condemnation? If the answer to such questions is no, the liberal maintains, then the sexual activity in question is perfectly acceptable from a moral point of view.

According to the liberal, then, we must conclude that nonmarital sex is, in many cases, morally acceptable. Sexual partners may share some degree of mutual affection or love, or they may merely share a mutual desire to attain sexual satisfaction. The sexual interaction may be heterosexual or homosexual. Or there may be no *inter*action at all; the sexual activity may be masturbation. But what about the morality of adultery, an especially noteworthy type of nonmarital sex? As the marriage bond is usually understood, the liberal might respond, there is present in cases of adultery a distinctive ground of moral condemnation. To the extent that marriage involves a pledge of sexual exclusivity, as is typically the case, then adulterous behavior seems to involve a serious breaking of trust. However, the liberal would insist, if marriage partners have entered into a so-called open marriage, with no pledge of sexual exclusivity, then this special ground of moral condemnation evaporates.

If the liberal approach to sexual morality is correct, it is nevertheless important to recognize that some particular sexual involvement could be morally acceptable and yet unwise or imprudent, that is, not in a person's best long-term interests. An individual, for example, might very well decide to steer clear of casual sex, not because it is immoral but because of a conviction (perhaps based on past experience) that it does not produce personal happiness.

THE SEX WITH LOVE APPROACH

There is one additional point of view on sexual morality that is sufficiently common to warrant explicit recognition. One may, after all, find conventional sexual morality unwarranted and yet be inclined to stop short of granting moral approval to the promiscuity that is found morally acceptable on the liberal view. This intermediate point of view can be identified as the *sex with love* approach. Defenders of this approach typically insist that sex without love reduces a humanly significant activity to a merely mechanical performance, which in turn leads to the disintegration (fragmentation) of the human personality. They differ among themselves, however, as to whether the love necessary to warrant a sexual relationship must be an *exclusive* love or whether it may be a *nonexclusive* love. Those who argue that it must be exclusive nevertheless grant that *successive* sexual liaisons are not objectionable. Those who argue that the love may be nonexclusive necessarily presume that a person is capable of simultaneously loving several persons. On their view, even *simultaneous* love affairs are not objectionable. Whether exclusive or nonexclusive love is taken to be the relevant standard, proponents of the sex with love approach usually argue that their view allows for sexual freedom in a way that avoids the alleged dehumanizing effects of mere promiscuity. Where sex and love remain united, it is argued, there is no danger of dehumanization and psychological disintegration. The liberal might respond: If psychological disintegration is a justifiable fear, which can be doubted, such a consideration shows not that sex without love is immoral but only that it is imprudent.

HOMOSEXUALITY, MORALITY, AND THE LAW

Are homosexual acts immoral? While the advocate of conventional sexual morality vigorously condemns them, the liberal typically maintains that homosexual acts are no more immoral in themselves than heterosexual acts. There are, however, a substantial number of people who reject conventional sexual morality but nevertheless remain morally opposed to homosexual acts. Are such people correct in thinking that homosexual acts are morally problematic in a way that heterosexual acts are not? A homosexual, in the most generic sense, is a person (male or female) whose dominant sexual preference is for a person of the same sex. In common parlance, however, the term *homosexual* is often taken to designate a male, whereas the term *lesbian* is used to designate a female. It is apparently true that male homosexual acts occasion a higher degree of societal indignation than female homosexual acts, but it is implausible to believe that there is any morally relevant difference between the two.

There is no lack of invective against homosexuality and homosexual acts. For example, the following claims are often asserted: (1) Homosexual acts are repulsive and highly offensive. (2) Homosexuality as a way of life is totally given over to promiscuity and is little susceptible of enduring human relationships. (3) Homosexuals make the streets unsafe for our children. (4) Homosexuality is a perversion, a sin against nature. (5) If homosexual acts are tolerated, the stability of family life will be threatened and the social fabric will be undermined.

It is important to assess the extent to which such claims support the view that homosexual acts are morally objectionable. With regard to (1), it may in fact be true that many people find homosexual acts repulsive and offensive, but it is also true that many people find eating liver repulsive and offensive, and no one thinks that this fact establishes the conclusion that eating liver is morally objectionable. With regard to (2), it may be true that many homosexuals are promiscuous, but it can be argued that society's attitude toward homosexuality is responsible for making homosexual relationships extremely difficult to sustain. With regard to (3), it may be true that *some* homosexuals prey upon children (as do some heterosexuals), and surely this is morally reprehensible, but still we find ourselves left with the more typical case in which homosexual relations take place between consenting adults.

Although the "unnaturalness argument" (4) is sometimes employed against such "perversions" as masturbation and (heterosexual) oral-genital sex practices, it is especially prominent as an argument against homosexual acts. In one of this chapter's selections, Mike W. Martin critically analyzes the claim that homosexual acts are immoral because they are unnatural. His analysis suggests the conclusion that homosexual acts are not *unnatural* in any morally relevant sense.

In the final reading of this chapter, John Arthur takes issue, among other things, with argument (5). Whereas proponents of (5) assert that homosexual acts cannot be tolerated because they have a destructive impact on the social fabric, Arthur insists that there is no sound basis for the belief that the practice of homosexuality constitutes a threat to the institutions of marriage and family. Moreover, in response to (5), it could be argued that societal acceptance of homosexuals and homosexual acts would, on balance, have beneficial rather than detrimental social consequences.

One of the central goals of the "gay liberation" movement is to achieve the decriminalization of homosexual acts *between consenting adults in private.* Presently, however, homosexual acts (even between consenting adults in private) remain criminal offenses in many states. These states have statutes that are often referred to as sodomy statutes. In the law, *sodomy* is roughly synonymous with "unnatural sex practices" or "crimes against nature." Accordingly, sodomy statutes typically prohibit both oral and anal intercourse, as well as other "crimes against nature," such as bestiality, that is, sexual intercourse with animals. Although sodomy statutes apply to heterosexuals as well as homosexuals, they are usually enforced—if they are enforced at all—only against (male) homosexuals.

The United States Supreme Court upheld the constitutionality of Georgia's sodomy statute in *Bowers v. Hardwick* (1986), and the majority opinion in this case is reprinted in this chapter. Arthur is very critical of the Court's decision in *Bowers.* He presents a systematic response to the arguments made by the state of Georgia in defense of its sodomy statute. In particular, Arthur contends that Georgia's sodomy statute is not a reasonable response to the public health danger posed by AIDS.

SEXUAL MORALITY AND FEMINIST CRITIQUE

Feminists typically renounce conventional sexual morality. A central feminist goal is to eradicate structures of oppression (see Chapter 6 for an extensive discussion of the concept of oppression), and feminists ordinarily consider conventional sexual morality an oppressive value system. For one thing, according to many feminists, this traditional standard embodies a norm of "compulsory heterosexuality" and thus is oppressive to lesbians and gay males. Further, many feminists would say, conventional sexual morality is systematically linked with the traditional concept of marriage and traditional sex roles and thus is deeply implicated in the patriarchal oppression of women. A related point is embodied in the feminist complaint against the "double standard" often associated with conventional sexual morality. The concern here is that conventional sexual morality has been put forth as a standard for both men and women but only women have really been expected to follow it.

What attitude might feminists take toward the liberal view of sexual morality? Two prominent feminist philosophers write:

> According to liberals . . . , consenting adults should be free to express and explore their sexuality in whatever way they choose within the context of a mature and private relationship. Some feminists share the liberal view, but others argue that liberals are blind to the unequal economic and social realities that form the context in which this so-called free sexual expression occurs. In addition, feminists disagree strongly over whether certain sexual practices are so inherently degrading to women that they should not be tolerated under any conditions.[5]

The moral legitimacy of sadomasochistic sexual practices is an example of an issue that occasions strong disagreement among feminists. Some feminists argue that sadomasochistic sexual practices are morally objectionable even if they are genuinely consensual. The implications of eroticizing dominance/subordination relationships are a principal concern in this regard.

Even feminists who are somewhat sympathetic to the emphasis placed by the liberal tradition on the moral legitimacy of consensual sexual interactions often insist that this emphasis must be corrected or qualified in certain ways. For example, many feminists would challenge the idea that sexual relationships can be genuinely consensual if there are significant social inequalities between the two sexual partners. In particular, it is said, the relative lack of power that typically characterizes women relative to men in a patriarchal society creates a significant obstacle to women giving genuine consent to heterosexual interactions. Another challenge to the liberal tradition is presented by Robin West in this chapter. Her point is not that background social forces tend to undermine the possibility of women giving genuine consent to heterosexual interactions, but rather that underlying social realities often result in women's being significantly harmed by heterosexual interactions, even when these interactions are essentially consensual.

Thomas A. Mappes

---

[5]Alison M. Jaggar and Paula S. Rothenberg, *Feminist Frameworks,* 3rd ed. (New York: McGraw-Hill, 1993), p. 286.

Morality and Human Sexuality

Vincent C. Punzo

Vincent C. Punzo is professor of philosophy at St. Louis University. His published articles include "Reason in Morals" and "Natural Law Ethics: Immediate or Mediated Naturalism." Punzo is also the author of *Reflective Naturalism: An Introduction to Moral Philosophy* (1969), from which this selection is excerpted.

Punzo begins by arguing that there is a morally significant difference between sexual intercourse and other types of human activity. Then, emphasizing the historical aspect of the human self, he constructs an argument against premarital sexual intercourse. Marriage, in his view, is constituted by a mutual and total commitment. Apart from this framework of commitment, he argues, sexual unions are "morally deficient because they lack existential integrity." Although Punzo is essentially a proponent of conventional sexual morality, he understands marriage in such a way that he does not condemn "preceremonial" intercourse. He insists that the commitment constitutive of marriage can exist prior to and apart from any legal or ceremonial formalities.

If one sees man's moral task as being simply that of not harming anyone, that is if one sees this task in purely negative terms, he will certainly not accept the argument to be presented in the following section. However, if one accepts the notion of the morality of aspiration, if one accepts the view that man's moral task involves the positive attempt to live up to what is best in man, to give reality to what he sees to be the perfection of himself as a human subject, the argument may be acceptable.

SEXUALITY AND THE HUMAN SUBJECT

[Prior discussion] has left us with the question as to whether sexual intercourse is a type of activity that is similar to choosing a dinner from a menu. This question is of utmost significance in that one's view of the morality of premarital intercourse seems to depend on the significance that one gives to the sexual encounter in human life. Those such as [John] Wilson and [Eustace] Chesser who see nothing immoral about the premarital character of sexual intercourse seem to see sexual intercourse as being no different from myriad of other purely aesthetic matters. This point is seen in Chesser's questioning of the reason for demanding permanence in the relationship of sexual partners when we do not see such permanence as being important to other human relationships.[1] It is also seen in his asking why we raise a moral issue about premarital coition when two people may engage in it, with the resulting social and psychological consequences being no different than if they had gone to a movie.[2]

Wilson most explicitly makes a case for the view that sexual intercourse does not differ significantly from other human activities. He holds that people think that there is a logical difference between the question "Will you engage in sexual intercourse with me?" and the question, "Will you play tennis with me?" only because they are influenced by the acquisitive character of contemporary society.[3] Granted that the two questions may be identical from the purely formal perspective of logic, the ethician must move beyond this perspective to a consideration of their content. Men and women find themselves involved in many different relationships: for example, as buyer-seller, employer-employee, teacher-student, lawyer-client, and partners or competitors in certain games such as tennis or bridge. Is there any morally significant difference between these relationships and sexual intercourse? We cannot examine all the possible relationships into which a man and woman can enter, but we will consider the employer-employee relationship in order to get some perspective on the distinctive character of the sexual relationship.

A man pays a woman to act as his secretary. What rights does he have over her in such a situation? The woman agrees to work a certain number of hours during the day taking dictation, typing letters, filing reports, arranging appointments and flight schedules, and greeting clients and competitors. In short, we can say that the man has rights to certain of the woman's services or skills. The use of the word "services" may lead some to conclude that this relationship is not significantly different from the relationship between a prostitute and her client in that the prostitute also offers her "services."

It is true that we sometimes speak euphemistically of a prostitute offering her services to a man for a sum of money, but if we are serious about our quest for the difference between the sexual encounter and other types of human relationships, it is necessary to drop euphemisms and face the issue directly. The man and woman who engage in sexual intercourse are giving their bodies, the most intimate physical expression of themselves, over to the other. Unlike the man who plays tennis with a woman, the man who has sexual relations with her has literally entered her. A man and woman engaging in sexual intercourse have united themselves as intimately and as totally as is physically possible for two human beings. Their union is not simply a union of organs, but is as intimate and as total a physical union of two selves as is possible of achievement. Granted the character of this union, it seems strange to imply that there is no need for a man and a woman to give any more thought to the question of whether they should engage in sexual intercourse than to the question of whether they should play tennis.

In opposition to Wilson, I think that it is the acquisitive character of our society that has blinded us to the distinction between the two activities. Wilson's and Chesser's positions seem to imply that exactly the same moral considerations ought to apply to a situation in which a housewife is bartering with a butcher for a few pounds of pork chops and the situation in which two human beings are deciding whether sexual intercourse ought to be an ingredient of their relationship. So long as the butcher does not put his thumb on the scale in the weighing process, so long as he is truthful in stating that the meat is actually pork, so long as the woman pays the proper amount with the proper currency, the trade is perfectly moral. Reflecting on sexual intercourse from the same sort of economic perspective, one can say that so long as the sexual partners are truthful in reporting their freedom from contagious venereal diseases and so long as they are truthful in reporting that they are interested in the activity for the mere pleasure of it or to try out their sexual techniques, there is nothing immoral about such activity. That in the one case pork chops are being exchanged for money whereas in the other the decision concerns the most complete and intimate merging of one's self with another makes no difference to the moral evaluation of the respective cases.

It is not surprising that such a reductionistic outlook should pervade our thinking on sexual matters, since in our society sexuality is used to sell everything from shave cream to underarm deodorants, to soap, to mouthwash, to cigarettes, and to auto-mobiles. Sexuality has come to play so large a role in our commercial lives that it is not surprising that our sexuality should itself come to be treated as a commodity gov-erned by the same moral rules that govern any other economic transaction.

Once sexuality is taken out of this commercial framework, once the character of the sexual encounter is faced directly and squarely, we will come to see that Doctor Mary Calderone has brought out the type of questions that ought to be asked by those contemplating the introduction of sexual intercourse into their relationships: "How many times, and how casually, are you willing to invest a portion of your total self, and to be the custodian of a like investment from the other person, without the sure-ness of knowing that these investments are being made for keeps?"[4] These questions come out of the recognition that the sexual encounter is a definitive experience, one in which the physical intimacy and merging involves also a merging of the non-physical dimensions of the partners. With these questions, man moves beyond the negative concern with avoiding his or another's physical and psychological harm to the question of what he is making of himself and what he is contributing to the ex-istential formation of his partner as a human subject.

If we are to make a start toward responding to Calderone's questions we must cease talking about human selfhood in abstraction. The human self is an historical as well as a physical being. He is a being who is capable of making at least a portion of his past an object of his consciousness and thus is able to make this past play a conscious role in his present and in his looking toward the future. He is also a being who looks to the future, who faces tomorrow with plans, ideals, hopes, and fears. The very being of a human self involves his past and his movement toward the future. Moreover, the human self is not completely shut off in his own past and future. Men and women are capable of consciously and purposively uniting themselves in a common career and venture. They can commit themselves to sharing the future with another, shar-ing it in all its aspects—in its fortunes and misfortunes, in its times of happiness and times of tragedy. Within the lives of those who have so committed themselves to each other, sexual intercourse is a way of asserting and confirming the fullness and to-tality of their mutual commitment.

Unlike those who have made such a commitment and who come together in the sexual act in the fullness of their selfhood, those who engage in premarital sexual unions and who have made no such commitment act as though they can amputate their bodily existence and the most intimate physical expression of their selfhood from their existence as historical beings. Granting that there may be honesty on the verbal level in that two people engaging in premarital intercourse openly state that they are interested only in the pleasure of the activity, the fact remains that such unions are morally deficient because they lack existential integrity in that there is a total merging and union on a physical level, on the one hand, and a conscious decision not to unite any other dimension of themselves, on the other hand. Their sexual union thus involves a "depersonalization" of their bodily existence, an attempt to cut off the most intimate physical expression of their respective selves from their very selfhood. The mutual agreement of premarital sex partners is an agreement to merge with the other not as a self, but as a body which one takes unto oneself, which one possesses in a most intimate and total fashion for one's own pleasure or designs, allowing the other to treat oneself in the same way. It may be true that no physical or psychological harm may result from such unions, but such partners have failed to existentially incorporate human sexuality, which is at the very least the most intimate physical expression of the human self, into the character of this selfhood.

In so far as premarital sexual unions separate the intimate and total physical union that is sexual intercourse from any commitment to the self in his historicity, human sexuality, and consequently the human body, have been fashioned into external things or objects to be handed over totally to someone else, whenever one feels that he can get possession of another's body, which he can use for his own purposes.[5] The human body has thus been treated no differently from the pork chops spoken of previously or from any other object or commodity, which human beings exchange and haggle over in their day-to-day transactions. One hesitates to use the word that might be used to capture the moral value that has been sacrificed in premarital unions because in our day the word has taken on a completely negative meaning at best, and, at worst, it has become a word used by "sophisticates" to mock or deride certain attitudes toward human sexuality. However, because the word "chastity" has been thus abused is no reason to leave it in the hands of those who have misrepresented the human value to which it gives expression.

The chaste person has often been described as one intent on denying his sexuality. The value of chastity as conceived in this section is in direct opposition to this description. It is the unchaste person who is separating himself from his sexuality, who is willing to exchange human bodies as one would exchange money for tickets to a baseball game—honestly and with no commitment of self to self. Against this alienation of one's sexuality from one's self, an alienation that makes one's sexuality an object, which is to be given to another in exchange for his objectified sexuality, chastity affirms the integrity of the self in his bodily and historical existence. The sexuality of man is seen as an integral part of his subjectivity. Hence, the chaste man rejects depersonalized sexual relations as a reduction of man in his most intimate physical being to the status of an object or pure instrument for another. He asserts that man is a subject and end in himself, not in some trans-temporal, nonphysical world, but in the historical-physical world in which he carries on his moral task and where he finds his fellow man. He will not freely make of himself in his bodily existence a thing to be handed over to another's possession, nor will he ask that another treat his own body in this way. The total physical intimacy of sexual intercourse will be an expression of total union with the other self on all levels of their beings.

Seen from this perspective, chastity is one aspect of man's attempt to attain existential integrity, to accept his body as a dimension of his total personality.

In concluding this section, it should be noted that I have tried to make a case against the morality of premarital sexual intercourse even in those cases in which the partners are completely honest with each other. There is reason to question whether the complete honesty, to which those who see nothing immoral in such unions refer, is as a matter of fact actually found very often among premarital sex partners. We may well have been dealing with textbook cases which present these unions in their best light. One may be pardoned for wondering whether sexual intercourse often occurs under the following conditions: "Hello, my name is Josiah. I am interested in having a sexual experience with you. I can assure you that I am good at it and that I have no communicable disease. If it sounds good to you and if you have taken the proper contraceptive precautions, we might have a go at it. Of course, I want to make it clear to you that I am interested only in the sexual experience and that I have no intention of making any long-range commitment to you." If those, who defend the morality of premarital sexual unions so long as they are honestly entered into, think that I have misrepresented what they mean by honesty, then they must specify what they mean by an honest premarital union. . . .

MARRIAGE AS A TOTAL HUMAN COMMITMENT

The preceding argument against the morality of premarital sexual unions was not based on the view that the moral character of marriage rests on a legal certificate or on a legal or religious ceremony. The argument was not directed against "preceremonial" intercourse, but against premarital intercourse. Morally speaking, a man and woman are married when they make the mutual and total commitment to share the problems and prospects of their historical existence in the world. . . .

. . . A total commitment to another means a commitment to him in his historical existence. Such a commitment is not simply a matter of words or of feelings, however strong. It involves a full existential sharing on the part of two beings of the burdens, opportunities, and challenges of their historical existence.

Granted the importance that the character of their commitment to each other plays in determining the moral quality of a couple's sexual encounter, it is clear that there may be nothing immoral in the behavior of couples who engage in sexual intercourse before participating in the marriage ceremony. For example, it is foolish to say that two people who are totally committed to each other and who have made all the arrangements to live this commitment are immoral if they engage in sexual intercourse the night before the marriage ceremony. Admittedly this position can be abused by those who have made a purely verbal commitment, a commitment, which will be carried out in some vague and ill-defined future. At some time or other, they will unite their two lives totally by setting up house together and by actually undertaking the task of meeting the economic, social, legal, medical responsibilities that are involved in living this commitment. Apart from the reference to a vague and amorphous future time when they will share the full responsibility for each other, their commitment presently realizes itself in going to dances, sharing a box of popcorn at

Saturday night movies, and sharing their bodies whenever they can do so without taking too great a risk of having the girl become pregnant.

Having acknowledged that the position advanced in this section can be abused by those who would use the word "commitment" to rationalize what is an interest only in the body of the other person, it must be pointed out that neither the ethician nor any other human being can tell two people whether they actually have made the commitment that is marriage or are mistaking a "warm glow" for such a commitment. There comes a time when this issue falls out of the area of moral philosophy and into the area of practical wisdom. . . .

The characterization of marriage as a total commitment between two human beings may lead some to conclude that the marriage ceremony is a wholly superfluous affair. It must be admitted that people may be morally married without having engaged in a marriage ceremony. However, to conclude from this point that the ceremony is totally meaningless is to lose sight of the social character of human beings. The couple contemplating marriage do not exist in a vacuum, although there may be times when they think they do. Their existences reach out beyond their union to include other human beings. By making their commitment a matter of public record, by solemnly expressing it before the law and in the presence of their respective families and friends and, if they are religious people, in the presence of God and one of his ministers, they sink the roots of their commitment more deeply and extensively in the world in which they live, thus taking steps to provide for the future growth of their commitment to each other. The public expression of this commitment makes it more fully and more explicitly a part of a couple's lives and of the world in which they live. . . .

NOTES

1 Eustace Chesser, *Unmarried Love* (New York: Pocket Books, 1965), p. 29.
2 *Ibid.,* pp. 35–36, see also p. 66.
3 John Wilson, *Logic and Sexual Morality* (Baltimore, Md.: Penguin Books, 1965). See footnote 1, p. 67.
4 Mary Steichen Calderone, "The Case for Chastity," *Sex in America,* ed. by Henry Anatole Grunwald (New York: Bantam Books, 1964), p. 147.
5 The psychoanalyst Rollo May makes an excellent point in calling attention to the tendency in contemporary society to exploit the human body as if it were only a machine. Rollo May, "The New Puritanism," *Sex in America,* pp. 161–164.

QUESTIONS

1 Could the idea of existential integrity be developed in such a way as to provide a justification for the sex with love approach instead of conventional sexual morality?
2 Punzo says that no one is capable of telling "two people whether they actually have made the commitment that is marriage or are mistaking a 'warm glow' for such a commitment." What factors should a couple consider in attempting to resolve this question?

Sexual Morality and the Concept of Using
Another Person

Thomas A. Mappes

Thomas A. Mappes is professor of philosophy at Frostburg State University, Maryland. He is the author of "What Is Personal Ethics and Should We Be Teaching More of It?" and the coauthor of "Patient Choices, Family Interests, and Physician Obligations." He is also coeditor of *Biomedical Ethics* (4th ed., 1996).

Advocating a liberal approach to sexual morality, Mappes attempts to determine the conditions under which someone would be guilty of *sexually* using another person. On his view, the morally significant sense of "using another person" is best understood in reference to the notion of voluntary informed consent. Accordingly, his central thesis is that one person (A) is guilty of sexually using another person (B) "if and only if A intentionally acts in a way that violates the requirement that B's sexual interaction with A be based on B's voluntary informed consent." Mappes emphasizes the importance of deception and coercion as mechanisms for the sexual using of another person, but he also insists that such using can result from "taking advantage of someone's desperate situation."

The central tenet of *conventional* sexual morality is that nonmarital sex is immoral. A somewhat less restrictive sexual ethic holds that *sex without love* is immoral. If neither of these positions is philosophically defensible, and I would contend that neither is, it does not follow that there are no substantive moral restrictions on human sexual interaction. *Any* human interaction, including sexual interaction, may be judged morally objectionable to the extent that it transgresses a justified moral rule or principle. The way to construct a detailed account of sexual morality, it would seem, is simply to work out the implications of relevant moral rules or principles in the area of human sexual interaction.

As one important step in the direction of such an account, I will attempt to work out the implications of an especially relevant moral principle, the principle that it is wrong for one person to use another person. However ambiguous the expression "using another person" may seem to be, there is a determinate and clearly specifiable sense according to which using another person is morally objectionable. Once this morally significant sense of "using another person" is identified and explicated, the concept of using another person can play an important role in the articulation of a defensible account of sexual morality.

I THE MORALLY SIGNIFICANT SENSE OF "USING ANOTHER PERSON"

Historically, the concept of using another person is associated with the ethical system of Immanuel Kant. According to a fundamental Kantian principle, it is morally wrong for A to use B *merely as a means* (to achieve A's ends). Kant's principle does not rule out A using B as a means, only A using B *merely* as a means, that is, in a way incompatible with respect for B as a person. In the ordinary course of life, it is surely unavoidable (and morally unproblematic) that each of us in numerous ways uses others as a means to achieve our various ends. A college teacher uses students as a means to achieve his or her livelihood. A college student uses instructors as a means of gaining knowledge and skills. Such human interactions, presumably based on the voluntary participation of the respective parties, are quite compatible with the idea of respect for persons. But respect for persons entails that each of us recognize the rightful authority of other persons (as rational beings) to conduct their individual lives as they see fit. We may legitimately recruit others to participate in the satisfaction of our personal ends, but they are used merely as a means whenever we undermine the voluntary or informed character of their consent to interact with us in some desired way. A coerces B at knife point to hand over $200. A uses B merely as a means. If A had requested of B a gift of $200, leaving B free to determine whether or not to make the gift, A would have proceeded in a manner compatible with respect for B as a person. C deceptively rolls back the odometer of a car and thereby manipulates D's decision to buy the car. C uses D merely as a means.

On the basis of these considerations, I would suggest that the morally significant sense of "using another person" is best understood by reference to the notion of *voluntary informed consent.* More specifically, A immorally uses B if and only if A intentionally acts in a way that violates the requirement that B's involvement with A's ends be based on B's voluntary informed consent. If this account is correct, using another person (in the morally significant sense) can arise in at least two important ways: via *coercion,* which is antithetical to voluntary consent, and via *deception,* which undermines the informed character of voluntary consent.

The notion of voluntary informed consent is very prominent in the literature of biomedical ethics and is systematically related to the much emphasized notion of (patient) autonomy. We find in the famous words of Supreme Court Justice Cardozo a ringing affirmation of patient autonomy. "Every human being of adult years and sound mind has a right to determine what shall be done with his own body." Because respect for individual autonomy is an essential part of respect for persons, if medical professionals (and biomedical researchers) are to interact with their patients (and research subjects) in an acceptable way, they must respect individual autonomy. That is, they must respect the self-determination of the patient/subject, the individual's right to determine what shall be done with his or her body. This means that they must not act in a way that violates the requirement of voluntary informed consent. Medical procedures must not be performed without the consent of competent patients; research on human subjects must not be carried out without the consent of the subjects involved. Moreover, consent must be voluntary; coercion undermines individual autonomy. Consent must also be informed; lying or withholding relevant information undercuts rational decision making and thereby undermines individual autonomy.

To further illuminate the concept of using that has been proposed, I will consider in greater detail the matter of research involving human subjects. In the sphere of researcher-subject interaction, just as in the sphere of human sexual interaction, there is ample opportunity for immorally using another person. If a researcher is engaged in a study that involves human subjects, we may presume that the "end" of the researcher is the successful completion of the study. (The researcher may desire this particular end for any number of reasons: the speculative understanding it will provide, the technology it will make possible, the eventual benefit of humankind, increased status in the scientific community, a raise in pay, etc.) The work, let us presume, strictly requires the use (employment) of human research subjects. The researcher, however, immorally uses other people only if he or she intentionally acts in a way that violates the requirement that the participation of research subjects be based on their voluntary informed consent.

Let us assume that in a particular case participation as a research subject involves some rather significant risks. Accordingly, the researcher finds that potential subjects are reluctant to volunteer. At this point, if an unscrupulous researcher is willing to resort to the immoral using of other people (to achieve his or her own ends), two manifest options are available—deception and coercion. By way of deception, the researcher might choose to lie about the risks involved. For example, potential subjects could be explicitly told that there are no significant risks associated with research participation. On the other hand, the researcher could simply withhold a full disclosure of risks. Whether pumped full of false information or simply deprived of relevant information, the potential subject is intentionally deceived in such a way as to be led to a decision that furthers the researcher's ends. In manipulating the decision making process of the potential subject in this way, the researcher is guilty of immorally using another person.

To explain how an unscrupulous researcher might immorally use another person via coercion, it is helpful to distinguish two basic forms of coercion.[1] "Occurrent" coercion involves the use of physical force. "Dispositional" coercion involves the threat of harm. If I am forcibly thrown out of my office by an intruder, I am the victim of occurrent coercion. If, on the other hand, I leave my office because an intruder has threatened to shoot me if I do not leave, I am the victim of dispositional coercion. The victim of occurrent coercion literally has no choice in what happens. The victim of dispositional coercion, in contrast, does intentionally choose a certain course of action. However, one's choice, in the face of the threat of harm, is less than fully voluntary.

It is perhaps unlikely that even an unscrupulous researcher would resort to any very explicit measure of coercion. Deception, it seems, is less risky. Still, it is well known that Nazi medical experimenters ruthlessly employed coercion. By way of occurrent coercion, the Nazis literally forced great numbers of concentration camp victims to participate in experiments that entailed their own death or dismemberment. And if some concentration camp victims "volunteered" to participate in Nazi research to avoid even more unspeakable horrors, clearly we must consider them victims of dispositional coercion. The Nazi researchers, employing coercion, immorally used other human beings with a vengeance.

II DECEPTION AND SEXUAL MORALITY

To this point, I have been concerned to identify and explicate the morally significant sense of "using another person." On the view proposed, A immorally uses B if and only if A intentionally acts in a way that violates the requirement that B's involvement with A's ends be based on B's voluntary informed consent. I will now apply this account to the area of human sexual interaction and explore its implications. For economy of expression in what follows, "using" (and its cognates) is to be understood as referring only to the morally significant sense.

If we presume a state of affairs in which A desires some form of sexual interaction with B, we can say that this desired form of sexual interaction with B is A's end. Thus A sexually *uses* B if and only if A intentionally acts in a way that violates the requirement that B's sexual interaction with A be based on B's voluntary informed consent. It seems clear then that A may sexually use B in at least two distinctive ways, (1) via coercion and (2) via deception. However, before proceeding to discuss deception and then the more problematic case of coercion, one important point must be made. In emphasizing the centrality of coercion and deception as mechanisms for the sexual using of another person, I have in mind sexual interaction with a fully competent adult partner. We should also want to say, I think, that sexual interaction with a child inescapably involves the sexual using of another person. Even if a child "consents" to sexual interaction, he or she is, strictly speaking, incapable of *informed* consent. It's a matter of being *incompetent* to give consent. Similarly, to the extent that a mentally retarded person is rightly considered incompetent, sexual interaction with such a person amounts to the sexual using of that person, unless someone empowered to give "proxy consent" has done so. (In certain circumstances, sexual involvement might be in the best interests of a mentally retarded person.) We can also visualize the case of an otherwise fully competent adult temporarily disordered by drugs or alcohol. To the extent that such a person is rightly regarded as temporarily incompetent, winning his or her "consent" to sexual interaction could culminate in the sexual using of that person.

There are a host of clear cases in which one person sexually uses another precisely because the former employs deception in a way that undermines the informed character of the latter's consent to sexual interaction. Consider this example. One person, A, has decided, as a matter of personal prudence based on past experience, not to become sexually involved outside the confines of a loving relationship. Another person, B, strongly desires a sexual relationship with A but does not love A. B, aware of A's unwillingness to engage in sex without love, professes love for A, thereby hoping to win A's consent to a sexual relationship. B's ploy is successful; A consents. When the smoke clears and A becomes aware of B's deception, it would be both appropriate and natural for A to complain, "I've been used."

In the same vein, here are some other examples. (1) Mr. A is aware that Ms. B will consent to sexual involvement only on the understanding that in time the two will be married. Mr. A has no intention of marrying Ms. B but says that he will. (2) Ms. C has herpes and is well aware that Mr. D will never consent to sex if he knows of her condition. When asked by Mr. D, Ms. C denies that she has herpes. (3). Mr. E knows that Ms. F will not consent to sexual intercourse in the absence of responsible birth control measures. Mr. E tells Ms. F that he has had a vasectomy, which is not the case. (4) Ms. G knows that Mr. H. would not consent to sexual involvement with a married woman. Ms. G is married but tells Mr. H that she is single. (5)

Ms. I is well aware that Ms. J is interested in a stable lesbian relationship and will not consent to become sexually involved with someone who is bisexual. Ms. I tells Ms. J that she is exclusively homosexual, whereas the truth is that she is bisexual.

If one person's consent to sex is predicated on false beliefs that have been intentionally and deceptively inculcated by one's sexual partner in an effort to win the former's consent, the resulting sexual interaction involves one person sexually using another. In each of the above cases, one person explicitly *lies* to another. False information is intentionally conveyed to win consent to sexual interaction, and the end result is the sexual using of another person.

As noted earlier, however, lying is not the only form of deception. Under certain circumstances, the simple withholding of information can be considered a form of deception. Accordingly, it is possible to sexually use another person not only by (deceptively) lying about relevant facts but also by (deceptively) not disclosing relevant facts. If A has good reason to believe that B would refuse to consent to sexual interaction should B become aware of certain factual information, and if A withholds disclosure of this information in order to enhance the possibility of gaining B's consent, then, if B does consent, A sexually uses B via deception. One example will suffice. Suppose that Mr. A meets Ms. B in a singles bar. Mr. A realizes immediately that Ms. B is the sister of Ms. C, a woman that Mr. A has been sexually involved with for a long time. Mr. A, knowing that it is very unlikely that Ms. B will consent to sexual interaction if she becomes aware of Mr. A's involvement with her sister, decides not to disclose this information. If Ms. B eventually consents to sexual interaction, since her consent is the product of Mr. A's deception, it is rightly thought that she has been sexually used by him.

III COERCION AND SEXUAL MORALITY

We have considered the case of deception. The present task is to consider the more difficult case of coercion. Whereas deception functions to undermine the *informed* character of voluntary consent (to sexual interaction), coercion either obliterates consent entirely (the case of occurrent coercion) or undermines the voluntariness of consent (the case of dispositional coercion).

Forcible rape is the most conspicuous, and most brutal, way of sexually using another person via coercion.[2] Forcible rape may involve either occurrent coercion or dispositional coercion. A man who rapes a woman by the employment of sheer physical force, by simply overpowering her, employs occurrent coercion. There is literally no sexual *interaction* in such a case; only the rapist performs an action. In no sense does the woman consent to or participate in sexual activity. She has no choice in what takes place, or rather, physical force results in her choice being simply beside the point. The employment of occurrent coercion for the purpose of rape "objectifies" the victim in the strongest sense of that term. She is treated like a physical object. One does not interact with physical objects; one acts upon them. In a perfectly ordinary (not the morally significant) sense of the term, we "use" physical objects. But when the victim of rape is treated as if she were a physical object, there we have one of the most vivid examples of the immoral using of another person.

Frequently, forcible rape involves not occurrent coercion (or not *only* occurrent coercion) but dispositional coercion.[3] In dispositional coercion, the relevant factor is not physical force but the threat of harm. The rapist threatens his victim with immediate and serious bodily harm. For example, a man threatens to kill or beat a woman if she resists his sexual demands. She "consents," that is, she submits to his demands. He may demand only passive participation (simply not struggling against him) or he may demand some measure of active participation. Rape that employs dispositional coercion is surely just as wrong as rape that employs occurrent coercion, but there is a notable difference in the mechanism by which the rapist uses his victim in the two cases. With occurrent coercion, the victim's consent is entirely bypassed. With dispositional coercion, the victim's consent is not bypassed. It is coerced. Dispositional coercion undermines the *voluntariness* of consent. The rapist, by employing the threat of immediate and serious bodily harm, may succeed in bending the victim's will. He may gain the victim's "consent." But he uses another person precisely because consent is coerced.

The relevance of occurrent coercion is limited to the case of forcible rape. Dispositional coercion, a notion that also plays an indispensable role in an overall account of forcible rape, now becomes our central concern. Although the threat of immediate and serious bodily harm stands out as the most brutal way of coercing consent to sexual interaction, we must not neglect the employment of other kinds of threats to this same end. There are numerous ways in which one person can effectively harm, and thus effectively threaten, another. Accordingly, for example, consent to sexual interaction might be coerced by threatening to damage someone's reputation. If a person consents to sexual interaction to avoid a threatened harm, then that person has been sexually used (via dispositional coercion). In the face of a threat, of course, it remains possible that a person will refuse to comply with another's sexual demands. It is probably best to describe this sort of situation as a case not of coercion, which entails the *successful* use of threats to gain compliance, but of *attempted* coercion. Of course, the moral fault of an individual emerges with the *attempt* to coerce. A person who attempts murder is morally blameworthy even if the attempt fails. The same is true for someone who fails in an effort to coerce consent to sexual interaction.

Consider now each of the following cases:

Case 1   Mr. Supervisor makes a series of increasingly less subtle sexual overtures to Ms. Employee. These advances are consistently and firmly rejected by Ms. Employee. Eventually, Mr. Supervisor makes it clear that the granting of "sexual favors" is a condition of her continued employment.

Case 2   Ms. Debtor borrowed a substantial sum of money from Mr. Creditor, on the understanding that she would pay it back within one year. In the meantime, Ms. Debtor has become sexually attracted to Mr. Creditor, but he does not share her interest. At the end of the one-year period, Mr. Creditor asks Ms. Debtor to return the money. She says she will be happy to return the money so long as he consents to sexual interaction with her.

Case 3   Mr. Theatergoer has two tickets to the most talked-about play of the season. He is introduced to a woman whom he finds sexually attractive and who shares his interest in the theater. In the course of their conversation, she expresses disappointment that the play everyone is talking about is sold out; she would love to see it. At this point, Mr. Theatergoer suggests that she be his guest at the theater. "Oh, by the way," he says, "I always expect sex from my dates."

Case 4 Ms. Jetsetter is planning a trip to Europe. She has been trying for some time to develop a sexual relationship with a man who has shown little interst in her. She knows, however, that he has always wanted to go to Europe and that it is only lack of money that has deterred him. Ms. Jetsetter proposes that he come along as her traveling companion, all expenses paid, on the express understanding that sex is part of the arrangement.

Cases 1 and 2 involve attempts to sexually use another person whereas cases 3 and 4 do not. To see why this is so, it is essential to introduce a distinction between two kinds of proposals, viz., the distinction between *threats* and *offers*.[4] The logical form of a threat differs from the logical form of an offer in the following way. Threat: "If you *do not* do what I am proposing you do, I will bring about an *undesirable consequence* for you." Offer: "If you *do* what I am proposing you do, I will bring about a *desirable consequence* for you." The person who makes a threat attempts to gain compliance by attaching an undesirable consequence to the alternative of noncompliance. This person attempts to *coerce* consent. The person who makes an offer attempts to gain compliance by attaching a desirable consequence to the alternative of compliance. This person attempts not to coerce but to *induce* consent.

Since threats are morally problematic in a way that offers are not, it is not uncommon for threats to be advanced in the language of offers. Threats are represented as if they were offers. An armed assailant might say, "I'm going to make you an *offer*. If you give me your money, I will allow you to go on living." Though this proposal on the surface has the logical form of an offer, it is in reality a threat. The underlying sense of the proposal is this: "If you do not give me your money, I will kill you." If, in a given case, it is initially unclear whether a certain proposal is to count as a threat or an offer, ask the following question. Does the proposal in question have the effect of making a person *worse off upon noncompliance?* The recipient of an offer, upon noncompliance, *is not worse off* than he or she was before the offer. In contrast, the recipient of a threat, upon noncompliance, *is worse off* than he or she was before the threat. Since the "offer" of our armed assailant has the effect, upon noncompliance, of rendering its recipient worse off (relative to the preproposal situation of the recipient), the recipient is faced with a threat, not an offer.

The most obvious way for a coercer to attach an undesirable consequence to the path of noncompliance is by threatening to render the victim of coercion materially worse off than he or she has heretofore been. Thus a person is threatened with loss of life, bodily injury, damage to property, damage to reputation, etc. It is important to realize, however, that a person can also be effectively coerced by being threatened with the withholding of something (in some cases, what we would call a "benefit") to which the person is entitled. Suppose that A is mired in quicksand and is slowly but surely approaching death. When B happens along, A cries out to B for assistance. All B need do is throw A a rope. B is quite willing to accommodate A, "provided you pay me $100,000 over the next ten years." Is B making A an offer? Hardly! B, we must presume, stands under a moral obligation to come to the aid of a person in serious distress, at least when such assistance entails no significant risk, sacrifice of time, etc. A is entitled to B's assistance. Thus, in reality, B attaches an undesirable consequence to A's noncompliance with the proposal that A pay B $100,000. A is undoubtedly better off that B has happened along, but A is not rendered better off *by B's proposal.* Before B's proposal, A legitimately expected assistance from B, "no strings attached." In attaching a very unwelcome string, B's proposal effectively renders A worse off. What B proposes, then, is not an offer of assistance. Rather, B threatens A with the withholding of something (assistance) that A is entitled to have from B.

Since threats have the effect of rendering a person worse off upon noncompliance, it is ordinarily the case that a person does not welcome (indeed, despises) them. Offers, on the other hand, are ordinarily welcome to a person. Since an offer provides no penalty for noncompliance with a proposal but only an inducement for compliance, there is *in principle* only potential advantage in being confronted with an offer. In real life, of course, there are numerous reasons why a person may be less than enthusiastic about being presented with an offer. Enduring the presentation of trivial offers does not warrant the necessary time and energy expenditures. Offers can be both annoying and offensive; certainly this is true of some sexual offers. A person might also be unsettled by an offer that confronts him or her with a difficult decision. All this, however, is compatible with the fact that an offer is fundamentally welcome to a rational person in the sense that the *content* of an offer necessarily widens the field of opportunity and thus provides, in principle, only potential advantage.

With the distinction between threats and offers clearly in view, it now becomes clear why cases 1 and 2 do indeed involve attempts to sexually use another person whereas cases 3 and 4 do not. Cases 1 and 2 embody threats, whereas cases 3 and 4 embody offers. In case 1, Mr. Supervisor proposes sexual interaction with Ms. Employee and, in an effort to gain compliance, threatens her with the loss of her job. Mr. Supervisor thereby attaches an undesirable consequence to one of Ms. Employee's alternatives, the path of noncompliance. Typical of the threat situation, Mr. Supervisor's proposal has the effect of rendering Ms. Employee worse off upon noncompliance. Mr. Supervisor is attempting via (dispositional) coercion to sexually use Ms. Employee. The situation in case 2 is similar. Ms. Debtor, as *she* might be inclined to say, "offers" to pay Mr. Creditor the money she owes him *if* he consents to sexual interaction with her. In reality, Ms. Debtor is threatening Mr. Creditor, attempting to coerce his consent to sexual interaction, attempting to sexually use him. Though Mr. Creditor is not now in possession of the money Ms. Debtor owes him, he is *entitled* to receive it from her at this time. She threatens to deprive him of something to which he is entitled. Clearly, her proposal has the effect of rendering him worse off upon noncompliance. Before her proposal, he had the legitimate expectation, "no strings attached," of receiving the money in question.

Cases 3 and 4 embody offers; neither involves an attempt to sexually use another person. Mr. Theatregoer simply provides an inducement for the woman he has just met to accept his proposal of sexual interaction. He offers her the opportunity to see the play that everyone is talking about. In attaching a desirable consequence to the alternative of compliance, Mr. Theatregoer in no way threatens or attempts to coerce his potential companion. Typical of the offer situation, his proposal does not have the effect of rendering her worse off upon noncompliance. She now has a new opportunity; if she chooses to forgo this opportunity, she is no worse off. The situation in case 4 is similar. Ms. Jetsetter provides an inducement for a man that she is interested in to accept her proposal of sexual involvement. She offers him the opportunity to see Europe, without expense, as her traveling companion. Before Ms. Jetsetter's proposal, he had no prospect of a European trip. If he chooses to reject her proposal, he is no worse off than he has heretofore been. Ms. Jetsetter's proposal embodies an offer, not a threat. She cannot be accused of attempting to sexually use her potential traveling companion.

Consider now two further cases, 5 and 6, each of which develops in the following way. Professor Highstatus, a man of high academic accomplishment, is sexually attracted to a student in one of his classes. He is very anxious to secure her consent to sexual interaction. Ms. Student, confused and unsettled by his sexual advances, has begun to practice "avoidance behavior." To the extent that it is possible, she goes out of her way to avoid him.

Case 5   Professor Highstatus tells Ms. Student that, though her work is such as to entitle her to a grade of B in the class, she will be assigned a D unless she consents to sexual interaction.

Case 6   Professor Highstatus tells Ms. Student that, though her work is such as to entitle her to a grade of B, she will be assigned an A if she consents to sexual interaction.

It is clear that case 5 involves an attempt to sexually use another person. Case 6, however, at least at face value, does not. In case 5, Professor Highstatus *threatens* to deprive Ms. Student of the grade she deserves. In case 6, he *offers* to assign her a grade that is higher than she deserves. In case 5, Ms. Student would be worse off upon noncompliance with Professor Highstatus' proposal. In case 6, she would not be worse off upon noncompliance with his proposal. In saying that case 6 does not involve an attempt to sexually use another person, it is not being asserted that Professor Highstatus is acting in a morally legitimate fashion. In offering a student a higher grade than she deserves, he is guilty of abusing his institutional authority. He is under an obligation to assign the grades that students earn, as defined by the relevant course standards. In case 6, Professor Highstatus is undoubtedly acting in a morally reprehensible way, but in contrast to case 5, where it is fair to say that he both abuses his institutional authority *and* attempts to sexually use another person, we can plausibly say that in case 6 his moral failure is limited to abuse of his institutional authority.

There remains, however, a suspicion that case 6 might after all embody an attempt to sexually use another person. There is no question that the literal content of what Professor Highstatus conveys to Ms. Student has the logical form of an offer and not a threat. Still, is it not the case that Ms. Student may very well feel threatened? Professor Highstatus, in an effort to secure consent to sexual interaction, has announced that he will assign Ms. Student a higher grade than she deserves. Can she really turn him down without substantial risk? Is he not likely to retaliate? If she spurns him, will he not lower her grade or otherwise make it harder for her to succeed in her academic program? He does, after all, have power over her. Will he use it to her detriment? Surely he is not above abusing his institutional authority to achieve his ends; this much is abundantly clear from his willingness to assign a grade higher than a student deserves.

Is Professor Highstatus naive to the threat that Ms. Student may find implicit in the situation? Perhaps. In such a case, if Ms. Student reluctantly consents to sexual interaction, we may be inclined to say that he has *unwittingly* used her. More likely, Professor Highstatus is well aware of the way in which Ms. Student will perceive his proposal. He knows that threats need not be verbally expressed. Indeed, it may even be the case that he consciously exploits his underground reputation. "Everyone knows what happens to the women who reject Professor Highstatus's little offers." To the extent, then, that Professor Highstatus intends to convey a threat in case 6, he is attempting via coercion to sexually use another person.

Many researchers "have pointed out the fact that the possibility of sanctions for noncooperation is implicit in all sexual advances across authority lines, as between teacher and student."[5] I do not think that this consideration should lead us to the conclusion that a person with an academic appointment is obliged in all circumstances to refrain from attempting to initiate sexual involvement with one of his or her students. Still, since even "good faith" sexual advances may be ambiguous in the eyes of a student, it is an interesting question what precautions an instructor must take to avoid unwittingly coercing a student to consent to sexual interaction.

Much of what has been said about the professor/student relationship in an academic setting can be applied as well to the supervisor/subordinate relationship in an employment setting. A manager who functions within an organizational structure is required to evaluate fairly his or her subordinates according to relevant corporate or institutional standards. An unscrupulous manager, willing to abuse his or her institutional authority in an effort to win the consent of a subordinate to sexual interaction, can advance threats and/or offers related to the managerial task of employee evaluation. An employee whose job performance is entirely satisfactory can be threatened with an unsatisfactory performance rating, perhaps leading to termination. An employee whose job performance is excellent can be threatened with an unfair evaluation, designed to bar the employee from recognition, merit pay, consideration for promotion, etc. Such threats, when made in an effort to coerce employee consent to sexual interaction, clearly embody the attempt to sexually use another person. On the other hand, the manager who (abusing his or her institutional authority) offers to provide an employee with an inflated evaluation as an inducement for consent to sexual interaction does not, at face value, attempt to sexually use another person. Of course, all of the qualifications introduced in the discussion of case 6 above are applicable here as well.

IV   THE IDEA OF A COERCIVE OFFER

In section III, I have sketched an overall account of sexually using another person *via coercion*. In this section, I will consider the need for modifications or extensions of the suggested account. As before, certain case studies will serve as points of departure.

Case 7   Ms. Starlet, a glamorous, wealthy, and highly successful model, wants nothing more than to become a movie superstar. Mr. Moviemogul, a famous producer, is very taken with Ms. Starlet's beauty. He invites her to come to his office for a screen test. After the screen test, Mr. Moviemogul tells Ms. Starlet that he is prepared to make her a star, on the condition that she agree to sexual involvement with him. Ms. Starlet finds Mr. Moviemogul personally repugnant, she is not at all sexually attracted to him. With great reluctance, she agrees to his proposal.

Has Mr. Moviemogul sexually used Ms. Starlet? No. He has made her an offer that she has accepted, however reluctantly. The situation would be quite different if it were plausible to believe that she was, before acceptance of his proposal, *entitled* to his efforts to make her a star. Then we could read case 7 as amounting to his threatening to deprive her of something to which she was entitled. But what conceivable grounds could be found for the claim that Mr. Moviemogul, before Ms. Starlet's acceptance of his proposal, is under an obligation to make her a star? He does not threaten her; he makes her an offer. Even if there are other good grounds for morally condemning his action, it is a mistake to think that he is guilty of coercing consent.

But some would assert that Mr. Moviemogul's offer, on the grounds that it confronts Ms. Starlet with an overwhelming inducement, is simply an example of a *coercive offer.* The more general claim at issue is that offers are coercive precisely inasmuch as they are extremely enticing or seductive. Though there is an important reality associated with the notion of a coercive offer, a reality that must shortly be confronted, we ought not embrace the view that an offer is coercive merely because it is extremely enticing or seductive. Virginia Held is a leading proponent of the view under attack here. She writes:

> A person unable to spurn an offer may act as unwillingly as a person unable to resist a threat. Consider the distinction between rape and seduction. In one case constraint and threat are operative, in the other inducement and offer. If the degree of inducement is set high enough in the case of seduction, there may seem to be little difference in the extent of coercion involved. In both cases, persons may act against their own wills.[6]

Certainly a rape victim who acquiesces at knife point is forced to act *against her will.* Does Ms. Starlet, however, act against her will? We have said that she consents "with great reluctance" to sexual involvement, but she does not act against her will. She *wants* very much to be a movie star. I might want very much to be thin. She regrets having to become sexually involved with Mr. Moviemogul as a means of achieving what she wants. I might regret very much having to go on a diet to lose weight. If we say that Ms. Starlet acts against her will in case 7, then we must say that I am acting against my will in embracing "with great reluctance" the diet I despise.

A more important line of argument against Held's view can be advanced on the basis of the widely accepted notion that there is a moral presumption against coercion. Held herself embraces this notion and very effectively clarifies it:

> . . . although coercion is not *always* wrong (quite obviously: one coerces the small child not to run across the highway, or the murderer to drop his weapon), there is a presumption against it. . . . This has the standing of a fundamental moral principle. . . .

What can be concluded at the moral level is that we have a *prima facie* obligation not to employ coercion.[7] [all italics hers]

But it would seem that acceptance of the moral presumption against coercion is not compatible with the view that offers become coercive precisely inasmuch as they become extremely enticing or seductive. Suppose you are my neighbor and regularly spend your Saturday afternoon on the golf course. Suppose also that you are a skilled gardener. I am anxious to convince you to do some gardening work for me and it must be done this Saturday. I offer you $100, $200, $300, . . . in an effort to make it worth your while to sacrifice your recreation and undertake my gardening. At some point, my proposal becomes very enticing. Yet, at the same time in no sense is my proposal becoming morally problematic. If my proposal were becoming coercive, surely our moral sense would be aroused.

Though it is surely not true that the extremely enticing character of an offer is sufficient to make it coercive, we need not reach the conclusion that no sense can be made out of the notion of a coercive offer. Indeed, there is an important social reality that the notion of a coercive offer appears to capture, and insight into this reality can be gained by simply taking note of the sort of case that most draws us to the language of "coercive offer." Is it not a case in which the recipient of an offer is in circumstances of genuine need, and acceptance of the offer seems to present the only realistic possibility for alleviating the need? Assuming that this sort of case is the heart of the matter, it seems that we cannot avoid introducing some sort of distinction between *genuine needs* and *mere wants*. Though the philosophical difficulties involved in drawing this distinction are not insignificant, I nevertheless claim that we will not achieve any clarity about the notion of a coercive offer, at least in this context, except in reference to it. Whatever puzzlement we may feel with regard to the host of borderline cases that can be advanced, it is nevertheless true, for example, that I *genuinely need* food and that I *merely want* a backyard tennis court. In the same spirit, I think it can be acknowledged by all that Ms. Starlet, though she *wants* very much to be a star, does not in any relevant sense *need* to be a star. Accordingly, there is little plausibility in thinking that Mr. Moviemogul makes her a coercive offer. The following case, in contrast, can more plausibly be thought to embody a coercive offer.

Case 8 Mr. Troubled is a young widower who is raising his three children. He lives in a small town and believes that it is important for him to stay there so that his children continue to have the emotional support of other family members. But economic times are tough. Mr. Troubled has been laid off from his job and has not been able to find another. His unemployment benefits have ceased and his relatives are in no position to help him financially. If he is unable to come up with the money for his mortgage payments, he will lose his rather modest house. Ms. Opportunistic lives in the same town. Since shortly after the death of Mr. Troubled's wife, she has consistently made sexual overtures in his direction. Mr. Troubled, for his part, does not care for Ms. Opportunistic and has made it clear to her that he is not interested in sexual involvement with her. She, however, is well aware of his present difficulties. To win his consent to a sexual affair, Ms. Opportunistic offers to make mortgage payments for Mr. Troubled on a continuing basis.

Is Ms. Opportunistic attempting to sexually use Mr. Troubled? The correct answer is yes, even though we must first accept the conclusion that her proposal embodies an offer and not a threat. If Ms. Opportunistic were threatening Mr. Troubled, her proposal would have the effect of rendering him worse off upon noncompliance. But this is not the case. If he rejects her proposal, his situation will not worsen; he will simply remain, as before, in circumstances of extreme need. It might be objected at this point that Ms. Opportunistic does in fact threaten Mr. Troubled. She threatens to deprive him of something to which he is entitled, namely, the alleviation of a genuine need. But this approach is defensible only if, before acceptance of her proposal, he is entitled to have his needs alleviated *by her.* And whatever Mr. Troubled and his children are entitled to from their society as a whole—they are perhaps slipping through the "social safety net"—it cannot be plausibly maintained that Mr. Troubled is entitled to have his mortgage payments made *by Ms. Opportunistic.*

Yet, though she does not threaten him, she is attempting to sexually use him. How can this conclusion be reconciled with our overall account of sexually using another person? First of all, I want to suggest that nothing hangs on whether or not we decide to call Ms. Opportunistic's offer "coercive." More important than the label "coercive offer" is an appreciation of the social reality that inclines us to consider the label appropriate. The label most forcefully asserts itself when we reflect on what Mr. Troubled is likely to say after accepting the offer. "I really had no choice." "I didn't want to accept her offer but what could I do? I have my children to think about." Both Mr. Troubled and Ms. Starlet (in our previous case) *reluctantly* consented to sexual interaction, but I think it can be agreed that Ms. Starlet had a choice in a way that Mr. Troubled did not. Mr. Troubled's choice was *severely constrained by his needs,* whereas Ms. Starlet's was not. As for Ms. Opportunistic, it seems that we might describe her approach as in some sense exploiting or taking advantage of Mr. Troubled's desperate situation. It is not so much, as we would say in the case of threats, that she coerces him or his consent, but rather that she achieves her aim of winning consent by taking advantage of the fact that he is already "under coercion," that is, his choice is severely constrained by his need. If we choose to describe what has taken place as a "coercive offer," we should remember that Mr. Troubled is "coerced" (constrained) by his own need or perhaps by preexisting factors in his situation rather than by Ms. Opportunistic or her offer.

Since it is not quite right to say that Ms. Opportunistic is attempting to coerce Mr. Troubled, even if we are prepared to embrace the label "coercive offer," we cannot simply say, as we would say in the case of threats, that she is attempting to sexually use him *via coercion.* The proper account of the way in which Ms. Opportunistic attempts to sexually use Mr. Troubled is somewhat different. Let us say simply that she attempts to sexually use him *by taking advantage of his desperate situation.* The sense behind this distinctive way of sexually using someone is that a person's choice situation can sometimes be subject to such severe prior constraints that the possibility of *voluntary* consent to sexual interaction is precluded. A advances an offer calculated to gain B's reluctant consent to sexual interaction by confronting B, who has no apparent way of alleviating a genuine need, with an opportunity to do so, but makes this opportunity contingent upon consent to sexual interaction. In such a case, should we not say simply that B's need, when coupled with a lack of viable alternatives, results in B being incapable of *voluntarily* accepting A's offer? Thus A, in making an offer which B "cannot refuse," although not coercing B, nevertheless does intentionally act in a way that violates the requirement that B's sexual interaction with A be based upon B's voluntary informed consent. Thus A sexually uses B.

The central claim of this paper is that A sexually uses B if and only if A intentionally acts in a way that violates the requirement that B's sexual interaction with A be based on B's voluntary informed consent. Clearly, deception and coercion are important mechanisms whereby sexual using takes place. But consideration of case 8 has led us to the identification of yet another mechanism. In summary, then, limiting attention to cases of sexual interaction with a fully competent adult partner, A can sexually use B not only (1) by deceiving B or (2) by coercing B but also (3) by taking advantage of B's desperate situation.

NOTES

1 I follow here an account of coercion developed by Michael D. Bayles in "A Concept of Coercion," in J. Roland Pennock and John W. Chapman, eds., *Coercion: Nomos XIV* (Chicago: Aldine-Atherton, 1972), pp. 16–29.
2 Statutory rape, sexual relations with a person under the legal age of consent, can also be construed as the sexual using of another person. In contrast to forcible rape, however, statutory rape need not involve coercion. The victim of statutory rape may freely "consent" to sexual interaction but, at least in the eyes of the law, is deemed incompetent to consent.
3 A man wrestles a woman to the ground. She is the victim of occurrent coercion. He threatens to beat her unless she submits to his sexual demands. Now she becomes the victim of dispositional coercion.
4 My account of this distinction largely derives from Robert Nozick, "Coercion," in Sidney Morgenbesser, Patrick Suppes, and Morton White, eds., *Philosophy, Science, and Method* (New York: St. Martin's Press, 1969), pp. 440–472, and from Michael D. Bayles, "Coercive Offers and Public Benefits," *The Personalist* 55, no. 2 (Spring 1974), 139–144.
5 The National Advisory Council on Women's Educational Programs, *Sexual Harassment: A Report on the Sexual Harassment of Students* (August 1980), p. 12.
6 Virginia Held, "Coercion and Coercive Offers," in *Coercion: Nomos XIV,* p. 58.
7 *Ibid.,* pp. 61, 62.

QUESTIONS

1 Is there a morally relevant sense of *sexually* using another person that is not captured by reference to the notion of voluntary informed consent?
2 What is promiscuity? Is promiscuity immoral?
3 Is prostitution immoral?

The Harms of Consensual Sex

Robin West

Robin West is professor of law at Georgetown University Law Center. She is the author of *Narrative, Authority, and Law* (1993) and *Progressive Constitutionalism: Reconstructing the Fourteenth Amendment* (1994). Her many law journal articles include "Reconstructing Liberty" and "Jurisprudence and Gender."

West argues that heterosexual transactions—even when consensual—are frequently harmful to women. In her view, the harms of consensual sex include injuries to a woman's self-assertiveness, to her sense of self-possession, to her autonomy, and to her integrity. West also argues that the harms of consensual sex are frequently unnoticed or not taken seriously, and she suggests several reasons why this is the case. Among other things, she maintains that both liberal feminist rape reform efforts and radical feminist theory have unwittingly contributed to an underacknowledgment of the harms of consensual sex.

Are consensual, non-coercive, non-criminal, and even non-tortious, heterosexual transactions ever harmful to women? I want to argue briefly that many (not all) consensual sexual transactions are, and that accordingly we should open a dialogue about what those harms might be. Then I want to suggest some reasons those harms may be difficult to discern, even by the women sustaining them, and lastly two ways in which the logic of feminist legal theory and practice itself might undermine their recognition.

Let me assume what many women who are or have been heterosexually active surely know to be true from their own experience, and that is that some women occasionally, and many women quite frequently, consent to sex even when they do not desire the sex itself, and accordingly have a good deal of sex that, although consensual, is in no way pleasurable. Why might a woman consent to sex she does not desire? There are, of course, many reasons. A woman might consent to sex she does not want because she or her children are dependent upon her male partner for economic sustenance, and she must accordingly remain in his good graces. A woman might consent to sex she does not want because she rightly fears that if she does not her partner will be put into a foul humor, and she simply decides that tolerating the undesired sex is less burdensome than tolerating the foul humor. A woman might consent to sex she does not want because she has been taught and has come to believe that it is her lot in life to do so, and that she has no reasonable expectation of attaining her own pleasure through sex. A woman might consent to sex she does not want because she rightly fears that her refusal to do so will lead to an outburst of violent behavior some time following—only if the violence or overt threat of violence is *very* close to the sexual act will this arguably constitute a rape. A woman may con-

Reprinted with permission of the American Philosophical Association from *APA Newsletters,* vol. 94, Spring 1995, pp. 52–55.

sent to sex she does not desire because she *does* desire a friendly man's protection against the very real threat of non-consensual violent rape by other more dangerous men, and she correctly perceives, or intuits, that to gain the friendly man's protection, she needs to give him in exchange for that protection, the means to his own sexual pleasure. A woman, particularly a young woman or teenager, may consent to sex she does not want because of peer expectations that she be sexually active, or because she cannot bring herself to hurt her partner's pride, or because she is uncomfortable with the prospect of the argument that might ensue, should she refuse.

These transactions may well be rational—indeed in some sense they all are. The women involved all trade sex for something they value more than they value what they have given up. But that doesn't mean that they are not harmed. Women who engage in unpleasurable, undesired, but consensual sex may sustain real injuries to their sense of selfhood, in at least four distinct ways. First, they may sustain injuries to their capacities for self-assertion: the "psychic connection," so to speak, between pleasure, desire, motivation, and action is weakened or severed. *Acting* on the basis of our own felt pleasures and pains is an important component of forging our own way in the world—of "asserting" our "selves." Consenting to *un*pleasurable sex— acting in spite of displeasure—threatens that means of self-assertion. Second, women who consent to undesired sex may injure their sense of self-*possession.* When we consent to undesired penetration of our physical bodies we have in a quite literal way constituted ourselves as what I have elsewhere called "giving selves"—selves who cannot be violated, because they have been defined as (and define themselves as) being "for others." Our bodies to that extent no longer belong to ourselves. Third, when women consent to undesired and unpleasurable sex because of their felt or actual dependency upon a partner's affection or economic status, they injure their sense of autonomy: they have thereby neglected to take whatever steps would be requisite to achieving the self-sustenance necessary to their independence. And fourth, to the extent that these unpleasurable and undesired sexual acts are followed by contrary to fact claims that they enjoyed the whole thing—what might be called "hedonic lies"—women who engage in them do considerable damage to their sense of integrity.

These harms—particularly if multiplied over years or indeed over an entire adulthood—may be quite profound, and they certainly may be serious enough to outweigh the momentary or day-to-day benefits garnered by each individual transaction. Most debilitating, though, is their circular, self-reinforcing character: the more thorough the harm—the deeper the injury to self-assertiveness, self-possession, autonomy and integrity—the greater the likelihood that the woman involved will indeed *not* experience these harms as harmful, or as painful. A woman utterly lacking in self-assertiveness, self-possession, a sense of autonomy, or integrity will not experience the activities in which she engages that reinforce or constitute those qualities *as harmful,* because she, to that degree, lacks a self-asserting, self-possessed self who *could* experience those activities as a threat to her selfhood. But the fact that she does not experience these activities as harms certainly does not mean that they are not harmful. Indeed, that they are not felt as harmful is a consequence of the harm they have already caused. This phenomenon, of course, renders the "rationality" of these transactions tremendously and even tragically misleading. Although these women may be making rational calculations in the context of the particular decision facing them, they are by making those calculations, sustaining deeper and to some degree unfelt harms that undermine the very qualities that constitute the capacity for rationality being exercised.

Let me quickly suggest some reasons that these harms go so frequently unnoticed—or are simply not taken seriously—and then suggest in slightly more detail some ways that feminist legal theory and practice may have undermined their recognition. The first reason is cultural. There is a deep-seated U.S. cultural tendency to equate the legal with the good, or harmless: we are, for better or worse, an anti-moralistic, anti-authoritarian, and anti-communitarian people. When combined with the sexual revolution of the 1960s, this provides a powerful cultural explanation for our tendency to shy away from a sustained critique of the harms of consensual sex. Any suggestion that legal transactions to which individuals freely consent may be harmful, and hence *bad,* will invariably be met with skepticism—*particularly* where those transactions are sexual in nature. This tendency is even further underscored by more contemporary postmodern skeptical responses to claims asserting the pernicious consequences of false consciousness.

Second, at least our legal-academic discourses, and no doubt academic political discourses as well, have been deeply transformed by the "exchange theory of value," according to which, if I exchange A for B voluntarily, then I simply must be better off after the exchange than before, having, after all, agreed to it. If these exchanges *are* the source of value, then it is of course impossible to ground a *value* judgment that some voluntary exchanges are harmful. Although stated baldly this theory of value surely has more critics than believers, it nevertheless in some way perfectly captures the modern zeitgeist. It is certainly, for example, the starting and ending point of normative analysis for many, and perhaps most, law students. Obviously, given an exchange theory of value, the harms caused by consensual sexual transactions simply fade away into definitional oblivion.

Third, the exchange theory of value is underscored, rather than significantly challenged, by the continuing significance of liberal theory and ideology in academic life. To the degree that liberalism still rules the day, we continue to valorize individual choice against virtually anything with which it might seem to be in conflict, from communitarian dialogue to political critique, and continue to perceive these challenges to individual primacy as somehow on a par with threats posed by totalitarian statist regimes.

Fourth, and perhaps most obvious, the considerable harms women sustain from consensual but undesired sex must be downplayed if the considerable pleasure men reap from heterosexual transactions is morally justified—*whatever* the relevant moral theory. Men do have a psycho-sexual stake in insisting that voluntariness alone ought be sufficient to ward off serious moral or political inquiry into the value of consensual sexual transactions.

Let me comment in a bit more detail on a further reason why these harms seem to be underacknowledged, and that has to do with the logic of feminist legal theory, and the efforts of feminist practitioners, in the area of rape law reform. My claim is that the theoretical conceptualizations of sex, rape, force, and violence that underscore both liberal and radical legal feminism undermine the effort to articulate the harms that might be caused by consensual sexuality. I will begin with liberal feminism and then turn to radical feminism.

First, and entirely to their credit, liberal feminist rape law reformers have been on the forefront of efforts to stiffen enforcement of the existing criminal sanction against rape, and to extend that sanction to include non-consensual sex which presently is not cognizable legally as rape but surely should be. This effort is to be applauded, but it has the *almost* inevitable consequence of valorizing, celebrating, or, to use the critical term, "legitimating" consensual sexual transactions. If rape is bad *because* it is non-consensual—which is increasingly the dominant liberal-feminist position on the badness of rape—then it seems to follow that *consensual* sex must be good because it is consensual. But appearances can be misleading, and this one certainly is. That non-consensual transactions—rape, theft, slavery—are bad because non-consensual, does *not* imply the value, worth or goodness of their consensual counterparts—sex, property, or work. It only follows that consensual sex, property, or work are not bad in the ways that non-consensual transactions are bad; they surely may be bad for some other reason. We need to explore, in the case of sex (as well as property and work) what those other reasons might be. Non-consensuality does not exhaust the types of harm we inflict on each other in social interactions, nor does consensuality exhaust the list of benefits.

That the liberal-feminist argument for extending the criminal sanction against rape to include non-consensual sex *seems* to imply the positive value of consensual sex is no doubt in part simply a reflection of the powers of the forces enumerated above—the cultural, economic, and liberal valorization of individualism against communal and authoritarian controls. Liberal feminists can obviously not be faulted for that phenomenon. What I want to caution against, is simply the ever present temptation to *trade* on those cultural and academic forces in putting forward arguments for reform of rape law. We need not trumpet the glories of consensual sex *in order to* make out a case for strengthening the criminal sanction against coercive sex. Coercion, violence, and the fear under which women live because of the threat of rape are sufficient evils to sustain the case for strengthening and extending the criminal law against those harms. We need not and should not supplement the argument with the unnecessary and unwarranted celebration of consensual sex—which whatever the harms caused by coercion, does indeed carry its own harms.

Ironically, radical feminist rhetoric—which *is* aimed at highlighting the damage and harm done to women by ordinary, "normal" heterosexual transactions—*also* indirectly burdens the attempt to articulate the harms done to women by consensual heterosexual transactions, although it does so in a very different way. Consider the claim, implicit in a good deal of radical feminist writing, explicit in some, that "all sex is rape," and compare it for a moment with the rhetorical Marxist claim that "all property is theft." Both claims are intended to push the reader or listener to a reexamination of the ordinary, and both do so by blurring the distinction between consent and coercion. Both seem to share the underlying premise that which is co-erced—and perhaps *only* that which is coerced—is bad, or as a strategic matter, is going to be perceived as bad. Both want us to reexamine the value of that which we normally think of as good or at least unproblematic because of its apparent consen-suality—heterosexual transactions in the first case, property transactions in the sec-ond—and both do so by putting into doubt the reality of that apparent consensual-ity.

But there is a very real difference in the historical context and hence the practi-cal consequences of these two rhetorical claims. More specifically, there are two per-nicious, or at least counter-productive consequences of the feminist claim which are not shared, at least to the same degree, by the marxist. First, and as any number of liberal feminists have noted, the radical feminist equation of sex and rape runs the risk of undermining parallel feminist efforts in a way not shared by the marxist equa-tion of property and theft. Marxists are for the most part not engaged in the project of attempting to extend the existing laws against *theft* so as to embrace non-consensual market transactions that are currently not covered by the laws against lar-ceny and embezzlement. Feminists, however, *are* engaged in a parallel effort to ex-tend the existing laws against rape to include all non-consensual sex, and as a result, the radical feminist equation of rape and sex is indeed undermining. The claim that all sex is in effect non-consensual runs the real risk of "trivializing," or at least con-fusing, the feminist effort at rape reform so as to include all truly non-consensual sexual transactions.

There is, though, a second cost to the radical feminist rhetorical claim, which I hope these comments have by now made clear. The radical feminist equation of rape and sex, no less than the liberal rape reform movement, gets its rhetorical force by trading on the liberal, normative-economic, and cultural assumptions that whatever is coercive is bad, and whatever is non-coercive is morally non-problematic. It has the effect, then, of further burdening the articulation of harms caused by consensual sex by forcing the characterization of those harms into a sort of "descriptive funnel" of non-consensuality. It requires us to say, in other words, that consensual sex is harm-ful, if it is, only because or to the extent that it shares in the attributes of non-consensual sex. But this might not be true—the harms caused by consensual sex might be just as important, just as serious, but nevertheless *different* from the harms caused by non-consensual sex. If so, then women are disserved, rather than served, by the equation of rape and sex, even were that equation to have the rhetorical ef-fect its espousers clearly desire.

Liberal feminist rape reform efforts and radical feminist theory both, then, in dif-ferent ways, undermine the effort to articulate the distinctive harms of consensual sex; the first by indirectly celebrating the value of consensual sex, and the latter by at least rhetorically denying the existence of the category. Both, then, in different ways, underscore the legitimation of consensual sex effectuated by non-feminist cul-tural and academic forces. My conclusion is simply that feminists could counter these trends in part by focusing attention on the harms caused women by consensual sex-uality. . . .

QUESTIONS

1 Do women frequently consent to sex that is undesired and unpleasant? Do men ever consent to sex that is undesired and unpleasant?
2 How significant are the harms of consensual sex for women? What social changes would help to eradicate or minimize these harms?
3 Does West provide an adequate overall account of the reasons why the harms of consensual sex frequently go unnoticed?

Homosexuality and Homophobia

Mike W. Martin

Mike W. Martin is professor of philosophy at Chapman University. He is the coauthor of *Ethics in Engineering* (1983) and the author of *Self-Deception and Morality* (1986), *Virtuous Giving: Philanthropy, Voluntary Service, and Caring* (1994), and *Everyday Morality: An Introduction to Applied Ethics* (2d ed., 1995).

Martin is unsympathetic to the view that homosexual acts are immoral. In response to the claim that homosexual acts are unnatural and therefore immoral because they cannot result in procreation, he suggests that there are no good reasons for believing that all nonreproductive sex acts are morally objectionable. Martin also considers other senses of "unnatural" but concludes that it is doubtful that there is any morally relevant sense in which homosexuality or homosexual acts are unnatural. After providing a brief discussion of what he calls the "mystery and risk" argument, Martin concludes with some reflections on homophobia.

Homosexuality is the sexual orientation in which one's primary attraction is to members of one's own sex. Gays are men primarily attracted to men, and lesbians are women primarily attracted to women. In heterosexuality the primary sexual attraction is to members of the opposite sex, and in bisexuality the attraction is to both men and women. Sexual orientation is defined by predominant patterns of sexual desires, emotions, fantasies, behavior, and the cues or stimuli that lead to sexual arousal. Sexual orientation differs from biological sex type (male versus female) and gender identity (one's conviction of being male or female and masculine or feminine).[1] It also differs from sex roles, that is, the social roles conventionally expected for men and women (as defined by physique, voice, clothing, personality, occupation, parenting styles, and so on).

Classical Greek culture accepted male homosexuality, but most Western societies have treated homosexuals with contempt and oppression. For a long while, homo-

Reprinted with permission of Wadsworth Publishing Co. from Mike W. Martin, *Everyday Morality* (1995), pp. 245–253.

sexuality was viewed as a sickness, and today many people continue to condemn homosexual acts as deeply immoral. [Here] we discuss whether those negative attitudes are justified or whether they are based on ignorance, prejudice, and fear, that is, homophobia. Homophobia is the excessive and unjustified fear and hatred of homosexuality, homosexual acts, and homosexuals. Often, homophobia leads to acts of prejudice and persecution: ridicule, discrimination, support of social policies that oppress homosexuals, and violence against gays and lesbians. Is homosexuality immoral, or is hatred of homosexuality an irrational prejudice (homophobic)? Is the moral problem homosexuality or homophobia? [Here] we consider the arguments on each side of this issue.

CLOSETS AND COMING OUT

. . . Negative social attitudes lead many homosexuals to live "closeted" lives of sexual isolation, loneliness, fear, and frustration. Not only does this compound the normal difficulties associated with finding sexual partners, it also encourages short-lived affairs rather than long-term relationships, which are publicly visible and hence dangerous in a climate of social oppression of homosexuality. Public affirmation of a homosexual identity—"coming out"—usually incurs the risk of reprisals: rejection, derisive laughter, physical assault, and violation of rights in gaining and retaining employment, in buying or renting homes, and in purchasing life insurance.

Social pressure also can make it difficult to "come out to oneself," that is, to acknowledge and affirm to oneself one's sexual orientation. Whatever one's sexual identity, adolescence is a turbulent time in terms of awakening to, accepting, and expressing one's sexuality. For gays and lesbians, however, the obstacles are multiplied. . . .

THE REPRODUCTIVE PURPOSE OF SEX

Is there anything immoral about homosexual acts? One view, held by the Catholic church and some other major religions, is that homosexuality is *unnatural* in that it departs from (or "perverts") the proper role of sex in human life. Sex is properly viewed as the means of procreation—of having children. Because homosexual acts do not have the potential to generate children, they constitute a misuse of sex and are therefore immoral. According to Leviticus in the Old Testament, homosexual acts are an abomination warranting death by stoning.[2] And according to Romans in the New Testament, homosexuals are guilty of a "vile affection" that alters "the natural use [of sex] into that which is against nature"[3] (although it is noteworthy that Jesus never himself condemns or even mentions homosexuality).

If homosexual acts are immoral simply because they cannot lead to children, then it follows that all other kinds of sexual acts that cannot lead to children are also immoral. Masturbation and heterosexual intercourse using contraceptives, for example, would also have to be condemned. If we leave aside certain religious views, it is hard to see how such acts could be immoral; and if we accept that masturbation and sexual intercourse using effective contraception are not inherently immoral, the statement that all nonreproductive sex is immoral becomes false. Therefore, the mere fact that homosexual acts cannot generate children does not make them immoral.

This type of argument is known as *reductio ad absurdum* (reduction to absurdity), which is an attempt to refute a view by showing that it entails a falsehood, drawing on the logical point that true views do not entail falsehoods. The argument should be convincing for anyone who believes that masturbation and the use of birth control devices are not immoral per se. What could be said, however, to persuade someone who does not hold these beliefs?

For example, Saint Thomas Aquinas would not be convinced by the *reductio ad absurdum* argument. According to him, all use of sex except for procreation is immoral:

> The emission of semen ought to be so ordered that it will result in both the production of the proper offspring and in the upbringing of this offspring.
>
> It is evident from this that every emission of semen, in such a way that generation cannot follow, is contrary to the good for man. And if this be done deliberately, it must be a sin. . . . For which reason, sins of this type are called contrary to nature.[4]

In fact, Aquinas believed that masturbation and homosexuality constituted sins even worse than heterosexual rape, because rape could at least generate children. Today, the Catholic church does not share that view, nor does it agree with Aquinas that the *sole* legitimate use of sex is procreation: Sex also should express love. Nevertheless, the official Catholic view concurs with Aquinas that masturbation, use of contraceptives in heterosexual sex, and homosexual acts are all immoral for the same reason: They are not the type of acts that can lead to reproduction.

One way to proceed at this point is to argue that masturbation is surely morally permissible when it leads to pleasure and has no bad side effects; and that intercourse with contraceptives is morally permissible and often desirable when it supports loving relationships and yields no harmful side effects (as are other nonreproductive sex acts based on mutual consent, such as oral sex). Support for this view seems to be offered, at least on the surface, by utilitarianism (in emphasizing mutual pleasure and happiness), duty ethics (in emphasizing mutual respect and autonomous consent of adults), and rights ethics (in emphasizing freedom that does not harm others).

Let us shift the burden of proof, however, by asking whether there are any good reasons for believing that nonreproductive sex is bad. What could be morally objectionable about using sex solely to express affection and love, at least within long-term relationships . . . ? Doesn't sex have several natural and legitimate uses in addition to procreation, enabling us, for instance, to obtain pleasure, relieve stress, strengthen self-esteem, show affection, and express love?

Notice that the question about moral reasons does not disappear if we appeal to God or stipulate that "natural" means "what God commands" and "unnatural" means what God forbids. Even if we set aside religious disagreements about what God commands and whether God exists, . . . [i]t makes sense to ask *why* God commands certain things rather than others. Presumably, a morally perfect being would make commandments on the basis of good moral reasons rather than on whim or from prejudice.

Are there any good reasons to believe that a morally perfect being would forbid all nonreproductive types of sex acts? This is essentially the same question as above: Are there any good reasons for believing that all nonreproductive sex acts are bad? This question will be left as a discussion topic.

OTHER SENSES OF "UNNATURAL"

If we set aside the senses of "unnatural sex" that mean "nonprocreative" and "contrary to God's commands," are there any other senses in which homosexuality is unnatural—senses that have some moral relevance? The words *natural* and *unnatural* do have other meanings, but it is doubtful that they have any moral significance or relevance for thinking about homosexuality.

First, one could define *natural* in terms of "the *primary* biological function." Thus, the natural function of the digestive system and of eating is to provide nutrition for the body; similarly, the natural function of genitals and sexual intercourse is procreation. If we adopt this definition, nonreproductive sex is unnatural (assuming the most important evolutionary role of sex is reproduction); but even though this may be true, critics argue that it is morally irrelevant to the topic of homosexuality. Just because the primary function of the digestive system and of eating is nutrition, it does not follow that it is immoral sometimes to eat just for pleasure or during an enjoyable luncheon with a friend or spouse, even though one is not hungry or in need of food. Similarly, even if the primary biological purpose of sex is procreation, it does not follow that it is bad to use sex solely for pleasure or for expressing love.

Second, *natural* might mean "healthy," both mentally and physically. Is homosexuality a mental illness? Here the expert testimony of health professionals is relevant (if not decisive). Before 1974, the American Psychiatric Association (APA) viewed homosexuality as a mental disorder and listed it as such in its *Diagnostic and Statistical Manual of Mental Disorders*. In 1974, however, the APA acknowledged that it had made a mistake and emended the *Manual*. Did the mistake arise because psychiatrists misinterpreted the anxieties they sometimes observed in homosexuals as symptoms of an illness rather than as largely the product of special societal pressures on homosexuals? Did the mistake perhaps express homophobia among health professionals of the time? Today, most health professionals—the vast majority—do not view homosexuality as unhealthy. Insofar as homosexuals suffer from any greater anxiety or depression, the cause is now understood to be society's rejection of homosexuality.

The physical health of many gays, of course, has been devastated by AIDS. Homosexuality is not, however, the cause of AIDS, and homosexual acts by themselves do not cause AIDS. AIDS is spread by the failure to use precautions (especially condoms) during homosexual *or* heterosexual intercourse (as well as by the shared use of needles by drug addicts and transfusions of contaminated blood).

Third, some people see a kind of naturalness in how genitals "fit together" during heterosexual intercourse. Here *natural* seems to mean "geometrically complementary." Is the notion of genital geometry, however, relevant to the debate over homosexuality as unnatural? Or does it express a heterosexual bias against homosexual experiences, especially in view of the fact that the alleged geometrical problem is never voiced by homosexuals?

Fourth, *natural* might mean "common" or "usual." Again, critics argue that this sense is also irrelevant morally. The fact that most people are heterosexual does not make it immoral to be in a sexual minority. If it did, then by analogy all left-handed people would be immoral too, because they represent a minority orientation to space and activities; likewise, windsurfing would constitute an immoral use of the sea.

Fifth, *natural* might be used to characterize something that "feels natural," in the sense that it is based on an inclination that one feels and with which one identifies. True, many heterosexuals do lack or are uncomfortable about homosexual impulses, which seem alien and repulsive, but isn't this only a statement about heterosexual tastes and orientation, a statement that lacks moral force? To illustrate, many people are repelled at the thought of eating snails, but it does not follow that a passion for escargot is immoral. Tastes in food, wine, books, and friends—and sex—involve deep feelings that can be as strong as moral emotions. For this reason, it is sometimes easy to confuse issues of taste and morality, but they are distinct.

Sixth, *natural* might be defined as that which conforms to the appropriate roles for men and women. Homosexuality, it is claimed, is morally objectionable because gays tend to be effeminate in gesture and voice, violating masculine role models; conversely, lesbians tend to be unfeminine. Critics point out that this argument falsely stereotypes the mannerisms of gays and lesbians, most of whom do not fit this profile. (For example, Rock Hudson was gay but not effeminate.) The argument also assumes that all males and all females have a moral obligation to fit a particular gender role, and it apparently misappropriates the word *natural* by applying it to what are primarily socially created (not naturally created) sex roles.

PROMISCUITY

Another stereotypic view of gays—that all gays are promiscuous due to something inherent in male homosexuality—merits a separate discussion. Whereas lesbians tend not to be promiscuous, there are in fact gay men who have many hundreds of sexual partners during a lifetime. Yet most gays have fewer partners than this stereotype suggests, and of course many heterosexual males are also promiscuous, and have sex as often as they can find a willing partner.

Nevertheless, Roger Scruton argues that male homosexuality *tends* to encourage promiscuity and thereby discourages long-term love relationships of the kind he values. According to Scruton, all males have a strong natural tendency to sexual predation, which means they will desire many sexual partners during a lifetime. This instinct is tamed through attraction to the "mystery" of the opposite sex. Because members of the opposite sex are radically unlike oneself (physically, mentally), in pursuing sexual relationships with them one knowingly undertakes great risks—the risks of the unknown. These risks encourage commitment and fidelity that form the basis for long-term relationships grounded in erotic love.

> The opening of the self to the mystery of another gender, thereby taking responsibility for an experience which one does not wholly understand, is a feature of sexual maturity, and

one of the fundamental motives tending towards commitment. This exposure to something unknown can resolve itself, finally, only in a mutual vow. Only in a vow is the trust created which protects the participants from the threat of betrayal. Without the fundamental experience of the otherness of the sexual partner, an important component in erotic love is therefore put in jeopardy. For the homosexual, who knows intimately in himself the generality that he finds in the other, there may be a diminished sense of risk. The move out of the self may be less adventurous, the help of the other [within a long-term relationship] less required.[5]

In short, Scruton thinks that mystery heightens risk, and risk encourages the partners to make a mutual commitment that sustains them in taking the risk. Homosexual relationships offer less mystery because the participants are already familiar with the gender of their partners; therefore, the need for commitment is decreased, and promiscuity is encouraged.

Is this a sound argument? Scruton is sensitive to one difficulty: If the argument works for gays, why should it not also work for lesbians? Lesbian promiscuity is rare, and Scruton implies that the real problem lies in the sexual predatoriness of all males. But his "mystery of the opposite sex" argument seems to imply that lesbians would be less inclined to form commitments than other women, and no evidence supports that conclusion. A second difficulty is that the promiscuity of some gays can be explained in another way, which Scruton does not consider. As previously mentioned, the harsh social condemnations of homosexuality have made it very risky (often dangerous) for gays to be identified publicly, which discourages open, long-term relationships and encourages brief and secretive sexual encounters.

In assessing the "mystery and risk" argument, two further points need to be considered. There may be deep mysteries (and unknowns worth exploring) between any two lovers, whatever their sexual orientation. Were society to remove its taboo on homosexuality, couldn't the emotional and intellectual differences between two individuals suffice to encourage trust and commitment? Furthermore, shouldn't heterosexuals allow the possibility that homosexuality may contain its own domains of new and "mysterious" experience for those who choose to explore it? In this connection, consider the words of the poet and feminist Adrienne Rich concerning lesbian experience:

> Lesbian existence comprises both the breaking of a taboo and the rejection of a compulsory way of life. It is also a direct or indirect attack on male right of access to women. But it is more than these. . . . I perceive the lesbian experience as being, like motherhood, a profoundly *female* experience, with particular oppressions, meanings, and potentialities.[6]

HOMOPHOBIA AND SEXUAL TASTES

At this point we leave for discussion whether there are any convincing moral reasons against homosexuality. Let us conclude with some comments about homophobia. Whatever one's considered views about homosexuality, it is one thing to believe that homosexual acts are bad; it is quite another to hate, detest, degrade, and condone repression of homosexual persons.

Not everyone who objects to homosexuality (perhaps because of religious beliefs) is homophobic. They might object to hatred of homosexuals as much as they object to homosexuality itself. Many people, however, feel justified in "putting down" gays and lesbians in a variety of ways, ranging from tasteless jokes and derisive laughter to indifference to their legal rights. Is this not a form of prejudice as bad as prejudice based on race, religion, or physique?

Imagine someone arguing that the hatred involved in homophobia is no more immoral than hatred involved in other phobias. According to this argument, it is not immoral to have and to act upon phobias about spiders or snakes, about open spaces or closed spaces, or about heights and airplane rides. Similarly, nothing is immoral about hating gays and lesbians (whatever the moral status of homosexual acts). In fact, this argument is based on a weak analogy. Homophobia is directed toward people, not animals, spaces, special locations, or modes of transportation. The argument is akin to the assertion that one is not a racist, rather one simply has a phobia about black or Jewish people.

Consider another argument that appeals to the right to pursue one's own tastes. Just as we have tastes in food, sex, and clothing, we all have tastes in the kinds of people with whom we interact. Some people, so the argument goes, are uncomfortable with gay people and have a right to dislike them, avoid them, and joke about them. We do, of course, have a right to pursue our tastes, including those concerning people; but there are limits to those rights, and they do not justify violating the rights of others.

An equally important point is this: The existence of a right to pursue a taste does not imply that the taste is "all right" (i.e., morally permissible). The right to pursue our tastes implies that others should not attempt to coerce us to act otherwise; our tastes and actions may nevertheless be objectionable because they are prejudiced. Hatred of all homosexuals is a form of dismissing and shutting out people on the basis of one of their attributes, their sexual orientation. In that respect, at least, it is similar to racism and sexism. . . .

NOTES

1 Frederick Suppe, "Curing Homosexuality," in R. Baker and F. Elliston (eds.), *Philosophy and Sex,* rev. ed. (Buffalo, NY: Prometheus, 1984), pp. 394–395.
2 Lev. 18:22, King James version.
3 Rom. 1:26–27, King James version.
4 Saint Thomas Aquinas, *On the Truth of the Catholic Faith,* Book 3: *Providence,* Part 1, trans. V. J. Bourke (New York: Doubleday, 1956). Quoted in R. Baker and F. Elliston (eds.), *Philosophy and Sex,* rev. ed. (Buffalo, NY: Prometheus, 1984), p. 15.
5 Roger Scruton, *Sexual Desire: A Moral Philosophy of the Erotic* (New York: Free Press, 1986), pp. 307–308.
6 Adrienne Rich, "Compulsory Heterosexuality and Lesbian Existence," *SIGNS: Journal of Women in Culture and Society,* vol. 5 (1980). Reprinted in C. R. Stimpson and E. Spector (eds.), *Women: Sex and Sexuality* (Chicago: University of Chicago Press, 1980), pp. 81–82.

QUESTIONS

1 Are homosexual acts unnatural? Are they immoral?
2 What are the psychological and societal roots of homophobia?

Majority Opinion in *Bowers v. Hardwick*

Justice Byron R. White

Byron R. White, associate justice of the United States Supreme Court, is a graduate of Yale Law School. In private practice until 1960, he served as United States deputy attorney general (1961–1962) and was appointed to the Supreme Court in 1962.

In this case, a male homosexual (Hardwick) challenged the constitutionality of the Georgia sodomy statute. The Federal District Court sided with Bowers (the attorney general of Georgia) and dismissed Hardwick's suit "for failure to state a claim." The Court of Appeals reversed the decision of the District Court, but the United States Supreme Court agreed with the District Court and reversed the judgment of the Court of Appeals.

Justice White, writing the majority opinion in a five-to-four decision, argues against the view that the Constitution confers upon homosexuals a fundamental right to engage in sodomy. He also rejects (1) the view that consensual sodomy is constitutionally protected so long as it occurs in the privacy of the home and (2) the view that majority sentiments about the immorality of sodomy provide an inadequate basis for sodomy statutes.

In August 1982, respondent Hardwick (hereafter respondent) was charged with violating the Georgia statute criminalizing sodomy[1] by committing that act with another adult male in the bedroom of respondent's home. After a preliminary hearing, the District Attorney decided not to present the matter to the grand jury unless further evidence developed.

Respondent then brought suit in the Federal District Court, challenging the constitutionality of the statute insofar as it criminalized consensual sodomy. He asserted that he was a practicing homosexual, that the Georgia sodomy statute, as administered by the defendants, placed him in imminent danger of arrest, and that the statute for several reasons violates the Federal Constitution. The District Court granted the defendants' motion to dismiss for failure to state a claim. . . .

A divided panel of the Court of Appeals for the Eleventh Circuit reversed. . . . The court went on to hold that the Georgia statute violated respondent's fundamental rights because his homosexual activity is a private and intimate association that is beyond the reach of state regulation by reason of the Ninth Amendment and the Due Process Clause of the Fourteenth Amendment. The case was remanded for trial, at which, to prevail, the State would have to prove that the statute is supported by a compelling interest and is the most narrowly drawn means of achieving that end.

. . . We agree with petitioner that the Court of Appeals erred, and hence reverse its judgment.

This case does not require a judgment on whether laws against sodomy between consenting adults in general, or between homosexuals in particular, are wise or desirable. It raises no question about the right or propriety of state legislative decisions

United States Supreme Court. 478 U.S. 186 (1986).

to repeal their laws that criminalize homosexual sodomy, or of state-court decisions invalidating those laws on state constitutional grounds. The issue presented is whether the Federal Constitution confers a fundamental right upon homosexuals to engage in sodomy and hence invalidates the laws of the many States that still make such conduct illegal and have done so for a very long time. The case also calls for some judgment about the limits of the Court's role in carrying out its constitutional mandate.

We first register our disagreement with the Court of Appeals and with respondent that the Court's prior cases have construed the Constitution to confer a right of privacy that extends to homosexual sodomy and for all intents and purposes have decided this case. . . . [These cases have been] described as dealing with child rearing and education; with family relationships; with procreation; with marriage; with contraception; and with abortion. [The cases dealing with contraception and abortion] were interpreted as construing the Due Process Clause of the Fourteenth Amendment to confer a fundamental individual right to decide whether or not to beget or bear a child.

Accepting the decisions in these cases and the above description of them, we think it evident that none of the rights announced in those cases bears any resemblance to the claimed constitutional right of homosexuals to engage in acts of sodomy that is asserted in this case. No connection between family, marriage, or procreation on the one hand and homosexual activity on the other has been demonstrated, either by the Court of Appeals or by respondent. Moreover, any claim that these cases nevertheless stand for the proposition that any kind of private sexual conduct between consenting adults is constitutionally insulated from state proscription is unsupportable. . . .

Precedent aside, however, respondent would have us announce, as the Court of Appeals did, a fundamental right to engage in homosexual sodomy. This we are quite unwilling to do. It is true that despite the language of the Due Process Clauses of the Fifth and Fourteenth Amendments, which appears to focus only on the processes by which life, liberty, or property is taken, the cases are legion in which those Clauses have been interpreted to have substantive content, subsuming rights that to a great extent are immune from federal or state regulation or proscription. Among such cases are those recognizing rights that have little or no textual support in the constitutional language. . . .

Striving to assure itself and the public that announcing rights not readily identifiable in the Constitution's text involves much more than the imposition of the Justices' own choice of values on the States and the Federal Government, the Court has sought to identify the nature of the rights qualifying for heightened judicial protection. In *Palko* v. *Connecticut* (1937), it was said that this category includes those fundamental liberties that are "implicit in the concept of ordered liberty," such that "neither liberty nor justice would exist if [they] were sacrificed." A different description of fundamental liberties appeared in *Moore* v. *East Cleveland* (1977), where they are characterized as those liberties that are "deeply rooted in this Nation's history and tradition."

It is obvious to us that neither of these formulations would extend a fundamental right to homosexuals to engage in acts of consensual sodomy. Proscriptions against that conduct have ancient roots. Sodomy was a criminal offense at common law and was forbidden by the laws of the original 13 States when they ratified the Bill of Rights. In 1868, when the Fourteenth Amendment was ratified, all but 5 of the 37 States in the Union had criminal sodomy laws. In fact, until 1961, all 50 States outlawed sodomy, and today, 24 States and the District of Columbia continue to provide criminal penalties for sodomy performed in private and between consenting adults. Against this background, to claim that a right to engage in such conduct is "deeply rooted in this Nation's history and tradition" or "implicit in the concept of ordered liberty" is, at best, facetious.

Nor are we inclined to take a more expansive view of our authority to discover new fundamental rights imbedded in the Due Process Clause. The Court is most vulnerable and comes nearest to illegitimacy when it deals with judge-made constitutional law having little or no cognizable roots in the language or design of the Constitution. . . .

Respondent, however, asserts that the result should be different where the homosexual conduct occurs in the privacy of the home. He relies on *Stanley* v. *Georgia* (1969), where the Court held that the First Amendment prevents conviction for possessing and reading obscene material in the privacy of one's home: "If the First Amendment means anything, it means that a State has no business telling a man, sitting alone in his house, what books he may read or what films he may watch."

Stanley did protect conduct that would not have been protected outside the home, and it partially prevented the enforcement of state obscenity laws; but the decision was firmly grounded in the First Amendment. The right pressed upon us here has no similar support in the text of the Constitution, and it does not qualify for recognition under the prevailing principles for construing the Fourteenth Amendment. Its limits are also difficult to discern. Plainly enough, otherwise illegal conduct is not always immunized whenever it occurs in the home. Victimless crimes, such as the possession and use of illegal drugs, do not escape the law where they are committed at home. *Stanley* itself recognized that its holding offered no protection for the possession in the home of drugs, firearms, or stolen goods. And if respondent's submission is limited to the voluntary sexual conduct between consenting adults, it would be difficult, except by fiat, to limit the claimed right to homosexual conduct while leaving exposed to prosecution adultery, incest, and other sexual crimes even though they are committed in the home. We are unwilling to start down that road.

Even if the conduct at issue here is not a fundamental right, respondent asserts that there must be a rational basis for the law and that there is none in this case other than the presumed belief of a majority of the electorate in Georgia that homosexual sodomy is immoral and unacceptable. This is said to be an inadequate rationale to support the law. The law, however, is constantly based on notions of morality, and if all laws representing essentially moral choices are to be invalidated under the Due Process Clause, the courts will be very busy indeed. Even respondent makes no such claim, but insists that majority sentiments about the morality of homosexuality should be declared inadequate. We do not agree, and are unpersuaded that the sodomy laws of some 25 States should be invalidated on this basis.

Accordingly, the judgment of the Court of Appeals is *Reversed.*

NOTE

1 Georgia Code Ann. § 16-6-2 (1984) provides, in pertinent part, as follows: "(a) A person commits the offense of sodomy when he performs or submits to any sexual act involving the sex organs of one person and the mouth or anus of another. . . . (b) A person convicted of the offense of sodomy shall be punished by imprisonment for not less than one nor more than 20 years. . . ."

QUESTIONS

1 Concerned with the constitutionality of the Georgia sodomy statute, Justice White writes, "This case does not require a judgment on whether laws against sodomy between consenting adults in general, or between homosexuals in particular, are wise or desirable." As a matter of social policy, are such laws well advised?
2 Opponents of the decriminalization of homosexual sodomy sometimes argue as follows: It is necessary that homosexual sodomy, even between consenting adults in private, be considered a criminal offense; toleration of homosexual sodomy would lead to long-term consequences disastrous for society. Is this a sound argument?

Privacy, Homosexuality, and the Constitution

John Arthur

John Arthur is professor of philosophy and director, Program in Philosophy, Politics, and Law, Binghamton University—SUNY. He is the author of *The Unfinished Constitution: Philosophy and Constitutional Practice* (1989), the editor of *Morality and Moral Controversies* (3d ed., 1993), and the coeditor of *Readings in the Philosophy of Law* (2d ed., 1993).

Arthur reviews both the majority opinion of Justice White and the dissenting opinion of Justice Blackmun in the case of *Bowers v. Hardwick* (1986). He then considers and rejects the arguments made by the state of Georgia (represented by Attorney General Michael Bowers) in support of its sodomy statute. Georgia claims that homosexual sodomy is not protected by the constitutional right of privacy because this right protects only activities compatible with the traditional values of marriage and family. Georgia also claims that homosexual sodomy poses a threat to the institutions of marriage and family. Arthur advances counterarguments to both of these claims. He also rejects two other arguments made by Georgia: (1) that sodomy is immoral because it is unnatural and (2) that Georgia's sodomy statute is a reasonable response to the public health danger posed by AIDS. Arthur maintains that the first argument is medically, psychologically, and philosophically unsound. He counters the second argument with the contention that sodomy laws are not only ineffective but also counterproductive as a public health measure.

. . . Georgia law defines *sodomy* as submitting to or committing "any act involving the sex organs of one person and the anus or mouth of another." Sodomy is a criminal act in Georgia, whatever the sexes of the actors; violators are subject to prison terms of one to ten years. Michael Hardwick had been at a bar where police, in an effort to harass gays, had arrested him for displaying an open beer bottle. Unaware that Hardwick had paid the fine, an officer went to his house to collect. A friend of Hardwick let him in, and the officer observed Hardwick in the bedroom having sex with another man. After about a minute the officer arrested Hardwick and took him to jail, where he spent one night. When the jailer locked Michael Hardwick up, he told the others in the cell that they would enjoy themselves, because Hardwick had been arrested for sodomy. Although the prosecutor chose not to present the case to a grand jury, Hardwick nonetheless challenged the constitutionality of the statute.

A federal appeals court held that the Fourteenth Amendment protected privacy, including sexual freedom. The Court did not, however, demand that the statute be overturned; it merely held that the state of Georgia must demonstrate before a federal judge that the law served a compelling state interest. It was only that decision—that Georgia would be required to defend its sodomy law—which the Supreme Court reviewed.

Immediately after hearing the case, Justice Powell indicated that he would join four others in requiring review of the statute. But he later changed his mind, and in a 5-to-4 opinion the court upheld the Georgia law. (Powell said in a speech three years later, however, that he had again changed his mind and would now vote to overturn the law.)

Writing for the majority, Justice White stated that:

> Respondent would have us announce, as the Court of Appeals did, a fundamental right to engage in homosexual sodomy. This we are quite unwilling to do. . . . In *Palko v. Connecticut,* it was said that fundamental liberties are "implicit in the concept of ordered liberty," such that "neither liberty nor justice would exist if [they] were sacrificed." A different description of fundamental liberties appeared in *Moore v. East Cleveland,* where they are characterized as those liberties that are "deeply rooted in this Nation's history and tradition." . . .
>
> Proscriptions against that conduct have ancient roots. Sodomy was a criminal offense at common law and was forbidden by the laws of the original thirteen States when they ratified the Bill of Rights. In 1868, when the Fourteenth Amendment was ratified, all but 5 of the 37 States in the Union had criminal sodomy laws. In fact, until 1961, all States outlawed sodomy, and today, 24 States and the District of Columbia continue to provide criminal penalties for sodomy performed in private and between consenting adults. Against this background, to claim that a right to engage in such conduct is "deeply rooted in this Nation's history and tradition" or "implicit in the concept of ordered liberty" is, at best, facetious. . . .
>
> Plainly enough, otherwise illegal conduct is not always immunized whenever it occurs in the home. Victimless crimes, such as the possession and use of illegal drugs do not escape the law where they are committed at home. . . . And if respondent's submission is limited to the voluntary sexual conduct between consenting adults, it would be difficult, except by fiat, to limit the claimed right to homosexual conduct while leaving exposed to

prosecution adultery, incest, and other sexual crimes even though they are committed in the home. We are unwilling to start down that road.[1]

Justice White argues that in previous cases the right to privacy revolved around marriage, family, and home, and that therefore homosexual sodomy does not fall within its scope. In short, Georgia's statute does not implicate any Fourteenth Amendment rights because only liberties that are fundamental or deeply rooted in our traditions are protected, and to make such a claim about sodomy is "at best facetious." Sodomy is not part of the traditional respect accorded the family, nor is it part of the basic liberties guaranteed by the Constitution.

Justice Blackmun, in dissent, argues that White has misunderstood the issue by focusing on the narrow question of sodomy instead of the principles that underlie the Court's earlier cases. In past privacy cases, he writes,

> [T]he Court has proceeded along two somewhat distinct, albeit complementary, lines. First, it has recognized a privacy interest with reference to certain decisions that are properly for the individual to make. E.g., [*Roe* (right to abortion), *Pierce* (right to send children to private schools)]. Second, it has recognized a privacy interest with reference to certain places without regard for the particular activities in which the individuals who occupy them are engaged. The case before us implicates both the decisional and the spatial aspects of the right to privacy. . . .
>
> [The] fact that individuals define themselves in a significant way through their intimate sexual relationships with others suggests, in a Nation as diverse as ours, that there may be many "right" ways of conducting those relationships, and that much of the richness of a relationship will come from the freedom an individual has to choose the form and nature of these intensely personal bonds. [The] Court claims that its decision today merely refuses to recognize a fundamental right to engage in homosexual sodomy; what the Court really has refused to recognize is the fundamental interest all individuals have in controlling the nature of their intimate associations with others.
>
> The behavior for which Hardwick faces prosecution occurred in his own home, a place to which the Fourth Amendment attaches special significance. The Court's treatment of this aspect of the case is symptomatic of its overall refusal to consider the broad principles that have informed our treatment of privacy in specific cases. Just as the right to privacy is more than the mere aggregation of a number of entitlements to engage in specific behavior, so too, protecting the physical integrity of the home is more than merely a means of protecting specific activities that often take place there. . . .
>
> I cannot agree that either the length of time a majority has held its convictions or the passions with which it defends them can withdraw legislation from the Court's scrutiny. [It] is precisely because the issue raised by this case touches the heart of what makes individuals what they are that we should be especially sensitive to the rights of those whose choices upset the majority. . . .
>
> The mere knowledge that other individuals do not adhere to one's value system cannot be a legally cognizable interest, let alone an interest that can justify invading the houses, hearts, and minds of citizens who choose to live their lives differently.[2]

Justice Blackmun claims privacy has both a decisional and a spatial aspect. Some personal decisions are of such fundamental importance to the personal lives of individuals that they demand a compelling state interest before they can be restricted. The choice of a sexual partner is such a decision, Blackmun said, and is therefore included within the principles already enunciated by the Court. Privacy also has a spatial dimension: it matters where the law intrudes. Georgia's statute reaches into an area that the Constitution takes special care to shield from government: the home. *Bowers* therefore lies at the intersection of two important constitutional principles: protection of personal choices and protection of the sanctity of the home.

Justice Blackmun goes on to reject arguments advanced by Georgia to justify its restriction of Hardwick's liberty. There is no evidence, he says, that the public health is protected by the law, nor can the law be defended on grounds of society's right to protect moral decency. Hardwick's behavior took place in private, out of sight of people who find it offensive. In fact, he concludes, the statute is nothing more than an effort to dictate "private morality."

The disagreement between White and Blackmun turns in large measure on the same issues that divided Douglas and Harlan in *Griswold* [*v. Connecticut* (1965)]. For White the majority is justified in enforcing its conception of the good life when, as in *Bowers,* it relies on the traditional values of family and marriage. Georgia's statute, however, does not present the conflict between tradition and the will of the legislature that Harlan saw in *Griswold.* Blackmun adopts the alternative view that government should aspire to neutrality and respect the rights of those who "choose to live their lives differently," especially when the issue involves sexual identity and personality to the extent that this does. Neither traditional disapproval of the practice nor legislative enactments, even if they reflect majority will, can justify intrusion into this private decision.

Blackmun would not say, however, that any conception of the good should be protected merely because it involves personal, sexual decisions. Rape, even if done in privacy, must be criminalized. How, then, are we to assess the risks to society that homosexuality may pose? In his brief, Georgia Attorney General Michael Bowers gave two arguments in support of the claim that the legislature acted reasonably in banning sodomy. The first argument goes to support the contention, adopted by White, that privacy protects traditional values of family and marriage and therefore does not provide protection to homosexual conduct. The attorney general wrote that traditionally the Court has

> recognized the right of individuals to be free from governmental intrusion in decisions relating to marriage and family life, and used as a guide the teachings of history and the basic values of society to conclude that the Constitution protects the sanctity of the family, even the extended family, "precisely because the institution of the family is deeply rooted in this nation's history and tradition. It is through the family that we inculcate and pass down many of our most cherished values, moral and cultural" [*Moore v. East Cleveland* (1977)]. . . . The statute most certainly does not interfere with personal decisions concerning marriage or family life.[3]

Not only is homosexuality beyond the bounds of the family, but it poses a danger to that institution. Georgia's law, he wrote, reflects the view that

> Homosexual sodomy is the anathema of the basic units of our society—marriage and the family. To decriminalize or artificially withdraw the public's expression of its disdain for this conduct does not uplift sodomy, but rather demotes these sacred institutions to merely

other alternative lifestyles. If the legal distinctions between the intimacies of marriage and homosexual sodomy are lost, it is certainly possible to make the assumption, perhaps unprovable at this time, that the order of society, our way of life, could be changed in a harmful way. The states have a legitimate and, it is argued, compelling interest in the protection of the organization of society.[4]

On what grounds might a legislator or judge believe that decriminalizing homosexuality would endanger the family, our society, and "our way of life"? The American Psychological Association and the American Public Health Association filed an amicus curiae ("friend of the court") brief that argued against Georgia.[5] In that brief they pointed out that from 70 to 80 percent of gay men and lesbian women live as couples, despite the lack of social and legal encouragement. Equally important,

> Couplehood, either as a reality or an aspiration, is as strong among gay people as it is among heterosexuals. Principal concerns for all types of couples include equity, loyalty, stability, intimacy, and love. The nontraditional couples also often make substantial commitments to each other and in many cases stay together for decades.[6]

Many heterosexual couples marry and maintain a "family" despite the absence of children; why, then, are homosexual couples who wish to do the same a threat to "the order of society, our way of life"? It is not clear that Georgia's law is consistent with the family values it purports to support. If the point of giving marriage special protection is to enable people to achieve bonds of love, intimacy, and commitment, then why should the fact that the partners are of different sexes be crucial? Oddly enough, Justice Powell, who provided the last-minute fifth vote in *Bowers,* had written an opinion just a few years earlier that indicated sympathy with people living in the "nontraditional" family. *Moore v. East Cleveland*[7] (1977) invalidated a Cleveland zoning law that limited occupancy within a dwelling to a single family. The ordinance defined "family" so narrowly that it prevented Mrs. Moore from living with her two grandsons. Powell wrote in *Moore:*

> Whether or not such a family is established because of personal tragedy, the choice of relatives in this degree of kinship to live together may not lightly be denied by the State. [*Pierce*] The Constitution prevents East Cleveland from standardizing its children—and its adults—by forcing all to live in certain narrowly defined family patterns.[8]

Justice White, who wrote the *Bowers* opinion, dissented in *Moore.* So although there is no evidence that they even considered the fact of homosexual families, those on the Court who believed that laws should promote family values should also have considered the real meaning behind that ideal. If the point is to facilitate intimacy, stability, and family life, they should oppose sodomy laws making such values harder for homosexuals to realize. In fact, as we have seen, the evidence indicates that homosexuals seek relationships that are for all intents and purposes familial; the underlying purpose is identical to that of heterosexuals, and often even includes raising children. So besides Blackmun's objection to the majority in *Bowers,* there is also a potentially powerful conservative attack on Georgia's law that sees the law as discouraging creation of stable families and undermining the same family values as Harlan invoked in *Griswold.*

Nor can it be maintained that homosexuality threatens the traditional family because it is contagious. Homosexuality is widely practiced in all societies, whether homosexuals are admired, ignored, or repressed.[9] And sexual preference, as opposed to sexual acts, is not something we choose. Estimates are that anywhere from 5 to 25 million Americans are homosexual in the sense that they are primarily or exclusively attracted to members of their own sex rather than of the opposite sex. Whether heterosexual or homosexual, we discover our sexual orientation rather as we discover that we are either right or left handed. Only a small fraction of those who find themselves attracted to people of the same sex could have their preference modified through therapy, perhaps no more than the percentage of heterosexuals whose preference would be changed.

The idea that sodomy laws protect heterosexual marriage is thus mistaken on two counts. Such laws do not reduce homosexual orientation of adults, and even if they did normal contact with homosexual adults does not affect the sexual orientation of others.[10] Homosexuals pose no threat to the institution of marriage and family; and allowing them to create families would arguably promote rather than hinder those values.

Georgia made two additional arguments in its brief: that sodomy is "immoral" and that [its sodomy law] is a reasonable response to the public health dangers posed by acquired immune deficiency syndrome (AIDS). I will look at each in turn.

Homosexual sodomy, the state claimed, is "purely an unnatural means of satisfying an unnatural lust, which has been declared by Georgia to be morally wrong."[11] Again, however, both the medical and psychological evidence, as well as philosophical reflection, show this argument to be mistaken. Although the case was widely thought to involve only homosexuality, Georgia also criminalizes oral and anal intercourse between heterosexual couples. The law was passed at a time when such behavior was thought wrong regardless of the sex of those who do it. Today, however, sodomy is widely practiced among heterosexual as well as homosexual couples, and for exactly the same reasons. In a study cited in the American Psychological Association's brief, approximately 90 percent of heterosexual couples were found to engage in oral sex; another study found that 25 percent of all heterosexual married couples had engaged in anal intercourse within the past year.[12] Indeed, said the brief, such forms of intercourse are often recommended as a means to improve sexual function and health. Nor is there evidence that homosexuality causes mental illness or is associated with other emotional illnesses. Medical professionals are in wide agreement with the American Psychiatric Associations's 1977 finding that "homosexuality per se implies no impairment in judgment, stability, reliability or general social or vocational capabilities . . . homosexuality does not constitute any form of mental disease."[13]

In what sense, then, is sodomy "unnatural" and therefore morally wrong? Is it unnatural only when done by people of the same sex? Certainly it is not unnatural in the sense that it is uncommon, nor does the mere fact that it is not the most common form of sexual practice—if indeed it isn't—have anything to do with its being moral. Lying is far more common than viola playing, though that hardly makes the former moral and the latter not. Perhaps the real point is that homosexuality and sodomy are contrary to the "natural" purpose of sexual organs. If the true purpose of sex is reproduction, which can only occur through sexual intercourse between people of the opposite sex, then sodomy is contrary to nature and thus wrong. Much traditionally condoned sexual activity, however, also has nothing to do with reproduction: kissing, hugging, sex done with contraceptives, and sexual intercourse when either partner is infertile. And the other purposes that these activities serve, including expression of love or commitment, are achieved by homosexuals and heterosexuals alike. There's also the question of why it should matter that people use sex for purposes other than the one biology seems to prescribe. Besides hearing, people use ears to support eyeglasses and earrings, though it seems a bit harsh to condemn them for it. The claim that sodomy is immoral cannot withstand scrutiny. It is not uncommon, and even if it were that is no ground for condemnation. Nor is it unnatural in any morally relevant sense.

Georgia might also have based its criminalization of homosexuality on religion, claiming for example that it is condemned in the Bible. One problem with this, of course, is that the First Amendment guarantees religious freedom, promising that government will neither establish religion nor prevent its free exercise. The fact that homosexuality is condemned by one religion, or even all, would not, standing alone, justify its criminalization. Another argument would appeal simply to the disgust and homophobia that many Americans feel. Indeed, it seems impossible to explain the justices' decision in *Bowers* without appreciating the extent of homophobia in this culture. But that argument—that society can express its irrational dislike of minorities—would also find few supporters on the Court, at least until it were dressed up in more acceptable terms.

Public health, and especially the threat of AIDS, is another matter. Here, finally, is an argument that does not obviously rest on antiquated medicine, special psychology, or bad philosophy: AIDS is a major health problem. One of the two most common ways it is spread—anal intercourse—is a frequent practice of homosexual men. So perhaps Georgia's statute can be justified as a public health measure, though AIDS was clearly not what the legislature had in mind when the law was passed in 1816.

In fact, however, the evidence is overwhelming that sodomy laws not only are ineffective as a public health measure but are counterproductive. First, Georgia enforced its sodomy law only against homosexuals, making the statute doubly defective as a public health effort. It is too broad because it condemns oral sex, and there is no indication that people who practice oral sex, whatever the sexes of their partners, risk spreading AIDS. As it was actually enforced, the statute is also too narrow because it condemns anal intercourse only among homosexuals, despite the fact that the AIDS virus pays no attention to the sex of the person it infects. If the statute really were an attempt to prevent the spread of the disease then it would criminalize all and only anal intercourse, outlawing it between heterosexuals and homosexuals alike, without criminalizing other forms of homosexual conduct.

But even if it were meant as an attack on AIDS rather than homosexuals, health officials agree that criminalizing homosexuality makes the task of preventing the spread of AIDS much more difficult. There are many reasons for this. Antihomosexual statutes discourage accurate reporting and testing, requiring those who seek treatment to become prisoners. Sick people may not get treatment and are deterred from taking the tests that would tell them if they are likely to infect others.

Sodomy laws also frustrate researchers, making it more difficult for them to get the accurate information that is essential to fighting the disease effectively. Researchers initially found it difficult to explain why Haitians were a high-risk group, for example, because of the fears of those who were afflicted to report that they were either gay or intravenous drug users. Efforts at prevention are also hampered by sodomy laws. Condoms are extremely effective in limiting the spread of AIDS, yet government often finds it difficult to reconcile condemning sodomy through law with helping men practice it safely.

As a public health measure, Georgia's law is both badly drawn and counterproductive. This point is important because statutes limiting liberty must be closely tailored to meet their objectives. Even state laws that do not involve any fundamental right such as privacy must have at least a "rational basis" if the Supreme Court is to uphold them, although this test gives wide latitude to a legislature. Georgia's law not only fails the former test, of unduly infringing liberty, but is also arguably so irrational, counterproductive, and dangerous that it fails even the latter, "rational basis" test.

The *Bowers* decision did not meet with widespread approval, as the majority may have hoped. Many newspapers expressed surprise that the Court would allow Georgia to regulate consensual adult sexual activity in the bedroom. By ignoring the scientific and psychological evidence while adopting the state's homophobic moral arguments, the Court lost an opportunity to introduce a degree of thoughtful discussion to an important topic, contributed to the discrimination that homosexuals suffer, and added to the burdens facing responsible public health officials in trying to combat AIDS.

NOTES

1   106 S. Ct. 2846 (1986).
2   Ibid.
3   Brief of Attorney General Michael Bowers, in *Bowers v. Hardwick* (1985), at 30, 32.
4   *Bowers* Brief, at 37–38.
5   Brief of Amici Curiae American Psychological Association and American Public Health Association in Support of Respondent, *Bowers v. Hardwick* (1985), hereafter APA Brief.
6   APA Brief (1985), at 14.
7   431 U.S. 494 (1977).
8   *Moore v. East Cleveland,* 431 U.S. 494 (1977).
9   APA Brief, at 7.
10   APA Brief, at 28.
11   *Bowers* Brief, at 27.
12   APA Brief, at 6.
13   Resolution of the American Psychiatric Association, December 15, 1973, quoted in APA Brief, at 9.

QUESTIONS

1 How is the constitutional right of privacy best understood? Is it best understood as protecting homosexual sodomy?

2 Does homosexual sodomy pose a threat to the institutions of marriage and family?

3 Can Georgia's sodomy statute be justified as a public health measure directed against the spread of AIDS?

SUGGESTED ADDITIONAL READINGS FOR CHAPTER 4

BAKER, ROBERT, and FREDERICK ELLISTON: *Philosophy and Sex,* new rev. ed. Buffalo, N.Y.: Prometheus, 1984. This anthology contains a number of articles relevant to the topic of sexual morality.

BELLIOTTI, RAYMOND A.: *Good Sex: Perspectives on Sexual Ethics.* Lawrence: University Press of Kansas, 1993. Belliotti discusses mainstream philosophical views of sexual morality, considers Marxist and feminist perspectives, and then constructs his own theory, which he calls "sexual morality in five tiers."

CAMERON, PAUL: "A Case Against Homosexuality." *Human Life Review,* vol. 4, Summer 1978, pp. 17–49. As a psychologist, Cameron introduces empirical data about homosexuality. He contends that homosexuality is an undesirable life-style and argues against the liberalization of social policy (regarding homosexuality).

FERGUSON, ANN: *Blood at the Root: Motherhood, Sexuality and Male Dominance.* London: Pandora, 1989. In Chapter 10, entitled "A Transitional Feminist Sexual Morality," Ferguson employs feminist criteria to sort sexual practices into three categories: basic (i.e., unproblematic), risky, and forbidden.

JAGGAR, ALLISON M., and PAULA S. ROTHENBERG: *Feminist Frameworks: Alternative Theoretical Accounts of the Relations between Women and Men,* 3d ed. New York: McGraw-Hill, 1993. One section of this anthology (pp. 448–513) provides a collection of feminist perspectives on issues of sexuality.

KLEPPER, HOWARD: "Sexual Exploitation and the Value of Persons." *Journal of Value Inquiry,* vol. 27, December 1993, pp. 479–486. Klepper argues that the concept of sexually using another person cannot be reduced entirely to violations of the requirement of voluntary informed consent.

PIERCE, CHRISTINE: "AIDS and *Bowers v. Hardwick." Journal of Social Philosophy,* vol. 20, Winter 1989, pp. 21–32. Pierce contends that natural law arguments have aggravated the AIDS crisis by leading to both bad science and bad law. She presents an extensive critique of the Supreme Court's holding in *Bowers v. Hardwick.*

TAYLOR, RICHARD: *Having Love Affairs.* Buffalo, N.Y., Prometheus, 1982. Taylor rejects the idea that adultery is immoral. He also emphasizes the values served by love affairs and defends their moral legitimacy.

VANNOY, RUSSELL: *Sex Without Love: A Philosophical Exploration.* Buffalo, N.Y.: Prometheus, 1980. Vannoy defends sex without love: "I conclude, therefore, that on the whole, sex with a humanistic non-lover is far preferable to sex with an erotic lover." Both Chapter 1, "Sex with Love vs. Sex without Love" (pp. 7–29), and Chapter 4, "Types of Sexual Philosophy: A Summary" (pp. 118–127), are especially relevant to the topic of sexual morality.

WASSERSTROM, RICHARD: "Is Adultery Immoral?" In Richard Wasserstrom, ed., *Today's Moral Problems,* 3d ed. New York: Macmillan, 1985. This helpful article investigates the various arguments that can plausibly be made in support of the claim that adultery is immoral. Wasserstrom's analysis is especially valuable in focusing attention on the presuppositions of such arguments.

WHITELEY, C. H., and W. N. WHITELEY: *Sex and Morals.* New York: Basic, 1967. This book as a whole is useful, but chapter 5, on "Unfruitful Sex," is especially germane. In this chapter, the authors examine the morality of masturbation, homosexual behavior, and other types of sexual activity that cut off the possibility of procreation.

CHAPTER 5

Pornography, Hate Speech, and Censorship

Efforts to place legal restrictions on the flow of pornographic material typically give rise to complaints of unwarranted censorship and unjustified intrusion into individual liberty. Proposals to regulate hate speech, whether on college campuses or in society more generally, typically give rise to similar complaints. This chapter deals first with the issue of restricting access to pornography and then with the issue of regulating hate speech.

Is a government justified in limiting the access of *consenting adults* to pornographic materials? Censorship laws, in their most common form, seek to limit access to pornographic materials by prohibiting their distribution, sale, or exhibition. However, it is also possible for censorship laws to prohibit the production of pornography or even its possession.

COMMISSION REPORTS ON PORNOGRAPHY

In 1967, the Congress of the United States, labeling the traffic in obscene and pornographic materials "a matter of national concern," established the Commission on Obscenity and Pornography. This advisory commission, whose members were appointed by President Lyndon Johnson in January 1968, was charged with initiating a thorough study of obscenity and pornography and, on the basis of such a study, submitting recommendations for the regulation of obscene and pornographic materials. In September 1970 the Commission transmitted its final report to the President and the Congress. Its fundamental recommendation was that all legislation prohibiting the sale, exhibition, or distribution of sexual materials to *consenting adults* be repealed. However, the Commission recommended the continuation of legislation intended to protect nonconsenting adults from being confronted with sexually explicit material through public displays and unsolicited mailings. It also recommended the continuation of legislation prohibiting the commercial distribution of certain sexual material to juveniles. The Commission based its fundamental recommendation largely, though not exclusively, on its central factual finding: There is no evidence to support the contention that exposure to explicit sexual materials plays a significant role in the causation of either social harms (via antisocial behavior) or individual harms (such as severe emotional disturbance).

The report of the Commission on Obscenity and Pornography was unwelcome in many quarters. To begin with, only twelve of the Commission's eighteen members voted in support of its fundamental recommendation. In fact, the report itself features a substantial minority report that questions the factual findings as well as the recommendations of the Commission. President Richard Nixon contended that the report was completely unsatisfactory. Many members of Congress were also displeased, and there was a substantial public outcry that the conclusions of the Commission were "morally bankrupt." As a result, there was no significant movement to implement its fundamental recommendation.

In Spring 1985, responsive to a request by President Ronald Reagan, Attorney General Edwin Meese III named an eleven-member commission to *reexamine* the problem of pornography in American society. The Attorney General's Commission on Pornography submitted its final report in July 1986. With regard to the issue of the harmfulness of pornography, some of the factual findings of this second commission (which will be called "the 1986 Commission") stand in stark contrast to the central factual finding of the earlier commission (which will be called "the 1970 Commission"). The 1986 Commission, employing the word "pornography" to refer to material that is "predominantly sexually explicit and intended primarily for the purpose of sexual arousal," thought it important to distinguish among (1) violent pornography, (2) nonviolent but degrading pornography, and (3) nonviolent and nondegrading pornography. The Commission concluded that both category (1) and category (2) materials, but *not* category (3) materials, bear a causal relationship to undesirable attitudinal changes and acts of sexual violence. The thinking of the Commission on these matters is exhibited in an excerpt from the *Final Report* that is reprinted in this chapter.

The 1970 Commission, convinced of the essential harmlessness of pornography, embraced an explicit anticensorship stance. In contrast, the 1986 Commission was fundamentally procensorship and endorsed (and in fact called for vigorous enforcement of) already existing laws that criminalize the sale, distribution, or exhibition of *legally obscene* pornographic materials. The relevant standard of legal obscenity—a category that does not enjoy First Amendment protection—was first enunciated by the Supreme Court in *Miller v. California* (1973). In accordance with "the Miller standard," material is legally obscene if three conditions are satisfied:

(a) . . . "the average person, applying contemporary community standards," would find that the work, taken as a whole, appeals to the prurient interest; (b) . . . the work depicts or describes, in a patently offensive way, sexual conduct specifically defined by the applicable state law; and (c) . . . the work, taken as a whole, lacks serious literary, artistic, political, or scientific value.[1]

[1]United States Supreme Court, 413 U.S. 15, 24.

The 1986 Commission also called special attention to the problem of child pornography. Since the production of child pornography typically entails the sexual abuse of children, the Commission pointed out that there is a distinctive and compelling rationale for laws that prohibit the production, as well as the sale, exhibition, or distribution, of child pornography.

The 1986 Commission reported that pornography in American society had undergone significant changes in the sixteen years that had passed between the two commission reports. Its finding was that pornography had become increasingly violent, increasingly degrading, and increasingly pervasive. Whether pornography has become even more violent and degrading since 1986 is perhaps difficult to say, but computer-generated images and internet transmission seem to leave little doubt that pornography has become even more pervasive in American society.

LIBERTY-LIMITING PRINCIPLES

Laws limiting the access of consenting adults to pornographic materials, like all prohibitive laws, inevitably involve limitation of individual liberty. Accordingly, one way of providing a framework for our discussion is to take notice of the kinds of grounds that may be advanced to justify the limitation of individual liberty. Four suggested liberty-limiting principles are especially noteworthy:[2]

1 The harm principle—Individual liberty is justifiably limited to prevent *harm to others.*

2 The principle of legal paternalism—Individual liberty is justifiably limited to prevent *harm to self.*

3 The principle of legal moralism—Individual liberty is justifiably limited to prevent *immoral behavior.*

4 The offense principle—Individual liberty is justifiably limited to prevent *offense to others.*

The *harm principle* is the most widely accepted liberty-limiting principle. Few will dispute that the law is within its proper bounds when it restricts actions whereby one person causes harm to others. (The category of *harm to others* is understood as encompassing not only personal injury but also damage to the general welfare of society.) What remains a lively source of debate is whether any, or all, of the other suggested principles are legitimate liberty-limiting principles. According to John Stuart Mill (1806–1873), only the harm principle is a legitimate liberty-limiting principle. Some brief excerpts from his famous essay *On Liberty* appear in this chapter. Although Mill need not be read as unsympathetic to the offense principle, he clearly and vigorously rejects both the principle of legal paternalism and the principle of legal moralism.

According to the *principle of legal paternalism,* the law may justifiably be invoked to prevent self-harm, and thus "to protect individuals from themselves." Supporters

---

[2]Joel Feinberg's discussion of such principles served as a guide for the formulations adopted here. *Social Philosophy* (Englewood Cliffs, N.J.: Prentice-Hall, 1973), chap. 2.

of this principle think that the law rightfully serves much as a benevolent parent who limits his or her child's liberty in order to save the child from harm. Others, of course, often in the spirit of Mill, hotly contest the legitimacy of the principle of legal paternalism. It is said, for example, that government does not have the right to meddle in the private life of its citizens. Though there is little doubt that there are presently numerous paternalistic features in our legal system, their justifiability remains a disputed issue. The widespread law that requires motorcyclists to wear protective head gear is one apparent example of a paternalistic law.

According to the *principle of legal moralism,* the law may justifiably be invoked to prevent immoral behavior or, as it is often expressed, to "enforce morals." Such things as kidnapping, murder, and fraud are undoubtedly immoral, but there would seem to be no need to appeal to the principle of legal moralism to justify laws against them. An appeal to the harm principle already provides a widely accepted independent justification. As a result, the principle of legal moralism usually comes to the fore only when so-called victimless crimes are under discussion. Is it justifiable to legislate against homosexual relations, gambling, and smoking marijuana simply on the grounds that such activities are thought to be morally unacceptable? There are many such laws, and presumably they are intended to enforce conventional morality, but some people continue to call for their repeal on the grounds that the principle of legal moralism is an unacceptable liberty-limiting principle. To accept the principle of legal moralism, in Mill's words, is tantamount to permitting a "tyranny of the majority."

According to the *offense principle,* the law may justifiably be invoked to prevent "offensive" behavior in public. "Offensive" behavior is understood as behavior that causes shame, embarrassment, discomfort, etc., to be experienced by onlookers. The offense principle, unlike the other principles under discussion here, is not ordinarily advanced to justify laws that would limit the access of *consenting* adults to pornographic materials. However, this principle is sometimes advanced to justify laws that protect *nonconsenting* adults from "offensive" displays of pornography.

IS THE CENSORSHIP OF PORNOGRAPHY JUSTIFIED?

Arguments in support of laws that would limit the access of consenting adults to pornographic materials can conveniently be organized by reference to the liberty-limiting principles on which they are based.

The most important procensorship argument is based on the *harm principle.* It is asserted that exposure to pornography is a significant causal factor in sex-related crimes such as rape. Defenders of this thesis sometimes argue for their claim by citing examples of persons exposed to pornographic material who subsequently commit sex-related crimes. Such examples, however, fail to establish that the crime, which *follows* exposure to pornography, is a *causal result* of exposure to pornography. Indeed, the 1970 Commission reported that there is no evidence to support such a causal connection. On the other hand, the 1986 Commission surveyed the available evidence and reported the existence of a causal connection between exposure to certain kinds of pornography (namely, *violent* pornography and *degrading* pornography) and acts of sexual violence. All of these matters continue to be hotly debated. However, since the harm principle is a widely accepted liberty-limiting principle, a formidable argument for censorship emerges to the extent that a causal connection between the use of pornography (or certain kinds of pornography) and antisocial be-havior can be established.

A second procensorship argument is based on the *principle of legal paternalism.* It is said that those exposed to pornography will be harmed by such exposure. They will, it is thought, develop or reinforce emotional problems; they will render them-selves incapable of love and other human relationships necessary for a happy and satisfying life. In a more abstract and possibly rhetorical version of this argument, it is alleged that frequent exposure to pornography "depersonalizes" or "dehuman-izes," and presumably such effects are at least in a broad sense harmful to the indi-vidual. The argument based on the principle of legal paternalism is answered in two ways: (1) The alleged self-harm does not occur. (2) Regardless of the truth or falsity of the claim of self-harm, the principle of legal paternalism is not an acceptable liberty-limiting principle.

A third procensorship argument is based on the *principle of legal moralism.* It is claimed that there is a widespread consensus to the effect that pornography is morally repugnant.[3] Inasmuch as the principle of legal moralism seems to allow a commu-nity to enforce its moral convictions, it follows that the access of consenting adults to pornographic materials may rightfully be restricted. The argument based on the principle of legal moralism is answered in two ways: (1) The alleged consensus of moral opinion is nonexistent. (2) Regardless of the truth or falsity of the claim of an existing moral consensus, the principle of legal moralism is not an acceptable liberty-limiting principle.

The overall case against laws limiting the access of consenting adults to porno-graphic materials typically takes the following form: The principle of legal paternal-ism is an unacceptable liberty-limiting principle; the government should not meddle in the private affairs of its citizens since such meddling is likely to produce more harm than it prevents. The principle of legal moralism is also an unacceptable liberty-limiting principle; to enforce the moral views of the majority is, in effect, to allow a "tyranny of the majority." A government can rightfully restrict the activity of con-senting adults only on the grounds that such activity is *harmful to others.* At the pre-sent time, however, it has not been established that the access of consenting adults to pornographic materials presents a "clear and present danger." Thus censorship, es-pecially in view of the administrative nightmares it is likely to generate and the very real possibility that the power of the censor will be abused, is clearly unwarranted.

FEMINISM AND PORNOGRAPHY

In recent years, an important new critique of pornography has arisen from a femi-nist point of view. In contrast to more traditional critics of pornography, feminists do not ordinarily object to the sexual explicitness that is found in pornography.

---

[3]The morality of pornography is an important ethical issue in its own right. To some extent, of course, one's moral assessment of pornography will be a function of one's views on sexual morality in general.

Rather, their concern is rooted in the fact that pornography typically portrays *women* in a degrading and dehumanizing way. Related to this central concern is a distinction that feminists ordinarily draw between *pornography* (which is morally and socially problematic) and *erotica* (which is not).

In one of this chapter's selections, Helen E. Longino defines pornography as "material that explicitly represents or describes degrading and abusive sexual behavior so as to endorse and/or recommend the behavior as described." Because pornography is *injurious* to women in a number of related ways, she maintains, its production and distribution are justifiably subject to control. In essence, then, Longino presents a procensorship argument based on the harm principle. However, not all feminists advocate the censorship of pornography. In another of this chapter's selections, Mark R. Wicclair vigorously defends an anticensorship stance within the framework of feminism. He emphasizes the values associated with the principle of freedom of expression and calls attention to the detrimental side effects of censorship. He also maintains, against the procensorship feminist, that the connection between pornography and harm to women is too speculative to warrant incurring the social costs of censorship.

REGULATING HATE SPEECH

In *On Liberty,* John Stuart Mill constructs a famous case for the free expression of opinion.[4] With regard to factual, scientific, philosophical, religious, moral, and political matters, he argues for complete freedom of expression. His underlying claim is that societal attempts to suppress unpopular and unorthodox opinions are more productive of harm than are the unregulated opinions themselves. On the other hand, Mill is not committed to the view that no restrictions whatsoever on expressions of opinion are justified. Sometimes expressions of opinion are overtly harmful to others (e.g., when speech is used to incite violence), and in such cases the harm principle would allow restrictions.

Hate speech, perhaps especially the use of slurs and epithets, confronts contemporary society with a profound dilemma. Should people be free to make racist, sexist, and homophobic statements? Should people be free to confront others directly with the hateful venom of slurs and epithets? On the one hand, freedom of expression is a deeply held value, enshrined in the First Amendment of the United States Constitution. On the other hand, not only do all morally sensitive people find hate speech offensive but, more importantly, the victims of hate speech are left to deal with its psychological fallout. Are the psychological harms produced by hate speech significant enough to override the presumption we ordinarily give to the principle of free expression? Are they sufficient to justify legal restrictions?

In one of this chapter's selections, Andrew Altman provides an extensive analysis of the issue of hate-speech regulation on college campuses. He acknowledges that hate speech can cause serious psychological harms but does not believe that such

---

[4]The account of Mill's thinking provided in this paragraph follows Feinberg's analysis in "Limits to the Free Expression of Opinion," in Joel Feinberg and Hyman Gross, eds., *Philosophy of Law* (Belmont, Calif.: Wadsworth, 1995), pp. 262–264.

harms can serve to justify hate-speech regulation, at least within the theoretical framework he identifies as *liberalism*. Altman focuses attention on one distinctive type of hate speech, characterized by the fact that a person is treated as a moral subordinate, that is, as having inferior moral status. It is this narrowly drawn class of hate speech—involving what he calls "the speech-act wrong of subordination"—that he believes can justifiably be targeted for regulation. Altman is unsympathetic to sweeping hate-speech regulation but he does essentially endorse the sort of narrowly drawn hate-speech rules that were introduced at Stanford University.

It is unclear whether any form of campus hate-speech regulation can be drafted in a way that will ultimately withstand constitutional scrutiny on First Amendment grounds. To date, courts have been generally unsympathetic to campus hate-speech codes. For example, both a University of Michigan code and a University of Wisconsin System code have been struck down in federal court, and in February 1995 even the narrowly drawn Stanford code was declared unconstitutionally overbroad by the Superior Court of Santa Clara County (California).[5]

Whether hate-speech regulation is discussed specifically in reference to college campuses or more broadly in reference to society as a whole, ethical evaluation is frequently intertwined with First Amendment analysis. *Village of Skokie v. National Socialist Party of America,* an important freedom-of-expression case decided by the Illinois Supreme Court in 1978, is included in this chapter. In *Skokie,* the Court ruled that the American Nazi Party could not be prevented from displaying the swastika (which can be understood as hate speech against Jews) during the course of a planned demonstration in a predominantly Jewish community. In one other selection in this chapter, Charles R. Lawrence III analyzes the impact of face-to-face racial insults on those who are subjected to them. He argues that such insults are undeserving of First Amendment protection.

Thomas A. Mappes

[5]*Corry v. Stanford University,* No. 94-740309 (Santa Clara County, February 27, 1995).

On Liberty

John Stuart Mill

John Stuart Mill (1806–1873) is known primarily as an advocate of utilitarianism. Unlike most contemporary philosophers, Mill was not an academician. He had a successful career with the British East India Company and served one term as a Member of Parliament. Mill's most important works include *Utilitarianism, On Liberty,* and the feminist classic, *The Subjection of Women.*

Reprinted from the original edition of *On Liberty* (London, 1859).

In these excerpts from his classic work *On Liberty* (1859), Mill first contends that society is warranted in restricting individual liberty only if an action is harmful to others, never because an action in one way or another is harmful to the person who performs the action. He clearly rejects both the principle of legal paternalism and the principle of legal moralism. Mill argues on utilitarian grounds for an exclusive adherence to the harm principle, holding that society will be better off by tolerating all expressions of individual liberty that involve no harm to others, rather than by "compelling each to live as seems good to the rest." Mill also constructs, again on a utilitarian foundation, an overall argument for the free expression of opinion.

. . . The object of this Essay is to assert one very simple principle, as entitled to govern absolutely the dealings of society with the individual in the way of compulsion and control, whether the means used be physical force in the form of legal penalties, or the moral coercion of public opinion. That principle is, that the sole end for which mankind are warranted, individually or collectively, in interfering with the liberty of action of any of their number, is self-protection. That the only purpose for which power can be rightfully exercised over any member of a civilized community, against his will, is to prevent harm to others. His own good, either physical or moral, is not a sufficient warrant. He cannot rightfully be compelled to do or forbear because it will be better for him to do so, because it will make him happier, because, in the opinions of others, to do so would be wise, or even right. These are good reasons for remonstrating with him, or reasoning with him, or persuading him, or entreating him, but not for compelling him, or visiting him with any evil in case he do otherwise. To justify that, the conduct from which it is desired to deter him, must be calculated to produce evil to some one else. The only part of the conduct of any one, for which he is amenable to society, is that which concerns others. In the part which merely concerns himself, his independence is, of right, absolute. Over himself, over his own body and mind, the individual is sovereign.

It is, perhaps, hardly necessary to say that this doctrine is meant to apply only to human beings in the maturity of their faculties. We are not speaking of children, or of young persons below the age which the law may fix as that of manhood and womanhood. Those who are still in a state to require being taken care of by others, must be protected against their own actions as well as against external injury. . . .

. . . There is a sphere of action in which society, as distinguished from the individual, has, if any, only an indirect interest; comprehending all that portion of a person's life and conduct which affects only himself, or if it also affects others, only with their free, voluntary, and undeceived consent and participation. When I say only himself, I mean directly, and in the first instance: for whatever affects himself, may affect others *through* himself; and the objection which may be grounded on this contingency, will receive consideration in the sequel. This, then, is the appropriate region of human liberty. It comprises, first, the inward domain of consciousness; demanding liberty of conscience, in the most comprehensive sense; liberty of thought and feeling; absolute freedom of opinion and sentiment on all subjects, practical or speculative, scientific, moral, or theological. The liberty of expressing and publishing opinions may seem to fall under a different principle, since it belongs to that part of the conduct of an individual which concerns other people; but, being almost of as much importance as the liberty of thought itself, and resting in great part on the same reasons, is practically inseparable from it. Secondly, the principle requires liberty of tastes and pursuits; of framing the plan of our life to suit our own character; of doing as we like, subject to such consequences as may follow; without impediment from our fellow-creatures, so long as what we do does not harm them, even though they should think our conduct foolish, perverse, or wrong. Thirdly, from this liberty of each individual, follows the liberty, within the same limits, of combination among individuals; freedom to unite, for any purpose not involving harm to others: the persons combining being supposed to be of full age, and not forced or deceived.

No society in which these liberties are not, on the whole, respected, is free, whatever may be its form of government; and none is completely free in which they do not exist absolute and unqualified. The only freedom which deserves the name, is that of pursuing our own good in our own way, so long as we do not attempt to deprive others of theirs, or impede their efforts to obtain it. Each is the proper guardian of his own health, whether bodily, or mental and spiritual. Mankind are greater gainers by suffering each other to live as seems good to themselves, than by compelling each to live as seems good to the rest. . . .

OF THE LIBERTY OF THOUGHT AND DISCUSSION

. . . If all mankind minus one, were of one opinion, and only one person were of the contrary opinion, mankind would be no more justified in silencing that one person, than he, if he had the power, would be justified in silencing mankind. Were an opinion a personal possession of no value except to the owner; if to be obstructed in the enjoyment of it were simply a private injury, it would make some difference whether the injury was inflicted only on a few persons or on many. But the peculiar evil of silencing the expression of an opinion is, that it is robbing the human race; posterity as well as the existing generation; those who dissent from the opinion, still more than those who hold it. If the opinion is right, they are deprived of the opportunity of exchanging error for truth: if wrong, they lose, what is almost as great a benefit, the clearer perception and livelier impression of truth, produced by its collision with error.

It is necessary to consider separately these two hypotheses, each of which has a distinct branch of the argument corresponding to it. We can never be sure that the opinion we are endeavouring to stifle is a false opinion; and if we were sure, stifling it would be an evil still.

First: the opinion which it is attempted to suppress by authority may possibly be true. Those who desire to suppress it, of course deny its truth; but they are not infallible. They have no authority to decide the question for all mankind, and exclude every other person from the means of judging. To refuse a hearing to an opinion, because they are sure that it is false, is to assume that *their* certainty is the same thing as *absolute* certainty. All silencing of discussion is an assumption of infallibility. . . .

Let us now pass to the second division of the argument, and dismissing the supposition that any of the received opinions may be false, let us assume them to be true, and examine into the worth of the manner in which they are likely to be held, when their truth is not freely and openly canvassed. However unwillingly a person who has a strong opinion may admit the possibility that his opinion may be false, he ought to be moved by the consideration that however true it may be, if it is not fully, frequently, and fearlessly discussed, it will be held as a dead dogma, not a living truth. . . .

. . . If the cultivation of the understanding consists in one thing more than in another, it is surely in learning the grounds of one's own opinions. . . . He who knows only his own side of the case, knows little of that. His reasons may be good, and no one may have been able to refute them. But if he is equally unable to refute the reasons on the opposite side; if he does not so much as know what they are, he has no ground for preferring either opinion. . . . Nor is it enough that he should hear the arguments of adversaries from his own teachers, presented as they state them, and accompanied by what they offer as refutations. That is not the way to do justice to the arguments, or bring them into real contact with his own mind. He must be able to hear them from persons who actually believe them; who defend them in earnest, and do their very utmost for them. He must know them in their most plausible and persuasive form. . . .

. . . The fact . . . is, that not only the grounds of the opinion are forgotten in the absence of discussion, but too often the meaning of the opinion itself. The words which convey it, cease to suggest ideas, or suggest only a small portion of those they were originally employed to communicate. Instead of a vivid conception and a living belief, there remain only a few phrases retained by rote; or, if any part, the shell and husk only of the meaning is retained, the finer essence being lost. The great chapter in human history which this fact occupies and fills, cannot be too earnestly studied and meditated on. . . .

. . . We have hitherto considered only two possibilities: that the received opinion may be false, and some other opinion, consequently, true; or that, the received opinion being true, a conflict with the opposite error is essential to a clear apprehension and deep feeling of its truth. But there is a commoner case than either of these; when the conflicting doctrines, instead of being one true and the other false, share the truth between them; and the nonconforming opinion is needed to supply the remainder of the truth, of which the received doctrine embodies only a part. . . .

We have now recognised the necessity to the mental well-being of mankind (on which all their other well-being depends) of freedom of opinion, and freedom of the expression of opinion, on four distinct grounds; which we will now briefly recapitulate.

First, if any opinion is compelled to silence, that opinion may, for aught we can certainly know, be true. To deny this is to assume our own infallibility.

Secondly, though the silenced opinion be an error, it may, and very commonly does, contain a portion of truth; and since the general or prevailing opinion on any subject is rarely or never the whole truth, it is only by the collision of adverse opinions that the remainder of the truth has any chance of being supplied.

Thirdly, even if the received opinion be not only true, but the whole truth; unless it is suffered to be, and actually is, vigorously and earnestly contested, it will, by most of those who receive it, be held in the manner of a prejudice, with little comprehension or feeling of its rational grounds. And not only this, but, fourthly, the meaning of the doctrine itself will be in danger of being lost, or enfeebled, and deprived of its vital effect on the character and conduct: the dogma becoming a mere formal profession, inefficacious for good, but cumbering the ground, and preventing the growth of any real and heartfelt conviction, from reason or personal experience. . . .

QUESTIONS

1 Is it true, as Mill claims, that "Mankind are greater gainers by suffering each other to live as seems good to themselves, than by compelling each to live as seems good to the rest"?
2 Would you endorse an argument for the censorship of pornography based on the principle of legal paternalism? Would you endorse a procensorship argument based on the principle of legal moralism?
3 Does Mill provide a compelling case for the free expression of opinion?

The Question of Harm

The Attorney General's Commission on Pornography

The Attorney General's Commission on Pornography was formed by Attorney General Edwin Meese III in the Spring of 1985. This eleven-member group was chaired by Henry E. Hudson, who was at that time commonwealth attorney in Arlington County, Virginia. This selection is excerpted from the Commission's final report, which was submitted in July 1986.

In considering the question whether pornography is harmful, the 1986 Commission distinguishes among (1) violent pornography, (2) nonviolent but degrading pornography, and (3) nonviolent and nondegrading pornography. On its interpretation of the evidence, material in category (1) bears a causal relationship to undesirable attitudinal changes and to acts of sexual violence. The Commission also asserts that these same effects are causally connected with category (2) material. On the other hand, the Commission concludes that category (3) material does not bear a causal relationship to acts of sexual violence. In a brief reference to the category of child pornography, the Commission emphasizes the way in which the production of child pornography entails child abuse.

MATTERS OF METHOD

. . . The analysis of the hypothesis that pornography causes harm must start with the identification of hypothesized harms, proceed to the determination of whether those

Reprinted from *Final Report* (Washington, D.C.: United States Department of Justice, July 1986).

hypothesized harms are indeed harmful, and then conclude with the examination of whether a causal link exists between the material and the harm. When the consequences of exposure to sexually explicit material are not harmful, or when there is no causal relationship between exposure to sexually explicit material and some harmful consequence, then we cannot say that the sexually explicit material is harmful. But if sexually explicit material of some variety is causally related to, or increases the incidence of, some behavior that *is* harmful, then it is safe to conclude that the material is harmful. . . .

The Problem of Multiple Causation

The world is complex, and most consequences are "caused" by numerous factors. Are highway deaths caused by failure to wear seat belts, failure of the automobile companies to install airbags, failure of the government to require automobile companies to install airbags, alcohol, judicial leniency towards drunk drivers, speeding, and so on and on? Is heart disease caused by cigarette smoking, obesity, stress, or excess animal fat in our diets? As with most other questions of this type, the answers can only be "all of the above," and so too with the problem of pornography. We have concluded, for example, that some forms of sexually explicit material bear a causal relationship both to sexual violence and to sex discrimination, but we are hardly so naive as to suppose that were these forms of pornography to disappear the problems of sex discrimination and sexual violence would come to an end.

If this is so, then what does it mean to identify a causal relationship? It means that the evidence supports the conclusion that if there were none of the material being tested, then the incidence of the consequences would be less. We live in a world of multiple causation, and to identify a factor as a *cause* in such a world means only that if this factor were eliminated while everything else stayed the same then the problem would at least be lessened. In most cases it is impossible to say any more than this, although to say this is to say quite a great deal. But when we identify something as a cause, we do not deny that there are other causes, and we do not deny that some of these other causes might bear an even *greater* causal connection than does some form of pornography. That is, it may be, for example, and there is some evidence that points in this direction, that certain magazines focusing on guns, martial arts, and related topics bear a closer causal relationship to sexual violence than do some magazines that are, in a term we will explain shortly, "degrading." If this is true, then the amount of sexual violence would be reduced more by eliminating the weaponry magazines and keeping the degrading magazines than it would be reduced by eliminating the degrading magazines and keeping the weaponry magazines. . . .

OUR CONCLUSIONS ABOUT HARM

We present in the following sections our conclusions regarding the harms we have investigated with respect to the various subdividing categories we have found most useful. . . .

Sexually Violent Material

The category of material on which most of the evidence has focused is the category of material featuring actual or unmistakably simulated or unmistakably threatened violence presented in sexually explicit fashion with a predominant focus on the sexually explicit violence. Increasingly, the most prevalent forms of pornography, as well as an increasingly prevalent body of less sexually explicit material, fit this description. Some of this material involves sado-masochistic themes, with the standard accoutrements of the genre, including whips, chains, devices of torture, and so on. But another theme of some of this material is not sado-masochistic, but involves instead the recurrent theme of a man making some sort of sexual advance to a woman, being rebuffed, and then raping the woman or in some other way violently forcing himself on the woman. In almost all of this material, whether in magazine or motion picture form, the woman eventually becomes aroused and ecstatic about the initially forced sexual activity, and usually is portrayed as begging for more. There is also a large body of material, more "mainstream" in its availability, that portrays sexual activity or sexually suggestive nudity coupled with extreme violence, such as disfigurement or murder. The so-called "slasher" films fit this description, as does some material, both in films and in magazines, that is less or more sexually explicit than the prototypical "slasher" film.

It is with respect to material of this variety that the scientific findings and ultimate conclusions of the 1970 Commission are least reliable for today, precisely because material of this variety was largely absent from that Commission's inquiries. It is not, however, absent from the contemporary world, and it is hardly surprising that conclusions about this material differ from conclusions about material not including violent themes.

When clinical and experimental research has focused particularly on sexually violent material, the conclusions have been virtually unanimous. In both clinical and experimental settings, exposure to sexually violent materials has indicated an increase in the likelihood of aggression. More specifically, the research, which is described in much detail later in this Report, shows a causal relationship between exposure to material of this type and aggressive behavior towards women.

Finding a link between aggressive behavior towards women and sexual violence, whether lawful or unlawful, requires assumptions not found exclusively in the experimental evidence. We see no reason, however, not to make these assumptions. The assumption that increased aggressive behavior towards women is causally related, for an aggregate population, to increased sexual violence is significantly supported by the clinical evidence, as well as by much of the less scientific evidence. They are also to all of us assumptions that are plainly justified by our own common sense. This is not to say that all people with heightened levels of aggression will commit acts of sexual violence. But it is to say that over a sufficiently large number of cases we are confident in asserting that an increase in aggressive behavior directed at women will cause an increase in the level of sexual violence directed at women.

Thus we reach our conclusions by combining the results of the research with highly justifiable assumptions about the generalizability of more limited research results.

Since the clinical and experimental evidence supports the conclusion that there is a causal relationship between exposure to sexually violent materials and an increase in aggressive behavior directed towards women, and since we believe that an increase in aggressive behavior towards women will in a population increase the incidence of sexual violence in that population, we have reached the conclusion, unanimously and confidently, that the available evidence strongly supports the hypothesis that substantial exposure to sexually violent materials as described here bears a causal relationship to antisocial acts of sexual violence and, for some subgroups, possibly to unlawful acts of sexual violence.

Although we rely for this conclusion on significant scientific empirical evidence, we feel it worthwhile to note the underlying logic of the conclusion. The evidence says simply that the images that people are exposed to bears a causal relationship to their behavior. This is hardly surprising. What would be surprising would be to find otherwise, and we have not so found. We have not, of course, found that the images people are exposed to are a greater cause of sexual violence than all or even many other possible causes the investigation of which has been beyond our mandate. Nevertheless, it would be strange indeed if graphic representations of a form of behavior, especially in a form that almost exclusively portrays such behavior as desirable, did not have at least some effect on patterns of behavior.

Sexual violence is not the only negative effect reported in the research to result from substantial exposure to sexually violent materials. The evidence is also strongly supportive of significant attitudinal changes on the part of those with substantial exposure to violent pornography. These attitudinal changes are numerous. Victims of rape and other forms of sexual violence are likely to be perceived by people so exposed as more responsible for the assault, as having suffered less injury, and as having been less degraded as a result of the experience. Similarly, people with a substantial exposure to violent pornography are likely to see the rapist or other sexual offender as less responsible for the act and as deserving of less stringent punishment.

These attitudinal changes have been shown experimentally to include a larger range of attitudes than those just discussed. The evidence also strongly supports the conclusion that substantial exposure to violent sexually explicit material leads to a greater acceptance of the "rape myth" in its broader sense—that women enjoy being coerced into sexual activity, that they enjoy being physically hurt in sexual context, and that as a result a man who forces himself on a woman sexually is in fact merely acceding to the "real" wishes of the woman, regardless of the extent to which she seems to be resisting. The myth is that a woman who says "no" really means "yes," and that men are justified in acting on the assumption that the "no" answer is indeed the "yes" answer. We have little trouble concluding that this attitude is both pervasive and profoundly harmful, and that any stimulus reinforcing or increasing the incidence of this attitude is for that reason alone properly designated as harmful.

. . . All of the harms discussed here, including acceptance of the legitimacy of sexual violence against women but not limited to it, are more pronounced when the sexually violent materials depict the woman as experiencing arousal, orgasm, or other form of enjoyment as the ultimate result of the sexual assault. This theme, unfortunately very common in the materials we have examined, is likely to be the major, albeit not the only, component of what it is in the materials in this category that causes the consequences that have been identified. . . .

Nonviolent Materials Depicting Degradation, Domination, Subordination, or Humiliation

. . . It appears that effects similar to, although not as extensive as that involved with violent material, can be identified with respect to . . . degrading material, but that these effects are likely absent when neither degradation nor violence is present.

An enormous amount of the most sexually explicit material available, as well as much of the material that is somewhat less sexually explicit, is material that we would characterize as "degrading," the term we use to encompass the undeniably linked characteristics of degradation, domination, subordination, and humiliation. The degradation we refer to is degradation of people, most often women, and here we are referring to material that, although not violent, depicts people, usually women, as existing solely for the sexual satisfaction of others, usually men, or that depicts people, usually women, in decidedly subordinate roles in their sexual relations with others, or that depicts people engaged in sexual practices that would to most people be considered humiliating. Indeed, forms of degradation represent the largely predominant proportion of commercially available pornography.

With respect to material of this variety, our conclusions are substantially similar to those with respect to violent material, although we make them with somewhat less assumption than was the case with respect to violent material. The evidence, scientific and otherwise, is more tentative, but supports the conclusion that the material we describe as degrading bears some causal relationship to the attitudinal changes we have previously identified. That is, substantial exposure to material of this variety is likely to increase the extent to which those exposed will view rape or other forms of sexual violence as less serious than they otherwise would have, will view the victims of rape and other forms of sexual violence as significantly more responsible, and will view the offenders as significantly less responsible. We also conclude that the evidence supports the conclusion that substantial exposure to material of this type will increase acceptance of the proposition that women like to be forced into sexual practices, and, once again, that the woman who says "no" really means "yes."

. . . We believe we are justified in drawing the following conclusions: Over a large enough sample of population that believes that many women like to be raped, that believes that sexual violence or sexual coercion is often desired or appropriate, and that believes that sex offenders are less responsible for their acts, will commit more acts of sexual violence or sexual coercion than would a population holding these beliefs to a lesser extent.

. . . Thus, we conclude that substantial exposure to materials of this type bears some causal relationship to the level of sexual violence, sexual coercion, or unwanted sexual aggression in the population so exposed.

We need mention as well that our focus on these more violent or more coercive forms of actual subordination of women should not diminish what we take to be a necessarily incorporated conclusion: Substantial exposure to materials of this type bears some causal relationship to the incidence of various nonviolent forms of discrimination against or subordination of women in our society. To the extent that these materials create or reinforce the view that women's function is disproportionately to satisfy the sexual needs of men, then the materials will have pervasive effects on the treatment of women in society far beyond the incidence of identifiable acts of rape or other sexual violence. We obviously cannot here explore fully all the forms in which women are discriminated against in contemporary society. Nor can we explore all of the causes of that discrimination against women. But we feel confident in concluding that the view of women as available for sexual domination is one cause of that discrimination, and we feel confident as well in concluding that degrading material bears a causal relationship to the view that women ought to subordinate their own desires and beings to the sexual satisfaction of men. . . .

Non-Violent and Non-Degrading Materials

Our most controversial category has been the category of sexually explicit materials that are not violent and are not degrading as we have used that term. They are materials in which the participants appear to be fully willing participants occupying substantially equal roles in a setting devoid of actual or apparent violence or pain. This category is in fact quite small in terms of currently available materials. There is some, to be sure, and the amount may increase as the division between the degrading and the non-degrading becomes more accepted, but we are convinced that only a small amount of currently available highly sexually explicit material is neither violent nor degrading. We thus talk about a small category, but one that should not be ignored.

We have disagreed substantially about the effects of such materials, and that should come as no surprise. We are dealing in this category with "pure" sex, as to which there are widely divergent views in this society. That we have disagreed among ourselves does little more than reflect the extent to which we are representative of the population as a whole. In light of that disagreement, it is perhaps more appropriate to explain the various views rather than indicate a unanimity that does not exist, within this Commission or within society, or attempt the preposterous task of saying that some fundamental view about the role of sexuality and portrayals of sexuality was accepted or defeated by such-and-such vote. We do not wish to give easy answers to hard questions, and thus feel better with describing the diversity of opinion rather than suppressing part of it.

In examining the material in this category, we have not had the benefit of extensive evidence. Research has only recently begun to distinguish the non-violent but degrading from material that is neither violent nor degrading, and we have all relied on a combination of interpretation of existing studies that may not have drawn the same divisions, studies that did draw these distinctions, clinical evidence, interpretation of victim testimony, and our own perceptions of the effect of images on human behavior. Although the social science evidence is far from conclusive, we are, on the current state of the evidence, persuaded that material of this type does not bear a causal relationship to rape and other acts of sexual violence. . . .

That there does not appear from the social science evidence to be a causal link with sexual violence, however, does not answer the question of whether such materials might not themselves simply for some other reason constitute a harm in themselves, or bear a causal link to consequences other than sexual violence but still taken to be harmful. And it is here that we and society at large have the greatest differences in opinion.

One issue relates to materials that, although undoubtedly consensual and equal, depict sexual practices frequently condemned in this and other societies. In addition, level of societal condemnation varies for different activities; some activities are condemned by some people, but not by others. We have discovered that to some significant extent the assessment of the harmfulness of materials depicting such activities correlates directly with the assessment of the harmfulness of the activities themselves. Intuitively and not experimentally, we can hypothesize that materials portraying such an activity will either help to legitimize or will bear some causal relationship to that activity itself. With respect to these materials, therefore, it appears that a conclusion about the harmfulness of these materials turns on a conclusion about the harmfulness of the activity itself. As to this, we are unable to agree with respect to many of these activities. Our differences reflect differences now extant in society at large, and actively debated, and we can hardly resolve them here.

A larger issue is the very question of promiscuity. Even to the extent that the behavior depicted is not inherently condemned by some or any of us, the manner of presentation almost necessarily suggests that the activities are taking place outside of the context of marriage, love, commitment, or even affection. Again, it is far from implausible to hypothesize that materials depicting sexual activity without marriage, love, commitment, or affection bear some causal relationship to sexual activity without marriage, love, commitment, or affection. There are undoubtedly many causes for what used to be called the "sexual revolution," but it is absurd to suppose that depictions or descriptions of uncommitted sexuality were not among them. Thus, once again our disagreements reflect disagreements in society at large, although not to as great an extent. Although there are many members of this society who can and have made affirmative cases for uncommitted sexuality, none of us believes it to be a good thing. A number of us, however, believe that the level of commitment in sexuality is a matter of choice among those who voluntarily engage in the activity. Others of us believe that uncommitted sexual activity is wrong for the individuals involved and harmful to society to the extent of its prevalence. Our view of the ultimate harmfulness of much of this material, therefore, is reflective of our individual views about the extent to whether sexual commitment is purely a matter of individual choice. . . .

THE SPECIAL HORROR OF CHILD PORNOGRAPHY

What is commonly referred to as "child pornography" is not so much a form of pornography as it is a form of sexual exploitation of children. The distinguishing characteristic of child pornography, as generally understood, is that actual children are photographed while engaged in some form of sexual activity, either with adults or with other children. To understand the very idea of child pornography requires understanding the way in which real children, whether actually identified or not, are photographed, and understanding the way in which the use of real children in photographs creates a special harm largely independent of the kinds of concerns often expressed with respect to sexually explicit materials involving only adults.

Thus, the necessary focus of an inquiry into child pornography must be on the process by which children, from as young as one week up to the age of majority, are induced to engage in sexual activity of one sort or another, and the process by which children are photographed while engaging in that activity. The inevitably permanent record of that sexual activity created by a photograph is rather plainly a harm to the children photographed. But even if the photograph were never again seen, the very activity involved in creating the photograph is itself an act of sexual exploitation of children, and thus the issues related to the sexual abuse of children and those related to child pornography are inextricably linked. Child pornography necessarily includes the sexual abuse of a real child, and there can be no understanding of the special problem of child pornography until there is understanding of the special way in which child pornography *is* child abuse. . . .

QUESTIONS

1 Is it possible to provide a workable definition of "degrading pornography" or is this concept hopelessly subjective?
2 Which of the following, if any, would you endorse: (1) the censorship of violent pornography; (2) the censorship of nonviolent but degrading pornography; (3) the censorship of nonviolent and nondegrading pornography?
3 In *Ohio v. Osborne* (1990), the Supreme Court ruled that it is constitutional for states to prohibit by law even the private *possession* of child pornography. In view of the special evil of child pornography, would you endorse such a law?

Pornography, Oppression, and Freedom: A Closer Look

Helen E. Longino

Helen E. Longino is associate professor of philosophy at Rice University. Her published articles include "Evidence and Hypothesis" and "Can There Be a Feminist Science?" Longino is the coeditor of *Competition: A Feminist Taboo?* (1987) and the author of *Science as Social Knowledge: Values and Objectivity in Scientific Inquiry* (1990).

Longino constructs a case against pornography from a feminist point of view. She begins by defining pornography in such a way as to distinguish it from both erotica and moral realism; pornography is "material that explicitly represents or describes degrading and abusive sexual behavior so as to endorse and/or recommend the behavior as described." In Longino's view, pornography is immoral not because it is sexually explicit but because it typically portrays women in a degrading and dehumanizing way. She explicitly identifies a number of related ways in which pornography is injurious to women. Because of pornography's injurious character, she concludes, its production and distribution are justifiably subject to control.

I INTRODUCTION

The much-touted sexual revolution of the 1960's and 1970's not only freed various modes of sexual behavior from the constraints of social disapproval, but also made possible a flood of pornographic material. According to figures provided by WAVPM (Women Against Violence in Pornography and Media), the number of pornographic magazines available at newsstands has grown from zero in 1953 to forty in 1977, while sales of pornographic films in Los Angeles alone have grown from $15 million in 1969 to $85 million in 1976.[1]

Traditionally, pornography was condemned as immoral because it presented sexually explicit material in a manner designed to appeal to "prurient interests" or a "morbid" interest in nudity and sexuality, material which furthermore lacked any redeeming social value and which exceeded "customary limits of candor." While these phrases, taken from a definition of "obscenity" proposed in the 1954 American Law Institute's *Model Penal Code,*[2] require some criteria of application to eliminate vagueness, it seems that what is objectionable is the explicit description or representation of bodily parts or sexual behavior for the purpose of inducing sexual stimulation or pleasure on the part of the reader or viewer. This kind of objection is part of a sexual ethic that subordinates sex to procreation and condemns all sexual interactions outside of legitimated marriage. It is this code which was the primary target of the sexual revolutionaries in the 1960's, and which has given way in many areas to more open standards of sexual behavior.

One of the beneficial results of the sexual revolution has been a growing acceptance of the distinction between questions of sexual mores and questions of morality. This distinction underlies the old slogan, "Make love, not war," and takes harm to others as the defining characteristic of immorality. What is immoral is behavior which causes injury to or violation of another person or people. Such injury may be physical or it may be psychological. To cause pain to another, to lie to another, to hinder another in the exercise of her or his rights, to exploit another, to degrade another, to misrepresent and slander another are instances of immoral behavior. Masturbation or engaging voluntarily in sexual intercourse with another consenting adult of the same or the other sex, as long as neither injury nor violation of either individual or another is involved, are not immoral. Some sexual behavior is morally objectionable, but not because of its sexual character. Thus, adultery is immoral not because it involves sexual intercourse with someone to whom one is not legally married, but because it involves breaking a promise (of sexual and emotional fidelity to one's spouse). Sadistic, abusive, or forced sex is immoral because it injures and violates another.

The detachment of sexual chastity from moral virtue implies that we cannot condemn forms of sexual behavior merely because they strike us as distasteful or subversive of the Protestant work ethic, or because they depart from standards of behavior we have individually adopted. It has thus seemed to imply that no matter how offensive we might find pornography, we must tolerate it in the name of freedom from illegitimate repression. I wish to argue that this is not so, that pornography is immoral because it is harmful to people.

II WHAT IS PORNOGRAPHY?

I define pornography as *verbal or pictorial explicit representations of sexual behavior that,* in the words of the Commission on Obscenity and Pornography, *have as a distinguishing characteristic "the degrading and demeaning portrayal of the role and status of the human female . . . as a mere sexual object to be exploited and manipulated sexually."*[3] In pornographic books, magazines, and films, women are represented as passive and as slavishly dependent upon men. The role of female characters is limited to the provision of sexual services to men. To the extent that women's sexual pleasure is represented at all, it is subordinated to that of men and is never an end in itself as is the sexual pleasure of men. What pleases women is the use of their bodies to satisfy male desires. While the sexual objectification of women is common to all pornography, women are the recipients of even worse treatment in violent pornography, in which women characters are killed, tortured, gang-raped, mutilated, bound, and otherwise abused, as a means of providing sexual stimulation or pleasure to the male characters. It is this development which has attracted the attention of feminists and been the stimulus to an analysis of pornography in general.[4]

Not all sexually explicit material is pornography, nor is all material which contains representations of sexual abuse and degradation pornography.

A representation of a sexual encounter between adult persons which is characterized by mutual respect is, once we have disentangled sexuality and morality, not morally objectionable. Such a representation would be one in which the desires and experiences of each participant were regarded by the other participants as having a validity and a subjective importance equal to those of the individual's own desire and experiences. In such an encounter, each participant acknowledges the other participant's basic human dignity and personhood. Similarly, a representation of a nude human body (in whole or in part) in such a manner that the person shown maintains self-respect—e.g., is not portrayed in a degrading position—would not be morally objectionable. The educational films of the National Sex Forum, as well as a certain amount of erotic literature and art, fall into this category. While some erotic materials are beyond the standards of modesty held by some individuals, they are not for this reason immoral.

A representation of a sexual encounter which is not characterized by mutual respect, in which at least one of the parties is treated in a manner beneath her or his dignity as a human being, is no longer simple erotica. That a representation is of degrading behavior does not in itself, however, make it pornographic. Whether or not it is pornographic is a function of contextual features. Books and films may contain descriptions or representations of a rape in order to explore the consequences of such an assault upon its victim. What is being shown is abusive or degrading behavior which attempts to deny the humanity and dignity of the person assaulted, yet the context surrounding the representation, through its exploration of the consequences of the act, acknowledges and reaffirms her dignity. Such books and films, far from being pornographic, are (or can be) highly moral, and fall into the category of moral realism.

What makes a work a work of pornography, then, is not simply its representation of degrading and abusive sexual encounters, but its implicit, if not explicit, approval and recommendation of sexual behavior that is immoral, i.e., that physically or psychologically violates the personhood of one of the participants. Pornography, then, is verbal or pictorial material which represents or describes sexual behavior that is degrading or abusive to one or more of the participants *in such a way as to endorse the degradation.* The participants so treated in virtually all heterosexual pornography are women or children, so heterosexual pornography is, as a matter of fact, material which endorses sexual behavior that is degrading and/or abusive to women and children. As I use the term "sexual behavior," this includes sexual encounters between persons, behavior which produces sexual stimulation or pleasure for one of the participants, and behavior which is preparatory to or invites sexual activity. Behavior that is degrading or abusive includes physical harm or abuse, and physical or psychological coercion. In addition, behavior which ignores or devalues the real interests, desires, and experiences of one or more participants in any way is degrading. Finally, that a person has chosen or consented to be harmed, abused, or subjected to coercion does not alter the degrading character of such behavior.

Pornography communicates its endorsement of the behavior it represents by various features of the pornographic context: the degradation of the female characters is represented as providing pleasure to the participant males and, even worse, to the participant females, and there is no suggestion that this sort of treatment of others is inappropriate to their status as human beings. These two features are together sufficient to constitute endorsement of the represented behavior. The contextual features which make material pornographic are intrinsic to the material. In addition to these, extrinsic features, such as the purpose for which the material is presented—i.e., the sexual arousal/pleasure/satisfaction of its (mostly) male consumers—or an accompanying text, may reinforce or make explicit the endorsement. Representations which in and of themselves do not show or endorse degrading behavior may be put into a pornographic context by juxtaposition with others that are degrading, or by a text which invites or recommends degrading behavior toward the subject represented. In such a case the whole complex—the series of representations or representations with text—is pornographic.

The distinction I have sketched is one that applies most clearly to sequential material—a verbal or pictorial (filmed) story—which represents an action and provides a temporal context for it. In showing the before and after, a narrator or film-maker has plenty of opportunity to acknowledge the dignity of the person violated or clearly to refuse to do so. It is somewhat more difficult to apply the distinction to single still representations. The contextual features cited above, however, are clearly present in still photographs or pictures that glamorize degradation and sexual violence. Phonograph album covers and advertisements offer some prime examples of such glamorization. Their representations of women in chains (the Ohio Players), or bound by ropes and black and blue (the Rolling Stones) are considered high-quality commercial "art" and glossily prettify the violence they represent. Since the standard function of prettification and glamorization is the communication of desirability, these albums and ads are communicating the desirability of violence against women. Representations of women bound or chained, particularly those of women bound in such a way as to make their breasts, or genital or anal areas vulnerable to any passerby, endorse the scene they represent by the absence of any indication that this treatment of women is in any way inappropriate.

To summarize: Pornography is not just the explicit representation or description of sexual behavior, nor even the explicit representation or description of sexual behavior which is degrading and/or abusive to women. Rather, it is material that explicitly represents or describes degrading and abusive sexual behavior so as to endorse and/or recommend the behavior as described. The contextual features, moreover, which communicate such endorsement are intrinsic to the material; that is, they are features whose removal or alteration would change the representation or description.

This account of pornography is underlined by the etymology and original meaning of the word "pornography." *The Oxford English Dictionary* defines pornography as "Description of the life, manners, etc. of prostitutes and their patrons [from πόρνη (porne) meaning "harlot" and γράφειν (graphein) meaning "to write"]; hence the expression or suggestion of obscene or unchaste subjects in literature or art."[5]

Let us consider the first part of the definition for a moment. In the transactions between prostitutes and their clients, prostitutes are paid, directly or indirectly, for the use of their bodies by the client for sexual pleasure.[6] Traditionally males have obtained from female prostitutes what they could not or did not wish to get from their wives or women friends, who, because of the character of their relation to the male, must be accorded some measure of human respect. While there are limits to what treatment is seen as appropriate toward women as wives or women friends, the prostitute as prostitute exists to provide sexual pleasure to males. The female characters of contemporary pornography also exist to provide pleasure to males, but in the pornographic context no pretense is made to regard them as parties to a contractual arrangement. Rather, the anonymity of these characters makes each one Everywoman, thus suggesting not only that all women are appropriate subjects for the enactment of the most bizarre and demeaning male sexual fantasies, but also that this is their primary purpose. The recent escalation of violence in pornography—the presentation of scenes of bondage, rape, and torture of women for the sexual stimulation of the male characters or male viewers—while shocking in itself, is from this point of view merely a more vicious extension of a genre whose success depends on treating women in a manner beneath their dignity as human beings.

III PORNOGRAPHY: LIES AND VIOLENCE AGAINST WOMEN

What is wrong with pornography, then, is its degrading and dehumanizing portrayal of women (and *not* its sexual content). Pornography, by its very nature, requires that women be subordinate to men and mere instruments for the fulfillment of male fantasies. To accomplish this, pornography must lie. Pornography lies when it says that our sexual life is or ought to be subordinate to the service of men, that our pleasure consists in pleasing men and not ourselves, that we are depraved, that we are fit subjects for rape, bondage, torture, and murder. Pornography lies explicitly about women's sexuality, and through such lies fosters more lies about our humanity, our dignity, and our personhood.

Moreover, since nothing is alleged to justify the treatment of the female characters of pornography save their womanhood, pornography depicts all women as fit objects of violence by virtue of their sex alone. Because it is simply being female that, in the pornographic vision, justifies being violated, the lies of pornography are lies about all women. Each work of pornography is on its own libelous and defamatory, yet gains power through being reinforced by every other pornographic work. The sheer number of pornographic productions expands the moral issue to include not only assessing the morality or immorality of individual works, but also the meaning and force of the mass production of pornography.

The pornographic view of women is thoroughly entrenched in a booming portion of the publishing, film, and recording industries, reaching and affecting not only all who look to such sources for sexual stimulation, but also those of us who are forced into an awareness of it as we peruse magazines at newsstands and record albums in record stores, as we check the entertainment sections of city newspapers, or even as we approach a counter to pay for groceries. It is not necessary to spend a great deal of time reading or viewing pornographic material to absorb its male-centered definition of women. No longer confined within plain brown wrappers, it jumps out from billboards that proclaim "Live X-rated Girls!" or "Angels in Pain" or "Hot and Wild," and from magazine covers displaying a woman's genital area being spread open to the viewer by her own fingers.[7] Thus, even men who do not frequent pornographic shops and movie houses are supported in the sexist objectification of women by their environment. Women, too, are crippled by internalizing as self-images those that are presented to us by pornographers. Isolated from one another and with no source of support for an alternative view of female sexuality, we may not always find the strength to resist a message that dominates the common cultural media.

The entrenchment of pornography in our culture also gives it a significance quite beyond its explicit sexual messages. To suggest, as pornography does, that the primary purpose of women is to provide sexual pleasure to men is to deny that women are independently human or have a status equal to that of men. It is, moreover, to deny our equality at one of the most intimate levels of human experience. This denial is especially powerful in a hierarchical, class society such as ours, in which individuals feel good about themselves by feeling superior to others. Men in our society have a vested interest in maintaining their belief in the inferiority of the female sex, so that no matter how oppressed and exploited by the society in which they live and work, they can feel that they are at least superior to someone or some category of individuals—a woman or women. Pornography, by presenting women as wanton, depraved, and made for the sexual use of men, caters directly to that interest.[8] The very intimate nature of sexuality which makes pornography so corrosive also protects it from explicit public discussion. The consequent lack of any explicit social disavowal of the pornographic image of women enables this image to continue fostering sexist attitudes even as the society publicly proclaims its (as yet timid) commitment to sexual equality.

In addition to finding a connection between the pornographic view of women and the denial to us of our full human rights, women are beginning to connect the consumption of pornography with committing rape and other acts of sexual violence against women. Contrary to the findings of the Commission on Obscenity and Pornography a growing body of research is documenting (1) a correlation between exposure to representations of violence and the committing of violent acts generally, and (2) a correlation between exposure to pornographic materials and the committing of sexually abusive or violent acts against women.[9] While more study is needed to establish precisely what the causal relations are, clearly so-called hard-core pornography is not innocent.

From "snuff" films and miserable magazines in pornographic stores to *Hustler,* to phonograph album covers and advertisements, to *Vogue,* pornography has come to occupy its own niche in the communications and entertainment media and to acquire a quasi-institutional character (signaled by the use of diminutives such as "porn" or "porno" to refer to pornographic material, as though such familiar naming could take the hurt out). Its acceptance by the mass media, whatever the motivation, means a cultural endorsement of its message. As much as the materials themselves, the social tolerance of these degrading and distorted images of women in such quantities is harmful to us, since it indicates a general willingness to see women in ways incompatible with our fundamental human dignity and thus to justify treating us in those ways.[10] The tolerance of pornographic representations of the rape, bondage, and torture of women helps to create and maintain a climate more tolerant of the actual physical abuse of women.[11] The tendency on the part of the legal system to view the victim of a rape as responsible for the crime against her is but one manifestation of this.

In sum, pornography is injurious to women in at least three distinct ways:

1 Pornography, especially violent pornography, is implicated in the committing of crimes of violence against women.

2 Pornography is the vehicle for the dissemination of a deep and vicious lie about women. It is defamatory and libelous.

3 The diffusion of such a distorted view of women's nature in our society as it exists today supports sexist (i.e., male-centered) attitudes, and thus reinforces the oppression and exploitation of women.

Society's tolerance of pornography, especially pornography on the contemporary massive scale, reinforces each of these modes of injury: By not disavowing the lie, it supports the male-centered myth that women are inferior and subordinate creatures.

Thus, it contributes to the maintenance of a climate tolerant of both psychological and physical violence against women. . . .

CONCLUSION

I have defined pornography in such a way as to distinguish it from erotica and from moral realism, and have argued that it is defamatory and libelous toward women, that it condones crimes against women, and that it invites tolerance of the social, economic, and cultural oppression of women. The production and distribution of pornographic material is thus a social and moral wrong. Contrasting both the current volume of pornographic production and its growing infiltration of the communications media with the status of women in this culture makes clear the necessity for its control. . . .

Appeals for action against pornography are sometimes brushed aside with the claim that such action is a diversion from the primary task of feminists—the elimination of sexism and of sexual inequality. This approach focuses on the enjoyment rather than the manufacture of pornography, and sees it as merely a product of sexism which will disappear when the latter has been overcome and the sexes are socially and economically equal. Pornography cannot be separated from sexism in this way: Sexism is not just a set of attitudes regarding the inferiority of women but the behaviors and social and economic rules that manifest such attitudes. Both the manufacture and distribution of pornography and the enjoyment of it are instances of sexist behavior. The enjoyment of pornography on the part of individuals will presumably decline as such individuals begin to accord women their status as fully human. A cultural climate which tolerates the degrading representation of women is not a climate which facilitates the development of respect for women. Furthermore, the demand for pornography is stimulated not just by the sexism of individuals but by the pornography industry itself. Thus, both as a social phenomenon and in its effect on individuals, pornography, far from being a mere product, nourishes sexism. The campaign against it is an essential component of women's struggle for legal, economic, and social equality, one which requires the support of all feminists.[12]

NOTES

1 *Women Against Violence in Pornography and Media Newspage,* Vol. II, No. 5, June 1978; and Judith Reisman in *Women Against Violence in Pornography and Media Proposal.*

2 American Law Institute *Model Penal Code,* sec. 251.4.

3 *Report of the Commission on Obscenity and Pornography* (New York: Bantam Books, 1970), p. 239. The Commission, of course, concluded that the demeaning content of pornography did not adversely affect male attitudes toward women.

4 Among recent feminist discussions are Diana Russell, "Pornography: A Feminist Perspective" and Susan Griffin, "On Pornography," *Chrysalis,* Vol. I, No. 4, 1978; and Ann Garry, "Pornography and Respect for Women," *Social Theory and Practice,* Vol. 4, Spring 1978, pp. 395–421.

5 *The Oxford English Dictionary,* Compact Edition (London: Oxford University Press, 1971), p. 2242.

6 In talking of prostitution here, I refer to the concept of, rather than the reality of, prostitution. The same is true of my remarks about relationships between women and their husbands or men friends.

7 This was a full-color magazine cover seen in a rack at the check-out counter of a corner delicatessen.

8 Pornography thus becomes another tool of capitalism. One feature of some contemporary pornography—the use of Black and Asian women in both still photographs and films—exploits the racism as well as the sexism of its white consumers. For a discussion of the interplay between racism and sexism under capitalism as it relates to violent crimes against women, see Angela Y. Davis, "Rape, Racism, and the Capitalist Setting," *The Black Scholar,* Vol. 9, No. 7, April 1978.

9 Urie Bronfenbrenner, *Two Worlds of Childhood* (New York: Russell Sage Foundation, 1970); H. J. Eysenck and D. K. B. Nias, *Sex, Violence and the Media* (New York: St. Martin's Press, 1978); and Michael Goldstein, Harold Kant, and John Hartman, *Pornography and Sexual Deviance* (Berkeley: University of California Press, 1973); and the papers by Diana Russell, Pauline Bart, and Irene Diamond included in [Laura Lederer, ed., *Take Back the Night* (New York: William Morrow, 1980)].

10 This tolerance has a linguistic parallel in the growing acceptance and use of nonhuman nouns such as "chick," "bird," "filly," "fox," "doll," "babe," "skirt," etc., to refer to women, and of verbs of harm such as "fuck," "screw," "bang," to refer to sexual intercourse. See Robert Baker and Frederick Elliston, " 'Pricks' and 'Chicks': A Plea for Persons." *Philosophy and Sex* (Buffalo, N.Y.: Prometheus Books, 1975).

11 This is supported by the fact that in Denmark the number of rapes committed has increased while the number of rapes reported to the authorities has decreased over the past twelve years. See *WAVPM Newspage,* Vol. II, No. 5, June, 1978, quoting M. Harry, "Denmark Today—The Causes and Effects of Sexual Liberty" (paper presented to The Responsible Society, London, England, 1976). See also Eysenck and Nias, *Sex, Violence and the Media* (New York: St. Martin's Press, 1978), pp. 120–124.

12 Many women helped me to develop and crystallize the ideas presented in this paper. I would especially like to thank Michele Farrell, Laura Lederer, Pamela Miller, and Dianne Romain for their comments in conversation and on the first written draft. Portions of this material were presented orally to members of the Society for Women in Philosophy and to participants in the workshops on "What Is Pornography?" at the Conference on Feminist Perspectives on Pornography, San Francisco, November 17, 18, and 19, 1978. Their discussion was invaluable in helping me to see problems and to clarify the ideas presented here.

QUESTIONS

1 Do you accept Longino's suggested definition of pornography? Is there a better definition?

2 Emphasizing the injurious impact of pornography on women, Longino concludes that "its control is necessary." What specific controls on the production and distribution of pornography would you endorse?

Feminism, Pornography, and Censorship

Mark R. Wicclair

Mark R. Wicclair is professor of philosophy at West Virginia University. He is also adjunct professor of medicine and associate of the Center for Medical Ethics, University of Pittsburgh. Wicclair is the author of *Ethics and the Elderly* (1993). His published articles include "Patient Decision-Making Capacity and Risk" and "Preferential Treatment and Desert."

Wicclair operates with the definition of pornography suggested by Longino. He argues, however, that censorship of pornography is not a legitimate means to achieve the aims of feminism, nor even the most effective means. In his view, there is a strong presumption against censorship; this presumption is based on the principle of freedom of expression as well as the likely negative side effects of censorship. In rejecting the argument that censorship of pornography is a legitimate means of preventing harm to women, he claims that the connection between pornography and harm to women is too speculative to warrant incurring the costs of censorship. In addition to emphasizing the costs of censorship, Wicclair warns against overestimating its expected benefits. He concludes by presenting the procensorship feminist with a series of difficulties.

It is sometimes claimed that pornography is objectionable because it violates conventional standards of sexual morality. Although feminists tend to agree that pornography is objectionable, they reject this particular argument against it.[1] This argument is unacceptable to feminists because it is associated with an oppressive Puritanical sexual ethic that inhibits the sexual fulfillment of all people, but especially women. In order to understand why feminists find pornography objectionable, one has to keep in mind that they do not equate the terms "pornographic" and "sexually explicit." Rather, sexually explicit material is said to be "pornographic" only if it depicts and condones the exploitation, dehumanization, subordination, abuse, or denigration of women. By definition, then, all pornography is sexist and misogynistic. Some pornographic material has the additional feature of depicting and condoning acts of *violence* against women (e.g., rape, brutality, torture, sadism). Thus there is a world of difference between harmless "erotica" and pornography. Whereas erotica depicts sexual activity in a manner which is designed to produce sexual arousal and is therefore likely to be objectionable only to those who subscribe to a Puritanical sexual ethic, pornography is "material that explicitly represents or describes degrading and abusive sexual behavior so as to endorse and/or recommend the behavior as described."[2]

Despite the general agreement among feminists that pornography, understood in the way just described, is objectionable, they are sharply divided over the question of its *censorship.* Whereas some feminists find pornography to be so objectionable that they call for its censorship, others oppose this proposal.[3] I will argue that anyone who supports the aims of feminism and who seeks the liberation of all people should reject the censorship of pornography.[4]

When discussing censorship, it is important to keep in mind that there are very strong reasons to be wary of its use. In our society, the importance of the principle of freedom of expression—an anticensorship principle—is widely recognized. The ability to speak one's mind and to express ideas and feelings without the threat of legal penalties or government control is rightly perceived as an essential feature of a truly free society. Moreover, an environment that tolerates the expression of dif-fering views about politics, art, lifestyles, etc., encourages progress and aids in the search for truth and justice. In addition to the many important values associated with the principle of freedom of expression, it is also necessary to consider likely nega-tive side effects of censorship. There is a serious risk that once any censorship is al-lowed, the power to censor will, over time, expand in unintended and undesirable directions (the "slippery slope"). This is not mere speculation, for such an expan-sion of the power to censor is to be expected in view of the fact that it is extremely difficult, if not impossible, to formulate unequivocal and unambiguous criteria of cen-sorship. Then, too, the power to censor can all too easily be abused or misused. Even though it may arise in a genuine effort to promote the general welfare and to protect certain rights, officials and groups might use the power to censor as a means to ad-vance their own interests and values and to suppress the rights, interests, and values of others. Thus, given the value of freedom of expression and the many dangers as-sociated with censorship, there is a strong *prima facie* case against censorship. In other words, advocates of censorship have the burden of showing that there are suf-ficiently strong overriding reasons which would justify it in a specific area.

Like racist and antisemitic material, sexist and misogynistic films, books, and mag-azines surely deserve condemnation. But censorship is another matter. In view of the strength of the case against censorship in general, it is unwise to advocate it merely to prevent depicting morally objectionable practices in a favorable light. Fortunately, proponents of the censorship of pornography tend to recognize this, for they usually base their call for censorship on a claim about the *effects* of pornography. Pornog-raphy, it is held, is *injurious* or *harmful* to women because it fosters the objection-able practices that it depicts. Pornography generally is said to promote the exploita-tion, humiliation, denigration, subordination, etc., of women; and pornography that depicts acts of violence against women is said to cause murder, rape, assault, and other acts of violence. On the basis of the "harm principle"—a widely accepted prin-ciple that allows us to restrict someone's freedom in order to prevent harm to oth-ers—it would appear to be justified to override the principle of freedom of expres-sion and to restrict the freedom of would-be producers, distributors, sellers, exhibitors, and consumers of pornography. In short it seems that censorship of pornography is a legitimate means of preventing harm to women.

However, there are a number of problems associated with this attempt to justify censorship. To begin with, it is essential to recognize the important difference be-tween words and images, on the one hand, and actions, on the other hand. A would-be rapist poses a *direct* threat to his intended victim, and by stopping him, we pre-vent an act of violence. But if there is a connection between the depiction of a rape—even one which appears to condone it—and someone's committing an act of violence against a woman, the connection is relatively *indirect;* and stopping the production, distribution, sale, and exhibition of depictions of rape does not directly restrict the freedom of would-be rapists to commit acts of violence against women. In recognition of the important difference between restricting words and images and preventing harmful behavior, exceptions to the principle of freedom of expression are generally thought to be justified only if words or images present a "clear and present danger" of harm or injury. Thus, to cite a standard example, it is justified to stop someone from falsely shouting "Fire!" in a crowded theater, for this exclamation is likely to cause a panic that would result in serious injury and even death.

It is doubtful that pornography satisfies the "clear and present danger" condition. For there does not seem to be conclusive evidence that establishes its *causal* significance. Most studies are limited to violent pornography. And even though some of these studies do suggest a *temporary* impact on *attitudes* (e.g., those who view violent pornography may be more likely to express the view that women seek and "enjoy" violence), this does not show that viewing violent pornography causes violent *behavior.* Moreover, there is some evidence suggesting that the effect on attitudes is only temporary and that it can be effectively counteracted by additional information.[5]

But even if there is no conclusive evidence that pornography causes harm, is it not reasonable to "play it safe," and does this not require censorship? Unfortunately, the situation is not as simple as this question appears to suggest. For one thing, it is sometimes claimed that exposure to pornography has a "cathartic" effect and that it therefore produces a net *reduction* in harm to women. This claim is based upon two assumptions, neither of which has been proven to be false: (1) Men who are not already violence-prone are more likely to be "turned off" than to be "turned on" by depictions of rape, brutality, dismemberment, etc. (2) For men in the latter category, exposure to pornography can function as a substitute for actually causing harm. It is also necessary to recall that there are significant values associated with the principle of freedom of expression, and that a failure to observe it involves a number of serious dangers. Since censorship has costs which are substantial and not merely speculative, the more speculative the connection between pornography and harm to women, the less basis there is for incurring the costs associated with censorship.

Just as it is easy to overlook the negative side of censorship, it is also common to overplay its positive effects. Surely it would be foolish to think that outlawing anti-semitism in sexually explicit material would have halted the slaughter of Jews in Hitler Germany or that prohibiting racism in sexually explicit material would reduce the suffering of Blacks in South Africa. Similarly, in view of the violent nature of American society generally and the degree to which sexism persists to this day, it is unlikely that censorship of pornography by itself would produce any significant improvement in the condition of women in the United States. Fortunately, there are other, more effective and direct means of eliminating sexism than by censoring pornography. Passage and strict enforcement of the Equal Rights Amendment, electing feminists to local, state, and national political office, achieving genuine economic justice for women, and securing their reproductive freedom will do considerably more to foster the genuine liberation of women in the United States than will the censorship of pornography. With respect to rape and other acts of violence, it has often been noted that American society is extremely violent, and, sadly, there are no magic solutions to the problems of rape and violence. But the magnitude of the problem suggests that censoring pornography only addresses a symptom and not the underlying disease. Although there is still much dispute about the causes of violence generally and rape in particular, it is unlikely that there will be a serious reduction in acts of violence against women until there are rather drastic changes in the socioeconomic environment and in the criminal justice system.

Those who remain concerned about the possible contribution of pornography to violence and sexism should keep in mind that it can be "neutralized" in ways that avoid the dangers of censorship. One important alternative to government censorship is to help people understand why pornography is objectionable and why it and its message should be rejected. This can be accomplished by means of educational campaigns, discussions of pornography on radio and television and at public forums, letter writing, and educational picketing. In addition, attempts might be made to prevent or restrict the production, distribution, display, sale, and consumption of pornographic material by means of organized pickets, boycotts, and the like. Such direct measures by private citizens raise some troubling questions, but the dangers and risks which they pose are considerably less than those associated with government censorship.

There are several other reasons for questioning the view that the sexist and misogynistic nature of pornography justifies its censorship. Some of the more important of these include the following:

1 Although pornography depicts some practices that are both morally objectionable and illegal (e.g., rape, assault, torture), many of the practices depicted are morally repugnant *but do not break any law*. Thus, for example, our legal system does not explicitly prohibit men from treating women in a degrading or humiliating manner; and with some exceptions, it is not a crime to treat women exclusively as sex objects or to use them exclusively as means and not ends. But is it not odd to recommend making illegal the production, distribution, sale, and exhibition of materials that depict practices that are not themselves illegal?

2 It is essential that laws be clearly formulated and that vagueness be avoided. Vague laws can have a "chilling effect" on unobjectionable activities, and they tend to undermine the fair and effective enforcement of the law by giving police, prosecutors, and judges too much discretionary power. But those who call for the censorship of pornography on the grounds that it is sexist and misogynistic fail to recognize the difficulty of formulating laws which would have an acceptable degree of clarity and specificity. Proponents of censorship use terms like "degrading," "humiliating," "debasing," "exploitative," and "subordination of women." But these terms are far from unambiguous. In fact, they are highly subjective in the sense that different people have different criteria for deciding when something is degrading, humiliating, etc. For example, someone might think that the depiction of an unmarried female or a lesbian couple having and enjoying sex is "demeaning" or "debasing." Thus, in order to prevent censorship from being applied in unintended and undesirable ways, it is necessary to offer clear and unambiguous operational criteria for terms like "demeaning," "humiliating," etc. But the feasibility of articulating generally acceptable criteria of this sort remains highly doubtful.

3 Sexually explicit material that depicts violence against women or that depicts sexist practices is said to be subject to censorship only if it *condones* the objectionable practices. Thus, for example, news films, documentaries, and works which take a critical stance toward those practices are not to be censored. But it is exceedingly difficult in many cases to determine the "point of view" of films, books, photographs, etc.[6] If scholars who have advanced degrees in film, literature, and art can come to no general consensus about the "meaning" or "message" of certain works, is it plausible to think that prosecutors, judges, and juries are likely to fare any better?

4 Why call for the censorship of sexist and misogynistic books, magazines, films, and photographs only if they include an explicit depiction of *sexual activity?* There is no conclusive evidence showing that material that includes a depiction of sexual activity has a greater causal impact on attitudes and behavior.[7] Moreover, it will not do to claim that such material is not worthy of protection under the principle of freedom of expression. Surely, many works which include explicit depictions of sex are not totally devoid of significant and challenging ideas. Consequently, advocates of censorship are faced with a dilemma: Either they can call for the censorship of *all* material that contains objectionable images of women; or they can call for censorship only in the case of sexually explicit materials of that nature. If the first alternative is chosen, then given the pervasiveness of objectionable portrayals of women in art, literature, and the mass media, very little would be immune from censorship. But in view of the strong *prima facie* case against censorship, this seems unacceptable. On the other hand, if the second alternative is chosen, this invites the suspicion that the restriction to sexual material is based upon the very same Puritanical sexual ethic which feminists rightly tend to reject. I am not suggesting that feminists who call for censorship wish to champion sexual oppression. But it is noteworthy that many conservatives who generally do not support the aims of feminism align themselves with feminists who advocate censoring pornography.

5 Why call for censorship of materials only if they depict violence or other objectionable practices in relation to *women?* Wouldn't consistency require censoring *all* violence and material that portrays *anyone* in a derogatory light? But this is clearly unacceptable. For so much of our culture is permeated with images of violence and morally distasteful treatment of people that it is hard to think of many films, television programs, books, or magazines which would be totally immune from censorship. Censorship would be the rule rather than an exception, and such pervasive censorship is incompatible with a truly free society. It also won't do to limit censorship to members of historically oppressed groups (e.g., women, Blacks, Jews). First, it is very unlikely that such "preferential censorship" would be accepted by the majority for too long. Sooner or later others would object and/or press for protection too. Second, in view of the significant costs of censorship, even if it were limited to the protection of historically oppressed groups, it would not be justified unless there were a demonstrable "clear and present danger;" and this remains doubtful.

But what about the view that only pornography should be subject to censorship because *women need special protection?* This position is also unacceptable. For since men are victimized by acts of racism, antisemitism, and violence, and since there is no evidence to prove that depictions of objectionable practices have a greater effect on behavior in pornographic material than they do in nonpornographic material, this position seems to be based on the sexist assumption that women need greater protection than men because they are "naturally" more fragile and vulnerable.

I have tried to show that censorship of pornography is neither the most effective nor a legitimate means to achieve the aims of feminism. Much pornographic material is morally repugnant, but there are less costly ways to express one's moral outrage and to attempt to "neutralize" pornography than by censorship. Moreover, pornography is only a relatively minor manifestation of the sexist practices and institutions that still pervade our society. Hence, the genuine liberation of women—and men—is best served by directly attacking those oppressive practices and institutions. It may be easier to identify and attack pornography—and to win some battles—but the payoff would be slight, and the negative side effects would be substantial.

NOTES

1 Just as the civil rights movement in the United States in the 1950's and 1960's included many people who were not black, so one does not have to be a woman to be a feminist. As I am using the term, a feminist is any person who supports the fundamental goal of feminism: the liberation of women.

2 Helen E. Longino, "Pornography, Oppression, and Freedom: A Closer Look," in Laura Lederer, ed., *Take Back the Night* (New York: William Morrow and Company, Inc., 1980), p. 44. Longino also stipulates that the sexual activities depicted in pornography are degrading or abusive *to women.*

3 In response to the generally pro-censorship Women Against Violence in Pornography and Media, other feminists have organized the Feminist Anti-Censorship Taskforce.

4 Until recently, advocates of censorship have pressed for laws which prohibit or restrict the production, distribution, sale, and exhibition of pornographic material. However, pro-censorship feminists have hit upon a new strategy: Ordinances which stipulate that pornography is *sex discrimination,* enabling women to file sex discrimination lawsuits against producers, distributors, sellers, and exhibitors of pornography. Most of the criticisms of censorship which I discuss in this paper apply to both strategies.

5 For a discussion of research on the effects of pornography, see Edward Donnerstein and Neil Malamuth, eds., *Pornography and Sexual Aggression* (New York: Academic Press, 1984).

6 An informative illustration of how a film can resist unambiguous classification as either progressive or retrograde from a feminist perspective is provided in Lucy Fischer and Marcia Landy, *"The Eyes of Laura Mars: A Binocular Critique," Screen,* Vol. 23, Nos. 3–4 (September–October 1982).

7 In fact some researchers claim that the impact of depictions of violence is *greater* in material which is *not* pornographic. See, for example, the contribution of Edward Donnerstein and Daniel Linz to a section on pornography, "Pornography: Love or Death?" in *Film Comment,* vol. 20, No. 6 (December 1984), pp. 34–35.

QUESTIONS

1 Does the easy availability of pornography pose a "clear and present danger" to women?
2 Considering the aims of feminism, are feminists well advised to endorse the censorship of pornography?

Opinion in *Village of Skokie v. National Socialist Party of America*

Illinois Supreme Court

This case originated when the village of Skokie, a Chicago suburb with a predominantly Jewish population, attempted to block certain activities planned by the National Socialist Party of America in conjunction with a demonstration in Skokie. The circuit court of Cook County issued an injunction against (1) marching, walking, or parading while wearing the party uniform, (2) displaying the swastika, and (3) distributing pamphlets or displaying materials (e.g., slogans) that promote religious, ethnic, or racial hatred. An appellate court modified the original injunction so that party members were ordered only to refrain from displaying the swastika; the appellate court held the original injuction unconstitutional with regard to (1) and (3) above, but not with regard to (2). The Illinois Supreme Court affirmed the judgment of the appellate court with regard to (1) and (3) but reversed the judgment of the appellate court with regard to (2).

Referring to relevant decisions in the United States Supreme Court, the Illinois Supreme Court holds that display of the swastika is symbolic political speech and thus entitled to First Amendment protection. The Court argues that display of the swastika does not fall within the definition of "fighting words." The Court also argues that anticipation of a hostile audience cannot justify the prior restraint embodied in a court order against display of the swastika.

Plaintiff, the village of Skokie, filed a complaint in the circuit court of Cook County seeking to enjoin defendants, the National Socialist Party of America (the American Nazi Party) and 10 individuals as "officers and members" of the party, from engaging in certain activities while conducting a demonstration within the village. The circuit court issued an order enjoining certain conduct during the planned demonstration. The appellate court modified the injunction order, and, as modified, defendants are enjoined from "[i]ntentionally displaying the swastika on or off their persons, in the course of a demonstration, march, or parade." We allowed defendants' petition for leave to appeal.

The pleadings and the facts adduced at the hearing are fully set forth in the ap-

Illinois Supreme Court. 373 N.E.2d 21 (1978).

pellate court opinion, and only those matters necessary to the discussion of the issues will be repeated here. The facts are not disputed.

It is alleged in plaintiff's complaint that the "uniform of the National Socialist Party of America consists of the storm trooper uniform of the German Nazi Party embellished with the Nazi swastika"; that the plaintiff village has a population of about 70,000 persons of which approximately 40,500 persons are of "Jewish religion or Jewish ancestry" and of this latter number 5,000 to 7,000 are survivors of German concentration camps; that the defendant organization is "dedicated to the incitation of racial and religious hatred directed principally against individuals of Jewish faith or ancestry and non-Caucasians"; and that its members "have patterned their conduct, their uniform, their slogan and their tactics along the pattern of the German Nazi Party. . . ."

Defendants moved to dismiss the complaint. In an affidavit attached to defendants' motion to dismiss, defendant Frank Collin, who testified that he was "party leader," stated that on or about March 20, 1977, he sent officials of the plaintiff village a letter stating that the party members and supporters would hold a peaceable, public assembly in the village on May 1, 1977, to protest the Skokie Park District's requirement that the party procure $350,000 of insurance prior to the party's use of the Skokie public parks for public assemblies. The demonstration was to begin at 3 P.M., last 20 to 30 minutes, and consist of 30 to 50 demonstrators marching in single file, back and forth, in front of the village hall. The marchers were to wear uniforms which include a swastika emblem or armband. They were to carry a party banner containing a swastika emblem and signs containing such statements as "White Free Speech," "Free Speech for the White Man," and "Free Speech for White America." The demonstrators would not distribute handbills, make any derogatory statements directed to any ethnic or religious group, or obstruct traffic. They would cooperate with any reasonable police instructions or requests.

At the hearing on plaintiff's motion for an "emergency injunction" a resident of Skokie testified that he was a survivor of the Nazi holocaust. He further testified that the Jewish community in and around Skokie feels the purpose of the march in the "heart of the Jewish population" is to remind the two million survivors "that we are not through with you" and to show "that the Nazi threat is not over, it can happen again." Another resident of Skokie testified that as the result of defendants' announced intention to march in Skokie, 15 to 18 Jewish organizations, within the village and surrounding area, were called and a counterdemonstration of an estimated 12,000 to 15,000 people was scheduled for the same day. There was opinion evidence that defendants' planned demonstration in Skokie would result in violence.

The circuit court entered an order enjoining defendants from "marching, walking or parading in the uniform of the National Socialist Party of America; marching, walking or parading or otherwise displaying the swastika on or off their person; distributing pamphlets or displaying any materials which incite or promote hatred against persons of Jewish faith or ancestry or hatred against persons of any faith or ancestry, race or religion" within the village of Skokie. The appellate court, as earlier noted, modified the order so that defendants were enjoined only from intentional display of the swastika during the Skokie demonstration.

The appellate court opinion adequately discussed and properly decided those issues arising from the portions of the injunction order which enjoined defendants from marching, walking, or parading, from distributing pamphlets or displaying materials, and from wearing the uniform of the National Socialist Party of America. The only issue remaining before this court is whether the circuit court order enjoining defendants from displaying the swastika violates the first amendment rights of those defendants.

In defining the constitutional rights of the parties who come before this court, we are, of course, bound by the pronouncements of the United States Supreme Court in its interpretation of the United States Constitution. The decisions of that court, particularly *Cohen v. California* (1971), in our opinion compel us to permit the demonstration as proposed, including display of the swastika.

"It is firmly settled that under our Constitution the public expression of ideas may not be prohibited merely because the ideas are themselves offensive to some of their hearers," and it is entirely clear that the wearing of distinctive clothing can be symbolic expression of a thought or philosophy. The symbolic expression of thought falls within the free speech clause of the first amendment, and the plaintiff village has the heavy burden of justifying the imposition of a prior restraint upon defendants' right to freedom of speech.

The village of Skokie seeks to meet this burden by application of the "fighting words" doctrine first enunciated in *Chaplinsky v. New Hampshire* (1942). That doctrine was designed to permit punishment of extremely hostile personal communication likely to cause immediate physical response, "no words being 'forbidden except such as have a direct tendency to cause acts of violence by the persons to whom, individually, the remark is addressed.' " In *Cohen* the Supreme Court restated the description of fighting words as "those personally abusive epithets which, when addressed to the ordinary citizen, are, as a matter of common knowledge, inherently likely to provoke violent reaction." Plaintiff urges, and the appellate court has held, that the exhibition of the Nazi symbol, the swastika, addresses to ordinary citizens a message which is tantamount to fighting words. Plaintiff further asks this court to extend *Chaplinsky,* which upheld a statute punishing the use of such words, and hold that the fighting-words doctrine permits a prior restraint on defendants' symbolic speech. In our judgment we are precluded from doing so.

In *Cohen,* defendant's conviction stemmed from wearing a jacket bearing the words "Fuck the Draft" in a Los Angeles County courthouse corridor. The Supreme Court for reasons we believe applicable here refused to find that the jacket inscription constituted fighting words. That court stated:

> The constitutional right of free expression is powerful medicine in a society as diverse and populous as ours. It is designed and intended to remove governmental restraints from the arena of public discussion, putting the decision as to what views shall be voiced largely into the hands of each of us, in the hope that use of such freedom will ultimately produce a more capable citizenry and more perfect polity and in the belief that no other approach would comport with the premise of individual dignity and choice upon which our political system rests.
>
> To many, the immediate consequence of this freedom may often appear to be only ver-

bal tumult, discord, and even offensive utterance. These are, however, within established limits, in truth necessary side effects of the broader enduring values which the process of open debate permits us to achieve. That the air may at times seem filled with verbal cacophony is, in this sense not a sign of weakness but of strength. We cannot lose sight of the fact that, in what otherwise might seem a trifling and annoying instance of individual distasteful abuse of a privilege, these fundamental societal values are truly implicated. . . . "so long as the means are peaceful, the communication need not meet standards of acceptability."

Against this perception of the constitutional policies involved, we discern certain more particularized considerations that peculiarly call for reversal of this conviction. First, the principle contended for by the State seems inherently boundless. How is one to distinguish this from any other offensive word [emblem]? Surely the State has no right to cleanse public debate to the point where it is grammatically palatable to the most squeamish among us. Yet no readily ascertainable general principle exists for stopping short of that result were we to affirm the judgment below. For, while the particular four-letter word [emblem] being litigated here is perhaps more distasteful than most others of its genre, it is nevertheless often true that one man's vulgarity is another's lyric. Indeed, we think it is largely because governmental officials cannot make principled distinctions in this area that the Constitution leaves matters of taste and style so largely to the individual. . . .

Finally, and in the same vein, we cannot indulge the facile assumption that one can forbid particular words without also running a substantial risk of suppressing ideas in the process. Indeed, governments might soon seize upon the censorship of particular words [emblems] as a convenient guise for banning the expression of unpopular views. We have been able, as noted above, to discern little social benefit that might result from running the risk of opening the door to such grave results.

The display of the swastika, as offensive to the principles of a free nation as the memories it recalls may be, is symbolic political speech intended to convey to the public the beliefs of those who display it. It does not, in our opinion, fall within the definition of "fighting words," and that doctrine cannot be used here to overcome the heavy presumption against the constitutional validity of a prior restraint.

Nor can we find that the swastika, while not representing fighting words, is nevertheless so offensive and peace threatening to the public that its display can be enjoined. We do not doubt that the sight of this symbol is abhorrent to the Jewish citizens of Skokie, and that the survivors of the Nazi persecutions, tormented by their recollections, may have strong feelings regarding its display. Yet it is entirely clear that this factor does not justify enjoining defendants' speech. The *Cohen* court spoke to this subject:

Finally, in arguments before this Court much has been made of the claim that Cohen's distasteful mode of expression was thrust upon unwilling or unsuspecting viewers, and that the State might therefore legitimately act as it did in order to protect the sensitive from otherwise unavoidable exposure to appellant's crude form of protest. Of course, the mere presumed presence of unwitting listeners or viewers does not serve automatically to justify curtailing all speech capable of giving offense. While this Court has recognized that government may properly act in many situations to prohibit intrusion into the privacy of the home of unwelcome views and ideas which cannot be totally banned from the public dialogue, we have at the same time consistently stressed that "we are often 'captives' outside the sanctuary of the home and subject to objectionable speech." The ability of government, consonant with the Constitution, to shut off discourse solely to protect others from hearing it is, in other words, dependent upon a showing that substantial privacy interests are being invaded in an essentially intolerable manner. Any broader view of this authority would effectively empower a majority to silence dissidents simply as a matter of personal predilections.

Similarly, the Court of Appeals for the Seventh Circuit, in reversing the denial of defendant Collin's application for a permit to speak in Chicago's Marquette Park, noted that courts have consistently refused to ban speech because of the possibility of unlawful conduct by those opposed to the speaker's philosophy. . . .

Rockwell v. Morris (1961) also involved an American Nazi leader, George Lincoln Rockwell, who challenged a bar to his use of a New York City park to hold a public demonstration where anti-Semitic speeches would be made. Although approximately 2½ million Jewish New Yorkers were hostile to Rockwell's message, the court ordered that a permit to speak be granted, stating:

> A community need not wait to be subverted by street riots and storm troopers; but, also, it cannot, by its policemen or commissioners, suppress a speaker, in prior restraint, on the basis of news reports, hysteria, or inference that what he did yesterday, he will do today. Thus, too, if the speaker incites others to immediate unlawful action he may be punished—in a proper case, stopped when disorder actually impends; but this is not to be confused with unlawful action from others who seek unlawfully to suppress or punish the speaker.
>
> So, the unpopularity of views, their shocking quality, their obnoxiousness, and even their alarming impact is not enough. Otherwise, the preacher of any strange doctrine could be stopped; the anti-racist himself could be suppressed, if he undertakes to speak in "restricted" areas; and one who asks that public schools be open indiscriminately to all ethnic groups could be lawfully suppressed, if only he choose to speak where persuasion is needed most.

In summary, as we read the controlling Supreme Court opinions, use of the swastika is a symbolic form of free speech entitled to first amendment protections. Its display on uniforms or banners by those engaged in peaceful demonstrations cannot be totally precluded solely because that display may provoke a violent reaction by those who view it. Particularly is this true where, as here, there has been advance notice by the demonstrators of their plans so that they have become, as the complaint alleges, "common knowledge" and those to whom sight of the swastika banner or uniforms would be offense are forewarned and need not view them. A speaker who gives prior notice of his message has not compelled a confrontation with those who voluntarily listen.

As to those who happen to be in a position to be involuntarily confronted with the swastika, the following observations from *Erznoznik v. City of Jacksonville* (1975) are appropriate:

> The plain, if at all times disquieting, truth is that in our pluralistic society, constantly proliferating new and ingenious forms of expression, "we are inescapably captive audiences for many purposes." Much that we encounter offends our esthetic, if not our political and moral, sensibilities. Nevertheless, the Constitution does not permit government to decide which types of otherwise protected speech are sufficiently offensive to require protection for the unwilling listener or viewer. Rather, absent the narrow circumstances described

above [home intrusion or captive audience], the burden normally falls upon the viewer to "avoid further bombardment of [his] sensibilities simply by averting [his] eyes."

Thus by placing the burden upon the viewer to avoid further bombardment, the Supreme Court has permitted speakers to justify the initial intrusion into the citizen's sensibilities.

We accordingly, albeit reluctantly, conclude that the display of the swastika cannot be enjoined under the fighting-words exception to free speech, nor can anticipation of a hostile audience justify the prior restraint. Furthermore, *Cohen* and *Erznoznik* direct the citizens of Skokie that it is their burden to avoid the offensive symbol if they can do so without unreasonable inconvenience. Accordingly, we are constrained to reverse that part of the appellate court judgment enjoining the display of the swastika. That judgment is in all other respects affirmed.

QUESTIONS

1 What meaning does display of the swastika have for the Jewish community? Does display of the swastika constitute "fighting words"?
2 In your view, did the circuit court, the appellate court, or the Illinois Supreme Court provide the most defensible resolution of this case?

Racist Speech as the Functional Equivalent of Fighting Words

Charles R. Lawrence III

Charles R. Lawrence III is professor of law, Georgetown University Law Center. He is the coauthor of *The Bakke Case: The Politics of Inequality* (1979) and his many law journal articles include "The Epidemiology of Color-Blindness: Learning to Think and Talk about Race, Again."

Lawrence argues that face-to-face racial insults are unworthy of First Amendment protection. He gives two reasons: (1) Racial insults produce an immediate injury. (2) Racial insults typically have a preemptive effect on further speech and thus do not cohere with the underlying purpose of the First Amendment, which is presumably to foster the greatest amount of speech. Lawrence presents an analysis of the "speechlessness" often experienced by those subjected to racial insults. In his view, racial insults are less likely than other "fighting words" to produce violent responses, in part because of the relative powerlessness of those typically subjected to them. However, Lawrence argues that since racial insults function to inhibit speech as much or more than other "fighting words," they are best understood as the "functional equivalent" of fighting words.

Reprinted with permission of the author from "If He Hollers Let Him Go: Regulating Racist Speech on Campus," *Duke Law Journal,* vol. 1990. Copyright © 1990 Charles R. Lawrence III.

. . . When racist speech takes the form of face-to-face insults, catcalls, or other assaultive speech aimed at an individual or small group of persons, then it falls within the "fighting words" exception to first amendment protection. The Supreme Court has held [in *Chaplinsky v. New Hampshire* (1942)] that words that "by their very utterance inflict injury or tend to incite an immediate breach of the peace" are not constitutionally protected.

Face-to-face racial insults, like fighting words, are undeserving of first amendment protection for two reasons. The first reason is the immediacy of the injurious impact of racial insults. The experience of being called "nigger," "spic," "Jap," or "kike" is like receiving a slap in the face. The injury is instantaneous. There is neither an opportunity for intermediary reflection on the idea conveyed nor an opportunity for responsive speech. The harm to be avoided is both clear and present. The second reason that racial insults should not fall under protected speech relates to the purpose underlying the first amendment. If the purpose of the first amendment is to foster the greatest amount of speech, then racial insults disserve that purpose. Assaultive racist speech functions as a preemptive strike. The racial invective is experienced as a blow, not a proffered idea, and once the blow is struck, it is unlikely that dialogue will follow. Racial insults are undeserving of first amendment protection because the perpetrator's intention is not to discover truth or initiate dialogue but to injure the victim.

The fighting words doctrine anticipates that the verbal "slap in the face" of insulting words will provoke a violent response with a resulting breach of the peace. When racial insults are hurled at minorities, the response may be silence or flight rather than a fight, but the preemptive effect on further speech is just as complete as with fighting words. Women and minorities often report that they find themselves speechless in the face of discriminatory verbal attacks. This inability to respond is not the result of oversensitivity among these groups, as some individuals who oppose protective regulation have argued. Rather, it is the product of several factors, all of which reveal the non-speech character of the initial preemptive verbal assault. The first factor is that the visceral emotional response to personal attack precludes speech. Attack produces an instinctive, defensive psychological reaction. Fear, rage, shock, and flight all interfere with any reasoned response. Words like "nigger," "kike," and "faggot" produce physical symptoms that temporarily disable the victim, and the perpetrators often use these words with the intention of producing this effect. Many victims do not find words of response until well after the assault when the cowardly assaulter has departed.

A second factor that distinguishes racial insults from protected speech is the preemptive nature of such insults—the words by which to respond to such verbal attacks may never be forthcoming because speech is usually an inadequate response. When one is personally attacked with words that denote one's subhuman status and untouchability, there is little (if anything) that can be said to redress either the emotional or reputational injury. This is particularly true when the message and meaning of the epithet resonates with beliefs widely held in society. This preservation of widespread beliefs is what makes the face-to-face racial attack more likely to preempt speech than are other fighting words. The racist name-caller is accompanied by a cultural chorus of equally demeaning speech and symbols.

The subordinated victim of fighting words also is silenced by her relatively powerless position in society. Because of the significance of power and position, the categorization of racial epithets as "fighting words" provides an inadequate paradigm; instead one must speak of their "functional equivalent." The fighting words doctrine presupposes an encounter between two persons of relatively equal power who have been acculturated to respond to face-to-face insults with violence. The fighting words doctrine is a paradigm based on a white male point of view. In most situations, minorities correctly perceive that a violent response to fighting words will result in a risk to their own life and limb. Since minorities are likely to lose the fight, they are forced to remain silent and submissive. This response is most obvious when women submit to sexually assaultive speech or when the racist name-caller is in a more powerful position—the boss on the job or the mob. Certainly, we do not expect the black women crossing the Wisconsin campus to turn on their tormentors and pummel them. Less obvious, but just as significant, is the effect of pervasive racial and sexual violence and coercion on individual members of subordinated groups who must learn the survival techniques of suppressing and disguising rage and anger at an early age.

One of my students, a white, gay male, related an experience that is quite instructive in understanding the inadequacy and potential of the "fighting words" doctrine. In response to my request that students describe how they experienced the injury of racist speech, Michael told a story of being called "faggot" by a man on a subway. His description included all of the speech inhibiting elements I have noted previously. He found himself in a state of semi-shock, nauseous, dizzy, unable to muster the witty, sarcastic, articulate rejoinder he was accustomed to making. He suddenly was aware of the recent spate of gay-bashing in San Francisco, and how many of these had escalated from verbal encounters. Even hours later when the shock resided and his facility with words returned, he realized that any response was inadequate to counter the hundreds of years of societal defamation that one word—"faggot"—carried with it. Like the word "nigger" and unlike the word "liar," it is not sufficient to deny the truth of the word's application, to say, "I am not a faggot." One must deny the truth of the word's meaning, a meaning shouted from the rooftops by the rest of the world a million times a day. Although there are many of us who constantly and in myriad ways seek to counter the lie spoken in the meaning of hateful words like "nigger" and "faggot," it is a nearly impossible burden to bear when one encounters hateful speech face-to-face.

But there was another part of my discussion with Michael that is equally instructive. I asked if he could remember a situation when he had been verbally attacked with reference to his membership in a superordinate group. Had he ever been called a "honkie," a "chauvinist pig," or "mick"? (Michael is from a working class Irish family in Boston.) He said that he had been called some version of all three and that although he found the last one more offensive than the first two, he had not experienced—even in that subordinated role—the same disorienting powerlessness he had experienced when attacked for his membership in the gay community. The question of power, of the context of the power relationships within which speech takes place, must be considered as we decide how best to foster the freest and fullest dialogue within our communities. . . .

QUESTIONS

1 Does Lawrence provide a compelling analysis of the "speechlessness" often experienced by those who are subjected to racial insults?
2 Lawrence claims that "The fighting words doctrine is a paradigm based on a white male point of view." Do you agree?

Liberalism and Campus Hate Speech: A Philosophical Examination

Andrew Altman

Andrew Altman is associate professor of philosophy at George Washington University. His principal research interests are in the connection between legal and political philosophy, and he is the author of *Critical Legal Studies: A Liberal Critique* (1990) and *Arguing About Law: An Introduction to Legal Philosophy* (1996).

Altman engages the issue of campus hate-speech regulation. He argues, within the liberal tradition, in favor of a very narrow form of hate-speech regulation, but he does not base his argument on the psychological harms produced by hate speech. Rather, in conjunction with an analysis of the typical function of slurs and epithets, he develops the concept of "the speech-act wrong of subordination," and he endorses hate-speech regulation that targets this particular speech-act wrong. Although Altman concedes that any hate-speech regulation violates the important liberal principle of viewpoint-neutrality, he argues that hate-speech regulation targeting the speech-act wrong of subordination can accommodate the deeper liberal concerns underlying that principle.

INTRODUCTION

In recent years a vigorous public debate has developed over freedom of speech within the academic community. The immediate stimulus for the debate has been the enactment by a number of colleges and universities of rules against hate speech. While some have defended these rules as essential for protecting the equal dignity of all members of the academic community, others have condemned them as intolerable efforts to impose ideological conformity on the academy.

Liberals can be found on both sides of this debate. Many see campus hate-speech regulation as a form of illegitimate control by the community over individual liberty of expression. They argue that hate-speech rules violate the important liberal principle that any regulation of speech be viewpoint-neutral. But other liberals see hate-speech regulation as a justifiable part of the effort to help rid society of discrimina-

Reprinted with permission of the author and the publisher from *Ethics,* vol. 103 (January 1993), pp. 302–317. Copyright © 1993 by the University of Chicago.

tion and subordination based on such characteristics as race, religion, ethnicity, gender, and sexual preference.

In this article, I develop a liberal argument in favor of certain narrowly drawn rules prohibiting hate speech. The argument steers a middle course between those who reject all forms of campus hate-speech regulation and those who favor relatively sweeping forms of regulation. Like those who reject all regulation, I argue that rules against hate speech are not viewpoint-neutral. Like those who favor sweeping regulation, I accept the claim that hate speech can cause serious psychological harm to those at whom it is directed. However, I do not believe that such harm can justify regulation, sweeping or otherwise. Instead, I argue that some forms of hate speech inflict on their victims a certain kind of wrong, and it is on the basis of this wrong that regulation can be justified. The kind of wrong in question is one that is inflicted in virtue of the performance of a certain kind of speech-act characteristic of some forms of hate speech, and I argue that rules targeting this speech-act wrong will be relatively narrow in scope.[1]

HATE SPEECH, HARASSMENT, AND NEUTRALITY

Hate-speech regulations typically provide for disciplinary action against students for making racist, sexist, or homophobic utterances or for engaging in behavior that expresses the same kinds of discriminatory attitudes.[2] The stimulus for the regulations has been an apparent upsurge in racist, sexist, and homophobic incidents on college campuses over the past decade. The regulations that have actually been proposed or enacted vary widely in the scope of what they prohibit.

The rules at Stanford University are narrow in scope. They require that speech meet three conditions before it falls into the proscribed zone: the speaker must intend to insult or stigmatize another on the basis of certain characteristics such as race, gender, or sexual orientation; the speech must be addressed directly to those whom it is intended to stigmatize; and the speech must employ epithets or terms that similarly convey "visceral hate or contempt" for the people at whom it is directed.[3]

On the other hand, the rules of the University of Connecticut, in their original form, were relatively sweeping in scope. According to these rules, "Every member of the University is obligated to refrain from actions that intimidate, humiliate or demean persons or groups or that undermine their security or self-esteem." Explicitly mentioned as examples of proscribed speech were "making inconsiderate jokes . . . stereotyping the experiences, background, and skills of individuals, . . . imitating stereotypes in speech or mannerisms [and] attributing objections to any of the above actions to 'hypersensitivity' of the targeted individual or group."[4]

Even the narrower forms of hate-speech regulation, such as we find at Stanford, must be distinguished from a simple prohibition of verbal harassment. As commonly understood, harassment involves a pattern of conduct that is intended to annoy a person so much as to disrupt substantially her activities. No one questions the authority of universities to enact regulations that prohibit such conduct, whether the conduct be verbal or not. There are three principal differences between hate-speech rules and rules against harassment. First, hate-speech rules do not require a pattern of conduct: a single incident is sufficient to incur liability. Second, hate-speech rules describe the offending conduct in ways that refer to the moral and political viewpoint it expresses. The conduct is not simply annoying or disturbing; it is racist, sexist, or homophobic.

The third difference is tied closely to the second and is the most important one: rules against hate speech are not viewpoint-neutral. Such rules rest on the view that racism, sexism, and homophobia are morally wrong. The liberal principle of viewpoint-neutrality holds that those in authority should not be permitted to limit speech on the ground that it expresses a viewpoint that is wrong, evil, or otherwise deficient. Yet, hate-speech rules rest on precisely such a basis. Rules against harassment, on the other hand, are not viewpoint-based. Anyone in our society could accept the prohibition of harassment because it would not violate their normative political or moral beliefs to do so. The same cannot be said for hate-speech rules because they embody a view of race, gender, and homosexuality contrary to the normative viewpoints held by some people. . . .

. . . The fact is that any plausible justification of hate-speech regulation hinges on the premise that racism, sexism, and homophobia are wrong. Without that premise there would be no basis for arguing that the viewpoint-neutral proscription of verbal harassment is insufficient to protect the rights of minorities and women. The liberal who favors hate-speech regulations, no matter how narrowly drawn, must therefore be prepared to carve out an exception to the principle of viewpoint-neutrality.

THE HARMS OF HATE SPEECH

Many of the proponents of campus hate-speech regulation defend their position by arguing that hate speech causes serious harm to those who are the targets of such speech. Among the most basic of these harms are psychological ones. Even when it involves no direct threat of violence, hate speech can cause abiding feelings of fear, anxiety, and insecurity in those at whom it is targeted. As Mari Matsuda has argued, this is in part because many forms of such speech tacitly draw on a history of violence against certain groups.[5] The symbols and language of hate speech call up historical memories of violent persecution and may encourage fears of current violence. Moreover, hate speech can cause a variety of other harms, from feelings of isolation, to a loss of self-confidence, to physical problems associated with serious psychological disturbance.[6]

The question is whether or not the potential for inflicting these harms is sufficient ground for some sort of hate-speech regulation. As powerful as these appeals to the harms of hate speech are, there is a fundamental sticking point in accepting them as justification for regulation, from a liberal point of view. The basic problem is that the proposed justification sweeps too broadly for a liberal to countenance it. Forms of racist, sexist, or homophobic speech that the liberal is committed to protecting may cause precisely the kinds of harm that the proposed justification invokes.

The liberal will not accept the regulation of racist, sexist, or homophobic speech couched in a scientific, religious, philosophical, or political mode of discourse. The regulation of such speech would not merely carve out a minor exception to the principle of viewpoint-neutrality but would, rather, eviscerate it in a way unacceptable to any liberal. Yet, those forms of hate speech can surely cause in minorities the harms that are invoked to justify regulation: insecurity, anxiety, isolation, loss of self-confidence, and so on. Thus, the liberal must invoke something beyond these kinds of harm in order to justify any hate-speech regulation.

Liberals who favor regulation typically add to their argument the contention that the value to society of the hate speech they would proscribe is virtually nil, while scientific, religious, philosophical, and political forms of hate speech have at least some significant value. Thus, Mary Ellen Gale says that the forms she would prohibit "neither advance knowledge, seek truth, expose government abuses, initiate dialogue, encourage participation, further tolerance of divergent views, nor enhance the victim's individual dignity or self respect."[7] As an example of such worthless hate speech Gale cites an incident of white students writing a message on the mirror in the dorm room of blacks: "African monkeys, why don't you go back to the jungle."[8] But she would protect a great deal of racist or sexist speech, such as a meeting of neo-Nazi students at which swastikas are publicly displayed and speeches made that condemn the presence of Jews and blacks on campus.[9]

Although Gale ends up defending relatively narrow regulations, I believe liberals should be very hesitant to accept her argument for distinguishing regulable from nonregulable hate speech. One problem is that she omits from her list of the values that valuable speech serves one which liberals have long considered important, especially for speech that upsets and disturbs others. Such speech, it is argued, enables the speaker to "blow off steam" in a relatively nondestructive and nonviolent way. Calling particular blacks "African monkeys" might serve as a psychological substitute for harming them in a much more serious way, for example, by lynchings or beatings.

Gale could respond that slurring blacks might just as well serve as an encouragement and prelude to the more serious harms. But the same can be said of forms of hate speech that Gale would protect from regulation, for example, the speech at the neo-Nazi student meeting. Moreover, liberals should argue that it is the job of legal rules against assault, battery, conspiracy, rape, and so on to protect people from violence. It is, at best, highly speculative that hate speech on campus contributes to violence against minorities or women. And while the claim about blowing off steam is also a highly speculative one, the liberal tradition clearly puts a substantial burden of proof on those who would silence speech.

There is a more basic problem with any effort to draw the line between regulable and nonregulable hate speech by appealing to the value of speech. Such appeals invariably involve substantial departures from the principle of viewpoint-neutrality. There is no way to make differential judgments about the value of different types of hate speech without taking one or another moral and political viewpoint. . . .

I do not assume that the principle of viewpoint-neutrality is an absolute or ultimate one within the liberal framework. . . . Moreover, the viewpoint-neutrality principle itself rests on deeper liberal concerns which it is thought to serve. Ideally, a liberal argument for the regulation of hate speech would show that regulations can be developed that accommodate these deeper concerns and that simultaneously serve important liberal values. I believe that there is such a liberal argument. In order to show this, however, it is necessary to examine a kind of wrong committed by hate speakers that is quite different from the harmful psychological effects of their speech.

SUBORDINATION AND SPEECH ACTS

Some proponents of regulation claim that there is an especially close connection between hate speech and the subordination of minorities. Thus, Charles Lawrence contends, "all racist speech constructs the social reality that constrains the liberty of non-whites because of their race."[10] Along the same lines, Mari Matsuda claims, "racist speech is particularly harmful because it is a mechanism of subordination."[11]

The position of Lawrence and Matsuda can be clarified and elaborated using J. L. Austin's distinction between perlocutionary effects and illocutionary force.[12] The perlocutionary effects of an utterance consists of its causal effects on the hearer: infuriating her, persuading her, frightening her, and so on. The illocutionary force of an utterance consists of the kind of speech act one is performing in making the utterance: advising, warning, stating, claiming, arguing, and so on. Lawrence and Matsuda are not simply suggesting that the direct perlocutionary effects of racist speech constitute harm. Nor are they simply suggesting that hate speech can persuade listeners to accept beliefs that then motivate them to commit acts of harm against racial minorities. That again is a matter of the perlocutionary effects of hate speech. Rather, I believe that they are suggesting that hate speech can inflict a wrong in virtue of its illocutionary acts, the very speech acts performed in the utterances of such speech.

What exactly does this speech-act wrong amount to? My suggestion is that it is the wrong of treating a person as having inferior moral standing. In other words, hate speech involves the performance of a certain kind of illocutionary act, namely, the act of treating someone as a moral subordinate.

Treating persons as moral subordinates means treating them in a way that takes their interests to be intrinsically less important, and their lives inherently less valuable, than the interests and lives of those who belong to some reference group. There are many ways of treating people as moral subordinates that are natural as opposed to conventional: the status of these acts as acts of subordination depend solely on universal principles of morality and not on the conventions of a given society. Slavery and genocide, for example, treat people as having inferior moral standing simply in virtue of the affront of such practices to universal moral principles.

Other ways of treating people as moral subordinates have both natural and conventional elements. The practice of racial segregation is an example. It is subordinating because the conditions imposed on blacks by such treatment violate moral principles but also because the act of separation is a convention for putting the minority group in its (supposedly) proper, subordinate place.

I believe that the language of racist, sexist, and homophobic slurs and epithets provides wholly conventional ways of treating people as moral subordinates. Terms such as 'kike', 'faggot', 'spic', and 'nigger' are verbal instruments of subordination. They are used not only to express hatred or contempt for people but also to "put them in their place," that is, to treat them as having inferior moral standing.

It is commonly recognized that through language we can "put people down," to use the vernacular expression. There are many different modes of putting people down: putting them down as less intelligent or less clever or less articulate or less skillful. Putting people down in these ways is not identical to treating them as moral subordinates, and the ordinary put-down does not involve regarding someone as having inferior moral standing. The put-downs that are accomplished with the slurs and epithets of hate speech are different from the ordinary verbal put-down in that respect, even though both sorts of put-down are done through language.

I have contended that the primary verbal instruments for treating people as moral subordinates are the slurs and epithets of hate speech. In order to see this more clearly, consider the difference between derisively calling someone a "faggot" and saying to that person, with equal derision, "You are contemptible for being homosexual." Both utterances can treat the homosexual as a moral subordinate, but the former accomplishes it much more powerfully than the latter. This is, I believe, because the conventional rules of language make the epithet 'faggot' a term whose principal purpose is precisely to treat homosexuals as having inferior moral standing.

I do not believe that a clean and neat line can be drawn around those forms of hate speech that treat their targets as moral subordinates. Slurs and epithets are certainly used that way often, but not always, as is evidenced by the fact that sometimes victimized groups seize on the slurs that historically have subordinated them and seek to "transvalue" the terms. For example, homosexuals have done this with the term 'queer', seeking to turn it into a term of pride rather than one of subordination.

Hate speech in modes such as the scientific or philosophical typically would not involve illocutionary acts of moral subordination. This is because speech in those modes usually involves essentially different kinds of speech acts: describing, asserting, stating, arguing, and so forth. To assert or argue that blacks are genetically inferior to whites is not to perform a speech act that itself consists of treating blacks as inferior. Yet, language is often ambiguous and used for multiple purposes, and I would not rule out a priori that in certain contexts even scientific or philosophical hate speech is used in part to subordinate.

The absence of a neat and clean line around those forms of hate speech that subordinate through speech acts does not entail that it is futile to attempt to formulate regulations that target such hate speech. Rules and regulations rarely have an exact fit with what they aim to prevent: over- and underinclusiveness are pervasive in any system of rules that seeks to regulate conduct. The problem is to develop rules that have a reasonably good fit. Later I argue that there are hate-speech regulations that target subordinating hate speech reasonably well. But first I must argue that such speech commits a wrong that may be legitimately targeted by regulation.

SPEECH-ACT WRONG

I have argued that some forms of hate speech treat their targets as moral subordinates on account of race, gender, or sexual preference. Such treatment runs counter to the central liberal idea of persons as free and equal. To that extent, it constitutes a wrong, a speech-act wrong inflicted on those whom it addresses. However, it does not follow that it is a wrong that may be legitimately targeted by regulation. A liberal republic is not a republic of virtue in which the authorities prohibit every conceivable wrong. The liberal republic protects a substantial zone of liberty around the individual in which she is free from authoritative intrusion even to do some things that are wrong.

Yet, the wrongs of subordination based on such characteristics as race, gender, and sexual preference are not just any old wrongs. Historically, they are among the principal wrongs that have prevented—and continue to prevent—Western liberal democracies from living up to their ideals and principles. As such, these wrongs are especially appropriate targets of regulation in our liberal republic. Liberals recognize the special importance of combating such wrongs in their strong support for laws prohibiting discrimination in employment, housing, and public accommodations. And even if the regulation of speech-act subordination on campus is not regarded as mandatory for universities, it does seem that the choice of an institution to regulate that type of subordination on campus is at least justifiable within a liberal framework.

In opposition, it may be argued that subordination is a serious wrong that should be targeted but that the line should be drawn when it comes to subordination through speech. There, viewpoint-neutrality must govern. But I believe that the principle of viewpoint-neutrality must be understood as resting on deeper liberal concerns. Other things being equal, a departure from viewpoint-neutrality will be justified if it can accommodate these deeper concerns while at the same time serving the liberal principle of the equality of persons.

The concerns fall into three basic categories. First is the Millian idea that speech can promote individual development and contribute to the public political dialogue, even when it is wrong, misguided, or otherwise deficient. Second is the Madisonian reason that the authorities cannot be trusted with formulating and enforcing rules that silence certain views: they will be too tempted to abuse such rules in order to promote their own advantage or their own sectarian viewpoint. Third is the idea that any departures from viewpoint-neutrality might serve as precedents that could be seized upon by would-be censors with antiliberal agendas to further their broad efforts to silence speech and expression.

These concerns that underlie viewpoint-neutrality must be accommodated for hate-speech regulation to be justifiable from a liberal perspective. But that cannot be done in the abstract. It needs to be done in the context of a particular set of regulations. In the next section, I argue that there are regulations that target reasonably well those forms of hate speech that subordinate, and in the following section I argue that such regulations accommodate the concerns that underlie the liberal endorsement of the viewpoint-neutrality principle.

TARGETING SPEECH-ACT WRONG

If I am right in thinking that the slurs and epithets of hate speech are the principal instruments of the speech-act wrong of treating someone as a moral subordinate and that such a wrong is a legitimate target of regulation, then it will not be difficult to formulate rules that have a reasonably good fit with the wrong they legitimately seek to regulate. In general, what are needed are rules that prohibit speech that (*a*) employs slurs and epithets conventionally used to subordinate persons on account of their race, gender, religion, ethnicity, or sexual preference, (*b*) is addressed to particular persons, and (*c*) is expressed with the intention of degrading such persons on account of their race, gender, religion, ethnicity, or sexual preference. With some modification, this is essentially what one finds in the regulations drafted by Grey for Stanford.[13]

Restricting the prohibition to slurs and epithets addressed to specific persons will capture many speech-act wrongs of subordination. But it will not capture them all. Slurs and epithets are not necessary for such speech acts, as I conceded earlier. In addition, it may be possible to treat someone as a moral subordinate through a speech act, even though the utterance is not addressing that person. However, prohibiting more than slurs and epithets would run a high risk of serious overinclusiveness, capturing much speech that performs legitimate speech acts such as stating and arguing. And prohibiting all use of slurs and epithets, whatever the context, would mandate a degree of intrusiveness into the private lives of students that would be difficult for liberals to license.

The regulations should identify examples of the kinds of terms that count as epithets or slurs conventionally used to perform speech acts of subordination. This is required in order to give people sufficient fair warning. But because the terms of natural languages are not precise, univocal, and unchanging, it is not possible to give an exhaustive list, nor is it mandatory to try. Individuals who innocently use an epithet that conventionally subordinates can plead lack of the requisite intent.

The intent requirement is needed to accommodate cases in which an epithet or slur is not used with any intent to treat the addressee as a moral subordinate. These cases cover a wide range, including the efforts of some minorities to capture and transvalue terms historically used to subordinate them. There are several different ways in which the required intent could be described: the intent to stigmatize or to demean or to insult or to degrade and so on. I think that 'degrade' does the best job of capturing the idea of treating someone as a moral subordinate in language the average person will find familiar and understandable. 'Insult' does the poorest job and should be avoided. Insulting someone typically does not involve treating the person as a moral subordinate. Rather, it involves putting someone down in other ways: as less skillful, less intelligent, less clever, and the like.

The regulations at some universities extend beyond what I have defended and prohibit speech that demeans on the basis of physical appearance. I do not believe that such regulations can be justified within the liberal framework I have developed here. Speech can certainly be used to demean people based on physical appearance. 'Slob', 'dog', 'beast', 'pig': these are some examples of terms that are used in such verbal put-downs. But I do not believe that they are used to treat people as moral subordinates, and thus the terms do not inflict the kind of speech-act wrong that justifies the regulation of racist, sexist, or homophobic slurs and epithets.

It should not be surprising that terms which demean on the basis of appearance do not morally subordinate, since the belief that full human moral standing depends on good looks is one that few people, if any, hold.[14] The terms that put people down for their appearance are thus fundamentally different from racist, sexist, or homophobic slurs and epithets. The latter terms do reflect beliefs that are held by many about the lower moral standing of certain groups.

ACCOMMODATING LIBERAL CONCERNS

I have argued that regulations should target those forms of hate speech that inflict the speech-act wrong of subordination on their victims. This wrong is distinct from the psychological harm that hate speech causes. In targeting speech-act subordination, the aim of regulation is not to prohibit speech that has undesirable psychological effects on individuals but, rather, to prohibit speech that treats people as moral subordinates. To target speech that has undesirable psychological effects is invariably to target certain ideas, since it is through the communication of ideas that the psychological harm occurs. In contrast, targeting speech-act subordination does not target ideas. Any idea would be free from regulation as long as it was expressed through a speech act other than one which subordinates: stating, arguing, claiming, defending, and so on would all be free of regulation.

Because of these differences, regulations that target speech-act subordination can accommodate the liberal concerns underlying viewpoint-neutrality, while regulations that sweep more broadly cannot. Consider the important Millian idea that individual development requires that people be left free to say things that are wrong and to learn from their mistakes. Under the sort of regulation I endorse, people would be perfectly free to make racist, sexist, and homophobic assertions and arguments and to learn of the deficiencies of their views from the counterassertions and counterarguments of others. And the equally important Millian point that public dialogue gains even through the expression of false ideas is accommodated in a similar way. Whatever contribution a racist viewpoint can bring to public discussion can be made under regulations that only target speech-act subordination.

The liberal fear of trusting the authorities is somewhat more worrisome. Some liberals have argued that the authorities cannot be trusted with impartial enforcement of hate-speech regulations. Nadine Strossen, for example, claims that the hate-speech regulations at the University of Michigan have been applied in a biased manner, punishing the racist and homophobic speech of blacks but not of whites.[15] Still, it is not at all clear that the biased application of rules is any more of a problem with rules that are not viewpoint-neutral than with those that are. A neutral rule against harassment can also be enforced in a racially discriminatory manner. There is no reason to think a priori that narrowly drawn hate-speech rules would be any more liable to such abuse. Of course, if it did turn out that there was a pervasive problem with the biased enforcement of hate-speech rules, any sensible liberal would advocate rescinding them. But absent a good reason for thinking that this is likely to happen—not just that it could conceivably happen—the potential for abusive enforcement is no basis for rejecting the kind of regulation I have defended.

Still remaining is the problem of precedent: even narrowly drawn regulations targeting only speech-act subordination could be cited as precedent for more sweeping, antiliberal restrictions by those at other universities or in the community at large who are not committed to liberal values. In response to this concern, it should be argued that narrowly drawn rules will not serve well as precedents for would-be censors with antiliberal agendas. Those who wish to silence socialists, for example, on the ground that socialism is as discredited as racism will find scant precedential support from regulations that allow the expression of racist opinions as long as they are not couched in slurs and epithets directed at specific individuals.

There may be some precedent-setting risk in such narrow regulations. Those who wish to censor the arts, for example, might draw an analogy between the epithets that narrow hate-speech regulations proscribe and the "trash" they would proscribe: both forms of expression are indecent, ugly, and repulsive to the average American, or so the argument might go.

Yet, would-be art censors already have precedents at their disposal providing much closer analogies in antiobscenity laws. Hate-speech regulations are not likely to give would-be censors of the arts any additional ammunition. To this, a liberal opponent of any hate-speech regulation might reply that there is no reason to take the risk. But the response will be that there is a good reason, namely, to prevent the wrong of speech-act subordination that is inflicted by certain forms of hate speech.

CONCLUSION

There is a defensible liberal middle ground between those who oppose all campus hate-speech regulation and those who favor the sweeping regulation of such speech. But the best defense of this middle ground requires the recognition that speech acts of subordination are at the heart of the hate-speech issue. Some forms of hate speech do wrong to people by treating them as moral subordinates. This is the wrong that can and should be the target of campus hate-speech regulations.

NOTES

1 In a discussion of the strictly legal issues surrounding the regulation of campus hate speech, the distinction between private and public universities would be an important one. The philosophical considerations on which this article focuses, however, apply both to public and private institutions.

2 In this article I will focus on the restriction of racist (understood broadly to include anti-Semitic), sexist, and homophobic expression. In addition to such expression, regulations typically prohibit discriminatory utterances based on ethnicity, religion, and physical appearance. The argument I develop in favor of regulation applies noncontroversially to ethnicity and religion, as well as to race, gender, and sexual preference. But in a later section I argue against the prohibition of discriminatory remarks based on appearance. . . .

3 The full text of the Stanford regulations is in Thomas Grey, "Civil Rights v. Civil Liberties: The Case of Discriminatory Verbal Harassment," *Social Philosophy and Policy* 8 (1991): 106–7.

4 The University of Connecticut's original regulations are found in the pamphlet "Protect Campus Pluralism," published under the auspices of the Department of Student Affairs, the Dean of Students Office, and the Division of Student Affairs and Services. The regulations have since been rescinded in response to a legal challenge and replaced by ones

similar to those in effect at Stanford. See *University of Connecticut Student Handbook* (Storrs: University of Connecticut, 1990–91), p. 62.

5 Mari Matsuda, "Legal Storytelling: Public Response to Racist Speech: Considering the Victim's Story," *Michigan Law Review* 87 (1989): 2329–34, 2352.

6 See Richard Delgado, "Words That Wound: A Tort Action for Racial Insults, Epithets and Name-Calling," *Harvard Civil Rights–Civil Liberties Law Review* 17 (1982): 137, 146.

7 Mary Ellen Gale, "Reimagining the First Amendment: Racist Speech and Equal Liberty," *St. John's Law Review* 65 (1991): 179–80.

8 Ibid., p. 176.

9 Ibid.

10 Charles Lawrence, "If He Hollers Let Him Go: Regulating Racist Speech on Campus," *Duke Law Journal* (1990), p. 444.

11 Matsuda, p. 2357.

12 J. L. Austin, *How to Do Things with Words* (New York: Oxford University Press, 1962), pp. 98 ff. . . .

13 Stanford describes the intent that is needed for a hate speaker to be liable as the intent to insult or stigmatize. My reservations about formulating the requisite intent in terms of 'insult' are given below.

14 Some people believe that being overweight is the result of a failure of self-control and thus a kind of moral failing. But that is quite different from thinking that the rights and interests of overweight people are morally less important than those of people who are not overweight. . . .

15 Nadine Strossen, "Regulating Racist Speech on Campus: A Modest Proposal?" *Duke Law Journal* (1990), pp. 557–58. . . .

QUESTIONS

1 How significant are the psychological harms produced by hate speech? Do these harms provide a sufficient basis for hate-speech regulation?

2 Does Altman provide an adequate theoretical basis for hate-speech regulation?

3 Do you agree with Altman that hate-speech regulation targeting the speech-act wrong of subordination can accommodate the liberal concerns underlying the principle of viewpoint-neutrality?

SUGGESTED ADDITIONAL READINGS FOR CHAPTER 5

BAIRD, ROBERT M., and STUART E. ROSENBAUM, eds.: *Pornography: Private Right or Public Menace?* Buffalo, N.Y.: Prometheus, 1991. This anthology provides articles written from feminist, libertarian, and religious perspectives. It also includes sections dealing with the two commission reports and "the causal issue."

BERGER, FRED R., ed.: *Freedom of Expression.* Belmont, Calif.: Wadsworth, 1980. Several articles in this collection deal with the philosophical basis of the right of free expression. Other articles deal with more concrete freedom-of-expression issues.

COPP, DAVID, and SUSAN WENDELL, eds.: *Pornography and Censorship.* Buffalo, N.Y.: Prometheus, 1983. Part I of this anthology contains a number of excellent philosophical essays. Part II contains essays by social scientists on the question of whether the wide availability of pornography has harmful consequences. Part III contains judicial opinions.

Doe v. University of Michigan. 721 F. Supp. 852 (E.D.Mich. 1989). At issue in this case was the constitutionality of a very restrictive hate-speech code. The code was struck down as vague and overbroad.

FEINBERG, JOEL: *Social Philosophy.* Englewood Cliffs, N.J.: Prentice-Hall, 1973. Chapters 2 and 3 of this book provide a very helpful discussion of liberty-limiting principles.

GATES, HENRY LOUIS, JR., et al.: *Speaking of Race, Speaking of Sex: Hate Speech, Civil Rights, and Civil Liberties.* New York: New York University Press, 1994. The six authors who contribute articles to this collection are generally critical of proposals to regulate hate speech.

HILL, JUDITH M.: "Pornography and Degradation." *Hypatia,* vol. 2, Summer 1987, pp. 39–54. Hill analyzes the concept of degradation and argues that the pornography industry degrades all women by perpetuating derogatory myths about them.

LEDERER, LAURA, ed.: *Take Back the Night: Women on Pornography.* New York: Morrow, 1980. This anthology provides an overall indictment of pornography from a feminist point of view.

MATSUDA, MARI J., CHARLES R. LAWRENCE III, RICHARD DELGADO, and KIMBERLE WILLIAMS CRENSHAW: *Words that Wound: Critical Race Theory, Assaultive Speech, and the First Amendment.* Boulder, Col.: Westview Press, 1993. Each of the authors, all of whom are advocates for the regulation of racially abusive hate speech, contributes a long essay. The authors identify themselves as two African Americans, a Chicano, and an Asian American, and they say that the view they collectively defend is "grounded in our experiences as people of color."

SOBLE, ALAN: "Pornography: Defamation and the Endorsement of Degradation." *Social Theory and Practice,* vol. 11, Spring 1985, pp. 61–87. Soble critiques and rejects two arguments commonly made by feminists (e.g., Longino) against pornography. He finds unsound both (1) the argument that pornography defames women and (2) the argument that pornography endorses the degradation of women.

CHAPTER 6

Sexism, Racism, and Oppression

Many of the issues discussed in Chapters 7, 8, and 9 involve questions of justice. Are affirmative action programs unjust? Are governmental domestic welfare programs unjust to those who have to pay for them through taxes? Does justice require the redistribution of wealth from the more technologically advanced countries in the northern part of the globe to those in the southern hemisphere? The chapters dealing specifically with affirmative action, economic justice, and world hunger contain articles that respond to their respective questions from a variety of perspectives. But some theorists argue that adequate responses to questions of justice require an understanding of the concept of oppression and of the ways that oppressive social structures are inimical to justice. Thus in this chapter the central questions are the following: What is the nature of oppression? Why is it wrong? What are racism and sexism? Are racism and sexism forms of oppression?

WHAT IS OPPRESSION?

As normally understood, *oppression* is not a value-neutral term. To say that one person oppresses another or that an institution systematically oppresses some people is to express a criticism of the oppressor or institutional practice. Of course, not every constraint or limitation can correctly be described as oppressive. Chapter 5, for example, presents arguments regarding justifiable limitations on individual freedom. When laws are passed threatening individuals with harm if they harm others, those laws can be seen as constraining. But it would be a mistake to claim that the very existence of such laws is a form of oppression. Parents limit their children's freedom in all sorts of ways for their own good, but requiring their children to do a reasonable amount of school work instead of playing baseball all the time can hardly be seen as a form of oppression. Thus whatever oppression is, it cannot be identified simply with constraints or limitations imposed on individuals by either other individuals or social structures.

Traditionally, oppression has been understood as the abuse of power by a ruling group and hence treated as synonymous with tyranny or despotism. On this understanding of oppression, a powerful group deliberately adopts policies intended to subjugate another group. The now disbanded system of apartheid in South Africa provides one example of this kind of oppression. The writers in this chapter, however, share a common concern with oppression understood in a sense which may, but need not, involve the conscious and intentional subjugation of one group by another. Their focus is on the way that economic, political, and cultural institutions systematically function to disadvantage certain groups even in well-intentioned societies. On this approach to oppression, all oppression involves two characteristics. First, a person is not oppressed as a *particular individual* but as a *member of a specific group*. So one's treatment is due not to one's personal characteristics but to the characteristics attributed to one's group. Second, oppression is systematic. As Kenneth Clatterbaugh explains in material not included in this chapter,

> Oppression of a group is systematic; that is, it exists throughout a society, usually over a substantial period of time, and the institutions of society interlock and reinforce each other in ways that create and maintain the oppression. For example, oppressed groups may be denied access to valuable resources of the society and in turn their lack of such resources may be used as evidence that they should continue to be denied access. Thus, the practice feeds the justification and the justification supports the practice.[1]

In her article on oppression in this chapter, Marilyn Frye also stresses the systematic character of oppression when she speaks of a structure of forces and barriers that function to oppress women. On this view, oppression results from everyday practices embodied in unquestioned norms and habits. Within this framework, individuals who contribute to maintaining and reproducing oppression are often simply doing their jobs and do not even see themselves as part of a system of oppression.

Iris M. Young maintains in this chapter that it is not possible to give a general definition of oppression. She grants that all oppressed people have something in common: they all suffer some inhibition of their ability to develop and exercise their capacities and express their needs, thoughts, and feelings. Beyond this, however, we cannot identify an attribute or set of attributes that all oppressed people have in common. Rather, there are different forms of oppression: exploitation, marginalization, powerlessness, cultural imperialism, and systematic violence. The first three involve relations of power and oppression that result from the social division of labor. (Young's discussion of exploitation is particularly relevant to Kai Nielsen's criticisms of capitalism in Chapter 8.) Cultural imperialism involves the acceptance of one group's experiences, values, goals, and achievements as universal. These norms are then used in judging members of other groups as deviant and inferior. Finally, systematic violence against individuals because of their group membership is seen as a form of oppression. Members of such groups share the knowledge that they may be victims of violence solely on the basis of their group identity. Young brings out the ways that these different forms of oppression intersect so that some groups can be

---

[1]Kenneth Clatterbaugh, "The Oppression Debate in Sexual Politics," in Larry May and Robert A. Strikwerda, eds., *Rethinking Masculinity* (Lanham, Md.: Rowman and Littlefield, 1992), p. 171.

judged to be more oppressed than others even though no one definition of oppression is possible.

Clatterbaugh, in one of this chapter's readings, rejects Young's claim regarding the impossibility of a general definition of oppression. He defines oppression as the systematic dehumanization of an identifiable target human group. Members of target groups are dehumanized insofar as they are perceived as not possessing those characteristics that society values as important to being a human being. Social structures are oppressive, then, if they assume, promote, or treat the target groups as if they were defective in the valued human abilities, needs, wants, or achievements.

Clatterbaugh's definition can be seen as complementing Young's analysis. For example, is it always correct to say that because workers in a capitalist system are exploited they are oppressed? Some individuals in the system may be highly paid, may hold a great deal of power over others, may enjoy a great deal of social prestige, and may be members of the dominant social group. Are such individuals rightly considered oppressed? Using Clatterbaugh's understanding of oppression as involving systematic dehumanization, we may be able to distinguish between those cases of exploitation or marginalization that result in oppression and those that do not. Clatterbaugh himself uses his account of oppression to argue that in our society men are not oppressed simply by virtue of being men. They may be oppressed because they are gay or because they are part of some other oppressed group, but not simply because they are men.

SEXISM AND RACISM

If we accept Young's and Clatterbaugh's conceptions of oppression, are racism and sexism forms of oppression? To answer this question it is necessary to look at some of the ways *racism* and *sexism* as well as their cognates are used. On one understanding of racism and sexism, individuals are described as racist or sexist when they are prejudiced against members of a particular group or when they engage in discriminatory behavior on the basis of such prejudices. On this understanding of racism and sexism, a black might be described as racist in respect to whites and a woman might be described as sexist in regard to men. A woman might be accused of sexism, for example, if she refused to hire a man as a department secretary based on her belief that men are incapable of the kind of sensitivity and cooperativeness required by the job. If we understand racism and sexism in this way, not all instances of racism or sexism would be seen as forms of oppression as this concept is understood by Young and Clatterbaugh.

Some theorists would argue, however, that it is simply incorrect to characterize the above sorts of attitudes and behavior as racist or sexist. Some of these attitudes may be deplorable and some of the acts unjust, but in their view, prejudice and unjust discrimination are not sufficient to qualify as racism or sexism. Gloria Yamato in this chapter, for example, defines racism as the systematic, institutionalized mistreatment of one group of people by another based on racial heritage. Since historically such treatment of blacks and other groups in our society has involved the kind of dehumanization discussed by Clatterbaugh, given Yamato's definition of racism,

racism certainly can be considered a form of oppression. It is important to note that the emphasis is on the systematic and institutionalized nature of racism. As with the discussion of oppression, when writers in this chapter discuss racism and sexism, they are not so much concerned with prejudiced attitudes or individual acts of discrimination as with the sorts of social structures and practices that function in interrelated ways to disadvantage certain groups while empowering others. In her analysis of sexism, for example, Frye focuses on the deeply ingrained cultural and economic structures that enforce gender differentiations which divide the species into dominators and subordinates on the basis of sex. Thus, as understood by Frye and Yamato, sexism and racism are forms of oppression.[2]

At issue in this chapter, however, is not the correct use of the words "racism" and "sexism" and their cognates. At issue is the relation between racism and sexism on the one hand and oppression on the other. If we understand *racism* and *sexism* in the first way described above, then not all cases of racism or sexism are cases of oppression, as the writers in this chapter describe oppression. On Yamato's and Frye's conceptions of racism and sexism, however, racism and sexism are forms of oppression.

Jane S. Zembaty

[2]One of the central goals of feminism is the eradication of *patriarchal* oppression—the oppression of women by men. In chapter 1, Susan Sherwin argues that patriarchal opposition to abortion is part and parcel of patriarchal oppression. In Chapter 11, Karen J. Warren argues that there are important connections between the patriarchal domination of women and the human domination of nonhuman nature.

Sexism

Marilyn Frye

Marilyn Frye is professor of philosophy at Michigan State University. She is the author of *Some Reflections on Separatism and Power* (1981), *The Politics of Reality: Essays in Feminist Theory* (1983), from which this selection is excerpted, and *Willful Virgin: Essays in Feminism, 1976–1992* (1992).

According to Frye, if we are to understand sexism, we must focus not simply on individual acts but on the larger social context. She is concerned with the ways that cultural and economic structures create gender insofar as they enforce elaborate and rigid patterns of sex-marking and sex-announcing behavior. Frye labels these structures "sexist" insofar as they divide the species into dominators and subordinates on the basis of sex. On her analysis, individual acts are sexist when they reinforce and support these structures.

Reprinted with permission of The Crossing Press from Marilyn Frye, *The Politics of Reality: Essays in Feminist Theory* (1983).

The first philosophical project I undertook as a feminist was that of trying to say carefully and persuasively what sexism is, and what it is for someone, some institution or some act to be sexist. This project was pressed on me with considerable urgency because, like most women coming to a feminist perception of themselves and the world, I was seeing sexism everywhere and trying to make it perceptible to others. I would point out, complain and criticize, but most frequently my friends and colleagues would not see that what I declared to be sexist was sexist, or at all objectionable.

As the critic and as the initiator of the topic, I was the one on whom the burden of proof fell—it was I who had to explain and convince. Teaching philosophy had already taught me that people cannot be persuaded of things they are not ready to be persuaded of; there are certain complexes of will and prior experience which will inevitably block persuasion, no matter the merits of the case presented. I knew that even if I could explain fully and clearly what I was saying when I called something sexist, I would not necessarily be able to convince various others of the correctness of this claim. But what troubled me enormously was that I could not explain it in any way which satisfied *me*. It is this sort of moral and intellectual frustration which, in my case at least, always generates philosophy.

The following was the product of my first attempt to state clearly and explicitly what sexism is:

> The term 'sexist' in its core and perhaps most fundamental meaning is a term which characterizes anything whatever which creates, constitutes, promotes or exploits any irrelevant or impertinent marking of the distinction between the sexes.[1]

When I composed this statement, I was thinking of the myriads of instances in which persons of the two sexes are treated differently, or behave differently, but where nothing in the real differences between females and males justifies or explains the difference of treatment or behavior. I was thinking, for instance, of the tracking of boys into Shop and girls into Home Ec, where one can see nothing about boys or girls considered in themselves which seems to connect essentially with the distinction between wrenches and eggbeaters. I was thinking also of sex discrimination in employment—cases where someone otherwise apparently qualified for a job is not hired because she is a woman. But when I tried to put this definition of 'sexist' to use, it did not stand the test.

Consider this case: If a company is hiring a supervisor who will supervise a group of male workers who have always worked for male supervisors, it can scarcely be denied that the sex of a candidate for the job is relevant to the candidate's prospects of moving smoothly and successfully into an effective working relationship with the supervisees (though the point is usually exaggerated by those looking for excuses not to hire women). Relevance is an intrasystematic thing. The patterns of behavior, attitude and custom within which a process goes on determine what is relevant to what in matters of describing, predicting or evaluating. In the case at hand, the workers' attitudes and the surrounding customs of the culture make a difference to how they interact with their supervisor and, in particular, *make* the sex of the supervisor a relevant factor in predicting how things will work out. So then, if the company hires a man, in preference to a more experienced and knowledgeable woman, can we explain our objection to the decision by saying it involved distinguishing on the basis of sex when sex is irrelevant to the ability to do the job? No: sex is relevant here.

So, what did I mean to say about 'sexist'? I was thinking that in a case of a candidate for a supervisory job, the reproductive capacity of the candidate has nothing to do with that person's knowing what needs to be done and being able to give properly timed, clear and correct directions. What I was picturing was a situation purified of all sexist perception and reaction. But, of course. *If* the whole context were not sexist, sex would not be an issue in such a job situation; indeed, it might go entirely unnoticed. It is precisely the fact that the sex of the candidate *is* relevant that is the salient symptom of the sexism of the situation.

I had failed, in that first essay, fully to grasp or understand that the locus of sexism is primarily in the system or framework, not in the particular act. It is not accurate to say that what is going on in cases of sexism is that distinctions are made on the basis of sex when sex is irrelevant; what is wrong in cases of sexism is, in the first place, that sex *is* relevant; and then that the making of distinctions on the basis of sex reinforces the patterns which make it relevant.

In sexist cultural/economic systems, sex is always relevant. To understand what sexism is, then, we have to step back and take a larger view.

Sex-identification intrudes into every moment of our lives and discourse, no matter what the supposedly primary focus or topic of the moment is. Elaborate, systematic, ubiquitous and redundant marking of a distinction between two sexes of humans and most animals is customary and obligatory. One *never* can ignore it.

Examples of sex-marking behavior patterns abound. A couple enters a restaurant; the headwaiter or hostess addresses the man and does not address the woman. The physician addresses the man by surname and honorific (Mr. Baxter, Rev. Jones) and addresses the woman by given name (Nancy, Gloria). You congratulate your friend— a hug, a slap on the back, shaking hands, kissing; one of the things which determines which of these you do is your friend's sex. In everything one does one has two complete repertoires of behavior, one for interactions with women and one for interactions with men. Greeting, storytelling, ordergiving and order-receiving, negotiating, gesturing deference or dominance, encouraging, challenging, asking for information: one does all of these things differently depending upon whether the relevant others are male or female.

That this is so has been confirmed in sociological and socio-linguistic research, but it is just as easily confirmed in one's own experience. To discover the differences in how you greet a woman and how you greet a man, for instance, just observe yourself, paying attention to the following sorts of things: frequency and duration of eye contact, frequency and type of touch, tone and pitch of voice, physical distance maintained between bodies, how and whether you smile, use of slang or swear words, whether your body dips into a shadow curtsy or bow. That I have two repertoires for handling introductions to people was vividly confirmed for me when a student introduced me to his friend, Pat, and I really could not tell what sex Pat was. For a moment I was stopped cold, completely incapable of action. I felt myself helplessly caught between two paths—the one I would take if Pat were female and the

one I would take if Pat were male. Of course the paralysis does not last. One is rescued by one's ingenuity and good will; one can invent a way to behave as one says
"How do you do?" to a human being. But the habitual ways are not for humans: they
are one way for women and another for men.

Interlaced through all our behavior is our speaking—our linguistic behavior.
Third person singular pronouns mark the sex of their referents. The same is true for
a huge range of the nouns we use to refer to people ('guy', 'boy', 'lady', 'salesman',
etc., and all the terms which covertly indicate the sex of the referent, like 'pilot',
'nurse', etc.), and the majority of given proper names ('Bob', 'Gwen', etc.). In
speaking, one constantly marks the sexes of those one speaks about. . . .

The pressure on each of us to guess or determine the sex of everybody else both
generates and is exhibited in a great pressure on each of us to *inform* everybody all
the time of our sex. For, if you strip humans of most of their cultural trappings, it is
not always that easy to tell without close inspection which are female, which are male.
The tangible and visible physical differences between the sexes are not particularly
sharp or numerous. Individual variation along the physical dimensions we think of
as associated with maleness and femaleness are great, and the differences between
the sexes could easily be obscured by bodily decoration, hair removal and the like.
One of the shocks, when one does mistake someone's sex, is the discovery of how
easily one can be misled. We could not ensure that we could identify people by their
sex virtually any time and anywhere under any conditions if they did not announce
themselves, did not *tell* us in one way or another.

We do not, in fact, announce our sexes "in one way or another." We announce
them in a thousand ways. We deck ourselves from head to toe with garments and
decorations which serve like badges and buttons to announce our sexes. For every
type of occasion there are distinct clothes, gear and accessories, hairdos, cosmetics
and scents, labeled as "ladies' " or "men's" and labeling us as females or males, and
most of the time most of us choose, use, wear or bear the paraphernalia associated
with our sex. It goes below the skin as well. There are different styles of gait, gesture, posture, speech, humor, taste and even of perception, interest and attention that
we learn as we grow up to be women or to be men and that label and announce us
as women or as men. It begins early in life: even infants in arms are color coded.

That we wear and bear signs of our sexes, and that this is compulsory, is made
clearest in the relatively rare cases when we do not do so, or not enough. Responses
ranging from critical to indignant to hostile meet mothers whose small children are
not immediately sex-identifiable, and hippies used to be accosted on the streets (by
otherwise reserved and polite people) with criticisms and accusations when their
clothing and style gave off mixed and contradictory sex-announcements. Anyone in
any kind of job placement service and any Success Manual will tell you that you cannot expect to get or keep a job if your clothing or personal style is ambiguous in its
announcement of your sex. You don't go to a job interview wearing the other sex's
shoes and socks. . . .

The intense demand for marking and for asserting what sex each person is adds
up to a strenuous requirement that there *be* two distinct and sharply dimorphic sexes.
But, in reality, there are not. There are people who fit on a biological spectrum be-

tween two not-so-sharply defined poles. In about 5 percent of live births, possibly more, the babies are in some degree and way not perfect exemplars of male and female. There are individuals with chromosome patterns other than XX or XY and individuals whose external genitalia at birth exhibit some degree of ambiguity. There are people who are chromosomally "normal" who are at the far ends of the normal spectra of secondary sex characteristics—height, musculature, hairiness, body density, distribution of fat, breast size, etc.—whose overall appearance fits the norm of people whose chromosomal sex is the opposite of theirs.

These variations not withstanding, persons (mainly men, of course) with the power to do so actually *construct* a world in which men are men and women are women and there is nothing in between and nothing ambiguous; they do it by chemically and/or surgically altering people whose bodies are indeterminate or ambiguous with respect to sex. Newborns with "imperfectly formed" genitals are immediately "corrected" by chemical or surgical means, children and adolescents are given hormone "therapies" if their bodies seem not to be developing according to what physicians and others declare to be the norm for what has been declared to be that individual's sex. Persons with authority recommend and supply cosmetics and cosmetic regimens, diets, exercises and all manner of clothing to revise or disguise the too-hairy lip, the too-large breast, the too-slender shoulders, the too-large feet, the too-great or too-slight stature. Individuals whose bodies do not fit the picture of exactly two sharply dimorphic sexes are often enough quite willing to be altered or veiled for the obvious reason that the world punishes them severely for their failure to be the "facts" which would verify the doctrine of two sexes. The demand that the world be a world in which there are exactly two sexes is inexorable, and we are all compelled to answer to it emphatically, unconditionally, repetitiously and unambiguously.

Even being physically "normal" for one's assigned sex is not enough. One must *be* female or male, actively. Again, the costumes and performances. Pressed to acting feminine or masculine, one colludes (co-lude: play along) with the doctors and counselors in the creation of a world in which the apparent dimorphism of the sexes is so extreme that one can only think there is a great gulf between female and male, that the two are, essentially and fundamentally and naturally, utterly different. One helps to create a world in which it seems to us that we *could* never mistake a woman for a man or a man for a woman. We never need worry.

Along with all the making, marking and announcing of sex-distinction goes a strong and visceral feeling or attitude to the effect that sex-distinction is the most important thing in the world: that it would be the end of the world if it were not maintained, clear and sharp and rigid; that a sex-dualism which is rooted in the nature of the beast is absolutely crucial and fundamental to all aspects of human life, human society and human economy. Where feminism is perceived as a project of blurring this distinction, antifeminist rhetoric is vivid with the dread that the world will end if the feminists have their way. Some feminists' insistence that the feminist goal is *not* a "unisex" society is defensive in a way that suggests they too believe that culture or civilization would not survive blurring the distinction. I think that one of the sources of the prevalence and profundity of this conviction and dread is our immersion in the very behavior patterns I have been discussing.

It is a general and obvious principle of information theory that when it is very, very important that certain information be conveyed, the suitable strategy is redundancy. If a message *must* get through, one sends it repeatedly and by as many means or media as one has at one's command. On the other end, as a receiver of information, if one receives the same information over and over, conveyed by every medium one knows, another message comes through as well, and implicitly: the message that this information is very, very important. The enormous frequency with which information about people's sexes is conveyed conveys implicitly the message that this topic is enormously important. I suspect that this is the single topic on which we most frequently receive information from others throughout our entire lives. If I am right, it would go part way to explaining why we end up with an almost irresistible impression, unarticulated, that the matter of people's sexes is the most important and most fundamental topic in the world.

We exchange sex-identification information, along with the implicit message that it is very important, in a variety of circumstances in which there really is no concrete or experientially obvious point in having the information. There are reasons, as this discussion has shown, why you should want to know whether the person filling your water glass or your tooth is male or female and why that person wants to know what you are, but those reasons are woven invisibly into the fabric of social structure and they do not have to do with the bare mechanics of things being filled. Furthermore, the same culture which drives us to this constant information exchange also simultaneously enforces a strong blanket rule requiring that the simplest and most nearly definitive physical manifestations of sex difference be hidden from view in all but the most private and intimate circumstances. The double message of sex-distinction and its pre-eminent importance is conveyed, in fact, in part *by* devices which systematically and deliberately cover up and hide from view the few physical things which do (to a fair extent) distinguish two sexes of humans. The messages are overwhelmingly dissociated from the concrete facts they supposedly pertain to, and from matrices of concrete and sensible reasons and consequences. . . .

If one is made to feel that a thing is of prime importance, but common sensory experience does not connect it with things of obvious concrete and practical importance, then there is mystery, and with that a strong tendency to the construction of mystical or metaphysical conceptions of its importance. If it is important, but not of mundane importance, it must be of transcendent importance. All the more so if it is *very* important.

This matter of our sexes must be very profound indeed if it must, on pain of shame and ostracism, be covered up and must, on pain of shame and ostracism, be boldly advertised by every means and medium one can devise.

There is one more point about redundancy that is worth making here. If there is one thing more effective in making one believe a thing than receiving the message repetitively, it is rehearsing it repetitively. Advertisers, preachers, teachers, all of us in the brainwashing professions, make use of this apparently physical fact of human psychology routinely. The redundancy of sex-marking and sex-announcing serves not only to make the topic seem transcendently important, but to make the sex-duality it advertises seem transcendently and unquestionably *true*. . . .

Sex-marking and sex-announcing are equally compulsory for males and females; but that is as far as equality goes in this matter. The meaning and import of this behavior is profoundly different for women and for men.

Whatever features an individual male person has which tend to his social and economic disadvantage (his age, race, class, height, etc.), one feature which never tends to his disadvantage in the society at large is his maleness. The case for females is the mirror image of this. Whatever features an individual female person has which tend to her social and economic advantage (her age, race, etc.), one feature which always tends to her disadvantage is her femaleness. Therefore, when a male's sex-category is the thing about him that gets first and most repeated notice, the thing about him that is being framed and emphasized and given primacy is a feature which in general is an asset to him. When a female's sex-category is the thing about her that gets first and most repeated notice, the thing about her that is being framed and emphasized and given primacy is a feature which in general is a liability to her. Manifestations of this divergence in the meaning and consequences of sex-announcement can be very concrete.

Walking down the street in the evening in a town or city exposes one to some risk of assault. For males the risk is less; for females the risk is greater. If one announces oneself male, one is presumed by potential assailants to be more rather than less likely to defend oneself or be able to evade the assault and, if the male-announcement is strong and unambiguous, to be a noncandidate for sexual assault. If one announces oneself female, one is presumed by potential assailants to be less rather than more likely to defend oneself or to evade the assault and, if the female-announcement is strong and unambiguous, to be a prime candidate for sexual assault. Both the man and the woman "announce" their sex through style of gait, clothing, hair style, etc., but they are not equally or identically affected by announcing their sex. The male's announcement tends toward his protection or safety, and the female's announcement tends toward her victimization. It could not be more immediate or concrete; the meaning of the sex-identification could not be more different.

The sex-marking behavioral repertoires are such that in the behavior of almost all people of both sexes addressing or responding to males (especially within their own culture/race) generally is done in a manner which suggests basic respect, while addressing or responding to females is done in a manner that suggests the females' inferiority (condescending tones, presumptions of ignorance, overfamiliarity, sexual aggression, etc.). So, when one approaches an ordinary well-socialized person in such cultures, if one is male, one's own behavioral announcement of maleness tends to evoke supportive and beneficial response and if one is female, one's own behavioral announcement of femaleness tends to evoke degrading and detrimental response.

The details of the sex-announcing behaviors also contribute to the reduction of women and the elevation of men. The case is most obvious in the matter of clothing. As feminists have been saying for two hundred years or so, ladies' clothing is generally restrictive, binding, burdening and frail; it threatens to fall apart and/or to uncover something that is supposed to be covered if you bend, reach, kick, punch or run. It typically does not protect effectively against hazards in the environment, nor permit the wearer to protect herself against the hazards of the human environment.

Men's clothing is generally the opposite of all this—sturdy, suitably protective, permitting movement and locomotion. The details of feminine manners and postures also serve to bind and restrict. To be feminine is to take up little space, to defer to others, to be silent or affirming of others, etc. It is not necessary here to survey all this, for it has been done many times and in illuminating detail in feminist writings. My point here is that though both men and women must behave in sex-announcing ways, the behavior which announces femaleness is in itself both physically and socially binding and limiting as the behavior which announces maleness is not.

The sex-correlated variations in our behavior tend systematically to the benefit of males and the detriment of females. The male, announcing his sex in sex-identifying behavior and dress, is both announcing and acting on his membership in a dominant caste—dominant within his subculture and to a fair extent across subcultures as well. The female, announcing her sex, is both announcing and acting on her membership in the subordinated caste. She is obliged to inform others constantly and in every sort of situation that she is to be treated as an inferior, without authority, assaultable. She cannot move or speak within the usual cultural norms without engaging in self-deprecation. The male cannot move or speak without engaging in self-aggrandizement. Constant sex-identification both defines and maintains the caste boundary without which there could not be a dominance-subordination structure. . . .

The cultural and economic structures which create and enforce elaborate and rigid patterns of sex-marking and sex-announcing behavior, that is, create gender as we know it, mold us as dominators and subordinates (I do not say "mold our minds" or "mold our personalities"). They construct two classes of animals, the masculine and the feminine, where another constellation of forces might have constructed three or five categories, and not necessarily hierarchically related. Or such a spectrum of sorts that we would not experience them as "sorts" at all.

The term 'sexist' characterizes cultural and economic structures which create and enforce the elaborate and rigid patterns of sex-marking and sex-announcing which divide the species, along lines of sex, into dominators and subordinates. Individual acts and practices are sexist which reinforce and support those structures, either as culture or as shapes taken on by the enculturated animals. Resistance to sexism is that which undermines those structures by social and political action and by projects of reconstruction and revision of ourselves.

NOTE

1 "Male Chauvinism—A Conceptual Analysis," *Philosophy and Sex,* edited by Robert Baker and Frederick Elliston (Prometheus Books, Buffalo, New York, 1975), p. 66. . . .

QUESTIONS

1 What kind of institutional changes would be necessary to eliminate sexism in our society?
2 Is sexism, as Frye describes it, a form of oppression?

Something about the Subject Makes It Hard to Name

Gloria Yamato

Gloria Yamato is a visual/performing/martial artist and office manager for American Friends Service Committee in Seattle. Her published articles include "Where Are All the Colored Folks?" and "Mixed Bloods, Half Breeds, Mongrels, Hybrids. . . ."

Yamato defines *oppression* as "the systematic, institutionalized mistreatment of one group of people by another for whatever reason." In keeping with this definition, she defines racism as "the systematic, institutionalized mistreatment of one group of people by another based on racial heritage." Yamato distinguishes and discusses four types of racism: (1) aware/blatant racism, (2) aware/covert racism, (3) unaware/unintentional racism, and (4) unaware/self-righteous racism. She is especially concerned with what she calls *internalized oppression*—the belief by those who are oppressed that their oppression is deserved, natural, and right.

Racism—simple enough in structure, yet difficult to eliminate. Racism—pervasive in the U.S. culture to the point that it deeply affects all the local town folk and spills over, negatively influencing the fortunes of folk around the world. Racism is pervasive to the point that we take many of its manifestations for granted, believing "that's life." Many believe that racism can be dealt with effectively in one hellifying workshop, or one hour-long heated discussion. Many actually believe this monster, racism, that has had at least a few hundred years to take root, grow, invade our space and develop subtle variations . . . this mind-funk that distorts thought and action, can be merely wished away. I've run into folks who really think that we can beat this devil, kick this habit, be healed of this disease in a snap. In a sincere blink of a well-intentioned eye, presto—poof—racism disappears. "I've dealt with my racism . . . (envision a laying on of hands) . . . Hallelujah! Now I can go to the beach." Well, fine. Go to the beach. In fact, why don't we all go to the beach and continue to work on the sucker over there? Cuz you can't even shave a little piece off this thing called racism in a day, or a weekend, or a workshop.

When I speak of *oppression,* I'm talking about the systematic, institutionalized mistreatment of one group of people by another for whatever reason. The oppressors are purported to have an innate ability to access economic resource, information, respect, etc., while the oppressed are believed to have a corresponding negative innate ability. The flip side of oppression is *internalized oppression.* Members of the target group are emotionally, physically, and spiritually battered to the point that they begin to actually believe that their oppression is deserved, is their lot in life, is natural and right, and that it doesn't even exist. The oppression begins to feel comfortable, familiar enough that when mean ol' Massa lay down de whip, we got's to pick up and whack ourselves and each other. Like a virus, it's hard to beat racism, because by the time you come up with a cure, it's mutated to a "new cure-resistant" form. One shot just won't get it. Racism must be attacked from many angles.

The forms of racism that I pick up on these days are 1) aware/blatant racism, 2) aware/covert racism, 3) unaware/unintentional racism, and 4) unaware/self-righteous racism. I can't say that I prefer any one form of racism over the others, because they all look like an itch needing a scratch. I've heard it said (and understandably so) that the aware/blatant form of racism is preferable if one must suffer it. Outright racists will, without apology or confusion, tell us that because of our color we don't appeal to them. If we so choose, we can attempt to get the hell out of their way before we get the sweat knocked out of us. Growing up, aware/covert racism is what I heard many of my elders bemoaning "up north," after having escaped the overt racism "down south." Apartments were suddenly no longer vacant or rents were outrageously high, when black, brown, red, or yellow persons went to inquire about them. Job vacancies were suddenly filled, or we were fired for very vague reasons. It still happens, though the perpetrators really take care to cover their tracks these days. They don't want to get gummed to death or slobbered on by the toothless laws that supposedly protect us from such inequities.

Unaware/unintentional racism drives usually tranquil white liberals wild when they get called on it, and confirms the suspicions of many people of color who feel that white folks are just plain crazy. It has led white people to believe that it's just fine to ask if they can touch my hair (while reaching). They then exclaim over how soft it is, how it does not scratch their hand. It has led whites to assume that bending over backwards and speaking to me in high-pitched (terrified), condescending tones would make up for all the racist wrongs that distort our lives. This type of racism has led whites right to my doorstep, talking 'bout, "We're sorry/we love you and want to make things right," which is fine, and further, "We're gonna give you the opportunity to fix it while we sleep. Just tell us what you need. 'Bye!!"—which *ain't* fine. With the best of intentions, the best of educations, and the greatest generosity of heart, whites, operating on the misinformation fed to them from day one, will behave in ways that are racist, will perpetuate racism by being "nice" the way we're taught to be nice. You can just "nice" somebody to death with naïveté and lack of awareness of privilege. Then there's guilt and the desire to end racism and how the two get all tangled up to the point that people, morbidly fascinated with their guilt, are immobilized. Rather than deal with ending racism, they sit and ponder their guilt and hope nobody notices how awful they are. Meanwhile, racism picks up momentum and keeps on keepin' on.

Now, the newest form of racism that I'm hip to is unaware/self-righteous racism. The "good white" racist attempts to shame Blacks into being blacker, scorns Japanese-Americans who don't speak Japanese, and knows more about the Chicano/a community than the folks who make up the community. They assign themselves as the "good whites," as opposed to the "bad whites," and are often so busy telling people of color what the issues in the Black, Asian, Indian, Latino/a communities should be that they don't have time to deal with their errant sisters and brothers in the white community. Which means that people of color are still left to deal with what the "good whites" don't want to . . . racism.

Internalized racism is what really gets in my way as a Black woman. It influences the way I see or don't see myself, limits what I expect of myself or others like me. It results in my acceptance of mistreatment, leads me to believe that being treated with less than absolute respect, at least this once, is to be expected because I am Black, because I am not white. "Because I am *(you fill in the color),* you think, "Life is going to be hard." The fact is life may be hard, but the color of your skin is not the cause of the hardship. The color of your skin may be used as an excuse to mistreat you, but there is no reason or logic involved in the mistreatment. If it seems that your color is the reason; if it seems that your ethnic heritage is the cause of the woe, it's because you've been deliberately beaten down by agents of a greedy system until you swallowed the garbage. That is the internalization of racism.

Racism is the systematic, institutionalized mistreatment of one group of people by another based on racial heritage. Like every other oppression, racism can be internalized. People of color come to believe misinformation about their particular ethnic group and thus believe that their mistreatment is justified. With that basic vocabulary, let's take a look at how the whole thing works together. Meet "the Ism Family," racism, classism, ageism, adultism, elitism, sexism, heterosexism, physicalism, etc. All these ism's are systematic, that is, not only are these parasites feeding off our lives, they are also dependent on one another for foundation. Racism is supported and reinforced by classism, which is given a foothold and a boost by adultism, which also feeds sexism, which is validated by heterosexism, and so it goes on. You cannot have the "ism" functioning without first effectively installing its flipside, the internalized version of the ism. Like twins, as one particular form of the ism grows in potency, there is a corresponding increasing in its internalized form within the population. Before oppression becomes a specific ism like racism, usually all hell breaks loose. War. People fight attempts to enslave them, or to subvert their will, or to take what they consider theirs, whether that is territory or dignity. It's true that the various elements of racism, while repugnant, would not be able to do very much damage, but for one generally overlooked key piece: power/privilege.

While in one sense we all have power we have to look at the fact that, in our society, people are stratified into various classes and some of these classes have more privilege than others. The owning class has enough power and privilege to not have to give a good whinney what the rest of the folks have on their minds. The power and privilege of the owning class provides the ability to pay off enough of the working class and offer that paid-off group, the middle class, just enough privilege to make it agreeable to do various and sundry oppressive things to other working-class and outright disenfranchised folk, keeping the lid on explosive inequities, at least for a minute. If you're at the bottom of this heap, and you believe the line that says you're there because that's all you're worth, it is at least some small solace to believe that there are others more worthless than you, because of their gender, race, sexual preference . . . whatever. The specific form of power that runs the show here is the power to intimidate. The power to take away the most lives the quickest, and back it up with legal and "divine" sanction, is the very bottom line. It makes the difference between who's holding the racism end of the stick and who's getting beat with it (or beating others as vulnerable as they are) on the internalized racism end of the stick. What I am saying is, while people of color are welcome to tear up their own neighborhoods and each other, everybody knows that you cannot do that to white folks without hell to pay. People of color can be prejudiced against one another and whites, but do not have an ice-cube's chance in hell of passing laws that will get whites sent to relocation camps "for their own protection and the security of the nation." People who have not thought about or refuse to acknowledge this imbalance of power/privilege often want to talk about the racism of people of color. But then that is one of the ways racism is able to continue to function. You look for someone to blame and you blame the victim, who will nine times out of ten accept the blame out of habit.

So, what can we do? Acknowledge racism for a start, even though and especially when we've struggled to be kind and fair, or struggled to rise above it all. It is hard to acknowledge the fact that racism circumscribes and pervades our lives. Racism must be dealt with on two levels, personal and societal, emotional and institutional. It is possible—and most effective—to do both at the same time. We must reclaim whatever delight we have lost in our own ethnic heritage or heritages. This so-called melting pot has only succeeded in turning us into fast food–gobbling "generics" (as in generic "white folks" who were once Irish, Polish, Russian, English, etc. and "black folks," who were once Ashanti, Bambara, Baule, Yoruba, etc.) Find or create safe places to actually *feel* what we've been forced to repress each time we were a victim of, witness to or perpetrator of racism, so that we do not continue, like puppets, to act out the past in the present and future. Challenge oppression. Take a stand against it. When you are aware of something oppressive going down, stop the show. At least call it. We become so numbed to racism that we don't even think twice about it, unless it is immediately life-threatening.

Whites who want to be allies to people of color: You can educate yourselves via research and observation rather than rigidly, arrogantly relying solely on interrogating people of color. Do not expect that people of color should teach you how to behave non-oppressively. Do not give into the pull to be lazy. Think, hard. Do not blame people of color for your frustration about racism, but do appreciate the fact that people of color will often help you get in touch with that frustration. Assume that your effort to be a good friend is appreciated, but don't expect or accept gratitude from people of color. Work on racism for your sake, not "their" sake. Assume that you are needed and capable of being a good ally. Know that you'll make mistakes and commit yourself to correcting them and continuing on as an ally, no matter what. Don't give up.

People of color, working through internalized racism: Remember always that you and others like you are completely worthy of respect, completely capable of achieving whatever you take a notion to do. Remember that the term "people of color" refers to a variety of ethnic and cultural backgrounds. These various groups have been oppressed in a variety of ways. Educate yourself about the ways different peoples have been oppressed and how they've resisted that oppression. Expect and insist that whites are capable of being good allies against racism. Don't give up. Resist the pull to give out the "people of color seal of approval" to aspiring white allies. A moment of appreciation is fine, but more than that tends to be less than helpful. Celebrate yourself. Celebrate yourself. Celebrate the inevitable end of racism.

QUESTIONS

1 If individuals do not think of themselves as oppressed, can it still be true that they are oppressed?
2 Is unaware racism worse than aware racism?

Oppression

Marilyn Frye

A biographical sketch of Marilyn Frye is found on p. 257.

Frye maintains that we need to distinguish between suffering and oppression. While it is true that both men and women suffer in all sorts of ways, women, unlike men, are oppressed in our society. In her view, oppression involves severe and systematically related limitations on one's choices. She describes the experience of oppression as one of "being caged in," with "all avenues, in every direction, . . . blocked or booby trapped."

It is a fundamental claim of feminism that women are oppressed. The word 'oppression' is a strong word. It repels and attracts. It is dangerous and dangerously fashionable and endangered. It is much misused, and sometimes not innocently.

The statement that women are oppressed is frequently met with the claim that men are oppressed too. We hear that oppressing is oppressive to those who oppress as well as to those they oppress. Some men cite as evidence of their oppression their much-advertised inability to cry. It is tough, we are told, to be masculine. When the stresses and frustrations of being a man are cited as evidence that oppressors are oppressed by their oppressing, the word 'oppression' is being stretched to meaninglessness; it is treated as though its scope includes any and all human experience of limitation or suffering, no matter the cause, degree or consequence. Once such usage has been put over on us, then if ever we deny that any person or group is oppressed, we seem to imply that we think they never suffer and have no feelings. We are accused of insensitivity; even of bigotry. For women, such accusation is particularly intimidating, since sensitivity is one of the few virtues that has been assigned to us.

Reprinted with permission of The Crossing Press from Marilyn Frye, *The Politics of Reality: Essays in Feminist Theory* (1983), pp. 1–7.

If we are found insensitive, we may fear we have no redeeming traits at all and perhaps are not real women. Thus are we silenced before we begin: the name of our situation drained of meaning and our guilt mechanisms tripped.

But this is nonsense. Human beings can be miserable without being oppressed, and it is perfectly consistent to deny that a person or group is oppressed without denying that they have feelings or that they suffer.

We need to think clearly about oppression, and there is much that mitigates against this. I do not want to undertake to prove that women are oppressed (or that men are not), but I want to make clear what is being said when we say it. We need this word, this concept, and we need it to be sharp and sure.

. . . The root of the word 'oppression' is the element 'press'. *The press of the crowd; pressed into military service; to press a pair of pants; printing press; press the button.* Presses are used to mold things or flatten them or reduce them in bulk, sometimes to reduce them by squeezing out the gasses or liquids in them. Something pressed is something caught between or among forces and barriers which are so related to each other that jointly they restrain, restrict or prevent the thing's motion or mobility. Mold. Immobilize. Reduce.

The mundane experience of the oppressed provides another clue. One of the most characteristic and ubiquitous features of the world as experienced by oppressed people is the double bind—situations in which options are reduced to a very few and all of them expose one to penalty, censure or deprivation. For example, it is often a requirement upon oppressed people that we smile and be cheerful. If we comply, we signal our docility and our acquiescence in our situation. We need not, then, be taken note of. We acquiesce in being made invisible, in our occupying no space. We participate in our own erasure. On the other hand, anything but the sunniest countenance exposes us to being perceived as mean, bitter, angry or dangerous. This means, at the least, that we may be found "difficult" or unpleasant to work with, which is enough to cost one one's livelihood; at worst, being seen as mean, bitter, angry or dangerous has been known to result in rape, arrest, beating and murder. One can only choose to risk one's preferred form and rate of annihilation.

Another example: It is common in the United States that women, especially younger women, are in a bind where neither sexual activity nor sexual inactivity is all right. If she is heterosexually active, a woman is open to censure and punishment for being loose, unprincipled or a whore. The "punishment" comes in the form of criticism, snide and embarrassing remarks, being treated as an easy lay by men, scorn from her more restrained female friends. She may have to lie and hide her behavior from her parents. She must juggle the risks of unwanted pregnancy and dangerous contraceptives. On the other hand, if she refrains from heterosexual activity, she is fairly constantly harassed by men who try to persuade her into it and pressure her to "relax" and "let her hair down"; she is threatened with labels like "frigid," "uptight," "man-hater," "bitch" and "cocktease." The same parents who would be disapproving of her sexual activity may be worried by her inactivity because it suggests she is not or will not be popular, or is not sexually normal. She may be charged with lesbianism. If a woman is raped, then if she has been heterosexually active she is subject to the presumption that she liked it (since her activity is presumed to show that she likes sex), and if she has not been heterosexually active, she is subject to the presumption that she liked it (since she is supposedly "repressed and frustrated"). Both heterosexual activity and heterosexual nonactivity are likely to be taken as proof that you wanted to be raped, and hence, of course, weren't *really* raped at all. You can't win. You are caught in a bind, caught between systematically related pressures.

Women are caught like this, too, by networks of forces and barriers that expose one to penalty, loss or contempt whether one works outside the home or not, is on welfare or not, bears children or not, raises children or not, marries or not, stays married or not, is heterosexual, lesbian, both or neither. Economic necessity; confinement to racial and/or sexual job ghettos; sexual harassment; sex discrimination; pressures of competing expectations and judgments about *women, wives* and *mothers* (in the society at large, in racial and ethnic subcultures and in one's own mind); dependence (full or partial) on husbands, parents or the state; commitment to political ideas; loyalties to racial or ethnic or other "minority" groups; the demands of self-respect and responsibilities to others. Each of these factors exists in complex tension with every other, penalizing or prohibiting all of the apparently available options. And nipping at one's heels, always, is the endless pack of little things. If one dresses one way, one is subject to the assumption that one is advertising one's sexual availability; if one dresses another way, one appears to "not care about oneself" or to be "unfeminine." If one uses "strong language," one invites categorization as a whore or slut; if one does not, one invites categorization as a "lady"—one too delicately constituted to cope with robust speech or the realities to which it presumably refers.

The experience of oppressed people is that the living of one's life is confined and shaped by forces and barriers which are not accidental or occasional and hence avoidable, but are systematically related to each other in such a way as to catch one between and among them and restrict or penalize motion in any direction. It is the experience of being caged in: all avenues, in every direction, are blocked or booby trapped.

Cages. Consider a birdcage. If you look very closely at just one wire in the cage, you cannot see the other wires. If your conception of what is before you is determined by this myopic focus, you could look at that one wire, up and down the length of it, and be unable to see why a bird would not just fly around the wire any time it wanted to go somewhere. Furthermore, even if, one day at a time, you myopically inspected each wire, you still could not see why a bird would have trouble going past the wires to get anywhere. There is no physical property of any one wire, *nothing* that the closest scrutiny could discover, that will reveal how a bird could be inhibited or harmed by it except in the most accidental way. It is only when you step back, stop looking at the wires one by one, microscopically, and take a macroscopic view of the whole cage, that you can see why the bird does not go anywhere; and then you will see it in a moment. It will require no great subtlety of mental powers. It is perfectly *obvious* that the bird is surrounded by a network of systematically related barriers, no one of which would be the least hindrance to its flight, but which, by their relations to each other, are as confining as the solid walls of a dungeon.

It is now possible to grasp one of the reasons why oppression can be hard to see and recognize: one can study the elements of an oppressive structure with great care and some good will without seeing the structure as a whole, and hence without seeing or being able to understand that one is looking at a cage and that there are people there who are caged, whose motion and mobility are restricted, whose lives are shaped and reduced.

The arresting of vision at a microscopic level yields such common confusion as that about the male door-opening ritual. This ritual, which is remarkably widespread across classes and races, puzzles many people, some of whom do and some of whom do not find it offensive. Look at the scene of the two people approaching a door. The male steps slightly ahead and opens the door. The male holds the door open while the female glides through. Then the male goes through. The door closes after them. "Now how," one innocently asks, "can those crazy womenslibbers say that is oppressive? The guy *removed* a barrier to the lady's smooth and unruffled progress." But each repetition of this ritual has a place in a pattern, in fact in several patterns. One has to shift the level of one's perception in order to see the whole picture.

The door-opening pretends to be a helpful service, but the helpfulness is false. This can be seen by noting that it will be done whether or not it makes any practical sense. Infirm men and men burdened with packages will open doors for able-bodied women who are free of physical burdens. Men will impose themselves awkwardly and jostle everyone in order to get to the door first. The act is not determined by convenience or grace. Furthermore, these very numerous acts of unneeded or even noisome "help" occur in counterpoint to a pattern of men not being helpful in many practical ways in which women might welcome help. What *women* experience is a world in which gallant princes charming commonly make a fuss about being helpful and providing small services when help and services are of little or no use, but in which there are rarely ingenious and adroit princes at hand when substantial assistance is really wanted either in mundane affairs or in situations of threat, assault or terror. There is no help with the (his) laundry; no help typing a report at 4:00 A.M.; no help in mediating disputes among relatives or children. There is nothing but advice that women should stay indoors after dark, be chaperoned by a man, or when it comes down to it, "lie back and enjoy it."

The gallant gestures have no practical meaning. Their meaning is symbolic. The door-opening and similar services provided are services which really are needed by people who are for one reason or another incapacitated—unwell, burdened with parcels, etc. So the message is that women are incapable. The detachment of the acts from the concrete realities of what women need and do not need is a vehicle for the message that women's actual needs and interests are unimportant or irrelevant. Finally, these gestures imitate the behavior of servants toward masters and thus mock women, who are in most respects the servants and caretakers of men. The message of the false helpfulness of male gallantry is female dependence, the invisibility or insignificance of women, and contempt for women.

One cannot see the meanings of these rituals if one's focus is riveted upon the individual event in all its particularity, including the particularity of the individual man's present conscious intentions and motives and the individual woman's conscious perception of the event in the moment. It seems sometimes that people take a deliberately myopic view and fill their eyes with things seen microscopically in order not to see macroscopically. At any rate, whether it is deliberate or not, people can and do fail to see the oppression of women because they fail to see macroscopically and hence fail to see the various elements of the situation as systematically related in larger schemes.

As the cageness of the birdcage is a macroscopic phenomenon, the oppressiveness of the situations in which women live our various and different lives is a macroscopic phenomenon. Neither can be *seen* from a microscopic perspective. But when you look macroscopically you can see it—a network of forces and barriers which are systematically related and which conspire to the immobilization, reduction and molding of women and the lives we live. . . .

QUESTIONS

1 Are there any good reasons for holding that men in our society are oppressed simply by virtue of being men and not because of their membership in a targeted group?

2 Can an action be sexist even though the individual who performs it sees it simply as a thoughtful or polite action?

Five Faces of Oppression

Iris M. Young

Iris M. Young is professor of public policy and international affairs at the University of Pittsburgh. She is the author of *Throwing Like a Girl and Other Essays in Feminist Philosophy and Social Theory* (1990) and *Justice and the Politics of Difference* (1990), from which this selection is excerpted. She is also the coeditor of *The Thinking Muse: Feminism and Modern French Philosophy* (1989).

In Young's view, all oppressed people have something in common: They all suffer some inhibition of their ability to develop and exercise their capacities and express their needs, thoughts, and feelings. However, no one set of criteria can be used to describe the condition of all those who are oppressed. Rather, oppression takes multiple forms: exploitation, marginalization, powerlessness, cultural imperialism, and systematic violence. In Young's view, the presence of even one of these five conditions is sufficient for calling a group oppressed.

Many people in the United States would not choose the term "oppression" to name injustice in our society. For contemporary emancipatory social movements, on the other hand—socialists, radical feminists, American Indian activists, Black activists, gay and lesbian activists—oppression is a central category of political discourse. Entering the political discourse in which oppression is a central category involves adopting a general mode of analyzing and evaluating social structures and practices which is incommensurate with the language of liberal individualism that dominates political discourse in the United States.

A major political project for those of us who identify with at least one of these movements must thus be to persuade people that the discourse of oppression makes sense of much of our social experience. We are ill prepared for this task, however, because we have no clear account of the meaning of oppression. While we find the term used often in the diverse philosophical and theoretical literature spawned by radical social movements in the United States, we find little direct discussion of the meaning of the concept as used by these movements.

In this [essay] I offer some explication of the concept of oppression as I understand its use by new social movements in the United States since the 1960s. My starting point is reflection on the conditions of the groups said by these movements to be oppressed: among others women, Blacks, Chicanos, Puerto Ricans and other Spanish-speaking Americans, American Indians, Jews, lesbians, gay men, Arabs, Asians, old people, working-class people, and the physically and mentally disabled. I aim to systematize the meaning of the concept of oppression as used by these diverse political movements, and to provide normative argument to clarify the wrongs the term names.

Obviously the above-named groups are not oppressed to the same extent or in the same ways. In the most general sense, all oppressed people suffer some inhibition of their ability to develop and exercise their capacities and express their needs, thoughts, and feelings. In that abstract sense all oppressed people face a common condition. Beyond that, in any more specific sense, it is not possible to define a single set of criteria that describe the condition of oppression of the above groups. Consequently, attempts by theorists and activists to discover a common description or the essential causes of the oppression of all these groups have frequently led to fruitless disputes about whose oppression is more fundamental or more grave. The contexts in which members of these groups use the term oppression to describe the injustices of their situation suggest that oppression names in fact a family of concepts and conditions, which I divide into five categories: exploitation, marginalization, powerlessness, cultural imperialism, and violence. . . .

THE FACES OF OPPRESSION

Exploitation

The central function of Marx's theory of exploitation is to explain how class structure can exist in the absence of legally and normatively sanctioned class distinctions. In precapitalist societies domination is overt and accomplished through directly political means. In both slave society and feudal society the right to appropriate the product of the labor of others partly defines class privilege, and these societies legitimate class distinctions with ideologies of natural superiority and inferiority.

Capitalist society, on the other hand, removes traditional juridically enforced class distinctions and promotes a belief in the legal freedom of persons. Workers freely contract with employers and receive a wage; no formal mechanisms of law or custom force them to work for that employer or any employer. Thus the mystery of capitalism arises: when everyone is formally free, how can there be class domination? Why do class distinctions persist between the wealthy, who own the means of production, and the mass of people, who work for them? The theory of exploitation answers this question.

Profit, the basis of capitalist power and wealth, is a mystery if we assume that in the market goods exchange at their values. The labor theory of value dispels this mystery. Every commodity's value is a function of the labor time necessary for its production. Labor power is the one commodity which in the process of being consumed produces new value. Profit comes from the difference between the value of the labor performed and the value of the capacity to labor which the capitalist purchases. Profit is possible only because the owner of capital appropriates any realized surplus value. . . .

Marx's theory of exploitation lacks an explicitly normative meaning, even though the judgment that workers are exploited clearly has normative as well as descriptive power in that theory. C. B. Macpherson (1973, chap. 3) reconstructs this theory of exploitation in a more explicitly normative form. The injustice of capitalist society consists in the fact that some people exercise their capacities under the control, according to the purposes, and for the benefit of other people. Through private ownership of the means of production, and through markets that allocate labor and the ability to buy goods, capitalism systematically transfers the powers of some persons to others, thereby augmenting the power of the latter. In this process of the transfer of powers, according to Macpherson, the capitalist class acquires and maintains an ability to extract benefits from workers. Not only are powers transferred from workers to capitalists, but also the powers of workers diminish by more than the amount of transfer, because workers suffer material deprivation and a loss of control, and hence are deprived of important elements of self-respect. Justice, then, requires eliminating the institutional forms that enable and enforce this process of transference and replacing them with institutional forms that enable all to develop and use their capacities in a way that does not inhibit, but rather can enhance, similar development and use in others.

The central insight expressed in the concept of exploitation, then, is that this oppression occurs through a steady process of the transfer of the results of the labor of one social group to benefit another. The injustice of class division does not consist only in the distributive fact that some people have great wealth while most people have little. Exploitation enacts a structural relation between social groups. Social rules about what work is, who does what for whom, how work is compensated, and the social process by which the results of work are appropriated operate to enact relations of power and inequality. These relations are produced and reproduced through a systematic process in which the energies of the have-nots are continuously expended to maintain and augment the power, status, and wealth of the haves. . . .

Feminists have had little difficulty showing that women's oppression consists partly in a systematic and unreciprocated transfer of powers from women to men.

Women's oppression consists not merely in an inequality of status, power, and wealth resulting from men's excluding them from privileged activities. The freedom, power, status, and self-realization of men is possible precisely because women work for them. Gender exploitation has two aspects, transfer of the fruits of material labor to men and transfer of nurturing and sexual energies to men.

Christine Delphy (1984), for example, describes marriage as a class relation in which women's labor benefits men without comparable remuneration. She makes it clear that the exploitation consists not in the sort of work that women do in the home, for this might include various kinds of tasks, but in the fact that they perform tasks for someone on whom they are dependent. Thus, for example, in most systems of agricultural production in the world, men take to market the goods women have produced, and more often than not men receive the status and often the entire income from this labor.

With the concept of sex-affective production, Ann Ferguson (1984; 1989, chap. 4) identifies another form of the transference of women's energies to men. Women provide men and children with emotional care and provide men with sexual satisfaction, and as a group receive relatively little of either from men. The gender socialization of women makes us tend to be more attentive to interactive dynamics than men, and makes women good at providing empathy and support for people's feelings and at smoothing over interactive tensions. Both men and women look to women as nurturers of their personal lives, and women frequently complain that when they look to men for emotional support they do not receive it. The norms of heterosexuality, moreover, are oriented around male pleasure, and consequently many women receive little satisfaction from their sexual interaction with men.

Most feminist theories of gender exploitation have concentrated on the institutional structure of the patriarchal family. Recently, however, feminists have begun to explore relations of gender exploitation enacted in the contemporary workplace and through the state. Carol Brown argues that as men have removed themselves from responsibility for children, many women have become dependent on the state for subsistence as they continue to bear nearly total responsibility for childrearing (Brown, 1981). This creates a new system of the exploitation of women's domestic labor mediated by state institutions, which she calls public patriarchy.

In twentieth-century capitalist economies the workplaces that women have been entering in increasing numbers serve as another important site of gender exploitation. David Alexander (1987) argues that typically feminine jobs involve gender-based tasks requiring sexual labor, nurturing, caring for others' bodies, or smoothing over workplace tensions. In these ways women's energies are expended in jobs that enhance the status of, please, or comfort others, usually men; and these gender-based labors of waitresses, clerical workers, nurses, and other caretakers often go unnoticed and undercompensated.

To summarize, women are exploited in the Marxist sense to the degree that they are wage workers. Some have argued that women's domestic labor also represents a form of capitalist class exploitation insofar as it is labor covered by the wages a family receives. As a group, however, women undergo specific forms of gender exploitation in which their energies and power are expended, often unnoticed and unacknowledged, usually to benefit men by releasing them for more important and creative work, enhancing their status or the environment around them, or providing them with sexual or emotional service.

Race is a structure of oppression at least as basic as class or gender. Are there, then, racially specific forms of exploitation? There is no doubt that racialized groups in the United States, especially Blacks and Latinos, are oppressed through capitalist superexploitation resulting from a segmented labor market that tends to reserve skilled, high-paying, unionized jobs for whites. There is wide disagreement about whether such superexploitation benefits whites as a group or only benefits the capitalist class and I do not intend to enter into that dispute here.

However one answers the question about capitalist superexploitation of racialized groups, is it possible to conceptualize a form of exploitation that is racially specific on analogy with the gender-specific forms just discussed? I suggest that the category of *menial* labor might supply a means for such conceptualization. In its derivation "menial" designates the labor of servants. Wherever there is racism, there is the assumption, more or less enforced, that members of the oppressed racial groups are or ought to be servants of those, or some of those, in the privileged group. In most white racist societies this means that many white people have dark- or yellow-skinned domestic servants, and in the United States today there remains significant racial structuring of private household service. But in the United States today much service labor has gone public: anyone who goes to a good hotel or a good restaurant can have servants. Servants often attend the daily—and nightly—activities of business executives, government officials, and other high-status professionals. In our society there remains strong cultural pressure to fill servant jobs—bellhop, porter, chambermaid, busboy, and so on—with Black and Latino workers. These jobs entail a transfer of energies whereby the servers enhance the status of the served.

Menial labor usually refers not only to service, however, but also to any servile, unskilled, low-paying work lacking in autonomy, in which a person is subject to taking orders from many people. Menial work tends to be auxiliary work, instrumental to the work of others, where those others receive primary recognition for doing the job. Laborers on a construction site, for example, are at the beck and call of welders, electricians, carpenters, and other skilled workers, who receive recognition for the job done. In the United States explicit racial discrimination once reserved menial work for Blacks, Chicanos, American Indians, and Chinese, and menial work still tends to be linked to Black and Latino workers. I offer this category of menial labor as a form of racially specific exploitation, as a provisional category in need of exploration. . . .

Marginalization

Increasingly in the United States racial oppression occurs in the form of marginalization rather than exploitation. Marginals are people the system of labor cannot or will not use. Not only in Third World capitalist countries, but also in most Western capitalist societies, there is a growing underclass of people permanently confined to lives of social marginality, most of whom are racially marked—Blacks or Indians in Latin America, and Blacks, East Indians, Eastern Europeans, or North Africans in Europe.

Marginalization is by no means the fate only of racially marked groups, however. In the United States a shamefully large proportion of the population is marginal: old people, and increasingly people who are not very old but get laid off from their jobs and cannot find new work; young people, especially Black or Latino, who cannot find first or second jobs; many single mothers and their children; other people involuntarily unemployed; many mentally and physically disabled people; American Indians, especially those on reservations.

Marginalization is perhaps the most dangerous form of oppression. A whole category of people is expelled from useful participation in social life and thus potentially subjected to severe material deprivation and even extermination. The material deprivation marginalization often causes is certainly unjust, especially in a society where others have plenty. Contemporary advanced capitalist societies have in principle acknowledged the injustice of material deprivation caused by marginalization, and have taken some steps to address it by providing welfare payments and services. The continuance of this welfare state is by no means assured, and in most welfare state societies, especially the United States, welfare redistributions do not eliminate large-scale suffering and deprivation.

Material deprivation, which can be addressed by redistributive social policies, is not, however, the extent of the harm caused by marginalization. Two categories of injustice beyond distribution are associated with marginality in advanced capitalist societies. First, the provision of welfare itself produces new injustice by depriving those dependent on it of rights and freedoms that others have. Second, even when material deprivation is somewhat mitigated by the welfare state, marginalization is unjust because it blocks the opportunity to exercise capacities in socially defined and recognized ways. I shall explicate each of these in turn.

Liberalism has traditionally asserted the right of all rational autonomous agents to equal citizenship. Early bourgeois liberalism explicitly excluded from citizenship all those whose reason was questionable or not fully developed, and all those not independent. Thus poor people, women, the mad and the feebleminded, and children were explicitly excluded from citizenship, and many of these were housed in institutions modeled on the modern prison: poorhouses, insane asylums, schools.

Today the exclusion of dependent persons from equal citizenship rights is only barely hidden beneath the surface. Because they depend on bureaucratic institutions for support or services, the old, the poor, and the mentally or physically disabled are subject to patronizing, punitive, demeaning, and arbitrary treatment by the policies and people associated with welfare bureaucracies. Being a dependent in our society implies being legitimately subject to the often arbitrary and invasive authority of social service providers and other public and private administrators, who enforce rules with which the marginal must comply, and otherwise exercise power over the conditions of their lives. In meeting needs of the marginalized, often with the aid of social scientific disciplines, welfare agencies also construct the needs themselves. Medical and social service professionals know what is good for those they serve, and the marginals and dependents themselves do not have the right to claim to know what is good for them. Dependency in our society thus implies, as it has in all liberal societies, a sufficient warrant to suspend basic rights to privacy, respect, and individual choice.

Although dependency produces conditions of injustice in our society, dependency in itself need not be oppressive. One cannot imagine a society in which some people would not need to be dependent on others at least some of the time: children, sick people, women recovering from childbirth, old people who have become frail, depressed or otherwise emotionally needy persons, have the moral right to depend on others for subsistence and support.

An important contribution of feminist moral theory has been to question the deeply held assumption that moral agency and full citizenship require that a person be autonomous and independent. Feminists have exposed this assumption as inappropriately individualistic and derived from a specifically male experience of social relations, which values competition and solitary achievement. Female experience of social relations, arising both from women's typical domestic care responsibilities and from the kinds of paid work that many women do, tends to recognize dependence as a basic human condition. Whereas on the autonomy model a just society would as much as possible give people the opportunity to be independent, the feminist model envisions justice as according respect and participation in decisionmaking to those who are dependent as well as to those who are independent. Dependency should not be a reason to be deprived of choice and respect, and much of the oppression many marginals experience would be lessened if a less individualistic model of rights prevailed.

Marginalization does not cease to be oppressive when one has shelter and food. Many old people, for example, have sufficient means to live comfortably but remain oppressed in their marginal status. Even if marginals were provided a comfortable material life within institutions that respected their freedom and dignity, injustices of marginality would remain in the form of uselessness, boredom, and lack of self-respect. Most of our society's productive and recognized activities take place in contexts of organized social cooperation, and social structures and processes that close persons out of participation in such social cooperation are unjust. Thus while marginalization definitely entails serious issues of distributive justice, it also involves the deprivation of cultural, practical, and institutionalized conditions for exercising capacities in a context of recognition and interaction. . . .

Powerlessness

As I have indicated, the Marxist idea of class is important because it helps reveal the structure of exploitation: that some people have their power and wealth because they profit from the labor of others. For this reason I reject the claim some make that a traditional class exploitation model fails to capture the structure of contemporary society. It remains the case that the labor of most people in the society augments the power of relatively few. Despite their differences from nonprofessional workers, most professional workers are still not members of the capitalist class. Professional labor either involves exploitative transfers to capitalists or supplies important conditions for such transfers. Professional workers are in an ambiguous class position, it is true, because . . . they also benefit from the exploitation of nonprofessional workers.

While it is false to claim that a division between capitalist and working classes no longer describes our society, it is also false to say that class relations have remained unaltered since the nineteenth century. An adequate conception of oppression cannot ignore the experience of social division reflected in the colloquial distinction between the "middle class" and the "working class," a division structured by the social division of labor between professionals and nonprofessionals. Professionals are privileged in relation to nonprofessionals, by virtue of their position in the division of labor and the status it carries. Nonprofessionals suffer a form of oppression in addition to exploitation, which I call powerlessness.

In the United States, as in other advanced capitalist countries, most workplaces are not organized democratically, direct participation in public policy decisions is rare, and policy implementation is for the most part hierarchical, imposing rules on bureaucrats and citizens. Thus most people in these societies do not regularly participate in making decisions that affect the conditions of their lives and actions, and in this sense most people lack significant power. At the same time, domination in modern society is enacted through the widely dispersed powers of many agents mediating the decisions of others. To that extent many people have some power in relation to others, even though they lack the power to decide policies or results. The powerless are those who lack authority or power even in this mediated sense, those over whom power is exercised without their exercising it; the powerless are situated so that they must take orders and rarely have the right to give them. Powerlessness also designates a position in the division of labor and the concomitant social position that allows persons little opportunity to develop and exercise skills. The powerless have little or no work autonomy, exercise little creativity or judgment in their work, have no technical expertise or authority, express themselves awkwardly, especially in public or bureaucratic settings, and do not command respect. Powerlessness names the oppressive situations Sennett and Cobb (1972) describe in their famous study of working-class men.

This powerless status is perhaps best described negatively: the powerless lack the authority, status, and sense of self that professionals tend to have. The status privilege of professionals has three aspects, the lack of which produces oppression for nonprofessionals.

First, acquiring and practicing a profession has an expansive, progressive character. Being professional usually requires a college education and the acquisition of a specialized knowledge that entails working with symbols and concepts. Professionals experience progress first in acquiring the expertise, and then in the course of professional advancement and rise in status. The life of the nonprofessional by comparison is powerless in the sense that it lacks this orientation toward the progressive development of capacities and avenues for recognition.

Second, while many professionals have supervisors and cannot directly influence many decisions or the actions of many people, most nevertheless have considerable day-to-day work autonomy. Professionals usually have some authority over others, moreover—either over workers they supervise, or over auxiliaries, or over clients.

Nonprofessionals, on the other hand, lack autonomy, and in both their working and their consumer-client lives often stand under the authority of professionals.

Though based on a division of labor between "mental" and "manual" work, the distinction between "middle class" and "working class" designates a division not only in working life, but also in nearly all aspects of social life. Professionals and non-professionals belong to different cultures in the United States. The two groups tend to live in segregated neighborhoods or even different towns, a process itself mediated by planners, zoning officials, and real estate people. The groups tend to have different tastes in food, decor, clothes, music, and vacations, and often different health and educational needs. Members of each group socialize for the most part with others in the same status group. While there is some intergroup mobility between generations, for the most part the children of professionals become professionals and the children of nonprofessionals do not.

Thus, third, the privileges of the professional extend beyond the workplace to a whole way of life. I call this way of life "respectability." To treat people with respect is to be prepared to listen to what they have to say or to do what they request because they have some authority, expertise, or influence. The norms of respectability in our society are associated specifically with professional culture. Professional dress, speech, tastes, demeanor, all connote respectability. Generally professionals expect and receive respect from others. In restaurants, banks, hotels, real estate offices, and many other such public places, as well as in the media, professionals typically receive more respectful treatment than nonprofessionals. For this reason nonprofessionals seeking a loan or a job, or to buy a house or a car, will often try to look "professional" and "respectable" in those settings.

The privilege of this professional respectability appears starkly in the dynamics of racism and sexism. In daily interchange women and men of color must prove their respectability. At first they are often not treated by strangers with respectful distance or deference. Once people discover that this woman or that Puerto Rican man is a college teacher or a business executive, however, they often behave more respectfully toward her or him. Working-class white men, on the other hand, are often treated with respect until their working-class status is revealed. . . .

Cultural Imperialism

Exploitation, marginalization, and powerlessness all refer to relations of power and oppression that occur by virtue of the social division of labor—who works for whom, who does not work, and how the content of work defines one institutional position relative to others. These three categories refer to structural and institutional relations that delimit people's material lives, including but not restricted to the resources they have access to and the concrete opportunities they have or do not have to develop and exercise their capacities. These kinds of oppression are a matter of concrete power in relation to others—of who benefits from whom, and who is dispensable.

Recent theorists of movements of group liberation, notably feminist and Black liberation theorists, have also given prominence to a rather different form of oppression, which following Lugones and Spelman (1983) I shall call cultural imperialism. To experience cultural imperialism means to experience how the dominant meanings of a society render the particular perspective of one's own group invisible at the same time as they stereotype one's group and mark it out as the Other.

Cultural imperialism involves the universalization of a dominant group's experience and culture, and its establishment as the norm. Some groups have exclusive or primary access to what Nancy Fraser (1987) calls the means of interpretation and communication in a society. As a consequence, the dominant cultural products of the society, that is, those most widely disseminated, express the experience, values, goals, and achievements of these groups. Often without noticing they do so, the dominant groups project their own experience as representative of humanity as such. Cultural products also express the dominant group's perspective on and interpretation of events and elements in the society, including other groups in the society, insofar as they attain cultural status at all.

An encounter with other groups, however, can challenge the dominant group's claim to universality. The dominant group reinforces its position by bringing the other groups under the measure of its dominant norms. Consequently, the difference of women from men, American Indians or Africans from Europeans, Jews from Christians, homosexuals from heterosexuals, workers from professionals, becomes reconstructed largely as deviance and inferiority. Since only the dominant group's cultural expressions receive wide dissemination, their cultural expressions become the normal, or the universal, and thereby the unremarkable. Given the normality of its own cultural expressions and identity, the dominant group constructs the differences which some groups exhibit as lack and negation. These groups become marked as Other.

The culturally dominated undergo a paradoxical oppression, in that they are both marked out by stereotypes and at the same time rendered invisible. As remarkable, deviant beings, the culturally imperialized are stamped with an essence. The stereotypes confine them to a nature which is often attached in some way to their bodies, and which thus cannot easily be denied. These stereotypes so permeate the society that they are not noticed as contestable. Just as everyone knows that the earth goes around the sun, so everyone knows that gay people are promiscuous, that Indians are alcoholics, and that women are good with children. White males, on the other hand, insofar as they escape group marking, can be individuals.

Those living under cultural imperialism find themselves defined from the outside, positioned, placed, by a network of dominant meanings they experience as arising from elsewhere, from those with whom they do not identify and who do not identify with them. Consequently, the dominant culture's stereotyped and inferiorized images of the group must be internalized by group members at least to the extent that they are forced to react to behavior of others influenced by those images. This creates for the culturally oppressed the experience that W.E.B. Du Bois called "double consciousness"—"this sense of always looking at one's self through the eyes of others, of measuring one's soul by the tape of a world that looks on in amused contempt and pity" (Du Bois, 1969 [1903], p. 45). Double consciousness arises when the oppressed subject refuses to coincide with these devalued, objectified, stereotyped visions of herself or himself. While the subject desires recognition as human, capable of activity, full of hope and possibility, she receives from the dominant culture only the judgment that she is different, marked, or inferior.

The group defined by the dominant culture as deviant, as a stereotyped Other, *is* culturally different from the dominant group, because the status of Otherness creates specific experiences not shared by the dominant group, and because culturally oppressed groups also are often socially segregated and occupy specific positions in the social division of labor. Members of such groups express their specific group experiences and interpretations of the world to one another, developing and perpetuating their own culture. Double consciousness, then, occurs because one finds one's being defined by two cultures: a dominant and a subordinate culture. Because they can affirm and recognize one another as sharing similar experiences and perspectives on social life, people in culturally imperialized groups can often maintain a sense of positive subjectivity.

Cultural imperialism involves the paradox of experiencing oneself as invisible at the same time that one is marked out as different. The invisibility comes about when dominant groups fail to recognize the perspective embodied in their cultural expressions as a perspective. These dominant cultural expressions often simply have little place for the experience of other groups, at most only mentioning or referring to them in stereotyped or marginalized ways. This, then, is the injustice of cultural imperialism: that the oppressed group's own experience and interpretation of social life finds little expression that touches the dominant culture, while that same culture imposes on the oppressed group its experience and interpretation of social life. . . .

Violence

Finally, many groups suffer the oppression of systematic violence. Members of some groups live with the knowledge that they must fear random, unprovoked attacks on their persons or property, which have no motive but to damage, humiliate, or destroy the person. In American society women, Blacks, Asians, Arabs, gay men, and lesbians live under such threats of violence, and in at least some regions Jews, Puerto Ricans, Chicanos, and other Spanish-speaking Americans must fear such violence as well. Physical violence against these groups is shockingly frequent. Rape Crisis Center networks estimate that more than one-third of all American women experience an attempted or successful sexual assault in their lifetimes. Manning Marable (1984, pp. 238–41) catalogues a large number of incidents of racist violence and terror against blacks in the United States between 1980 and 1982. He cites dozens of incidents of the severe beating, killing, or rape of Blacks by police officers on duty, in which the police involved were acquitted of any wrongdoing. In 1981, moreover, there were at least five hundred documented cases of random white teenage violence against Blacks. Violence against gay men and lesbians is not only common, but has been increasing in the last five years. While the frequency of physical attack on members of these and other racially or sexually marked groups is very disturbing, I also include in this category less severe incidents of harrassment, intimidation, or ridicule simply for the purpose of degrading, humiliating, or stigmatizing group members.

Given the frequency of such violence in our society, why are theories of justice usually silent about it? I think the reason is that theorists do not typically take such incidents of violence and harrassment as matters of social injustice. No moral theorist would deny that such acts are very wrong. But unless all immoralities are injustices, they might wonder, why should such acts be interpreted as symptoms of social injustice? Acts of violence or petty harrassment are committed by particular individuals, often extremists, deviants, or the mentally unsound. How then can they be said to involve the sorts of institutional issues I have said are properly the subject of justice?

What makes violence a face of oppression is less the particular acts themselves, though these are often utterly horrible, than the social context surrounding them, which makes them possible and even acceptable. What makes violence a phenomenon of social injustice, and not merely an individual moral wrong, is its systemic character, its existence as a social practice.

Violence is systemic because it is directed at members of a group simply because they are members of that group. Any woman, for example, has a reason to fear rape. Regardless of what a Black man has done to escape the oppressions of marginality or powerlessness, he lives knowing he is subject to attack or harrassment. The oppression of violence consists not only in direct victimization, but in the daily knowledge shared by all members of oppressed groups that they are *liable* to violation, solely on account of their group identity. Just living under such a threat of attack on oneself or family or friends deprives the oppressed of freedom and dignity, and needlessly expends their energy.

Violence is a social practice. It is a social given that everyone knows happens and will happen again. It is always at the horizon of social imagination, even for those who do not perpetrate it. According to the prevailing social logic, some circumstances make such violence more "called for" than others. The idea of rape will occur to many men who pick up a hitchhiking woman; the idea of hounding or teasing a gay man on their dorm floor will occur to many straight male college students. Often several persons inflict the violence together, especially in all-male groupings. Sometimes violators set out looking for people to beat up, rape, or taunt. This rule-bound, social, and often premeditated character makes violence against groups a social practice.

Group violence approaches legitimacy, moreover, in the sense that it is tolerated. Often third parties find it unsurprising because it happens frequently and lies as a constant possibility at the horizon of the social imagination. Even when they are caught, those who perpetrate acts of group-directed violence or harrassment often receive light or no punishment. To that extent society renders their acts acceptable.

An important aspect of random, systemic violence is its irrationality. Xenophobic violence differs from the violence of states or ruling-class repression. Repressive violence has a rational, albeit evil, motive: rulers use it as a coercive tool to maintain their power. Many accounts of racist, sexist, or homophobic violence attempt to explain its motivation as a desire to maintain group privilege or domination. I do not doubt that fear of violence often functions to keep oppressed groups subordinate, but I do not think xenophobic violence is rationally motivated in the way that, for example, violence against strikers is.

On the contrary, the violation of rape, beating, killing, and harrassment of women, people of color, gays, and other marked groups is motivated by fear or hatred of those groups. Sometimes the motive may be a simple will to power, to victimize those marked as vulnerable by the very social fact that they are subject to violence. If so, this motive is secondary in the sense that it depends on a social practice of group violence. Violence-causing fear or hatred of the other at least partly involves insecurities on the part of the violators; its irrationality suggests that unconscious processes are at work. . . .

Cultural imperialism, moreover, itself intersects with violence. The culturally imperialized may reject the dominant meanings and attempt to assert their own subjectivity, or the fact of their cultural difference may put the lie to the dominant culture's implicit claim to universality. The dissonance generated by such a challenge to the hegemonic cultural meanings can also be a source of irrational violence. . . .

APPLYING THE CRITERIA

Social theories that construct oppression as a unified phenomenon usually either leave out groups that even the theorists think are oppressed, or leave out important ways in which groups are oppressed. Black liberation theorists and feminist theorists have argued persuasively, for example, that Marxism's reduction of all oppressions to class oppression leaves out much about the specific oppression of Blacks and women. By pluralizing the category of oppression in the way explained in this chapter, social theory can avoid the exclusive and oversimplifying effects of such reductionism.

I have avoided pluralizing the category in the way some others have done, by constructing an account of separate systems of oppression for each oppressed group: racism, sexism, classism, heterosexism, ageism, and so on. There is a double problem with considering each group's oppression a unified and distinct structure or system. On the one hand, this way of conceiving oppression fails to accommodate the similarities and overlaps in the oppressions of different groups. On the other hand, it falsely represents the situation of all group members as the same.

I have arrived at the five faces of oppression—exploitation, marginalization, powerlessness, cultural imperialism, and violence—as the best way to avoid such exclusions and reductions. They function as criteria for determining whether individuals and groups are oppressed, rather than as a full theory of oppression. I believe that these criteria are objective. They provide a means of refuting some people's belief that their group is oppressed when it is not, as well as a means of persuading others that a group is oppressed when they doubt it. Each criterion can be operationalized; each can be applied through the assessment of observable behavior, status relationships, distributions, texts and other cultural artifacts. I have no illusions that such assessments can be value-neutral. But these criteria can nevertheless serve as means of evaluating claims that a group is oppressed, or adjudicating disputes about whether or how a group is oppressed.

The presence of any of these five conditions is sufficient for calling a group oppressed. But different group oppressions exhibit different combinations of these forms, as do different individuals in the groups. Nearly all, if not all, groups said by contemporary social movements to be oppressed suffer cultural imperialism. The other oppressions they experience vary. Working-class people are exploited and powerless, for example, but if employed and white do not experience marginalization and violence. Gay men, on the other hand, are not qua gay exploited or powerless, but they experience severe cultural imperialism and violence. Similarly, Jews and Arabs as groups are victims of cultural imperialism and violence, though many members of these groups also suffer exploitation or powerlessness. Old people are oppressed by marginalization and cultural imperialism, and this is also true of physically and mentally disabled people. As a group women are subject to gender-based exploitation, powerlessness, cultural imperialism, and violence. Racism in the United States condemns many Blacks and Latinos to marginalization, and puts many more at risk, even though many members of these groups escape that condition; members of these groups often suffer all five forms of oppression.

Applying these five criteria to the situation of groups makes it possible to compare oppressions without reducing them to a common essence or claiming that one is more fundamental than another. One can compare the ways in which a particular form of oppression appears in different groups. For example, while the operations of cultural imperialism are often experienced in similar fashion by different groups, there are also important differences. One can compare the combinations of oppressions groups experience, or the intensity of those oppressions. Thus with these criteria one can plausibly claim that one group is more oppressed than another without reducing all oppressions to a single scale. . . .

REFERENCES

Alexander, David. 1987. "Gendered Job Traits and Women's Occupations." Ph.D. dissertation, Economics, University of Massachusetts.

Brown, Carol. 1981. "Mothers, Fathers and Children: From Private to Public Patriarchy." In Lydia Sargent, ed., *Women and Revolution.* Boston: South End.

Delphy, Christine. 1984. *Close to Home: A Materialist Analysis of Women's Oppression.* Amherst: University of Massachusetts Press.

Du Bois, W.E.B. 1969 [1903]. *The Souls of Black Folk.* New York: New American Library.

Ferguson, Ann. 1984. "On Conceiving Motherhood and Sexuality: A Feminist Materialist Approach." In Joyce Trebilcot, ed., *Mothering: Essays in Feminist Theory.* Totowa, N.J.: Rowman and Allanheld.

————. 1989. *Blood at the Root.* London: Pandora.

Fraser, Nancy. 1987. "Social Movements vs. Disciplinary Bureaucracies: The Discourse of Social Needs." CHS Occasional Paper No. 8. Center for Humanistic Studies, University of Minnesota.

Lugones, Maria C., and Elizabeth V. Spelman. 1983. "Have We Got a Theory for You! Feminist Theory, Cultural Imperialism and the Demand for 'the Woman's Voice.' " *Women's Studies International Forum* 6:573–81.

Macpherson, C. B. 1973. *Democratic Theory: Essays in Retrieval.* Oxford: Oxford University Press.

Marable, Manning. 1984. *Race, Reform and Rebellion: The Second Reconstruction in Black America, 1945–82.* Jackson: University Press of Mississippi.

Sennett, Richard, and Jonathan Cobb. 1972. *The Hidden Injuries of Class.* New York: Vintage.

QUESTIONS

1 How do stereotypes function to reinforce oppression?
2 Is marginalization the most dangerous form of oppression?
3 Can social institutions that function to systematically oppress members of some groups be considered just?

The Oppression Debate in Sexual Politics

Kenneth Clatterbaugh

Kenneth Clatterbaugh is associate professor of philosophy at the University of Washington. He is the author of *Leibniz's Doctrine of Individual Accidents* (1973) and *Contemporary Perspectives on Masculinity: Men, Women, and Politics in Modern Society* (1990).

Clatterbaugh argues against the claim that in the United States today, men are oppressed simply in virtue of being men and not because they happen to be members of a targeted group (e.g., African Americans or gays). He begins by defending a specific conception of oppression: Oppression is the systematic *dehumanization* of an identifiable target human group. Using this definition, Clatterbaugh evaluates and rejects three arguments advanced to support the claim that men are oppressed: the socialization argument, the reversal argument, and the expendability argument.

THE "MAN QUESTION" IN FEMINISM

The "man question" in feminist theory is: "Where should men be located in feminist theory and practice? This question encompasses such issues as: "What are the roles of men in creating and maintaining women's social condition?" "What are the roles of men in helping to change women's social condition?" "What are the benefits and/or costs to women and men of these roles?" Of course each of these questions has a multitude of specific forms depending on the particular feminist theory.

The "man question" in feminist theory immediately translates for men into the "self question." How are men to think about themselves in relationship to feminist theory and practice?" One does not face this question only if one is a profeminist man. Antifeminist men and even those who seek some neutral ground must decide to which of the many conflicting feminist claims they should be opposed, be supportive, or be neutral.

I want to explore a particular version of the "self question," starting with the fundamental belief that the condition of women in modern society is best described as one of oppression. This version continues in holding that men collectively and indi-

Reprinted with permission of Rowman and Littlefield Publishers from *Rethinking Masculinity* (1992), edited by Larry May and Robert A. Strikwerda, pp. 169–171, 177–190.

vidually cause and maintain women's oppression; men are the oppressors. In contrast to women, men are not oppressed but privileged beneficiaries of women's oppression. And, because they benefit from women's oppression, men are unreliable allies in the struggle to end women's oppression.

To use the language of "oppression" is to use strong language; to be oppressed is more serious than to be discriminated against, treated unfairly, unequally, or unjustly, although it may well include all of these. And, to be an oppressor is a more serious moral flaw than to be the perpetrator of discrimination or unequal treatment, although an oppressor may well be guilty of these injustices as well. The remedy for oppression is also more threatening to the status quo; oppression demands radical solutions (revolutions of liberation) while inequality typically requires only reform.

To illustrate the greater seriousness of the oppression description of the condition of women let me contrast this view with the view that women's condition in society is one of simple inequality to men. According to the inequality description, most of the principles of distributive justice for our society are good principles, if only they were applied fairly for both men and women. Men are not at fault for having what they have if women are given equal access to what men have. There is even in this version a way of admitting that women are not equal *and at the same time* blaming women for their condition, namely, if only women would not choose to stay at home, avoid math courses, or take career breaks for child rearing then women would gain greater equality to men. Through such allowances even conservative men can be made comfortable with an inequality account. Oppression descriptions are, on the other hand, much more painful to men; they suggest that what men have gained has come at the expense of women and that fine tuning the system may not help much. These differences probably account for the fact that there is far more literature by men challenging the oppression story, and correspondingly more literature by men accepting the inequality story.

What is of interest in this paper is the specific counterclaim that men are oppressed. This claim is critical to two of the major challenges to the oppression story. First, men have claimed that both men and women are oppressed by a social system that neither created. Second, the more antifeminist challenge is that the story is reversed; it is men who are oppressed to a large extent by women who are not oppressed and who benefit from men's oppression. It is frequently this rejoinder that launches the oppression debate in sexual politics. My contribution to this debate shall be as follows. First, I defend a theory of oppression that seems to me to meet some obvious criteria of adequacy for such a theory. Second, I use that theory to give content to the rejoinder claim that men are oppressed. Third, I argue that the rejoinder claim that men are oppressed is not well-grounded. The usual arguments for this conclusion fail. In this essay nothing I say assumes that women are oppressed, although I believe that that is the true condition of women. Also, I shall not explore whether even if men are oppressed that gets men off the hook of being the oppressors of women. In fact, I doubt that such a fact would make men less culpable. . . .

TOWARD A THEORY OF SOCIAL OPPRESSION

Rosa Parks once observed that she refused to give up her seat on the bus because she just wanted to be treated like a human being. Academic philosophers from Kant to

Rawls have argued that everyone is entitled to equal respect as a human being. Similar themes have appealed to those who write about oppression. Leaving open what it means to treat someone as a human being, one suggestion is that it is oppressive to act in a systematically dehumanizing way toward an identifiable group of humans.

In *Pedagogy of the Oppressed,* Friere notes that "while both humanization and dehumanization are real alternatives, only the first is man's vocation. This vocation is constantly negated by . . . injustice, exploitation, oppression, and the violence of the oppressors."[1] Frye claims that women are not heard because they are excluded from the class of persons.[2] Daniel McGuire in setting out the criteria for those who are entitled to preferential treatment notes that one criterion is that prejudice against those who are so entitled has reached the level of depersonalization.[3] Sandra Lee Bartky notes that "psychological oppression is . . . separating of a person from some of the essential attributes of personhood."[4]

The common thread in each of these authors is the concept of *dehumanization* or *depersonalization.* The dehumanization theory that I shall develop holds that *oppression is the systematic dehumanization of an identifiable target human group.*[5] To dehumanize a group is to deny that the members of that group possess the complete range of human abilities, needs, wants, and achievements that are valued at that time as important to being a human being. It also counts as dehumanizing to treat, overtly or covertly, a human group as if its members lack the abilities, needs, wants, or achievements of a more complete human being. It is not important whether the members of a group are conceived as *non*human or *defectively* human. Of course, groups that are oppressed under one standard need not be oppressed under another. In fact there are some dramatic changes in history where a group that was not oppressed in one century was oppressed in the next.

Of course what constitutes a complete human being is a social construct, which is historically and culturally relative. It may not even be an accurate and complete account of what humans really are. I am not claiming that a group is oppressed just because the historical concept of a complete human being leaves out some abilities, needs, wants, and achievements that they in fact have. It is not a question of how well a group's perceived characteristics match their actual ones, but how well their perceived abilities, needs, wants, and achievements match what the broader society values as human.

A group is not oppressed if there are qualities included in being a human being that are denied of them and which they in fact lack. Thus, it is not oppressive to treat people who cannot walk as if they cannot walk, although it would be oppressive to deny that they have other human needs, for example, needs for privacy and dignity when they have such needs. Again, a group is not oppressed if there are qualities included in being a human that are denied of them and which society does *not* value as important to being human.

A social structure becomes oppressive under this definition, if it assumes, promotes, or treats the target population as if it is defective in any of the defining human abilities, needs, wants, or achievements. I use "social structure" in a very broad sense to include such items as social institutions, practices, policies, laws, humor, ideology, and work relations. Usually, when a group is oppressed in a society these social structures interlock and support each other. Thus, to take an example, if African-

American children are denied access to education and therefore do not achieve in academic pursuits, the systems interlock when lack of achievement justifies continued denial of opportunity. . . .

. . . Clearly there are those who are held up as more completely human, indeed as paradigm cases of human being. To this group is extended the full rights of citizenship and the responsibilities of business, government, morality, and politics. It is this group's standards of excellence that are embraced as the appropriate standards. And, it is this group's definitions that are used to determine the deficiencies of other groups (cultural imperialism). Thus, for example, Andrew Carnegie argues in *Triumphant Democracy* that "the defective classes" cannot be expected to overcome "their inherent lack of abilities."[6] Whereas people like himself, Anglo-Americans, are not defective in the above ways, in fact they exhibit the complements of these defects, namely, "genius," "ability," "concentration," "honesty," and even openmindedness.[7] . . .

ARE MEN OPPRESSED?

When we turn to the issue of whether men can claim oppression, we must make it clear what we are asking. We are not concerned with the question of whether or not men fall into targeted groups. Men clearly have been and are oppressed as African Americans, as Jews, as colonials in French Algeria. The question here is whether men, as men, have a claim to be oppressed in twentieth-century America? It is the arguments toward this conclusion that I shall now address.

There are three primary arguments to the conclusion that men are oppressed as men. The first is what I call the "socialization argument"; it holds that because men are socialized just as women are socialized, and since that socialization is oppressive for women, it is also oppressive for men. The second argument, which I shall call the "reversal argument," finds that the oppression of men benefits women and that women help to maintain it. Women are viewed as unreliable allies in the struggle to end men's oppression. This argument is the mirror image of the oppression story that is used to describe the condition of women. The final argument is the "expendability argument." Men's lives are seen as expendable in a way that women's lives are not; the usual evidence for this claim is drawn from images in fictive film, the draft laws, casualties of war, and even domestic violence statistics.

A   The Socialization Argument

The first argument has its beginnings in the liberal profeminist men's movement. According to liberal feminist analysis women are denied their full humanity by their restricted social role; profeminist men argued, similarly, that men, too were subjected to restricted social roles and thereby denied their full humanity. If such restriction is oppressive to women, then it is also oppressive to men. Many liberal profeminist men do not hesitate to draw this conclusion. They speak of the "oppressive, dehumanizing sex roles" that afflict men or "the oppression we feel by being forced to conform to the narrow and lonely roles of men in this society.[8] The Berkeley Men's Center

Manifesto declares that "we are oppressed by conditioning."[9] As long as women's subjugation to the feminine mystique was oppressive, men believed that they too were oppressed by the masculine mystique. This argument depends on the parallel between the social conditioning of women and that of men.

There are many grounds on which this argument may be criticized. It is not obvious that either masculinity or femininity is a unified role or that either is a role that cannot be readily altered to suit individual needs. In other words one or both of these roles, as normative, may be easily violated. Masculinity and femininity, either or both, may not even qualify as social roles; the norms that guide them may be too vague.

However, I wish to raise another concern. It is far from clear that the claim that "if the limitations of the feminine role are oppressive so are the limitations of the masculine role" is true or plausible. We have already noted that it does not seem to be plausible to view restriction (limitation) just by itself as oppressive. The reason is that members of privileged and dominant groups within society may be severely constrained in the social roles that they are allowed to play. Thus, if men are a privileged group within society and women are second-class citizens, they may both confront limitations, but for different reasons. Imagine a young boy who announces that he wants to be a nurse. While that occupation is less off limits today than it was a decade ago, it is easy to imagine that he will be told that the occupation is unworthy of him. Of course, he *could* be a nurse, if he tried, but doctors are more prestigious, better paid, and worthy of the challenge of being a man. A young girl who announces her intention to be a doctor may face a different set of objections. She is told that she *cannot* be a doctor; it requires abilities that she lacks, for example, a talent for science and mathematics, physical strength, or emotional toughness, and it may even cause her to miss her menstrual cycle. In fact Mary Roth Walsh tells a story very much like this one in her book *"Doctors Wanted: No Women Need Apply": Sexual Barriers in the Medical Profession, 1835–1975.*[10]

But the point is simple, to make the parallel one needs to show that the constraints put on men and women both derive from dehumanization as we have defined it. But if men are constrained because they are groomed for dominance and women are constrained because of a perceived lack of abilities, the former is not oppressive and the latter certainly is. And since there is a strong *prima facie* case that men are perceived as reservoirs of valued human traits, especially relative to women, it becomes incumbent on anyone using this argument to show that the source of constraint is the same in each case. The reason this argument has survived for the past twenty years is that those who offer it are satisfied to think of oppression only in terms of constraint. And, obviously, such a limited analysis does not get one to the conclusion that men too are oppressed.

B   The Reversal Argument

The 1980s saw a different kind of argument emerging. It abandoned the parallel and argued that the situations of men and women are sufficiently different that the oppression of men needs to be talked about in a new way. It has long been recognized within the writing about men that there are harms that come out of the masculine role. But it took a new argument to conclude from the harms of the masculine role to the conclusion that men are oppressed.

It was in *The Hazards of Being Male* that Herb Goldberg began to develop his case for men's oppression.[11] Goldberg and others were aware that masculinity, in most feminist analysis, was considered a dominating and privileged social role. This belief had also been held by the liberal and radical profeminist men who wrote on masculinity. Hence, Goldberg's first move is to argue that the feminist picture inverts reality. It is men who are underprivileged:

> By what perverse logic can the male continue to imagine himself "top dog"? Emotionally repressed, out of touch with his body, alienated and isolated from other men, terrorized by the fear of failure, afraid to ask for help, thrown out at a moment's notice . . . when all he knew was how to work. . . . The male has become an artist in the creation of many hidden ways of killing himself.[12]

Next, Goldberg tries to explain how it is that men and women are misinformed about male privilege. He suggests that masculinity is considered a privileged role because men are highly visible and socially successful; men are "the heroes, the studs, the providers, the warriors, the empire builders, the fearless ones."[13] The hidden nature of the male role makes the oppression of men different in kind from the oppression of women:

> Unlike some of the problems of women, the problems of men are not readily changed through legislation. The male has no apparent and clearly defined targets against which he can vent his rage. Yet he is oppressed by the cultural pressures that have denied him his feelings, by the mythology of the woman and the distorted and self-destructive way he sees and relates to her, by the urgency for him to "act like a man" . . . and by a generalized self-hate that causes him to feel comfortable only when he is functioning well in harness. . . .[14]

Finally, women, to their own advantage, play a significant role in keeping men in their oppressed situation by perpetuating the myth that men are "top dog" and that women are their victims. It is men who are the "oppressors," "abusers," "chauvinists," and "sexist pigs," and who have the perks in society.[15] These myths make men feel guilt and self-hate; the result is male subservience and blame rather than change.[16] Goldberg seems to believe, further, that women have already escaped their oppression; now they have the choice to be "wife, mother, or business executive."[17] Thus, women are liberated, but women's liberation requires that men stay in harness; otherwise a woman would not have a choice of being a wife and mother (with a man to provide).

This reversal argument has been advanced by many writers since Goldberg's original formulation. Roy Schenk in *The Other Side of the Coin: Causes and Consequences of Men's Oppression* identifies women as "society's agents in the oppression of us men."[18] Because women believe themselves to be morally superior, a belief that is widespread in society and that gives them great power over men, men cannot even protest this arrangement and consequently are left feeling anger, rage, and guilt. Women gain from this arrangement, and men lose.

Men Freeing Men: Exploding the Myth of the Traditional Male is a collection of writings that come out of the Free Men movement, of which Goldberg was a founder.[19] The authors in this book repeat this argument over and over in various formulations. Women have the real power but it benefits women to perpetuate the myth that men are the heavies and that men have the real power—they keep their options open and an income coming in.

This reversal argument can be challenged at several levels. Even a cursory look at the situation of women in society makes it problematic as to whether women really have a choice to be wife, mother, or executive. Further, feminists have long argued that women do not benefit when men are the provider. They do not benefit because they do not learn the skills to take care of themselves in divorce or death; they do not benefit because they are unable to fulfill many of their own desires to work; and they do not benefit by a system that puts control of salaries, wages, and work only in the hands of men; they do not benefit from dependency on men. These are elementary points in feminist theory, points that go back to Betty Friedan's *The Feminine Mystique.*

And, for all his efforts to illustrate the costs of masculinity, Goldberg has not shown that those costs are not the effects of privilege and dominance. It is not enough to say rhetorically: "how can the male continue to imagine himself 'top dog' " when he is subjected to a sufficiently long list of disorders. Profeminist male writers, whom Goldberg does not acknowledge, noted all of these harms in the early 1970s, yet they found them to be due to the competitive roles that dominant persons play in society. It is a twist of logic to try to argue, as Goldberg does, that because there are costs in having power, one does not have power. Shorter life expectancy, access to drugs, fear of failure, and disorders due to competitive activities may well be the costs for men in a society that privileges men. By itself the need to be in control of life, women, and work produces many of the harms that are so frequently mentioned, especially in a world where control is rarely possible. Until a sustained argument is made that shows that the afflictions of masculinity are *not* the result of trying to maintain power and advantage, there is no reason to allow the reversal argument to proceed. In its first premise this argument essentially begs the question; it assumes that the costs of masculinity are either due to oppression or that they constitute oppression simply because they are limiting.

In brief, if Goldberg is arguing directly from the costs of masculinity to the view that men are oppressed, then he begs the question and avoids the difficult issue as to whether these harms are in fact due to male dominance. If Goldberg is falling back on some generalized claim that men are oppressed because men do not control everything in their lives or that men are oppressed because men are constrained in their social roles, these arguments depend upon a seriously flawed theory of oppression, namely, oppression as limitation.

C   The Expendability Argument

The first two arguments really get to the conclusion that men are oppressed by using a notion of oppression by which everyone is oppressed, namely, oppression is limitation. The final argument that I now consider, at least, appears more compatible with the concept of oppression as dehumanization. The idea behind this argument is that violence against men is acceptable in our society (compared to violence against women or children). From this observation it is concluded that men's lives are valued less and therefore men are oppressed. The crucial premise of this argument is that violence against men is acceptable in our society. Usually this premise is defended by pointing out that only men are drafted, only men can serve in combat in a war, men are "killed" much more regularly in television and movies, and domestic violence against men is not treated as the serious social problem that domestic violence against women is.

> Asked about women in combat at her confirmation hearings, then–Supreme Court nominee Sandra Day O'Connor said she'd hate to see them come home in coffins. Why are men expendable in her eyes?[20]

> By *expecting* men to play life-threatening roles, we are less horrified when their lives are lost. By being less horrified, we can continue the assignment rather than look at our roles . . . *sponsoring* violence against men by turning to war films, murder mysteries, westerns, or TV movies in which men are killed routinely for our entertainment.[21]

> If . . . we turn to the only large nationally representative sample of spouse abuse . . . *we find that 12 percent of husbands were violent toward wives and 12 percent of wives were violent toward husbands.* A ratio of 1 to 1.[22]

Once again, however, there are a great many logical and factual questions that these arguments fail to address. The domestic violence studies that are used, over and over, are purely behavioristic; that is, they study how many times a spouse slammed a door, threw an object, threatened with a knife, etc. There is no effort to study the context in which these behaviors occurred. On a strictly behavioristic analysis, if x threatens y and y reacts by pulling a knife on x to protect her/his life, y is judged to be domestically violent in this situation. When aggression is factored in, however, and defensive behavior excluded, men are overwhelmingly more violent.

Those who offer the expendability argument never give a criterion for determining when a social practice is acceptable. Sometimes they even seem to slide from the fact that violence with men as victims is very widespread to the conclusion that it is acceptable or that men's lives are not valued. Surely some things that are widespread are acceptable, but not everything that is widespread is acceptable.

Finally, we again face the same serious oversight in this argument that occurred in the previous two arguments. Is the fact that only men are drafted and used in combat the result of valuing men's lives less or the result of a patriarchal society that through its institutions holds that only men are capable of being soldiers; only men have the courage, strength, and military intelligence to defend their country. Women, on the other hand, are the property and the spoils of war that victors take along with the roads, homes, farms, and factories of the vanquished. The historical rhetoric suggests the second hypothesis far more than the first. Add to this observation the fact that the military has provided a primary road of upward mobility for men through elaborate subsidizations in insurance, home loans, educational opportunities and monies, preferential hiring, and tax benefits. The military experience is one in which most men do *not* serve and in which *very few* men become "expendable." One cannot help but doubt that the military experience oppresses men as *men* when further facts are indicated, namely, that the men who serve in the front lines, the "cannon fodder" are overwhelmingly African American, Hispanic, and poor. If there is a case to be made it is that the history of the military is deeply patriarchal with most benefits, honor, and glory going to white men.

CONCLUSION

The arguments intended to show that men are oppressed have been offered almost exclusively by the men's rights perspective, even though the beginnings of this position are in the profeminist men's movement. These arguments are widespread and have found favor among many men and even some feminist women. Typically the notion of oppression in these arguments is a limitation theory of oppression. But oppression is not limitation. I have argued, instead, that social oppression is a systematic dehumanization of an identifiable group. Thus, it is a serious failure of these arguments that they fail to show that men as men are systematically dehumanized.

It is not hard to imagine a possible world in which men are systematically dehumanized. Imagine that our world is suddenly controlled by humanoid aliens who establish a new hegemony over the traits that are valued in human society. They reverse or revise the valued traits that have been held to belong especially to (white) males and for which white males have been socialized. An elaborate science develops that teaches that men are overly controlled by their genitals and the emotion of anger; their so-called rational abilities are now seen as rationalizations to support their biological and emotional demands. Male achievement in the arts, literature, philosophy, and sport are expunged from the pages of history and the media or treated as trivial accomplishments. The new set of valued traits installed as human making include many of the traits in which men have not traditionally excelled; for example, being a caregiver. A crisis ensues in which men lose confidence in themselves and strive to live up to the new concept although hardly any are seen as doing so. Men, by socialization, are simply not prepared to excel in this new world. As a result even when they are given the opportunity they do not fare nearly as well as the new humanoids and/or women. Men in fact do have the traits to excel in this world, but they are systematically kept from the kinds of achievements and opportunities to develop those abilities and when they do they are exceptionalized or ignored. In short, men are dehumanized and therefore oppressed.

The hypothetical world which I describe could come about; it could come about without an invasion of aliens. In fact, in our present world the standards are changing. The norms by which people are judged to be worthy are no longer so uniformly (white) male. It is this change that men fear and it is this changing standard that leaves some men less prepared for this world. Instead of welcoming a new and more humane conception of what is truly human, these men resist that change. They attack the revolutionaries as oppressors.

Feminist theorists have made the case that women are dehumanized; that is, women as an identifiable group are seen as defective relative to men whose talents and achievements constitute a norm. In fact, much of the history of Western science is a debate as to whether women have the requisite abilities, needs, wants, and achievements, be it in medicine, sports, artistic expression, music, religion, or science itself. On the negative side women have been found wanting by male political theorists, scientists, and political leaders; wanting in genius, creativity, spirituality, and political ability. On the positive side women have made important gains against their exclusion by simply demonstrating that they do have the requisite abilities and talents to do the very things from which they have been excluded. Feminists have also demanded a new set of valued traits for all persons; it is a set that is without preference for sex or race. Hopefully it is a conception that will not readily lend itself to the dehumanization of any group. . . .

NOTES

1 Paulo Friere, *Pedagogy of the Oppressed* (New York: The Continuum Publishing Corporation, 1970), p. 28.
2 Marilyn Frye, *The Politics of Reality: Essays in Feminist Theory* (Trumansburg, NY: The Crossing Press, 1993), p. 50.
3 Daniel C. Maguire, *A New American Justice: Ending White Male Monopolies* (Garden City, NY: Doubleday, 1980), pp. 129–30.
4 Sandra Lee Bartky, "On Psychological Oppression," *Philosophy for a New Generation,* eds. A. K. Bierman and James A. Gould (New York: Macmillan, 1981), pp. 418–29.
5 The dehumanization theory of oppression used in this essay was developed jointly with Mark Walstead. I owe Mark thanks for supporting me in this paper and making substantive theoretical and historical contributions.
6 Andrew Carnegie, *Triumphant Democracy* (New York: Scribner's 1893), p. 176.
7 Ibid., pp. 111, 113, 121, 122, 192, 200, 205.
8 Jeff Keith, "My Own Men's Liberation," *Men and Masculinity,* eds. Joseph H. Pleck and Jack Sawyer (New York: Prentice-Hall, 1974), pp. 81–88.
9 Berkeley Men's Center, "Berkeley Men's Center Manifesto," *Men and Masculinity,* eds. Joseph H. Pleck and Jack Sawyer (New York: Prentice-Hall, 1974), pp. 173–74.
10 Mary Roth Walsh, *"Doctors Wanted, No Women Need Apply": Sexual Barriers in the Medical Profession, 1835–1975* (New Haven: Yale University Press, 1977).
11 Herb Goldberg, *The Hazards of Being Male: Surviving the Myth of Masculine Privilege* (New York: Signet, 1976).
12 Ibid., pp. 181–82.
13 Ibid., p. 3.
14 Ibid., p. 4.
15 Ibid.; Herb Goldberg, *The New Male* (New York: Signet, 1979), p. 141.
16 Goldberg, *The Hazards of Being Male,* op. cit., p. 5.
17 Ibid., p. 2.
18 Roy Schenk, *The Other Side of the Coin: Causes and Consequences of Men's Oppression* (Madison, WI: Bioenergetics Press, 1982), p. 66.
19 Francis Baumli, ed., *Men Freeing Men: Exploding the Myth of the Traditional Male* (Jersey City, NJ: New Atlantis, 1985).
20 Dan Logan, "Woman in Combat," in Baumli, op. cit., p. 239.
21 Warren Farrell, *Why Men Are the Way They Are* (New York: McGraw-Hill, 1986), p. 229.
22 Ibid., p. 228.

QUESTIONS

1 Is any restriction or limitation a form of oppression?
2 What is dehumanization?

SUGGESTED ADDITIONAL READINGS FOR CHAPTER 6

BARTKY, SANDRA: *Femininity and Domination: Studies in the Phenomenology of Oppression.* New York: Routledge, 1990. Bartky analyzes the social construction of femininity and the ways that it oppresses women. According to her phenomenological analysis, women construct oppressive self-images as a result of working with the images and models of femininity available to them in their cultures.

BURGESS-JACKSON, KEITH: "On the Coerciveness of Sexist Socialization." *Public Affairs Quarterly,* vol. 9, January 1995, pp. 15–27. Burgess-Jackson argues that from a radical feminist point of view, the focus on coercion is misplaced.

CUDD, ANN: "Oppression by Choice." *Journal of Social Philosophy,* vol. 25, June 1994, pp. 22–44. Working with an account of oppression as a systematic institutionalized harm to a social group, Cudd argues against the view that choice negates oppression.

ELLIOT, PATRICIA: "More Thinking about Gender: A Response to Julie A. Nelson." *Hypatia,* vol. 9, Winter 1994, pp. 195–198. Elliott argues that those feminine qualities that have previously been devalued are the result of a sexist construction of gender categories. In her view, a nonsexist society would have no reason to preserve them.

GOLDBERG, DAVID THEO: "Racist Exclusions." *Philosophical Forum,* vol. 26, Fall 1994, pp. 1–32. After examining some current conceptions of racism, Goldberg provides his own reformulation of racism. On the basis of this reformulation, he assesses some of the more usual rationalizations for racism.

HACKER, ANDREW: *Two Nations: Black and White, Separate, Hostile, Unequal.* New York: Ballantine Books, 1992. Hacker advances statistical and other evidence to support his thesis that the United States is a society radically divided according to race. As part of his analysis of racial divisions, he argues that whites can never understand what it is to be black in the United States.

INGRAM, VIRGINIA: "Grounding Benefit in Responsibility." *Kinesis,* vol. 21, Fall 1994, pp. 4–12. Ingram focuses on the ways men benefit from the oppression of women and argues that in certain cases men ought to feel responsible for that oppression.

THALBERG, IRVING: "Visceral Racism." *The Monist,* Vol. 56, 1972, pp. 43–63. Thalberg describes and discusses what he calls "visceral racism"—a set of unacknowledged attitudes held by *unprejudiced* whites.

THOMAS, LAURENCE: "Sexism and Racism: Some Conceptual Differences." *Ethics,* vol. 90, January 1980, pp. 239–250. Thomas examines what he takes to be conceptual differences between racism and sexism.

WENDELL, SUSAN: "Oppression and Victimization; Choice and Responsibility." *Hypatia,* Fall 1990, pp. 15–46. Wendell discusses a cluster of problems for feminist theory and practice which concern responsibility and choice under conditions of oppression.

CHAPTER 7

Affirmative Action

Prior to the 1960s and 1970s, blatant racial discrimination was a fact of life for many minorities, especially blacks. The majority of blacks were in the lowest economic strata of American society due to various factors, including discrimination in housing, inferior education, and outright denial of access to most nonmenial positions as well as to union membership. Women, too, were blatantly discriminated against in many ways. Sexual discrimination was commonplace in the economic sphere, for example, and women's earning power was much less than that of men. Today the earnings gap between men and women is still very wide. While men predominate in the best-paying jobs, women, in disproportionate numbers, are clustered in the lowest-paying ones. In respect to blacks and other minorities, statistics show that whites predominate in the most desirable occupations while blacks and other minorities predominate in the least desirable and worst-paying ones.

There is widespread agreement today that the hiring and education practices of the past, which routinely disadvantaged women and blacks, as well as other minorities, were morally wrong. There is also widespread agreement about why this racial and sexual discrimination was wrong. However, there is widespread disagreement about the correct answers to the following sorts of questions. To what extent is sexual and racial discrimination an ongoing reality that continues to deny women, blacks, and other minority groups equal opportunities in education and employment? Does society owe a debt to groups whose members have been systematically denied equality of opportunity in the past? Must it rectify the wrongs resulting from past discrimination? Since equality of opportunity for all members of society is a worthy social goal, what social policies are most likely to eradicate the ongoing racial and sexual inequalities that work against this goal? This chapter focuses primarily on consideration of these sorts of questions.

THE WRONGNESS OF RACIAL AND SEXUAL DISCRIMINATION

Why are actions and practices that deny people various opportunities simply on the basis of their race or sex morally wrong? The usual answer is that such actions and practices violate the *principle of equality*. According to this principle, equals should be treated equally and unequals should be treated unequally, in proportion to their differences. This is sometimes called the "formal principle of justice." But what constitutes equality or inequality? In what ways must two individuals be alike before we can claim that they should receive the same treatment? In what ways must two individuals differ before we can claim that they should be accorded unequal treatment?

The usual way of answering these questions is to say that the differences between individuals must be *relevant* to the treatment in question. When a particular kind of employment is at issue, for example, it would seem that what is relevant is having the appropriate abilities, competencies, or skills. If Joe Smith and John Doe both apply for a job as lifeguard, a difference in their ethnic background seems to have no bearing on which of them should get the job. But if Joe is a nonswimmer and John an Olympic swimming champion, that difference between them is relevant to the hiring decision. On this line of reasoning, sex may be relevant when what is at issue is maternity leave. But it is not relevant when a choice is made between competing accountants, although mathematical ability is relevant. A qualified woman accountant who is not hired to fill an accounting position simply because of her sex is treated unjustly—she is denied an employment opportunity on the basis of a characteristic unrelated to the task in hand. When this happens, the principle of equality is clearly violated.

The discussion so far has focused on that part of the principle of equality that states that equals should be treated equality. But some unequal treatment is also in keeping with the principle of equality. Young children cannot be given the same rights and responsibilities as adults, for example. A five-year-old cannot be expected to take on responsibilities such as voting or signing binding contracts. This kind of unequal treatment of young children and adults is consistent with the principle of equality, since young children differ from adults in relevant respects. They are incapable of exercising the rational capacities needed to assume certain responsibilities.

To sum up, both institutional practices that treat equals equally and those that treat unequals unequally, in proportion to their differences, are morally correct according to the principle of equality. But when individuals are treated unequally on the basis of irrelevant characteristics, the principle of equality is clearly violated.

It is widely agreed that the racial and sexual discrimination practiced in the past was obviously unjust insofar as it involved gross violations of the principle of equality. For the same reason, it is also widely agreed that ongoing discrimination against minorities and women (unequal treatment on the basis of irrelevant grounds) is wrong. It also seems undeniable that past discrimination is to a large extent responsible for many of the racial and sexual inequalities existing today. Especially crucial to the perpetuation of racial and sexual inequalities are the existing economic and educational disadvantages that have resulted from past discrimination, as well as other factors resulting from this discrimination, such as the dearth of appropriate role models. What is a matter of great dispute, however, can be expressed in the following question: What obligations, if any, does society have to undo some of the self-perpetuating wrongs caused by past discrimination or to compensate women, blacks, and other minorities for burdens and injustices suffered due to sexism and racism?

Much of the contemporary controversy centers on certain hiring, promotion, and admission policies adopted by businesses and educational institutions, largely in response to government affirmative action requirements. But controversy also surrounds affirmative action programs instituted by the federal government itself. To understand these controversies, it is useful to look briefly at the ways in which the call for affirmative action has been understood and reflected in hiring, promotion, and admission policies as well as in federal government programs.

AFFIRMATIVE ACTION AND THE CONSTITUTION

Employers have responded to calls for affirmative action in various ways. Some have adopted practices of *passive nondiscrimination* that simply require all decisions about hiring and promotion to disregard race and sex. Note that passive nondiscrimination involves no compensation for past injustices. Nor does it help to undo the ongoing effects of past discrimination. The limitations of this approach are readily apparent, moreover, when we realize the extent to which seniority systems perpetuate old discriminatory patterns. Other employers have adopted measures that more accurately fall under the heading *affirmative action.* Some of these measures involve no more than making every effort to find women and minority applicants and to ensure that employment and promotion opportunities are highly visible. Here the pool of women and minority applicants may be enlarged, but they receive no preference when decisions are made about hiring and promotion. Other employers committed to affirmative action have attempted to go further by giving preference to women and minority applicants. The programs involved, often called "preferential treatment" programs, are the focal point of the moral debate about affirmative-action programs. Preferential treatment programs are of two types. The first type involves hard quotas or specific numerical goals. Such preferential treatment programs specify some set number or proportion of women and minority applicants who must be hired or promoted. The second type involves neither a hard quota nor a specific numerical goal, but nevertheless does require the preferential treatment of women and minority applicants.

Institutions of higher learning, such as law and medical schools, have also attempted to establish affirmative-action admissions policies, including preferential treatment programs. Some of these programs have led to landmark lawsuits. The first university preferential treatment case decided by the United States Supreme Court was *University of California v. Bakke* (1978). Alan Bakke, a white male, applied for admission to the University of California at Davis Medical School. The school, which had a hard quota preferential treatment admissions policy favoring minority students, had set aside 16 of its 100 places in the first-year class for those students. Admission was denied to Bakke, but it was granted to minority students whose college grade point averages (GPAs) and scores on the Medical College Admission Test (MCAT) were much lower than Bakke's. The trial court ruled that Bakke was a victim of *invidious* racial discrimination, and the Supreme Court of the State of California upheld that decision. The justices of the United States Supreme Court were divided four-to-four on the major issues in the case, with Justice Powell providing the decisive vote. Five justices, including Justice Powell, held that the quota system used by the University of California was unconstitutional and that Bakke must be admitted to the medical school. But four other justices along with Powell held that colleges and universities *can* consider race as a factor in the admissions process. Justice Powell's opinion cites a program instituted by Harvard University as an example of a constitutionally permissible admissions program, one which takes race into account in the interest of diversity but which does not automatically exclude non-minority applicants from a specific number of seats in the entering class:

> In recent years Harvard College has expanded the concept of diversity to include students from disadvantaged economic, racial and ethnic groups. Harvard College now recruits not only Californians or Louisianans but also blacks and Chicanos and other minority students. . . .
>
> In practice, this new definition of diversity has meant that race has been a factor in some admission decisions. When the Committee on Admissions reviews the large middle group of applicants who are admissible and deemed capable of doing good work in their courses, the race of an applicant may tip the balance in his favor just as geographic origin or a life spent on a farm may tip the balance in other candidates' cases. . . .
>
> In Harvard college admissions the Committee has not set target-quotas for the number of blacks, or of musicians, football players, physicists or Californians to be admitted in a given year. But that awareness [of the necessity of including more than a token number of black students] does not mean that the Committee sets a minimum number of blacks or of people from west of the Mississippi who are to be admitted. It means only that in choosing among thousands of applicants who are not only "admissible" academically but have other strong qualities, the Committee, with a number of criteria in mind, pays some attention to distribution among many types and categories of students.[1]

Subsequent to *Bakke* the United States Supreme Court has been confronted with a number of cases regarding affirmative action policies instituted by universities, businesses, unions, the federal government and others. It has accepted the use of racial classifications in some affirmative action programs. However, in many of its opinions, the Court has asserted the need for what it calls "strict scrutiny" in the case of all racial classifications, even those intended to advantage members of groups discriminated against. Strict scrutiny requires that all racial classifications receive detailed examination in regard to both their ends and means: (1) the racial classification must serve a compelling state interest; (2) the program must be narrowly tailored to serve that interest; and (3) the program must be a necessary means to the achievement of that interest. Repeatedly, however, various justices have argued for a weaker standard in the case of "benign" racial classifications, such as those embodied in affirmative action programs. In one case, *Metro Broadcasting v. FCC* (1990), the Court ruled that benign federal race-based policies should be subject to a lesser standard, intermediate scrutiny: Even measures involving benign federal racial classifications which "are not remedial in the sense of being designed to compensate victims of past governmental or societal discrimination are constitutionally permissible to the extent that they serve important governmental objectives within the power of

---

[1] United States Supreme Court, 438 U.S. 265 (1978).

Congress and are substantially related to achievement of those objectives."[2] The *Metro* decision was effectively overturned by the Supreme Court in *Adarand Constructors v. Federico Pena, Secretary of Transportation* (1995). The plurality opinion in *Adarand,* written by Justice Sandra Day O'Connor and partly reprinted in this chapter, reasserts the strict scrutiny requirement. The variety of positions taken by Supreme Court justices in respect to the constitutionality of "benign" racial classifications is reflected in excerpts from two other opinions in the *Adarand* case that are reprinted in this chapter. Justice Clarence Thomas rejects *all* racial classifications as unconstitutional while Justice John Paul Stevens, in a dissenting opinion, asserts that the Court's rulings must recognize the significant difference between invidious discrimination and remedial race-based preferences.

THE MORAL JUSTIFIABILITY OF PREFERENTIAL TREATMENT

In this chapter, our primary concern is not with the legal and constitutional issues raised by cases such as *Bakke, Metro,* and *Adarand* but with the *moral justifiability* of the sorts of preferential treatment programs that gave rise to these cases. One attempt to justify preferential treatment is primarily *backward-looking* insofar as it is based in the claim that *compensation* is due to groups whose members have been unjustly discriminated against in the past. This approach appeals to the *principle of compensatory justice,* which states that whenever an injustice has been committed, just compensation or reparation must be made to the injured parties. The principle of compensatory justice is implicitly invoked, for example, when the claim is made that American Indians must be compensated for the past deprivation of tribal land and water rights due to government exploitation. On this line of reasoning, preferential treatment programs that favor women, blacks, or other minorities are seen as compensatory in nature. Since their purpose is to make reparations for past injustices, these programs are morally justified by appeal to the principle of compensatory justice.

Many objections are raised against the compensatory approach. One objection appeals to the principle of equality. As noted above, the principle of equality is violated whenever individuals are denied equal treatment simply on the basis of generally irrelevant characteristics such as sex or race. This is what seems to have happened to Bakke and Adarand Constructors. They were not accorded the same treatment as members of the favored minority groups. Such unequal treatment is sometimes called "reverse discrimination." This label is used to describe actions or practices that discriminate against an individual or group, on the basis of some normally irrelevant characteristic, *because* preference is being given to members of previously discriminated against groups. In keeping with our earlier account of the principle of equality, reverse discrimination certainly appears to be morally wrong. Not everyone who rejects a compensatory justification of preferential treatment policies maintains that members of groups wronged by racial and sexual discrimination do not de-

---

[2]United States Supreme Court, 497 U.S. 547 (1990).

serve some sort of compensation. What those who reject this approach do maintain, however, is that preferential treatment in schooling and employment is a morally unacceptable means of providing that compensation because it violates the very principle of equality that is the basis of the claim that racial and sexual discrimination is morally wrong.

Other major objections to the compensatory approach include the following. First, individuals receiving preferential treatment may not themselves have actually suffered any unjust treatment. Second, individuals who lose out because others receive preferential treatment may themselves have been severely disadvantaged economically and socially. Third, if compensatory justice requires preferential treatment for individuals who have been treated unjustly in the past, then race or sex is irrelevant. What is relevant is past unjust treatment, and individuals who have been treated unjustly belong to both sexes and to many different ethnic and racial groups. Still another line of attack against the compensatory approach utilizes an infinite regress argument: Suppose we are required to give preference today to individuals belonging to groups that were discriminated against in the past in order to compensate them for past inequality of treatment. Will we be required to give compensatory preferential treatment in the future to members of groups denied equality of treatment by today's compensatory programs? And what about the compensation due to those treated unequally by those future programs?

Not everyone who defends preferential treatment adopts a compensatory stance. Many defenders utilize a consequentialist approach. One consequentialist line of argument is advanced and briefly discussed by Edwin C. Hettinger in this chapter. Hettinger questions an important presumption underlying many of the attacks on preferential treatment programs—the presumption that only those characteristics directly related to job performance are relevant in hiring and admissions decisions. He argues, in contrast, that the underlying purpose of a preferential treatment policy may render the race or sex of applicants a morally relevant characteristic. Take, for example, a specific preferential admissions policy whose purpose is to provide more role models for members of previously discriminated against groups in order to bring about a more sexually and racially egalitarian society. In light of this purpose, the sex or race of the applicants is a relevant characteristic. Thus admissions decisions made in accordance with this preferential treatment policy would not violate the principle of equality because that principle requires only that differential treatment not be based on irrelevant characteristics.

In contrast to compensatory approaches, which are backward-looking, consequentialist defenses of preferential treatment can be seen as both backward- and forward-looking. They can be seen as backward-looking because they identify past wrongs and argue for policies intended to rectify the ongoing effects of past injustices. They are forward-looking, however, insofar as they argue for preferential treatment as a necessary means to the achievement of a morally desirable social goal—a more egalitarian society free of racism and sexism. Hettinger's reasoning in this chapter exemplifies this consequentialist approach. In his view, if affirmative action practices help to eliminate the grave injustice of sexual and racial inequality, and thereby contribute to the achievement of a more egalitarian society, the social good achieved will far outweigh the relatively minor injustices resulting from reverse discrimination. Clearly, such consequentialist reasoning avoids some of the difficulties raised for the compensatory approach. On the consequentialist approach, for example, the question of whether or not a particular black woman who benefits from a preferential hiring decision was herself the direct victim of past discrimination becomes irrelevant. She is not being treated preferentially in order to compensate her for some specific wrong that she herself has suffered. Rather, the justification for the preferential treatment policy by which she benefits is its instrumental role in undoing the effects of past discrimination and bringing about a more egalitarian society.

Defenders of preferential treatment who depend on consequentialist arguments must pay special attention to *factual* issues. They must attempt to answer the following kinds of questions. Will preferential treatment programs in fact result in greater sexual and racial equality? Are preferential treatment programs necessary to prevent ongoing sexual and racial discrimination? Is discrimination, albeit often subtle, still so pervasive in our society that mandatory quota systems are required to eliminate continued discrimination against women and minorities? Will preferential treatment programs eventually result in greater equality of opportunity for everyone in society regardless of race or sex? A challenge to the consequentialist defense of preferential treatment is expressed, for example, in Shelby Steele's article in this chapter. Steele argues that blacks have more to lose than to gain by affirmative action programs. In contrast, Cornel West, in another reading in this chapter, sees such programs as necessary to ensure that persisting discriminatory practices are lessened. West maintains, however, that affirmative action, while necessary, will do little to alleviate the major problems currently faced by blacks. In his view, there are two major problems in the black community—too much poverty and too little self-love. West discusses what he identifies as black nihilism and some strategies for overcoming it.

Jane S. Zembaty

What Is Wrong with Reverse Discrimination?

Edwin C. Hettinger

Edwin C. Hettinger is associate professor of philosophy at the College of Charleston. His published articles include "The Responsible Use of Animals in Biomedical Research," "Justifying Intellectual Property," and "Valuing Predation in Rolston's *Environmental Ethics.*"

Hettinger adopts a consequentialist approach to the justification of reverse discrimination. He defends affirmative action practices that are committed to the

Reprinted with permission of the author from *Business & Professional Ethics Journal,* vol. 6 (Fall 1987), pp. 39–51.

hiring and admission of slightly less well qualified women or blacks rather than slightly more qualified white males. In Hettinger's view, such reverse discrimination is justified insofar as its ultimate goal is the eradication of sexual and/or racial inequality. Hettinger discusses and evaluates various objections to reverse discrimination and identifies the following two objections as morally troubling: (1) When reverse discrimination takes place, people are judged on the basis of involuntary characteristics—characteristics over which they have no control. (2) Job-seeking white males who are subject to reverse discrimination are not compensated for the sacrifices they make in bearing a disproportionate share of the costs of achieving an egalitarian society. In Hettinger's view, the problems pinpointed by these two objections are relatively minor, however, when weighed against the serious injustice of racial and sexual inequality.

Many people think it obvious that reverse discrimination is unjust. Calling affirmative action reverse discrimination itself suggests this. This discussion evaluates numerous reasons given for this alleged injustice. Most of these accounts of what is wrong with reverse discrimination are found to be deficient. The explanations for why reverse discrimination is morally troubling show only that it is unjust in a relatively weak sense. This result has an important consequence for the wider issue of the moral justifiability of affirmative action. If social policies which involve minor injustice are permissible (and perhaps required) when they are required in order to overcome much greater injustice, then the mild injustice of reverse discrimination is easily overridden by its contribution to the important social goal of dismantling our sexual and racial caste system.

By 'reverse discrimination' or 'affirmative action' I shall mean hiring or admitting a slightly less well qualified woman or black, rather than a slightly more qualified white male, for the purpose of helping to eradicate sexual and/or racial inequality, or for the purpose of compensating women and blacks for the burdens and injustices they have suffered due to past and ongoing sexism and racism. There are weaker forms of affirmative action, such as giving preference to minority candidates only when qualifications are equal, or providing special educational opportunities for youths in disadvantaged groups. This paper seeks to defend the more controversial sort of reverse discrimination defined above. I begin by considering several spurious objections to reverse discrimination. In the second part, I identify the ways in which this policy is morally troubling and then assess the significance of these negative features.

SPURIOUS OBJECTIONS

1 Reverse Discrimination as Equivalent to Racism and Sexism

In a discussion on national television, George Will, the conservative news analyst and political philosopher, articulated the most common objection to reverse discrimination. It is unjust, he said, because it is discrimination on the basis of race or sex. Reverse discrimination against white males is the same evil as traditional discrimination against women and blacks. The only difference is that in this case it is the white male who is being discriminated against. Thus if traditional racism and sexism are wrong and unjust, so is reverse discrimination, and for the very same reasons.

But reverse discrimination is not at all like traditional sexism and racism. The motives and intentions behind it are completely different, as are its consequences. Consider some of the motives underlying traditional racial discrimination. Blacks were not hired or allowed into schools because it was felt that contact with them was degrading, and sullied whites. These policies were based on contempt and loathing for blacks, on a feeling that blacks were suitable only for subservient positions and that they should never have positions of authority over whites. Slightly better qualified white males are not being turned down under affirmative action for any of these reasons. No defenders or practitioners of affirmative action (and no significant segment of the general public) think that contact with white males is degrading or sullying, that white males are contemptible and loathsome, or that white males—by their nature—should be subservient to blacks or women.

The consequences of these two policies differ radically as well. Affirmative action does not stigmatize white males; it does not perpetuate unfortunate stereotypes about white males; it is not part of a pattern of discrimination that makes being a white male incredibly burdensome. Nor does it add to a particular group's "already overabundant supply" of power, authority, wealth, and opportunity, as does traditional racial and sexual discrimination. On the contrary, it results in a more egalitarian distribution of these social and economic benefits. If the motives and consequences of reverse discrimination and of traditional racism and sexism are completely different, in what sense could they be morally equivalent acts? If acts are to be individuated (for moral purposes) by including the motives, intentions, and consequences in their description, then clearly these two acts are not identical.

It might be argued that although the motives and consequences are different, the act itself is the same: reverse discrimination is discrimination on the basis of race and sex, and this is wrong in itself independently of its motives or consequences. But discriminating (i.e., making distinctions in how one treats people) on the basis of race or sex is not always wrong, nor is it necessarily unjust. It is not wrong, for example, to discriminate against one's own sex when choosing a spouse. Nor is racial or sexual discrimination in hiring necessarily wrong. This is shown by Peter Singer's example in which a director of a play about ghetto conditions in New York City refuses to consider any white applicants for the actors because she wants the play to be authentic.[1] If I am looking for a representative of the black community, or doing a study about blacks and disease, it is perfectly legitimate to discriminate against all whites. Their whiteness makes them unsuitable for my (legitimate) purposes. Similarly, if I am hiring a wet-nurse, or a person to patrol the women's change rooms in my department store, discriminating against males is perfectly legitimate.

These examples show that racial and sexual discrimination are not wrong in themselves. This is not to say that they are never wrong; most often they clearly are. Whether or not they are wrong, however, depends on the purposes, consequences, and context of such discrimination.

2 Race and Sex as Morally Arbitrary and Irrelevant Characteristics

A typical reason given for the alleged injustice of all racial and sexual discrimination (including affirmative action) is that it is morally arbitrary to consider race or sex when hiring, since these characteristics are not relevant to the decision. But the above examples show that not all uses of race or sex as a criterion in hiring decisions are morally arbitrary or irrelevant. Similarly, when an affirmative action officer takes into account race and sex, use of these characteristics is not morally irrelevant or arbitrary. Since affirmative action aims to help end racial and sexual inequality by providing black and female role models for minorities (and non-minorities), the race and sex of the job candidates are clearly relevant to the decision. There is nothing arbitrary about the affirmative action officer focusing on race and sex. Hence, if reverse discrimination is wrong, it is not wrong for the reason that it uses morally irrelevant and arbitrary characteristics to distinguish between applicants.

3 Reverse Discrimination as Unjustified Stereotyping

It might be argued that reverse discrimination involves judging people by alleged average characteristics of a class to which they belong, instead of judging them on the basis of their individual characteristics, and that such judging on the basis of stereotypes is unjust. But the defense of affirmative action suggested in this paper does not rely on stereotyping. When an employer hires a slightly less well qualified woman or black over a slightly more qualified white male for the purpose of helping to overcome sexual and racial inequality, she judges the applicants on the basis of their individual characteristics. She uses this person's sex or skin color as a mechanism to help achieve the goals of affirmative action. Individual characteristics of the white male (his skin color and sex) prevent him from serving one of the legitimate goals of employment policies, and he is turned down on this basis.

Notice that the objection does have some force against those who defend reverse discrimination on the grounds of compensatory justice. An affirmative action policy whose purpose is to compensate women and blacks for past and current injustices judges that women and blacks on the average are owed greater compensation than are white males. Although this is true, opponents of affirmative action argue that some white males have been more severely and unfairly disadvantaged than some women and blacks. A poor white male from Appalachia may have suffered greater undeserved disadvantages than the upper-middle class woman or black with whom he competes. Although there is a high correlation between being female (or being black) and being especially owed compensation for unfair disadvantages suffered, the correlation is not universal.

Thus defending affirmative action on the grounds of compensatory justice may lead to unjust treatment of white males in individual cases. Despite the fact that certain white males are owed greater compensation than are some women or blacks, it is the latter that receive compensation. This is the result of judging candidates for jobs on the basis of the average characteristics of their class, rather than on the basis of their individual characteristics. Thus compensatory justice defenses of reverse discrimination may involve potentially problematic stereotyping. But this is not the defense of affirmative action considered here.

4 Failing to Hire the Most Qualified Person Is Unjust

One of the major reasons people think reverse discrimination is unjust is because they think that the most qualified person should get the job. But why should the most qualified person be hired?

A Efficiency   One obvious answer to this question is that one should hire the most qualified person because doing so promotes efficiency. If job qualifications are positively correlated with job performance, then the more qualified person will tend to do a better job. Although it is not always true that there is such a correlation, in general there is, and hence this point is well taken. There are short term efficiency costs of reverse discrimination as defined here.

Note that a weaker version of affirmative action has no such efficiency costs. If one hires a black or woman over a white male only in cases where qualifications are roughly equal, job performance will not be affected. Furthermore, efficiency costs will be a function of the qualifications gap between the black or woman hired, and the white male rejected: the larger the gap, the greater the efficiency costs. The existence of efficiency costs is also a function of the type of work performed. Many of the jobs in our society are ones which any normal person can do (e.g., assembly line worker, janitor, truck driver, etc.). Affirmative action hiring for these positions is unlikely to have significant efficiency costs (assuming whoever is hired is willing to work hard). In general, professional positions are the ones in which people's performance levels will vary significantly, and hence these are the jobs in which reverse discrimination could have significant efficiency costs.

While concern for efficiency gives us a reason for hiring the most qualified person, it in no way explains the alleged injustice suffered by the white male who is passed over due to reverse discrimination. If the affirmative action employer is treating the white male unjustly, it is not because the hiring policy is inefficient. Failing to maximize efficiency does not generally involve acting unjustly. For instance, a person who carries one bag of groceries at a time, rather than two, is acting inefficiently, though not unjustly.

It is arguable that the manager of a business who fails to hire the most qualified person (and thereby sacrifices some efficiency) treats the owners of the company unjustly, for their profits may suffer, and this violates one conception of the manager's fiduciary responsibility to the shareholders. Perhaps the administrator of a hospital who hires a slightly less well qualified black doctor (for the purposes of affirmative action) treats the future patients at that hospital unjustly, for doing so may reduce the level of health care they receive (and it is arguable that they have a legitimate expectation to receive the best health care possible for the money they spend). But neither of these examples of inefficiency leading to injustice concern the white male "victim" of affirmative action, and it is precisely this person who the opponents of reverse discrimination claim is being unfairly treated.

To many people, that a policy is inefficient is a sufficient reason for condemning it. This is especially true in the competitive and profit oriented world of business. However, profit maximization is not the only legitimate goal of business hiring policies (or other business decisions). Businesses have responsibilities to help heal society's ills, especially those (like racism and sexism) which they in large part helped to create and perpetuate. Unless one takes the implausible position that business' only legitimate goal is profit maximization, the efficiency costs of affirmative action are not an automatic reason for rejecting it. And as we have noted, affirmative action's efficiency costs are of no help in substantiating and explaining its alleged injustice to white males.

B The Most Qualified Person Has a Right to the Job   One could argue that the most qualified person for the job has a right to be hired in virtue of superior qualifications. On this view, reverse discrimination violates the better qualified white male's right to be hired for the job. But the most qualified applicant holds no such right. If you are the best painter in town, and a person hires her brother to paint her house, instead of you, your rights have not been violated. People do not have rights to be hired for particular jobs (though I think a plausible case can be made for the claim that there is a fundamental human right to employment). If anyone has a right in this matter, it is the employer. This is not to say, of course, that the employer cannot do wrong in her hiring decision; she obviously can. If she hires a white because she loathes blacks, she does wrong. The point is that her wrong does not consist in violating the right some candidate has to her job (though this would violate other rights of the candidate).

C   The Most Qualified Person Deserves the Job   It could be argued that the most qualified person should get the job because she deserves it in virtue of her superior qualifications. But the assumption that the person most qualified for a job is the one who most deserves it is problematic. Very often people do not deserve their qualifications, and hence they do not deserve anything on the basis of those qualifications. A person's qualifications are a function of at least the following factors: (a) innate abilities, (b) home environment, (c) socio-economic class of parents, (d) quality of the schools attended, (e) luck, and (f) effort or perseverance. A person is only responsible for the last factor on this list, and hence one only deserves one's qualifications to the extent that they are a function of effort.

It is undoubtedly often the case that a person who is less well qualified for a job is more deserving of the job (because she worked harder to achieve those lower qualifications) than is someone with superior qualifications. This is frequently true of women and blacks in the job market: they worked harder to overcome disadvantages most (or all) white males never faced. Hence, affirmative action policies which permit the hiring of slightly less well qualified candidates may often be more in line with considerations of desert than are the standard meritocratic procedures.

The point is not that affirmative action is defensible because it helps insure that more deserving candidates get jobs. Nor is it that desert should be the only or even the most important consideration in hiring decisions. The claim is simply that hiring the most qualified person for a job need not (and quite often does not) involve hiring the most deserving candidate. Hence the intuition that morality requires one to hire the most qualified people cannot be justified on the grounds that these people deserve to be hired.

D The Most Qualified Person Is Entitled to the Job One might think that although the most qualified person neither deserves the job nor has a right to the job, still this person is entitled to the job. By 'entitlement' in this context, I mean a natural and legitimate expectation based on a type of social promise. Society has implicitly encouraged the belief that the most qualified candidate will get the job. Society has set up a competition and the prize is a job which is awarded to those applying with the best qualifications. Society thus reneges on an implicit promise it has made to its members when it allows reverse discrimination to occur. It is dashing legitimate expectations it has encouraged. It is violating the very rules of a game it created.

Furthermore, the argument goes, by allowing reverse discrimination, society is breaking an explicit promise (contained in the Civil Rights Act of 1964) that it will not allow race or sex to be used against one of its citizens. Title VII of that Act prohibits discrimination in employment on the basis of race or sex (as well as color, religion, or national origin).

In response to this argument, it should first be noted that the above interpretation of the Civil Rights Act is misleading. In fact, the Supreme Court has interpreted the Act as allowing race and sex to be considered in hiring or admission decisions.[2] More importantly, since affirmative action has been an explicit national policy for the last twenty years (and has been supported in numerous court cases), it is implausible to argue that society has promised its members that it will not allow race or sex to outweigh superior qualifications in hiring decisions. In addition, the objection takes a naive and utopian view of actual hiring decisions. It presents a picture of our society as a pure meritocracy in which hiring decisions are based solely on qualifications. The only exception it sees to these meritocratic procedures is the unfortunate policy of affirmative action. But this picture is dramatically distorted. Elected government officials, political appointees, business managers, and many others clearly do not have their positions solely or even mostly because of their qualifications. Given the widespread acceptance in our society of procedures which are far from meritocratic, claiming that the most qualified person has a socially endorsed entitlement to the job is not believable.

5 Undermining Equal Opportunity for White Males

It has been claimed that the right of white males to an equal chance of employment is violated by affirmative action. Reverse discrimination, it is said, undermines equality of opportunity for white males.

If equality of opportunity requires a social environment in which everyone at birth has roughly the same chance of succeeding through the use of his or her natural talents, then it could well be argued that given the social, cultural, and educational disadvantages placed on women and blacks, preferential treatment of these groups brings us closer to equality of opportunity. White males are full members of the community in a way in which women and blacks are not, and this advantage is diminished by affirmative action. Affirmative action takes away the greater than equal opportunity white males generally have, and thus it brings us closer to a situation in which all members of society have an equal chance of succeeding through the use of their talents.

It should be noted that the goal of affirmative action is to bring about a society in which there is equality of opportunity for women and blacks without preferential treatment of these groups. It is not the purpose of the sort of affirmative action defended here to disadvantage white males in order to take away the advantage a sexist and racist society gives to them. But noticing that this occurs is sufficient to dispel the illusion that affirmative action undermines the equality of opportunity for white males.

LEGITIMATE OBJECTIONS

The following two considerations explain what is morally troubling about reverse discrimination.

1   Judging on the Basis of Involuntary Characteristics

In cases of reverse discrimination, white males are passed over on the basis of membership in a group they were born into. When an affirmative action employer hires a slightly less well qualified black (or woman), rather than a more highly qualified white male, skin color (or sex) is being used as one criterion for determining who gets a very important benefit. Making distinctions in how one treats people on the basis of characteristics they cannot help having (such as skin color or sex) is morally problematic because it reduces individual autonomy. Discriminating between people on the basis of features they can do something about is preferable, since it gives them some control over how others act towards them. They can develop the characteristics others use to give them favorable treatment and avoid those characteristics others use as grounds for unfavorable treatment.

For example, if employers refuse to hire you because you are a member of the American Nazi Party, and if you do not like the fact that you are having a hard time finding a job, you can choose to leave the party. However, if a white male is having trouble finding employment because slightly less well qualified women and blacks are being given jobs to meet affirmative action requirements, there is nothing he can do about this disadvantage, and his autonomy is curtailed.

Discriminating between people on the basis of their involuntary characteristics is morally undesirable, and thus reverse discrimination is also morally undesirable. Of course, that something is morally undesirable does not show that it is unjust, nor that it is morally unjustifiable.

How morally troubling is it to judge people on the basis of involuntary characteristics? Notice that our society frequently uses these sorts of features to distinguish between people. Height and good looks are characteristics one cannot do much about, and yet basketball players and models are ordinarily chosen and rejected on the basis of precisely these features. To a large extent our intelligence is also a feature beyond our control, and yet intelligence is clearly one of the major characteristics our society uses to determine what happens to people.

Of course there are good reasons why we distinguish between people on the basis of these sorts of involuntary characteristics. Given the goals of basketball teams, model agencies, and employers in general, hiring the taller, better looking, or more intelligent person (respectively) makes good sense. It promotes efficiency, since all these people are likely to do a better job. Hiring policies based on these involuntary characteristics serve the legitimate purposes of these businesses (e.g., profit and serving the public), and hence they may be morally justified despite their tendency to reduce the control people have over their own lives.

This argument applies to reverse discrimination as well. The purpose of affirmative action is to help eradicate racial and sexual injustice. If affirmative action policies help bring about this goal, then they can be morally justified despite their tendency to reduce the control white males have over their lives.

In one respect this sort of consequentialist argument is more forceful in the case of affirmative action. Rather than merely promoting the goal of efficiency (which is the justification for businesses hiring naturally brighter, taller, or more attractive individuals), affirmative action promotes the nonutilitarian goal of an egalitarian society. In general, promoting a consideration of justice (such as equality) is more important than is promoting efficiency or utility. Thus in terms of the importance of the objective, this consequentialist argument is stronger in the case of affirmative action. If one can justify reducing individual autonomy on the grounds that it promotes efficiency, one can certainly do so on the grounds that it reduces the injustice of racial and sexual inequality.

2   Burdening White Males without Compensation

Perhaps the strongest moral intuition concerning the wrongness of reverse discrimination is that it is unfair to job seeking white males. It is unfair because they have been given an undeserved disadvantage in the competition for employment; they have been handicapped because of something that is not their fault. Why should white males be made to pay for the sins of others?

It would be a mistake to argue for reverse discrimination on the grounds that white males deserve to be burdened and that therefore we should hire women and blacks even when white males are better qualified. Young white males who are now entering the job market are not more responsible for the evils of racial and sexual inequality than are other members of society. Thus, reverse discrimination is not properly viewed as punishment administered to white males.

The justification for affirmative action supported here claims that bringing about sexual and racial equality necessitates sacrifice on the part of white males who seek employment. An important step in bringing about the desired egalitarian society involves speeding up the process by which women and blacks get into positions of power and authority. This requires that white males find it harder to achieve these same positions. But this is not punishment for deeds done.

Thomas Nagel's helpful analogy is state condemnation of property under the right of eminent domain for the purpose of building a highway. Forcing some in the community to move in order that the community as a whole may benefit is unfair. Why should these individuals suffer rather than others? The answer is: Because they happen to live in a place where it is important to build a road. A similar response should be given to the white male who objects to reverse discrimination with the same "Why me?" question. The answer is: Because job seeking white males happen to be in the way of an important road leading to the desired egalitarian society. Job-seeking white males are being made to bear the brunt of the burden of affirmative action because of accidental considerations, just as are homeowners whose property is condemned in order to build a highway.[3]

This analogy is extremely illuminating and helpful in explaining the nature of reverse discrimination. There is, however, an important dissimilarity that Nagel does not mention. In cases of property condemnation, compensation is paid to the owner. Affirmative action policies, however, do not compensate white males for shouldering this burden of moving toward the desired egalitarian society. So affirmative action is unfair to job seeking white males because they are forced to bear an unduly large share of the burden of achieving racial and sexual equality without being compensated for this sacrifice. Since we have singled out job seeking white males from the larger pool of white males who should also help achieve this goal, it seems that some compensation from the latter to the former is appropriate.

This is a serious objection to affirmative action policies only if the uncompensated burden is substantial. Usually it is not. Most white male "victims" of affirmative action easily find employment. It is highly unlikely that the same white male will repeatedly fail to get hired because of affirmative action. The burdens of affirmative action should be spread as evenly as possible among all the job seeking white males. Furthermore, the burden job seeking white males face—of finding it somewhat more difficult to get employment—is inconsequential when compared to the burdens ongoing discrimination places on women and blacks. Forcing job seeking white males to bear an extra burden is acceptable because this is a necessary step toward achieving a much greater reduction in the unfair burdens our society places on women and blacks. If affirmative action is a necessary mechanism for a timely dismantlement of our racial and sexual caste system, the extra burdens it places on job seeking white males are justified.

Still the question remains: Why isn't compensation paid? When members of society who do not deserve extra burdens are singled out to sacrifice for an important community goal, society owes them compensation. This objection loses some of its force when one realizes that society continually places undeserved burdens on its members without compensating them. For instance, the burden of seeking efficiency is placed on the shoulders of the least naturally talented and intelligent. That one is born less intelligent (or otherwise less talented) does not mean that one deserves to have reduced employment opportunities, and yet our society's meritocratic hiring procedures make it much harder for less naturally talented members to find meaningful employment. These people are not compensated for their sacrifices either.

Of course, pointing out that there are other examples of an allegedly problematic social policy does not justify that policy. Nonetheless, if this analogy is sound, failing to compensate job-seeking white males for the sacrifices placed on them by reverse discrimination is not without precedent. Furthermore, it is no more morally troublesome than is failing to compensate less talented members of society for their undeserved sacrifice of employment opportunities for the sake of efficiency.

CONCLUSION

This article has shown the difficulties in pinpointing what is morally troubling about reverse discrimination. The most commonly heard objections to reverse discrimination fail to make their case. Reverse discrimination is not morally equivalent to traditional racism and sexism since its goals and consequences are entirely different, and the act of treating people differently on the basis of race or sex is not necessarily morally wrong. The race and sex of the candidates are not morally irrelevant in all hiring decisions, and affirmative action hiring is an example where discriminating on the basis of race or sex is not morally arbitrary. Furthermore, affirmative action can be defended on grounds that do not involve stereotyping. Though affirmative action hiring of less well qualified applicants can lead to short run inefficiency, failing to hire the most qualified applicant does not violate this person's rights, entitlements, or deserts. Additionally, affirmative action hiring does not generally undermine equal opportunity for white males.

Reverse discrimination is morally troublesome in that it judges people on the basis of involuntary characteristics and thus reduces the control they have over their lives. It also places a larger than fair share of the burden of achieving an egalitarian society on the shoulders of job seeking white males without compensating them for this sacrifice. But these problems are relatively minor when compared to the grave injustice of racial and sexual inequality, and they are easily outweighed if affirmative action helps alleviate this far greater injustice.

NOTES

I thank Cheshire Calhoun, Beverly Diamond, John Dickerson, Jasper Hunt, Glenn Lesses, Richard Nunan, and Martin Perlmutter for helpful comments.

1 Peter Singer, "Is Racial Discrimination Arbitrary?" *Philosophia,* vol. 8 (November 1978), pp. 185–203.

2 See Justice William Brennan's majority opinion in *United Steel Workers and Kaiser Aluminum v. Weber,* United States Supreme Court, *443 U.S. 193* (1979). See also Justice Lewis Powell's majority opinion in the *University of California v. Bakke,* United States Supreme Court, *438 U.S. 265* (1978).

3 Thomas Nagel, "A Defense of Affirmative Action" in *Ethical Theory and Business,* 2nd edition, ed. Tom Beauchamp and Norman Bowie (Englewood Cliffs, NJ: Prentice-Hall, 1983), p. 484.

QUESTIONS

1 Are there morally significant differences between reverse discrimination and traditional racism and sexism?
2 Do consequentialist considerations justify preferential treatment policies? Explain your reasoning.

Affirmative Action: The Price of Preference

Shelby Steele

Shelby Steele is professor of English at San Jose State University. He is the author of *The Content of Our Character: A New Vision of Race in America* (1990) and articles such as "Being Black and Feeling Blue."

Steele criticizes affirmative action programs that give preference to minority applicants. He argues that blacks have more to lose than to gain from preferential treatment. First, these programs do not address the underlying problem—the need to develop a formerly oppressed people so that they can achieve proportionate representation on their own. Second, they are demoralizing for blacks since the assumption underlying preferential treatment programs is the inferiority of the black applicants. Third, such programs encourage blacks to exploit their own past victimization. In Steele's view, affirmative action should not involve preferential treatment but should serve what he sees as the original purpose of affirmative action—enforcing equal opportunity and applying strong sanctions when actual discrimination is found.

In a few short years, when my two children will be applying to college, the affirmative action policies by which most universities offer black students some form of preferential treatment will present me with a dilemma. I am a middle-class black, a college professor, far from wealthy, but also well-removed from the kind of deprivation that would qualify my children for the label "disadvantaged." Both of them have endured racial insensitivity from whites. They have been called names, have suffered slights, and have experienced firsthand the peculiar malevolence that racism brings out in people. Yet, they have never experienced racial discrimination, have never been stopped by their race on any path they have chosen to follow. Still, their society now tells them that if they will only designate themselves as black on their college applications, they will likely do better in the college lottery than if they conceal this fact. I think there is something of a Faustian bargain in this.

Of course, many blacks and a considerable number of whites would say that I was sanctimoniously making affirmative action into a test of character. They would say that this small preference is the meagerest recompense for centuries of unrelieved oppression. And to these arguments other very obvious facts must be added. In America, many marginally competent or flatly incompetent whites are hired every-day—some because their white skin suits the conscious or unconscious racial pref-erence of their employer. The white children of alumni are often grandfathered into elite universities in what can only be seen as a residual benefit of historic white priv-ilege. Worse, white incompetence is always an individual matter, while for blacks it is often confirmation of ugly stereotypes. The Peter Principle was not conceived with only blacks in mind. Given that unfairness cuts both ways, doesn't it only bal-ance the scales of history that my children now receive a slight preference over whites? Doesn't this repay, in a small way, the systematic denial under which their grandfather lived out his days?

So, in theory, affirmative action certainly has all the moral symmetry that fair-ness requires—the injustice of historical and even contemporary white advantage is offset with black advantage; preference replaces prejudice, inclusion answers ex-clusion. It is reformist and corrective, even repentent and redemptive. And I would never sneer at these good intentions. Born in the late forties in Chicago, I started my education (a charitable term in this case) in a segregated school and suffered all the indignities that come to blacks in a segregated society. My father, born in the South, only made it to the third grade before the white man's fields took permanent prior-ity over his formal education. And though he educated himself into an advanced reader with an almost professorial authority, he could only drive a truck for a living and never earned more than ninety dollars a week in his entire life. So yes, it is cru-cial to my sense of citizenship, to my ability to identify with the spirit and the inter-ests of America, to know that this country, however imperfectly, recognizes its past sins and wishes to correct them.

Yet good intentions, because of the opportunity for innocence they offer us, are very seductive and can blind us to the effects they generate when implemented. In our society, affirmative action is, among other things, a testament to white goodwill and to black power, and in the midst of these heavy investments, its effects can be hard to see. But after twenty years of implementation, I think affirmative action has shown itself to be more bad than good and that blacks—whom I will focus on in this essay—now stand to lose more from it than they gain.

In talking with affirmative action administrators and with blacks and whites in general, it is clear that supporters of affirmative action focus on its good intentions while detractors emphasize its negative effects. Proponents talk about "diversity" and "pluralism"; opponents speak of "reverse discrimination," the unfairness of quotas and set-asides. It was virtually impossible to find people outside either camp. The closest I came was a white male manager at a large computer company who said, "I think it amounts to reverse discrimination, but I'll put up with a little of that for a little more diversity." I'll live with a little of the effect to gain a little of the inten-tion, he seemed to be saying. But this only makes him a halfhearted supporter of af-firmative action. I think many people who don't really like affirmative action sup-port it to one degree or another anyway.

I believe they do this because of what happened to white and black Americans in the crucible of the sixties when whites were confronted with their racial guilt and blacks tasted their first real power. In this stormy time white absolution and black power coalesced into virtual mandates for society. Affirmative action became a meeting ground for these mandates in the law, and in the late sixties and early seventies it underwent a remarkable escalation of its mission from simple anti-discrimination enforcement to social engineering by means of quotas, goals, timetables, set-asides and other forms of preferential treatment.

Legally, this was achieved through a series of executive orders and EEOC guidelines that allowed racial imbalances in the workplace to stand as proof of racial discrimination. Once it could be assumed that discrimination explained racial imbalances, it became easy to justify group remedies to presumed discrimination, rather than the normal case-by-case redress for proven discrimination. Preferential treatment through quotas, goals, and so on is designed to correct imbalances based on the assumption that they always indicate discrimination. This expansion of what constitutes discrimination allowed affirmative action to escalate into the business of social engineering in the name of anti-discrimination, to push society toward statistically proportionate racial representation, without any obligation of proving actual discrimination.

What accounted for this shift, I believe, was the white mandate to achieve a new racial innocence and the black mandate to gain power. Even though blacks had made great advances during the sixties without quotas, these mandates, which came to a head in the very late sixties, could no longer be satisfied by anything less than racial preferences. I don't think these mandates in themselves were wrong, since whites clearly needed to do better by blacks and blacks needed more real power in society. But, as they came together in affirmative action, their effect was to distort our understanding of racial discrimination in a way that allowed us to offer the remediation of preference on the basis of mere color rather than actual injury. By making black the color of preference, these mandates have reburdened society with the very marriage of color and preference (in reverse) that we set out to eradicate. The old sin is reaffirmed in a new guise.

But the essential problem with this form of affirmative action is the way it leaps over the hard business of developing a formerly oppressed people to the point where they can achieve proportionate representation on their own (given equal opportunity) and goes straight for the proportionate representation. This may satisfy some whites of their innocence and some blacks of their power, but it does very little to truly uplift blacks.

A white female affirmative action officer at an Ivy League university told me what many supporters of affirmative action now say: "We're after diversity. We ideally want a student body where racial and ethnic groups are represented according to their proportion in society." When affirmative action escalated into social engineering, diversity became a golden word. It grants whites an egalitarian fairness (innocence) and blacks an entitlement to proportionate representation (power). *Diversity* is a term that applies democratic principles to races and cultures rather than to citizens, despite the fact that there is nothing to indicate that real diversity is the same thing as proportionate representation. Too often the result of this on campuses (for example) has been a democracy of colors rather than of people, an artificial diversity that gives the appearance of an educational parity between black and white students that has not yet been achieved in reality. Here again, racial preferences allow society to leapfrog over the difficult problem of developing blacks to parity with whites and into a cosmetic diversity that covers the blemish of disparity—a full six years after admission, only about 26 percent of black students graduate from college.

Racial representation is not the same thing as racial development, yet affirmative action fosters a confusion of these very different needs. Representation can be manufactured; development is always hard-earned. However, it is the music of innocence and power that we hear in affirmative action that causes us to cling to it and to its distracting emphasis on representation. The fact is that after twenty years of racial preferences, the gap between white and black median income is greater than it was in the seventies. None of this is to say that blacks don't need policies that ensure our right to equal opportunity, but what we need more is the development that will let us take advantage of society's efforts to include us.

I think that one of the most troubling effects of racial preferences for blacks is a kind of demoralization, or put another way, an enlargement of self-doubt. Under affirmative action the quality that earns us preferential treatment is an implied inferiority. However this inferiority is explained—and it is easily enough explained by the myriad deprivations that grew out of our oppression—it is still inferiority. There are explanations, and then there is the fact. And the fact must be borne by the individual as a condition apart from the explanation, apart even from the fact that others like himself also bear this condition. In integrated situations where blacks must compete with whites who may be better prepared, these explanations may quickly wear thin and expose the individual to racial as well as personal self-doubt.

All of this is compounded by the cultural myth of black inferiority that blacks have always lived with. What this means in practical terms is that when blacks deliver themselves into integrated situations, they encounter a nasty little reflex in whites, a mindless, atavistic reflex that responds to the color black with alarm. Attributions may follow this alarm if the white cares to indulge them, and if they do, they will most likely be negative—one such attribution is intellectual ineptness. I think this reflex and the attributions that may follow it embarrass most whites today, therefore, it is usually quickly repressed. Nevertheless, on an equally atavistic level, the black will be aware of the reflex his color triggers and will feel a stab of horror at seeing himself reflected in this way. He, too, will do a quick repression, but a lifetime of such stabbings is what constitutes his inner realm of racial doubt.

The effects of this may be a subject for another essay. The point here is that the implication of inferiority that racial preferences engender in both the white and black mind expands rather than contracts this doubt. Even when the black sees no implication of inferiority in racial preferences, he knows that whites do, so that—consciously or unconsciously—the result is virtually the same. The effect of preferential treatment—the lowering of normal standards to increase black representation—puts blacks at war with an expanded realm of debilitating doubt, so that the doubt itself becomes an unrecognized preoccupation that undermines their ability to perform, especially in integrated situations. On largely white campuses, blacks are five times more likely to drop out than whites. Preferential treatment, no matter how it is justified in the light of day, subjects blacks to a midnight of self-doubt, and so often transforms their advantage into a revolving door.

Another liability of affirmative action comes from the fact that it indirectly encourages blacks to exploit their own past victimization as a source of power and privilege. Victimization, like implied inferiority, is what justifies preference, so that to receive the benefits of preferential treatment one must, to some extent, become invested in the view of one's self as a victim. In this way, affirmative action nurtures a victim-focused identity in blacks. The obvious irony here is that we become inadvertently invested in the very condition we are trying to overcome. Racial preferences send us the message that there is more power in our past suffering than our present achievements—none of which could bring us a *preference* over others.

When power itself grows out of suffering, then blacks are encouraged to expand the boundaries of what qualifies as racial oppression, a situation that can lead us to paint our victimization in vivid colors, even as we receive the benefits of preference. The same corporations and institutions that give us preference are also seen as our oppressors. At Stanford University minority students—some of whom enjoy as much as $15,000 a year in financial aid—recently took over the president's office demanding, among other things, more financial aid. The power to be found in victimization, like any power, is intoxicating and can lend itself to the creation of a new class of super-victims who can feel the pea of victimization under twenty mattresses. Preferential treatment rewards us for being underdogs rather than for moving beyond that status—a misplacement of incentives that, along with its deepening of our doubt, is more a yoke than a spur.

But, I think, one of the worst prices that blacks pay for preference has to do with an illusion. I saw this illusion at work recently in the mother of a middle-class black student who was going off to his first semester of college. "They owe us this, so don't think for a minute that you don't belong there." This is the logic by which many blacks, and some whites, justify affirmative action—it is something "owed," a form of reparation. But this logic overlooks a much harder and less digestible reality, that it is impossible to repay blacks living today for the historic suffering of the race. If all blacks were given a million dollars tomorrow morning it would not amount to a dime on the dollar of three centuries of oppression, nor would it obviate the residues of that oppression that we still carry today. The concept of historic reparation grows out of man's need to impose a degree of justice on the world that simply does not exist. Suffering can be endured and overcome, it cannot be repaid. Blacks cannot be repaid for the injustice done to the race, but we can be corrupted by society's guilty gestures of repayment.

Affirmative action is such a gesture. It tells us that racial preferences can do for us what we cannot do for ourselves. The corruption here is in the hidden incentive *not* to do what we believe preferences will do. This is an incentive to be reliant on others just as we are struggling for self-reliance. And it keeps alive the illusion that we can find some deliverance in repayment. The hardest thing for any sufferer to accept is that his suffering excuses him from very little and never has enough currency to restore him. To think otherwise is to prolong the suffering.

Several blacks I spoke with said they were still in favor of affirmative action because of the "subtle" discrimination blacks were subject to once on the job. One photojournalist said, "They have ways of ignoring you." A black female television producer said, "You can't file a lawsuit when your boss doesn't invite you to the insider meetings without ruining your career. So we still need affirmative action." Others mentioned the infamous "glass ceiling" through which blacks can see the top positions of authority but never reach them. But I don't think racial preferences are a protection against this subtle discrimination; I think they contribute to it.

In any workplace, racial preferences will always create two-tiered populations composed of preferreds and unpreferreds. This division makes automatic a perception of enhanced competence for the unpreferreds and of questionable competence for the preferreds—the former earned his way, even though others were given preference, while the latter made it by color as much as by competence. Racial preferences implicitly mark whites with an exaggerated superiority just as they mark blacks with an exaggerated inferiority. They not only reinforce America's oldest racial myth but, for blacks, they have the effect of stigmatizing the already stigmatized.

I think that much of the "subtle" discrimination that blacks talk about is often (not always) discrimination against the stigma of questionable competence that affirmative action delivers to blacks. In this sense, preferences scapegoat the very people they seek to help. And it may be that at a certain level employers impose a glass ceiling, but this may not be against the race so much as against the race's reputation for having advanced by color as much as by competence. Affirmative action makes a glass ceiling virtually necessary as a protection against the corruptions of preferential treatment. This ceiling is the point at which corporations shift the emphasis from color to competency and stop playing the affirmative action game. Here preference backfires for blacks and becomes a taint that holds them back. Of course, one could argue that this taint, which is, after all, in the minds of whites, becomes nothing more than an excuse to discriminate against blacks. And certainly the result is the same in either case—blacks don't get past the glass ceiling. But this argument does not get around the fact that racial preferences now taint this color with a new theme of suspicion that makes it even more vulnerable to the impulse in others to discriminate. In this crucial yet gray area of perceived competence, preferences make whites look better than they are and blacks worse, while doing nothing whatever to stop the very real discrimination that blacks may encounter. I don't wish to justify the glass ceiling here, but only to suggest the very subtle ways that affirmative action revives rather than extinguishes the old rationalizations for racial discrimination.

In education, a revolving door; in employment, a glass ceiling.

I believe affirmative action is problematic in our society because it tries to function like a social program. Rather than ask it to ensure equal opportunity we have demanded that it create parity between the races. But preferential treatment does not teach skills, or educate, or instill motivation. It only passes out entitlement by color, a situation that in my profession has created an unrealistically high demand for black professors. The social engineer's assumption is that this high demand will inspire more blacks to earn Ph.D.'s and join the profession. In fact, the number of blacks earning Ph.D.'s has declined in recent years. A Ph.D. must be developed from preschool on. He requires family and community support. He must acquire an entire system of values that enables him to work hard while delaying gratification. There are social programs, I believe, that can (and should) help blacks *develop* in all these areas, but entitlement by color is not a social program; it is a dubious reward for being black.

It now seems clear that the Supreme Court, in a series of recent decisions, is moving away from racial preferences. It has disallowed preferences except in instances of "identified discrimination," eroded the precedent that statistical racial imbalances are *prima facie* evidence of discrimination, and in effect granted white males the right to challenge consent degrees that use preference to achieve racial balances in the workplace. One civil rights leader said, "Night has fallen on civil rights." But I am not so sure. The effect of these decisions is to protect the constitutional rights of everyone rather than take rights away from blacks. What they do take away from blacks is the special entitlement to more rights than others that preferences always grant. Night has fallen on racial preferences, not on the fundamental rights of black Americans. The reason for this shift, I believe, is that the white mandate for absolution from past racial sins has weakened considerably during the eighties. Whites are now less willing to endure unfairness to themselves in order to grant special entitlements to blacks, even when these entitlements are justified in the name of past suffering. Yet the black mandate for more power in society has remained unchanged. And I think part of the anxiety that many blacks feel over these decisions has to do with the loss of black power they may signal. We had won a certain specialness and now we are losing it.

But the power we've lost by these decisions is really only the power that grows out of our victimization—the power to claim special entitlements under the law because of past oppression. This is not a very substantial or reliable power, and it is important that we know this so we can focus more exclusively on the kind of development that will bring enduring power. There is talk now that Congress will pass new legislation to compensate for these new limits on affirmative action. If this happens, I hope that their focus will be on development and anti-discrimination rather than entitlement, on achieving racial parity rather than jerry-building racial diversity.

I would also like to see affirmative action go back to its original purpose of enforcing equal opportunity—a purpose that in itself disallows racial preferences. We cannot be sure that the discriminatory impulse in America has yet been shamed into extinction, and I believe affirmative action can make its greatest contribution by providing a rigorous vigilance in this area. It can guard constitutional rather than racial rights, and help institutions evolve standards of merit and selection that are appropriate to the institution's needs yet as free of racial bias as possible (again, with the understanding that racial imbalances are not always an indication of racial bias). One of the most important things affirmative action can do is to define exactly what racial discrimination is and how it might manifest itself within a specific institution. The impulse to discriminate *is* subtle and cannot be ferreted out unless its many guises are made clear to people. Along with this there should be monitoring of institutions and heavy sanctions brought to bear when actual discrimination is found. This is the sort of affirmative action that America owes to blacks and to itself. It goes after the evil of discrimination itself, while preferences only sidestep the evil and grant entitlement to its *presumed* victims.

But if not preferences, then what? I think we need social policies that are committed to two goals: the educational and economic development of disadvantaged people, regardless of race, and the eradication from our society—through close monitoring and severe sanctions—of racial, ethnic, or gender discrimination. Preferences will not deliver us to either of these goals, since they tend to benefit those who are not disadvantaged—middle-class white women and middle-class blacks—and attack one form of discrimination with another. Preferences are inexpensive and carry the glamour of good intentions—change the numbers and the good deed is done. To be against them is to be unkind. But I think the unkindest cut is to bestow on children like my own an undeserved advantage while neglecting the development of those disadvantaged children on the East Side of my city who will likely never be in a position to benefit from a preference. Give my children fairness; give disadvantaged children a better shot at development—better elementary and secondary schools, job training, safer neighborhoods, better financial assistance for college, and so on. Fewer blacks go to college today than ten years ago; more black males of college age are in prison or under the control of the criminal justice system than in college. This despite racial preferences.

The mandates of black power and white absolution out of which preferences emerged were not wrong in themselves. What was wrong was that both races focused more on the goals of these mandates than on the means to the goals. Blacks can have no real power without taking responsibility for their own educational and economic development. Whites can have no racial innocence without earning it by eradicating discrimination and helping the disadvantaged to develop. Because we ignored the means, the goals have not been reached, and the real work remains to be done.

QUESTIONS

1 Has Steele given compelling reasons to support his claim that blacks have more to lose than to gain from preferential treatment programs?
2 What government policies should be adopted to further one of the goals that Steele sees as important—the educational and economic development of disadvantaged people?

Opinion in *Adarand Constructors v. Federico Pena, Secretary of Transportation*

Justice Sandra Day O'Connor

A biographical sketch of Justice Sandra Day O'Connor is found on p. 39.

Mountain Gravel & Construction Company received a federal agency contract for a highway construction project. It awarded a subcontract for guardrail work to Gonzales Construction Company, a Hispanic-owned company, which had been certified as a small disadvantaged business. Adarand Constructors, Inc., a white-owned highway construction company specializing in guardrail work had submitted the low bid. However, Mountain Gravel gave the subcontract to Gonzales because of financial incentives offered to companies receiving federal agency contracts who award subcontracts to small disadvantaged businesses. Adarand sued various federal officials, including Federico Pena, claiming that the race-based presumptions underlying such financial incentives violate the equal protection component of the Fifth Amendment's Due Process Clause. Both a district court and the Court of Appeals ruled against Adarand. The Court of Appeals, in assessing the constitutionality of the federal policy, used a lenient standard, citing two previous United States Supreme Court decisions, including *Metro Broadcasting, Inc. v. FCC,* which the Court of Appeals saw as requiring only intermediate, rather than strict, scrutiny for federal programs involving racial classifications.

   In this plurality opinion, O'Connor asserts that all race-based classifications involving unequal treatment must be subjected to the strictest judicial scrutiny— that is, they must be narrowly tailored measures that further compelling governmental interests. She rejects the weaker standard used by the Court of Appeals, thus overturning the U.S. Supreme Court's ruling in *Metro Broadcasting.* In reaching her conclusions, O'Connor asserts that consistency requires that all governmental racial classifications be subjected to the same strict standard.

Petitioner Adarand Constructors, Inc., claims that the Federal Government's practice of giving general contractors on government projects a financial incentive to hire subcontractors controlled by "socially and economically disadvantaged individuals," and in particular, the Government's use of race-based presumptions in identifying such individuals, violates the equal protection component of the Fifth Amendment's Due Process Clause. The Court of Appeals rejected Adarand's claim. We conclude, however, that courts should analyze cases of this kind under a different standard of review than the one the Court of Appeals applied. We therefore vacate the Court of Appeals' judgment and remand the case for further proceedings.

United States Supreme Court. 115 S.Ct. 2097 (1995).

I

In 1989, the Central Federal Lands Highway Division (CFLHD), which is part of the United States Department of Transportation (DOT), awarded the prime contract for a highway construction project in Colorado to Mountain Gravel & Construction Company. Mountain Gravel then solicited bids from subcontractors for the guardrail portion of the contract. Adarand, a Colorado-based highway construction company specializing in guardrail work, submitted the low bid. Gonzales Construction Company also submitted a bid.

The prime contract's terms provide that Mountain Gravel would receive additional compensation if it hired subcontractors certified as small businesses controlled by "socially and economically disadvantaged individuals," Gonzales is certified as such a business; Adarand is not. Mountain Gravel awarded the subcontract to Gonzales, despite Adarand's low bid, and Mountain Gravel's Chief Estimator has submitted an affidavit stating that Mountain Gravel would have accepted Adarand's bid, had it not been for the additional payment it received by hiring Gonzales instead. Federal law requires that a subcontracting clause similar to the one used here must appear in most federal agency contracts, and it also requires the clause to state that "[t]he contractor shall presume that socially and economically disadvantaged individuals include Black Americans, Hispanic Americans, Native Americans, Asian Pacific Americans, and other minorities, or any other individual found to be disadvantaged by the [Small Business] Administration pursuant to section 8(a) of the Small Business Act." Adarand claims that the presumption set forth in that statute discriminates on the basis of race in violation of the Federal Government's Fifth Amendment obligation not to deny anyone equal protection of the laws. . . .

After losing the guardrail subcontract to Gonzales, Adarand filed suit against various federal officials in the United States District Court for the District of Colorado, claiming that the race-based presumptions involved in the use of subcontracting compensation clauses violate Adarand's right to equal protection. The District Court granted the Government's motion for summary judgment. The Court of Appeals for the Tenth Circuit affirmed. It understood our decision in *Fullilove* v. *Klutznick* (1980) to have adopted "a lenient standard, resembling intermediate scrutiny, in assessing" the constitutionality of federal race-based action. Applying that "lenient standard," as further developed in *Metro Broadcasting, Inc.* v. *FCC* (1990), the Court of Appeals upheld the use of subcontractor compensation clauses. . . .

II

. . . In 1978, the Court confronted the question whether race-based governmental action designed to *benefit* . . . groups [that have suffered discrimination in our society] should . . . be subject to "the most rigid scrutiny." *Regents of Univ. of California* v. *Bakke* involved an equal protection challenge to a state-run medical school's practice of reserving a number of spaces in its entering class for minority students. The petitioners argued that "strict scrutiny" should apply only to "classifications that disadvantage 'discrete and insular minorities.' " *Bakke* did not produce an opinion for the Court, but Justice Powell's opinion announcing the Court's judgment rejected the argument. In a passage joined by Justice White, Justice Powell wrote that "[t]he guarantee of equal protection cannot mean one thing when applied to one individual and something else when applied to a person of another color." He concluded that "[r]acial and ethnic distinctions of any sort are inherently suspect and thus call for the most exacting judicial examination." On the other hand, four Justices in *Bakke* would have applied a less stringent standard of review to racial classifications "designed to further remedial purposes." . . .

Two years after *Bakke,* the Court faced another challenge to remedial race-based action, this time involving action undertaken by the Federal Government. In *Fullilove* v. *Klutznick* the Court upheld Congress' inclusion of a 10% set-aside for minority-owned businesses in the Public Works Employment Act of 1977. As in *Bakke,* there was no opinion for the Court. Chief Justice Burger, in an opinion joined by Justices White and Powell, observed that "[a]ny preference based on racial or ethnic criteria must necessarily receive a most searching examination to make sure that it does not conflict with constitutional guarantees." That opinion, however, "d[id] not adopt, either expressly or implicitly, the formulas of analysis articulated in such cases as [*Bakke*]." It employed instead a two-part test which asked, first, "whether the *objectives* of th[e] legislation are within the power of Congress," and second, "whether the limited use of racial and ethnic criteria, in the context presented, is a constitutionally permissible *means* for achieving the congressional objectives." . . . Justice Powell wrote separately to express his view that the plurality opinion had essentially applied "strict scrutiny" as described in his *Bakke* opinion—*i.e.,* it had determined that the set-aside was "a necessary means of advancing a compelling governmental interest." . . . Justice Stewart (joined by then JUSTICE REHNQUIST) dissented, arguing that the Constitution required the Federal Government to meet the same strict standard as the States when enacting racial classifications. . . . Justice Marshall (joined by Justices Brennan and Blackmun) concurred in the judgment, reiterating the view of four Justices in *Bakke* that any race-based governmental action designed to "remed[y] the present effects of past racial discrimination" should be upheld if it was "substantially related" to the achievement of an "important governmental objective"—*i.e.,* such action should be subjected only to what we now call "intermediate scrutiny."

In *Wygant* v. *Jackson Board of Ed.* (1986), the Court considered a Fourteenth Amendment challenge to another form of remedial racial classification. The issue in *Wygant* was whether a school board could adopt race-based preferences in determining which teachers to lay off. Justice Powell's plurality opinion observed that "the level of scrutiny does not change merely because the challenged classification operates against a group that historically has not been subject to governmental discrimination," and stated the two-part inquiry as "whether the layoff provision is supported by a compelling state purpose and whether the means chosen to accomplish that purpose are narrowly tailored." In other words, "racial classifications of any sort must be subjected to 'strict scrutiny.' " The plurality then concluded that the school board's interest in "providing minority role models for its minority students, as an attempt to alleviate the effects of societal discrimination," was not a compelling interest that could justify the use of a racial classification. It added that "[s]ocietal dis-

crimination, without more, is too amorphous a basis for imposing a racially classified remedy," and insisted instead that "a public employer . . . must ensure that, before it embarks on an affirmative-action program, it has convincing evidence that remedial action is warranted. That is, it must have sufficient evidence to justify the
conclusion that there has been prior discrimination." . . .

The Court's failure to produce a majority opinion in *Bakke, Fullilove,* and *Wygant*
left unresolved the proper analysis for remedial race-based governmental action. . . .

The Court resolved the issue, at least in part, in 1989. *Richmond* v. *J. A. Croson
Co.,* 488 U. S. 469 (1989), concerned a city's determination that 30% of its contracting work should go to minority-owned businesses. A majority of the Court in
Croson held that "the standard of review under the Equal Protection Clause is not
dependent on the race of those burdened or benefited by a particular classification,"
and that the single standard of review for racial classifications should be "strict
scrutiny." . . .

Despite lingering uncertainty in the details, however, the Court's cases through
Croson had established three general propositions with respect to governmental
racial classifications. First, skepticism: " '[a]ny preference based on racial or ethnic
criteria must necessarily receive a most searching examination.' " . . . Second, consistency: "the standard of review under the Equal Protection Clause is not dependent
on the race of those burdened or benefited by a particular classification," *i.e.,* all racial
classifications reviewable under the Equal Protection Clause must be strictly scrutinized. And third, congruence: "[e]qual protection analysis in the Fifth Amendment
area is the same as that under the Fourteenth Amendment." Taken together, these
three propositions lead to the conclusion that any person, of whatever race, has the
right to demand that any governmental actor subject to the Constitution justify any
racial classification subjecting that person to unequal treatment under the strictest
judicial scrutiny. Justice Powell's defense of this conclusion bears repeating here:

> "If it is the individual who is entitled to judicial protection against classifications based
> upon his racial or ethnic background because such distinctions impinge upon personal
> rights, rather than the individual only because of his membership in a particular group,
> then constitutional standards may be applied consistently. Political judgments regarding
> the necessity for the particular classification may be weighed in the constitutional balance,
> but the standard of justification will remain constant. This is as it should be, since those
> political judgments are the product of rough compromise struck by contending groups
> within the democratic process. When they touch upon an individual's race or ethnic back-
> ground, he is entitled to a judicial determination that the burden he is asked to bear on that
> basis is precisely tailored to serve a compelling governmental interest. The Constitution
> guarantees that right to every person regardless of his background."

A year later, however, the Court took a surprising turn. *Metro Broadcasting, Inc.*
v. *FCC* involved a Fifth Amendment challenge to two race-based policies of the Federal Communications Commission. In *Metro Broadcasting,* the Court repudiated the
long-held notion that "it would be unthinkable that the same Constitution would impose a lesser duty on the Federal Government" than it does on a State to afford equal
protection of the laws. It did so by holding that "benign" federal racial classifications need only satisfy intermediate scrutiny, even though *Croson* had recently concluded that such classifications enacted by a State must satisfy strict scrutiny.

"[B]enign" federal racial classifications, the Court said, "—even if those measures are not 'remedial' in the sense of being designed to compensate victims of past governmental or societal discrimination—are constitutionally permissible to the extent that they serve *important* governmental objectives within the power of Congress and are *substantially related* to achievement of those objectives." The Court did not explain how to tell whether a racial classification should be deemed "benign," other than to express "confiden[ce] that an 'examination of the legislative scheme and its history' will separate benign measures from other types of racial classifications."

Applying this test, the Court first noted that the FCC policies at issue did not serve as a remedy for past discrimination. Proceeding on the assumption that the policies were nonetheless "benign," it concluded that they served the "important governmental objective" of "enhancing broadcast diversity," and that they were "substantially related" to that objective. It therefore upheld the policies.

By adopting intermediate scrutiny as the standard of review for congressionally mandated "benign" racial classifications, *Metro Broadcasting* departed from prior cases in two significant respects. First, it turned its back on *Croson*'s explanation of why strict scrutiny of all governmental racial classifications is essential:

> "Absent searching judicial inquiry into the justification for such race-based measures, there is simply no way of determining what classifications are 'benign' or 'remedial' and what classifications are in fact motivated by illegitimate notions of racial inferiority or simple racial politics. Indeed, the purpose of strict scrutiny is to 'smoke out' illegitimate uses of race by assuring that the legislative body is pursuing a goal important enough to warrant use of a highly suspect tool. The test also ensures that the means chosen 'fit' this compelling goal so closely that there is little or no possibility that the motive for the classification was illegitimate racial prejudice or stereotype."

We adhere to that view today, despite the surface appeal of holding "benign" racial classifications to a lower standard, because "it may not always be clear that a so-called preference is in fact benign." "[M]ore than good motives should be required when government seeks to allocate its resources by way of an explicit racial classification system."

Second, *Metro Broadcasting* squarely rejected one of the three propositions established by the Court's earlier equal protection cases, namely, congruence between the standards applicable to federal and state racial classifications, and in so doing also undermined the other two—skepticism of all racial classifications, and consistency of treatment irrespective of the race of the burdened or benefited group. Under *Metro Broadcasting,* certain racial classifications ("benign" ones enacted by the Federal Government) should be treated less skeptically than others; and the race of the benefited group is critical to the determination of which standard of review to apply. *Metro Broadcasting* was thus a significant departure from much of what had come before it.

The three propositions undermined by *Metro Broadcasting* all derive from the basic principle that the Fifth and Fourteenth Amendments to the Constitution protect *persons,* not *groups.* It follows from that principle that all governmental action based on race—a *group* classification long recognized as "in most circumstances irrelevant and therefore prohibited"—should be subjected to detailed judicial inquiry to ensure that the *personal* right to equal protection of the laws has not been infringed. These ideas have long been central to this Court's understanding of equal protection, and holding "benign" state and federal racial classifications to different standards does not square with them. "[A] free people whose institutions are founded upon the doctrine of equality" should tolerate no retreat from the principle that government may treat people differently because of their race only for the most compelling reasons. Accordingly, we hold today that all racial classifications, imposed by whatever federal, state, or local governmental actor, must be analyzed by a reviewing court under strict scrutiny. In other words, such classifications are constitutional only if they are narrowly tailored measures that further compelling governmental interests. To the extent that *Metro Broadcasting* is inconsistent with that holding, it is overruled. . . .

Finally, we wish to dispel the notion that strict scrutiny is "strict in theory, but fatal in fact." The unhappy persistence of both the practice and the lingering effects of racial discrimination against minority groups in this country is an unfortunate reality, and government is not disqualified from acting in response to it. As recently as 1987, for example, every Justice of this Court agreed that the Alabama Department of Public Safety's "pervasive, systematic, and obstinate discriminatory conduct" justified a narrowly tailored race-based remedy. When race-based action is necessary to further a compelling interest, such action is within constitutional constraints if it satisfies the "narrow tailoring" test this Court has set out in previous cases.

III

Because our decision today alters the playing field in some important respects, we think it best to remand the case to the lower courts for further consideration in light of the principles we have announced. The Court of Appeals, following *Metro Broadcasting* and *Fullilove,* analyzed the case in terms of intermediate scrutiny. It upheld the challenged statutes and regulations because it found them to be "narrowly tailored to achieve [their] *significant governmental purpose* of providing subcontracting opportunities for small disadvantaged business enterprises." The Court of Appeals did not decide the question whether the interests served by the use of subcontractor compensation clauses are properly described as "compelling." It also did not address the question of narrow tailoring in terms of our strict scrutiny cases, by asking, for example, whether there was "any consideration of the use of race-neutral means to increase minority business participation" in government contracting or whether the program was appropriately limited such that it "will not last longer than the discriminatory effects it is designed to eliminate." . . .

QUESTIONS

1 Should federal affirmative action policies be subjected to a weaker standard of scrutiny than local and state government policies?
2 Is a need for minority role models a sufficient justification for at least some affirmative action policies?

Dissenting Opinion in *Adarand Constructors v. Federico Pena, Secretary of Transportation*

Justice John Paul Stevens

A biographical sketch of Justice John Paul Stevens is found on p. 110.

Stevens rejects the use of the strict scrutiny standard in the case of those racial classifications that are intended to benefit members of minority groups. Criticizing O'Connor's concept of consistency, he maintains that consistency does not justify treating differences as though they were similarities. Stevens emphasizes the importance of distinguishing between invidious discrimination and the kinds of remedial practices embodied in affirmative action policies.

Instead of deciding this case in accordance with controlling precedent, the Court today delivers a disconcerting lecture about the evils of governmental racial classifications. For its text the Court has selected three propositions, represented by the bywords "skepticism," "consistency," and "congruence." I shall comment on each of these propositions, then add a few words about *stare decisis,* and finally explain why I believe this Court has a duty to affirm the judgment of the Court of Appeals.

I

The Court's concept of skepticism is, at least in principle, a good statement of law and of common sense. Undoubtedly, a court should be wary of a governmental decision that relies upon a racial classification. "Because racial characteristics so seldom provide a relevant basis for disparate treatment, and because classifications based on race are potentially so harmful to the entire body politic," a reviewing court must satisfy itself that the reasons for any such classification are "clearly identified and unquestionably legitimate." . . . But, as the opinions in *Fullilove* demonstrate, substantial agreement on the standard to be applied in deciding difficult cases does not necessarily lead to agreement on how those cases actually should or will be resolved. In my judgment, because uniform standards are often anything but uniform, we should evaluate the Court's comments on "consistency," "congruence," and *stare decisis* with the same type of skepticism that the Court advocates for the underlying issue.

II

The Court's concept of "consistency" assumes that there is no significant difference between a decision by the majority to impose a special burden on the members of a minority race and a decision by the majority to provide a benefit to certain members

United States Supreme Court. 115 S.Ct. 2097 (1995).

of that minority notwithstanding its incidental burden on some members of the majority. In my opinion that assumption is untenable. There is no moral or constitutional equivalence between a policy that is designed to perpetuate a caste system and one that seeks to eradicate racial subordination. Invidious discrimination is an engine of oppression, subjugating a disfavored group to enhance or maintain the power of the majority. Remedial race-based preferences reflect the opposite impulse: a desire to foster equality in society. No sensible conception of the Government's constitutional obligation to "govern impartially" should ignore this distinction.

The consistency that the Court espouses would disregard the difference between a "No Trespassing" sign and a welcome mat. It would treat a Dixiecrat Senator's decision to vote against Thurgood Marshall's confirmation in order to keep African Americans off the Supreme Court as on a par with President Johnson's evaluation of his nominee's race as a positive factor. It would equate a law that made black citizens ineligible for military service with a program aimed at recruiting black soldiers. An attempt by the majority to exclude members of a minority race from a regulated market is fundamentally different from a subsidy that enables a relatively small group of newcomers to enter that market. An interest in "consistency" does not justify treating differences as though they were similarities.

The Court's explanation for treating dissimilar race-based decisions as though they were equally objectionable is a supposed inability to differentiate between "invidious" and "benign" discrimination. But the term "affirmative action" is common and well understood. Its presence in everyday parlance shows that people understand the difference between good intentions and bad. As with any legal concept, some cases may be difficult to classify, but our equal protection jurisprudence has identified a critical difference between state action that imposes burdens on a disfavored few and state action that benefits the few "in spite of" its adverse effects on the many.

Indeed, our jurisprudence has made the standard to be applied in cases of invidious discrimination turn on whether the discrimination is "intentional," or whether, by contrast, it merely has a discriminatory "effect." Surely this distinction is at least as subtle, and at least as difficult to apply as the usually obvious distinction between a measure intended to benefit members of a particular minority race and a measure intended to burden a minority race. A state actor inclined to subvert the Constitution might easily hide bad intentions in the guise of unintended "effects"; but I should think it far more difficult to enact a law intending to preserve the majority's hegemony while casting it plausibly in the guise of affirmative action for minorities.

Nothing is inherently wrong with applying a single standard to fundamentally different situations, as long as that standard takes relevant differences into account. For example, if the Court in all equal protection cases were to insist that differential treatment be justified by relevant characteristics of the members of the favored and disfavored classes that provide a legitimate basis for disparate treatment, such a standard would treat dissimilar cases differently while still recognizing that there is, after all, only one Equal Protection Clause. Under such a standard, subsidies for disadvantaged businesses may be constitutional though special taxes on such businesses would be invalid. But a single standard that purports to equate remedial preferences with invidious discrimination cannot be defended in the name of "equal protection."

Moreover, the Court may find that its new "consistency" approach to race-based classifications is difficult to square with its insistence upon rigidly separate categories for discrimination against different classes of individuals. For example, as the law currently stands, the Court will apply "intermediate scrutiny" to cases of invidious gender discrimination and "strict scrutiny" to cases of invidious race discrimination, while applying the same standard for benign classifications as for invidious ones. If this remains the law, then today's lecture about "consistency" will produce the anomalous result that the Government can more easily enact affirmative-action programs to remedy discrimination against women than it can enact affirmative-action pro grams to remedy discrimination against African Americans—even though the primary purpose of the Equal Protection Clause was to end discrimination against the former slaves. When a court becomes preoccupied with abstract standards, it risks sacrificing common sense at the altar of formal consistency.

As a matter of constitutional and democratic principle, a decision by representatives of the majority to discriminate against the members of a minority race is fundamentally different from those same representatives' decision to impose incidental costs on the majority of their constituents in order to provide a benefit to a disadvantaged minority. Indeed, as I have previously argued, the former is virtually always repugnant to the principles of a free and democratic society, whereas the latter is, in some circumstances, entirely consistent with the ideal of equality. By insisting on a doctrinaire notion of "consistency" in the standard applicable to all race-based governmental actions, the Court obscures this essential dichotomy.

III

The Court's concept of "congruence" assumes that there is no significant difference between a decision by the Congress of the United States to adopt an affirmative-action program and such a decision by a State or a municipality. In my opinion that assumption is untenable. It ignores important practical and legal differences between federal and state or local decisionmakers.

These differences have been identified repeatedly and consistently both in opinions of the Court and in separate opinions authored by members of today's majority. Thus, in *Metro Broadcasting, Inc.* v. *FCC,* in which we upheld a federal program designed to foster racial diversity in broadcasting, we identified the special "institutional competence" of our National Legislature. "It is of overriding significance in these cases," we were careful to emphasize, "that the FCC's minority ownership programs have been specifically approved—indeed, mandated—by Congress." We recalled the several opinions in *Fullilove* that admonished this Court to " 'approach our task with appropriate deference to the Congress, a co-equal branch charged by the Constitution with the power to "provide for the . . . general Welfare of the United States" and "to enforce, by appropriate legislation," the equal protection guarantees of the Fourteenth Amendment.' " . . .

. . . In his separate opinion in *Richmond* v. *J. A. Croson Co.,* JUSTICE SCALIA discussed the basis for this distinction. He observed that "it is one thing to permit racially based conduct by the Federal Government—whose legislative powers concerning matters of race were explicitly enhanced by the Fourteenth Amendment— and quite another to permit it by the precise entities against whose conduct in matters of race that Amendment was specifically directed. Continuing, JUSTICE SCALIA explained why a "sound distinction between federal and state (or local) action based on race rests not only upon the substance of the Civil War Amendments, but upon social reality and governmental theory."

> "What the record shows, in other words, is that racial discrimination against any group finds a more ready expression at the state and local than at the federal level. To the children of the Founding Fathers, this should come as no surprise. An acute awareness of the heightened danger of oppression from political factions in small, rather than large, political units dates to the very beginning of our national history." . . .

In my judgment, the Court's novel doctrine of "congruence" is seriously misguided. Congressional deliberations about a matter as important as affirmative action should be accorded far greater deference than those of a State or municipality.

IV

The Court's concept of *stare decisis* treats some of the language we have used in explaining our decisions as though it were more important than our actual holdings. In my opinion that treatment is incorrect.

This is the third time in the Court's entire history that it has considered the constitutionality of a federal affirmative-action program. On each of the two prior occasions, the first in 1980, *Fullilove* v. *Klutznick,* and the second in 1990, *Metro Broadcasting, Inc.* v. *FCC,* the Court upheld the program. Today the Court explicitly overrules *Metro Broadcasting* (at least in part), and undermines *Fullilove* by recasting the standard on which it rested and by calling even its holding into question. By way of explanation, JUSTICE O'CONNOR advises the federal agencies and private parties that have made countless decisions in reliance on those cases that "we do not depart from the fabric of the law; we restore it." A skeptical observer might ask whether this pronouncement is a faithful application of the doctrine of *stare decisis*. . . .

[V]

My skeptical scrutiny of the Court's opinion leaves me in dissent. The majority's concept of "consistency" ignores a difference, fundamental to the idea of equal protection, between oppression and assistance. The majority's concept of "congruence" ignores a difference, fundamental to our constitutional system, between the Federal Government and the States. And the majority's concept of *stare decisis* ignores the force of binding precedent. I would affirm the judgment of the Court of Appeals. . . .

QUESTIONS

1 Can you suggest any criteria that should be used to distinguish morally acceptable racial classifications from invidious and pernicious ones?
2 If there were no affirmative action programs, would the merit system be strictly applied in all hiring, promotions, and school admissions in the United States? If not, would injustice be rampant in hiring, etc.?

Concurring Opinion in *Adarand Constructors v. Federico Pena, Secretary of Transportation*

Justice Clarence Thomas

Justice Clarence Thomas, associate justice of the United States Supreme Court, is a graduate of Yale Law School. Prior to his appointment to the Supreme Court in 1991, he served as assistant secretary for civil rights, Department of Education, Washington, D.C. (1981–1982) and chair of the Equal Employment Opportunity Commission, Washington, D.C. (1982–1990).

Justice Thomas gives two grounds for rejecting Justice Stevens's contention that there is a relevant distinction between governmental racial classifications intended to oppress a minority and those intended to help members of groups considered disadvantaged. First, both of these violate the equal protection principle. Second, so-called "benign" racial discrimination leads to numerous adverse consequences, including the continuation of the belief in black inferiority.

I agree with the majority's conclusion that strict scrutiny applies to *all* government classifications based on race. I write separately, however, to express my disagreement with the premise underlying JUSTICE STEVENS' and JUSTICE GINSBURG's dissents: that there is a racial paternalism exception to the principle of equal protection. I believe that there is a "moral [and] constitutional equivalence" between laws designed to subjugate a race and those that distribute benefits on the basis of race in order to foster some current notion of equality. Government cannot make us equal; it can only recognize, respect, and protect us as equal before the law.

That these programs may have been motivated, in part, by good intentions cannot provide refuge from the principle that under our Constitution, the government may not make distinctions on the basis of race. As far as the Constitution is concerned, it is irrelevant whether a government's racial classifications are drawn by those who wish to oppress a race or by those who have a sincere desire to help those thought to be disadvantaged. There can be no doubt that the paternalism that appears to lie at the heart of this program is at war with the principle of inherent equality that underlies and infuses our Constitution. See Declaration of Independence ("We hold these truths to be self-evident, that all men are created equal, that they are endowed by their Creator with certain unalienable Rights, that among these are Life, Liberty, and the pursuit of Happiness").

These programs not only raise grave constitutional questions, they also undermine the moral basis of the equal protection principle. Purchased at the price of immeasurable human suffering, the equal protection principle reflects our Nation's understanding that such classifications ultimately have a destructive impact on the indi-

United States Supreme Court. 115 S.Ct. 2097 (1995).

vidual and our society. Unquestionably, "[i]nvidious [racial] discrimination is an engine of oppression." It is also true that "[r]emedial" racial preferences may reflect "a desire to foster equality in society." But there can be no doubt that racial paternalism and its unintended consequences can be as poisonous and pernicious as any other form of discrimination. So-called "benign" discrimination teaches many that because of chronic and apparently immutable handicaps, minorities cannot compete with them without their patronizing indulgence. Inevitably, such programs engender attitudes of superiority or, alternatively, provoke resentment among those who believe that they have been wronged by the government's use of race. These programs stamp minorities with a badge of inferiority and may cause them to develop dependencies or to adopt an attitude that they are "entitled" to preferences. . . .

In my mind, government-sponsored racial discrimination based on benign prejudice is just as noxious as discrimination inspired by malicious prejudice. In each instance, it is racial discrimination, plain and simple.

QUESTIONS

1 Justice Thomas, like Shelby Steele, discusses some possible bad consequences of affirmative action. What good consequences have resulted or might result from well-constructed affirmative action programs?
2 Do we need at least some affirmative action programs in order to curtail persisting discriminatory practices against members of certain groups?

Nihilism in Black America

Cornel West

Cornel West is professor of Afro-American studies and philosophy of religion at Harvard University. His books include *The Ethical Dimensions of Marxist Thought* (1991), *Prophetic Reflections: Notes on Race and Power in America* (1993), *Keeping Faith: Philosophy and Race in America* (1993), and *Race Matters* (1993).

In West's view, recent discussions of the problems facing African Americans conceal the most fundamental issue—nihilism within the black community itself. Nihilism, as he understands it, is the lived experience of coping with a life of horrifying meaninglessness, hopelessness, and lovelessness. To overcome nihilism in black America, West maintains, we need practices at the local level that will foster feelings of self-worth. In West's view, affirmative action programs will not provide any major solutions to black poverty. Nor are they sufficient as a means to the achievement of equality. However, affirmative action programs do play an important negative role—ensuring that persisting

discriminatory practices which increase black misery are abated—and hence
should be strengthened.

Recent discussions about the plight of African Americans—especially those at the
bottom of the social ladder—tend to divide into two camps. On the one hand, there
are those who highlight the *structural* constraints on the life chances of black people. Their viewpoint involves a subtle historical and sociological analysis of slavery, Jim Crowism, job and residential discrimination, skewed unemployment rates,
inadequate health care, and poor education. On the other hand, there are those who
stress the *behavioral* impediments on black upward mobility. They focus on the wan-
ing of the Protestant ethic—hard work, deferred gratification, frugality, and responsibility—in much of black America.

Those in the first camp—the liberal structuralists—call for full employment,
health, education, and child-care programs, and broad affirmative action practices.
In short, a new, more sober version of the best of the New Deal and the Great Society: more government money, better bureaucrats, and an active citizenry. Those in
the second camp—the conservative behaviorists—promote self-help programs, black
business expansion, and nonpreferential job practices. They support vigorous "free
market" strategies that depend on fundamental changes in how black people act and
live. To put it bluntly, their projects rest largely upon a cultural revival of the Protestant ethic in black America.

Unfortunately, these two camps have nearly suffocated the crucial debate that
should be taking place about the prospects for black America. This debate must go
far beyond the liberal and conservative positions in three fundamental ways. First,
we must acknowledge that structures and behavior are inseparable, that institutions
and values go hand in hand. How people act and live are shaped—though in no way
dictated or determined—by the larger circumstances in which they find themselves.
These circumstances can be changed, their limits attenuated, by positive actions to
elevate living conditions.

Second, we should reject the idea that structures are primarily economic and political creatures—an idea that sees culture as an ephemeral set of behavioral attitudes
and values. Culture is as much a structure as the economy or politics; it is rooted in
institutions such as families, schools, churches, synagogues, mosques, and communication industries (television, radio, video, music). Similarly, the economy and politics are not only influenced by values but also promote particular cultural ideals of
the good life and good society.

Third, and most important, we must delve into the depths where neither liberals
nor conservatives dare to tread, namely, into the murky waters of despair and dread
that now flood the streets of black America. To talk about the depressing statistics
of unemployment, infant mortality, incarceration, teenage pregnancy, and violent
crime is one thing. But to face up to the monumental eclipse of hope, the unprecedented collapse of meaning, the incredible disregard for human (especially black)
life and property in much of black America is something else.

The liberal/conservative discussion conceals the most basic issue now facing black America: *the nihilistic threat to its very existence.* This threat is not simply a matter of relative economic deprivation and political powerlessness—though economic well-being and political clout are requisites for meaningful black progress. It is primarily a question of speaking to the profound sense of psychological depression, personal worthlessness, and social despair so widespread in black America.

The liberal structuralists fail to grapple with this threat for two reasons. First, their focus on structural constraints relates almost exclusively to the economy and politics. They show no understanding of the structural character of culture. Why? Because they tend to view people in egoistic and rationalist terms according to which they are motivated primarily by self-interest and self-preservation. Needless to say, this is partly true about most of us. Yet, people, especially degraded and oppressed people, are also hungry for identity, meaning, and self-worth.

The second reason liberal structuralists overlook the nihilistic threat is a sheer failure of nerve. They hesitate to talk honestly about culture, the realm of meanings and values, because doing so seems to lend itself too readily to conservative conclusions in the narrow way Americans discuss race. If there is a hidden taboo among liberals, it is to resist talking *too much* about values because such discussions remove the focus from structures and especially because they obscure the positive role of government. But this failure by liberals leaves the existential and psychological realities of black people in the lurch. In this way, liberal structuralists neglect the battered identities rampant in black America.

As for the conservative behaviorists, they not only misconstrue the nihilistic threat but inadvertently contribute to it. This is a serious charge, and it rests upon several claims. Conservative behaviorists talk about values and attitudes as if political and economic structures hardly exist. They rarely, if ever, examine the innumerable cases in which black people do act on the Protestant ethic and still remain at the bottom of the social ladder. Instead, they highlight the few instances in which blacks ascend to the top, as if such success is available to all blacks, regardless of circumstances. Such a vulgar rendition of Horatio Alger in blackface may serve as a source of inspiration to some—a kind of model for those already on the right track. But it cannot serve as a substitute for serious historical and social analysis of the predicaments of and prospects for all black people, especially the grossly disadvantaged ones.

Conservative behaviorists also discuss black culture as if acknowledging one's obvious victimization by white supremacist practices (compounded by sexism and class condition) is taboo. They tell black people to see themselves as agents, not victims. And on the surface, this is comforting advice, a nice cliché for downtrodden people. But inspirational slogans cannot substitute for substantive historical and social analysis. While black people have never been simply victims, wallowing in self-pity and begging for white giveaways, they have been—and are—*victimized.* Therefore, to call on black people to be agents makes sense only if we also examine the dynamics of this victimization against which their agency will, in part, be exercised. What is particularly naive and peculiarly vicious about the conservative behavioral outlook is that it tends to deny the lingering effect of black history—a history inseparable from though not reducible to victimization. In this way, crucial and indispensable themes of self-help and personal responsibility are wrenched out of historical context and contemporary circumstances—as if it is all a matter of personal will.

This ahistorical perspective contributes to the nihilistic threat within black America in that it can be used to justify right-wing cutbacks for poor people struggling for decent housing, child care, health care, and education. As I pointed out above, the liberal perspective is deficient in important ways, but even so liberals are right on target in their critique of conservative government cutbacks for services to the poor. These ghastly cutbacks are one cause of the nihilist threat to black America.

The proper starting point for the crucial debate about the prospects for black America is an examination of the nihilism that increasingly pervades black communities. *Nihilism is to be understood here not as a philosophic doctrine that there are no rational grounds for legitimate standards or authority; it is, far more, the lived experience of coping with a life of horrifying meaninglessness, hopelessness, and (most important) lovelessness.* The frightening result is a numbing detachment from others and a self-destructive disposition toward the world. Life without meaning, hope, and love breeds a coldhearted, mean-spirited outlook that destroys both the individual and others.

Nihilism is not new in black America. The first African encounter with the New World was an encounter with a distinctive form of the Absurd. The initial black struggle against degradation and devaluation in the enslaved circumstances of the New World was, in part, a struggle against nihilism. In fact, the major enemy of black survival in America has been and is neither oppression nor exploitation but rather the nihilistic threat—that is, loss of hope and absence of meaning. For as long as hope remains and meaning is preserved, the possibility of overcoming oppression stays alive. The self-fulfilling prophecy of the nihilistic threat is that without hope there can be no future, that without meaning there can be no struggle.

The genius of our black foremothers and forefathers was to create powerful buffers to ward off the nihilistic threat, to equip black folk with cultural armor to beat back the demons of hopelessness, meaninglessness, and lovelessness. These buffers consisted of cultural structures of meaning and feeling that created and sustained communities; this armor constituted ways of life and struggle that embodied values of service and sacrifice, love and care, discipline and excellence. In other words, traditions for black surviving and thriving under usually adverse New World conditions were major barriers against the nihilistic threat. These traditions consist primarily of black religious and civic institutions that sustained familial and communal networks of support. If cultures are, in part, what human beings create (out of antecedent fragments of other cultures) in order to convince themselves not to commit suicide, then black foremothers and forefathers are to be applauded. In fact, until the early seventies black Americans had the lowest suicide rate in the United States. But now young black people lead the nation in suicides.

What has changed? What went wrong? The bitter irony of integration? The cumulative effects of a genocidal conspiracy? The virtual collapse of rising expectations after the optimistic sixties? None of us fully understands why the cultural structures that once sustained black life in America are no longer able to fend off the nihilistic threat. I believe that two significant reasons why the threat is more powerful now than ever before are the saturation of market forces and market moralities in black life and the present crisis in black leadership. The recent market-driven shattering of black civil society—black families, neighborhoods, schools, churches, mosques—leaves more and more black people vulnerable to daily lives endured with little sense of self and fragile existential moorings.

Black people have always been in America's wilderness in search of a promised land. Yet many black folk now reside in a jungle ruled by a cutthroat market morality devoid of any faith in deliverance or hope for freedom. Contrary to the superficial claims of conservative behaviorists, these jungles are not primarily the result of pathological behavior. Rather, this behavior is the tragic response of a people bereft of resources in confronting the workings of U.S. capitalist society. Saying this is not the same as asserting that individual black people are not responsible for their actions—black murderers and rapists should go to jail. But it must be recognized that the nihilistic threat contributes to criminal behavior. It is a threat that feeds on poverty and shattered cultural institutions and grows more powerful as the armors to ward against it are weakened.

But why is this shattering of black civil society occurring? What has led to the weakening of black cultural institutions in asphalt jungles? Corporate market institutions have contributed greatly to their collapse. By corporate market institutions I mean that complex set of interlocking enterprises that have a disproportionate amount of capital, power, and exercise a disproportionate influence on how our society is run and how our culture is shaped. Needless to say, the primary motivation of these institutions is to make profits, and their basic strategy is to convince the public to consume. These institutions have helped create a seductive way of life, a culture of consumption that capitalizes on every opportunity to make money. Market calculations and cost-benefit analyses hold sway in almost every sphere of U.S. society.

The common denominator of these calculations and analyses is usually the provision, expansion, and intensification of *pleasure*. Pleasure is a multivalent term; it means different things to many people. In the American way of life pleasure involves comfort, convenience, and sexual stimulation. Pleasure, so defined, has little to do with the past and views the future as no more than a repetition of a hedonistically driven present. This market morality stigmatizes others as objects for personal pleasure or bodily stimulation. Conservative behaviorists have alleged that traditional morality has been undermined by radical feminists and the cultural radicals of the sixties. But it is clear that corporate market institutions have greatly contributed to undermining traditional morality in order to stay in business and make a profit. The reduction of individuals to objects of pleasure is especially evident in the culture industries—television, radio, video, music—in which gestures of sexual foreplay and orgiastic pleasure flood the marketplace.

Like all Americans, African Americans are influenced greatly by the images of comfort, convenience, machismo, femininity, violence, and sexual stimulation that bombard consumers. These seductive images contribute to the predominance of the market-inspired way of life over all others and thereby edge out nonmarket values—

love, care, service to others—handed down by preceding generations. The predominance of this way of life among those living in poverty-ridden conditions, with a limited capacity to ward off self-contempt and self-hatred, results in the possible triumph of the nihilistic threat in black America.

A major contemporary strategy for holding the nihilistic threat at bay is a direct attack on the sense of worthlessness and self-loathing in black America. This *angst* resembles a kind of collective clinical depression in significant pockets of black America. The eclipse of hope and collapse of meaning in much of black America is linked to the structural dynamics of corporate market institutions that affect all Americans. Under these circumstances black existential *angst* derives from the lived experience of ontological wounds and emotional scars inflicted by white supremacist beliefs and images permeating U.S. society and culture. These beliefs and images attack black intelligence, black ability, black beauty, and black character daily in subtle and not-so-subtle ways. Toni Morrison's novel, *The Bluest Eye,* for example, reveals the devastating effect of pervasive European ideals of beauty on the self-image of young black women. Morrison's exposure of the harmful extent to which these white ideals affect the black self-image is a first step toward rejecting these ideals and overcoming the nihilistic self-loathing they engender in blacks.

The accumulated effect of the black wounds and scars suffered in a white-dominated society is a deep-seated anger, a boiling sense of rage, and a passionate pessimism regarding America's will to justice. Under conditions of slavery and Jim Crow segregation, this anger, rage, and pessimism remained relatively muted because of a well-justified fear of brutal white retaliation. The major breakthroughs of the sixties—more psychically than politically—swept this fear away. Sadly, the combination of the market way of life, poverty-ridden conditions, black existential *angst,* and the lessening of fear of white authorities has directed most of the anger, rage, and despair toward fellow black citizens, especially toward black women who are the most vulnerable in our society and in black communities. Only recently has this nihilistic threat—and its ugly inhumane outlook and actions—surfaced in the larger American society. And its appearance surely reveals one of the many instances of cultural decay in a declining empire.

What is to be done about this nihilistic threat? Is there really any hope, given our shattered civil society, market-driven corporate enterprises, and white supremacism? If one begins with the threat of concrete nihilism, then one must talk about some kind of *politics of conversion.* New models of collective black leadership must promote a version of this politics. Like alcoholism and drug addiction, nihilism is a disease of the soul. It can never be completely cured, and there is always the possibility of relapse. But there is always a chance for conversion—a chance for people to believe that there is hope for the future and a meaning to struggle. This chance rests neither on an agreement about what justice consists of nor on an analysis of how racism, sexism, or class subordination operate. Such arguments and analyses are indispensable. But a politics of conversion requires more. Nihilism is not overcome by arguments or analyses; it is tamed by love and care. Any disease of the soul must be conquered by a turning of one's soul. This turning is done through one's own affirmation of one's worth—an affirmation fueled by the concern of others. A love ethic must be at the center of a politics of conversion.

A love ethic has nothing to do with sentimental feelings or tribal connections. Rather it is a last attempt at generating a sense of agency among a downtrodden people. The best exemplar of this love ethic is depicted on a number of levels in Toni Morrison's great novel *Beloved.* Self-love and love of others are both modes toward increasing self-valuation and encouraging political resistance in one's community. These modes of valuation and resistance are rooted in a subversive memory—the best of one's past without romantic nostalgia—and guided by a universal love ethic. For my purposes here, *Beloved* can be construed as bringing together the loving yet critical affirmation of black humanity found in the best of black nationalist movements, the perennial hope against hope for trans-racial coalition in progressive movements, and the painful struggle for self-affirming sanity in a history in which the nihilistic threat *seems* insurmountable.

The politics of conversion proceeds principally on the local level—in those institutions in civil society still vital enough to promote self-worth and self-affirmation. It surfaces on the state and national levels only when grassroots democratic organizations put forward a collective leadership that has earned the love and respect of and, most important, has proved itself *accountable* to these organizations. This collective leadership must exemplify moral integrity, character, and democratic statesmanship within itself and within its organizations.

Like liberal structuralists, the advocates of a politics of conversion never lose sight of the structural conditions that shape the sufferings and lives of people. Yet, unlike liberal structuralism, the politics of conversion meets the nihilistic threat head-on. Like conservative behaviorism, the politics of conversion openly confronts the self-destructive and inhumane actions of black people. Unlike conservative behaviorists, the politics of conversion situates these actions within inhumane circumstances (but does not thereby exonerate them). The politics of conversion shuns the limelight—a limelight that solicits status seekers and ingratiates egomaniacs. Instead, it stays on the ground among the toiling everyday people, ushering forth humble freedom fighters—both followers and leaders—who have the audacity to take the nihilistic threat by the neck and turn back its deadly assaults. . . .

The fundamental crisis in black America is twofold: too much poverty and too little self-love. The urgent problem of black poverty is primarily due to the distribution of wealth, power, and income—a distribution influenced by the racial caste system that denied opportunities to most "qualified" black people until two decades ago.

The historic role of American progressives is to promote redistributive measures that enhance the standard of living and quality of life for the have-nots and have-too-littles. Affirmative action was one such redistributive measure that surfaced in the heat of battle in the 1960s among those fighting for racial equality. Like earlier *de facto* affirmative action measures in the American past—contracts, jobs, and loans to select immigrants granted by political machines; subsidies to certain farmers; FHA mortgage loans to specific home buyers; or GI Bill benefits to particular courageous Americans—recent efforts to broaden access to America's prosperity have been based upon preferential policies. Unfortunately, these policies always benefit middle-class Americans disproportionately. The political power of big business in big government circumscribes redistributive measures and thereby tilts these measures away from the have-nots and have-too-littles.

Every redistributive measure is a compromise with and concession from the caretakers of American prosperity—that is, big business and big government. Affirmative action was one such compromise and concession achieved after the protracted struggle of American progressives and liberals in the courts and in the streets. Visionary progressives always push for substantive redistributive measures that make opportunities available to the have-nots and have-too-littles, such as more federal support to small farmers, or more FHA mortgage loans to urban dwellers as well as suburban home buyers. Yet in the American political system, where the powers that be turn a skeptical eye toward any program aimed at economic redistribution, progressives must secure whatever redistributive measures they can, ensure their enforcement, then extend their benefits if possible.

If I had been old enough to join the fight for racial equality in the courts, the legislatures, and the board rooms in the 1960s (I *was* old enough to be in the streets), I would have favored—as I do now—a class-based affirmative action in principle. Yet in the heat of battle in American politics, a redistributive measure in principle with no power and pressure behind it means no redistributive measure at all. The prevailing discriminatory practices during the sixties, whose targets were working people, women, and people of color, were atrocious. Thus, an *enforceable* race-based—and later gender-based—affirmative action policy was the best possible compromise and concession.

Progressives should view affirmative action as neither a major solution to poverty nor a sufficient means to equality. We should see it as primarily playing a negative role—namely, to ensure that discriminatory practices against women and people of color are abated. Given the history of this country, it is a virtual certainty that without affirmative action racial and sexual discrimination would return with a vengeance. Even if affirmative action fails significantly to reduce black poverty or contributes to the persistence of racist perceptions in the workplace, without affirmative action black access to America's prosperity would be even more difficult to obtain and racism in the workplace would persist anyway.

This claim is not based on any cynicism toward my white fellow citizens; rather, it rests upon America's historically weak will toward racial justice and substantive redistributive measures. This is why an attack on affirmative action is an attack on redistributive efforts by progressives unless there is a real possibility of enacting and enforcing a more wide-reaching class-based affirmative action policy.

In American politics, progressives must not only cling to redistributive ideals, but must also fight for those policies that—out of compromise and concession—imperfectly conform to those ideals. Liberals who give only lip service to these ideals, trash the policies in the name of *realpolitik,* or reject the policies as they perceive a shift in the racial bellwether give up precious ground too easily. And they do so even as the sand is disappearing under our feet on such issues as regressive taxation, layoffs or takebacks from workers, and cutbacks in health and child care.

Affirmative action is not the most important issue for black progress in America, but it is part of a redistributive chain that must be strengthened if we are to confront and eliminate black poverty. If there were social democratic redistributive measures that wiped out black poverty, and if racial and sexual discrimination could be abated through the good will and meritorious judgments of those in power, affirmative action would be unnecessary. Although many of my liberal and progressive citizens view affirmative action as a redistributive measure whose time is over or whose life is no longer worth preserving, I question their view because of the persistence of discriminatory practices that increase black social misery, and the warranted suspicion that good will and fair judgment among the powerful does not loom as large toward women and people of color. . . .

QUESTIONS

1 Can you cite any evidence to support West's thesis that there is widespread nihilism among black Americans? Can you cite evidence against his claim?

2 Can you cite any evidence to support the view that the nihilism West describes is not limited to black Americans in our society?

SUGGESTED ADDITIONAL READINGS FOR CHAPTER 7

BEAUCHAMP, TOM L.: "The Justification of Reverse Discrimination." In William T. Blackstone and Robert Heslep, eds., *Social Justice and Preferential Treatment.* Athens: University of Georgia Press, 1976. Beauchamp offers a utilitarian argument in favor of policies productive of reverse discrimination in hiring. He proffers "factual evidence" to support his claim that such policies are a necessary means to achieve a morally desirable end—the demise of the continued discrimination against women and blacks.

COHEN, MARSHALL, THOMAS NAGEL, and THOMAS SCANLON, eds.: *Equality and Preferential Treatment.* Princeton, N.J.: Princeton University Press, 1977. This is an excellent collection of articles which, with one exception, originally appeared in different volumes of *Philosophy and Public Affairs.* The authors include Thomas Nagel, George Sher, Ronald Dworkin, Owen M. Fiss, Alan H. Goldman, Judith Jarvis Thomson, and Robert Simon. Ronald Dworkin's article, which was not originally published in *Philosophy and Public Affairs,* is especially interesting insofar as Dworkin compares and contrasts the issues raised by two important legal decisions—the first dealing with a 1945 admittance policy which denied a black man admittance to the University of Texas Law School, the second with a 1971 admissions policy which worked to keep a white male out of the University of Washington Law School.

EZORSKY, GERTRUDE: *Racism and Justice: The Case for Affirmative Action.* Ithaca, N.Y.: Cornell University Press, 1991. Ezorsky argues that in order to correct centuries of institutional racism directed at blacks, affirmative action has been and continues to be a necessary social policy.

GROSS, BARRY R., ed.: *Reverse Discrimination,* Buffalo, N.Y.: Prometheus, 1977. This anthology includes some well-known articles on the topic, including those of Sidney Hook, Lisa H. Newton, Bernard Boxhill, and Alan H. Goldman. The large collection of articles is organized into three sections, labeled "Facts and Polemics," "The Law," and "Value."

HELD, VIRGINIA: "Reasonable Progress and Self-Respect." *The Monist,* vol. 57, January 1973, pp. 12–27. Held focuses on two questions: How long is it reasonable to expect the victims of past discrimination to wait for a redress of their wrongs? What reasonable rate of progress would not involve a loss of self-respect?

NEWTON, LISA H.: "Reverse Discrimination as Unjustified." *Ethics,* vol. 83, July 1973, pp. 308–312. Newton argues that affirmative action policies are forms of reverse discrimination and hence unjust.

POJMAN, LOUIS P.: "The Moral Status of Affirmative Action." *Public Affairs Quarterly,* vol. 6, April 1992, pp. 181–206. Pojman offers a brief history of affirmative action. He then surveys the various arguments for and against it.

WARREN, MARY ANNE: "Secondary Sexism and Quota Hiring." *Philosophy and Public Affairs,* vol. 6, 1977, pp. 240–261. Warren argues that there exist certain discriminatory practices that although not explicitly based on sex, *de facto* discriminate against women. To counter this ongoing discrimination, she contends, minimum numerical quotas for the hiring and promotion of women are necessary.

WASSERSTROM, RICHARD: "A Defense of Programs of Preferential Treatment." *National Forum, The Phi Kappa Phi Journal,* vol. LVIII, Winter 1978, pp. 15–18. Wasserstrom primarily attacks two arguments against preferential treatment programs.

CHAPTER 8

Economic Justice and Welfare

Should everyone in an affluent society be guaranteed a minimum income? Should people be required to work for that income even if they do not want to work? Should they even be required to work at menial jobs they dislike? Is it morally correct to tax the income of those who work to provide incomes for those who do not? Questions such as these fall in the domain of economic justice. Answering them requires theorizing about what constitutes an economically just society. And this in turn involves us in questions about the part that a just government ought to play in the economic sphere and about the justifiable limits of government interference with individual liberty.

AN ECONOMICALLY JUST SOCIETY

In a short story called "The Babylon Lottery," Jorge Luis Borges describes a society in which all societal benefits and obligations are distributed solely on the basis of a periodic lottery. Simply as the result of chance, an individual may be a slave at one period, an influential government official the following period, and a person sentenced to jail the third one. When the temporary social and economic status of the individual is determined, no account is taken of the actual contribution the individual has made to society during a preceding period or of the individual's merit, effort, or need.[1] Such a situation strikes us as capricious. We are accustomed to think that there are some valid principles according to which a society's economic goods are distributed, even if we disagree about what principles ought to be operative in an economically just society. In the United States, for example, certain forms of government assistance such as Aid to Families with Dependent Children (AFDC) are sometimes said to be distributed on the basis of need; promotions in government offices and business firms are supposedly awarded on the basis of merit and achievement; and the high incomes of physicians and lawyers are assumed to be due them

---

[1]Jorge Luis Borges, "The Babylon Lottery," in *Ficciones* (New York: Grove Press, 1956).

344

on the basis of either the contribution they make to society or the effort they exert in preparing for their professions.

Whether, and to what extent, merit and achievement, need, effort, or productive contribution ought to be taken into account in the distribution of society's benefits are basic questions of economic justice. In responding to these questions, philosophers propose and defend various principles of economic justice. According to their proposals, the wealth of society ought to be distributed on the basis of one or more of the following principles.

1 To each individual an equal share
2 To each individual according to that individual's needs
3 To each individual according to that individual's ability, merit, or achievement
4 To each individual according to that individual's effort
5 To each individual according to that individual's actual productive contribution

We will briefly discuss the second principle since it is especially relevant to the readings in the chapter.

If distribution is to be made on the basis of needs, it is necessary to determine just what *needs* are to be considered. Are we to consider only essential or basic needs, such as the needs for food, clothing, shelter, and health care? Or are we to consider other human needs as well, such as the needs for aesthetic satisfaction and intellectual stimulation? Whether the principle of need is accepted as the sole determinant of a just economic distribution within the society or as only one of those determinants, we must select some way of ranking needs. If, on the one hand, the principle of need is the sole determinant of economic justice, we must first determine which needs take precedence—which needs must be satisfied before the satisfaction of other, less important needs is even considered. Then, if our society has the means to meet not only these basic needs but other less essential ones, we should find some way of ranking the latter. (For example, does an artist's need for subsidy take precedence over a scientist's need to satisfy his or her intellectual curiosity about the existence of life on Mars?) If, on the other hand, the principle of need is to be taken as only one of the determinants of economic justice, we ought to determine which needs must be satisfied before some other principle can be used as the basis for distributing the rest of society's wealth.

Note that if either or both of the first two principles are held to be the determinants of economic justice, the individual's own efforts, achievements, abilities, or productive contributions to society are not taken into account in determining that individual's benefits. When the claim is made, for example, that each family in a society ought to be guaranteed a minimum yearly income, the moral justification for this claim is often given either in terms of the principle of need or in terms of the conjunction of that principle and the principle of equal sharing: All human beings, just because they are human beings, are entitled to equal treatment in some important respects; they are entitled, for example, to have at least their most basic needs met by the society to which they belong.

Philosophers, economists, and others vehemently disagree about whether the principle of need (or the principle of need in conjunction with the principle of equal sharing) is a morally acceptable principle of economic justice. Their disagreements stem in large measure from their different conceptions of the moral ideal around which the institutions of any just society ought to be organized. To understand three of the major positions on the relation between need and economic justice, it is necessary to understand the part played by certain moral ideals in theories about (1) the morally correct role of the government in economic activity and (2) the justifiable limits of government interference with individual liberty.

LIBERTY, EQUALITY, NEED, AND GOVERNMENT INTERFERENCE

Two moral ideals, liberty and equality, are of key importance in conceptions of justice in general, and economic justice in particular. A *libertarian* or *individualist* conception of justice holds liberty to be the ultimate moral ideal. A *socialist* conception of justice takes social equality to be the ultimate ideal; and a *liberal* conception of justice tries to combine both equality and liberty into one ultimate moral ideal.

The Libertarian Conception of Justice

For the libertarian, a society is just when individual liberty is maximized. To understand the libertarian position on liberty, it is necessary to see that liberty is not synonymous with freedom. Freedom is the broader category; liberty is one aspect of freedom. If freedom is understood as the overall absence of constraint, liberty can be understood as the absence of a specific kind of constraint—*coercion,* the forceful and deliberate interference by human beings in the affairs of other human beings. Coercion can take two forms—either the direct use of physical force or the threat of harm, backed up by enforcement power. An example will illustrate why liberty is not synonymous with freedom. In some countries, citizens need a government permit to live and work in certain cities. Thus their freedom, more specifically their liberty, to go to live and work in those cities is restricted by coercion, the threat of harm should they disobey the rules. In the United States, citizens do not need such permits. There are no laws that threaten them with harm should they choose to move to New York City or Los Angeles. But not everyone who wants to do so is free to go to live and work in either city. All kinds of constraints may prevent it. Individuals may not have the money for transportation, for example, and this lack may limit their freedom to do what they wish to do. The jobs they are capable of doing may not be available and this lack, too, may prevent them from moving to the city of their choice. So individual freedom may be limited in many different ways. It is important to see that when libertarians advocate the maximization of liberty, they are not concerned with maximizing freedom in general. Their focus is on minimizing coercion, especially on minimizing the coercive interferences of governments.

On a libertarian view, individuals have certain moral rights to life, liberty, and property that any just society must recognize and respect. These rights are sometimes described as warnings against interference: If A has a right to X, no one should prevent A from pursuing X or deprive A of X, since A is entitled to it. According to a libertarian, the sole function of the government is to protect the individual's life, liberty, and property against force and fraud. Everything else in society is a matter of individual responsibility, decision, and action. Providing for the welfare of those who cannot or will not provide for themselves is not a morally justifiable function of government. To make such provisions, the government would have to take from some against their will in order to give to others. This is perceived as an unjustifiable coercive limitation on individual liberty. Individuals own their own bodies (or lives) and, therefore, the labor they exert. It follows, for the libertarian, that individuals have the right to whatever income or wealth their labor can earn in a free marketplace. Taxing some to give to others is analogous to robbery. John Hospers, who defends a libertarian position in this chapter, argues that laws requiring people to help one another (e.g., via welfare payments) rob Peter to pay Paul.

The Socialist Conception of Justice

A direct challenge to libertarians comes from those who defend a socialist conception of justice. There are many varieties of socialism. However, there are two common elements in socialist thought: (1) a commitment to the public ownership of the means of production and (2) a commitment to the ideal of equality. Equality is a complex ideal, including both the conception of moral equality and the conception of equality of condition. Moral equality is the belief that everyone's life matters equally. Equality of condition includes such ideals as equality of opportunity, the equal satisfaction of needs, and other factors which foster greater social equality. Since equality of condition is a central ideal, limitations on individual liberty, specifically on certain economic liberties, are seen as justified when they are necessary to promote equality. Socialists attack libertarian views on the primacy of liberty, in at least three ways. *First,* they offer defenses of their ideal of social equality. These take various forms and will not concern us here. *Second,* they point out the meaninglessness of libertarian rights to those who lack adequate food, shelter, health care, etc. For those who lack the money to buy the food and health care needed to sustain life, the libertarian right to life is an empty sham. The rights of liberty, such as the right to freedom of speech, are a joke to those who cannot exercise them because of economic considerations. *Third,* some defenders of socialism, such as Kai Nielsen in this chapter, argue that most people will have much more freedom in a socialist system than in a libertarian one because they will have more control over their economic lives. The freedom that the socialist wants to maximize, however, requires a society in which individuals have the greatest possible range of choices and not simply one in which government interference is minimal. It is important to recognize the difference between the socialist's conception of freedom and the libertarian's conception of liberty. Where libertarians stress liberty, understood as freedom from coercion, especially from government interference, socialists stress freedom from want. Where libertarians stress negative rights (rights not to be interfered with), socialists stress positive rights—rights *to* food, health care, productive work, etc. Where libertarians criticize socialism for the limitations it imposes on liberty, socialists criticize libertarianism for allowing gross inequalities among those who are *moral equals.*

The Liberal Conception of Justice

Like the socialist, the liberal rejects the libertarian conception of justice since that conception does not include what liberals perceive as a fundamental moral concern. Any purported conception of justice that does not require those who have more than enough to help those in need is morally unacceptable to liberals. Socialists and liberals also agree in recognizing the extent to which economic constraints in an industrial society effectively limit the exercise of libertarian rights by those lacking economic power. Unlike some socialists, however, liberals consider some of the libertarian's negative rights extremely important and advocate social institutions that do two important things—ensure certain basic liberties for all (e.g., freedom of speech) and yet provide for the economic needs of the disadvantaged members of society. Liberals also differ from socialists insofar as they do not advocate the public ownership of the means of production. Nor do liberals oppose all social and economic inequalities. Liberals disagree among themselves, however, concerning both the morally acceptable extent of such inequalities and their correct justification. A utilitarian committed to a liberal position might hold that inequalities are justified to the extent that allowing them maximizes the total amount of good in a society. If, for example, increased productivity depends on giving workers a significantly higher income than that given to those collecting welfare,[2] and if such incentive-stimulated productivity increases the total amount of good in a society, then the inequalities between the assembly-line worker and the welfare recipient would be justified for the utilitarian. A different approach, argued for by John Rawls,[3] maintains that only those inequalities of social goods are justified that will contribute to raising the position of the least-advantaged groups in the society. Here the concern is not with the total amount of good in a society but with the good of the least advantaged. In this view, income inequalities necessary for productivity gains are justified only if the productivity gains function to benefit those in the lowest economic strata.

Libertarianism, Liberalism, and Welfare

Some of the practical ramifications of the libertarian and liberal conceptions of justice are brought out in Trudy Govier's article in this chapter. Govier is concerned with the question, Should the needy have a legal right to welfare benefits? Working from a liberal point of view, Govier criticizes the libertarian (individualist) position on welfare. Her arguments for a legal right to welfare are based on both utilitarian and justice considerations. On Govier's analysis, the morally appropriate approach to welfare is what she calls the *permissive* approach. The permissive approach holds

---

[2]Just what constitutes *welfare* or a welfare program is a matter of dispute. Many would include a number of very different programs under this heading, e.g., unemployment benefits paid out of a fund supported by a mandatory payroll tax paid by employers, social security benefits paid out of a fund supported by a mandatory payroll tax paid by employers and employees, Medicaid programs paid out of state and federal funds, and AFDC paid out of state and federal funds. Usually, when what is at issue is a contrast between the incomes of workers and welfare recipients, the welfare in question includes such payments as AFDC, food stamps, and Medicaid.

[3]John Rawls, *A Theory of Justice* (Cambridge, Mass.: Harvard University Press, 1971).

that in societies with sufficient resources, the right to welfare should be unconditional. On this view, the right to receive benefits should not depend on one's attitude or behavior—on one's willingness to work, for example—but simply on need. Two other articles in this chapter also focus on issues regarding welfare, more particularly, the social-welfare system in the United States. Charles Murray argues that all social-welfare programs should be taken out of the hands of the federal government and left to local governments. Nancy Fraser is concerned with the way the welfare system interprets women's needs and the different assumptions underlying those social welfare programs whose primary recipients are women and those designed primarily with men in mind.

Jane S. Zembaty

What Libertarianism Is

John Hospers

John Hospers is professor emeritus of philosophy at the University of Southern California and past editor of *Pacific Philosophical Quarterly*. His books include *Human Conduct: Problems of Ethics* (1972), *Libertarianism: A Political Philosophy for Tomorrow* (1971), *Understanding the Arts* (1982), and *An Introduction to Philosophical Analysis* (3d ed., 1988).

Hospers defends two ideas central to libertarianism: (1) Individuals own their own lives. They, therefore, have the right to act as they choose unless their actions interfere with the liberty of others to act as they choose. (2) The only appropriate function of government is to protect human rights, understood as negative rights (i.e., rights of noninterference).

The political philosophy that is called libertarianism (from the Latin *libertas,* liberty) is the doctrine that every person is the owner of his own life, and that no one is the owner of anyone else's life; and that consequently every human being has the right to act in accordance with his own choices, unless those actions infringe on the equal liberty of other human beings to act in accordance with *their* choices.

There are several other ways of stating the same libertarian thesis:

1 *No one is anyone else's master, and no one is anyone else's slave.* Since I am the one to decide how my life is to be conducted, just as you decide about yours, I have no right (even if I had the power) to make you my slave and be your master, nor have you the right to become the master by enslaving me. Slavery is *forced* servitude, and since no one owns the life of anyone else, no one has the right to enslave

Reprinted with permission of Nelson-Hall Inc., Publishers from Tibor R. Machan, ed., *The Libertarian Alternative* (1974).

another. Political theories past and present have traditionally been concerned with who should be the master (usually the king, the dictator, or government bureaucracy) and who should be the slaves, and what the extent of the slavery should be. Libertarianism holds that no one has the right to use force to enslave the life of another, or any portion or aspect of that life.

2 *Other men's lives are not yours to dispose of.* I enjoy seeing operas; but operas are expensive to produce. Opera-lovers often say, "The state (or the city, etc.) should subsidize opera, so that we can all see it. Also it would be for people's betterment, cultural benefit, etc." But what they are advocating is nothing more or less than legalized plunder. They can't pay for the productions themselves, and yet they want to see opera, which involves a large number of people and their labor; so what they are saying in effect is, "Get the money through legalized force. Take a little bit more out of every worker's paycheck every week to pay for the operas we want to see." But I have no right to take by force from the workers' pockets to pay for what I want.

Perhaps it would be better if he *did* go to see opera—then I should try to convince him to go voluntarily. But to take the money from him forcibly, because in my opinion it would be good for *him,* is still seizure of his earnings, which is plunder.

Besides, if I have the right to force him to help pay for my pet projects, hasn't he equally the right to force me to help pay for his? Perhaps he in turn wants the government to subsidize rock-and-roll, or his new car, or a house in the country? If I have the right to milk him, why hasn't he the right to milk me? If I can be a moral cannibal, why can't he too?

We should beware of the inventors of utopias. They would remake the world according to their vision—with the lives and fruits of the labor of *other* human beings. Is it someone's utopian vision that others should build pyramids to beautify the landscape? Very well, then other men should provide the labor; and if he is in a position of political power, and he can't get men to do it voluntarily, then he must *compel* them to "cooperate"—i.e. he must enslave them.

A hundred men might gain great pleasure from beating up or killing just one insignificant human being; but other men's lives are not theirs to dispose of. "In order to achieve the worthy goals of the next five-year-plan, we must forcibly collectivize the peasants . . ."; but other men's lives are not theirs to dispose of. Do you want to occupy, rent-free, the mansion that another man has worked for twenty years to buy? But other men's lives are not yours to dispose of. Do you want operas so badly that everyone is forced to work harder to pay for their subsidization through taxes? But other men's lives are not yours to dispose of. Do you want to have free medical care at the expense of other people, whether they wish to provide it or not? But this would require them to work longer for you whether they want to or not, and other men's lives are not yours to dispose of.

> *The freedom to engage in any type of enterprise, to produce, to own and control property, to buy and sell on the free market, is derived from the rights to life, liberty, and property . . . which are stated in the Declaration of Independence . . . [but] when a government guarantees a "right" to an education or parity on farm products or a guaranteed annual income, it is staking a claim on the property of one group of citizens for the sake of another group. In short, it is violating one of the fundamental rights it was instituted to protect.*[1]

3 *No human being should be a nonvoluntary mortgage on the life of another.* I cannot claim your life, your work, or the products of your effort as mine. The fruit of one man's labor should not be fair game for every freeloader who comes along and demands it as his own. The orchard that has been carefully grown, nurtured, and harvested by its owner should not be ripe for the plucking for any bypasser who has a yen for the ripe fruit. The wealth that some men have produced should not be fair game for looting by government, to be used for whatever purposes its representatives determine, no matter what their motives in so doing may be. The theft of your money by a robber is not justified by the fact that he used it to help his injured mother.

It will already be evident that libertarian doctrine is embedded in a view of the rights of man. Each human being has the right to live his life as he chooses, compatibly with the equal right of all other human beings to live their lives as they choose.

All man's rights are implicit in the above statement. Each man has the right to life; any attempt by others to take it away from him, or even to injure him, violates this right, through the use of coercion against him. Each man has the right to liberty: to conduct his life in accordance with the alternatives open to him without coercive action by others. And every man has the right to property: to work to sustain his life (and the lives of whichever others he chooses to sustain, such as his family) and to retain the fruits of his labor.

People often defend the rights of life and liberty but denigrate property rights, and yet the right to property is as basic as the other two; indeed, without property rights no other rights are possible. Depriving you of property is depriving you of the means by which you live.

> *. . . All that which an individual possesses by right (including his life and property) are morally his to use, dispose of and even destroy, as he sees fit. If I own my life, then it follows that I am free to associate with whom I please and not to associate with whom I please. If I own my knowledge and services, it follows that I may ask any compensation I wish for providing them for another, or I may abstain from providing them at all, if I so choose. If I own my house, it follows that I may decorate it as I please and live in it with whom I please. If I control my own business, it follows that I may charge what I please for my products or services, hire whom I please and not hire whom I please. All that which I own in fact, I may dispose of as I choose to in reality. For anyone to attempt to limit my freedom to do so is to violate my rights.*
>
> *Where do my rights end? Where yours begin. I may do anything I wish with my own life, liberty and property without your consent; but I may do nothing with your life, liberty and property without your consent. If we recognize the principle of man's rights, it follows that the individual is sovereign of the domain of his own life and property, and is sovereign of no other domain. To attempt to interfere forcibly with another's use, disposal or destruction of his own property is to initiate force against him and to violate his rights.*

I have no right to decide how *you* should spend your time or your money. I can make that decision for myself, but not for you, my neighbor. I may deplore your choice of life-style, and I may talk with you about it provided you are willing to listen to me. But I have no right to use force to change it. Nor have I the right to decide how you should spend the money you have earned. I may appeal to you to give it to the Red Cross, and you may prefer to go to prizefights. But that is your decision, and however much I may chafe about it I do not have the right to interfere forcibly with it, for example by robbing you in order to use the money in accordance with *my* choices. (If I have the right to rob you, have you also the right to rob me?)

When I claim a right, I carve out a niche, as it were, in my life, saying in effect, "This activity I must be able to perform without interference from others. For you and everyone else, this is off limits." And so I put up a "no trespassing" sign, which marks off the area of my right. Each individual's right is his "no trespassing" sign in relation to me and others. I may not encroach upon his domain any more than he upon mine, without my consent. Every right entails a duty, true—but the duty is only that of *forbearance*—that is, of *refraining* from violating the other person's right. If you have a right to life, I have no right to take your life; if you have a right to the products of your labor (property), I have no right to take it from you without your consent. The non-violation of these rights will not guarantee you protection against natural catastrophes such as floods and earthquakes, but it will protect you against the aggressive activities *of other men.* And rights, after all, have to do with one's relations to other human beings, not with one's relations to physical nature.

Nor were these rights created by government; governments—some governments, obviously not all—*recognize* and *protect* the rights that individuals already have. Governments regularly forbid homicide and theft; and, at a more advanced stage, protect individuals against such things as libel and breach of contract. . . .

Government is the most dangerous institution known to man. Throughout history it has violated the rights of men more than any individual or group of individuals could do: it has killed people, enslaved them, sent them to forced labor and concentration camps, and regularly robbed and pillaged them of the fruits of their expended labor. Unlike individual criminals, government has the power to arrest and try; unlike individual criminals, it can surround and encompass a person totally, dominating every aspect of one's life, so that one has no recourse from it but to leave the country (and in totalitarian nations even that is prohibited). Government throughout history has a much sorrier record than any individual, even that of a ruthless mass murderer. The signs we see on bumper stickers are chillingly accurate: "Beware: the Government is Armed and Dangerous."

The only proper role of government, according to libertarians, is that of the protector of the citizen against aggression by other individuals. The government, of course, should never initiate aggression; its proper role is as the embodiment of the *retaliatory* use of force against anyone who initiates its use.

If each individual had constantly to defend himself against possible aggressors, he would have to spend a considerable portion of his life in target practice, karate exercises, and other means of self-defenses, and even so he would probably be helpless against groups of individuals who might try to kill, maim, or rob him. He would have little time for cultivating those qualities which are essential to civilized life, nor would improvements in science, medicine, and the arts be likely to occur. The function of government is to take this responsibility off his shoulders: the government undertakes to defend him against aggressors and to punish them if they attack him. When the government is effective in doing this, it enables the citizen to go about his business unmolested and without constant fear for his life. To do this, of course, government must have physical power—the police, to protect the citizen from aggression within its borders, and the armed forces, to protect him from aggressors outside. Beyond that, the government should not intrude upon his life, either to run his business, or adjust his daily activities, or prescribe his personal moral code.

Government, then, undertakes to be the individual's protector; but historically governments have gone far beyond this function. Since they already have the physical power, they have not hesitated to use it for purposes far beyond that which was entrusted to them in the first place. Undertaking initially to protect its citizens against aggression, it has often itself become an aggressor—a far greater aggressor, indeed, than the criminals against whom it was supposed to protect its citizens. Governments have done what no private citizen can do: arrest and imprison individuals without a trial and send them to slave labor camps. Government must have power in order to be effective—and yet the very means by which alone it can be effective make it vulnerable to the abuse of power, leading to managing the lives of individuals and even inflicting terror upon them.

What then should be the function of government? In a word, the *protection of human rights.*

1 *The right to life:* libertarians support all such legislation as will protect human beings against the use of force by others, for example, laws against killing, attempted killing, maiming, beating, and all kinds of physical violence.

2 *The right to liberty:* there should be no laws compromising in any way freedom of speech, of the press, and of peaceable assembly. There should be no censorship of ideas, books, films, or of anything else by government.

3 *The right to property:* libertarians support legislation that protects the property rights of individuals against confiscation, nationalization, eminent domain, robbery, trespass, fraud and misrepresentation, patent and copyright, libel and slander.

Someone has violently assaulted you. Should he be legally liable? Of course. He has violated one of your rights. He has knowingly injured you, and since he has initiated aggression against you he should be made to expiate.

Someone has negligently left his bicycle on the sidewalk where you trip over it in the dark and injure yourself. He didn't do it intentionally; he didn't mean you any harm. Should he be legally liable? Of course; he has, however unwittingly, injured you, and since the injury is caused by him and you are the victim, he should pay.

Someone across the street is unemployed. Should you be taxed extra to pay for his expenses? Not at all. You have not injured him, you are not responsible for the fact that he is unemployed (unless you are a senator or bureaucrat who agitated for further curtailing of business, which legislation passed, with the result that your neighbor was laid off by the curtailed business). You may voluntarily wish to help him out, or better still, try to get him a job to put him on his feet again; but since you have initiated no aggressive act against him, and neither purposely nor accidentally injured him in any way, you should not be legally penalized for the fact of his unemployment. (Actually, it is just such penalties that increase unemployment.)

One man, A, works hard for years and finally earns a high salary as a professional man. A second man, B, prefers not to work at all, and to spend wastefully what money he has (through inheritance), so that after a year or two he has nothing left. At the end of this time he has a long siege of illness and lots of medical bills to pay. He demands that the bills be paid by the government—that is, by the taxpayers of the land, including Mr. A.

But of course B has no such right. He chose to lead his life in a certain way—that was his voluntary decision. One consequence of that choice is that he must depend on charity in case of later need. Mr. A chose not to live that way. (And if everyone lived like Mr. B, on whom would he depend in case of later need?) Each has a right to live in the way he pleases, but each must live with the consequences of his own decision (which, as always, fall primarily on himself). He cannot, in time of need, claim A's beneficence as his right. . . .

Laws may be classified into three types: (1) laws protecting individuals against themselves, such as laws against fornication and other sexual behavior, alcohol, and drugs; (2) laws protecting individuals against aggressions by other individuals, such as laws against murder, robbery, and fraud; (3) laws requiring people to help one another; for example, all laws which rob Peter to pay Paul, such as welfare.

Libertarians reject the first class of laws totally. Behavior which harms no one else is strictly the individual's own affair. Thus, there should be no laws against becoming intoxicated, since whether or not to become intoxicated is the individual's own decision; but there should be laws against driving while intoxicated, since the drunken driver is a threat to every other motorist on the highway (drunken driving falls into type 2). Similarly, there should be no laws against drugs (except the prohibition of sale of drugs to minors) as long as the taking of these drugs poses no threat to anyone else. Drug addiction is a psychological problem to which no present solution exists. Most of the social harm caused by addicts, other than to themselves, is the result of thefts which they perform in order to continue their habit—and then the *legal* crime is the theft, not the addiction. The actual cost of heroin is about ten cents a shot; if it were legalized, the enormous traffic in illegal sale and purchase of it would stop, as well as the accompanying proselytization to get new addicts (to make more money for the pusher) and the thefts performed by addicts who often require eighty dollars a day just to keep up the habit. Addiction would not stop, but the crimes would: it is estimated that 75 percent of the burglaries in New York City today are performed by addicts, and all these crimes would be wiped out at one stroke through the legalization of drugs. (Only when the taking of drugs could be shown to constitute a threat to *others,* should it be prohibited by law. It is only laws protecting people against *themselves* that libertarians oppose.)

Laws should be limited to the second class only: aggression by individuals against other individuals. These are laws whose function is to protect human beings against encroachment by others; and this, as we have seen, is (according to libertarianism) the sole function of government.

Libertarians also reject the third class of laws totally: no one should be forced by law to help others, not even to tell them the time of day if requested, and certainly not to give them a portion of one's weekly paycheck. Governments, in the guise of humanitarianism, have given to some by taking from others (charging a "handling fee" in the process, which, because of the government's waste and inefficiency, sometimes is several hundred percent). And in so doing they have decreased incentive, violated the rights of individuals, and lowered the standard of living of almost everyone.

All such laws constitute what libertarians call *moral cannibalism*. A cannibal in the physical sense is a person who lives off the flesh of other human beings. A *moral* cannibal is one who believes he has a right to live off the "spirit" of other human beings—who believes that he has a moral claim on the productive capacity, time, and effort expended by others.

It has become fashionable to claim virtually everything that one needs or desires as one's *right*. Thus, many people claim that they have a right to a job, the right to free medical care, to free food and clothing, to a decent home, and so on. Now if one asks, apart from any specific context, whether it would be desirable if everyone had these things, one might well say yes. But there is a gimmick attached to each of them: *At whose expense?* Jobs, medical care, education, and so on, don't grow on trees. These are goods and services *produced only by men*. Who, then, is to provide them, and under what conditions?

If you have a right to a job, who is to supply it? Must an employer supply it even if he doesn't want to hire you? What if you are unemployable, or incurably lazy? (If you say "the government must supply it," does that mean that a job must be created for you which no employer needs done, and that you must be kept in it regardless of how much or little you work?) If the employer is forced to supply it at his expense even if he doesn't need you, then isn't *he* being enslaved to that extent? What ever happened to *his* right to conduct his life and his affairs in accordance with his choices?

If you have a right to free medical care, then, since medical care doesn't exist in nature as wild apples do, some people will have to supply it to you for free: that is, they will have to spend their time and money and energy taking care of you whether they want to or not. What ever happened to *their* right to conduct their lives as they see fit? Or do you have a right to violate theirs? Can there be a right to violate rights?

All those who demand this or that as a "free service" are consciously or unconsciously evading the fact that there is in reality no such thing as free services. All man-made goods and services are the result of human expenditure of time and effort. There is no such thing as "something for nothing" in this world. If you demand something free, you are demanding that other men give their time and effort to you without compensation. If they voluntarily choose to do this, there is no problem; but if you demand that they be *forced* to do it, you are interfering with their right not to do it if they so choose. "Swimming in this pool ought to be free!" says the indignant passerby. What he means is that others should build a pool, others should provide the materials, and still others should run it and keep it in functioning order, so that *he* can use it without fee. But what right has he to the expenditure of *their* time and effort? To expect something "for free" is to expect it *to be paid for by others* whether they choose to or not.

Many questions, particularly about economic matters, will be generated by the libertarian account of human rights and the role of government. Should government have no role in assisting the needy, in providing social security, in legislating minimum wages, in fixing prices and putting a ceiling on rents, in curbing monopolies, in erecting tariffs, in guaranteeing jobs, in managing the money supply? To these and all similar questions the libertarian answers with an unequivocal no.

"But then you'd let people go hungry!" comes the rejoinder. This, the libertarian insists, is precisely what would not happen; with the restrictions removed, the economy would flourish as never before. With the controls taken off business, existing enterprises would expand and new ones would spring into existence satisfying more and more consumer needs; millions more people would be gainfully employed instead of subsisting on welfare, and all kinds of research and production, released from the stranglehold of government, would proliferate, fulfilling man's needs and desires as never before. It has always been so whenever government has permitted men to be free traders on a free market. But *why* this is so, and how the free market is the best solution to all problems relating to the material aspect of man's life, is another and far longer story. . . .

NOTE

1 William W. Bayes, "What Is Property?" *The Freeman,* July 1970, p. 348.

QUESTIONS

1 Some libertarians argue that from a moral standpoint there is no difference between the actions of an ordinary thief and those of a government when it seizes money from some in order to support others. They assume that if the former are wrong, then so are the latter. Are they correct?
2 Do you agree that the government should have no role in assisting the needy? What reasons can you advance to defend your answer?

A Moral Case for Socialism

Kai Nielsen

Kai Nielsen is professor emeritus of philosophy at the University of Calgary, Canada. He is the author of *Equality and Liberty: A Defense of Radical Egalitarianism* (1985), *God, Scepticism and Modernity* (1989), and *Ethics without God* (1990).

Nielsen puts forth a moral case for socialism. He identifies and explicates a cluster of values that are basic to our culture—freedom and autonomy, equality, justice, rights, and democracy—and then compares "pure socialism" and "pure capitalism" in respect to these values. Nielsen concludes that a socialist system is much more likely to exemplify our basic values than a capitalist system.

Reprinted with permission from *Critical Review,* vol. 3, Summer/Fall 1989, pp. 542–552.

I

In North America socialism gets a bad press. It is under criticism for its alleged economic inefficiency and for its moral and human inadequacy. I want here to address the latter issue. Looking at capitalism and socialism, I want to consider, against the grain of our culture, what kind of moral case can be made for socialism.

The first thing to do, given the extensive, and, I would add, inexcusably extensive, confusions about this, is to say what socialism and capitalism are. That done I will then, appealing to a cluster of values which are basic in our culture, concerning which there is a considerable and indeed a reflective consensus, examine how capitalism and socialism fare with respect to these values. Given that people generally, at least in Western societies, would want it to be the case that these values have a stable exemplification in our social lives, it is appropriate to ask the question: which of these social systems is more likely stably to exemplify them? I shall argue, facing the gamut of a careful comparison in the light of these values, that, everything considered, socialism comes out better than capitalism. And this, if right, would give us good reason for believing that socialism is preferable—indeed morally preferable—to capitalism if it also turns out to be a feasible socio-economic system.

What, then, are socialism and capitalism? Put most succinctly, capitalism requires the existence of private *productive* property (private ownership of the means of production) while socialism works toward its abolition. What is essential for socialism is public ownership and control of the means of production and public ownership means just what it says: *ownership by the public.* Under capitalism there is a domain of private property rights in the means of production which are not subject to political determination. That is, even where the political domain is a democratic one, they are not subject to determination by the public; only an individual or a set of individuals who own that property can make the final determination of what is to be done with that property. These individuals make the determination and not citizens at large, as under socialism. In fully developed socialism, by contrast, there is, with respect to productive property, no domain which is not subject to political determination by the public, namely by the citizenry at large. Thus, where this public ownership and control is genuine, and not a mask for control by an elite of state bureaucrats, it will mean genuine popular and democratic control over productive property. What socialism is *not* is *state* ownership in the absence of, at the very least, popular sovereignty, i.e., genuine popular control over the state apparatus including any economic functions it might have.

The property that is owned in common under socialism is the means of existence—the productive property in the society. Socialism does not proscribe the ownership of private personal property, such as houses, cars, television sets and the like. It only proscribes the private ownership of the means of production.

The above characterizations catch the minimal core of socialism and capitalism, what used to be called the essence of those concepts. But beyond these core features, it is well, in helping us to make our comparison, to see some other important features which characteristically go with capitalism and socialism. Minimally, capitalism is private ownership of the means of production but it is also, at least characteristically, a social system in which a class of capitalists owns and controls the means of production and hires workers who, owning little or no means of production, sell their labor-power to some capitalist or other for a wage. This means that a capitalist society will be a class society in which there will be two principal classes: capitalists and workers. Socialism by contrast is a social system in which every able-bodied person is, was or will be a worker. These workers commonly own and control the means of production (this is the characteristic form of public ownership). Thus in socialism we have, in a perfectly literal sense, a classless society for there is no division between human beings along class lines.

There are both pure and impure forms of capitalism and socialism. The pure form of capitalism is competitive capitalism, the capitalism that Milton Friedman would tell us is the real capitalism while, he would add, the impure form is monopoly or corporate capitalism. Similarly the pure form of socialism is democratic socialism, with firm workers' control of the means of production and an industrial as well as a political democracy, while the impure form is state bureaucratic socialism.

Now it is a noteworthy fact that, to understate it, actually existing capitalisms and actually existing socialisms tend to be the impure forms. Many partisans of capitalism lament the fact that the actually existing capitalisms overwhelmingly tend to be forms of corporate capitalism where the state massively intervenes in the running of the economy. It is unclear whether anything like a fully competitive capitalism actually exists—perhaps Hong Kong approximates it—and it is also unclear whether many of the actual players in the major capitalist societies (the existing capitalists and their managers) want or even expect that it is possible to have laissez-faire capitalism again (if indeed we ever had it). Some capitalist societies are further down the corporate road than other societies, but they are all forms of corporate, perhaps in some instances even monopoly, capitalism. Competitive capitalism seems to be more of a libertarian dream than a sociological reality or even something desired by many informed and tough-minded members of the capitalist class. Socialism has had a similar fate. Its historical exemplifications tend to be of the impure forms, namely the bureaucratic state socialisms. Yugoslavia is perhaps to socialism what Hong Kong is to capitalism. It is a candidate for what might count as an exemplification, or at least a near approximation, of the pure form.

This paucity of exemplifications of pure forms of either capitalism or socialism raises the question of whether the pure forms are at best unstable social systems and at worse merely utopian ideals. I shall not try directly to settle that issue here. What I shall do instead is to compare *models* with *models*. In asking about the moral case for socialism, I shall compare forms that a not inconsiderable number of the theoretical protagonists of each take to be pure forms but which are still, they believe, historically feasible. But I will also be concerned to ask whether these models—these pure forms—can reasonably be expected to come to have a home. If they are not historically feasible models, then, even if we can make a good theoretical moral case for them, we will have hardly provided a good moral case for socialism or capitalism. To avoid bad utopianism we must be talking about forms which could be on the historical agenda. (I plainly here do not take "bad utopianism" to be pleonastic.)

II

Setting aside for the time being the feasibility question, let us compare the pure forms of capitalism and socialism—that is to say, competitive capitalism and democratic socialism—as to how they stand with respect to sustaining and furthering the values of freedom and autonomy, equality, justice, rights and democracy. My argument shall be that socialism comes out better with respect to those values.

Let us first look at freedom and autonomy. An autonomous person is a person who is able to set her ends for herself and in optimal circumstances is able to pursue those ends. But freedom does not only mean being autonomous; it also means the absence of unjustified political and social interference in the pursuit of one's ends. Some might even say that it is just the absence of interference with one's ends. Still it is self-direction—autonomy—not non-interference which is *intrinsically* desirable. Non-interference is only valuable where it is an aid to our being able to do what we want and where we are sufficiently autonomous to have some control over our wants.

How do capitalism and socialism fare in providing the social conditions which will help or impede the flourishing of autonomy? Which model society would make for the greater flourishing of autonomy? My argument is (a) that democratic social-ism makes it possible for more people to be more fully autonomous than would be autonomous under capitalism; and (b) that democratic socialism also interferes less in people's exercise of their autonomy than any form of capitalism. All societies limit liberty by interfering with people doing what they want to do in some ways, but the restrictions are more extensive, deeper and more undermining of autonomy in cap-italism than in democratic socialism. Where there is private ownership of produc-tive property, which, remember, is private ownership of the means of life, it cannot help but be the case that a few (the owning and controlling capitalist class) will have, along with the managers beholden to them, except in periods of revolutionary tur-moil, a firm control, indeed a domination, over the vast majority of people in the so-ciety. The capitalist class with the help of their managers determines whether work-ers (taken now as individuals) can work, how they work, on what they work, the conditions under which they work and what is done with what they produce (where they are producers) and what use is made of their skills and the like. As we move to welfare state capitalism—a compromise still favoring capital which emerged out of long and bitter class struggles—the state places some restrictions on some of these powers of capital. Hours, working conditions and the like are controlled in certain ways. Yet whether workers work and continue to work, how they work and on what, what is done with what they produce, and the rationale for their work are not deter-mined by the workers themselves but by the owners of capital and their managers; this means a very considerable limitation on the autonomy and freedom of workers. Since workers are the great majority, such socio-economic relations place a very con-siderable limitation on human freedom and indeed on the very most important free-dom that people have, namely their being able to live in a self-directed manner, when compared with the industrial democracy of democratic socialism. Under capitalist arrangements it simply cannot fail to be the case that a very large number of people will lose control over a very central set of facets of their lives, namely central aspects of their work and indeed in many instances, over their very chance to be able to work.

Socialism would indeed prohibit capitalist acts between consenting adults; the capitalist class would lose its freedom to buy and sell and to control the labor market. There should be no blinking at the fact that socialist social relations would impose some limitations on freedom, for there is, and indeed can be, no society without norms and some sanctions. In any society you like there will be some things you are at liberty to do and some things that you may not do. However, democratic socialism must bring with it an industrial democracy where workers by various democratic procedures would determine how they are to work, on what they are to work, the hours of their work, under what conditions they are to work (insofar as this is alterable by human effort at all), what they will produce and how much, and what is to be done with what they produce. Since, instead of there being "private ownership of the means of production," there is in a genuinely socialist society "public ownership of the means of production," the means of life are owned by everyone and thus each person has a *right* to work: she has, that is, a right to the means of life. It is no longer the private preserve of an individual owner of capital but it is owned in common by us all. This means that each of us has an equal right to the means of life. Members of the capitalist class would have a few of their liberties restricted, but these are linked with owning and controlling capital and are not the important civil and political liberties that we all rightly cherish. Moreover, the limitation of the capitalist liberties to buy and sell and the like would make for a more extensive liberty for many, many more people.

One cannot respond to the above by saying that workers are free to leave the working class and become capitalists or at least petty bourgeoisie. They may indeed all in theory, taken *individually,* be free to leave the working class, but if many in fact try to leave the exits will very quickly become blocked. Individuals are only free on the condition that the great mass of people, taken collectively, are not. We could not have capitalism without a working class and the working class is not free within the capitalist system to cease being wage laborers. We cannot all be capitalists. A people's capitalism is nonsense. Though a petty commodity production system (the family farm writ large) is a logical possibility, it is hardly a stable empirical possibility and, what is most important for the present discussion, such a system would not be a capitalist system. Under capitalism, most of us, if we are to find any work at all, will just have to sell (or *perhaps* "rent" is the better word) our labor-power as a commodity. Whether you sell or rent your labor power or, where it is provided, you go on welfare, you will not have much control over areas very crucial to your life. If these are the only feasible alternatives facing the working class, working class autonomy is very limited indeed. But these are the only alternatives under capitalism.

Capitalist acts between consenting adults, if they become sufficiently widespread, lead to severe imbalances in power. These imbalances in power tend to undermine autonomy by creating differentials in wealth and control between workers and capitalists. Such imbalances are the name of the game for capitalism. Even if we (perversely I believe) call a system of petty commodity production capitalism, we still must say that such a socio-economic system is inherently unstable. Certain individuals would win out in this exchanging of commodities and in fairly quick order it would lead to a class system and the imbalances of power—the domination of the many by the few—that I take to be definitive of capitalism. By abolishing capitalist acts between consenting adults, then (but leaving personal property and civil and political liberties untouched), socialism protects more extensive freedoms for more people and in far more important areas of their lives.

III

So democratic socialism does better regarding the value that epitomizes capitalist pride (*hubris,* would, I think, be a better term), namely autonomy. It also does better, I shall now argue, than capitalism with respect to another of our basic values, namely democracy. Since this is almost a corollary of what I have said about autonomy I can afford to be briefer. In capitalist societies, democracy must simply be *political* democracy. There can in the nature of the case be no genuine or thorough workplace democracy. When we enter the sphere of production, capitalists and not workers own, and therefore at least ultimately control, the means of production. While capitalism, as in some workplaces in West Germany and Sweden, sometimes can be pressured into allowing an ameliorative measure of worker control, once ownership rights are given up, we no longer have private productive property but public productive property (and in that way social ownership): capitalism is given up and we have socialism. However, where worker control is restricted to a few firms, we do not yet have socialism. What makes a system socialist or capitalist depends on what happens across the whole society, not just in isolated firms. Moreover, managers can become very important within capitalist firms, but as long as ownership, including the ability to close the place down and liquidate the business, rests in the hands of capitalists we can have no genuine workplace democracy. Socialism, in its pure form, carries with it, in a way capitalism in any form cannot, workplace democracy. (That some of the existing socialisms are anything but pure does not belie this.)

Similarly, whatever may be said of existing socialisms or at least of some existing socialisms, it is not the case that there is anything in the very idea of socialism that militates against political as well as industrial democracy. Socialists are indeed justly suspicious of some of the tricks played by parliamentary democracy in bourgeois countries, aware of its not infrequent hypocrisy and the limitations of its stress on purely legal and formal political rights and liberties. Socialists are also, without at all wishing to throw the baby out with the bath water, rightly suspicious of any simple reliance on majority rule, unsupplemented by other democratic procedures and safeguards. But there is nothing in socialist theory that would set it against political democracy and the protection of political and civil rights; indeed there is much in socialism that favors them, namely its stress on both autonomy and equality.

The fact that political democracy came into being and achieved stability within capitalist societies may prove something about conditions necessary for its coming into being, but it says nothing about capitalism being necessary for sustaining it. In

Chile, South Africa and Nazi Germany, indeed, capitalism has flourished without the protection of civil and political rights or anything like a respect for the democratic tradition. There is nothing structural in socialism that would prevent it from continuing those democratic traditions or cherishing those political and civil rights. That something came about under certain conditions does not establish that these conditions are necessary for its continued existence. That men initially took an interest in chess does not establish that women cannot quite naturally take an interest in it as well. When capitalist societies with long-flourishing democratic traditions move to socialism there is no reason at all to believe that they will not continue to be democratic. (Where societies previously had no democratic tradition or only a very weak one, matters are more problematic.)

IV

I now want to turn to a third basic value, equality. In societies across the political spectrum, *moral* equality (the belief that everyone's life matters equally) is an accepted value. Or, to be somewhat cynical about the matter, at least lip service is paid to it. But even this lip service is the compliment that vice pays to virtue. That is to say, such a belief is a deeply held considered conviction in modernized societies, though it has not been at all times and is not today a value held in all societies. This is most evident concerning moral equality.

While this value is genuinely held by the vast majority of people in capitalist societies, it can hardly be an effective or functional working norm where there is such a diminishment of autonomy as we have seen obtains unavoidably in such societies. Self-respect is deeply threatened where so many people lack effective control over their own lives, where there are structures of domination, where there is alienated labor, where great power differentials and differences in wealth make for very different (and often very bleak) life chances. For not inconsiderable numbers, in fact, it is difficult to maintain self-respect under such conditions unless they are actively struggling against the system. And, given present conditions, fighting the system, particularly in societies such as the United States, may well be felt to be a hopeless task. Under such conditions any real equality of opportunity is out of the question. And the circumstances are such, in spite of what is often said about these states, that equality of condition is an even more remote possibility. But without at least some of these things moral equality cannot even be approximated. Indeed, even to speak of it sounds like an obscene joke given the social realities of our lives.

Although under welfare-state capitalism some of the worst inequalities of capitalism are ameliorated, workers still lack effective control over their work, with repercussions in political and public life as well. Differentials of wealth cannot but give rise to differentials in power and control in politics, in the media, in education, in the direction of social life and in what options get seriously debated. The life chances of workers and those not even lucky enough to be workers (whose ranks are growing and will continue to grow under capitalism) are impoverished compared to the life chances of members of the capitalist class and its docile professional support stratum.

None of these equality-undermining features would obtain under democratic socialism. Such societies would, for starters, be classless, eliminating the power and control differentials that go with the class system of capitalism. In addition to political democracy, industrial democracy and all the egalitarian and participatory control that goes with that would, in turn, reinforce moral equality. Indeed it would make it possible where before it was impossible. There would be a commitment under democratic socialism to attaining or at least approximating, as far as it is feasible, equality of condition; and this, where approximated, would help make for real equality of opportunity, making equal life chances something less utopian than it must be under capitalism.

In fine, the very things, as we have seen, that make for greater autonomy under socialism than under capitalism, would, in being more equally distributed, make for greater equality of condition, greater equality of opportunity and greater moral equality in a democratic socialist society than in a capitalist one. These values are values commonly shared by both capitalistically inclined people and those who are socialistically inclined. What the former do not see is that in modern industrial societies, democratic socialism can better deliver these goods than even progressive capitalism.

There is, without doubt, legitimate worry about bureaucratic control under socialism. But that is a worry under any historically feasible capitalism as well, and it is anything but clear that state bureaucracies are worse than great corporate bureaucracies. Indeed, if socialist bureaucrats were, as the socialist system requires, really committed to production for needs and to achieving equality of condition, they might, bad as they are, be the lesser of two evils. But in any event democratic socialism is not bureaucratic state socialism, and there is no structural reason to believe that it must—if it arises in a society with skilled workers committed to democracy—give rise to bureaucratic state socialism. There will, inescapably, be some bureaucracy, but in a democratic socialist society it must and indeed will be controlled. This is not merely a matter of optimism about the will of socialists, for there are more mechanisms for democratic control of bureaucracy within a democratic socialism that is both a political and an industrial democracy, than there can be under even the most benign capitalist democracies—democracies which for structural reasons can never be industrial democracies. If, all that notwithstanding, bureaucratic creepage is inescapable in modern societies, then that is just as much a problem for capitalism as for socialism.

The underlying rationale for production under capitalism is profit and capital accumulation. Capitalism is indeed a marvelous engine for building up the productive forces (though clearly at the expense of considerations of equality and autonomy). We might look on it, going back to earlier historical times, as something like a forced march to develop the productive forces. But now that the productive forces in advanced capitalist societies are wondrously developed, we are in a position to direct them to far more humane and more equitable uses under a socio-economic system whose rationale for production is to meet human needs (the needs of everyone as far as this is possible). This egalitarian thrust, together with the socialists' commitment to attaining, as far as that is possible, equality of condition, makes it clear that socialism will produce more equality than capitalism.

V

In talking about autonomy, democracy and equality, we have, in effect, already been talking about justice. A society or set of institutions that does better in these respects than another society will be a more just society than the other society.

Fairness is a less fancy name for justice. If we compare two societies and the first is more democratic than the second; there is more autonomy in the first society than in the second; there are more nearly equal life chances in the first society than in the second and thus greater equality of opportunity; if, without sacrifice of autonomy, there is more equality of condition in the first society than in the second; and if there is more moral equality in the first society than in the second, then we cannot but conclude that the first society is a society with more fairness than the second and, thus, that it is the more just society. But this is exactly how socialism comes out vis-à-vis even the best form of capitalism.

A society which undermines autonomy, heels in democracy (where democracy is not violating rights), makes equality impossible to achieve and violates rights cannot be a just society. If, as I contend, that is what capitalism does, and cannot help doing, then a capitalist society cannot be a just society. Democratic socialism, by contrast, does not need to do any of those things, and we can predict that it would not, for there are no structural imperatives in democratic socialism to do so and there are deep sentiments in that tradition urging us not to do so. I do not for a moment deny that there are similar sentiments for autonomy and democracy in capitalist societies, but the logic of capitalism, the underlying structures of capitalist societies— even the best of capitalist societies—frustrate the realization of the states of affairs at which those sympathies aim. A radical democrat with a commitment to human rights, to human autonomy and moral equality and fair equality of opportunity ought to be a democratic socialist and a firm opponent of capitalism—even a capitalism with a human face.

QUESTIONS

1 Does Nielsen provide good arguments in support of his claim that a socialist system makes it possible for more people to be more fully autonomous than a capitalist system?
2 What arguments, if any, could Hospers offer to refute Nielsen's claim that a socialist system is more democratic than a capitalist system?

A Proposal for Public Welfare

Charles Murray

Charles Murray is Bradley Fellow at the Manhattan Institute for Policy Research. He is the author of *Losing Ground: American Social Policy 1950–1980* (1984), from which this selection is excerpted, and *In Pursuit of Happiness and Good Government* (1988). He is also the coauthor of *The Bell Curve: Intelligence and Class Structure in American Life* (1994).

Murray argues that we should scrap the entire federal welfare and income support structure for working-aged persons, including Aid to Families with Dependent Children (AFDC), Medicaid, food stamps, unemployment insurance, and workers compensation. He asks the reader to participate in a thought experiment about the possible consequences that would result if his proposal were adopted. Murray does not take a libertarian stance, that is, he does not argue that it is always inappropriate for governments to provide the above sort of help. Rather, he maintains that any such provisions should be determined at the local government level.

I begin with the proposition that it is within our resources to do enormous good for some people quickly. We have available to us a program that would convert a large proportion of the younger generation of hardcore unemployed into steady workers making a living wage. The same program would drastically reduce births to single teenage girls. It would reverse the trendline in the breakup of poor families. It would measurably increase the upward socioeconomic mobility of poor families. These improvements would affect some millions of persons.

All these are results that have eluded the efforts of the social programs installed since 1965, yet, from everything we know, there is no real question about whether they would occur under the program I propose. A wide variety of persuasive evidence from our own culture and around the world, from experimental data and longitudinal studies, from theory and practice, suggests that the program would achieve such results.

The proposed program, our final and most ambitious thought experiment, consists of scrapping the entire federal welfare and income-support structure for working-aged persons, including AFDC, Medicaid, Food Stamps, Unemployment Insurance, Worker's Compensation, subsidized housing, disability insurance, and the rest. It would leave the working-aged person with no recourse whatsoever except the job market, family members, friends, and public or private locally funded services. It is the Alexandrian solution: cut the knot, for there is no way to untie it.

It is difficult to examine such a proposal dispassionately. Those who dislike paying for welfare are for it without thinking. Others reflexively imagine bread lines and people starving in the streets. But as a means of gaining fresh perspective on the problem of effective reform, let us consider what this hypothetical society might look like.

A large majority of the population is unaffected. A surprising number of the huge American middle and working classes go from birth to grave without using any social welfare benefits until they receive their first Social Security check. Another portion of the population is technically affected, but the change in income is so small or so sporadic that it makes no difference in quality of life. A third group comprises persons who have to make new arrangements and behave in different ways. Sons and daughters who fail to find work continue to live with their parents or relatives or friends. Teenaged mothers have to rely on support from their parents or the father of the child and perhaps work as well. People laid off from work have to use their own savings or borrow from others to make do until the next job is found. All these changes involve great disruption in expectations and accustomed roles.

Along with the disruptions go other changes in behavior. Some parents do not want their young adult children continuing to live off their income, and become quite insistent about their children learning skills and getting jobs. This attitude is most prevalent among single mothers who have to depend most critically on the earning power of their offspring.

Parents tend to become upset at the prospect of a daughter's bringing home a baby that must be entirely supported on an already inadequate income. Some become so upset that they spend considerable parental energy avoiding such an eventuality. Potential fathers of such babies find themselves under more pressure not to cause such a problem, or to help with its solution if it occurs.

Adolescents who were not job-ready find they are job-ready after all. It turns out that they can work for low wages and accept the discipline of the workplace if the alternative is grim enough. After a few years, many—not all, but many—find that they have acquired salable skills, or that they are at the right place at the right time, or otherwise find that the original entry-level job has gradually been transformed into a secure job paying a decent wage. A few—not a lot, but a few—find that the process leads to affluence.

Perhaps the most rightful, deserved benefit goes to the much larger population of low-income families who have been doing things right all along and have been punished for it: the young man who has taken responsibility for his wife and child even though his friends with the same choice have called him a fool; the single mother who has worked full time and forfeited her right to welfare for very little extra money; the parents who have set an example for their children even as the rules of the game have taught their children that the example is outmoded. For these millions of people, the instantaneous result is that no one makes fun of them any longer. The longer-term result will be that they regain the status that is properly theirs. They will not only be the bedrock upon which the community is founded (which they always have been), they will be recognized as such. The process whereby they regain their position is not magical, but a matter of logic. When it becomes highly dysfunctional for a person to be dependent, status will accrue to being independent, and in fairly short order. Noneconomic rewards will once again reinforce the economic rewards of being a good parent and provider.

The prospective advantages are real and extremely plausible. In fact, if a government program of the traditional sort (one that would "do" something rather than simply get out of the way) could *as plausibly* promise these advantages, its passage would be a foregone conclusion. Congress, yearning for programs that are not retreads of failures, would be prepared to spend billions. Negative side-effects (as long as they were the traditionally acceptable negative side-effects) would be brushed aside as trivial in return for the benefits. For let me be quite clear: I am not suggesting that we dismantle income support for the working-aged to balance the budget or punish welfare cheats. I am hypothesizing, with the advantage of powerful collateral evidence, that the lives of large numbers of poor people would be radically changed for the better.

There is, however, a fourth segment of the population yet to be considered, those who are pauperized by the withdrawal of government supports and unable to make alternate arrangements: the teenaged mother who has no one to turn to; the incapacitated or the inept who are thrown out of the house; those to whom economic conditions have brought long periods in which there is no work to be had; those with illnesses not covered by insurance. What of these situations?

The first resort is the network of social services. Poor communities in our hypothetical society are still dotted with storefront health clinics, emergency relief agencies, employment services, legal services. They depend for support on local taxes or local philanthropy, and the local taxpayers and philanthropists tend to scrutinize them rather closely. But, by the same token, they also receive considerably more resources than they formerly did. The dismantling of the federal services has poured tens of billions of dollars back into the private economy. Some of that money no doubt has been spent on Mercedes and summer homes on the Cape. But some has been spent on capital investments that generate new jobs. And some has been spent on increased local services to the poor, voluntarily or as decreed by the municipality. In many cities, the coverage provided by this network of agencies is more generous, more humane, more wisely distributed, and more effective in its results than the services formerly subsidized by the federal government.

But we must expect that a large number of people will fall between the cracks. How might we go about trying to retain the advantages of a zero-level welfare system and still address the residual needs?

As we think about the nature of the population still in need, it becomes apparent that their basic problem in the vast majority of the cases is the lack of a job, and this problem is temporary. What they need is something to tide them over while finding a new place in the economy. So our first step is to re-install the Unemployment Insurance program in more or less its previous form. Properly administered, unemployment insurance makes sense. Even if it is restored with all the defects of current practice, the negative effects of Unemployment Insurance *alone* are relatively minor. Our objective is not to wipe out chicanery or to construct a theoretically unblemished system, but to meet legitimate human needs without doing more harm than good. Unemployment Insurance is one of the least harmful ways of contributing to such ends. Thus the system has been amended to take care of the victims of short-term swings in the economy.

Who is left? We are now down to the hardest of the hard core of the welfare-dependent. They have no jobs. They have been unable to find jobs (or have not tried to find jobs) for a longer period of time than the unemployment benefits cover. They have no families who will help. They have no friends who will help. For some reason, they cannot get help from local services or private charities except for the soup kitchen and a bed in the Salvation Army hall.

What will be the size of this population? We have never tried a zero-level federal welfare system under conditions of late-twentieth-century national wealth, so we cannot do more than speculate. But we may speculate. Let us ask of whom the population might consist and how they might fare.

For any category of "needy" we may name, we find ourselves driven to one of two lines of thought. Either the person is in a category that is going to be at the top of the list of services that localities vote for themselves, and at the top of the list of private services, or the person is in a category where help really is not all that essential or desirable. The burden of the conclusion is not that every single person will be taken care of, but that the extent of resources to deal with needs is likely to be very great—not based on wishful thinking, but on extrapolations from reality.

To illustrate, let us consider the plight of the stereotypical welfare mother—never married, no skills, small children, no steady help from a man. It is safe to say that, now as in the 1950s, there is no one who has less sympathy from the white middle class, which is to be the source of most of the money for the private and local services we envision. Yet this same white middle class is a soft touch for people trying to make it on their own, and a soft touch for "deserving" needy mothers—AFDC was one of the most widely popular of the New Deal welfare measures, intended as it was for widows with small children. Thus we may envision two quite different scenarios.

In one scenario, the woman is presenting the local or private sector with this proposition: "Help me find a job and day-care for my children, and I will take care of the rest." In effect, she puts herself into the same category as the widow and the deserted wife—identifies herself as one of the most obviously deserving of the deserving poor. Welfare mothers who want to get into the labor force are likely to find a wide range of help. In the other scenario, she asks for an outright and indefinite cash grant—in effect, a private or local version of AFDC—so that she can stay with the children and not hold a job. In the latter case, it is very easy to imagine situations in which she will not be able to find a local service or a private philanthropy to provide the help she seeks. The question we must now ask is: What's so bad about that? If children were always better off being with their mother all day and if, by the act of giving birth, a mother acquired the inalienable right to be with the child, then her situation would be unjust to her and injurious to her children. Neither assertion can be defended, however—especially not in the 1980s, when more mothers of all classes work away from the home than ever before, and even more especially not in view of the empirical record for the children growing up under the current welfare system. Why should the mother be exempted by the system from the pressures that must affect everyone else's decision to work?

As we survey these prospects, important questions remain unresolved. The first of these is why, if federal social transfers are treacherous, should locally mandated transfers be less so? Why should a municipality be permitted to legislate its own AFDC or Food Stamp program if their results are so inherently bad?

Part of the answer lies in conceptions of freedom. I have deliberately avoided raising them—the discussion is about how to help the disadvantaged, not about how to help the advantaged cut their taxes, to which arguments for personal freedom somehow always get diverted. Nonetheless, the point is valid: Local or even state systems leave much more room than a federal system for everyone, donors and recipients alike, to exercise freedom of choice about the kind of system they live under. Laws are more easily made and changed, and people who find them unacceptable have much more latitude in going somewhere more to their liking.

But the freedom of choice argument, while legitimate, is not necessary. We may put the advantages of local systems in terms of the Law of Imperfect Selection. A federal system must inherently employ very crude, inaccurate rules for deciding who gets what kind of help. . . . At the opposite extreme—a neighbor helping a neighbor, a family member helping another family member—the law loses its validity nearly altogether. Very fine-grained judgments based on personal knowledge are being made about specific people and changing situations. In neighborhoods and small cities, the procedures can still bring much individualized information to bear on decisions. Even systems in large cities and states can do much better than a national system; a decaying industrial city in the Northeast and a booming sunbelt city of the same size can and probably should adopt much different rules about who gets what and how much.

A final and equally powerful argument for not impeding local systems is diversity. We know much more in the 1980s than we knew in the 1960s about what does not work. We have a lot to learn about what *does* work. Localities have been a rich source of experiments. Marva Collins in Chicago gives us an example of how a school can bring inner-city students up to national norms. Sister Falaka Fattah in Philadelphia shows us how homeless youths can be rescued from the streets. There are numberless such lessons waiting to be learned from the diversity of local efforts. By all means, let a hundred flowers bloom, and if the federal government can play a useful role in lending a hand and spreading the word of successes, so much the better.

The ultimate unresolved question about our proposal to abolish income maintenance for the working-aged is how many people will fall through the cracks. In whatever detail we try to foresee the consequences, the objection may always be raised: We cannot be *sure* that everyone will be taken care of in the degree to which we would wish. But this observation by no means settles the question. If one may point in objection to the child now fed by Food Stamps who would go hungry, one may also point with satisfaction to the child who would have an entirely different and better future. Hungry children should be fed; there is no argument about that. It is no less urgent that children be allowed to grow up in a system free of the forces that encourage them to remain poor and dependent. If a strategy reasonably promises to remove those forces, after so many attempts to "help the poor" have failed, it is worth thinking about.

But that rationale is too vague. Let me step outside the persona I have employed and put the issue in terms of one last intensely personal hypothetical example. Let us suppose that you, a parent, could know that tomorrow your own child would be made an orphan. You have a choice. You may put your child with an extremely poor family, so poor that your child will be badly clothed and will indeed sometimes be hungry. But you also know that the parents have worked hard all their lives, will make sure your child goes to school and studies, and will teach your child that independence is a primary value. Or you may put your child with a family with parents who have never worked, who will be incapable of overseeing your child's education—but who have plenty of food and good clothes, provided by others. If the choice about where one would put one's own child is as clear to you as it is to me, on what grounds does one justify support of a system that, indirectly but without doubt, makes the other choice for other children? The answer that "What we really want is a world where that choice is not forced upon us" is no answer. We have tried to have it that way. We failed. Everything we know about why we failed tells us that more of the same will not make the dilemma go away. . . .

QUESTIONS

1 What advantages, if any, does a local system of welfare provision have over a federal system?
2 What disadvantages, if any, does a local system of welfare provision have over a federal system?

Women, Welfare, and the Politics of Need Interpretation

Nancy Fraser

Nancy Fraser is professor of political science at the New School for Social Research. She is the coeditor of *Revaluing French Feminism: Critical Essays on Difference, Agency, and Culture* (1992) as well as the author of *Unruly Practices: Power, Discourse, and Gender in Contemporary Social Theory* (1989), from which this selection is excerpted.

Fraser divides social-welfare programs into two subsystems, one oriented to individuals and the other to households. She brings out some of the assumptions concerning the sexual division of labor that distinguish these two types of programs. In her view, programs oriented to individuals, which treat recipients as rights holders, were established primarily with men in mind. In contrast, programs oriented to households, which treat recipients as dependent clients, were designed primarily with women in mind.

1

Long before the emergence of welfare states, governments have defined legally se-
cured arenas of societal action. In so doing, they have at the same time codified corresponding patterns of agency or social roles. Thus, early modern states defined an
economic arena and the corresponding role of an economic person capable of entering into contracts. More or less at the same time, they codified the "private sphere"
of the household and the role of head of the household. Somewhat later, governments
were led to secure a sphere of political participation and the corresponding role of
citizen with (limited) political rights. In each of these cases, the original and paradigmatic subject of the newly codified social role was male. Only secondarily, and
much later, was it conceded that women, too, could occupy these subject-positions,
without, however, entirely dispelling the association with masculinity.

Matters are different, however, with the contemporary welfare state. When this
type of government defined a new arena of activity—call it "the social"—and a new
societal role—the welfare client—it included women among its original and paradigmatic subjects. Today, in fact, women have become the principal subjects of the
welfare state. On the one hand, they make up the overwhelming majority both of program recipients and of paid social-service workers. On the other hand, they are the
wives, mothers, and daughters whose unpaid activities and obligations are redefined
as the welfare state increasingly oversees forms of caregiving. Since this benefi-
ciary/social worker/caregiver nexus of roles is constitutive of the social-welfare
arena, one might even call this arena a feminized terrain.

A brief statistical overview confirms women's greater involvement with and dependence on the U.S. social-welfare system. Consider, first, women's greater dependence as program clients and beneficiaries. In each of the major "means-tested"
programs in the U.S., women and the children for whom they are responsible now
comprise the overwhelming majority of clients. For example, more than 81 percent
of households receiving Aid to Families with Dependent Children (AFDC) are
headed by women, more than 60 percent of families receiving food stamps or Medicaid are headed by women, and 70 percent of all households in publicly owned or
subsidized housing are headed by women. High as they are, these figures actually
underestimate the representation of women. As Barbara Nelson notes, in the androcentric reporting system, households counted as female-headed contain by definition no healthy adult men.[1] But healthy adult women live in most households counted
as male-headed. Such women may directly or indirectly receive benefits going to
"male-headed" households, but they are invisible in the statistics, even though they
usually do the work of securing and maintaining program eligibility.

Women also predominate in the major U.S. "age-tested" programs. For example,
61.6 percent of all adult beneficiaries of Social Security are women, and 64 percent
of those covered by Medicare are women. In sum, because women as a group are
significantly poorer than men—indeed, women now compose nearly two-thirds of
all U.S. adults below the official poverty line—and because women tend to live longer
than men, women depend more on the social-welfare system as clients and beneficiaries.

But this is not the whole story. Women also depend more on the social-welfare system as paid human-service workers—a category of employment that includes education and health as well as social work and services administration. In 1980, 70 percent of the 17.3 million paid jobs in this sector in the U.S. were held by women. This accounts for one-third of U.S. women's total paid employment and a full 80 percent of all professional jobs held by women. The figures for women of color are even higher than this average, since 37 percent of their total paid employment and 82.4 percent of their professional employment is in this sector. It is a distinctive feature of the U.S. social-welfare system—as opposed to, say, the British and Scandinavian systems—that only 3 percent of these jobs are in the form of direct federal government employment. The rest are in state and local government, in the "private non-profit" sector, and in the "private" sector. However, the more decentralized and privatized character of the U.S. system does not make paid welfare workers any less vulnerable in the face of federal program cuts. On the contrary, the level of federal social-welfare spending affects the level of human-service employment in *all* sectors. State and local government jobs depend on federal and federally financed state and local government contracts, and private profit and nonprofit jobs depend on federally financed transfer payments to individuals and households for the purchase in the market of services like health care. Thus, reductions in social spending mean the loss of jobs for women. Moreover, as Barbara Ehrenreich and Frances Fox Piven note, this loss is not compensated when spending is shifted to the military, since only one-half of 1 percent of the entire female paid workforce is employed in work on military contracts. In fact, one study they cite estimates that with each one-billion-dollar increase in military spending, ninety-five hundred jobs are lost to women.[2]

Finally, women are subjects of and subject to the social-welfare system in their traditional capacity as unpaid caregivers. It is well known that the sexual division of labor assigns women primary responsibility for the care of those who cannot care for themselves. (I leave aside women's traditional obligations to provide personal services to adult males—husbands, fathers, grown sons, lovers—who can very well care for themselves.) Such responsibility includes child care, of course, but also care for sick and/or elderly relatives, often parents. For example, a British study conducted in 1975 and cited by Hilary Land found that three times as many elderly people live with married daughters as with married sons and that those without a close female relative were more likely to be institutionalized, irrespective of degree of infirmity.[3] Thus, as unpaid caregivers, women are more directly affected than men by the level and character of government social services for children, the sick, and the elderly.

As clients, paid human-service workers and unpaid caregivers, then, women are the principal subjects of the social-welfare system. It is as if this branch of the state were in effect a Bureau of Women's Affairs.

2

Of course, the welfare system does not deal with women on women's terms. On the contrary, it has its own characteristic ways of interpreting women's needs and positioning women as subjects. In order to understand these, we need to examine how gender norms and meanings are encoded in the structure of the U.S. social-welfare system.

This issue is quite complicated. On the one hand, nearly all U.S. social-welfare programs are officially gender-neutral. Nevertheless, the system as a whole is a dual or two-tiered one, and it has an unmistakable gender subtext. One set of programs is oriented to *individuals* and tied to participation in the paid work force—for example, unemployment insurance and Social Security. This set of programs is designed to supplement and compensate for the primary market in paid labor power. A second set of programs is oriented to *households* and tied to combined household income—for example, AFDC, food stamps, and Medicaid. This set of programs is designed to compensate for what are considered to be family failures, in particular the absence of a male breadwinner.

What integrates the two sets of programs is a common core of assumptions concerning the sexual division of labor, domestic and nondomestic. It is assumed that families do or should contain one primary breadwinner who is male and one unpaid domestic worker (homemaker and mother) who is female. It is further assumed that when a woman undertakes paid work outside the home, this is or should be in order to supplement the male breadwinner's wage and neither does nor should override her primary housewifely and maternal responsibilities. It is assumed, in other words, that society is divided into two separate spheres of home and outside work and that these are women's and men's spheres, respectively.

These assumptions are increasingly counterfactual. At present, fewer than 15 percent of U.S. families conform to the normative ideal of a domicile shared by a husband who is the sole breadwinner, a wife who is a full-time homemaker, and their offspring. Nonetheless, the "separate spheres" norms determine the structure of the social-welfare system. They determine that it contain one subsystem related to the primary labor market and another subsystem related to the family or household. Moreover, they determine that these subsystems be gender-linked, that the primary-labor-market-related system be implicitly "masculine" and the family-related system be implicitly "feminine." Consequently, the normative, ideal-typical recipient of primary-labor-market-oriented programs is a (white) male, whereas the normative, ideal-typical adult client of household-based programs is a female.

This gender subtext of the U.S. welfare system is confirmed when we take a second look at participation figures. Consider again the figures just cited for the "feminine" or family-based programs, which I referred to earlier as "means-tested" programs: more than 81 percent of households receiving AFDC are female-headed, as are more than 70 percent of those receiving housing assistance and more than 60 percent of those receiving Medicaid and food stamps. Now recall that these figures do not compare female *individuals* with male *individuals* but, rather, female-headed *households* with male-headed *households*. They therefore confirm four things: (1) these programs have a distinctive administrative identity in that their recipients are not individualized but *familialized;* (2) they serve what are considered to be defective families, overwhelmingly families without a male breadwinner; (3) the ideal-typical (adult) client is female; and (4) she makes her claim for benefits on the basis of her status as an unpaid domestic worker, a homemaker, and mother, not as a paid worker based in the labor market.

Now, contrast this with the case of a typical labor-market-based and thus "masculine" program, namely, unemployment insurance. Here the percentage of female claimants drops to 38 percent, a figure that contrasts female and male *individuals,* as opposed to female-headed and male-headed households. As Diana Pearce notes, this drop reflects at least two different circumstances.[4] First, and most straightforwardly, it reflects women's lower rate of participation in the paid work force. Second, it reflects the fact that many women wageworkers are not eligible to participate in this program, for example, paid household service workers, part-time workers, pregnant workers, and workers in the "irregular economy" such as prostitutes, babysitters, and home typists. The exclusion of these female wageworkers testifies to the existence of a gender-segmented labor market, divided into "primary" and "secondary" employment. It reflects the more general assumption that women's earnings are "merely supplementary," not on a par with those of the primary (male) breadwinner. Altogether, then, the figures tell us four things about programs like unemployment insurance: (1) they are administered in a way that *individualizes* rather than *familializes* recipients; (2) they are designed to compensate primary-labor-market effects, such as the temporary displacement of a primary breadwinner; (3) the ideal-typical recipient is male; and (4) he makes his claim on the basis of his identity as a paid worker, not as an unpaid domestic worker or parent.

One final example will round out the picture. The Social Security system of retirement insurance presents the interesting case of a hermaphrodite or androgyne. I shall soon show that this system has a number of characteristics of "masculine" programs in virtue of its link to participation in the paid work force. However, it is also internally dualized and gendered, and thus stands as a microcosm of the entire dual benefit welfare system. Consider that whereas a majority—61.6 percent—of adult beneficiaries are female, only somewhat more than half of these—or 33.3 percent of all recipients—claim benefits on the basis of their own paid work records. The remaining female recipients claim benefits on the basis of their husbands' records, that is, as wives or unpaid domestic workers. By contrast, virtually no male recipients claim benefits as husbands. On the contrary, they claim benefits as paid workers, a labor-market-located as opposed to family-located identity. So the Social Security system is hermaphroditic or androgynous; it is internally divided between family-based, "feminine" benefits, on the one hand, and labor-market-based, "masculine" benefits, on the other hand. Thus, it too gets its structure from gender norms and assumptions.

3

So far, I have established the dualistic structure of the U.S. social-welfare system and the gender subtext of that dualism. Now I can better tease out the system's implicit norms and tacit assumptions by examining its mode of operation. To see how welfare programs interpret women's needs, we must consider what benefits consist

in. To see how programs position women as subjects, we need to examine administrative practices. In general, we shall see that the "masculine" and "feminine" subsystems are not only separate but also unequal.

Consider that the "masculine" social-welfare programs are social insurance
schemes. They include unemployment insurance, Social Security (retirement insurance), Medicare (age-tested health insurance), and Supplemental Social Security Insurance (disability insurance for those with paid work records). These programs are
contributory (wageworkers and their employers pay into trust funds), they are administered on a national basis, and benefit levels are uniform across the country.
Though bureaucratically organized and administered, they require less, and less demeaning, effort on the part of beneficiaries in qualifying and maintaining eligibility
than do "feminine" programs. They are far less subject to intrusive controls and in
most cases lack the dimension of surveillance. They also tend to require less of beneficiaries in the way of actual efforts to collect their benefits, with the notable exception of unemployment insurance.

In sum, "masculine" social insurance schemes position recipients primarily as
rights-bearers. The beneficiaries of these programs are in the main not stigmatized.
Neither administrative practice nor popular discourse constitutes them as "on the
dole." They are constituted rather as receiving what they deserve; what they, in "partnership" with their employers, have already "paid in" for; what they, therefore, have
a *right* to. Moreover, these beneficiaries are also positioned as *purchasing consumers.* They often receive cash as opposed to "in kind" benefits and so are positioned as having "the liberty to strike the best bargain they can in purchasing services of their choice on the open market." In sum, these beneficiaries are what C. B.
MacPherson calls "possessive individuals."[5] Proprietors of their own persons who
have freely contracted to sell their labor power, they become participants in social
insurance schemes and, thence, paying consumers of human services. They therefore qualify as *social citizens* in virtually the fullest sense that term can acquire within
the framework of a male-dominated, capitalist society.

All this stands in stark contrast to the "feminine" sector of the U.S. social-welfare
system. This sector consists of relief programs, such as AFDC, food stamps, Medicaid, and public-housing assistance. These programs are not contributory but are financed out of general tax revenues (usually with one-third of the funds coming from
the federal government and two-thirds coming from the states); and they are not administered federally but rather by the states. As a result, benefit levels vary dramatically, though they are everywhere inadequate, deliberately pegged below the official poverty line. The relief programs are notorious for the varieties of administrative
humiliation they inflict upon clients. They require considerable work in qualifying
and maintaining eligibility, and they have a heavy component of surveillance.

These programs do not in any meaningful sense position their subjects as rights-
bearers. Far from being considered as having a right to what they receive, recipients
are defined as "beneficiaries of governmental largess" or "clients of public charity."
Moreover, their actual treatment fails to live up to even that definition, since they
are treated as "chiselers," "deviants," and "human failures." In the androcentric administrative framework, "welfare mothers" are considered not to work and so are

sometimes required—that is to say, coerced—to "work off" their benefits via "work-fare." They thus become inmates of what Diana Pearce calls a "workhouse without walls."[6] Indeed, the only sense in which the category of rights is relevant to these clients' situation is the somewhat dubious one according to which they are entitled to treatment governed by the standards of formal bureaucratic procedural rational-ity. But if that right is construed as protection from administrative caprice, then even it is widely and routinely disregarded.

Moreover, recipients of public relief are generally not positioned as purchasing consumers. A significant portion of their benefits is "in kind," and what cash they receive comes already carved up and earmarked for specific, administratively des-ignated purposes. These recipients are therefore essentially *clients,* a subject-position that carries far less power and dignity in capitalist societies than does the alternative position of purchaser. In these societies, to be a client (in the sense relevant to relief recipients) is to be an abject dependent. Indeed, this sense of the term carries con-notations of a fall from autonomy, as when we speak, for example, of "the client states of empires or superpowers." As clients, then, recipients of relief are *the negatives of possessive individuals.* Largely excluded from the market both as workers and as con-sumers, claiming benefits not as individuals but as members of "failed" families, these recipients are effectively denied the trappings of social citizenship as it is defined within male-dominated, capitalist societies.

Clearly, this system creates a double bind for women raising children without a male breadwinner. By failing to offer these women day care for their children, job training, a job that pays a "family wage;" or some combination of these, it constructs them exclusively as mothers. As a consequence, it interprets their needs as maternal needs and their sphere of activity as that of "the family." Now, according to the ide-ology of separate spheres, this should be an honored social identity. Yet the system does not honor these women. On the contrary, instead of providing them a guaran-teed income equivalent to a family wage as a matter of right, it stigmatizes, humili-ates, and harasses them. In effect, it decrees simultaneously that these women must be and yet cannot be normative mothers.

Moreover, the way in which the U.S. social-welfare system interprets "maternity" and "the family" is both race-specific and culture-specific. The bias is made plain in Carol Stack's study, *All Our Kin.*[7] Stack analyzes domestic arrangements of very poor black welfare recipients in a midwestern city. Where conservative ideologues see the "disorganization of *the* black family," she finds complex, highly organized kinship structures. These include kin-based networks of resource pooling and exchange, which enable those in direst poverty to survive economically and communally. The networks organize delayed exchanges or "gifts," in Mauss's sense,[8] of prepared meals, food stamps, cooking, shopping, groceries, furniture, sleeping space, cash (in-cluding wages and AFDC allowances), transportation, clothing, child care, even children. They span several physically distinct households and so transcend the prin-cipal administrative category that organizes relief programs. It is significant that Stack took great pains to conceal the identities of her subjects, even going so far as to dis-guise the identity of their city. The reason, though unstated, is obvious: these peo-ple would lose their benefits if program administrators learned that they did not uti-lize them within the confines and boundaries of a "household."

We can summarize the separate and unequal character of the two-tiered, gender-linked, race- and culture-biased U.S. social-welfare system in the following formulas: Participants in the "masculine" subsystem are positioned as *rights-bearing beneficiaries* and *purchasing consumers of services,* thus as *possessive individuals.* Participants in the "feminine" subsystem, on the other hand, are positioned as *dependent clients,* or *the negatives of possessive individuals. . . .*

NOTES

1 Barbara J. Nelson, "Women's Poverty and Women's Citizenship: Some Political Consequences of Economic Marginality," *Signs: Journal of Women in Culture and Society* 10, no. 2 (Winter 1984).
2 Barbara Ehrenreich and Frances Fox Piven, "The Feminization of Poverty," *Dissent* 31, no. 2 (Spring 1984), 162–70.
3 Hilary Land, "Who Cares for the Family?" *Journal of Social Policy* 7, no. 3 (July 1978), 257–84.
4 Diana Pearce, "Women, Work, and Welfare: The Feminization of Poverty," in *Working Women and Families,* ed. Karen Wolk Feinstein (Beverly Hills, Calif., 1979).
5 C. B. MacPherson, *The Political Theory of Possessive Individualism: Hobbes to Locke* (New York, 1964).
6 Pearce, "Women, Work, and Welfare."
7 Carol B. Stack, *All Our Kin: Strategies for Survival in a Black Community* (New York, 1974).
8 Marcel Mauss, *The Gift: Forms and Functions of Exchange in Archaic Societies,* trans. Ian Cunnison (New York, 1967).

QUESTIONS

1 What differences in social-welfare programs would result if they were designed by women on women's terms?
2 Does fairness require us to design social-welfare programs that reject the traditional assumptions about the sexual division of labor?

The Right to Eat and the Duty to Work

Trudy Govier

Trudy Govier is a philosopher who lives in Calgary, Canada. She is the author of *Problems in Argument Analysis and Evaluation* (1987) and *God, the Devil, and the Perfect Pizza: Ten Philosophical Questions* (1989) as well as the editor of *Selected Issues in Logic and Communication* (1988).

Govier focuses on issues arising out of the question, "Should the needy have a legal right to welfare benefits?" She first examines three positions that could be

Reprinted with permission of the publisher from *Philosophy of the Social Sciences,* vol. 5 (1975), pp. 125–143.

adopted in response: (1) the individualist (libertarian) position; (2) the permissive position; and (3) the puritan position. She proceeds to evaluate the three positions' policies regarding welfare on the basis of both utilitarian considerations and considerations of social justice. Govier concludes that permissivism is superior from both standpoints.

Although the topic of welfare is not one with which philosophers have often con-cerned themselves, it is a topic which gives rise to many complex and fascinating questions—some in the area of political philosophy, some in the area of ethics, and some of a more practical kind. The variety of issues related to the subject of welfare makes it particularly necessary to be clear just which issue one is examining in a dis-cussion of welfare. In a recent book on the subject, Nicholas Rescher asks:

> In what respects and to what extent is society, working through the instrumentality of the state, responsible for the welfare of its members? What demands for the promotion of his welfare can an individual reasonably make upon his society? These are questions to which no answer can be given in terms of some *a priori* approach with reference to universal ul-timates. Whatever answer can appropriately be given will depend, in the final analysis, on what the society decides it should be.[1]

Rescher raises this question only to avoid it. His response to his own question is that a society has all and only those responsibilities for its members that it thinks it has. Although this claim is trivially true as regards legal responsibilities, it is inad-equate from a moral perspective. If one imagines the case of an affluent society which leaves the blind, the disabled, and the needy to die of starvation, the incompleteness of Rescher's account becomes obvious. In this imagined case one is naturally led to raise the question as to whether those in power ought to supply those in need with the necessities of life. Though the needy have no legal right to welfare benefits of any kind, one might very well say that they ought to have such a right. It is this claim which I propose to discuss here.[2]

I shall approach this issue by examining three positions which may be adopted in response to it. These are:

1 *The Individualist Position:* Even in an affluent society, one ought not to have any legal right to state-supplied welfare benefits.

2 *The Permissive Position:* In a society with sufficient resources, one ought to have an unconditional legal right to receive state supplied welfare benefits. (That is, one's right to receive such benefits ought not to depend on one's behaviour; it should be guaranteed.)

3 *The Puritan Position:* In a society with sufficient resources one ought to have a legal right to state-supplied welfare benefits; this right ought to be conditional, how-ever, on one's willingness to work.

But before we examine these positions, some preliminary clarification must be attempted. . . .

Welfare systems are state-supported systems which supply benefits, usually in the form of cash income, to those who are in need. Welfare systems thus exist in the sort of social context where there is some private ownership of property. If no one owned anything individually (except possibly his own body), and all goods were considered to be the joint property of everyone, then this type of welfare system could not exist. A state might take on the responsibility for the welfare of its citizens, but it could not meet this responsibility by distributing a level of cash income which such citizens would spend to purchase the goods essential for life. The welfare systems which exist in the western world do exist against the background of extensive private ownership of property. It is in this context that I propose to discuss moral questions about having a right to welfare benefits. By setting out my questions in this way, I do not intend to endorse the institution of private property, but only to discuss questions which many people find real and difficult in the context of the social organization which they actually do experience. The present analysis of welfare is intended to apply to societies which *(a)* have the institution of private property, if not for means of production, at least for some basic good; and *(b)* possess sufficient resources so that it is at least possible for every member of the society to be supplied with the necessities of life.

1   The Individualist View

It might be maintained that a person in need has no legitimate moral claim on those around him and that the hypothetical inattentive society which left its blind citizens to beg or starve cannot rightly be censured for doing so. This view, which is dramatically at odds with most of contemporary social thinking, lives on in the writings of Ayn Rand and her followers.[3] The Individualist sets a high value on uncoerced personal choice. He sees each person as a responsible agent who is able to make his own decisions and to plan his own life. He insists that with the freedom to make decisions goes responsibility for the consequences of those decisions. A person has every right, for example, to spend ten years of his life studying Sanskrit—but if, as a result of this choice, he is unemployable, he ought not to expect others to labour on his behalf. No one has a proper claim on the labour of another, or on the income ensuing from that labour, unless he can repay the labourer in a way acceptable to that labourer himself. Government welfare schemes provide benefits from funds gained largely by taxing earned income. One cannot "opt out" of such schemes. To the Individualist, this means that a person is forced to work part of his time for others.

Suppose that a man works forty hours and earns two hundred dollars. Under modern-day taxation, it may well be that he can spend only two-thirds of that money as he chooses. The rest is taken by government and goes to support programmes which the working individual may not himself endorse. The beneficiaries of such programmes—those beneficiaries who do not work themselves—are as though they have slaves working for them. Backed by the force which government authorities can command, they are able to exist on the earnings of others. Those who support them do not do so voluntarily, out of charity; they do so on government command.

> Someone across the street is unemployed. Should you be taxed extra to pay for his expenses? Not at all. You have not injured him, you are not responsible for the fact that he

is unemployed (unless you are a senator or bureaucrat who agitated for further curtailing of business which legislation passed, with the result that your neighbour was laid off by the curtailed business). You may voluntarily wish to help him out, or better still, try to get him a job to put him on his feet again; but since you have initiated no aggressive act against him, and neither purposefully nor accidentally injured him in any way, you should not be legally penalized for the fact of his unemployment.[4]

The Individualist need not lack concern for those in need. He may give generously to charity; he might give more generously still, if his whole income were his to use, as he would like it to be. He may also believe that, as a matter of empirical fact, existing government programmes do not actually help the poor. They support a cumbersome bureaucracy and they use financial resources which, if untaxed, might be used by those with initiative to pursue job-creating endeavours. The thrust of the Individualist's position is that each person owns his own body and his own labour; thus each person is taken to have a virtually unconditional right to the income which that labour can earn him in a free market place.[5] For anyone to pre-empt part of a worker's earnings without that worker's voluntary consent is tantamount to robbery. And the fact that the government is the intermediary through which this deed is committed does not change its moral status one iota.

On an Individualist's view, those in need should be cared for by charities or through other schemes to which contributions are voluntary. Many people may wish to insure themselves against unforeseen calamities and they should be free to do so. But there is no justification for non-optional government schemes financed by taxpayers' money. . . .

2   The Permissive View

Directly contrary to the Individualist view of welfare is what I have termed the Permissive view. According to this view, in a society which has sufficient resources so that everyone could be supplied with the necessities of life, every individual ought to be given the legal right to social security, and this right ought not to be conditional in any way upon an individual's behavior. *Ex hypothesi* the society which we are discussing has sufficient goods to provide everyone with food, clothing, shelter and other necessities. Someone who does without these basic goods is scarcely living at all, and a society which takes no steps to change this state of affairs implies by its inaction that the life of such a person is without value. It does not execute him; but it may allow him to die. It does not put him in prison; but it may leave him with a life of lower quality than that of some prison inmates. A society which can rectify these circumstances and does not can justly be accused of imposing upon the needy either death or lifelong deprivation. And those characteristics which make a person needy—whether they be illness, old age, insanity, feeblemindedness, inability to find paid work, or even poor moral character—are insufficient to make him deserve the fate to which an inactive society would in effect condemn him. One would not be executed for inability or failure to find paid work; neither should one be allowed to die for this misfortune or failing.

A person who cannot or does not find his own means of social security does not thereby forfeit his status as a human being. If other human beings, with physical, mental and moral qualities different from his, are regarded as having the right to life and to the means of life, then so too should he be regarded. A society which does not accept the responsibility for supplying such a person with the basic necessities of life is, in effect, endorsing a difference between its members which is without moral justification. . . .

The adoption of a Permissive view of welfare would have significant practical implications. If there were a legal right, unconditional upon behaviour, to a specified level of state-supplied benefits, then state investigation of the prospective welfare recipient could be kept to a minimum. Why he is in need, whether he can work, whether he is willing to work, and what he does while receiving welfare benefits are on this view quite irrelevant to his right to receive those benefits. A welfare recipient is a person who claims from his society that to which he is legally entitled under a morally based welfare scheme. The fact that he makes this claim licenses no special state or societal interference with his behaviour. If the Permissive view of welfare were widely believed, then there would be no social stigma attached to being on welfare. There is such a stigma, and many long-term welfare recipients are considerably demoralized by their dependent status.[6] These facts suggest that the Permissive view of welfare is not widely held in our society.

3   The Puritan View

This view of welfare rather naturally emerges when we consider that no one can have a right to something without someone else's, or some group of other persons', having responsibilities correlative to this right. In the case in which the right in question is a legal right to social security, the correlative responsibilities may be rather extensive. They have been deemed responsibilities of "the state." The state will require resources and funds to meet these responsibilities, and these do not emerge from the sky miraculously, or zip into existence as a consequence of virtually effortless acts of will. They are taken by the state from its citizens, often in the form of taxation on earned income. The funds given to the welfare recipient and many of the goods which he purchases with these funds are produced by other members of society, many of whom give a considerable portion of their time and their energy to this end. If a state has the moral responsibility to ensure the social security of its citizens then all the citizens of that state have the responsibility to provide state agencies with the means to carry out their duties. This responsibility, in our present contingent circumstances, seems to generate an obligation to *work*.

A person who works helps to produce the goods which all use in daily living and, when paid, contributes through taxation to government endeavours. The person who does not work, even though able to work, does not make his contribution to social efforts towards obtaining the means of life. He is not entitled to a share of the goods produced by others if he chooses not to take part in their labours. Unless he can show that there is a moral justification for his not making the sacrifice of time and energy which others make, he has no legitimate claim to welfare benefits. If he is disabled or unable to obtain work, he cannot work; hence he has no need to justify his failure to work. But if he does choose not to work, he would have to justify his choice by saying "others should sacrifice their time and energy for me; I have no need to sacrifice time and energy for them." This principle, a version of what Rawls refers to as a free-rider's principle, simply will not stand up to criticism.[7] To deliberately avoid working and benefit from the labours of others is morally indefensible.

Within a welfare system erected on these principles, the right to welfare is conditional upon one's satisfactorily accounting for his failure to obtain the necessities of life by his own efforts. Someone who is severely disabled mentally or physically, or who for some other reason cannot work, is morally entitled to receive welfare benefits. Someone who chooses not to work is not. The Puritan view of welfare is a kind of compromise between the Individualist view and the Permissive view. . . .

The Puritan view of welfare, based as it is on the inter-relation between welfare and work, provides a rationale for two connected principles which those establishing welfare schemes in Canada and in the United States seem to endorse. First of all, those on welfare should never receive a higher income than the working poor. Secondly, a welfare scheme should, in some way or other, incorporate incentives to work. These principles, which presuppose that it is better to work than not to work, emerge rather naturally from the contingency which is at the basis of the Puritan view: the goods essential for social security are products of the labour of some members of society. If we wish to have a continued supply of such goods, we must encourage those who work to produce them. . . .

APPRAISAL OF POLICIES: SOCIAL CONSEQUENCES AND SOCIAL JUSTICE

In approaching the appraisal of prospective welfare policies under these two aspects I am, of course, making some assumptions about the moral appraisal of suggested social policies. Although these cannot possibly be justified here, it may be helpful to articulate them, at least in a rough way.

Appraisal of social policies is in part teleological. To the extent that a policy, P, increases the total human welfare more than does an alternative policy, P′, P is a better social policy than P′. Or, if P leaves the total human welfare as it is, while P′ diminishes it, then to that extent, P is a better social policy than P′. Even this skeletal formulation of the teleological aspect of appraisal reveals why appraisal cannot be entirely teleological. We consider total consequences—effects upon the total of "human well-being" in a society. But this total is a summation of consequences on different individuals. It includes no judgements as to how far we allow one individual's well-being to decrease while another's increases, under the same policy. Judgements relating to the latter problems are judgements about social justice.

In appraising social policies we have to weigh up considerations of total well-being against considerations of justice. Just how this is to be done, precisely, I would not pretend to know. However, the absence of precise methods does not mean that we should relinquish attempts at appraisal: some problems are already with us, and thought which is necessarily tentative and imprecise is still preferable to no thought at all.

1   Consequences of Welfare Schemes

First, let us consider the consequences of the non-scheme advocated by the Individualist. He would have us abolish all non-optional government programmes which have as their goal the improvement of anyone's personal welfare. This rejection extends to health schemes, pension plans and education, as well as to welfare and unemployment insurance. So following the Individualist would lead to very sweeping changes.

The Individualist will claim (as do Hospers and Ayn Rand) that on the whole his non-scheme will bring beneficial consequences. He will admit, as he must, that there are people who would suffer tremendously if welfare and other social security programmes were simply terminated. Some would even die as a result. We cannot assume that spontaneously developing charities would cover every case of dire need. Nevertheless the Individualist wants to point to benefits which would accrue to businessmen and to working people and their families if taxation were drastically cut. It is his claim that consumption would rise, hence production would rise, job opportunities would be extended, and there would be an economic boom, if people could only spend all their earned income as they wished. This boom would benefit both rich and poor.

There are significant omissions which are necessary in order to render the Individualist's optimism plausible. Either workers and businessmen would have insurance of various kinds, or they would be insecure in their prosperity. If they did have insurance to cover health problems, old age and possible job loss, then they would pay for it; hence they would not be spending their whole earned income on consumer goods. Those who run the insurance schemes could, of course, put this money back into the economy—but government schemes already do this. The economic boom under Individualism would not be as loud as originally expected. Furthermore the goal of increased consumption-increased productivity must be questioned from an ecological viewpoint: many necessary materials are available only in limited quantities.

Finally, a word about charity. It is not to be expected that those who are at the mercy of charities will benefit from this state, either materially or psychologically. Those who prosper will be able to choose between giving a great deal to charity and suffering from the very real insecurity and guilt which would accompany the existence of starvation and grim poverty outside their padlocked doors. It is to be hoped that they would opt for the first alternative. But, if they did, this might be every bit as expensive for them as government-supported benefit schemes are now. If they did not give generously to charity, violence might result. However one looks at it, the consequences of Individualism are unlikely to be good.

Welfare schemes operating in Canada today are almost without exception based upon the principles of the Puritan view. To see the consequences of that type of welfare scheme we have only to look at the results of our own welfare programmes. Taxation to support such schemes is high, though not so intolerably so as to have led to widescale resentment among taxpayers. Canadian welfare programmes are attended by complicated and often cumbersome bureaucracy, some of which results from the interlocking of municipal, provincial and federal governments in the administration and financing of welfare programmes. The cost of the programmes is no doubt increased by this bureaucracy; not all the tax money directed to welfare programmes goes to those in need. Puritan welfare schemes do not result in social catastrophe or in significant business stagnation—this much we know, because we already live with such schemes. Their adverse consequences, if any, are felt primarily not by society generally nor by businessmen and the working segment of the public, but rather by recipients of welfare.

Both the Special Senate Committee Report on Poverty and the Real Poverty Report criticize our present system of welfare for its demoralization of recipients, who often must deal with several levels of government and are vulnerable to arbitrary interference on the part of administering officials. Welfare officials have the power to check on welfare recipients and cut off or limit their benefits under a large number of circumstances. The dangers to welfare recipients in terms of anxiety, threats to privacy and loss of dignity are obvious. According to the Senate Report, the single aspect shared by all Canada's welfare systems is "a record of failure and insufficiency, of bureaucratic rigidities that often result in the degradation, humiliation and alienation of recipients."[8] The writers of this report cite many instances of humiliation, leaving the impression that these are too easily found to be "incidental aberrations."[9] Concern that a welfare recipient either be unable to work or be willing to work (if unemployed) can easily turn into concern about how he spends the income supplied him, what his plans for the future are, where he lives, how many children he has. And the rationale underlying the Puritan scheme makes the degradation of welfare recipients a natural consequence of welfare institutions. Work is valued and only he who works is thought to contribute to society. Welfare recipients are regarded as parasites and spongers—so when they are treated as such, this is only what we should have expected. Being on welfare in a society which thinks and acts in this fashion can be psychologically debilitating. Welfare recipients who are demoralized by their downgraded status and relative lack of personal freedom can be expected to be made less capable of self-sufficiency. To the extent that this is so, welfare systems erected on Puritan principles may defeat their own purposes.

In fairness, it must be noted here that bureaucratic checks and controls are not a feature only of Puritan welfare systems. To a limited extent, Permissive systems would have to incorporate them too. Within those systems, welfare benefits would be given only to those whose income was inadequate to meet basic needs. However, there would be no checks on "willingness to work," and there would be no need for welfare workers to evaluate the merits of the daily activities of recipients. If a Permissive guaranteed income system were administered through income tax returns, everyone receiving the basic income and those not needing it paying it back in taxes, then the special status of welfare recipients would fade. They would no longer be singled out as a special group within the population. It is to be expected that living solely on government-supplied benefits would be psychologically easier in that type of situation.

Thus it can be argued that for the recipients of welfare, a Permissive scheme has more advantages than a Puritan one. This is not a very surprising conclusion. The

Puritan scheme is relatively disadvantageous to recipients, and Puritans would acknowledge this point; they will argue that the overall consequences of Permissive schemes are negative in that these schemes benefit some at too great a cost to others. (Remember, we are not yet concerned with the *justice* of welfare policies, but solely with their consequences as regards *total* human well-being within the society in question.) The concern which most people have regarding the Permissive scheme relates to its costs and its dangers to the "work ethic." It is commonly thought that people work only because they have to work to survive in a tolerable style. If a guaranteed income scheme were adopted by the government, this incentive to work would disappear. No one would be faced with the choice between a nasty and boring job and starvation. Who would do the nasty and boring jobs then? Many of them are not eliminable and they have to be done somehow, by someone. Puritans fear that a great many people—even some with relatively pleasant jobs—might simply cease to work if they could receive non-stigmatized government money to live on. If this were to happen, the permissive society would simply grind to a halt.

In addressing these anxieties about the consequences of Permissive welfare schemes, we must recall that welfare benefits are set to ensure only that those who do not work have a bearable existence, with an income sufficient for basic needs, and that they have this income regardless of why they fail to work. Welfare benefits will not finance luxury living for a family of five! If jobs are adequately paid so that workers receive more than the minimum welfare income in an earned salary, then there will still be a financial incentive to take jobs. What guaranteed income schemes will do is to raise the salary floor. This change will benefit the many non-unionized workers in service and clerical occupations.

Furthermore it is unlikely that people work solely due to (i) the desire for money and the things it can buy and (ii) belief in the Puritan work ethic. There are many other reasons for working, some of which would persist in a society which had adopted a Permissive welfare system. Most people are happier when their time is structured in some way, when they are active outside their own homes, when they feel themselves part of an endeavor whose purposes transcend their particular egotistic ones. Women often choose to work outside the home for these reasons as much as for financial ones. With these and other factors operating I cannot see that the adoption of a Permissive welfare scheme would be followed by a level of slothfulness which would jeopardize human well-being.

Another worry about the Permissive scheme concerns cost. It is difficult to comment on this in a general way, since it would vary so much from case to case. Of Canada at the present it has been said that a guaranteed income scheme administered through income tax would cost less than social security payments administered through the present bureaucracies. It is thought that this saving would result from a drastic cut in administrative costs. The matter of the work ethic is also relevant to the question of costs. Within a Puritan framework it is very important to have a high level of employment and there is a tendency to resist any reorganization which results in there being fewer jobs available. Some of these proposed reorganizations would save money; strictly speaking we should count the cost of keeping jobs which are objectively unnecessary as part of the cost of Puritanism regarding welfare.

In summary, we can appraise Individualism, Puritanism and Permissivism with respect to their anticipated consequences, as follows: Individualism is unacceptable; Puritanism is tolerable, but has some undesirable consequences for welfare recipients; Permissivism appears to be the winner. Worries about bad effects which Permissive welfare schemes might have due to high costs and (alleged) reduced work-incentives appear to be without solid basis.

2   Social Justice under Proposed Welfare Schemes

We must now try to consider the merits of Individualism, Puritanism and Permissivism with regard to their impact on the distribution of the goods necessary for well-being. [Robert] Nozick has argued against the whole conception of a distributive justice on the grounds that it presupposes that goods are like manna from heaven: we simply get them and then have a problem—to whom to give them. According to Nozick we know where things come from and we do not have the problem of to whom to give them. There is not really a problem of distributive justice, for there is no central distributor giving out manna from heaven! It is necessary to counter Nozick on this point since his reaction to the (purported) problems of distributive justice would undercut much of what follows.[10]

There is a level at which Nozick's point is obviously valid. If A discovers a cure for cancer, then it is A and not B or C who is responsible for this discovery. On Nozick's view this is taken to imply that A should reap any monetary profits which are forthcoming; other people will benefit from the cure itself. Now although it cannot be doubted that A is a bright and hardworking person, neither can it be denied that A and his circumstances are the product of many co-operative endeavours: schools and laboratories, for instance. Because this is so, I find Nozick's claim that "we know where things come from" unconvincing at a deeper level. Since achievements like A's presuppose extensive social co-operation, it is morally permissible to regard even the monetary profits accruing from them as shareable by the "owner" and society at large.

Laws support existing income levels in many ways. Governments specify taxation so as to further determine net income. Property ownership is a legal matter. In all these ways people's incomes and possibilities for obtaining income are affected by deliberate state action. It is always possible to raise questions about the moral desirability of actual conventional arrangements. Should university professors earn less than lawyers? More than waitresses? Why? Why not? Anyone who gives an account of distributive justice is trying to specify principles which will make it possible to answer questions such as these, and nothing in Nozick's argument suffices to show that the questions are meaningless or unimportant.

Any human distribution of anything is unjust insofar as differences exist for no good reason. If goods did come like manna from heaven and the Central Distributor gave A ten times more than B, we should want to know why. The skewed distribution might be deemed a just one if A's needs were objectively ten times greater than B's, or if B refused to accept more than his small portion of goods. But if no reason at all could be given for it, or if only an irrelevant reason could be given (e.g.,

A is blue-eyed and B is not), then it is an unjust distribution. All the views we have expounded concerning welfare permit differences in income level. Some philosophers would say that such differences are never just, although they may be necessary, for historical or utilitarian reasons. Whether or not this is so, it is admittedly very difficult to say just what would constitute a good reason for giving A a higher income than B. Level of need, degree of responsibility, amount of training, unpleasantness of work—all these have been proposed and all have some plausibility. We do not need to tackle all this larger problem in order to consider justice under proposed welfare systems. For we can deal here solely with the question of whether everyone should receive a floor level of income; decisions on this matter are independent of decisions on overall equality or principles of variation among incomes above the floor. The Permissivist contends that all should receive at least the floor income; the Individualist and the Puritan deny this. All would claim justice for their side.

The Individualist attempts to justify extreme variations in income, with some people below the level where they can fulfill their basic needs, with reference to the fact of people's actual accomplishments. This approach to the question is open to the same objections as those which have already been raised against Nozick's non-manna-from-heaven argument, and I shall not repeat them here. Let us move on to the Puritan account. It is because goods emerge from human efforts that the Puritan advances his view of welfare. He stresses the unfairness of a system which would permit some people to take advantage of others. A Permissive welfare system would do this, as it makes no attempt to distinguish between those who choose not to work and those who cannot work. No one should be able to take advantage of another under the auspices of a government institution. The Puritan scheme seeks to eliminate this possibility, and for that reason, Puritans would allege, it is a more just scheme than the Permissive one.

Permissivists can best reply to this contention by acknowledging that any instance of free-riding would be an instance where those working were done an injustice, but by showing that any justice which the Puritan preserves by eliminating free-riding is outweighted by *injustice* perpetrated elsewhere. Consider the children of the Puritan's free-riders. They will suffer greatly for the "sins" of their parents. Within the institution of the family, the Puritan cannot suitably hurt the guilty without cruelly depriving the innocent. There is a sense, too, in which Puritanism does injustice to the many people on welfare who are not free-riders. It perpetuates the opinion that they are non-contributors to society and this doctrine, which is over-simplified if not downright false, has a harmful effect upon welfare recipients.

Social justice is not simply a matter of the distribution of goods, or the income with which goods are to be purchased. It is also a matter of the protection of rights. Western societies claim to give their citizens equal rights in political and legal contexts; they also claim to endorse the larger conception of a right to life. Now it is possible to interpret these rights in a limited and formalistic way, so that the duties correlative to them are minimal. On the limited, or negative, interpretation, to say that A has a right to life is simply to say that others have a duty not to interfere with A's attempts to keep himself alive. This interpretation of the right to life is compatible with Individualism as well as with Puritanism. But it is an inadequate interpretation of the right to life and of other rights. A right to vote is meaningless if one is starving and unable to get to the polls; a right to equality before the law is meaningless if one cannot afford to hire a lawyer. And so on.

Even a Permissive welfare scheme will go only a very small way towards protecting people's rights. It will amount to a meaningful acknowledgement of a right to life, by ensuring income adequate to purchase food, clothing and shelter—at the very least. These minimum necessities are presupposed by all other rights a society may endorse in that their possession is a precondition of being able to exercise these other rights. Because it protects the rights of all within a society better than do Puritanism and Individualism, the Permissive view can rightly claim superiority over the others with regard to justice.

NOTES

1 Nichols Rescher, *Welfare: Social Issues in Philosophical Perspective,* p. 114.
2 One might wish to discuss moral questions concerning welfare in the context of natural rights doctrines. Indeed, Article 22 of the United Nations Declaration of Human Rights states, "Everyone, as a member of society, has the right to social security and is entitled, through national effort and international cooperation and in accordance with the organization and resources of each State, to the economic, social and cultural rights indispensable for his dignity and the free development of his personality." I make no attempt to defend the right to welfare as a natural right. Granting that rights imply responsibilities or duties and that "ought" implies "can," it would only be intelligible to regard the right to social security as a natural right if all states were able to ensure the minimum well-being of their citizens. This is not the case. And a natural right is one which is by definition supposed to belong to all human beings simply in virtue of their status as human beings. The analysis given here in the permissive view is compatible with the claim that all human beings have a *prima facie* natural right to social security. It is not, however, compatible with the claim that all human beings have a natural right to social security if this right is regarded as one which is so absolute as to be inviolable under any and all conditions.
3 See, for example, Ayn Rand's *Atlas Shrugged, The Virtue of Selfishness* and *Capitalism: the Unknown Ideal.*
4 John Hospers, *Libertarianism: A Political Philosophy for Tomorrow,* p. 67.
5 I say virtually unconditional, because an Individualist such as John Hospers sees a legitimate moral role for government in preventing the use of force by some citizens against others. Since this is the case, I presume that he would also regard as legitimate such taxation as was necessary to support this function. Presumably that taxation would be seen as consented to by all, on the grounds that all "really want" government protection.
6 Ian Adams, William Cameron, Brian Hill, and Peter Penz, *The Real Poverty Report,* pp. 167–187.
7 See *A Theory of Justice,* pp. 124, 136. Rawls defines the free-rider as one who relies on the principle "everyone is to act justly except for myself, if I choose not to," and says that his position is a version of egoism which is eliminated as a morally acceptable principle by formal constraints. This conclusion regarding the tenability of egoism is one which I accept and which is taken for granted in the present context.
8 *Senate Report on Poverty,* p. 73.

9 The Hamilton Public Welfare Department takes automobile license plates from recipients, making them available again only to those whose needs meet with the Department's approval. (*Real Poverty Report,* p. 186.) The *Globe and Mail* for 12 January 1974 reported that welfare recipients in the city of Toronto are to be subjected to computerized budgeting. In the summer of 1973, the two young daughters of an Alabama man on welfare were sterilized against their own wishes and without their parents' informed consent. (See *Time,* 23 July 1973.)

10 Robert Nozick, "Distributive Justice," *Philosophy and Public Affairs,* Fall 1973.

QUESTIONS

1 Which of the three approaches to welfare described by Govier (individualist, permissive, puritan) is found in our society?

2 Govier finds the permissive position superior to the others on the basis of both utilitarian and justice considerations. What arguments could an individualist offer to rebut Govier's arguments? What arguments could an advocate of the puritan position offer to counter Govier's?

SUGGESTED ADDITIONAL READINGS FOR CHAPTER 8

ARTHUR, JOHN, and WILLIAM H. SHAW, eds.: *Justice and Economic Distribution,* 2d ed. Englewood Cliffs, N.J.: Prentice-Hall, 1991. This collection includes excerpts from John Rawls's *A Theory of Justice* and Robert Nozick's *Anarchy, State, and Utopia,* contemporary presentations of the utilitarian approach, and recent essays on economic justice.

FRIEDMAN, MILTON: *Capitalism and Freedom.* Chicago: University of Chicago Press, 1962. For Friedman, an economist and libertarian, the ethical principle governing the distribution of income in a free society is "to each according to what he or the instruments he owns produces." He sees economic freedom as a necessary condition for political freedom.

HARRINGTON, MICHAEL: *Socialism.* New York: Saturday Review Press, 1970, 1972. Harrington explores various "socialisms"—positions which he considers antisocialist. He presents his account of socialism as a possible alternative to both communism and the welfare state.

HELD, VIRGINIA, ed.: *Property, Profits, and Economic Justice.* Belmont, Calif.: Wadsworth, 1980. This is an excellent collection of readings centering on questions about our rights and interests in acquiring and holding property and in increasing or limiting profits.

KYMLICKA, WILL: *Contemporary Political Philosophy.* Oxford: Oxford University Press, 1990. Kymlicka discusses the competing views of justice and community advanced by the major schools in contemporary political theory.

NIELSEN, KAI: *Equality and Liberty: A Defense of Radical Egalitarianism,* Totowa, N.J.: Rowman & Littlefield, 1984. Nielsen defends the egalitarian ideal that is at the basis of socialist thinking.

NOZICK, ROBERT: *Anarchy, State, and Utopia.* New York: Basic, 1974. This book has engendered a great deal of discussion among philosophers concerned with distributive justice. Nozick, who endorses the libertarian conception of justice, holds the libertarian ideal to be exemplified by the principle, "from each as he chooses, to each as he is chosen."

OKIN, SUSAN MOLLER: *Justice, Gender, and the Family.* New York: Basic, 1989. Okin argues that without a just family structure there will not be a just society. She criticizes various contemporary Anglo-American theories of justice such as those of Robert Nozick and John Rawls for their androcentrism. However, Okin finds Rawls's veil of ignorance useful in developing a theory of justice within the family.

RAWLS, JOHN: "Justice as Fairness." *Philosophical Review,* vol. 67, April 1958, pp. 164–194. In this article, Rawls offers a definition of justice in terms of two principles, which he maintains all rational, self-interested persons would agree are in the equal interests of all. He argues (1) that everyone has the right to equal liberty and (2) that differences of wealth and privilege are justified only if everyone is free to compete for them and if everyone benefits from them.

————: *Political Liberalism.* New York: Columbia University Press, 1993. This book brings together essays which were written by Rawls over a twenty-year period. In these essays, Rawls moves beyond the near-universal moral theory of social and economic justice developed in his earlier works to a political theory of the modern liberal state with its pluralism and toleration.

————: *A Theory of Justice.* Cambridge, Mass.: Harvard University Press, 1971. This is a more developed discussion of the position Rawls presents in "Justice as Fairness." It is a seminal work that has stimulated a great deal of discussion among philosophers.

SHUE, HENRY: *Basic Rights: Subsistence, Affluence, and U.S. Foreign Policy.* Princeton, N.J.: Princeton University Press, 1980. Shue argues that there is at least one small set of economic rights, subsistence rights, that have equal priority with the highest-ranked political rights.

CHAPTER 9

World Hunger and Global Justice

In the world today, widespread hunger is an undeniable fact. Famines are commonplace in Africa and Southeast Asia, and, for many people in very diverse places on the globe, malnutrition is an everyday fact of life. Very few of the victims of famine and malnutrition actually "die of hunger"; but they die of illnesses, such as flu and intestinal problems, which they could have survived if they had not been weakened by hunger. The victims are often very old or very young. Aftereffects for those who survive are often tragic and long-lasting. A large number of children are stunted in growth and suffer incapacitating brain damage as a result of malnutrition. Whole populations are permanently weakened, listless, and lethargic, lacking the energy for any economic advances that might help prevent future famines. From a moral point of view, what should affluent countries (or their people) do to prevent such devastating hunger and malnutrition? What *can* they do? As the readings in this chapter show, answers concerning the moral *obligations* of more affluent individuals and nations in regard to world hunger are intertwined with answers concerning the *causes of world hunger* and *effective ways of eliminating those causes.* As we shall see, discussion of these issues also involves claims about the requirements of global justice.

NEO-MALTHUSIANISM

One answer regarding the causes of world hunger is offered by people labeled "neo-Malthusians." Following Thomas Robert Malthus (1766–1834), they identify the cause as *overpopulation.* For Malthus, unrestricted population growth necessarily outstrips economic growth, especially the growth in food supplies. This, in turn, *necessarily* results in famines. Uncontrolled fertility is the cause of poverty, and poverty is the cause of the miseries of the poor, including starvation. It has been shown that Malthus was wrong in certain respects, since in many countries the economic growth rate, including the growth in food supplies, has far outstripped the population growth rate. But contemporary neo-Malthusians hold that the economic growth rate cannot be sustained. They offer different reasons in support of this view (e.g., political or technical ones), but they all agree that continued economic growth is impossible. Having identified overpopulation as *the cause* of scarcity, neo-Malthusians locate the solution to problems of world hunger in population control. Optimistic neo-Malthusians hold that birth-control measures can eventually succeed in curbing population growth sufficiently to avert future famines. Pessimistic neo-Malthusians hold that serious political and psychological obstacles to planned population-control measures make famines inevitable in some countries. They predict that these famines will in turn effectively curb unmaintainable population growth unless those in more affluent countries intervene. Some pessimistic neo-Malthusians, including Garrett Hardin in this chapter, use their Malthusian analyses of world hunger to support claims about what more affluent individuals and nations *ought* to do regarding the needs of potential famine victims. The expressions "ethics of triage" and "lifeboat ethics" are often applied to the ethical approaches advocated by pessimistic neo-Malthusians.

The expression "method of triage" was first used to describe the French approach to their wounded in the First World War. The wounded were sorted into three categories. Those with the slightest injuries were given quick first aid. Those who could not be helped were simply allowed to die. Those in between received the most intensive medical care. Analogously, applying the method of triage to countries having serious food problems involves classifying them into three groups. The first group consists of countries that will survive even without aid. The second group consists of countries that will survive—given sufficient aid—because they are prepared to do what is necessary to bring their food resources and populations into line. Countries in the second group ought to be given the necessary aid. The third group consists of countries whose problems are insoluble in the long run because they are not willing to adopt the necessary population-control measures. According to the ethics of triage, countries in the third group should receive no help. Thus, the proponents of the ethics of triage argue that the affluent should help only those potential victims of famine and malnutrition who reside in countries that are effectively trying to bring population size into line with the country's food supply.[1]

The argument for the moral correctness of the ethics of triage is a consequentialist one and depends on the correctness of the following factual claim: Economic aid to countries with long-run insoluble problems is only a stopgap measure that in the long run will have highly undesirable consequences. Aid to societies in group 3, it is said, may alleviate current suffering, but it will cause more long-term suffering for the members of both the needy and affluent countries. Suffering will increase because economic aid will enable more people to survive and reproduce. If no real attempt is made to control population growth, the ever increasing population will make ever increasing demands on the world food supply. These demands will have a strong adverse effect on the quality of the life led by future members of today's more affluent societies. In time, it will be impossible even for the members of the once affluent countries to survive. If help is withheld from the countries in group 3, however, one of two things will follow. Either the needy countries will instigate mea-

---

[1]See especially Paul and William Paddock, *Famine—1975!* (Boston: Little, Brown, 1968).

sures to limit their populations in keeping with their own resources, or else nature itself through famine and disease will decimate the population to the appropriate level. In effect, those who argue in this way maintain that responsibilities and rights go hand in hand. People in the afflicted societies cause their own problems by having too many children. They are entitled to have their most basic needs met by more affluent individuals and societies only if they accept a crucial responsibility—the responsibility for limiting their fertility sufficiently so that they do not continue to place an ever growing burden on the world's food resources.

Garrett Hardin's lifeboat-ethics argument echoes some of the major contentions of the ethics of triage. Comparing nations to boats, Hardin maintains that many countries have outstripped their "carrying capacity." He advances a consequentialist argument to support his claim that the affluent *ought not* help those in the overpopulating countries. In Hardin's view, the long-range effects of food aid will be not only harmful but disastrous for everyone. They will be disastrous for countries whose fertility rates remain uncontrolled by either human planning or nature, since future generations in these countries will suffer massive starvation and profound misery. They will be disastrous for the human species as a whole, since the eventual outcome may be the elimination of the species. Hardin sees no real need to use the method of triage in making decisions about which countries should be given aid. If giving food to *any* overpopulated country does more harm than good, he argues, that food should not be given. For Hardin, "the question of triage does not even arise."[2]

NON-MALTHUSIAN ALTERNATIVES AND GLOBAL JUSTICE

Criticisms of neo-Malthusians take many forms. Some critics, for example, attack the *moral* claims of pessimistic neo-Malthusians. Rejecting the consequentialist approach to the moral dilemma, they maintain that no matter what the long-term consequences might be, we have an obligation to meet the most basic need of *existing* persons—the need for food. The most prominent attacks against Malthusianism, however, center around rejections of some or all of the Malthusian claims regarding the causes and/or the inevitability of famine and malnutrition in needy, developing countries. The counteranalyses offered reject the neo-Malthusian contention that the necessary economic growth is impossible. On these analyses, economic growth in the developing countries *themselves* is both possible and an essential part of the solution to problems of world hunger. Two major lines of argument emerge in these counteranalyses.

The first counteranalysis focuses on identifying the causes of high fertility rates among the poor in developing countries. Only if we understand why the poor have high rates of reproduction can we help to instigate and support social practices which will tend to end the cycle of poverty, high birth rates, and starvation which neo-Malthusians see as inevitable. Against the pessimistic neo-Malthusians, proponents of this analysis argue that famines and malnutrition are not inevitable. Against the

---

[2]Garrett Hardin, "Carrying Capacity as an Ethical Concept," in George R. Lucas, Jr., and Thomas W. Ogletree, eds., *Lifeboat Ethics* (New York: Harper & Row, 1976), p. 131.

optimistic neo-Malthusians, they argue that planned birth-control practices backed by government policies are not the solution. Ironically, the major factors influencing high fertility rates are identified as hunger and poverty. The Presidential Commission on World Hunger makes the point succinctly:

> Where hunger and poverty prevail, the population growth rate is more likely to increase than to decrease. Under inequitable social and economic conditions, a poor couple's desire for many children is a response to high infant mortality, the need for extra hands to help earn the family's daily bread, and the hope of support in old age. The key to reducing family size is to improve the social conditions which make large families a reasonable option.[3]

On this analysis, eradicating famine and malnutrition requires social and economic changes in the developing countries themselves, changes which would eliminate some of the gross inequalities of wealth and property in these countries. Without the recommended changes, it is argued, economic growth, including growth in the food supply, will not take place, population growth will not be slowed, and the tragic cycle will be repeated indefinitely.

Some of those who utilize this first approach against neo-Malthusians argue that the practices of members of more affluent nations prevent some of the poorest countries from increasing their own food supply. The identified culprits include multinational agribusinesses based in Western societies. It is charged that these multinationals have shifted the production of luxury items for the Western market from the highly industrialized countries to underdeveloped ones where cheap land and labor are available. As a result, the land in needy, underdeveloped countries is used to produce cash crops—crops that can be sold to members of the more affluent countries—while the food that is needed for the home market remains unproduced. In addition, it is argued that the international economic order favors the affluent, industrialized nations and is shaped by their needs. It is the affluent, industrialized societies that largely determine the prices for both the manufactured goods which developing nations must import and the agricultural products that the needy countries export. To the extent that the practices of those in affluent societies work against the potential self-sufficiency and real economic growth of developing countries, they help create and perpetuate the cycle of poverty, high fertility rates, and hunger.

The second counteranalysis advanced against neo-Malthusian reasoning comes from Marxists and other socialists and incorporates some of the elements of the first counteranalysis. Socialists reject both the contention that overpopulation is the cause of scarcity in the world and the contention that the requisite economic growth is impossible. They identify capitalism as the major cause of worldwide scarcity. Agreeing with the kinds of claims just discussed concerning the negative impact of multinational corporations on the economic growth of developing countries, they see a socialist economic system as the only solution to the problem of world hunger.[4] Kai

---

[3]The Presidential Commission on World Hunger, *Overcoming World Hunger: The Challenge Ahead* (1980), p. 26.

[4]See, for example, Howard L. Parsons, "Malthusianism and Socialism" in *Revolutionary World,* special issue, "Self, Global Issues, and Ethics," vols. 21/22 (1977).

Nielsen, a socialist, argues along these lines in this chapter as he identifies poverty and certain economic policies as the basic causes of famines.

In Nielsen's view, *global justice* requires the massive redistribution of resources from the affluent northern hemisphere to the southern hemisphere. In arguing to this conclusion, Nielsen discusses and rejects the following view: The very idea of global justice is incoherent, because questions of justice can be coherently raised only within individual societies or between societies that are similarly situated and in a condition of actual cooperative reciprocity, since only under this condition is there a possibility of reciprocal advantage. On Nielsen's account, a necessary condition for raising questions of justice is not *actual* cooperative reciprocity and the possibility of reciprocal advantage, but *moral* reciprocity, in which all human beings are treated as moral equals. Working with the idea of moral reciprocity, Nielsen argues that global justice is a coherent notion. Some of the arguments Nielsen advances to support his claim that global justice requires a massive redistribution of resources from North to South are similar to those in his article in Chapter 8. The material presented in the introduction to that chapter regarding negative and positive rights and the socialist conceptions of justice and freedom is also relevant here.

In another reading in this chapter, Richard T. De George also appeals to considerations of global justice, which he sees as a basis for poor countries to demand aid in the name of their citizens from rich countries. Unlike socialists, De George does not argue against either capitalism or the private ownership of the means of production. However, he does maintain that all human beings have the right to what is necessary for living in dignity and that this right takes precedence over property rights.

WHAT OUGHT WE TO DO?

What responsibilities do we as individuals have toward potential and actual famine victims? As the above discussion shows, our answers may depend on what we take to be a correct analysis of the causes of famine and malnutrition in the world. But if we set aside the kind of factual questions discussed above, we can still ask questions about the basis of a possible *moral obligation* that we as individuals might have to prevent starvation and malnutrition among the needy. Peter Singer, a utilitarian, argues for such a moral obligation. Utilitarianism holds that an action or practice is morally correct only if it is likely to produce the greatest balance of good over evil, everyone considered. Proceeding in a utilitarian spirit, Singer argues for an obligation to famine victims on the basis of the following principle: Persons are morally required to prevent something bad from happening if they can do so "without sacrificing anything of comparable moral significance." In Singer's view, even a weaker version of this principle is sufficient to establish a moral obligation to aid the victims of severe famines.

Jane S. Zembaty

Why Should the United States Be Concerned?

The Presidential Commission on World Hunger

In 1978 President Jimmy Carter appointed a Presidential Commission on World Hunger, chaired by Ambassador Sol Linowitz. The Commission was charged with the following tasks: (1) to identify the basic causes of domestic and international hunger and malnutrition; (2) to assess past and present national programs and policies that affect hunger and malnutrition; (3) to review existing studies and research on hunger; (4) to recommend to the President and Congress specific actions to create a coherent national food and hunger policy; and (5) to help implement those recommendations and focus public attention on food and hunger issues. This selection is excerpted from the Commission's final report, *Overcoming World Hunger: The Challenge Ahead.*

The Commission's major recommendation is that the elimination of hunger should be the primary focus of the United States government in its relationship with developing countries. The Commission bases its recommendations on the following reasons: (1) the moral obligation to overcome hunger, based on two universal values—respect for human dignity and social justice; (2) the dependence of national security on the economic well-being of the developing countries; and (3) the dependence of the economic vitality of the United States on a healthy international economy.

The major recommendation of the Presidential Commission on World Hunger is that the United States make the elimination of hunger the primary focus of its relations with the developing world—with all that implies for U.S. policy toward development assistance, trade, foreign investment and foreign affairs. In the Commission's view, there are significant reasons for the United States to place the elimination of hunger at the top of its list of global concerns.

MORAL OBLIGATION AND RESPONSIBILITY

Moral obligation alone would justify giving highest priority to the task of overcoming hunger. Even now, millions of human beings live on the edge of starvation—in conditions of subhuman poverty that, if we think about them at all, must fill us with shame and horror. We see this now most poignantly in famine conditions, but it is a fact of life every day for half a billion people. At least one out of every eight men, women and children on earth suffers malnutrition severe enough to shorten life, stunt physical growth, and dull mental ability.

Whether one speaks of human rights or basic human needs, the right to food is the most basic of all. Unless that right is first fulfilled, the protection of other human rights becomes a mockery for those who must spend all their energy merely to maintain life itself. The correct moral and ethical position on hunger is beyond debate.

Reprinted from *Overcoming World Hunger: The Challenge Ahead* (Washington, D.C.: Government Printing Office, 1980).

The major world religions and philosophical systems share two universal values: respect for human dignity and a sense of social justice. Hunger is the ultimate affront to both. Unless all governments begin now to act upon their rhetorical commitments to ending hunger, the principle that human life is sacred, which forms the very underpinnings of human society, will gradually but relentlessly erode. By concentrating its international efforts on the elimination of hunger, the United States would provide the strongest possible demonstration of its renewed dedication to the cause of human rights.

Moral obligation includes responsibility. In the Commission's view, the United States has a special capability and hence a special responsibility to lead the campaign against world hunger. The United States is by far the most powerful member of the world's increasingly interdependent food system. It harvests more than half the grain that crosses international borders. Its corporations dominate world grain trade. Its grain reserves are the largest on earth. Because of its agricultural productivity, its advanced food technology, and its market power, the United States inevitably exerts a major influence on all aspects of the international food system.

Global interdependence in food means that two straight years of bad harvests in any of the major grain-producing nations of the world could precipitate another global food crisis like the one that occurred in 1972–74. Recurrent crises of this nature could bring widespread famine and political disorder to the developing countries and would severely disrupt a fragile world economy already weakened by energy shortages and rampant inflation. U.S. policies will have a major role in determining whether or not this scenario will be played out.

American policies and resources also hold the key to solving that continuing world food crisis embodied in the swelling ranks of the chronically malnourished. To these hungry millions, it makes no difference whether such policies are made by choice or inertia, by acts of commission or acts of omission. In view of the undeniable influence that this nation's actions will have on world hunger, the Commission urges immediate yet careful long-range planning to assure that U.S. policy truly helps rather than harms the world's hungry people. Delay will only make the same ends more difficult and expensive to accomplish, and will not lift responsibility from the United States.

The Commission does not mean to imply that the United States alone can solve the world hunger problem. All nations, including those of the developing world, must make the conquest of hunger a common cause. However, the Commission is persuaded that unless the United States plays a major role by increasing its own commitment and action toward this goal, no effective and comprehensive global program to combat hunger is likely to be undertaken in the foreseeable future. Moreover, once its own commitment is clear, the United States will be in a particularly strong position to encourage others to do more. The Commission believes that the United States is uniquely situated to influence the fate of millions who do not get enough to eat.

NATIONAL SECURITY

The Commission believes that promoting economic development in general, and overcoming hunger in particular, are tasks far more critical to the U.S. national security than most policymakers acknowledge or even believe. Since the advent of nuclear weapons most Americans have been conditioned to equate national security with the strength of strategic military forces. The Commission considers this prevailing belief to be a simplistic illusion. Armed might represents merely the physical aspect of national security. Military force is ultimately useless in the absence of the global security that only coordinated international progress toward social justice can bring. . . .

ECONOMIC INTEREST

The Commission also finds compelling economic reasons for the United States to focus on the elimination of hunger. The United States can maintain its own economic vitality only within a healthy international economy whose overall strength will increase as each of its component parts becomes more productive, more equitable and more internationally competitive. To sustain a healthy global economy, the purchasing power of today's poor people must rise substantially, in order to set in motion that mutually reinforcing exchange of goods, services and commodities which provides the foundation for viable economic partnership and growth. . . .

[Thus we conclude that there] are compelling moral, economic and national security reasons for the United States Government to make the elimination of hunger the central focus of its relations with the developing world. . . .

QUESTIONS

1 According to the Commission, there are compelling *economic* reasons for the United States to focus on the elimination of hunger in its relations with developing countries. If this is correct, what evidence can be given to support it?
2 It has been said that the United States cannot solve the problem of world hunger; it *is* the problem. What reasons could be offered to support such a contention?

Famine, Affluence, and Morality

Peter Singer

Peter Singer is professor of philosophy and director of the Centre for Human Bioethics at Monash University, Victoria, Australia. He is the author of such books as *Animal Liberation* (2d ed., 1990) and *How Are We to Live? Ethics in an Age of Self-Interest* (1995). His edited works include *A Companion to Ethics* (1991) and *Ethics* (1994).

Singer expresses concern over the fact that while members of the more affluent nations spend money on trivia, people in the needier nations are starving. He argues that it is morally wrong not to prevent suffering whenever one can do so without sacrificing anything morally significant. Giving aid to the victims of famine can prevent such suffering. Even if giving requires a drastic reduction in the standard of living of the members of the more affluent societies, the latter are morally required to meet at least the basic need for food of people who will otherwise starve to death.

As I write this, in November 1971, people are dying in East Bengal from lack of food, shelter, and medical care. The suffering and death that are occurring there now are not inevitable, not unavoidable in any fatalistic sense of the term. Constant poverty, a cyclone, and a civil war have turned at least nine million people into destitute refugees; nevertheless, it is not beyond the capacity of the richer nations to give enough assistance to reduce any further suffering to very small proportions. The decisions and actions of human beings can prevent this kind of suffering. Unfortunately, human beings have not made the necessary decisions. At the individual level, people have, with very few exceptions, not responded to the situation in any significant way. Generally speaking, people have not given large sums to relief funds; they have not written to their parliamentary representatives demanding increased government assistance; they have not demonstrated in the streets, held symbolic fasts, or done anything else directed toward providing the refugees with the means to satisfy their essential needs. At the government level, no government has given the sort of massive aid that would enable the refugees to survive for more than a few days. Britain, for instance, has given rather more than most countries. It has, to date, given £14,750,000. For comparative purposes, Britain's share of the nonrecoverable development costs of the Anglo-French Concorde project is already in excess of £275,000,000, and on present estimates will reach £440,000,000. The implication is that the British government values a supersonic transport more than thirty times as highly as it values the lives of the nine million refugees. Australia is another country which, on a per capita basis, is well up in the "aid to Bengal" table. Australia's aid, however, amounts to less than one-twelfth of the cost of Sydney's new opera house. The total amount given, from all sources, now stands at about £65,000,000. The estimated cost of keeping the refugees alive for one year is £464,000,000. Most of the refugees have now been in the camps for more than six months. The World Bank has said that India needs a minimum of £300,000,000 in assistance from other countries before the end of the year. It seems obvious that assistance on this scale will not be forthcoming. India will be forced to choose between letting the refugees starve or diverting funds from her own development program, which will mean that more of her own people will starve in the future.[1]

   These are the essential facts about the present situation in Bengal. So far as it concerns us here, there is nothing unique about this situation except its magnitude. The Bengal emergency is just the latest and most acute of a series of major emergencies in various parts of the world, arising both from natural and from man-made causes. There are also many parts of the world in which people die from malnutrition and lack of food independent of any special emergency. I take Bengal as my example only because it is the present concern, and because the size of the problem has ensured that it has been given adequate publicity. Neither individuals nor governments can claim to be unaware of what is happening there.

What are the moral implications of a situation like this? In what follows, I shall argue that the way people in relatively affluent countries react to a situation like that in Bengal cannot be justified; indeed, the whole way we look at moral issues—our moral conceptual scheme—needs to be altered, and with it, the way of life that has come to be taken for granted in our society.

In arguing for this conclusion I will not, of course, claim to be morally neutral. I shall, however, try to argue for the moral position that I take, so that anyone who accepts certain assumptions, to be made explicit, will, I hope, accept my conclusion.

I begin with the assumption that suffering and death from lack of food, shelter, and medical care are bad. I think most people will agree about this, although one may reach the same view by different routes. I shall not argue for this view. People can hold all sorts of eccentric positions, and perhaps from some of them it would not follow that death by starvation is in itself bad. It is difficult, perhaps impossible, to refute such positions, and so for brevity I will henceforth take this assumption as accepted. Those who disagree need read no further.

My next point is this: if it is in our power to prevent something bad from happening, without thereby sacrificing anything of comparable moral importance, we ought, morally, to do it. By "without sacrificing anything of comparable moral importance" I mean without causing anything else comparably bad to happen, or doing something that is wrong in itself, or failing to promote some moral good, comparable in significance to the bad thing that we can prevent. This principle seems almost as uncontroversial as the last one. It requires us only to prevent what is bad, and not to promote what is good, and it requires this of us only when we can do it without sacrificing anything that is, from the moral point of view, comparably important. I could even, as far as the application of my argument to the Bengal emergency is concerned, qualify the point so as to make it: if it is in our power to prevent something very bad from happening, without thereby sacrificing anything morally significant, we ought, morally, to do it. An application of this principle would be as follows: if I am walking past a shallow pond and see a child drowning in it, I ought to wade in and pull the child out. This will mean getting my clothes muddy, but this is insignificant, while the death of the child would presumably be a very bad thing.

The uncontroversial appearance of the principle just stated is deceptive. If it were acted upon, even in its qualified form, our lives, our society, and our world would be fundamentally changed. For the principle takes, firstly, no account of proximity or distance. It makes no moral difference whether the person I can help is a neighbor's child ten yards from me or a Bengali whose name I shall never know, ten thousand miles away. Secondly, the principle makes no distinction between cases in which I am the only person who could possibly do anything and cases in which I am just one among millions in the same position.

I do not think I need to say much in defense of the refusal to take proximity and distance into account. The fact that a person is physically near to us, so that we have personal contact with him, may make it more likely that we *shall* assist him, but this does not show that we *ought* to help him rather than another who happens to be further away. If we accept any principle of impartiality, universalizability, equality, or whatever, we cannot discriminate against someone merely because he is far away from us (or we are far away from him). Admittedly, it is possible that we are in a better position to judge what needs to be done to help a person near to us than one far away, and perhaps also to provide the assistance we judge to be necessary. If this were the case, it would be a reason for helping those near to us first. This may once have been a justification for being more concerned with the poor in one's own town than with famine victims in India. Unfortunately for those who like to keep their moral responsibilities limited, instant communication and swift transportation have changed the situation. From the moral point of view, the development of the world into a "global village" has made an important, though still unrecognized, difference to our moral situation. Expert observers and supervisors, sent out by famine relief organizations or permanently stationed in famine-prone areas, can direct our aid to a refugee in Bengal almost as effectively as we could get it to someone in our own block. There would seem, therefore, to be no possible justification for discriminating on geographical grounds.

There may be a greater need to defend the second implication of my principle— that the fact that there are millions of other people in the same position, in respect to the Bengali refugees, as I am, does not make the situation significantly different from a situation in which I am the only person who can prevent something very bad from occurring. Again, of course, I admit that there is a psychological difference between the cases; one feels less guilty about doing nothing if one can point to others, similarly placed, who have also done nothing. Yet this can make no real difference to our moral obligations. Should I consider that I am less obliged to pull the drowning child out of the pond if on looking around I see other people, no further away than I am, who have also noticed the child but are doing nothing? One has only to ask this question to see the absurdity of the view that numbers lessen obligation. It is a view that is an ideal excuse for inactivity; unfortunately most of the major evils—poverty, overpopulation, pollution—are problems in which everyone is almost equally involved.

The view that numbers do make a difference can be made plausible if stated in this way: if everyone in circumstances like mine gave £5 to the Bengal Relief Fund, there would be enough to provide food, shelter, and medical care for the refugees; there is no reason why I should give more than anyone else in the same circumstances as I am; therefore I have no obligation to give more than £5. Each premise in this argument is true, and the argument looks sound. It may convince us, unless we notice that it is based on a hypothetical premise, although the conclusion is not stated hypothetically. The argument would be sound if the conclusion were: if everyone in circumstances like mine were to give £5, I would have no obligation to give more than £5. If the conclusion were so stated, however, it would be obvious that the argument has no bearing on a situation in which it is not the case that everyone else gives £5. This, of course, is the actual situation. It is more or less certain that not everyone in circumstances like mine will give £5. So there will not be enough to provide the needed food, shelter, and medical care. Therefore by giving more than £5 I will prevent more suffering than I would if I gave just £5.

It might be thought that this argument has an absurd consequence. Since the situation appears to be that very few people are likely to give substantial amounts, it follows that I and everyone else in similar circumstances ought to give as much as possible, that is, at least up to the point at which by giving more one would begin to cause serious suffering for oneself and one's dependents—perhaps even beyond this point to the point of marginal utility, at which by giving more one would cause oneself and one's dependents as much suffering as one would prevent in Bengal. If everyone does this, however, there will be more than can be used for the benefit of the refugees, and some of the sacrifice will have been unnecessary. Thus, if everyone does what he ought to do, the result will not be as good as it would be if everyone did a little less than he ought to do, or if only some do all that they ought to do.

The paradox here arises only if we assume that the actions in question—sending money to the relief funds—are performed more or less simultaneously, and are also unexpected. For if it is to be expected that everyone is going to contribute something, then clearly each is not obliged to give as much as he would have been obliged to had others not been giving too. And if everyone is not acting more or less simultaneously, then those giving later will know how much more is needed, and will have no obligation to give more than is necessary to reach this amount. To say this is not to deny the principle that people in the same circumstances have the same obligations, but to point out that the fact that others have given, or may be expected to give, is a relevant circumstance: those giving after it has become known that many others are giving and those giving before are not in the same circumstances. So the seemingly absurd consequence of the principle I have put forward can occur only if people are in error about the actual circumstances—that is, if they think they are giving when others are not, but in fact they are giving when others are. The result of everyone doing what he really ought to do cannot be worse than the result of everyone doing less than he ought to do, although the result of everyone doing what he reasonably believes he ought to do could be.

If my argument so far has been sound, neither our distance from a preventable evil nor the number of other people who, in respect to that evil, are in the same situation as we are, lessens our obligation to mitigate or prevent that evil. I shall therefore take as established the principle I asserted earlier. As I have already said, I need to assert it only in its qualified form: if it is in our power to prevent something very bad from happening, without thereby sacrificing anything else morally significant, we ought, morally, to do it.

The outcome of this argument is that our traditional moral categories are upset. The traditional distinction between duty and charity cannot be drawn, or at least, not in the place we normally draw it. Giving money to the Bengal Relief Fund is regarded as an act of charity in our society. The bodies which collect money are known as "charities." These organizations see themselves in this way—if you send them a check, you will be thanked for your "generosity." Because giving money is regarded as an act of charity, it is not thought that there is anything wrong with not giving. The charitable man may be praised, but the man who is not charitable is not condemned. People do not feel in any way ashamed or guilty about spending money on new clothes or a new car instead of giving it to famine relief. (Indeed, the alternative does not occur to them.) This way of looking at the matter cannot be justified. When we buy new clothes not to keep ourselves warm but to look "well-dressed" we are not providing for any important need. We would not be sacrificing anything significant if we were to continue to wear our old clothes, and give the money to famine relief. By doing so, we would be preventing another person from starving. It follows from what I have said earlier that we ought to give money away, rather than spend it on clothes which we do not need to keep us warm. To do so is not charitable, or generous. Nor is it the kind of act which philosophers and theologians have called "supererogatory"—an act which it would be good to do, but not wrong not to do. On the contrary, we ought to give the money away, and it is wrong not to do so.

I am not maintaining that there are no acts which are charitable, or that there are no acts which it would be good to do but not wrong not to do. It may be possible to redraw the distinction between duty and charity in some other place. All I am arguing here is that the present way of drawing the distinction, which makes it an act of charity for a man living at the level of affluence which most people in the "developed nations" enjoy to give money to save someone else from starvation, cannot be supported. It is beyond the scope of my argument to consider whether the distinction should be redrawn or abolished altogether. There would be many other possible ways of drawing the distinction—for instance, one might decide that it is good to make other people as happy as possible, but not wrong not to do so.

Despite the limited nature of the revision in our moral conceptual scheme which I am proposing, the revision would, given the extent of both affluence and famine in the world today, have radical implications. These implications may lead to further objections, distinct from those I have already considered. I shall discuss two of these.

One objection to the position I have taken might be simply that it is too drastic a revision of our moral scheme. People do not ordinarily judge in the way I have suggested they should. Most people reserve their moral condemnation for those who violate some moral norm, such as the norm against taking another person's property. They do not condemn those who indulge in luxury instead of giving to famine relief. But given that I did not set out to present a morally neutral description of the way people make moral judgments, the way people do in fact judge has nothing to do with the validity of my conclusion. My conclusion follows from the principle which I advanced earlier, and unless that principle is rejected, or the arguments shown to be unsound, I think the conclusion must stand, however strange it appears. . . .

The second objection to my attack on the present distinction between duty and charity is one which has from time to time been made against utilitarianism. It follows from some forms of utilitarian theory that we all ought, morally, to be working full time to increase the balance of happiness over misery. The position I have taken here would not lead to this conclusion in all circumstances, for if there were no bad occurrences that we could prevent without sacrificing something of comparable moral importance, my argument would have no application. Given the present conditions in many parts of the world, however, it does follow from my argument that we ought, morally, to be working full time to relieve great suffering of the sort that occurs as a result of famine or other disasters. Of course, mitigating circumstances can be adduced—for instance, that if we wear ourselves out through over-work, we shall be less effective than we would otherwise have been. Nevertheless, when all considerations of this sort have been taken into account, the conclusion re-mains: we ought to be preventing as much suffering as we can without sacrificing something else of comparable moral importance. This conclusion is one which we may be reluctant to face. I cannot see, though, why it should be regarded as a criti-cism of the position for which I have argued, rather than a criticism of our ordinary standards of behavior. Since most people are self-interested to some degree, very few of us are likely to do everything that we ought to do. It would, however, hardly be honest to take this as evidence that it is not the case that we ought to do it. . . .

The conclusion reached earlier [raises] the question of just how much we all ought to be giving away. One possibility, which has already been mentioned, is that we ought to give until we reach the level of marginal utility—that is, the level at which, by giving more, I would cause as much suffering to myself or my dependents as I would relieve by my gift. This would mean, of course, that one would reduce oneself to very near the material circumstances of a Bengali refugee. It will be re-called that earlier I put forward both a strong and a moderate version of the princi-ple of preventing bad occurrences. The strong version, which required us to prevent bad things from happening unless in doing so we would be sacrificing something of a comparable moral significance, does seem to require reducing ourselves to the level of marginal utility. I should also say that the strong version seems to me to be the correct one. I proposed the more moderate version—that we should prevent bad oc-currences unless, to do so, we had to sacrifice something morally significant—only in order to show that even on this surely undeniable principle a great change in our way of life is required. On the more moderate principle, it may not follow that we ought to reduce ourselves to the level of marginal utility, for one might hold that to reduce oneself and one's family to this level is to cause something significantly bad to happen. Whether this is so I shall not discuss, since, as I have said, I can see no good reason for holding the moderate version of the principle rather than the strong version. Even if we accepted the principle only in its moderate form, however, it should be clear that we would have to give away enough to ensure that the consumer society, dependent as it is on people spending on trivia rather than giving to famine relief, would slow down and perhaps disappear entirely. There are several reasons why this would be desirable in itself. The value and necessity of economic growth are now being questioned not only by conservationists, but by economists as well.[2] There is no doubt, too, that the consumer society has had a distorting effect on the goals and purposes of its members. Yet looking at the matter purely from the point of view of overseas aid, there must be a limit to the extent to which we should de-liberately slow down our economy; for it might be the case that if we gave away, say, forty percent of our Gross National Product, we would slow down the economy so much that in absolute terms we would be giving less than if we gave twenty-five percent of the much larger GNP that we would have if we limited our contribution to this smaller percentage.

I mention this only as an indication of the sort of factor that one would have to take into account in working out an ideal. Since Western societies generally consider one percent of the GNP an acceptable level for overseas aid, the matter is entirely academic. Nor does it affect the question of how much an individual should give in a society in which very few are giving substantial amounts.

It is sometimes said, though less often now than it used to be, that philosophers have no special role to play in public affairs, since most public issues depend primarily on an assessment of facts. On questions of fact, it is said, philosophers as such have no special expertise, and so it has been possible to engage in philosophy without committing oneself to any position on major public issues. No doubt there are some issues of social policy and foreign policy about which it can truly be said that a really expert assessment of the facts is required before taking sides or acting, but the issue of famine is surely not one of these. The facts about the existence of suffering are beyond dispute. Nor, I think, is it disputed that we can do something about it, either through orthodox methods of famine relief or through population control or both. This is therefore an issue on which philosophers are competent to take a position. The issue is one which faces everyone who has more money than he needs to support himself and his dependents, or who is in a position to take some sort of political action. These categories must include practically every teacher and student of philosophy in the universities of the Western world. If philosophy is to deal with matters that are relevant to both teachers and students, this is an issue that philosophers should discuss.

Discussion, though, is not enough. What is the point of relating philosophy to public (and personal) affairs if we do not take our conclusions seriously? In this instance, taking our conclusion seriously means acting upon it. The philosopher will not find it any easier than anyone else to alter his attitudes and way of life to the extent that, if I am right, is involved in doing everything that we ought to be doing. At the very least, though, one can make a start. The philosopher who does so will have to sacrifice some of the benefits of the consumer society, but he can find compensation in the satisfaction of a way of life in which theory and practice, if not yet in harmony, are at least coming together.

NOTES

1 There was also a third possibility: that India would go to war to enable the refugees to return to their lands. Since I wrote this paper, India has taken this way out. The situation is no longer that described above, but this does not affect my argument, as the next paragraph indicates.
2 See, for instance, John Kenneth Galbraith, *The New Industrial State* (Boston, 1967); and E. J. Mishan, *The Costs of Economic Growth* (London, 1967).

QUESTIONS

1 Think about the following claim: Contributing to famine relief is not a moral obligation which we must perform if we are to act in a morally correct way, but an act of charity which we may or may not perform. Can you offer any arguments to defend it?
2 Singer says, "we ought to be preventing as much suffering as we can without sacrificing something else of comparable moral importance." What moral considerations would outweigh the obligation Singer claims we have to aid famine victims?

Living on a Lifeboat

Garrett Hardin

Garrett Hardin is professor of biology at the University of California, Santa Barbara. His many books include *Filters against Folly: How to Survive Despite Economists, Ecologists, and the Merely Eloquent* (1985) and *Living Within Limits: Ecology, Economics, and Population Taboos* (1993).

Using the metaphor of a lifeboat, Hardin argues that the time may have come to refuse aid in the form of food to needy countries which do not accept the responsibility for limiting their population growth. He maintains that adherence to the principle "From each according to his ability; to each according to his need" will have strong adverse effects. Bolstered by our aid, needy countries will continue their irresponsible policies in regard to food production and population growth. Furthermore, the food we supply will enable these populations to continue to increase. This in the long run will jeopardize the survival of the human species.

No generation has viewed the problem of the survival of the human species as seriously as we have. Inevitably, we have entered this world of concern through the door of metaphor. Environmentalists have emphasized the image of the earth as a spaceship—Spaceship Earth. Kenneth Boulding (1966) is the principal architect of this metaphor. It is time, he says, that we replace the wasteful "cowboy economy" of the past with the frugal "spaceship economy" required for continued survival in the limited world we now see ours to be. The metaphor is notably useful in justifying pollution control measures.

Unfortunately, the image of a spaceship is also used to promote measures that are suicidal. One of these is a generous immigration policy, which is only a particular instance of a class of policies that are in error because they lead to the tragedy of the commons (Hardin 1968). These suicidal policies are attractive because they mesh with what we unthinkingly take to be the ideals of "the best people." What is missing in the idealistic view is an insistence that rights and responsibilities must go together. The "generous" attitude of all too many people results in asserting inalienable rights while ignoring or denying matching responsibilities.

For the metaphor of a spaceship to be correct the aggregate of people on board would have to be under unitary sovereign control (Ophuls 1974). A true ship always has a captain. It is conceivable that a ship could be run by a committee. But it could not possibly survive if its course were determined by bickering tribes that claimed rights without responsibilities.

What about Spaceship Earth? It certainly has no captain, and no executive committee. The United Nations is a toothless tiger, because the signatories of its charter

Reprinted, with permission, from the October 1974 issue of *BioScience,* © American Institute of Biological Sciences.

wanted it that way. The spaceship metaphor is used only to justify spaceship demands on common resources without acknowledging corresponding spaceship responsibilities.

An understandable fear of decisive action leads people to embrace "incrementalism"—moving toward reform in tiny stages. As we shall see, this strategy is counterproductive in the area discussed here if it means accepting rights before responsibilities. Where human survival is at stake, the acceptance of responsibilities is a precondition to the acceptance of rights, if the two cannot be introduced simultaneously.

LIFEBOAT ETHICS

Before taking up certain substantive issues let us look at an alternative metaphor, that of a lifeboat. In developing some relevant examples the following numerical values are assumed. Approximately two-thirds of the world is desperately poor, and only one-third is comparatively rich. The people in poor countries have an average per capita GNP (Gross National Product) of about $200 per year; the rich, of about $3,000. (For the United States it is nearly $5,000 per year.) Metaphorically, each rich nation amounts to a lifeboat full of comparatively rich people. The poor of the world are in other, much more crowded lifeboats. Continuously, so to speak, the poor fall out of their lifeboats and swim for a while in the water outside, hoping to be admitted to a rich lifeboat, or in some other way to benefit from the "goodies" on board. What should the passengers on a rich lifeboat do? This is the central problem of "the ethics of a lifeboat."

First we must acknowledge that each lifeboat is effectively limited in capacity. The land of every nation has a limited carrying capacity. The exact limit is a matter for argument, but the energy crunch is convincing more people every day that we have already exceeded the carrying capacity of the land. We have been living on "capital"—stored petroleum and coal—and soon we must live on income alone.

Let us look at only one lifeboat—ours. The ethical problem is the same for all, and is as follows. Here we sit, say 50 people in a lifeboat. To be generous, let us assume our boat has a capacity of 10 more, making 60. (This, however, is to violate the engineering principle of the "safety factor." A new plant disease or a bad change in the weather may decimate our population if we don't preserve some excess capacity as a safety factor.)

The 50 of us in the lifeboat see 100 others swimming in the water outside, asking for admission to the boat, or for handouts. How shall we respond to their calls? There are several possibilities.

One. We may be tempted to try to live by the Christian ideal of being "our brother's keeper," or by the Marxian ideal (Marx 1875) of "from each according to his abilities, to each according to his needs." Since the needs of all are the same, we take all the needy into our boat, making a total of 150 in a boat with a capacity of 60. The boat is swamped, and everyone drowns. Complete justice, complete catastrophe.

Two. Since the boat has an unused excess capacity of 10, we admit just 10 more to it. This has the disadvantage of getting rid of the safety factor, for which action we will sooner or later pay dearly. Moreover, *which* 10 do we let in? "First come, first served?" The best 10? The neediest 10? How do we *discriminate?* And what do we say to the 90 who are excluded?

Three. Admit no more to the boat and preserve the small safety factor. Survival of the people in the lifeboat is then possible (though we shall have to be on our guard against boarding parties).

The last solution is abhorrent to many people. It is unjust, they say. Let us grant that it is.

"I feel guilty about my good luck," say some. The reply to this is simple: *Get out and yield your place to others.* Such a selfless action might satisfy the conscience of those who are addicted to guilt but it would not change the ethics of the lifeboat. The needy person to whom a guilt-addict yields his place will not himself feel guilty about his sudden good luck. (If he did he would not climb aboard.) The net result of conscience-stricken people relinquishing their unjustly held positions is the elimination of their kind of conscience from the lifeboat. The lifeboat, as it were, purifies itself of guilt. The ethics of the lifeboat persist, unchanged by such momentary aberrations.

This then is the basic metaphor within which we must work out our solutions. Let us enrich the image step by step with substantive additions from the real world.

REPRODUCTION

The harsh characteristics of lifeboat ethics are heightened by reproduction, particularly by reproductive differences. The people inside the lifeboats of the wealthy nations are doubling in numbers every 87 years; those outside are doubling every 35 years, on the average. And the relative difference in prosperity is becoming greater.

Let us, for a while, think primarily of the U.S. lifeboat. As of 1973 the United States had a population of 210 million people, who were increasing by 0.8% per year, that is, doubling in number every 87 years.

Although the citizens of rich nations are outnumbered two to one by the poor, let us imagine an equal number of poor people outside our lifeboat—a mere 210 million poor people reproducing at a quite different rate. If we imagine these to be the combined populations of Colombia, Venezuela, Ecuador, Morocco, Thailand, Pakistan, and the Philippines, the average rate of increase of the people "outside" is 3.3% per year. The doubling time of this population is 21 years.

Suppose that all these countries, and the United States, agreed to live by the Marxian ideal, "to each according to his needs," the ideal of most Christians as well. Needs, of course, are determined by population size, which is affected by reproduction. Every nation regards its rate of reproduction as a sovereign right. If our lifeboat were big enough in the beginning it might be possible to live *for a while* by Christian-Marxian ideals. *Might.*

Initially, in the model given, the ratio of non-Americans to Americans would be one to one. But consider what the ratio would be 87 years later. By this time Americans would have doubled to a population of 420 million. The other group (doubling every 21 years) would now have swollen to 3,540 million. Each American would have more than eight people to share with. How could the lifeboat possibly keep afloat?

All this involves extrapolation of current trends into the future, and is consequently suspect. Trends may change. Granted: but the change will not necessarily be favorable. If—as seems likely—the rate of population increase falls faster in the ethnic group presently inside the lifeboat than it does among those now outside, the future will turn out to be even worse than mathematics predicts, and sharing will be even more suicidal.

RUIN IN THE COMMONS

The fundamental error of the sharing ethics is that it leads to the tragedy of the commons. Under a system of private property the man (or group of men) who own property recognize their responsibility to care for it, for if they don't they will eventually suffer. A farmer, for instance, if he is intelligent, will allow no more cattle in a pasture than its carrying capacity justifies. If he overloads the pasture, weeds take over, erosion sets in, and the owner loses in the long run.

But if a pasture is run as a commons open to all, the right of each to use it is not matched by an operational responsibility to take care of it. It is no use asking independent herdsmen in a commons to act responsibly, for they dare not. The considerate herdsman who refrains from overloading the commons suffers more than a selfish one who says his needs are greater. (As Leo Durocher says, "Nice guys finish last.") Christian-Marxian idealism is counterproductive. That it *sounds* nice is no excuse. With distribution systems, as with individual morality, good intentions are no substitute for good performance.

A social system is stable only if it is insensitive to errors. To the Christian-Marxian idealist a selfish person is a sort of "error." Prosperity in the system of the commons cannot survive errors. If *everyone* would only restrain himself, all would be well; but it takes *only one less than everyone* to ruin a system of voluntary restraint. In a crowded world of less than perfect human beings—and we will never know any other—mutual ruin is inevitable in the commons. This is the core of the tragedy of the commons. . . .

WORLD FOOD BANKS

In the international arena we have recently heard a proposal to create a new commons, namely an international depository of food reserves to which nations will contribute according to their abilities, and from which nations may draw according to their needs. Nobel laureate Norman Borlaug has lent the prestige of his name to this proposal.

A world food bank appeals powerfully to our humanitarian impulses. We remember John Donne's celebrated line, "Any man's death diminishes me." But before we rush out to see for whom the bell tolls let us recognize where the greatest political push for international granaries comes from, lest we be disillusioned later.

Our experience with Public Law 480 clearly reveals the answer. This was the law that moved billions of dollars worth of U.S. grain to food-short, population-long countries during the past two decades. When P.L. 480 first came into being, a headline in the business magazine *Forbes* (Paddock 1970) revealed the power behind it: "Feeding the World's Hungry Millions: How it will mean billions for U.S. business."

And indeed it did. In the years 1960 to 1970 a total of $7.9 billion was spent on the "Food for Peace" program, as P.L. 480 was called. During the years of 1948 to 1970 an additional $49.9 billion were extracted from American taxpayers to pay for other economic aid programs, some of which went for food and food-producing machinery. (This figure does *not* include military aid.) That P.L. 480 was a give-away program was concealed. Recipient countries went through the motions of paying for P.L. 480 food—with IOU's. In December 1973 the charade was brought to an end as far as India was concerned when the United States "forgave" India's $3.2 billion debt (Anonymous 1974). Public announcement of the cancellation of the debt was delayed for two months: one wonders why. . . .

What happens if some organizations budget for emergencies and others do not? If each organization is solely responsible for its own well-being, poorly managed ones will suffer. But they should be able to learn from experience. They have a chance to mend their ways and learn to budget for infrequent but certain emergencies. The weather, for instance, always varies and periodic crop failures are certain. A wise and competent government saves out of the production of the good years in anticipation of bad years that are sure to come. This is not a new idea. The Bible tells us that Joseph taught this policy to Pharaoh in Egypt more than 2,000 years ago. Yet it is literally true that the vast majority of the governments of the world today have no such policy. They lack either the wisdom or the competence, or both. Far more difficult than the transfer of wealth from one country to another is the transfer of wisdom between sovereign powers or between generations.

"But it isn't their fault! How can we blame the poor people who are caught in an emergency? Why must we punish them?" The concepts of blame and punishment are irrelevant. The question is, what are the operational consequences of establishing a world food bank? If it is open to every country every time a need develops, slovenly rulers will not be motivated to take Joseph's advice. Why should they? Others will bail them out whenever they are in trouble.

Some countries will make deposits in the world food bank and others will withdraw from it: there will be almost no overlap. Calling such a depository-transfer unit a "bank" is stretching the metaphor of *bank* beyond its elastic limits. The proposers, of course, never call attention to the metaphorical nature of the word they use.

THE RATCHET EFFECT

An "international food bank" is really, then, not a true bank but a disguised oneway transfer device for moving wealth from rich countries to poor. In the absence of such a bank, in a world inhabited by individually responsible sovereign nations, the population of each nation would repeatedly go through a cycle of the sort shown in Figure 1. P_2 is greater than P_1, either in absolute numbers or because a deterioration of

Fig. 1

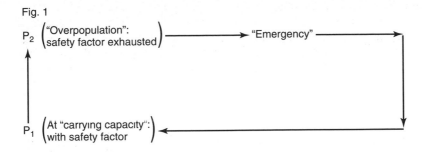

the food supply has removed the safety factor and produced a dangerously low ratio of resources to population. P_2 may be said to represent a state of overpopulation, which becomes obvious upon the appearance of an "accident," e.g., a crop failure. If the "emergency" is not met by outside help, the population drops back to the "normal" level—the "carrying capacity" of the environment—or even below. In the absence of population control by a sovereign, sooner or later the population grows to P_2 again and the cycle repeats. The long-term population curve (Hardin 1966) is an irregularly fluctuating one, equilibrating more or less about the carrying capacity.

A demographic cycle of this sort obviously involves great suffering in the restrictive phase, but such a cycle is normal to any independent country with inadequate population control. The third century theologian Tertullian (Hardin 1969) expressed what must have been the recognition of many wise men when he wrote: "The scourges of pestilence, famine, wars, and earthquakes have come to be regarded as a blessing to overcrowded nations, since they serve to prune away the luxuriant growth of the human race."

Only under a strong and farsighted sovereign—which theoretically could be the people themselves, democratically organized—can a population equilibrate at some set point below the carrying capacity, thus avoiding the pains normally caused by periodic and unavoidable disasters. For this happy state to be achieved it is necessary that those in power be able to contemplate with equanimity the "waste" of surplus food in times of bountiful harvests. It is essential that those in power resist the temptation to convert extra food into extra babies. On the public relations level it is necessary that the phrase "surplus food" be replaced by "safety factor."

But wise sovereigns seem not to exist in the poor world today. The most anguishing problems are created by poor countries that are governed by rulers insufficiently wise and powerful. If such countries can draw on a world food bank in times of "emergency," the population *cycle* of Figure 1 will be replaced by the population *escalator* of Figure 2. The input of food from a food bank acts as the pawl of a ratchet, preventing the population from retracing its steps to a lower level. Reproduction pushes the population upward, inputs from the world bank prevent its moving downward. Population size escalates, as does the absolute magnitude of "accidents" and "emergencies." The process is brought to an end only by the total collapse of the whole system, producing a catastrophe of scarcely imaginable proportions.

Fig. 2

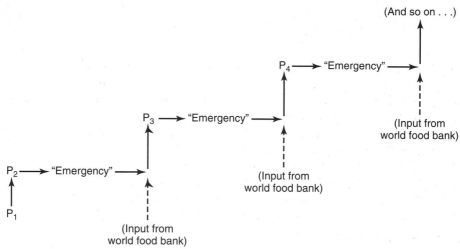

Such are the implications of the well-meant sharing of food in a world of irresponsible reproduction. . . .

To be generous with one's own possessions is one thing; to be generous with posterity's is quite another. This, I think, is the point that must be gotten across to those who would, from a commendable love of distributive justice, institute a ruinous system of the commons. . . .

If the argument of this essay is correct, so long as there is no true world government to control reproduction everywhere it is impossible to survive in dignity if we are to be guided by Spaceship ethics. Without a world government that is sovereign in reproductive matters mankind lives, in fact, on a number of sovereign lifeboats. For the foreseeable future survival demands that we govern our actions by the ethics of a lifeboat. Posterity will be ill served if we do not.

REFERENCES

Anonymous. 1974. *Wall Street Journal* 19 Feb.

Boulding, K. 1966. The economics of the coming spaceship earth. In H. Jarrett, ed. *Environmental Quality in a Growing Economy.* Johns Hopkins Press, Baltimore.

Hardin, G. 1966. Chap. 9 in *Biology: Its Principles and Implications,* 2nd ed. Freeman, San Francisco.

————. 1968. The tragedy of the commons. *Science* 162: 1243–1248.

————. 1969. Page 18 in *Population, Evolution, and Birth Control,* 2nd ed. Freeman, San Francisco.

Marx, K. 1875. *Critique of the Gotha program.* Page 388 in R. C. Tucker, ed. *The Marx-Engels Reader,* Norton, N.Y., 1972.

Ophuls, W. 1974. The scarcity society. *Harpers* 248 (1487): 47–52.

Paddock, W. C. 1970. How green is the green revolution? *Bioscience* 20: 897–902.

QUESTIONS

1 What evidence is available to support the claim that the resources of the world will not be able to save all the poor countries? If it cannot be conclusively proved that all the poor countries cannot be saved, can a moral justification be given for refusing to aid famine victims in all those countries?

2 Suppose that it is highly unlikely that all the nations in the world can be saved. Which would be the better moral choice: (1) to deliberately cut off aid to those least likely to survive in order to ensure the survival of the others or (2) to continue our aid despite our awareness of the consequences which will probably follow?

Global Justice, Capitalism and the Third World

Kai Nielsen

A biographical sketch of Kai Nielsen is found on p. 356.

Nielsen argues that justice requires an extensive redistribution of resources from the northern to the southern hemisphere to correct the current imbalance in the distribution of benefits and burdens between the North and the South. He first criticizes neo-Malthusian arguments advanced in support of the thesis that a massive global redistribution of resources would impoverish the North. He then argues against those who hold that questions of justice appropriately arise only within particular societies or between societies which are similarly situated and in a condition of mutual cooperation. Nielsen maintains that since justice as fair reciprocity requires treating all human beings as equals, global justice requires a correction of the great disparities between North and South. Finally, Nielsen maintains, bringing about the necessary correction requires the collective ownership and control of the means of production.

SOME FACTS ABOUT FAMINE

Let us start with some stark empirical realities. Approximately 10,000 people starve every day. There was a severe drought last year (1983) in Africa and about 20 million people, spread through eighteen countries, face severe shortages of food: shortages that will in some instances bring on starvation and in others, for very many people, will bring about debilitating malnutrition—a malnutrition that sometimes will permanently and seriously damage them. The Brandt Report of 1980 estimates that 800 million people cannot afford an adequate diet. This means that millions are constantly hungry, that millions suffer from deficiency diseases and from infections that they could resist with a more adequate diet. Approximately 15 million children die each year from the combined effects of malnutrition and infection. In some areas of

Reprinted with permission of the publisher from *International Justice and the Third World* (Routledge, 1992), edited by Robin Attfield and Barry Wilins.

the world half the children born will die before their fifth birthday. Life for not a few of us in the industrially developed world is indeed, in various ways, grim. But our level of deprivation hardly begins to approximate to the level of poverty and utter misery that nearly 40 per cent of the people in the Third World face.

As Robert McNamara, who is surely no spokesman for the left, put it, there are these masses of 'severely deprived human beings struggling to survive in a set of squalid and degraded circumstances almost beyond the power of sophisticated imaginations and privileged circumstances to conceive'.[1] Human misery is very much concentrated in the southern hemisphere (hereafter 'the South') and by any reasonable standard of justice there is a global imbalance of the benefits and burdens of life—the resources available to people—that calls for an extensive redistribution of resources from the industrial countries of the northern hemisphere ('the North') to the South.

This, of course, assumes that there is something properly called global justice and this, in certain quarters, will be resisted as a mirage or as being an incoherent conception. We can properly speak of justice within a society with a common labour market, but we cannot speak of justice for the world community as a whole. We cannot say, some claim, of the world community as a whole that it is just or unjust. Justice is only possible, the claim goes, where there are common bonds of reciprocity. There are no such bonds between a Taude of Highland New Guinea and a farmer in Manitoba. In general there are no such bonds between people at great distances from each other and with no cultural ties, so, given what justice is, we cannot correctly speak of global justice. I think this is a mistaken way of construing things and I shall return to it in a moment.

The call for a massive redistribution of resources also assumes, what neo-Malthusians will not grant, namely that we can carry this out without still greater harm resulting. Part of the demand for the redistribution of resources is in the redistribution of food and in the resources (including the technology and the technological know-how) to realize agricultural potential. Neo-Malthusians believe that this redistribution, at least for the worst-off parts of the Third World, is suicidal.

It is a moral truism, but for all of that true, that it would be better, if no greater harm would follow from our achieving it, if we had a world in which no one starved and no one suffered from malnutrition. But, some neo-Malthusians argue, greater harm would in fact follow if starvation were prevented in the really desperate parts of the world, for with the world's extensive population-explosion resulting from improved medicine and the like, the earth, if population growth is not severely checked, will exceed its carrying capacity. An analogy is made with a lifeboat. Suppose the sea is full of desperate swimmers and the only available lifeboat can only take on a certain number. It has, after all, a very definite carrying capacity. If too many are taken on the lifeboat it will swamp and everyone will drown. So the thing is not to go beyond the maximum carrying capacity of the lifeboat.

We are, neo-Malthusians claim, in a similar position *vis-à-vis* the earth. It is like a lifeboat and if the population goes out of control and gets too large in relation to the carrying capacity of the earth there will be mass starvation and an unsettlement bringing on a suffering vastly exceeding the already terrible suffering that is upon us. Sometimes our choices are between evils and, where this is so, the rational and morally appropriate choice is to choose the lesser evil. It may be true that we may never do evil that good may come, but faced with the choice between two certain evils we should choose the lesser evil. Better four dead than twenty. But, some neo-Malthusians claim, *vis-à-vis* famine relief, this is just the terrible situation we are in.

Parts of the earth have already, they claim, exceeded their carrying capacity. The population there is too great for the region to yield enough food for its expanding population. Yet it is in the poorer parts of the world that the population continues to swell and, it is terrible but still necessary to recognize, it is the above horrendous situation that we are facing in many parts of the world.

Neo-Malthusians maintain that if we do not check this population explosion in a rather drastic way the whole earth will in time be in the desperate position of the Sahel. Redistributive reform is soft-hearted and soft-headed, encouraging the poor to increase their numbers and with that to increase the sum total of misery in the world.

I shall talk about neo-Malthusianism first and then . . . turn to a consideration of whether we have a coherent conception of global justice. Neo-Malthusianism, I shall argue, is a pseudo-realism making dramatics out of a severe and tragic morality of triage when the facts in the case will not rationally warrant such dramatics—will not warrant in these circumstances a morality of triage.

In the first place, while lifeboats have a determinate carrying capacity, we have no clear conception of what this means with respect to the earth. What population density makes for commodious living is very subjective indeed; technological innovations continually improve crop yield and could do so even more adequately if more scientific effort were set in that direction.

Second, for the foreseeable future we have plenty of available fertile land and the agricultural potential adequately to feed a very much larger world population than we actually have. Less than half of the available fertile land of the world is being used for any type of food production. In Africa, for example, as everyone knows, there are severe famine conditions and radical underdevelopment, but African agriculture has been declining for the last twenty years. Farmers are paid as little as possible; masses of people have gone into the large urban centres where industrialization is going on. Domestic food production is falling while a lot of food is imported at prices that a very large number of people in the Third World cannot afford to pay. Yet Africa has half the unused farm land in the world. If it were only utilized, Africa could readily feed itself and be a large exporter of food. The principal problem is not overpopulation or even drought but man-made problems. . . .

Third, the land that is used is very frequently used in incredibly inefficient ways. The *latifundia* system in Latin America is a case in point. In Latin America as a whole, and by conservative estimates, landless families form 40 per cent of all farm families. One per cent of all farm families control, again by conservative estimates, 50 per cent of all farm land. This landed elite has incredible power in Latin America and they use this power to keep the peasantry poor, disorganized and dependent. The *latifundia* system is an autocratic system, but—and this is what is most relevant for our purposes—it is also a very inefficient system of agricultural production. The landowner, not infrequently through his farm manager, has firm control over the run-ning of the farm and over the destinies of his farm labourers. The *latifundios* are very large estates and the land on them is underworked. Much of it is used for pasture. Only 4 per cent of all the land in large estates is actually in crops. There is more fal-low land, that is land not even used for pasture but held idle, than there is land in crops. If the *latifundia* land were redistributed to peasants and they were allowed to work it intensively and particularly if they formed into peasant co-operatives, the food production would be increased enormously. Again, it isn't the lack of land or the size of the population that is the problem but the way the land is used.

Fourth, there is the problem of cash crops: crops such as peanuts, strawberries, bananas, mangoes, artichokes, and the like. Key farm land, once used by local resi-dents for subsistence farming, is now used for these cash crops, driving subsistence farmers off the best land into increasingly marginal land and, in many instances, forc-ing them to purchase food at very high prices, prices they often cannot afford to pay. The result has been increasing malnutrition and starvation and impoverishment. Pre-viously in New Guinea most of the tribal peoples had a reasonably adequate diet. Now, with the incursion of the multinationals and the introduction of cash crops, se-vere malnutrition is rife. The good land is used for cash crops and the farming for local consumption is on the marginal land. Mexican peasants, to take another ex-ample, did reasonably well on a staple diet of corn and beans. With the advent of multinational food producers, they became a rural, but typically underemployed, pro-letariat, in one not atypical instance, planting, harvesting and processing in freezing plants strawberries for export and importing food to replace the staple food they had previously grown themselves. The catch was that the food they purchased was typ-ically less nutritious and was at prices they could hardly afford. Again, in those Mex-ican communities malnutrition is rife but the principal cause here, just as in New Guinea, is in the socio-economic system and not in droughts or population explo-sion.

In fine, against neo-Malthusians, it is not the case that the basic cause of famine is the failure of the food supply relative to the population. Rather the basic cause of famine is poverty and certain economic policies. People who are not poor are not hungry. We look at North–South imbalance and it is plain as anything can be that this is the result of the workings of the world economic system and a clear indicator of that is the food economy. A stark difference between North and South is in the vast malnutrition and starvation which are principally a phenomenon of the South. But these famine conditions result from the working of the economic system in al-locating the ability of people to acquire goods.[2] As Amartya Sen has shown for the great Bengal famine of 1943–4, a famine in which around 3 million people died, it was not the result of any crop failure or population explosion.[3] In 1942 there had been an extraordinary harvest but the 1943 crop was only somewhat lower and was in fact higher than the crop of 1941 which was not a famine year. Sen's figures show that the 1943 crop was only 10 per cent less than the average of the five preceding years. Yet 1943 was a famine year of gigantic proportions. Why? The answer lies in peo-ple's economic position.[4] People have entitlements to a range of goods that they can acquire. Whether they have such entitlements, whether they can command the goods they need, depends on the workings of the economic system. Given—to take a current (1983) example—the minimum wage in Brazil (something for which approximately a third of the workforce labours), if that situation persists, many workers will not have the entitlement to the food they need to survive. In fact, right now a day's wage enables them only to command a kilo of beans. They can, that is, only purchase a kilo of beans for a day's work at the minimum wage. So people in such circumstances, understandably, reasonably and indeed rightly, take considerable risks to loot supermarkets and the like. People starve when their entitlements are not sufficiently large to buy the food necessary to keep them alive. That, to return to Sen's example of the great famine in Bengal, is precisely what happened in Bengal in 1943–4 and is happening again in Brazil and, with greater severity, in a not inconsiderable number of other places.

The food available to people is a matter of income distribution and that, in the capitalist system, is fundamentally rooted in their ability to provide services that people in the economy are willing to pay for. In poorer countries for many people about two-thirds of their total income goes for expenditures on food. Where there is some rapid industrialization newly employed workers are likely, with increased entitlements, to spend more on food. This, under a capitalist system, will force food prices up and it is very likely as a result that the entitlements of very poor agricultural labourers—labourers who own no land and have only their labour power to sell—will fall, until, even with a constant supply of food in their environment, they will no longer be able to purchase food to meet their minimum needs. Where people are on the margin of sustainable life, a famine may be created by such an increase of demand with little or no decline in the food supply. What we need to recognize is that hunger, malnutrition and famine are fundamentally questions of distribution of income and the entitlements to food. And here, of course, we have plainly questions of justice and, I shall argue below, questions of global justice. But in trying to achieve a moral assessment of what should be done in the face of such extensive starvation and malnutrition, neo-Malthusian accounts are very wide of the mark, principally because of their failure to understand what causes and sustains such misery. . . .

GLOBAL JUSTICE AND THE THIRD WORLD

. . . There are some who would maintain that talk of justice can only coherently be applied within particular societies or at best between societies similarly situated and in a condition of mutual co-operation. I want to show why this doctrine is false and why it is quite morally imperative for us to speak of global justice and injustice and to characterize these notions in a perspicuous fashion.

Those who would argue against extending justice arguments into a North–South context, and into the international arena generally, will argue that when we talk about what is to be done here we need to recognize that we are beyond the circumstances of justice. For considerations of justice coherently to arise there must, between the people involved, (a) be a rough equality in the powers and capacities of persons, (b) be a situation where people do co-operate but largely on the basis of reciprocal advantage and (c) be a situation where all parties are in a condition of moderate scarcity.[5] It is, many have argued, only in such circumstances that issues of justice are at home. Only in such circumstances, the claim goes, can we appeal to principles of justice to adjudicate conflicting claims on moderately scarce goods. For principles of justice to function, there must be enough reciprocity around for people to find some balance of reciprocal advantage. If they cannot find that, they have no basis for regulating their conduct in accordance with the principles of justice.

However, if these really are the circumstances of justice, it looks at least as if we can have no global justice, for the richest nations do not seem to be related to the poorest ones in such a way that the rich nations secure a reciprocal advantage if justice is done. It very likely makes more sense for them to go on cruelly exploiting the poor nations as they have done in the past. There is, in short, in most circumstances at least, little in it for them if they would do what, in circumstances of greater equality, we would uncontroversially say is the just thing to do.

The mistake here, I believe, is in sticking with the existence of a skein of actual co-operative reciprocity as essential for the circumstances of justice. The world is certainly not a co-operative scheme. We do not have in place internationally schemes for mutual support. It is even rather far-fetched, given the class nature of our own societies, to regard discrete societies as co-operative partnerships, but certainly the world is not. We do not have in place there the co-operative reciprocal interdependency which, some say, is essential for justice.

However, this condition for the very possibility of justice is too strong. That this is so can be seen from the following considerations. There is a worldwide network of international trade; poor countries stand to rich countries in complex relations of interdependence, indeed in an interdependency relation that places poor countries in a position of dependence. The rich nations, functioning as instruments for gigantic capitalist enterprises, have dominated and exploited underdeveloped countries using their resources and markets on unfair terms. Between North and South—between rich and poor nations—there are conflicts of interest and competing claims under conditions not so far from moderate scarcity such that conditions giving scope for arguments of justice obtain. In intra-state situations we do not need conditions of actual reciprocity of mutual advantage for issues of justice to be in place. The Australian Aborigine population could be too small, too weak and too marginal to mainstream life in Australia for the non-Aboriginal population to gain any advantage from *not* seizing their lands and driving them from them without any compensation. But such an action would not only be plainly wrong; it would be grossly unjust. Yet it is quite possible that the non-Aboriginal population would stand to gain rather than lose from such an action. Still, that would not make such an action one whit the less unjust. What we need to invoke instead is a *moral reciprocity* not resting on actual schemes of co-operation for mutual advantage but instead on a broadly Kantian conception of moral equality in which justice requires that we all treat each other as equals, namely, we are to treat all people as persons and in doing so treat them as we would reasonably wish to be treated ourselves.[6] In other words, we must, in reasoning justly, be willing to universalize and to engage in role reversal. It does not take much moral imagination for us, if we are relatively privileged members of the so-called First World, to realize that we would not wish to live the marginal existence of many people in the Third World. We would, that is, not wish to starve or have our children starve or to be in one way or another crippled by malnutrition or live, where this could be avoided, without anything like an adequate education or without adequate housing and the like. We would not accept role reversal here. If our feet, that is, were in their shoes, we would not take as morally tolerable, where such conditions could be avoided, such conditions of life for ourselves. But there is no relevant difference here between ourselves and them. If, in such circumstances, we would not will it for ourselves, we cannot will it for them either.

In the light of our conception of the moral equality of people, we could not accept such inequalities as just. . . . However, the injustice . . . is even more evident if we develop a conception of justice as fair reciprocity. People, through conquest, domination and exploitation, have been made worse off than they were before these relations were brought into place. They have been driven into bargains they would not have made if they had not been driven to the wall. They are plainly being coerced and they are surely not being treated as moral equals.

If we start with an idea of moral reciprocity in which all human beings are treated as equals, we cannot accept the relations that stand between North and South as something that has even the simulacrum of justice. But any tolerably adequate understanding of what morality requires of us will not allow us to accept anything less than a commitment to relations of moral equality. Starting from there we can see that global justice is a plain extension of domestic justice when we remember that in the international arena as well as in the domestic arena we stand (a) in conditions of interdependence, (b) in conditions of moderate scarcity (if we pool our resources) and (c) in conditions where our interests sometimes conflict. Moreover, by any plausible principles of global justice we might enunciate, the relations between North and South are so unjust that extensive redistributions of resources are in order. Whatever critical standards we use to regulate conflicting claims over scarce goods, we cannot, if we have any tolerably good knowledge of the facts in the case and a sense of fairness, but think the present relations are unjust and require rectification. There is not even in the various states of the North a fair access to basic natural and cultural resources, but viewed globally to speak of anything like a fair access to basic natural and cultural resources, where people are being treated as equals, can be nothing but a cruel and rather stupid joke.

If we start from a premise of *moral* equality as the vast majority of social theorists and moral philosophers right across the political spectrum do . . . we will believe that the interest of everyone matters and matters equally. There is no not believing in that, if we believe in *moral* equality.

For liberal egalitarians, such as Ronald Dworkin, this will involve a commitment to attain, not equality of condition but equality of resources, while for a radical egalitarian it will involve, as well, under conditions of productive abundance, a commitment to try to move as close as we reasonably can to an equality of condition. While rejecting all such egalitarian readings of *moral* equality, Nozick, with most other philosophers and economists on the right, thinks of moral equality as consisting most essentially in protecting individual rights to non-interference. Individuals in a just social order must be protected in their rights peacefully to pursue their own interests without interference from government, church or anyone else. Even if the kind of redistribution from North to South I am advocating did not bring about financial hara-kiri for people in the North, it would still involve an interference with their right peacefully to pursue their own interests where they are not harming anyone. Thus such a redistribution would still be wrong.

There are at least two responses that should be made here. The first is to assert that such capitalist behaviour has in fact harmed people. Sometimes this has been intentional, often not. But in any event, harm has been done. . . . But in our historical circumstances this is unnecessary for we could have an economic system whose underlying rationale was production to meet human needs and which was controlled democratically. Moreover, we now have the technical capacity to develop our productive powers so that the needs of people could be met. But the capitalist order has been massively supported in a very large part of the North and a not inconsiderable number of people in the North have been the beneficiaries of a socio-economic order that did so exploit. (Of course, there are others in the North who are just victims of that order.) This being so, even Nozickian notions of justice in rectification would require redistribution between North and South.

However, a second response seems to me more fundamental, less puritanical and less concerned with blaming people. To see best what is at issue we should proceed rather indirectly. We not only have rights to non-interference, we also have rights to fair co-operation and these rights can conflict. A very important liberty is the liberty to be able to guide one's own life in accordance with one's own unmystified preferences. Central to liberty is the capacity and opportunity to make rational choices and to be able to act on those rational choices.[7] This is much broader than to construe liberty as simply the absence of restrictions or interference, though it certainly includes that. What is vital to see here is that liberty will not be adequately protected if we limit our rights to the protection of rights to non-interference. We must also give central weight to the rights of fair co-operation. If the right of all to effective participation in government and, more generally, to effective direction of their lives is to be attained, there must be in place in our social organizations a respect for the right of everyone to fair co-operation. It is, of course, evident that respect for this right is not very widespread in the world. It will not only not be in place where there is subordination and domination, it will also not be effective where there is widespread starvation, malnutrition, exploitation and ignorance. What is unavoidable is that in class-based societies rights to fair co-operation and rights to non-interference will conflict. To move towards correcting the imbalances between North and South, we will have to move to a collective ownership and control of the means of production, for otherwise economic power becomes concentrated in the hands of a few and they will dominate and exploit others. But moving to collective ownership will in turn have the effect of overriding the rights to non-interference of Horatio Alger types who, capitalistically inclined, seek to acquire productive property through hard work and honest bargains. (It is hardly accurate or fair to say that there are no capitalists like that, particularly small capitalists.) In following their entirely peaceful interests—they have no wish to dominate or impoverish anyone—they wish to invest, buy and sell, and own productive property. If we are to protect their rights to non-interference, these activities can hardly be stopped, but if they are allowed to go on, the institutional stage is set, whatever the particular agent's own inclinations may be, for the undermining of rights to fair co-operation. So we have a fundamental clash of rights: rights of non-subordination with rights to non-interference.

To overcome the great disparities between North and South, even to put an end to the conditions of immiseration in the South—starvation, malnutrition, lack of work, extreme poverty—there would have to be significant and varied redistribution from North to South. In doing this we would have to give rather more weight to the rights of fair co-operation than to rights of non-interference. But—and here is what is alleged to be the catch—there is no significant consensus concerning which rights are to be overriding when they conflict.

I think that there would be a consensus if we came to command a clear view of these rights and their relations, along with some other powerful moral considerations, and came, as well, to command a clear view of the relevant social realities. Surely people have a right to pursue their interests without interference. But there are interests and interests. (Indeed, rights are most paradigmatically linked to our vital interests.) There is, among these interests, our interest in maintaining our bodily and moral integrity. To require, for example, that a person (say, a quite ordinary person), quite against her wishes, donate a kidney to keep someone alive whose value to the society is extensive is, that fact notwithstanding, still an intolerable intrusion on that involuntary donor's bodily integrity; to require a person to give up her religion or political convictions to enhance social harmony or even peace is another intolerable intrusion in that person's life—it simply runs roughshod over her civil liberties. But the interference with the peaceful pursuit of a person's interests that would go with a collective ownership of the means of production would not touch such vital interests. Rather what would be touched is her freedom to buy and sell, to invest and to bequeath *productive* property. But these interests are not nearly as vital as the above type of interests which genuinely are vital for our personal integrity. When the price for overriding those less vital interests is, as it is in the North–South situation, the overcoming of starvation, malnutrition, domination, subordination, great poverty and ignorance (certainly vital interests for any person), there is no serious doubt about in which direction the trade-offs should go. That there is not a massive consensus about this results, I believe, not from deeply embedded moral differences between people but from disputes or at least from different beliefs about what is in fact the case and about what in fact can come to be the case.[8] Ideological mystification leads us to believe that there is nothing significant that could be done about these matters or nothing that could be done short of impoverishing us all or undermining our civil liberties. But that is just ideological mystification. . . .

NOTES

1 Robert McNamara as cited by Peter Singer, *Practical Ethics,* London: Cambridge University Press, 1979, p. 159.

2 Amartya Sen, *Poverty and Famines: An Essay on Entitlement and Deprivation,* Oxford: Clarendon Press, 1981; Kenneth J. Arrow, 'Why people go hungry', *New York Review of Books,* XXIX, 12, 15 July 1982, pp. 24–6.

3 Sen, op. cit., pp. 52–83.

4 Ibid.

5 David Hume, *A Treatise of Human Nature,* ed. L. A. Selby-Bigge, Oxford: Clarendon Press, 1964, pp. 485–95; John Rawls, *A Theory of Justice,* Cambridge, MA: Harvard University Press, 1971, pp. 126–30; Brian Barry, 'Circumstances of justice and future generations', in R. I. Sikora and Brian Barry (eds), *Obligations to Future Generations,* Philadelphia, PA: Temple University Press, 1978, pp. 204–48.

6 David A. J. Richards, 'International distributive justice', in Roland J. Pennock and John W. Chapman (eds), *Nomos,* XXIV, New York: New York University Press, 1982, pp. 275–95; Thomas Nagel, *Mortal Questions,* Cambridge: Cambridge University Press, 1979, pp. 111–12.

7 Richard Norman, 'Liberty, equality, property', *Aristotelian Society,* supplementary volume, LV, 1981, pp. 199–202.

8 This is powerfully argued by Andrew Collier in 'Scientific socialism and the question of socialist values', in Kai Nielsen and Steven Patten (eds), *Marx and Morality,* Guelph, Ontario: Canadian Association for Publishing in Philosophy, 1981, pp. 121–54.

QUESTIONS

1 Has Nielsen presented a compelling case against neo-Malthusian claims regarding the causes of famine and malnutrition?

2 Are the kinds of gross inequalities of income and wealth Nielsen describes incompatible with the conception of human beings as moral equals?

Property and Global Justice

Richard T. De George

Richard T. De George is professor of philosophy at the University of Kansas. He is the author of *The Nature and Limits of Authority* (1985), *Business Ethics* (3rd ed., 1990), and *Competing with Integrity in International Business* (1993).

De George examines two apparently conflicting answers to the question, "Who rightly owns the resources of the world?" While seeing some value in both answers, De George criticizes both views and argues that the issue is one of basic human rights and not one of property. Fundamental to his reasoning is the claim that basic human rights take precedence over property rights. Basic rights or entitlements held by all persons include "the right to life, the right to respect, the right to satisfy their basic needs, and the right to access to what is necessary to develop their potentialities." De George maintains that global justice provides a

Reprinted with permission from *Philosophy in Context,* vol. 15 (1985), pp. 34–40, 42.

basis for poor countries to demand aid from rich countries in the name of their citizens, and he examines some of the obstacles to the achievement of global justice.

Who properly owns the resources of the world? The question is being increasingly raised and stridently answered. Yet, despite the question's simple appearance, it is a complex one to which no easy answer is both appropriate and possible.

The question of who rightly owns the natural resources of the world is sometimes considered a question about property. The moral intuitions of many people facing the question in this form are ambivalent. On the one hand, the natural resources of most of the world have been divided up and nations and individuals seem to hold legitimate claims to what they have. On the other hand, the resources of the world can be said to belong to everyone; the world is mankind's to use, and it seems appropriate that all mankind benefit from its riches. Both intuitions have a certain amount of force to them and articulate spokesm[e]n have defended them. Can the two intuitions be reconciled, or can the force of each at least be given its due? I shall argue that these intuitions can be reconciled if we interpret the original question not as one about property, but as a question of rights and of equal access to the resources of the world.

THE STATUS QUO VIEW OF RESOURCES

The first intuition is embodied in the common-sense view that the resources of the world have already been divided up. Governments, corporations, and individuals own them. It is futile to inquire about the original allocation of resources or to deny the reality of present ownership. However resources are defined, property comes into existence only in society and always in a certain socio-economic system. The world is divided into countries, each of which makes territorial claims. Most of these are not challenged by others, even though a few areas and borders are in dispute. Each of the countries has within it some government and some economic order. Ownership means different things in different societies, and claims and rights are treated differently in different countries. In some, individuals or groups are allowed to own land, minerals, factories; in others only the government owns these. In all systems, however, some food and some goods are produced and distributed; some services are available and enjoyed. Each system has a mechanism for deciding when the ownership rights it recognizes have been violated, and procedures for deciding how to allocate them when there is a dispute. Justice, according to this view, means abiding by the rules and procedures governing those within the system. This is usually equated with legality.

Thus, the oil in the Soviet Union belongs to the Soviet Union, the oil in the United States belongs to the United States, the oil in Arabia belongs to Arabia, and the oil in Mexico belongs to Mexico. In each of these countries, the oil may be further divided and the legal property rights assigned. In all the countries individuals wishing gasoline for a car must pay for it. Any attempt to claim that Mexico's oil does not belong to Mexico but to all the people of the earth would be met with immediate, fierce, and legitimate resistance. For according to the rules by which Mexico and the whole rest of the world abide, the oil is Mexico's.

The question of ownership, allocation, and use of natural resources on a global scale does not, as the Marxist asserts, hinge on private versus social ownership. Rich countries include some that are socialist as well as so-called capitalist ones, just as the poor countries include both. The Soviet Union has and claims the oil in the Soviet Union in the same way that the United States claims the oil in the United States. Chad, which has no oil, has a recognized claim on neither Soviet nor American oil. The legitimacy of any claim it may have is not dependent on the presence or absence of private property, nor on the presence or absence of social property. Nor is the issue of the allocation of goods and resources primarily an issue of power, although it is frequently put in that mode. If power were truly in the hands of the people of either the United States or the Soviet Union, it is not clear that the approach of either to the Third World countries or of the Third World countries to them would be different from what it is now.

The status quo view resists any property claims by resource-poor countries on the resources of other countries.

THE UNIVERSAL OWNERSHIP VIEW

The status quo view is attacked, however, by those who claim that the present division of the world's resources is unjust. The distribution of resources is arbitrary. Some countries have very few while others have a great many. The second intuition with which we started now comes into play. From a moral point of view the natural distribution can be taken as the starting point; but it must be corrected. Originally the goods of the earth belonged in common to all, and all people retain a claim on the earth's resources despite arbitrary divisions and allocations that some people have introduced.

What does it mean, however, to say that the resources of the earth belong to everyone? In one sense something can belong to everyone if each person has a right to its use and no one has a right to exclude anyone else from its use. Thus a public park might be said to belong to all the people. Anyone who wants can use the park as a park. But there are limits on the use one can make of it; and the obligation to maintain it must somehow be assigned.

A second sense in which all land, resources, and productive property may belong to everyone is the sense in which each has the equal right to appropriate and use, and in the process consume, the item in question. If everyone in a society owns the wheat grown in that country, then everyone has a claim on an equal or fair share of the grain. The grain does not belong to the farmers who grow it or to the people who process it or to those who distribute it. It belongs to all and all are entitled to a fair, and other things being the same, an equal share. This would also be true of the mineral resources of a land.

Yet it would be a vacuous right or type of ownership if the iron in the ground belonged to everyone and this meant that everyone had the right to go to where it is, dig it up, and use it. Most people do not live near iron deposits, and do not need iron ore. What they need and want are products made from iron. Their ownership of the iron in the ground, to be effective, must mean a right or claim on that iron such that they eventually get the iron products they need. In practice this will mean that some people will have the right and obligation to mine the ore, to smelt it, to process it, to turn it into goods. At each stage only certain people will have the right to access and to work on the material. It is unlikely that anyone who wished, anywhere along the line, could take what he wanted because everything belongs to everyone. One reason is that since there is scarcity, although everything may belong to everyone in the society, it must be apportioned so that each gets his fair share. To allow anyone to take anything at any time would interfere with the fair allocation. In this sense, saying that everything belongs to everyone means that each of us has a certain claim on a certain portion of what is available.

Clearly if we are to have a society of any complexity, there will have to be rules and regulations about allocation, production, work, and the distribution of goods. How allocation, production, and distribution are to be carried out in a society in which all property is socially owned is far from clear, since thus far socially owned property has been more or less equal to government-owned property. Whether on a large scale there is any alternative, such as true social ownership without government, is at best problematic. But even if it were achieved, individuals would still have different bundles of rights with respect to different goods.

Defenders of the universal ownership view have no clear plan for world-wide redistribution; but they defend the need for this redistribution nonetheless. They argue that national sovereignty stands in the way of a world-wide just distribution of natural resources. Hence, sovereignty is to this extent morally arbitrary and should be superseded. The argument, even if it could be made out, is not soon to be accepted by the people of any country today—rich or poor. Nor is it clear what would replace national sovereignty and how a just allocation of natural resources would be accomplished without sovereign states.

JUSTICE AND THE CONTENDING INTUITIONS

Each of the positions characterized by the conflicting intuitions contains a view of property and a view of justice. The strength of the first intuition stems from its correct description of the existing division of the resources of the world, the existence of sovereign states, and the allocation of property rights within each of them. Just as the notion of what property is depends on the bundle of rights recognized within a society, so the notion of what constitutes justice with respect to property depends on the structures of a given society. The weakness of the position is that its notions hinge on the status quo of each nation; because it is difficult to extrapolate from these to any global notion of property or justice does not mean any such view is nonsense. The strength of the universal ownership view is its moral insight that natural resources are distributed by nature arbitrarily and that such arbitrariness does not morally justify ownership claims. There *is* a sense in which the world and its resources belong to everyone. The weakness of the position is that in the concrete it is difficult to give much meaning to the universal ownership claims, and in today's world there is no agreed upon sense of justice on a global scale that can be used as a basis for reallocation.

The conflict of these two intuitions necessitates a closer look at both justice and property claims if we are to find a way out of the dilemma they pose.

Justice can be defined initially, following Aristotle, as giving each person his due. What constitutes one's due may be decided in many ways. If we speak of justice within a system, as the status quo position does, justice is in part determined by the rules of the society, which make certain kinds of transactions possible. If the rules set up a system whereby one pays for goods, then it is just to give someone the equivalent value for the goods received. Justice in this sense is similar to property in that it exists within a given system at a specific time and place.

Yet we can say of some systems that they are unjust. Thus we can say slavery is unjust because it deprives human beings of the freedom and dignity they are due as human beings. Whether or not ancient slavery could be justified, at the present time slavery cannot be justified. Within the slave system some transactions were considered fair or just and one might even speak of the just or fair price for a given slave.

Since it is possible to make some judgments about systems or societies irrespective of the social system from which we speak, it may be possible to make global judgments of justice.

Commutative justice governs transactions between individuals within a society, and transactions between individuals or groups of different societies, as well as international trade. Commutative justice consists of two sides freely trading equals for equals. Injustice consists either of one side's forcing an exchange or of trading unequals. One form of such injustice is exploitation, which might be practiced either within a society or by one society or people on another.

Compensatory justice consists in making compensation for a previous harm or injustice. Thus the victims of exploitation deserve compensation for the harm they have suffered. This is true within a society as well as between societies.

Both of these types of justice are compatible with the status quo and with the existence of nation states. Both can be applied internationally. Neither is directly pertinent to the question of who properly owns the resources of the world. That question falls under the domain of distributive justice.

Distributive justice in its most commonly used sense consists of a government or society distributing in some fair way benefits and burdens to its members. It is because its members are united by common bonds, social structures, culture, and government that within a society both benefits and burdens are distributed. Different societies, which distribute benefits and burdens in different ways through a variety of background institutions, might each realize distributive justice to a rather high degree. The distribution in contemporary societies is typically governed by law and administered by government.

While commutative and compensatory justice operate both within and between societies (we can call the latter international justice), distributive justice to the extent that it requires global background distributive institutions does not operate on a global scale because there are insufficient background institutions and no distribution mechanism for distributing benefits and burdens on a global scale. Under the present division of the world into nation states, the status quo view correctly says that there is no distributive justice on a global level—nor is there any global distributive injustice—since the conditions for any redistribution are lacking. This is a descriptive statement. Yet there is a sense in which we can say that just as burdens and benefits are distributed within a society, so they *should* be distributed globally. In that sense we can say there should be global distributive justice. This is very close to the claim that the resources of the world by right belong to everyone. Yet there are important differences.

THE RIGHT TO UNIVERSAL ACCESS

Although the natural distribution of resources is arbitrary, from a moral point of view what is done with the resources is not arbitrary. The riches of the earth should be used for the benefit of all. This is a correct insight of the universal ownership view. But the heart of the dispute between rich and poor countries does not hinge on the ownership of land or resources, even though it is sometimes couched in those terms. Ownership and property claims obscure rather than clarify what is really at issue. The question to whom the resources of the world properly belong, as it is frequently posed today, is a rhetorical question. The question is not really about property but about human rights.

Each just society should recognize the fun[d]amental respect due to each human being as a member of the society and their fundamental equality as moral beings. All persons deserve and are entitled to what is necessary for living in dignity. Their basic entitlements are the right to life, the right to respect, the right to satisfy their basic needs, and the right to access to what is necessary to develop their potentialities. These rights are not maximal ideals but minimal entitlements. Fulfillment of these basic rights is compatible with different societies being at different stages of development and enjoying different standards of living.

These basic rights, moreover, take precedence over property rights, however defined or specified. The reason is that the right to life and minimal sustenance at the human level are more fundamental than property.

What I have a right to, and what all others have the right to, is what is necessary for subsistence and for as much beyond that as fair structures allow me and them access. Members of underdeveloped countries have a right to the same as I do. Their structures do not presently allow them as much access. It would be pointless, however, to claim that they each had a right to as much oil as I do, even if they have no need or use for oil. They have a right to access when they have need. This point is often distorted into a claim that those of us with present needs are immoral if we use oil in certain ways, because by our using it now we will deprive others from using it when they have sufficiently developed to have needs similar to ours.

The claim is confused because it assumes that each person has a certain permanent claim on natural resources, rather than on the right to a certain level of life and equality of access. Acknowledging that the waste of unrenewable natural resources is immoral is consistent with the legitimacy of some people using more than others because of their real present needs, even if those needs are at a higher level than those of other people.

No one should seriously hold that each person has the right to a certain amount of land or of oil and that, as the population of the globe increases, the amount of land or of oil to which we are each entitled diminishes accordingly. Basically the moral concern of most people expressed in the intuition of universal ownership is properly translated into a claim that either all should have equal or that all should have an adequate standard of living. That latter claim, rather than a specific claim about ownership, whether it be private or social, is the fundamental one.

Against whom does one appropriately exercise these basic rights? In an abstract sense one exercises them against all other human beings. In a negative sense this means that no one should be kept from taking the means necessary to preserve his life and developing his capacities. But this negative sense is not enough in a society of scarcity. Does anyone in a positive sense have the obligation to implement those basic rights for others? This positive, as opposed to negative, obligation depends first of all on the fulfillment by the right-holder of the prior obligation to work if he is capable of doing so, to take care of himself, to expend his energy to learn, and so on. Positive obligations of others arise to the extent that the right-holder's own initiatives are inadequate because of the lack of resources, skill, energy, or other necessary factors.

The individual person properly exercises his basic rights first against members of his own society. It is with them that he has the closest social relations, it is with them that he can most readily share benefits and burdens. The obligation to help those in need in a society falls on the other members of the society. These obligations might be met individually or within a family or social unit; usually in organized societies today other general obligations of mutual aid are structured through government.

Just as individuals, who through no fault of their own are unable to secure the means of satisfying their basic needs, have a claim on their fellow citizens, mediated through government, so, if their fellow citizens and government cannot satisfy their basic needs, the individuals have a claim on other people. Just as the individual has a stronger claim on those with whom he forms a closer community than on the larger community, so on the global level one's claim would fall first on those other peoples with whom one has closer ties and, if they are unable to help, then on those further removed who are able to help. Rights that all human beings have *qua* human being may thus impose obligations on other human beings in foreign lands.

The same foundation for distributive justice on the national level exists on the global level. But the implementation on the global level encounters many difficulties.

When one's society can satisfy its citizens' right to food and the wherewithal for development but does not, the claim of individuals to outside help becomes an individual one on the part of the citizens; it is not the claim of one society or nation on another. As individual, however, the claim is not addressed to other nations as such, and can only be vaguely addressed to other individuals. Their response is limited in many ways—by lack of knowledge, by lack of wherewithal to make the needed goods available, and perhaps by the state structure itself, which often precludes individuals from dealing directly with other individuals. Other mediating groups may or may not be successful.

If we consider the legitimate government of a nation as an actor on the global stage, its main function on the dominant view is *internal* to the nation. Externally it represents the collective body, interacts with other governments, and protects and promotes the interests of its people individually and collectively. It is not established by the people of one nation primarily to help people of other nations. What a government can appropriately do for people of other lands with its resources, natural or monetary, obtained through taxation or derived directly from production, is limited. One can give away one's own money or goods if one chooses. One cannot give away the money and goods of others in the same manner. Such money and goods can be used to fulfill obligations but not, without proper consent, to be charitable. A government uses public monies appropriately to fulfill its own obligations and the obligations of those it represents. This includes seeing to the welfare of all within its jurisdiction. However, the American welfare system does not extend to those in other countries; nor do similar systems in other countries apply to the population of the United States. A government's obligation with respect to other people or peoples is to do them no unjustifiable harm. Its positive obligations to them, if it has any, are a function of the obligations of its members to help others. If the people within a country have the obligation to help foreign people, they may use the mechanism of government and taxes to fulfill that obligation. The government then acts for the people to fullfill the people's (individual or collective) obligation, not its own. If a country owns the productive resources within its borders, then it may allocate a certain amount to fulfill the obligation of its people to others in need. . . .

[CONCLUSION]

Global justice forms a basis for poor countries in the name of their citizens to demand aid from rich countries, acting as mediators for their citizens. The demands of distributive justice on the global level, however, are much weaker than the demands of distributive justice that take place within a given society. On the national level distributive justice does not end with simply fulfilling minimal needs and providing equal access. The reason for the difference is that within a society social structures make possible the sharing of both burdens and benefits through organized and accepted social institutions. The members of a society are related in many more ways than are the people of the world.

Even on this minimalist level global justice is difficult—sometimes impossible—to implement even where the will to do so is present because of the lack of global background institutions. In cases of short-term famine and natural disasters there are mechanisms through which the International Red Cross and UN agencies help the stricken country and people with aid; but such agencies are dependent on good will and charity and there is no effective mechanism for proportioning the amount of aid each country should give or of assessing each country its fair share. In cases of chronic malnutrition and severe deprivation of natural resources the situation is even worse.

National sovereignty is one of the central factors preventing the implementation of global justice. The developed nations refuse to recognize any superior international body that has the right to tax them for purposes of redistribution to other countries and to those suffering severe deprivation of their basic needs. Underdeveloped nations are just as reluctant as developed nations to give up their sovereignty and, as recipients of aid, they are reluctant to allow outsiders to dictate how such aid is to be used. This they consider an incursion into their internal affairs.

If we assume that in the present day more harm than good is achieved by attempting forcibly to violate national sovereignty even to achieve the good of helping those in need, the problems associated with implementing global justice are multiplied.

The demands of global justice are actual moral demands on people today. The immediate responsibility of those able to do so, individually and collectively, is not only to respond to them as best they can but also creatively and generously to work towards developing the necessary global implementing organizations and apparatus. Even if people do so, the result will be less than the full global justice possible if all mankind were a single unified society. Nonetheless even if the possibility of developing such a society in the near future is slim, the demands of global justice on at least the minimal level are actual and present. Respon[d]ing to them is a present actual moral demand that should be widely articulated and met, rather than, as is too often the case, either ignored or denied.

QUESTIONS

1 Does De George provide an accurate account of the strengths and weaknesses of the "status quo" view and of the "universal ownership" view?
2 Both Nielsen and De George reject the view that it makes no sense to speak of global justice. Do you agree with them that it does make sense to speak of global justice?

SUGGESTED ADDITIONAL READINGS FOR CHAPTER 9

AIKEN, WILLIAM, and HUGH LAFOLLETTE, eds.: *World Hunger and Moral Obligation.* Englewood Cliffs, N.J.: Prentice-Hall, 1977. With the exception of Joseph Fletcher, a theologian, and Garrett Hardin, a biologist, all the authors in this collection are philosophers. The writers examine various issues raised by the central question, "What moral responsibility do affluent nations (or the people in them) have to the starving masses?" The article by Peter Singer which is reprinted in this chapter is also reprinted in this volume and is followed by a postscript in which Singer (1) presents some later thoughts on the topic and (2) responds to some critics.

BELSEY, ANDREW: "World Poverty, Justice and Equality." In Robin Attfield, ed., *International Justice and the Third World.* New York: Routledge, 1992. Belsey argues against the claim that the special obligations that inhabitants of affluent countries have to people who are geographically or genetically closer to them override the interests of people in the Third World.

BROWN, PETER G., and HENRY SHUE, eds.: *Food Policy.* New York: Free Press, 1977. This book is designed to provide a foundation for a reflective appraisal of questions about the moral obligation of the agriculturally affluent in regard to world hunger. The articles, which were all written specifically for this volume, are divided into four sections: (1) "Needs and Obligations," (2) "Responsibilities in the Public Sector," (3) "Responsibilities in the Private Sector," and (4) "Reducing Dependence."

EBERSTADT, NICK: "Myths of the Food Crisis." *New York Review of Books,* February 19, 1976, pp. 32–37. Eberstadt attacks the myths about world hunger which distort our perception of the problems and lead to the pessimism exemplified by Garrett Hardin.

LAPPÉ, FRANCES MOORE, and JOSEPH COLLINS: *World Hunger: Twelve Myths.* New York: Grove, 1986. Lappé and Collins criticize both some of the common beliefs about the causes of world hunger and some present approaches to its alleviation.

LUCAS, GEORGE R., JR.: "African Famine: New Economic and Ethical Perspectives." *Journal of Philosophy,* vol. 87, November 1990, pp. 629–641. Lucas examines the causes of the recurrent episodes of famine in Ethiopia, the Sudan, and other nations of the sub-Saharan African "Sahel Region." He argues against the claim that these episodes are caused by severe drought, by resulting destruction of agricultural capability, by "desertification," or by war.

LUPER-FOY, STEVEN, ed.: *Problems of International Justice.* Boulder, Colo., and London: Westview, 1988. Part One of this book is devoted to the topic of world resources and distributive justice. It includes articles on the general issue of international distributive justice and on the specific issue of the obligation to help the needy.

MURDOCH, WILLIAM W., and ALLAN OATEN: "Population and Food: Metaphors and the Reality." *Bioscience,* September 9, 1975, pp. 561–567. Murdoch and Oaten criticize Garrett Hardin's lifeboat, commons, and ratchet metaphors and bring out various factors, other than food supply, that affect population growth.

O'NEILL, ONORA: "Justice, Gender, and International Boundaries." In Martha Nussbaum, ed., *The Quality of Life.* New York: Oxford University Press, 1993. O'Neill argues that an account of justice can combine abstract principles with consideration of differences in their application. She illustrates her claim by an account of the case of poor women in impoverished economies.

RACHELS, JAMES: "Killing and Starving to Death." *Philosophy,* vol. 54, April 1979, pp. 159–171. Rachels, attacking the view that killing is worse than letting die, argues that letting die is just as bad as killing. For Rachels our duty not to let people die from starvation is as strong as our duty not to kill them.

WOGAMAN, J. PHILIP, ed.: *The Population Crisis and Moral Responsibility.* Washington, D.C.: Public Affairs Press, 1973. This anthology emphasizes theological perspectives but contains articles by ethicists and population experts as well. The various articles are collected in four separate sections: (1) the moral basis of policy objectives, (2) the moral responsibility of government, (3) moral analysis of policy proposals, and (4) moral responsibility of religious communities.

CHAPTER 10

Animals

Human beings are responsible for a great deal of animal suffering. We use animals in experiments, raise and slaughter animals for food, and hunt and kill animals, sometimes merely for sport. Our treatment of animals raises numerous moral questions, some of which are discussed in this chapter.

SPECIESISM AND THE MORAL STATUS OF ANIMALS

In a now well-known book, *Animal Liberation,* Peter Singer, a utilitarian, forcefully calls attention to the suffering that human beings routinely inflict on nonhuman animals. (Utilitarianism is discussed in the introduction to Chapter 9.) In order to satisfy human desires for meat, we raise animals in such a way that their short lives are dominated by pain and suffering. In order to obtain information, purportedly for the benefit of humans, we devise experimental projects that involve the infliction of intense pain on animals. Our experimentation on animals and our meat-eating habits are paradigm examples, for Singer, of morally unacceptable practices in regard to animals. Because Singer finds human beings so willing to subordinate important animal interests (e.g., an interest in avoiding suffering) to much less important human interests, he charges the human community with *speciesism.* In an excerpt from *Animal Liberation* reprinted in this chapter, Singer defines speciesism as a "prejudice or attitude of bias toward the interests of members of one's own species and against those of members of other species." Singer uses the term "speciesism" in order to emphasize the similarities between sexist and racist practices on the one hand, and our treatment of animals on the other. In Singer's view, it is just as wrong to discriminate against animals because of their species as it is to discriminate against women because of their sex and blacks because of their race.

Singer's arguments, in effect, attribute moral status to animals. An entity has moral status if it is due moral consideration in its own right and not simply because of its relations to other beings. Some philosophers have argued that animals have no moral status. In their view, any obligations we have regarding animals are based on the interests or rights of human beings. If we have an obligation not to mistreat dogs, for example, it may be because the mistreatment of dogs causes suffering to human beings, many of whom sympathetically identify with the suffering of animals. Singer, in contrast, appeals directly to animal interests in condemning much of our current use of animals. He holds, in effect, that sentience is the relevant criterion in determining whether an entity has moral status. Sentience can be described as the capacity to have conscious experiences such as pleasure and pain. *All* sentient beings, Singer maintains, have interests, including an interest in avoiding pain and suffering. A fundamental principle of morality—*the principle of equal consideration of interests*—requires us to give equal consideration to the interests of all beings affected by our decisions. Animals, like human beings, are sentient beings with an interest in avoiding pain and suffering. Hence, we violate a fundamental principle of morality when we make decisions about the use of animals in experiments if we consider only human interests and fail to give equal consideration to the interests that animals have in avoiding suffering.

Whereas Singer focuses on animal *interests* as he advances a utilitarian line of reasoning, Tom Regan in this chapter focuses on animal *rights* as he advances his attack on speciesism. On Regan's analysis, animals, like humans, are bearers of rights because animals, like humans, have inherent value. To have inherent value, Regan maintains, an entity must be a conscious creature whose welfare is valuable or important to it, so that its having value is not dependent on its usefulness to others. Since animals are creatures of this sort, they have rights that must be respected. Regan rejects the view that animals, while having some inherent value, have less inherent value than human beings. In his view, all entities that have inherent value have it equally, and have an equal right to be treated with respect. Any attempt to specify a difference (e.g., rationality) between human beings and animals that would purport to justify the attribution of lesser inherent value to the latter would require us to attribute a lesser degree of inherent value to some "nonparadigm" human beings (e.g., the severely brain-damaged) if we are to be consistent in our moral reasoning. The same problem is faced, Regan maintains, by those who attempt to specify some criterion that rights holders must possess (e.g., the capacity for autonomy) that would exclude animals from the class of entities having rights.

Regan's claim that animals have rights is attacked by Carl Cohen in this chapter. Cohen's position rests on his conception of rights as claims or potential claims within a community of moral agents. Moral agency presupposes a capacity for free moral judgment and for exercising and responding to moral claims. To be a moral agent, one must have a capacity to understand the rules of duty that govern all members of the human community and to act in accordance with these rules. Only human beings have the relevant capacities. Hence, for Cohen, only human beings have moral rights. Cohen rejects Regan's contention that any criterion that might be used to exclude all animals from the class of entities having rights would also require us to exclude nonparadigm humans. In Cohen's view, although animals cannot have rights because they lack the relevant capacities, nonparadigm humans who also lack the relevant capacities (e.g., the severely mentally retarded) do have rights. In his view, such nonparadigmatic humans are still the bearers of rights because they belong to a species whose members are normally capable of moral reasoning. Cohen does not deny that animals have some sort of moral status. He grants that we do have some obligations to animals, including an obligation not to cause them needless suffering. In contrast to Singer, however, Cohen maintains that it is wrong to give animal and human interests equal consideration. Whatever moral status animals have because of their sentience, it is significantly less than that of human beings.

The question of possible differences in the moral status of human beings and animals is addressed by Mary Anne Warren in this chapter's final reading. A distinction made in the introduction to Chapter 1 between full moral status and partial moral status is useful here. Entities have full moral status if they have the same rights as paradigmatic (i.e., normal adult) human beings. They have partial moral status if their rights are lesser in some sense than those of paradigmatic humans. In comparing and contrasting human and animal rights, Warren effectively ascribes partial moral status to animals. According to her analysis, animal and human rights differ in respect to both their content and their strength (i.e., in the strength of the reasons required to override them). Warren holds that sentience is the basis for at least some rights. Thus she rejects Cohen's conception of rights. Warren argues, however, that moral agency (moral autonomy), as well as other differences between humans and animals, may be a basis for attributing stronger rights to human beings than to animals. In respect to nonparadigmatic humans, Warren advances reasons to support her claim that we can consistently grant them the same rights as those of paradigmatic humans while attributing only lesser rights to animals.

VEGETARIANISM

Is the human interest in eating meat sufficiently important to justify our practice of raising and slaughtering animals? Intertwined with this question is the issue of a vegetarian diet. Advocates of vegetarianism offer diverse arguments to support their position. Some advocate a vegetarian diet simply because they believe it to be superior in terms of health benefits. If a vegetarian diet does offer special health advantages (a controversial claim), then each individual, as a matter of personal prudence, would be well advised to adopt it. Apart from this *prudential argument,* many vegetarians advance *moral arguments* in defense of their diet. One common moral argument, closely related to the considerations developed in Chapter 9, is based on the fact that hunger, malnutrition, and starvation seriously threaten many people in our world. It is morally indefensible, the argument goes, to waste desperately needed protein by feeding our grain to animals whom we then eat. Eight pounds of protein in the form of grain are necessary on the average to produce one pound of protein in the form of meat. Since this process is so inefficient, we are morally obliged to adopt a vegetarian diet so that our protein resources in the form of grain can be shared with those who desperately need help. Though this particular moral argument is not without force, it would not seem to establish a need for a completely vegetarian diet. It may well be that world hunger could effectively be alleviated if people in affluent countries simply consumed *less meat.*

Probably the most important moral arguments advanced in defense of a vegetarian diet are those that take account of the impact of meat production on the animals themselves. Two lines of argument in this category may be distinguished. (1) Although it is not necessarily wrong to kill animals for food (assuming the killing is relatively painless), it is morally indefensible to subject them to the cruelty of "factory farming." Since the meat available in our society is produced in just this way, we are morally obliged not to eat it. R. G. Frey, in a reading in this chapter, labels this *the argument from pain and suffering.* (2) It is morally wrong to kill animals for food, however painless the killing; animals, like human beings, have a right to life. Regan's approach in this chapter exemplifies this second line of reasoning, which Frey labels *the argument from moral rights.* A different approach to vegetarianism, also discussed by Frey, is related to material in Chapter 11. On this approach, what is required is a fundamental shift in our attitudes toward animals and the rest of the natural world, such that any eating of animal flesh is morally unacceptable, regardless of how animals are raised or killed.

ANIMAL EXPERIMENTATION

The use of animals in scientific experimentation intended to benefit human beings raises its own set of troubling questions. Is there any need to use animals in experimentation intended to benefit human beings? If there is a genuine need, can this provide a moral justification for the resulting pain, or even death, of animals? It is possible to distinguish four major lines of reasoning on the morality of animal experimentation. (1) Animal experimentation is never justified because using animals in this way is inconsistent with treating them with the respect due to entities having inherent worth. Entities of this sort cannot be used merely as things for others' benefit. Just as the use of human beings in experiments without their informed consent violates their right to be treated with the respect due those with inherent value, so, too, does the use of animals in experiments conducted in order to benefit humans. This first line of reasoning is in keeping with Regan's position. (2) Animal experimentation is justified only in those cases where we would be willing to conduct the same experiments on brain-damaged human subjects. This is Singer's claim. The underlying reasoning here may be expressed as follows: There may be relevant differences between "normal, adult" humans and animals that would justify our using the latter, but not the former in some experiments—those that might be essential to save human lives or prevent great suffering. However, animals and certain nonparadigm humans do not differ in relevant respects. Hence we are justified in using the former in experiments only where we are justified in using the latter. (3) Given sufficiently important human interests, the presumption against using animals as experimental subjects may be overridden. Although animals, because of their sentience, have rights that must be taken into account, serious human interests can override them. The rights of nonparadigm humans cannot be overridden on the same grounds, however, since their rights are grounded not only in sentience but in other considerations. Warren's article exemplifies this third line of argument. (4) Animal experimentation for the benefit of humans is justifiable simply by appeal to human rights and interests. However, although animals do not have rights, not every experiment using animals is morally acceptable. If the same results could be achieved by using alternative methods (e.g., computer simulation), for example, then it would be morally wrong to conduct an experiment that inflicts needless suffering on animals. Cohen accepts this fourth position. He states, however, that it would be a mistake to think that alternative techniques could shortly replace most of the present experimentation using live animals as subjects.

Jane S. Zembaty

All Animals Are Equal

Peter Singer

A biographical sketch of Peter Singer is found on p. 398.

Singer rejects speciesism, which he defines as a prejudice or attitude of bias in favor of the interests of members of one's own species and against those of members of other species. In his view, speciesism is analogous to racism and sexism. Just as we have a moral obligation to give equal consideration to the interests of all human beings, regardless of sex or skin color, so, too, we have a moral obligation to give equal consideration to the interests of animals. Insofar as animals, like humans, have the capacity to suffer, they have an interest in not suffering. Not to take that interest into account is speciesist and immoral. Singer attacks our current practice of using animals in experiments that frequently inflict tremendous suffering, often for very trivial reasons. As a guiding principle for determining when an experiment using animals might be morally justifiable, Singer suggests that an experiment is justifiable only if it is so important that the use of brain-damaged humans would also be justifiable.

"Animal Liberation" may sound more like a parody of other liberation movements than a serious objective. The idea of "The Rights of Animals" actually was once used to parody the case for women's rights. When Mary Wollstonecraft, a forerunner of today's feminists, published her *Vindication of the Rights of Woman* in 1792, her views were widely regarded as absurd, and before long an anonymous publication appeared entitled *A Vindication of the Rights of Brutes.* The author of this satirical work (now known to have been Thomas Taylor, a distinguished Cambridge philosopher) tried to refute Mary Wollstonecraft's arguments by showing that they could be carried one stage further. If the argument for equality was sound when applied to women, why should it not be applied to dogs, cats, and horses? The reasoning seemed to hold for these "brutes" too; yet to hold that brutes had rights was manifestly absurd. Therefore the reasoning by which this conclusion had been reached must be unsound, and if unsound when applied to brutes, it must also be unsound when applied to women, since the very same arguments had been used in each case.

Reprinted with permission of the author from *Animal Liberation,* New York Review, second edition (1990), pp. 1–9, 36–37, 40, 81–83, 85–86.

In order to explain the basis of the case for the equality of animals, it will be help-ful to start with an examination of the case for the equality of women. Let us assume that we wish to defend the case for women's rights against the attack by Thomas Tay-lor. How should we reply?

One way in which we might reply is by saying that the case for equality between men and women cannot validly be extended to nonhuman animals. Women have a right to vote, for instance, because they are just as capable of making rational deci-sions about the future as men are; dogs, on the other hand, are incapable of under-standing the significance of voting, so they cannot have the right to vote. There are many other obvious ways in which men and women resemble each other closely, while humans and animals differ greatly. So, it might be said, men and women are similar beings and should have similar rights, while humans and nonhumans are dif-ferent and should not have equal rights.

The reasoning behind this reply to Taylor's analogy is correct up to a point, but it does not go far enough. There are obviously important differences between hu-mans and other animals, and these differences must give rise to some differences in the rights that each have. Recognizing this evident fact, however, is no barrier to the case for extending the basic principle of equality to nonhuman animals. The differ-ences that exist between men and women are equally undeniable, and the support-ers of Women's Liberation are aware that these differences may give rise to differ-ent rights. Many feminists hold that women have the right to an abortion on request. It does not follow that since these same feminists are campaigning for equality be-tween men and women they must support the right of men to have abortions too. Since a man cannot have an abortion, it is meaningless to talk of his right to have one. Since dogs can't vote, it is meaningless to talk of their right to vote. There is no reason why either Women's Liberation or Animal Liberation should get involved in such nonsense. The extension of the basic principle of equality from one group to another does not imply that we must treat both groups in exactly the same way, or grant ex-actly the same rights to both groups. Whether we should do so will depend on the nature of the members of the two groups. The basic principle of equality does not require equal or identical *treatment;* it requires equal consideration. Equal consid-eration for different beings may lead to different treatment and different rights.

So there is a different way of replying to Taylor's attempt to parody the case for women's rights, a way that does not deny the obvious differences between human beings and nonhumans but goes more deeply into the question of equality and con-cludes by finding nothing absurd in the idea that the basic principle of equality ap-plies to so-called brutes. At this point such a conclusion may appear odd; but if we examine more deeply the basis on which our opposition to discrimination on grounds of race or sex ultimately rests, we will see that we would be on shaky ground if we were to demand equality for blacks, women, and other groups of oppressed humans while denying equal consideration to nonhumans. To make this clear we need to see, first, exactly why racism and sexism are wrong. When we say that all human beings, whatever their race, creed, or sex, are equal, what is it that we are asserting? Those who wish to defend hierarchical, inegalitarian societies have often pointed out that by whatever test we choose it simply is not true that all humans are equal. Like it or not we must face the fact that humans come in different shapes and sizes; they come with different moral capacities, different intellectual abilities, different amounts of benevolent feeling and sensitivity to the needs of others, different abilities to communicate effectively, and different capacities to experience pleasure and pain. In short, if the demand for equality were based on the actual equality of all human beings, we would have to stop demanding equality.

Still, one might cling to the view that the demand for equality among human beings is based on the actual equality of the different races and sexes. Although, it may be said, humans differ as individuals, there are no differences between the races and sexes as such. From the mere fact that a person is black or a woman we cannot infer anything about that person's intellectual or moral capacities. This, it may be said, is why racism and sexism are wrong. The white racist claims that whites are superior to blacks, but this is false; although there are differences among individuals, some blacks are superior to some whites in all of the capacities and abilities that could conceivably be relevant. The opponent of sexism would say the same: a person's sex is no guide to his or her abilities, and this is why it is unjustifiable to discriminate on the basis of sex.

The existence of individual variations that cut across the lines of race or sex, however, provides us with no defense at all against a more sophisticated opponent of equality, one who proposes that, say, the interests of all those with IQ scores below 100 be given less consideration than the interests of those with ratings over 100. Perhaps those scoring below the mark would, in this society, be made the slaves of those scoring higher. Would a hierarchical society of this sort really be so much better than one based on race or sex? I think not. But if we tie the moral principle of equality to the factual equality of the different races or sexes, taken as a whole, our opposition to racism and sexism does not provide us with any basis for objecting to this kind of inegalitarianism.

There is a second important reason why we ought not to base our opposition to racism and sexism on any kind of factual equality, even the limited kind that asserts that variations in capacities and abilities are spread evenly among the different races and between the sexes: we can have no absolute guarantee that these capacities and abilities really are distributed evenly, without regard to race or sex, among human beings. So far as actual abilities are concerned there do seem to be certain measurable differences both among races and between sexes. These differences do not, of course, appear in every case, but only when averages are taken. More important still, we do not yet know how many of these differences are really due to the different genetic endowments of the different races and sexes, and how many are due to poor schools, poor housing, and other factors that are the result of past and continuing discrimination. Perhaps all of the important differences will eventually prove to be environmental rather than genetic. Anyone opposed to racism and sexism will certainly hope that this will be so, for it will make the task of ending discrimination a lot easier; nevertheless, it would be dangerous to rest the case against racism and sexism on the belief that all significant differences are environmental in origin. The opponent of, say, racism who takes this line will be unable to avoid conceding that if differences in ability did after all prove to have some genetic connection with race, racism would in some way be defensible.

Fortunately there is no need to pin the case for equality to one particular outcome of a scientific investigation. The appropriate response to those who claim to have found evidence of genetically based differences in ability among the races or between the sexes is not to stick to the belief that the genetic explanation must be wrong, whatever evidence to the contrary may turn up; instead we should make it quite clear that the claim to equality does not depend on intelligence, moral capacity, physical strength, or similar matters of fact. Equality is a moral idea, not an assertion of fact. There is no logically compelling reason for assuming that a factual difference in ability between two people justifies any difference in the amount of consideration we give to their needs and interests. *The principle of the equality of human beings is not a description of an alleged actual equality among humans: it is a prescription of how we should treat human beings.*

Jeremy Bentham, the founder of the reforming utilitarian school of moral philosophy, incorporated the essential basis of moral equality into his system of ethics by means of the formula: "Each to count for one and none for more than one." In other words, the interests of every being affected by an action are to be taken into account and given the same weight as the like interests of any other being. A later utilitarian, Henry Sidgwick, put the point in this way: "The good of any one individual is of no more importance, from the point of view (if I may say so) of the Universe, than the good of any other." More recently the leading figures in contemporary moral philosophy have shown a great deal of agreement in specifying as a fundamental presupposition of their moral theories some similar requirement that works to give everyone's interests equal consideration—although these writers generally cannot agree on how this requirement is best formulated.[1]

It is an implication of this principle of equality that our concern for others and our readiness to consider their interests ought not to depend on what they are like or on what abilities they may possess. Precisely what our concern or consideration requires us to do may vary according to the characteristics of those affected by what we do: concern for the well-being of children growing up in America would require that we teach them to read; concern for the well-being of pigs may require no more than that we leave them with other pigs in a place where there is adequate food and room to run freely. But the basic element—the taking into account of the interests of the being, whatever those interests may be—must, according to the principle of equality, be extended to all beings, black or white, masculine or feminine, human or nonhuman.

Thomas Jefferson, who was responsible for writing the principle of the equality of men into the American Declaration of Independence, saw this point. It led him to oppose slavery even though he was unable to free himself fully from his slaveholding background. He wrote in a letter to the author of a book that emphasized the notable intellectual achievements of Negroes in order to refute the then common view that they had limited intellectual capacities:

> Be assured that no person living wishes more sincerely than I do, to see a complete refutation of the doubts I myself have entertained and expressed on the grade of understanding allotted to them by nature, and to find that they are on a par with ourselves . . . but whatever be their degree of talent it is no measure of their rights. Because Sir Isaac New-

ton was superior to others in understanding, he was not therefore lord of the property or persons of others.[2]

Similarly, when in the 1850s the call for women's rights was raised in the United States, a remarkable black feminist named Sojourner Truth made the same point in more robust terms at a feminist convention:

> They talk about this thing in the head; what do they call it? ["Intellect," whispered someone nearby.] That's it. What's that got to do with women's rights or Negroes' rights? If my cup won't hold but a pint and yours holds a quart, wouldn't you be mean not to let me have my little half-measure full?[3]

It is on this basis that the case against racism and the case against sexism must both ultimately rest; and it is in accordance with this principle that the attitude that we may call "speciesism," by analogy with racism, must also be condemned. Speciesism—the word is not an attractive one, but I can think of no better term—is a prejudice or attitude of bias in favor of the interests of members of one's own species and against those of members of other species. It should be obvious that the fundamental objections to racism and sexism made by Thomas Jefferson and Sojourner Truth apply equally to speciesism. If possessing a higher degree of intelligence does not entitle one human to use another for his or her own ends, how can it entitle humans to exploit nonhumans for the same purpose?[4]

Many philosophers and other writers have proposed the principle of equal consideration of interests, in some form or other, as a basic moral principle; but not many of them have recognized that this principle applies to members of other species as well as to our own. Jeremy Bentham was one of the few who did realize this. In a forward-looking passage written at a time when black slaves had been freed by the French but in the British dominions were still being treated in the way we now treat animals, Bentham wrote:

> The day *may* come when the rest of the animal creation may acquire those rights which never could have been withholden from them but by the hand of tyranny. The French have already discovered that the blackness of the skin is no reason why a human being should be abandoned without redress to the caprice of a tormentor. It may one day come to be recognized that the number of the legs, the villosity of the skin, or the termination of the *os sacrum* are reasons equally insufficient for abandoning a sensitive being to the same fate. What else is it that should trace the insuperable line? Is it the faculty of reason, or perhaps the faculty of discourse? But a full-grown horse or dog is beyond comparison a more rational, as well as a more conversable animal, than an infant of a day or a week or even a month, old. But suppose they were otherwise, what would it avail? The question is not, Can they *reason?* nor Can they *talk?* but, Can they *suffer?*[5]

In this passage Bentham points to the capacity for suffering as the vital characteristic that gives a being the right to equal consideration. The capacity for suffering—or more strictly, for suffering and/or enjoyment or happiness—is not just another characteristic like the capacity for language or higher mathematics. Bentham is not saying that those who try to mark "the insuperable line" that determines whether the interests of a being should be considered happen to have chosen the wrong characteristic. By saying that we must consider the interests of all beings with the capacity for suffering or enjoyment Bentham does not arbitrarily exclude from consideration any interests at all—as those who draw the line with reference to the possession of reason or language do. The capacity for suffering and enjoyment is *a prerequisite for having interests at all,* a condition that must be satisfied before we can speak of interests in a meaningful way. It would be nonsense to say that it was not in the interests of a stone to be kicked along the road by a schoolboy. A stone does not have interests because it cannot suffer. Nothing that we can do to it could possibly make any difference to its welfare. The capacity for suffering and enjoyment is, however, not only necessary, but also sufficient for us to say that a being has interests—at an absolute minimum, an interest in not suffering. A mouse, for example, does have an interest in not being kicked along the road, because it will suffer if it is.

Although Bentham speaks of "rights" in the passage I have quoted, the argument is really about equality rather than about rights. Indeed, in a different passage, Bentham famously described "natural rights" as "nonsense" and "natural and imprescriptable rights" as "nonsense upon stilts." He talked of moral rights as a shorthand way of referring to protections that people and animals morally ought to have; but the real weight of the moral argument does not rest on the assertion of the existence of the right, for this in turn has to be justified on the basis of the possibilities for suffering and happiness. In this way we can argue for equality for animals without getting embroiled in philosophical controversies about the ultimate nature of rights.

In misguided attempts to refute the arguments of this book, some philosophers have gone to much trouble developing arguments to show that animals do not have rights.[6] They have claimed that to have rights a being must be autonomous, or must be a member of a community, or must have the ability to respect the rights of others, or must possess a sense of justice. These claims are irrelevant to the case for Animal Liberation. The language of rights is a convenient political shorthand. It is even more valuable in the era of thirty-second TV news clips than it was in Bentham's day; but in the argument for a radical change in our attitude to animals, it is in no way necessary.

If a being suffers there can be no moral justification for refusing to take that suffering into consideration. No matter what the nature of the being, the principle of equality requires that its suffering be counted equally with the like suffering—insofar as rough comparisons can be made—of any other being. If a being is not capable of suffering, or of experiencing enjoyment or happiness, there is nothing to be taken into account. So the limit of sentience (using the term as a convenient if not strictly accurate shorthand for the capacity to suffer and/or experience enjoyment) is the only defensible boundary of concern for the interests of others. To mark this boundary by some other characteristic like intelligence or rationality would be to mark it in an arbitrary manner. Why not choose some other characteristic, like skin color?

Racists violate the principle of equality by giving greater weight to the interests of members of their own race when there is a clash between their interests and the interests of those of another race. Sexists violate the principle of equality by favoring the interests of their own sex. Similarly, speciesists allow the interests of their own species to override the greater interests of members of other species. The pattern is identical in each case.

ANIMALS AND RESEARCH

Most human beings are speciesists. . . . Ordinary human beings—not a few exceptionally cruel or heartless humans, but the overwhelming majority of humans—take an active part in, acquiesce in, and allow their taxes to pay for practices that require the sacrifice of the most important interests of members of other species in order to promote the most trivial interests of our own species. . . .

The practice of experimenting on nonhuman animals as it exists today throughout the world reveals the consequences of speciesism. Many experiments inflict severe pain without the remotest prospect of significant benefits for human beings or any other animals. Such experiments are not isolated instances, but part of a major industry. In Britain, where experimenters are required to report the number of "scientific procedures" performed on animals, official government figures show that 3.5 million scientific procedures were performed on animals in 1988.[7] In the United States there are no figures of comparable accuracy. Under the Animal Welfare Act, the U.S. secretary of agriculture publishes a report listing the number of animals used by facilities registered with it, but this is incomplete in many ways. It does not include rats, mice, birds, reptiles, frogs, or domestic farm animals used for experimental purposes; it does not include animals used in secondary schools; and it does not include experiments performed by facilities that do not transport animals interstate or receive grants or contracts from the federal government.

In 1986 the U.S. Congress Office of Technology Assessment (OTA) published a report entitled "Alternatives to Animal Use in Research, Testing and Education." The OTA researchers attempted to determine the number of animals used in experimentation in the U.S. and reported that "estimates of the animals used in the United States each year range from 10 million to upwards of 100 million." They concluded that the estimates were unreliable but their best guess was "at least 17 million to 22 million."[8]

This is an extremely conservative estimate. In testimony before Congress in 1966, the Laboratory Animal Breeders Association estimated that the number of mice, rats, guinea pigs, hamsters, and rabbits used for experimental purposes in 1965 was around 60 million.[9] In 1984 Dr. Andrew Rowan of Tufts University School of Veterinary Medicine estimated that approximately 71 million animals are used each year. In 1985 Rowan revised his estimates to distinguish between the number of animals produced, acquired, and actually used. This yielded an estimate of between 25 and 35 million animals used in experiments each year.[10] (This figure omits animals who die in shipping or are killed before the experiment begins.) A stock market analysis of just one major supplier of animals to laboratories, the Charles River Breeding Laboratory, stated that this company alone produced 22 million laboratory animals annually.[11]

The 1988 report issued by the Department of Agriculture listed 140,471 dogs, 42,271 cats, 51,641 primates, 431,457 guinea pigs, 331,945 hamsters, 459,254 rabbits, and 178,249 "wild animals": a total of 1,635,288 used in experimentation. Remember that this report does not bother to count rats and mice, and covers at most an estimated 10 percent of the total number of animals used. Of the nearly 1.6 million animals reported by the Department of Agriculture to have been used for experimental purposes, over 90,000 are reported to have experienced "unrelieved pain or distress." Again, this is probably at most 10 percent of the total number of animals suffering unrelieved pain and distress—and if experimenters are less concerned about causing unrelieved pain to rats and mice than they are to dogs, cats, and primates, it could be an even smaller proportion.

Other developed nations all use large numbers of animals. In Japan, for example, a very incomplete survey published in 1988 produced a total in excess of eight million.[12] . . .

Among the tens of millions of experiments performed, only a few can possibly be regarded as contributing to important medical research. Huge numbers of animals are used in university departments such as forestry and psychology; many more are used for commercial purposes, to test new cosmetics, shampoos, food coloring agents, and other inessential items. All this can happen only because of our prejudice against taking seriously the suffering of a being who is not a member of our own species. Typically, defenders of experiments on animals do not deny that animals suffer. They cannot deny the animals' suffering, because they need to stress the similarities between humans and other animals in order to claim that their experiments may have some relevance for human purposes. The experimenter who forces rats to choose between starvation and electric shock to see if they develop ulcers (which they do) does so because the rat has a nervous system very similar to a human being's, and presumably feels an electric shock in a similar way.

There has been opposition to experimenting on animals for a long time. This opposition has made little headway because experimenters, backed by commercial firms that profit by supplying laboratory animals and equipment, have been able to convince legislators and the public that opposition comes from uninformed fanatics who consider the interests of animals more important than the interests of human beings. But to be opposed to what is going on now it is not necessary to insist that all animal experiments stop immediately. All we need to say is that experiments serving no direct and urgent purpose should stop immediately, and in the remaining fields of research, we should whenever possible, seek to replace experiments that involve animals with alternative methods that do not. . . .

When are experiments on animals justifiable? Upon learning of the nature of many of the experiments carried out, some people react by saying that all experiments on animals should be prohibited immediately. But if we make our demands as absolute as this, the experimenters have a ready reply: Would we be prepared to let thousands of humans die if they could be saved by a single experiment on a single animal?

This question is, of course, purely hypothetical. There has never been and never could be a single experiment that saved thousands of lives. The way to reply to this hypothetical question is to pose another: Would the experimenters be prepared to carry out their experiment on a human orphan under six months old if that were the only way to save thousands of lives?

If the experimenters would not be prepared to use a human infant then their readiness to use nonhuman animals reveals an unjustifiable form of discrimination on the basis of species, since adult apes, monkeys, dogs, cats, rats, and other animals are more aware of what is happening to them, more self-directing, and, so far as we can tell, at least as sensitive to pain as a human infant. (I have specified that the human infant be an orphan, to avoid the complications of the feelings of parents. Specifying the case in this way is, if anything, overgenerous to those defending the use of nonhuman animals in experiments, since mammals intended for experimental use are usually separated from their mothers at an early age, when the separation causes distress for both mother and young.)

So far as we know, human infants possess no morally relevant characteristic to a higher degree than adult nonhuman animals, unless we are to count the infants' potential as a characteristic that makes it wrong to experiment on them. Whether this characteristic should count is controversial—if we count it, we shall have to condemn abortion along with experiments on infants, since the potential of the infant and the fetus is the same. To avoid the complexities of this issue, however, we can alter our original question a little and assume that the infant is one with irreversible brain damage so severe as to rule out any mental development beyond the level of a six-month-old infant. There are, unfortunately, many such human beings, locked away in special wards throughout the country, some of them long since abandoned by their parents and other relatives, and, sadly, sometimes unloved by anyone else. Despite their mental deficiencies, the anatomy and physiology of these infants are in nearly all respects identical with those of normal humans. If, therefore, we were to force-feed them with large quantities of floor polish or drip concentrated solutions of cosmetics into their eyes [as has been done in experiments using animals], we would have a much more reliable indication of the safety of these products for humans than we now get by attempting to extrapolate the results of tests on a variety of other species. . . .

So whenever experimenters claim that their experiments are important enough to justify the use of animals, we should ask them whether they would be prepared to use a brain-damaged human being at a similar mental level to the animals they are planning to use. I cannot imagine that anyone would seriously propose carrying out the experiments described in this chapter on brain-damaged human beings. Occasionally it has become known that medical experiments have been performed on human beings without their consent; one case did concern institutionalized intellectually disabled children, who were given hepatitis. When such harmful experiments on human beings become known, they usually lead to an outcry against the experimenters, and rightly so. They are, very often, a further example of the arrogance of the research worker who justifies everything on the grounds of increasing knowledge. But if the experimenter claims that the experiment is important enough to justify inflicting suffering on animals, why is it not important enough to justify inflicting suffering on humans at the same mental level? What difference is there between the two? Only that one is a member of our species and the other is not? But to appeal to that difference is to reveal a bias no more defensible than racism or any other form of arbitrary discrimination. . . .

We have still not answered the question of when an experiment might be justifiable. It will not do to say "Never!" Putting morality in such black-and-white terms is appealing, because it eliminates the need to think about particular cases; but in extreme circumstances, such absolutist answers always break down. Torturing a human being is almost always wrong, but it is not absolutely wrong. If torture were the only way in which we could discover the location of a nuclear bomb hidden in a New York City basement and timed to go off within the hour, then torture would be justifiable. Similarly, if a single experiment could cure a disease like leukemia, that experiment would be justifiable. But in actual life the benefits are always more remote, and more often than not they are nonexistent. So how do we decide when an experiment is justifiable?

We have seen that experimenters reveal a bias in favor of their own species whenever they carry out experiments on nonhumans for purposes that they would not think justified them in using human beings, even brain-damaged ones. This principle gives us a guide toward an answer to our question. Since a speciesist bias, like a racist bias, is unjustifiable, an experiment cannot be justifiable unless the experiment is so important that the use of a brain-damaged human would also be justifiable.

This is not an absolutist principle. I do not believe that it could never be justifiable to experiment on a brain-damaged human. If it really were possible to save several lives by an experiment that would take just one life, and there were no other way those lives could be saved, it would be right to do the experiment. But this would be an extremely rare case. Admittedly, as with any dividing line, there would be a gray area where it was difficult to decide if an experiment could be justified. But we need not get distracted by such considerations now. . . . We are in the midst of an emergency in which appalling suffering is being inflicted on millions of animals for purposes that on any impartial view are obviously inadequate to justify the suffering. When we have ceased to carry out all those experiments, then there will be time enough to discuss what to do about the remaining ones which are claimed to be essential to save lives or prevent greater suffering. . . .

NOTES

1 For Bentham's moral philosophy, see his *Introduction to the Principles of Morals and Legislation,* and for Sidgwick's see *The Methods of Ethics,* 1907 (the passage is quoted from the seventh edition; reprint, London: Macmillan, 1963), p. 382. As examples of leading contemporary moral philosophers who incorporate a requirement of equal consideration of interests, see R. M. Hare, *Freedom and Reason* (New York: Oxford University Press, 1963), and John Rawls, *A Theory of Justice* (Cambridge: Harvard University Press, Belknap Press, 1972). For a brief account of the essential agreement on this issue between these and other positions, see R. M. Hare, "Rules of War and Moral Reasoning," *Philosophy and Public Affairs* 1 (2) (1972).

2 Letter to Henry Gregoire, February 25, 1809.

3 Reminiscences by Francis D. Gage, from Susan B. Anthony, *The History of Woman Suffrage,* vol. 1; the passage is to be found in the extract in Leslie Tanner, ed., *Voices From Women's Liberation* (New York: Signet, 1970).

4 I owe the term "speciesism" to Richard Ryder. It has become accepted in general use since the first edition of this book, and now appears in *The Oxford English Dictionary,* second edition (Oxford: Clarendon Press, 1989).

5 *Introduction to the Principles of Morals and Legislation,* chapter 17.
6 See M. Levin, "Animal Rights Evaluated," *Humanist* 37:14–15 (July/August 1977); M. A. Fox, "Animal Liberation: A Critique," *Ethics* 88: 134–138 (1978); C. Perry and G. E. Jones, "On Animal Rights," *International Journal of Applied Philosophy* 1: 39–57 (1982).
7 *Statistics of Scientific Procedures on Living Animals, Great Britain, 1988,* Command Paper 743 (London: Her Majesty's Stationery Office, 1989).
8 U.S. Congress Office of Technology Assessment, *Alternatives to Animal Use in Research, Testing and Education* (Washington, D.C.: Government Printing Office, 1986), p. 64.
9 Hearings before the Subcommittee on Livestock and Feed Grains of the Committee on Agriculture, U.S. House of Representatives, 1966, p. 63.
10 See A. Rowan, *Of Mice, Models and Men* (Albany: State University of New York Press, 1984), p. 71; his later revision is in a personal communication to the Office of Technology Assessment; see *Alternatives to Animal Use in Research, Testing and Education,* p. 56.
11 OTA, *Alternatives to Animal Use in Research, Testing and Education,* p. 56.
12 *Experimental Animals* 37: 105 (1988).

QUESTIONS

1 Is speciesism analogous to sexism and racism? Why or why not?
2 Has Singer advanced convincing reasons in support of the claim that an experiment using animals cannot be justifiable unless the experiment is so important that the use of a brain-damaged human would also be justifiable?

The Case for Animal Rights

Tom Regan

Tom Regan is professor of philosophy at North Carolina State University, Raleigh. He is the author of *The Case for Animal Rights* (1983), editor of *Animal Sacrifices: Religious Perspectives on the Use of Animals in Science* (1986), and coeditor of *Animal Rights and Human Obligations* (2d ed., 1989).

Like Singer, Regan attacks speciesism. In his view, animals, like humans, have rights which are violated when they are not treated with the respect due to beings who have inherent value. Regan maintains not only that animals, like humans, have inherent value but also that all beings that have inherent value have it equally. In his view, any attempt to specify some characteristic such as intelligence as a basis for attributing a lesser degree of inherent value to animals

Reprinted with permission of Basil Blackwell, Inc. from *In Defense of Animals* (1985), edited by Peter Singer, pp. 13–15, 21–25.

must be rejected since consistency in our moral reasoning would require us to attribute a lesser degree of inherent value to some human beings. Regan concludes by calling for the abolition of all scientific experiments using animals and the dissolution of all commercial animal agriculture.

I regard myself as an advocate of animal rights—as a part of the animal rights movement. That movement, as I conceive it, is committed to a number of goals, including:

- the total abolition of the use of animals in science;
- the total dissolution of commercial animal agriculture;
- the total elimination of commercial and sport hunting and trapping.

There are, I know, people who profess to believe in animal rights but do not avow these goals. Factory farming, they say, is wrong—it violates animals' rights—but traditional animal agriculture is all right. Toxicity tests of cosmetics on animals violate their rights, but important medical research—cancer research, for example—does not. The clubbing of baby seals is abhorrent, but not the harvesting of adult seals. I used to think I understood this reasoning. Not any more. You don't change unjust institutions by tidying them up.

What's wrong—fundamentally wrong—with the way animals are treated isn't the details that vary from case to case. It's the whole system. The forlornness of the veal calf is pathetic, heart wrenching; the pulsing pain of the chimp with electrodes planted deep in her brain is repulsive; the slow, tortuous death of the racoon caught in the leg-hold trap is agonizing. But what is wrong isn't the pain, isn't the suffering, isn't the deprivation. These compound what's wrong. Sometimes—often—they make it much, much worse. But they are not the fundamental wrong.

The fundamental wrong is the system that allows us to view animals as *our resources,* here for *us*—to be eaten, or surgically manipulated, or exploited for sport or money. Once we accept this view of animals—as our resources—the rest is as predictable as it is regrettable. Why worry about their loneliness, their pain, their death? Since animals exist for us, to benefit us in one way or another, what harms them really doesn't matter—or matters only if it starts to bother us, makes us feel a trifle uneasy when we eat our veal escalope, for example. So, yes, let us get veal calves out of solitary confinement, give them more space, a little straw, a few companions. But let us keep our veal escalope.

But a little straw, more space and a few companions won't eliminate—won't even touch—the basic wrong that attaches to our viewing and treating these animals as our resources. A veal calf killed to be eaten after living in close confinement is viewed and treated in this way: but so, too, is another who is raised (as they say) 'more humanely'. To right the wrong of our treatment of farm animals requires more than making rearing methods 'more humane'; it requires the total dissolution of commercial animal agriculture.

How we do this, whether we do it or, as in the case of animals in science, whether and how we abolish their use—these are to a large extent political questions. People must change their beliefs before they change their habits. Enough people, especially those elected to public office, must believe in change—must want it—before we will have laws that protect the rights of animals. This process of change is very complicated, very demanding, very exhausting, calling for the efforts of many hands in education, publicity, political organization and activity, down to the licking of envelopes and stamps. As a trained and practising philosopher, the sort of contribution I can make is limited but, I like to think, important. The currency of philosophy is ideas—their meaning and rational foundation—not the nuts and bolts of the legislative process, say, or the mechanics of community organization. That's what I have been exploring over the past ten years or so in my essays and talks and, most recently, in my book, *The Case for Animal Rights.* I believe the major conclusions I reach in the book are true because they are supported by the weight of the best arguments. I believe the idea of animal rights has reason, not just emotion, on its side.

In the space I have at my disposal here I can only sketch, in the barest outline, some of the main features of the book. Its main themes—and we should not be surprised by this—involve asking and answering deep, foundational moral questions about what morality is, how it should be understood and what is the best moral theory, all considered. I hope I can convey something of the shape I think this theory takes. . . .

What to do? Where to begin? . . . Suppose we consider that you and I, for example, do have value as individuals—what we'll call *inherent value.* To say we have such value is to say that we are something more than, something different from, mere receptacles. Moreover, to ensure that we do not pave the way for such injustices as slavery or sexual discrimination, we must believe that all who have inherent value have it equally, regardless of their sex, race, religion, birthplace and so on. Similarly to be discarded as irrelevant are one's talents or skills, intelligence and wealth, personality or pathology, whether one is loved and admired or despised and loathed. The genius and the retarded child, the prince and the pauper, the brain surgeon and the fruit vendor, Mother Teresa and the most unscrupulous used-car salesman—all have inherent value, all possess it equally, and all have an equal right to be treated with respect, to be treated in ways that do not reduce them to the status of things, as if they existed as resources for others. My value as an individual is independent of my usefulness to you. Yours is not dependent on your usefulness to me. For either of us to treat the other in ways that fail to show respect for the other's independent value is to act immorally, to violate the individual's rights.

Some of the rational virtues of this view—what I call the rights view—should be evident. . . . For example, the rights view *in principle* denies the moral tolerability of any and all forms of racial, sexual or social discrimination; and . . . this view *in principle* denies that we can justify good results by using evil means that violate an individual's rights—denies, for example, that it could be moral to kill my Aunt Bea to harvest beneficial consequences for others. That would be to sanction the disrespectful treatment of the individual in the name of the social good, something the rights view will not—categorically will not—ever allow.

The rights view, I believe, is rationally the most satisfactory moral theory. It surpasses all other theories in the degree to which it illuminates and explains the foundation of our duties to one another—the domain of human morality. On this score it has the best reasons, the best arguments, on its side. Of course, if it were possible to show that only human beings are included within its scope, then a person like myself, who believes in animal rights, would be obliged to look elsewhere.

But attempts to limit its scope to humans only can be shown to be rationally defective. Animals, it is true, lack many of the abilities humans possess. They can't read, do higher mathematics, build a bookcase or make *baba ghanoush*. Neither can many human beings, however, and yet we don't (and shouldn't) say that they (these humans) therefore have less inherent value, less of a right to be treated with respect, than do others. It is the *similarities* between those human beings who most clearly, most non-controversially have such value (the people reading this, for example), not our differences, that matter most. And the really crucial, the basic similarity is simply this: we are each of us the experiencing subject of a life, a conscious creature having an individual welfare that has importance to us whatever our usefulness to others. We want and prefer things, believe and feel things, recall and expect things. And all these dimensions of our life, including our pleasure and pain, our enjoyment and suffering, our satisfaction and frustration, our continued existence or our untimely death—all make a difference to the quality of our life as lived, as experienced, by us as individuals. As the same is true of those animals that concern us (the ones that are eaten and trapped, for example), they too must be viewed as the experiencing subjects of a life, with inherent value of their own.

Some there are who resist the idea that animals have inherent value. 'Only humans have such value,' they profess. How might this narrow view be defended? Shall we say that only humans have the requisite intelligence, or autonomy, or reason? But there are many, many humans who fail to meet these standards and yet are reasonably viewed as having value above and beyond their usefulness to others. Shall we claim that only humans belong to the right species, the species *Homo sapiens?* But this is blatant speciesism. Will it be said, then, that all—and only—humans have immortal souls? Then our opponents have their work cut out for them. I am myself not ill-disposed to the proposition that there are immortal souls. Personally, I profoundly hope I have one. But I would not want to rest my position on a controversial ethical issue on the even more controversial question about who or what has an immortal soul. That is to dig one's hole deeper, not to climb out. Rationally, it is better to resolve moral issues without making more controversial assumptions than are needed. The question of who has inherent value is such a question, one that is resolved more rationally without the introduction of the idea of immortal souls than by its use.

Well, perhaps some will say that animals have some inherent value, only less than we have. Once again, however, attempts to defend this view can be shown to lack rational justification. What could be the basis of our having more inherent value than animals? Their lack of reason, or autonomy, or intellect? Only if we are willing to make the same judgement in the case of humans who are similarly deficient. But it is not true that such humans—the retarded child, for example, or the mentally deranged—have less inherent value than you or I. Neither, then, can we rationally sustain the view that animals like them in being the experiencing subjects of a life have less inherent value. *All* who have inherent value have it *equally,* whether they be human animals or not.

Inherent value, then, belongs equally to those who are the experiencing subjects of a life. Whether it belongs to others—to rocks and rivers, trees and glaciers, for example—we do not know and may never know. But neither do we need to know, if we are to make the case for animal rights. We do not need to know, for example, how many people are eligible to vote in the next presidential election before we can know whether I am. Similarly, we do not need to know how many individuals have inherent value before we can know that some do. When it comes to the case for animal rights, then, what we need to know is whether the animals that, in our culture, are routinely eaten, hunted and used in our laboratories, for example, are like us in being subjects of a life. And we do know this. We do know that many—literally, billions and billions—of these animals are the subjects of a life in the sense explained and so have inherent value if we do. And since, in order to arrive at the best theory of our duties to one another, we must recognize our equal inherent value as individuals, reason—not sentiment, not emotion—reason compels us to recognize the equal inherent value of these animals and, with this, their equal right to be treated with respect.

That, *very* roughly, is the shape and feel of the case for animal rights. Most of the details of the supporting argument are missing. They are to be found in the book to which I alluded earlier. Here, the details go begging, and I must, in closing, limit myself to [one] final point. . . .

Having set out the broad outlines of the rights view, I can now say why its implications for farming and science, among other fields, are both clear and uncompromising. In the case of the use of animals in science, the rights view is categorically abolitionist. Lab animals are not our tasters; we are not their kings. Because these animals are treated routinely, systematically as if their value were reducible to their usefulness to others, they are routinely, systematically treated with a lack of respect, and thus are their rights routinely, systematically violated. This is just as true when they are used in trivial, duplicative, unnecessary or unwise research as it is when they are used in studies that hold out real promise of human benefits. We can't justify harming or killing a human being (my Aunt Bea, for example) just for these sorts of reason. Neither can we do so even in the case of so lowly a creature as a laboratory rat. It is not just refinement or reduction that is called for, not just larger, cleaner cages, not just more generous use of anaesthetic or the elimination of multiple surgery, not just tidying up the system. It is complete replacement. The best we can do when it comes to using animals in science is—not to use them. That is where our duty lies, according to the rights view.

As for commercial animal agriculture, the rights view takes a similar abolitionist position. The fundamental moral wrong here is not that animals are kept in stressful close confinement or in isolation, or that their pain and suffering, their needs and preferences are ignored or discounted. All these *are* wrong, of course, but they are not the fundamental wrong. They are symptoms and effects of the deeper, systematic wrong that allows these animals to be viewed and treated as lacking independent value, as resources for us—as, indeed, a renewable resource. Giving farm animals more space, more natural environments, more companions does not right the fundamental wrong, any more than giving lab animals more anaesthesia or bigger, cleaner cages would right the fundamental wrong in their case. Nothing less than the total dissolution of commercial animal agriculture will do this, just as, for similar reasons I won't develop at length here, morality requires nothing less than the total elimination of hunting and trapping for commercial and sporting ends. The rights view's implications, then, as I have said, are clear and uncompromising. . . .

QUESTIONS

1 Do all sentient beings have the same inherent value? Why or why not?
2 Is it always wrong to use animals in experiments intended to benefit human beings?

Moral Vegetarianism and the Argument from Pain and Suffering

R. G. Frey

R. G. Frey is professor of philosophy at Bowling Green State University. He is the author of *Interests and Rights: The Case against Animals* (1980) and *Rights, Killing, and Suffering: Moral Vegetarianism and Applied Ethics* (1983), from which this selection is excerpted. His coedited works include *Value, Welfare, and Morality* (1993).

Frey identifies three arguments advanced by proponents of moral vegetarianism: the argument from moral rights, the argument from killing, and the argument from pain and suffering. Frey argues that Singer and others who advance these kinds of arguments are committed only to conditional vegetarianism. That is, they are committed to the view that the wrongness of using animals for food is conditional on whether our treatment of animals in converting them into food violates their moral right to life and/or freedom from unnecessary suffering. The argument from pain and suffering, in particular, would have no force if animal raising and slaughtering practices were changed so as to eliminate both. In contrast, according to unconditional vegetarianism it is always wrong to eat animals, irrespective of how they are raised or killed. This type of vegetarianism is rooted in a way of life—one which involves an attempt to live in harmony with everything else in the world, encroaching as little as possible on other creatures and things.

By moral vegetarianism, then, I have in mind those cases for vegetarianism which locate the moral basis for boycotting meat in our treatment of animals in rearing and converting them into food.

Modern proponents of vegetarianism on this basis have relied principally upon three arguments to show that eating meat is wrong.

Reprinted with permission of Blackwell Publishers from R. G. Frey, *Rights, Killing, and Suffering* (1983), pp. 27, 21–23, 30–35.

The Argument from Moral Rights   This is the view that our present treatment of animals in converting them into food violates their moral right to life and/or freedom from unnecessary suffering. It is wrong to eat meat, then, because animals' moral rights have been violated in the course of their reaching our tables.

The Argument from Killing   This is the view that it is wrong to kill animals or to kill them for food, except, if at all, under conditions which few of us can pretend to be in.[1] It is wrong to eat meat because animals have undergone the irretrievable wrong of being killed, in the course of becoming food for human consumption.

The Argument from Pain and Suffering   This is the view . . . that it is wrong to eat meat, because factory-farmed (and perhaps even some traditionally-farmed) animals have suffered a good deal and, thus, been wrongly treated, in the course of being turned into food. . . .

THE ARGUMENT FROM PAIN AND SUFFERING

This argument, championed by Peter Singer in *Animal Liberation*[2] and *Practical Ethics,*[3] by Stephen Clark in *The Moral Status of Animals,*[4] and by many others, moves either directly or indirectly to moral vegetarianism from the pain and suffering which animals undergo in being bred, raised, and slaughtered for food. . . .

The argument from pain and suffering, of course, has a past; its use by Singer and others is but the most recent among several. The significance it has come to have, especially under the stimulus of *Animal Liberation,* stems from its application to intensive methods of food production, to factory or commercial farming. What Singer, amongst others, has done is to give the argument new and important life, by describing how some aspects of intensive farming involve animal suffering and then using the argument to combat these farming practices.

I do not believe it betrays undue sensitivity to find certain practices employed on factory farms profoundly disturbing. To put no finer point on the matter, there are practices afoot on them, pre-eminently in the cases of laying hens and veal calves, of which we cannot be proud. Even if such practices are necessary to sustain the level of profits by which farmers, their families, the meat industry as a whole, and, through it, a very great many others prosper, we still do well not to be proud of having to resort to them. Some might suggest that the great pleasure human beings receive from consuming veal more than outweighs the suffering (no grain, no straw-bedding, no exercise, perpetual confinement in tiny slatted stalls, little muscle-growth, induced iron-deficiency and anemia, almost no daylight, tethered to prevent seeking iron and exercise)[5] which these calves undergo in reaching the table. Even so, treatment such as this is not the sort of thing in which, morally, we take pride; and if it is something required in order to sustain a level or style of life to which we have become accustomed, we still do well to be disturbed that this is so.

As information about the treatment of, for example, veal calves has been more widely disseminated, more people have come to see this treatment as wrong. But this is by no means the end or even the essence of the matter for Singer; for it is central to his position—in fact, it seems the main feature of his position—that moral vegetarianism is *the means by which each of us* can move directly to eliminate the pains of food animals. Once we come to see our treatment of veal calves as wrong, vegetarianism is seen by Singer as the means by which each of us can do something about this treatment. This emerges very clearly from the central argument of *Animal Liberation.*

Animals can suffer, and since they can suffer, they have interests. In view of this fact, the moral principle of the equal consideration of interests applies to them, and this means that we are not morally justified in setting aside, ignoring, or otherwise devaluing their interests. This, however, is precisely what some factory farming practices, with their accompaniment of animal suffering, appear to involve, and the immorality which this represents is, if anything, accentuated by the fact that we do not need meat in order to survive and to lead healthy lives.

We can, on the other hand, do something about this situation: by boycotting meat, we can draw down market forces upon the head of the factory farmer and so reduce or eliminate the suffering of food animals. When demand slackens, prices fall; when prices fall, profits diminish; and when profits diminish, the factory farmer has less capital to re-invest in food stock. (The same is true for farmers who employ traditional methods of farming.) By becoming a vegetarian, then, each of us hits directly and immediately at factory farming; for in giving up meat, we reduce the number of food animals bred and raised for market and thereby total animal suffering. Accordingly, a genuine concern for the interests of animals and so with a diminution in their suffering requires that we cease rearing animals for food and cease eating them.

The picture one carries away from Singer's book, then, is that becoming a moral vegetarian is the means by which each of us can reduce animal suffering and so help in the effort to right a wrong. Once we have identified certain farming practices as wrong, we can use vegetarianism as the tool, as the direct and immediate means for eliminating or mitigating those practices. What is more, this means is relatively painless on us, given that there are wholesome and nutritious alternatives to meat readily available. . . .

TWO CONCEPTIONS OF THE STATUS OF VEGETARIANISM

There is a curious feature of the arguments from moral rights, killing, and pain and suffering that I am sure many readers have noticed. It consists in the fact that, even if we were to regard the arguments as completely successful, they would by no means bar or eliminate all meat-eating. In this can be found the basis for distinguishing two very different conceptions of the status of vegetarianism.

Partial and Absolute Exclusions

When I first arrived at Oxford from Virginia, I became friendly with a mathematician from Calcutta. He was a vegetarian and abstained from all meat. Meals in college were very unpleasant for him, since they invariably featured meat dishes, and what vegetables there were were unappetizing, always the same, and—the great English gastronomic failure—overcooked. He regarded eating meat as an abomination;

there were no circumstances—apart, perhaps from direst necessity, and even this was uncertain—in which he would allow it to be right. Eating meat was simply excluded from consideration, and there was an end to it.

The arguments from moral rights, killing, and pain and suffering do not have the same absolutely dismissive effect. The reason is that the objections which they severally pose are not actually to eating animals but to the treatment animals receive in the course of being converted into food. The result is obvious: to animals which have not undergone the treatment in question, the arguments do not apply. Thus, since the argument from moral rights makes the wrongness of violating animals' moral rights crucial, it places no objection in the way of eating meat from animals whose rights have not been violated. Someone who is a vegetarian solely on the basis of this argument, then, has no reason *per se* to abstain from such meat, any more than someone who is a vegetarian on the basis of the argument from pain and suffering has any reason *per se* to abstain from eating the flesh of animals who have not been cruelly treated in being turned into food. This does not mean, of course, that these individuals will eat the meat in question, only that they must have one more shot in their lockers, if they are going to abstain on principle from this meat as well.

To my Indian friend, this situation would appear very strange indeed. For here are purported vegetarians who, *prima facie,* have no reason not to eat this meat. *He* does not eat meat at all; eating meat is quite excluded from consideration, whether the animal has had its rights violated or been killed or been made to suffer, or whether it has simply fallen from the heavens at one's feet or miraculously appeared in one's cooking pot. To him, it would be exceedingly peculiar to think that his vegetarianism required him to look carefully into the question of whether this chicken has had its rights violated, or had dropped dead from heart seizure, or had not suffered at some point in the past, as if one as opposed to some other answer would make it right for him to eat meat. The plain fact is that, so far as *his* vegetarianism is concerned, such questions are beside the point. Conversely, to the proponents of the three arguments, these questions are very much to the point, and their vegetarianism is conditioned by the responses given in their respective cases.

To this Indian, then, proponents of the three arguments appear more exercised by rights, killing, and suffering than by eating animals. What the arguments make out to be morally wrong is not actually eating animals but violating their alleged moral rights or killing them or making them suffer. Do none of these things, and the wrongness of eating meat vanishes. Here, then, are vegetarians of whom vegetarianism is only demanded if animals are treated one way rather than another. (In the case of the argument from pain and suffering, this result gives rise to a view which *prima facie* seems very strange. For there seems something odd indeed about a view which says in effect that when animals are (treated in such a way as to be) miserable they may not be eaten but when they are (treated in such a way as to be) happy and content they may be eaten. One's natural inclination would be to say the opposite, that when animals are contented, their lives are a benefit to them and that then, if ever, vegetarianism is demanded of us. . . .

Conditional and Unconditional Conceptions

If we think of the position of this Indian mathematician as unconditional vegetarianism and that of the proponents of the three arguments as conditional vegetarianism, then how might we characterize the essential difference between these two conceptions of vegetarianism?

In his paper 'Utilitarianism and vegetarianism',[6] Peter Singer objects to Cora Diamond's claim[7] that his position yields the curious result that it is perfectly permissible to eat animals which are accident victims:

> Why is this curious? It is only curious on the assumption that vegetarians must think it *always* wrong to eat meat. No doubt some vegetarians are moral absolutists, just as there are absolute pacifists, absolute anti-abortionists and absolute truth-tellers who would never tell a lie. I reject all these forms of moral absolutism.[8]

Doubtless Singer would regard unconditional vegetarians as absolutists, and doubtless there is a significant difference between my Indian friend and Singer on this score. But the suggestion of the above passage—that some people think it always wrong to eat meat, whereas others, including Singer, think it only sometimes wrong—is not quite explicit as to the full difference between them.

If we think in terms of a distinction between unconditional and conditional vegetarianism, then the point I was making earlier can be put this way: when conditions of food animal treatment are one way rather than another, conditional vegetarianism ceases to have a ground, the result of which is, in the circumstances, to remove from conditional vegetarians their reason for abstaining from meat. When conditions are one way rather than another, vegetarianism is pointless; for the whole point of conditional vegetarianism is to improve the conditions in which animals are bred, raised, and slaughtered for food, and if conditions are already of the appropriate sort, then there is no point in adopting vegetarianism as the tactic by which to make them of that sort. Here, it seems to me, is encapsulated the essence of conditional vegetarianism: it is a tactic by means of which one hopes to improve the treatment of food animals. This is especially clear in the case of Singer, who . . . regards vegetarianism based upon the argument from pain and suffering as the means by which to combat the pains of factory-farmed animals.

At the core of conditional vegetarianism, then, is a conception of vegetarianism as a tactic for combating the treatment or pains of food animals. But tactics are appropriate to circumstances, and a change in circumstances can, as we have seen, render one's tactics pointless. In the case of a conditional vegetarian, to persist in abstaining from meat, even when circumstances are of the desired sort, becomes a needless gesture.

Accordingly, to say merely that what separates my Indian friend from Singer is a form of absolutism, to say merely that conditional vegetarianism is limited (or applies only in respect of some animals) whereas unconditional vegetarianism is unlimited, leaves out any mention of the tactical conception of vegetarianism, which essentially defines the conditional position. This omission is of the utmost importance; for no one even remotely in sympathy with the views of my Indian friend could accept such a conception of vegetarianism. To this Indian, vegetarianism is some-thing quite different: it represents a decision about how he will live in the world, a decision tantamount in part to the adoption of a way of life, for a world which con-tains a multiplicity of creatures and things, each as much a part of the whole as he is. It represents an attempt to live in harmony with the creatures and things he finds around him and to encroach on them as little as they on the whole encroach on him. It represents an effort to see himself as part of the world, and not a world—and law—unto himself. So far as I can see, nothing could be further from a tactical conception of vegetarianism than this conception of how we shall live in a world where we are but part of the whole, of which conception vegetarianism is a constituent.

(Someone armed with such a conception of vegetarianism is very likely to find Singer's emphasis upon pain rather puzzling. For though my Indian friend is not in-different to the pains of animals, it is not by virtue of the fact that they can feel pain that he thinks they warrant and obtain his respect. If asked whether it was because animals can feel pain that he tries to live in harmony with them, as one part of na-ture with another, he would, I think, view both the question and the questioner with deep puzzlement, not least because many portions of the whole of which he sees him-self as a part *cannot* feel pain. In time, I believe he would come to think that only someone with a particular theory would seize upon pain in this way and elevate it or its avoidance to supreme importance in ethics.)

I myself am as much opposed to moral absolutisms as is Singer and, I suspect, for many of the same reasons. I have used the example of this Indian mathematician simply in order to bring out the tactical conception of vegetarianism, which lies at the heart of conditional vegetarianism, especially that of Singer.

Counter-Argument and Competing Tactics

Apart from the fact that, as we have seen, some vegetarians reject the tactical con-ception of vegetarianism, this conception is exposed to counter-arguments of a spe-cific type. If we stick with Singer as our example, then these counter-arguments stem directly from the literature on utilitarianism.

The specific type of counter-argument is this: if vegetarianism is a tactic for com-bating the pains of food animals, then this tactic ceases to have any point whatever, if we develop ways of breeding, raising, and slaughtering animals painlessly. In this eventuality, we could eat all the meat we liked, and Singer would have no ground for complaint.

It will be claimed, however, that there is no meat available from animals which have not, in particular, been reared by painful methods. To this, there are three re-sponses.

First, it is factually false; there are millions upon millions of animals presently being farmed but not factory-farmed. It is both tempting to argue and not obviously wrong to suggest that because traditional farming methods are held, even by vege-tarians, to be vastly less painful than intensive ones, the argument from pain and suf-fering does not provide a reason for abstaining from the flesh of traditionally-farmed animals. . . .

Second, not all intensively farmed animals suffer to anything like the degree of veal calves, or have the same methods of production used upon them. To give but a single example, in the United States, dairy cows are commercially farmed, and when their days as milk-producers come to an end, they are sent to slaughter. However, their lives are by no means as miserable as those of veal calves.

Third, if we focus solely upon factory-farmed animals, then we can see clearly to what the tactical conception of vegetarianism finally exposes Singer. For just as not eating meat is a tactic for dealing with the pains of food animals, so, too, is the package involving, among other things, maintaining and expanding traditional farming techniques, progressivly eliminating painful practices in intensive farming, and funding research into and developing pain-killing drugs. As tactics, both are on all fours; one is not *per se* more morally correct than the other. Moreover, the latter tactic has two further attractions: first, it enables us not only to deal with animal pain but also to retain our present, meat-based diet intact, and second, it enables us to meet the claim that the heavy demand for meat today can only be satisfied by intensive methods of production.

In this way, vegetarianism, Singer's tactic, is confronted with competition. That is, we are confronted with different tactics for combating the pains of food animals, and the central issue between them becomes simply the degree of effectiveness in achieving this end. The determination of which of two tactics is more effective in lessening animal pain is not a piece of theory but a matter of fact. If technological developments succeed in the encompassing way the one tactic envisages, then it may well be, on grounds of effectiveness, the preferred one, as new and better pain-killers, administered painlessly, reach more and more animals. This very real possibility cannot be eliminated *a priori* through any theoretical considerations. This is especially true for utilitarians such as Singer, for whom it must always remain a contingent affair whether the implementation of one policy has consequences which, in comparison with those of the implementation of another, make it the preferred or right policy. Effectiveness, then, is everything, and vegetarianism must confront and defeat (or at least not be defeated by) one after another competitor on this score; it by no means is *obviously* the most effective tactic for reducing the pains of food animals, so that all potential competitors can be ignored *ab initio.* . . .

To my Indian friend, of course, all this squabbling over effectiveness is beside the point; for whether it is Singer or his opponent who has the more effective means for coming to grips with animal pain, eating meat remains an abomination, and that is that.

NOTES

1 I have in mind conditions of necessity, where the killing and eating of animals is necessary for our survival.

2 Peter Singer, *Animal Liberation,* London, Jonathan Cape, 1976.

3 Peter Singer, *Practical Ethics,* Cambridge, Cambridge University Press, 1980.

4 Stephen Clark, *The Moral Status of Animals,* Oxford, Clarendon Press, 1977.

5 Slaughter normally occurs anywhere from 12 to 15 weeks of this treatment.

6 Peter Singer, 'Utilitarianism and vegetarianism,' *Philosophy and Public Affairs,* vol. 9, 1980, pp. 325–37.

7 Cora Diamond, 'Eating meat and eating people,' *Philosophy,* vol. 53, 1978, pp. 465–479.

8 Singer, 'Utilitarianism and vegetarianism,' pp. 327–8; italics in original.

QUESTIONS

1 Is Frey correct in his claim that Singer is committed only to conditional vegetarianism?

2 Would Regan agree with Frey's understanding of the argument from moral rights?

3 Are we morally obliged to become vegetarians?

The Case for the Use of Animals in Biomedical Research

Carl Cohen

Carl Cohen is professor of philosophy at the Residential College at the University of Michigan. He is the author of *Four Systems* (1982) and coauthor of *Introduction to Logic* (8th ed., 1990). His numerous articles include "Militant Morality: Civil Disobedience and Bioethics."

Cohen, identifying himself as a speciesist, attacks both Singer and Regan and defends the use of animals in biomedical research. Against Regan, Cohen argues that animals have no rights, since they lack the capacities for free moral judgment and for exercising or responding to moral claims. Against Singer, he maintains that speciesism is not analogous to racism and sexism and that all sentient beings do not have equal moral standing. Furthermore, Cohen argues, we have an obligation to enlarge the use of animals in research in the interest of protecting potential human subjects. In his view, although we do have obligations to animals, they have no rights against us on which research can infringe.

Using animals as research subjects in medical investigations is widely condemned on two grounds: first, because it wrongly violates the *rights* of animals,[1] and second, because it wrongly imposes on sentient creatures much avoidable *suffering.*[2] Neither of these arguments is sound. The first relies on a mistaken understanding of rights; the second relies on a mistaken calculation of consequences. Both deserve definitive dismissal.

WHY ANIMALS HAVE NO RIGHTS

A right, properly understood, is a claim, or potential claim, that one party may exercise against another. The target against whom such a claim may be registered can

Reprinted with permission from *The New England Journal of Medicine,* vol. 315 (October 2, 1986), pp. 865–870.

be a single person, a group, a community, or (perhaps) all humankind. The content of rights claims also varies greatly: repayment of loans, nondiscrimination by employers, noninterference by the state, and so on. To comprehend any genuine right fully, therefore, we must know *who* holds the right, *against whom* it is held, and *to what* it is a right.

Alternative sources of rights add complexity. Some rights are grounded in constitution and law (e.g., the right of an accused to trial by jury); some rights are moral but give no legal claims (e.g., my right to your keeping the promise you gave me); and some rights (e.g., against theft or assault) are rooted both in morals and in law.

The differing targets, contents, and sources of rights, and their inevitable conflict, together weave a tangled web. Notwithstanding all such complications, this much is clear about rights in general: they are in every case claims, or potential claims, within a community of moral agents. Rights arise, and can be intelligibly defended, only among beings who actually do, or can, make moral claims against one another. Whatever else rights may be, therefore, they are necessarily human; their possessors are persons, human beings.

The attributes of human beings from which this moral capability arises have been described variously by philosophers, both ancient and modern: the inner consciousness of a free will (Saint Augustine[3]); the grasp, by human reason, of the binding character of moral law (Saint Thomas[4]); the self-conscious participation of human beings in an objective ethical order (Hegel[5]); human membership in an organic moral community (Bradley[6]); the development of the human self through the consciousness of other moral selves (Mead[7]); and the underivative, intuitive cognition of the rightness of an action (Prichard[8]). Most influential has been Immanuel Kant's emphasis on the universal human possession of a uniquely moral will and the autonomy its use entails.[9] Humans confront choices that are purely moral; humans—but certainly not dogs or mice—lay down moral laws, for others and for themselves. Human beings are self-legislative, morally *auto-nomous*.

Animals (that is, nonhuman animals, the ordinary sense of that word) lack this capacity for free moral judgment. They are not beings of a kind capable of exercising or responding to moral claims. Animals therefore have no rights, and they can have none. This is the core of the argument about the alleged rights of animals. The holders of rights must have the capacity to comprehend rules of duty, governing all including themselves. In applying such rules, the holders of rights must recognize possible conflicts between what is in their own interest and what is just. Only in a community of beings capable of self-restricting moral judgments can the concept of a right be correctly invoked.

Humans have such moral capacities. They are in this sense self-legislative, are members of communities governed by moral rules, and do possess rights. Animals do not have such moral capacities. They are not morally self-legislative, cannot possibly be members of a truly moral community, and therefore cannot possess rights. In conducting research on animal subjects, therefore, we do not violate their rights, because they have none to violate.

To animate life, even in its simplest forms, we give a certain natural reverence. But the possession of rights presupposes a moral status not attained by the vast majority of living things. We must not infer, therefore, that a live being has, simply in being alive, a "right" to its life. The assertion that all animals, only because they are alive and have interests, also possess the "right to life"[10] is an abuse of that phrase, and wholly without warrant.

It does not follow from this, however, that we are morally free to do anything we please to animals. Certainly not. In our dealings with animals, as in our dealings with other human beings, we have obligations that do not arise from claims against us based on rights. Rights entail obligations, but many of the things one ought to do are in no way tied to another's entitlement. Rights and obligations are not reciprocals of one another, and it is a serious mistake to suppose that they are.

Illustrations are helpful. Obligations may arise from internal commitments made: physicians have obligations to their patients not grounded merely in their patients' rights. Teachers have such obligations to their students, shepherds to their dogs, and cowboys to their horses. Obligations may arise from differences of status: adults owe special care when playing with young children, and children owe special care when playing with young pets. Obligations may arise from special relationships: the payment of my son's college tuition is something to which he may have no right, although it may be my obligation to bear the burden if I reasonably can; my dog has no right to daily exercise and veterinary care, but I do have the obligation to provide these things for her. Obligations may arise from particular acts or circumstances: one may be obliged to another for a special kindness done, or obliged to put an animal out of its misery in view of its condition—although neither the human benefactor nor the dying animal may have had a claim of right.

Plainly, the grounds of our obligations to humans and to animals are manifold and cannot be formulated simply. Some hold that there is a general obligation to do no gratuitous harm to sentient creatures (the principle of nonmaleficence); some hold that there is a general obligation to do good to sentient creatures when that is reasonably within one's power (the principle of beneficence). In our dealings with animals, few will deny that we are at least obliged to act humanely—that is, to treat them with the decency and concern that we owe, as sensitive human beings, to other sentient creatures. To treat animals humanely, however, is not to treat them as humans or as the holders of rights.

A common objection, which deserves a response, may be paraphrased as follows:

> If having rights requires being able to make moral claims, to grasp and apply moral laws, then many humans—the brain-damaged, the comatose, the senile—who plainly lack those capacities must be without rights. But that is absurd. This proves [the critic concludes] that rights do not depend on the presence of moral capacities.[1,10]

This objection fails; it mistakenly treats an essential feature of humanity as though it were a screen for sorting humans. The capacity for moral judgment that distinguishes humans from animals is not a test to be administered to human beings one by one. Persons who are unable, because of some disability, to perform the full moral functions natural to human beings are certainly not for that reason ejected from the moral community. The issue is one of kind. Humans are of such a kind that they may be the subject of experiments only with their voluntary consent. The choices they make freely must be respected. Animals are of such a kind that it is impossible for them, in principle, to give or withhold voluntary consent or to make a moral choice. What humans retain when disabled, animals have never had.

A second objection, also often made, may be paraphrased as follows:

> Capacities will not succeed in distinguishing humans from the other animals. Animals also reason; animals also communicate with one another; animals also care passionately for their young; animals also exhibit desires and preferences.[11,12] Features of moral relevance—rationality, interdependence, and love—are not exhibited uniquely by human beings. Therefore [this critic concludes], there can be no solid moral distinction between humans and other animals.[10]

This criticism misses the central point. It is not the ability to communicate or to reason, or dependence on one another, or care for the young, or the exhibition of preference, or any such behavior that marks the critical divide. Analogies between human families and those of monkeys, or between human communities and those of wolves, and the like, are entirely beside the point. Patterns of conduct are not at issue. Animals do indeed exhibit remarkable behavior at times. Conditioning, fear, instinct, and intelligence all contribute to species survival. Membership in a community of moral agents nevertheless remains impossible for them. Actors subject to moral judgment must be capable of grasping the generality of an ethical premise in a practical syllogism. Humans act immorally often enough, but only they—never wolves or monkeys—can discern, by applying some moral rule to the facts of a case, that a given act ought or ought not to be performed. The moral restraints imposed by humans on themselves are thus highly abstract and are often in conflict with the self-interest of the agent. Communal behavior among animals, even when most intelligent and most endearing, does not approach autonomous morality in this fundamental sense.

Genuinely moral acts have an internal as well as an external dimension. Thus, in law, an act can be criminal only when the guilty deed, the actus reus, is done with a guilty mind, mens rea. No animal can ever commit a crime; bringing animals to criminal trial is the mark of primitive ignorance. The claims of moral right are similarly inapplicable to them. Does a lion have a right to eat a baby zebra? Does a baby zebra have a right not to be eaten? Such questions, mistakenly invoking the concept of right where it does not belong, do not make good sense. Those who condemn biomedical research because it violates "animal rights" commit the same blunder.

IN DEFENSE OF "SPECIESISM"

Abandoning reliance on animal rights, some critics resort instead to animal sentience—their feelings of pain and distress. We ought to desist from the imposition of pain insofar as we can. Since all or nearly all experimentation on animals does impose pain and could be readily forgone, say these critics, it should be stopped. The ends sought may be worthy, but those ends do not justify imposing agonies on humans, and by animals the agonies are felt no less. The laboratory use of animals (these critics conclude) must therefore be ended—or at least very sharply curtailed.

Argument of this variety is essentially utilitarian, often expressly so[13]; it is based on the calculation of the net product, in pains and pleasures, resulting from experiments on animals. Jeremy Bentham, comparing horses and dogs with other sentient creatures, is thus commonly quoted: "The question is not, Can they reason? nor Can they talk? but, Can they suffer?"[14]

Animals certainly can suffer and surely ought not to be made to suffer needlessly. But in inferring, from these uncontroversial premises, that biomedical research causing animal distress is largely (or wholly) wrong, the critic commits two serious errors.

The first error is the assumption, often explicitly defended, that all sentient animals have equal moral standing. Between a dog and a human being, according to this view, there is no moral difference; hence the pains suffered by dogs must be weighed no differently from the pains suffered by humans. To deny such equality, according to this critic, is to give unjust preference to one species over another; it is "speciesism." The most influential statement of this moral equality of species was made by Peter Singer:

> The racist violates the principle of equality by giving greater weight to the interests of members of his own race when there is a clash between their interests and the interests of those of another race. The sexist violates the principle of equality by favoring the interests of his own sex. Similarly the speciesist allows the interests of his own species to override the greater interests of members of other species. The pattern is identical in each case.[2]

This argument is worse than unsound; it is atrocious. It draws an offensive moral conclusion from a deliberately devised verbal parallelism that is utterly specious. Racism has no rational ground whatever. Differing degrees of respect or concern for humans for no other reason than that they are members of different races is an injustice totally without foundation in the nature of the races themselves. Racists, even if acting on the basis of mistaken factual beliefs, do grave moral wrong precisely because there is no morally relevant distinction among the races. The supposition of such differences has led to outright horror. The same is true of the sexes, neither sex being entitled by right to greater respect or concern than the other. No dispute here.

Between species of animate life, however—between (for example) humans on the one hand and cats or rats on the other—the morally relevant differences are enormous, and almost universally appreciated. Humans engage in moral reflection; humans are morally autonomous; humans are members of moral communities, recognizing just claims against their own interest. Human beings do have rights; theirs is a moral status very different from that of cats or rats.

I am a speciesist. Speciesism is not merely plausible; it is essential for right conduct, because those who will not make the morally relevant distinctions among species are almost certain, in consequence, to misapprehend their true obligations. The analogy between speciesism and racism is insidious. Every sensitive moral judgment requires that the differing natures of the beings to whom obligations are owed be considered. If all forms of animate life—or vertebrate animal life?—must be treated equally, and if therefore in evaluating a research program the pains of a rodent count equally with the pains of a human, we are forced to conclude (1) that neither humans nor rodents possess rights, or (2) that rodents possess all the rights that humans possess. Both alternatives are absurd. Yet one or the other must be swallowed if the moral equality of all species is to be defended.

Humans owe to other humans a degree of moral regard that cannot be owed to animals. Some humans take on the obligation to support and heal others, both humans and animals, as a principal duty in their lives; the fulfillment of that duty may require the sacrifice of many animals. If biomedical investigators abandon the effective pursuit of their professional objectives because they are convinced that they may not do to animals what the service of humans requires, they will fail, objectively, to do their duty. Refusing to recognize the moral differences among species is a sure path to calamity. (The largest animal rights group in the country is People for the Ethical Treatment of Animals; its codirector, Ingrid Newkirk, calls research using animal subjects "fascism" and "supremacism." "Animal liberationists do not separate out the *human* animal," she says, "so there is no rational basis for saying that a human being has special rights. A rat is a pig is a dog is a boy. They're all mammals."[15])

Those who claim to base their objection to the use of animals in biomedical research on their reckoning of the net pleasures and pains produced make a second error, equally grave. Even if it were true—as it is surely not—that the pains of all animate beings must be counted equally, a cogent utilitarian calculation requires that we weigh all the consequences of the use, and of the nonuse, of animals in laboratory research. Critics relying (however mistakenly) on animal rights may claim to ignore the beneficial results of such research, rights being trump cards to which interest and advantage must give way. But an argument that is explicitly framed in terms of interest and benefit for all over the long run must attend also to the disadvantageous consequences of not using animals in research, and to all the achievements attained and attainable only through their use. The sum of the benefits of their use is utterly beyond quantification. The elimination of horrible disease, the increase of longevity, the avoidance of great pain, the saving of lives, and the improvement of the quality of lives (for humans and for animals) achieved through research using animals is so incalculably great that the argument of these critics, systematically pursued, establishes not their conclusion but its reverse: to refrain from using animals in biomedical research is, on utilitarian grounds, morally wrong.

When balancing the pleasures and pains resulting from the use of animals in research, we must not fail to place on the scales the terrible pains that would have resulted, would be suffered now, and would long continue had animals not been used. Every disease eliminated, every vaccine developed, every method of pain relief devised, every surgical procedure invented, every prosthetic device implanted—indeed, virtually every modern medical therapy is due, in part or in whole, to experimentation using animals. Nor may we ignore, in the balancing process, the predictable gains in human (and animal) well-being that are probably achievable in the future but that will not be achieved if the decision is made now to desist from such research or to curtail it.

Medical investigators are seldom insensitive to the distress their work may cause animal subjects. Opponents of research using animals are frequently insensitive to the cruelty of the results of the restrictions they would impose.[2] Untold numbers of human beings—real persons, although not now identifiable—would suffer grievously as the consequence of this well-meaning but shortsighted tenderness. If the morally relevant differences between humans and animals are borne in mind, and if all relevant considerations are weighed, the calculation of long-term consequences must give overwhelming support for biomedical research using animals.

CONCLUDING REMARKS

Substitution

The humane treatment of animals requires that we desist from experimenting on them if we can accomplish the same result using alternative methods—in vitro experimentation, computer simulation, or others. Critics of some experiments using animals rightly make this point.

It would be a serious error to suppose, however, that alternative techniques could soon be used in most research now using live animal subjects. No other methods now on the horizon—or perhaps ever to be available—can fully replace the testing of a drug, a procedure, or a vaccine, in live organisms. The flood of new medical possibilities being opened by the successes of recombinant DNA technology will turn to a trickle if testing on live animals is forbidden. When initial trials entail great risks, there may be no forward movement whatever without the use of live animal subjects. In seeking knowledge that may prove critical in later clinical applications, the unavailability of animals for inquiry may spell complete stymie. In the United States, federal regulations require the testing of new drugs and other products on animals, for efficacy and safety, before human beings are exposed to them.[16,17] We would not want it otherwise.

Every advance in medicine—every new drug, new operation, new therapy of any kind—must sooner or later be tried on a living being for the first time. That trial, controlled or uncontrolled, will be an experiment. The subject of that experiment, if it is not an animal, will be a human being. Prohibiting the use of live animals in biomedical research, therefore, or sharply restricting it, must result either in the blockage of much valuable research or in the replacement of animal subjects with human subjects. These are the consequences—unacceptable to most reasonable persons—of not using animals in research.

Reduction

Should we not at least reduce the use of animals in biomedical research? No, we should increase it, to avoid when feasible the use of humans as experimental subjects. Medical investigations putting human subjects at some risk are numerous and greatly varied. The risks run in such experiments are usually unavoidable, and (thanks to earlier experiments on animals) most such risks are minimal or moderate. But some experimental risks are substantial.

When an experimental protocol that entails substantial risk to humans comes before an institutional review board, what response is appropriate? The investigation, we may suppose, is promising and deserves support, so long as its human subjects are protected against unnecessary dangers. May not the investigators be fairly asked, Have you done all that you can to eliminate risk to humans by the extensive testing of that drug, that procedure, or that device on animals? To achieve maximal safety for humans we are right to require thorough experimentation on animal subjects before humans are involved.

Opportunities to increase human safety in this way are commonly missed; trials in which risks may be shifted from humans to animals are often not devised, sometimes not even considered. Why? For the investigator, the use of animals as subjects is often more expensive, in money and time, than the use of human subjects. Access to suitable human subjects is often quick and convenient, whereas access to appropriate animal subjects may be awkward, costly, and burdened with red tape. Physician-investigators have often had more experience working with human beings and know precisely where the needed pool of subjects is to be found and how they may be enlisted. Animals, and the procedures for their use, are often less familiar to these investigators. Moreover, the use of animals in place of humans is now more likely to be the target of zealous protests from without. The upshot is that humans are sometimes subjected to risks that animals could have borne, and should have borne, in their place. To maximize the protection of human subjects, I conclude, the wide and imaginative use of live animal subjects should be encouraged rather than discouraged. This enlargement in the use of animals is our obligation.

Consistency

Finally, inconsistency between the profession and the practice of many who oppose research using animals deserves comment. This frankly ad hominem observation aims chiefly to show that a coherent position rejecting the use of animals in medical research imposes costs so high as to be intolerable even to the critics themselves.

One cannot coherently object to the killing of animals in biomedical investigations while continuing to eat them. Anesthetics and thoughtful animal husbandry render the level of actual animal distress in the laboratory generally lower than that in the abattoir. So long as death and discomfort do not substantially differ in the two contexts, the consistent objector must not only refrain from all eating of animals but also protest as vehemently against others eating them as against others experimenting on them. No less vigorously must the critic object to the wearing of animal hides in coats and shoes, to employment in any industrial enterprise that uses animal parts, and to any commercial development that will cause death or distress to animals.

Killing animals to meet human needs for food, clothing, and shelter is judged entirely reasonable by most persons. The ubiquity of these uses and the virtual universality of moral support for them confront the opponent of research using animals with an inescapable difficulty. How can the many common uses of animals be judged morally worthy, while their use in scientific investigation is judged unworthy?

The number of animals used in research is but the tiniest fraction of the total used to satisfy assorted human appetites. That these appetites, often base and satisfiable in other ways, morally justify the far larger consumption of animals, whereas the quest for improved human health and understanding cannot justify the far smaller, is wholly implausible. Aside from the numbers of animals involved, the distinction in terms of worthiness of use, drawn with regard to any single animal, is not defensible. A given sheep is surely not more justifiably used to put lamb chops on the supermarket counter than to serve in testing a new contraceptive or a new prosthetic device. The needless killing of animals is wrong; if the common killing of them for our food or convenience is right, the less common but more humane uses of animals in the service of medical science are certainly not less right.

Scrupulous vegetarianism, in matters of food, clothing, shelter, commerce, and recreation, and in all other spheres, is the only fully coherent position the critic may adopt. At great human cost, the lives of fish and crustaceans must also be protected, with equal vigor, if speciesism has been forsworn. A very few consistent critics adopt this position. It is the reductio ad absurdum of the rejection of moral distinctions between animals and human beings.

Opposition to the use of animals in research is based on arguments of two different kinds—those relying on the alleged rights of animals and those relying on the consequences for animals. I have argued that arguments of both kinds must fail. We surely do have obligations to animals, but they have, and can have, no rights against us on which research can infringe. In calculating the consequences of animal research, we must weigh all the long-term benefits of the results achieved—to animals and to humans—and in that calculation we must not assume the moral equality of all animate species.

REFERENCES

1 Regan T. The case for animal rights. Berkeley, Calif.: University of California Press, 1983.
2 Singer P. Animal liberation. New York: Avon Books, 1977.
3 St. Augustine. Confessions. Book Seven. 397 A.D. New York: Pocketbooks, 1957:104–26.
4 St. Thomas Aquinas. Summa theologica. 1273 A.D. Philosophic texts. New York: Oxford University Press, 1960:353–66.
5 Hegel GWF. Philosophy of right. 1821. London: Oxford University Press, 1952:105–10.
6 Bradley FH. Why should I be moral? 1876. In: Melden AI, ed. Ethical theories. New York: Prentice-Hall, 1950:345–59.
7 Mead GH. The genesis of the self and social control. 1925. In: Reck AJ, ed. Selected writings. Indianapolis: Bobbs-Merrill, 1964:264–93.
8 Prichard HA. Does moral philosophy rest on a mistake? 1912. In: Cellars W, Hospers J, eds. Readings in ethical theory. New York: Appleton-Century-Crofts, 1952:149–63.
9 Kant I. Fundamental principles of the metaphysic of morals. 1785. New York: Liberal Arts Press, 1949.
10 Rollin BE. Animal rights and human morality. New York: Prometheus Books, 1981.
11 Hoff C. Immoral and moral uses of animals. N Engl J Med 1980; 302:115–8.
12 Jamieson D. Killing persons and other beings. In: Miller HB, Williams WH, eds. Ethics and animals. Clifton, N.J.: Humana Press, 1983:135–46.
13 Singer P. Ten years of animal liberation. New York Review of Books. 1985; 31:46–52.

14 Bentham J. Introduction to the principles of morals and legislation. London: Athlone Press, 1970.
15 McCabe K. Who will live, who will die? Washingtonian Magazine. August 1986:115.
16 U.S. Code of Federal Regulations, Title 21, Sect. 505(i). Food, drug, and cosmetic regulations.
17 U.S. Code of Federal Regulations, Title 16, Sect. 1500.40–2. Consumer product regulations.

QUESTIONS

1 Is speciesism a morally defensible position?
2 Do animals have rights?

Human and Animal Rights Compared

Mary Anne Warren

A biographical sketch of Mary Anne Warren is found on p. 10.

Along with Singer and Regan, Warren ascribes moral status to animals. In her view, animals, as sentient beings, do have rights. Her major concern, however, is with bringing out the *differences* between the rights of animals and those of human beings and with providing a justification for those differences. On Warren's account, the rights of animals and humans differ in respect to both their *content* and their *strength*—that is, in the strength of the reasons that are necessary to override them. Two reasons support the view that these differences are not arbitrary. (1) Human desires and interests are more extensive than those of animals, calling for differences in both the extent and strength of human rights. (2) The human capacity for moral autonomy, while not a necessary condition for having rights, can provide a reason for according somewhat stronger rights to human beings than to animals. Warren concludes by discussing the case of nonparadigm humans, who may not have a capacity for moral autonomy, and yet, unlike animals, have the *same* basic moral rights as paradigm humans, according to her analysis. She does not assert that animals and nonparadigm humans differ in their intrinsic value. Rather, both have intrinsic value and possess certain rights by virtue of their sentience. However, Warren argues, there are additional reasons, such as the value that nonparadigm humans have for paradigm humans, for ascribing stronger rights to nonparadigm humans than to animals.

None of the animal liberationists have thus far provided a clear explanation of how and why the moral status of (most) animals differs from that of (most) human be-

Reprinted with permission of the author from *Environmental Philosophy: A Collection of Readings* (Penn State University Press, 1983), edited by Robert Elliot and Arran Gare, pp. 112, 115–123.

ings; and this is a point which must be clarified if their position is to be made fully persuasive. That there is such a difference seems to follow from some very strong moral intuitions which most of us share. A man who shoots squirrels for sport may or may not be acting reprehensibly; but it is difficult to believe that his actions should be placed in *exactly* the same moral category as those of a man who shoots women, or black children, for sport. So too it is doubtful that the Japanese fishermen who slaughtered dolphins because the latter were thought to be depleting the local fish populations were acting quite *as* wrongly as if they had slaughtered an equal number of their human neighbours for the same reason. . . . There are two dimensions in which we may find differences between the rights of human beings and those of animals. The first involves the *content* of those rights, while the second involves their strength; that is, the strength of the reasons which are required to override them.

Consider, for instance, the right to liberty. The *human* right to liberty precludes imprisonment without due process of law, even if the prison is spacious and the conditions of confinement cause no obvious physical suffering. But it is not so obviously wrong to imprison animals, especially when the area to which they are confined provides a fair approximation of the conditions of their natural habitat, and a reasonable opportunity to pursue the satisfactions natural to their kind. Such conditions, which often result in an increased lifespan, and which may exist in wildlife sanctuaries or even well-designed zoos, need not frustrate the needs or interests of animals in any significant way, and thus do not clearly violate their rights. Similarly treated human beings, on the other hand (e.g., native peoples confined to prison-like reservations), do tend to suffer from their loss of freedom. Human dignity and the fulfillment of the sorts of plans, hopes and desires which appear (thus far) to be uniquely human, require a more extensive freedom of movement than is the case with at least many nonhuman animals. Furthermore, there are aspects of human freedom, such as freedom of thought, freedom of speech and freedom of political association, which simply do not apply in the case of animals.

Thus, it seems that the human right to freedom is more extensive; that is, it precludes a wider range of specific ways of treating human beings than does the corresponding right on the part of animals. The argument cuts both ways, of course. *Some* animals, for example, great whales and migratory birds, may require at least as much physical freedom as do human beings if they are to pursue the satisfactions natural to their kind, and this fact provides a moral argument against keeping such creatures imprisoned. And even chickens may suffer from the extreme and unnatural confinement to which they are subjected on modern "factory farms". Yet it seems unnecessary to claim for *most* animals a right to a freedom quite as broad as that which we claim for ourselves.

Similar points may be made with respect to the right to life. Animals, it may be argued, lack the cognitive equipment to value their lives in the way that human beings do. Ruth Cigman argues that animals have *no* right to life because death is no misfortune for them.[1] In her view, the death of an animal is not a misfortune, because animals have no desires which are *categorical;* that is which do not "merely presuppose being alive (like the desire to eat when one is hungry), but rather answer the question whether one wants to remain alive".[2] In other words, animals appear to lack the sorts of long-range hopes, plans, ambitions and the like, which give human beings such a powerful interest in continued life. Animals, it seems, take life as it comes and do not specifically desire that it go on. True, squirrels store nuts for the winter and deer run from wolves; but these may be seen as instinctive or conditioned responses to present circumstances, rather than evidence that they value life as such.

These reflections probably help to explain why the death of a sparrow seems less tragic than that of a human being. Human lives, one might say, have greater intrinsic value, because they are worth more *to their possessors.* But this does not demonstrate that no nonhuman animal has *any* right to life. Premature death may be a less *severe* misfortune for sentient nonhuman animals than for human beings, but it is a misfortune nevertheless. In the first place, it is a misfortune in that it deprives them of whatever pleasures the future might have held for them, regardless of whether or not they ever *consciously anticipated* those pleasures. The fact that they are not here afterwards, to *experience* their loss, no more shows that they have not lost anything than it does in the case of humans. In the second place, it is (possibly) a misfortune in that it frustrates whatever future-oriented desires animals *may* have, unbeknownst to us. Even now, in an age in which apes have been taught to use simplified human languages and attempts have been made to communicate with dolphins and whales, we still know very little about the operation of nonhuman minds. We know much too little to assume that nonhuman animals never consciously pursue relatively distant future goals. To the extent that they do, the question of whether such desires provide them with *reasons for living* or merely *presuppose* continued life, has no satisfactory answer, since they cannot contemplate these alternatives—or, if they can, we have no way of knowing what their conclusions are. All we know is that the more intelligent and psychologically complex an animal is, the more *likely* it is that it possesses specifically future-oriented desires, which would be frustrated even by *painless* death.

For these reasons, it is premature to conclude from the apparent intellectual inferiority of nonhuman animals that they have no right to life. A more plausible conclusion is that animals do have a right to life but that it is generally somewhat weaker than that of human beings. It is, perhaps, weak enough to enable us to justify killing animals when we have no other ways of achieving such vital goals as feeding or clothing ourselves, or obtaining knowledge which is necessary to save human lives. Weakening their right to life in this way does not render meaningless the assertion that they have such a right. For the point remains that *some* serious justification for the killing of sentient nonhuman animals is always necessary; they may not be killed merely to provide amusement or minor gains in convenience.

If animals' rights to liberty and life are somewhat weaker than those of human beings, may we say the same about their right to *happiness;* that is, their right not to be made to suffer needlessly or to be deprived of the pleasures natural to their kind? If so, it is not immediately clear why. There is little reason to suppose that pain or suffering are any less unpleasant for the higher animals (at least) than they are for us. Our large brains *may* cause us to experience pain more intensely than do most animals, and *probably* cause us to suffer more from the anticipation or remembrance of pain. These facts might tend to suggest that pain is, on the whole, a worse experience for us than for them. But it may also be argued that pain may be *worse* in some respects for nonhuman animals, who are presumably less able to distract themselves from it by thinking of something else, or to comfort themselves with the knowledge that it is temporary. Brigid Brophy points out that "pain is likely to fill the sheep's whole capacity for experience in a way it seldom does in us, whose intellect and imagination can create breaks for us in the immediacy of our sensations."[3]

The net result of such contrasting considerations is that we cannot possibly claim to know whether pain is, on the whole, worse for us than for animals, or whether their pleasures are any more or any less intense than ours. Thus, while we may justify assigning them a somewhat weaker right to life or liberty, on the grounds that they desire these goods less intensely than we do, we cannot discount their rights to freedom from needlessly inflicted pain or unnatural frustration on the same basis. There may, however, be *other* reasons for regarding all of the moral rights of animals as somewhat less stringent than the corresponding human rights.

A number of philosophers who deny that animals have moral rights point to the fact that nonhuman animals evidently lack the capacity for moral autonomy. Moral autonomy is the ability to act as a moral agent; that is, to act on the basis of an understanding of, and adherence to, moral rules or principles. H.J. McCloskey, for example, holds that "it is the capacity for moral autonomy . . . that is basic to the possibility of possessing a right".[4] McCloskey argues that it is inappropriate to ascribe moral rights to any entity which is not a moral agent, or *potentially* a moral agent, because a right is essentially an entitlement granted to a moral agent, licensing him or her to *act* in certain ways and to *demand* that other moral agents refrain from interference. For this reason, he says, "Where there is no possibility of [morally autonomous] action, potentially or actually . . . and where the being is not a member of a kind which is normally capable of [such] action, we withhold talk of rights."[5]

If moral autonomy—or being *potentially* autonomous, or a member of a kind which is *normally* capable of autonomy—is a necessary condition for having moral rights, then probably no nonhuman animal can qualify. For moral autonomy requires such probably uniquely human traits as "the capacity to be critically self-aware, manipulate concepts, use a sophisticated language, reflect, plan, deliberate, choose, and accept responsibility for acting".[6]

But why, we must ask, should the capacity for autonomy be regarded as a precondition for possessing moral rights? Autonomy is clearly crucial for the *exercise* of many human moral or legal rights, such as the right to vote or to run for public office. It is less clearly relevant, however, to the more basic human rights, such as the right to life or to freedom from unnecessary suffering. The fact that animals, like many human beings, cannot *demand* their moral rights (at least not in the words of any conventional human language) seems irrelevant. For, as Joel Feinberg points out, the interests of non-morally autonomous human beings may be defended by others, for example, in legal proceedings; and it is not clear why the interests of animals might not be represented in a similar fashion.[7]

It is implausible, therefore, to conclude that because animals lack moral autonomy they should be accorded *no moral rights whatsoever*. Nevertheless, it may be argued that the moral autonomy of (most) human beings provides a second reason, in addition to their more extensive interests and desires, for according somewhat *stronger* moral rights to human beings. The fundamental insight behind contractualist theories of morality is that, for morally autonomous beings such as ourselves, there is enormous mutual advantage in the adoption of a moral system designed to protect each of us from the harms that might otherwise be visited upon us by others. Each of us ought to accept and promote such a system because, to the extent that others also accept it, we will all be safer from attack by our fellows, more likely to receive assistance when we need it, and freer to engage in individual as well as co-operative endeavours of all kinds.

Thus, it is the possibility of *reciprocity* which motivates moral agents to extend *full and equal* moral rights, in the first instance, only to other moral agents. I respect your rights to life, liberty and the pursuit of happiness in part because you are a sentient being, whose interests have intrinsic moral significance. But I respect them as *fully equal to my own* because I hope and expect that you will do the same for me. Animals, insofar as they lack the degree of rationality necessary for moral autonomy, cannot agree to respect our interests as equal in moral importance to their own, and neither do they expect or demand such respect from us. Of course, domestic animals may expect to be fed, etc. But they do not, and cannot, expect to be treated as moral equals, for they do not understand that moral concept or what it implies. Consequently, it is neither pragmatically feasible nor morally obligatory to extend to them the same *full and equal* rights which we extend to human beings.

Is this a speciesist conclusion? Defenders of a more extreme animal-rights position may point out that this argument, from the lack of moral autonomy, has exactly the same form as that which has been used for thousands of years to rationalize denying equal moral rights to women and members of "inferior" races. Aristotle, for example, argued that women and slaves are naturally subordinate beings, because they lack the capacity for moral autonomy and self-direction;[8] and contemporary versions of this argument, used to support racist or sexist conclusions, are easy to find. Are we simply repeating Aristotle's mistake, in a different context?

The reply to this objection is very simple: animals, unlike women and slaves, really *are* incapable of moral autonomy, at least to the best of our knowledge. Aristotle certainly *ought* to have known that women and slaves are capable of morally autonomous action; their capacity to use moral language alone ought to have alerted him to this likelihood. If comparable evidence exists that (some) nonhuman animals are moral agents we have not yet found it. The fact that some apes (and, possibly, some **cetaceans**) are capable of learning radically simplified human languages, the terms of which refer primarily to objects and events in their immediate environment, in no way demonstrates that they can understand abstract moral concepts, rules or principles, or use this understanding to regulate their own behaviour.

On the other hand, this argument implies that if we *do* discover that certain nonhuman animals are capable of moral autonomy (which is certainly not impossible), then we ought to extend full and equal moral rights to those animals. Furthermore, if we someday encounter extraterrestrial beings, or build robots, **androids** or supercomputers which function as self-aware moral agents, then we must extend full and equal moral rights to these as well. Being a member of the human species is not a necessary condition for the possession of full "human" rights. Whether it is nevertheless a *sufficient* condition is the question to which we now turn.

THE MORAL RIGHTS OF NONPARADIGM HUMANS

If we are justified in ascribing somewhat different, and also somewhat stronger, moral rights to human beings than to sentient but non-morally autonomous animals, then what are we to say of the rights of human beings who happen not to be capable of moral autonomy, perhaps not even potentially? Both Singer and Regan have argued that if any of the superior intellectual capacities of normal and mature human beings are used to support a distinction between the moral status of *typical,* or paradigm, human beings, and that of animals, then consistency will require us to place certain "nonparadigm" humans, such as infants, small children and the severely retarded or incurably brain damaged, in the same inferior moral category.[9] Such a result is, of course, highly counterintuitive.

Fortunately, no such conclusion follows from the autonomy argument. There are many reasons for extending strong moral rights to nonparadigm humans; reasons which do not apply to most nonhuman animals. Infants and small children are granted strong moral rights in part because of their *potential* autonomy. But *potential* autonomy, as I have argued elsewhere,[10] is not in itself a sufficient reason for the ascription of full moral rights; if it were, then not only human foetuses (from conception onwards) but even ununited human sperm-egg pairs would have to be regarded as entities with a right to life the equivalent of our own—thus making not only abortion, but any intentional failure to procreate, the moral equivalent of murder. Those who do not find this extreme conclusion acceptable must appeal to reasons other than the *potential* moral autonomy of infants and small children to explain the strength of the latter's moral rights.

One reason for assigning strong moral rights to infants and children is that they possess not just *potential* but *partial* autonomy, and it is not clear how much of it they have at any given moment. The fact that, unlike baby chimpanzees, they are already learning the things which will enable them to *become* morally autonomous, makes it likely that their minds have more subtleties than their speech (or the lack of it) proclaims. Another reason is simply that most of us tend to place a very high value on the lives and well-being of infants. Perhaps we are to some degree "programmed" by nature to love and protect them; perhaps our reasons are somewhat egocentric; or perhaps we value them for their potential. Whatever the explanation, the fact that we do feel this way about them is in itself a valid reason for extending to them stronger moral and legal protections than we extend to nonhuman animals, even those which may have just as well or better-developed psychological capacities. A third, and perhaps the most important, reason is that if we did *not* extend strong moral rights to infants, far too few of them would ever *become* responsible, morally autonomous adults; too many would be treated "like animals" (i.e., in ways that it is generally wrong to treat even animals), and would consequently become socially crippled, antisocial or just very unhappy people. If any part of our moral code is to remain intact, it seems that infants and small children *must* be protected and cared for.

Analogous arguments explain why strong moral rights should also be accorded to other nonparadigm humans. The severely retarded or incurably senile, for instance, may have no potential for moral autonomy, but there are apt to be friends, relatives or other people who care what happens to them. Like children, such individuals may have more mental capacities than are readily apparent. Like children, they are more apt to achieve, or return to moral autonomy if they are valued and well cared for. Furthermore, any one of us may someday become mentally incapacitated to one degree or another, and we would all have reason to be anxious about our own futures if such incapacitation were made the basis for denying strong moral rights.

There are, then, sound reasons for assigning strong moral rights even to human beings who lack the mental capacities which justify the general distinction between human and animal rights. Their rights are based not only on the value which they themselves place upon their lives and well-being, but also on the value which other human beings place upon them.

But is this a valid basis for the assignment of moral rights? . . . Regan argues that we cannot justify the ascription of stronger rights to nonparadigm humans than to nonhuman animals in the way suggested, because "what underlies the ascription of rights to any given X is that X has value independently of anyone's valuing X".[11] After all, we do not speak of expensive paintings or gemstones as having rights, although many people value them and have good reasons for wanting them protected.

There is, however, a crucial difference between a rare painting and a severely retarded or senile human being; the latter not only has (or may have) value for other human beings but *also* has his or her own needs and interests. It may be this which leads us to say that such individuals have intrinsic value. The sentience of nonparadigm humans, like that of sentient nonhuman animals, gives them a place in the sphere of rights holders. So long as the moral rights of all sentient beings are given due recognition, there should be no objection to providing some of them with *additional* protections, on the basis of our interests as well as their own. Some philosophers speak of such additional protections, which are accorded to X on the basis of interests other than X's own, as *conferred* rights, in contrast to *natural* rights, which are entirely based upon the properties of X itself. But such "conferred" rights are not necessarily any weaker or less binding upon moral agents than are "natural" rights. Infants, and most other nonparadigm humans have the *same* basic moral rights that the rest of us do, even though the reasons for ascribing those rights are somewhat different in the two cases. . . .

NOTES

1 Ruth Cigman, "Death, Misfortune, and Species Inequality", *Philosophy and Public Affairs* 10, no. 1 (Winter 1981): p. 48.

2 Ibid., pp. 57–58. The concept of a categorical desire is introduced by Bernard Williams, "The Makropoulous Case", in his *Problems of the Self* (Cambridge: Cambridge University Press), 1973.

3 Brigid Brophy, "In Pursuit of a Fantasy," in *Animals, Men and Morals,* ed. Stanley and Rosalind Godlovitch (New York: Taplinger Publishing Co., 1972), p. 129.

4 H. J. McCloskey, "Moral Rights and Animals", *Inquiry* 22, nos. 1–2 (1979): 31.
5 Ibid., p. 29.
6 Michael Fox, "Animal Liberation: A Critique", *Ethics* 88, no. 2 (January 1978): 111.
7 Joel Feinberg, "The Rights of Animals and Unborn Generations," in *Philosophy and Environmental Crisis,* ed. William T. Blackstone (Athens, Ga.: University of Georgia Press), 1974, pp. 46–47.
8 Aristotle, *Politics* I. 1254, 1260, and 1264.
9 Peter Singer, *Animal Liberation: A New Ethics for Our Treatment of Animals* (New York: Avon, 1975), pp. 75–76; Tom Regan, "One Argument Concerning Animal Rights," *Inquiry* 22, nos. 1–2 (1979): 189–217.
10 Mary Anne Warren, "Do Potential People Have Moral Rights?", *Canadian Journal of Philosophy* 7, no. 2 (June 1977): 275–89.
11 Regan, "One Argument Concerning Animal Rights", p. 189.

QUESTIONS

1 Is Warren correct in making the following claim? If we someday encounter extraterrestrial beings, or build robots, androids, or supercomputers which function as self-aware moral agents, then we must extend full and equal moral rights to these.
2 What human needs, if any, are sufficiently important to warrant the infliction of pain and suffering on animals?

SUGGESTED ADDITIONAL READINGS FOR CHAPTER 10

DEGRAZIA, DAVID: "The Moral Status of Animals and Their Use in Research: A Philosophical Review." *Kennedy Institute of Ethics Journal,* vol. 1, March 1991, pp. 48–70. DeGrazia gives a philosophical review of (1) leading theories concerning the moral status of animals, (2) important theoretical issues on which more progress needs to be made, and (3) applications to the setting of animal research.

DOMBROWSKI, DANIEL A.: *The Philosophy of Vegetarianism.* Amherst: University of Massachusetts Press, 1984. This book provides an interesting historical background for contemporary philosophical discussions of vegetarianism. Its critical examination focuses primarily on ancient Greek sources, from the early poetic tradition of Hesiod and Homer down to the neoplatonists in the Christian era.

FEINBERG, JOEL: "The Rights of Animals and Unborn Generations." In William Blackstone, ed., *Philosophy and Environmental Crisis.* Athens: University of Georgia Press, 1974. On Feinberg's analysis of the concept of a right, only those beings who are capable of having interests can meaningfully be said to have rights. Individual animals are such beings.

FREY, R. G.: *Interests and Rights: The Case against Animals.* Oxford: Clarendon, 1980. In Frey's view, animals do not have interests, and thus they do not have moral rights. Accordingly, he contends, arguments for vegetarianism that are based on the claim that animals have moral rights are unsound.

MILLER, HARLAN B., and WILLIAM H. WILLIAMS, eds.: *Ethics and Animals.* Clifton, N.J.: Humana, 1983. This collection of articles focuses on the morality of human treatment of nonhuman animals. Among the topics covered are animal rights to life, killing animals for food, hunting, and animal experimentation.

REGAN, TOM: *The Case for Animal Rights.* Berkeley, Calif.: University of California Press,

1983. Regan argues that animals have a basic moral right to respectful treatment. He derives the following conclusions: (1) vegetarianism is obligatory; (2) hunting and trapping are wrong; (3) the use of animals in science is impermissible.

————, and PETER SINGER, eds.: *Animal Rights and Human Obligations,* 2d ed. Englewood Cliffs, N.J.: Prentice-Hall, 1989. This very useful anthology begins with a section on animals in the history of Western thought. Some of the other sections are "Animal Rights," "Killing and the Value of Life," "The Treatment of Farm Animals," and "The Treatment of Animals in Science."

ROLLIN, BERNARD E.: *The Unheeded Cry: Animal Consciousness, Animal Pain and Science.* Oxford: Oxford University Press, 1989. Rollin provides a study of American and European attitudes toward animal consciousness and their relation to scientific experimentation using animals, beginning with George Romanes in the nineteenth century. Also included is an extensive bibliography beginning with citations from 1879.

SECHZER, JERI A.: *The Role of Animals in Biomedical Research.* New York: The New York Academy of Sciences, 1983. This issue of the *Annals of the New York Academy of Sciences* (vol. 406) contains papers, discussions, and summaries on a wide range of topics dealing with animal experimentation. Topics include the methodologies employed as well as some of the relevant ethical and public policy issues.

SINGER, PETER: *Animal Liberation,* 2d ed. New York: New York Review, 1990. Singer advances a vigorous critique of our present attitudes toward animals and our dealings with them. He also provides a wealth of relevant factual material.

CHAPTER 11

The Environment

Much of our traditional thinking about morality is *anthropocentric*—that is, it assumes that moral obligation is essentially a function of *human* interests. Increasingly, however, anthropocentric approaches to morality are being challenged. Many thinkers concerned with our moral obligations with respect to the environment, like many of those concerned with our obligations with respect to animals, question whether an anthropocentric ethic can provide an adequate basis for all our moral obligations, including environmental ones. This chapter focuses on our moral obligations with respect to the environment and the appropriate moral foundation for those obligations.

THE BASIS FOR OUR MORAL OBLIGATIONS
REGARDING THE ENVIRONMENT

We are becoming increasingly aware of the extent to which human activities pollute and destroy the natural environment. Most reflective people would agree that much of this pollution and destruction is morally wrong. Philosophers and other writers who are concerned with environmental issues disagree, however, about *why* it is morally wrong, for example, to pollute the environment, destroy wilderness areas, or contribute to the destruction of species. What is the basis of our moral obligations regarding the natural environment? Three fundamentally different approaches can be distinguished in reference to this question: (1) anthropocentric approaches, (2) sentientist approaches, and (3) biocentric or ecocentric approaches.

Anthropocentric Approaches

On an anthropocentric approach, our obligations regarding the environment are to be determined solely on the basis of human interests. It seems clear, for example, that we can appeal to human interests in order to ground a prima facie duty not to pollute the environment—that is, a duty not to pollute unless there are overriding moral considerations. Human welfare, in fact human life, crucially depends on such necessities as breathable air, drinkable water, and eatable food. Thus, in the absence of overriding moral considerations, pollution is morally unacceptable precisely because it is damaging to the public welfare. On an alternative construal, still using an anthropocentric approach, the prima facie duty not to pollute may be understood as based on a basic human right, the right to a livable environment. Thus we can assert, with some confidence, that there is a prima facie duty not to pollute. We are left, however, with the problem of weighing the collective human interest in a nonpolluted environment against competing human interests, often economic in nature.

The following schematic example illustrates some of the complexities that confront us when environmental and economic interests clash. An industrial plant, representing a (small, large, massive) financial investment, producing a product that is (unessential, very desirable, essential) to society, and providing a (small, large, enormous) number of jobs, pollutes the environment in a (minor, substantial, major) way. In which of these several cases is the continued operation of the plant morally unacceptable? Certainly the general public interest in the quality of the environment must be recognized. But what about the economic interests of owners, employees, and potential customers? In sum, how is the collective human interest in a nonpolluted environment to be equitably weighed against competing economic interests? At this point, some ethicists tend to appeal to the kind of cost–benefit analyses that characterize utilitarian thinking. William F. Baxter, who defends an anthropocentric ethical stance in this chapter, adopts this cost–benefit approach in arguing for "optimal pollution"—pollution whose harms are outweighed by various human interests, including economic and aesthetic ones.

An anthropocentric moral stance can be taken on other environmental issues as well. For example, it can be argued that the preservation of wilderness serves numerous human interests, and these interests can be viewed as the basis for an obligation to preserve wilderness areas. In this vein, it is pointed out that many people find communing with nature in wilderness areas to be an important source of aesthetic experience and spiritual renewal, that wilderness areas provide significant recreational opportunities for human beings, that the biodiversity stockpiled in wilderness areas can be of great human benefit in connection with the search for substances that have medicinal value, and so on.

Those who believe that an anthropocentric approach is capable of providing an adequate foundation for our obligations with regard to the environment usually insist on the importance of considering a wide range of human interests, not just economic interests, and they also usually insist on taking seriously the interests of future generations of human beings, not just the interests of presently existing human beings. Since human well-being is so intimately intertwined with the well-being of the environment, they point out, we must resist forces of environmental degradation; otherwise, sooner or later, the possibility of human beings leading healthy and happy lives will be severely compromised.

Sentientist Approaches

On a *sentientist* approach, the interests of sentient beings determine our obligations regarding the environment. All sentient beings (not just human beings) are seen as having inherent (intrinsic) value and not merely instrumental value. As the distinction between inherent and instrumental value is usually drawn, some things are valuable as a *means* to some valued end; thus their value is instrumental. Other things are valuable in themselves and thus are said to have inherent or intrinsic value. (Singer in Chapter 10 takes a sentientist approach insofar as he uses sentience as the criterion for determining what sorts of things are entitled to an equal consideration of their interests.) Since sentient beings include human beings, it can be argued on a sentientist approach just as on an anthropocentric one that, for example, mountains, forests, and snail darters should be preserved because of their aesthetic value to human beings. But insofar as nonhuman animals are also sentient beings, a sentientist would insist that animal interests must also be considered when determining our environmental obligations. Bernard E. Rollin's reasoning in this chapter illustrates sentientist thinking. Rollin maintains that we might have a moral obligation to preserve some natural habitat that is of no value to human beings if its destruction would harm some nonhuman animals.

Biocentric (Ecocentric) Approaches

In recent years various writers have argued for an even more radical revision of traditional approaches to morality than that proposed by sentientists. In fact, sentientism is sometimes criticized as analogous to racism and speciesism insofar as all three can be viewed as giving unjustified preference to one's own "kind." John Rodman, who coined the term "sentientism," criticizes the sentientist approach as follows:

> The rest of nature is left in a state of thinghood, having no intrinsic worth, acquiring instrumental value only as resources for the well-being of an elite of sentient beings. Homocentrist rationalism has widened out into a kind of zoocentrist sentientism. . . . If it would seem arbitrary to a visitor from Mars to find one species claiming a monopoly of intrinsic value by virtue of its allegedly exclusive possession of reason, free will, soul, or some other occult quality, would it not seem almost as arbitrary to find that same species claiming a monopoly of intrinsic value for itself and those species most resembling it . . . by virtue of their common and allegedly exclusive possession of sentience?[1]

Aldo Leopold (1887–1948), whose famous essay "The Land Ethic" is partially reprinted in this chapter, argues for a more revolutionary environmental ethic. Insisting that moral consideration must be extended to all of nature, he writes:

> The land ethic simply enlarges the boundaries of the community to include soils, waters, plants, and animals, or collectively the land. . . . In short, a land ethic changes the role of *Homo sapiens* from conqueror of the land-community to plain member and citizen of it. It implies respect for his fellow-members, and also respect for the community as such. . . . A thing is right when it tends to preserve the integrity, stability, and beauty of the biotic community. It is wrong when it tends otherwise.[2]

[1] John Rodman, "The Liberation of Nature?" *Inquiry*, vol. 20, 1977, p. 91.
[2] Aldo Leopold, "The Land Ethic," in *A Sand County Almanac* (New York: Oxford University Press, 1966), pp. 219, 220, 240.

Leopold's approach to our moral obligations with regard to the environment is some-times said to involve a *biotic* view ("biotic" means "relating to life"), and is, there-fore, called *biocentric*. Proponents of a biocentric ethic consider all life to be inher-ently valuable, and they often understand "life" in such a broad sense that it includes even things that are not themselves living organisms, such as rivers, landscapes, ecosystems, and "the living earth." To the extent that biocentric approaches attach moral standing to ecosystems, they may also be labeled *ecocentric*.³ (An *ecosystem* can be defined as a unit made up of a community of living things taken in conjunc-tion with the nonliving factors of its environment.)

Leopold's land ethic provides one important articulation of a biocentric point of view. Another well-known expression of a biocentric point of view can be located in a school of thought known as *deep ecology*. Deep ecology is principally defined in reference to the writings of Arne Naess, Bill Devall, and George Sessions. Naess is a Norwegian philosopher, and the other two writers are Americans. In one of this chapter's readings, Devall and Sessions present the worldview of deep ecology in contrast to the "dominant worldview."

Proponents of deep ecology often contrast their approach with what they call *shal-low ecology*, and they identify shallow ecology with anthropocentric approaches, which are committed to constructing an account of environmental obligations solely in reference to human interests and concerns. At any rate, deep ecology firmly re-jects both anthropocentric and sentientist approaches to environmental obligations. It calls for a radical, fundamental revision in our attitude toward the natural world. Naess and Sessions write:

> The well-being and flourishing of human and nonhuman Life on Earth have value in them-selves (synonyms: intrinsic value, inherent value). These values are independent of the use-fulness of the nonhuman world for human purposes. . . . Richness and diversity of life forms contribute to the realization of these values and are also values in themselves. . . . Humans have no right to reduce this richness and diversity except to satisfy *vital* needs.⁴

CRITICISMS OF BIOCENTRIC APPROACHES

Two articles in this chapter incorporate criticisms of biocentric approaches. Rollin argues that moral consideration is appropriately extended to individual animals but not to other natural entities. Thus he claims that neither nonsentient natural objects (e.g., plants and rivers) nor "quasi-abstract entities, such as species and ecosys-

---

³Although the biocentric approaches explicitly discussed in this chapter are correctly labeled *eco-centric*, there is no necessary connection between biocentrism and ecocentrism. Indeed, one position in environmental ethics is called *biocentric individualism*. On this view, moral consideration is to be ex-tended to all *individual* living things but it is not to be extended (at least not directly extended) to ecosys-tems or the biosphere as a whole. See, for example, Paul W. Taylor, *Respect for Nature: A Theory of Environmental Ethics* (Princeton, N.J.: Princeton University Press, 1986).

⁴These statements are part of a platform of the deep ecology movement originally formulated by Naess and Sessions in 1984. The platform as a whole is included—under the heading "Basic Principles of Deep Ecology"—in the selection by Devall and Sessions in this chapter.

tems," possess intrinsic value. In his view, an adequate environmental ethic can be based solely on the instrumental value that other natural entities have for sentient creatures. Thus the paradoxes and difficulties that arise when intrinsic value is attributed to nonsentient natural objects and quasi-abstract entities can be avoided.

Ramachandra Guha argues in this chapter from a Third World perspective. He presents a wide-ranging critique of what he calls the *American* deep ecology movement. Guha rejects the anthropocentric–biocentric distinction that he identifies as a central tenet of American deep ecology. He maintains that the distinction is of little use in helping us to understand the dynamics of environmental degradation. Guha argues for what he considers a much more radical approach to environmental issues—an approach that he sees as exemplified in countries such as Germany and India. This approach emphasizes the need to change the sociopolitical basis of the consumerism and militarism that, on his view, are responsible for so much of the destruction of the environment. Thus, Guha's approach is "radical" in a different way than are biocentric approaches. Biocentric approaches are radical insofar as they call for a revolutionary revision of our fundamental moral categories. Guha's approach is politically radical, however, insofar as it calls for a rethinking of some of our fundamental sociopolitical institutions.

ECOLOGICAL FEMINISM

Ecological feminism (ecofeminism), another emerging school of thought in environmental ethics, is radical in its own way. Karen J. Warren, a philosopher and prominent ecofeminist, presents a discussion of ecological feminism in this chapter's final reading. In her words, "ecological feminism is the position that there are important connections . . . between the domination of women and the domination of nature." Although both deep ecologists and ecofeminists typically decry conceptual systems that provide a justification for the human domination of the natural world, ecofeminists characteristically believe that an adequate environmental ethic cannot be constructed without recognizing the connections between the "twin" dominations—the domination of nature and the patriarchal domination of women.

Thomas A. Mappes
Jane S. Zembaty

People or Penguins: The Case for Optimal Pollution

William F. Baxter

William F. Baxter is William Benjamin Scott and Luna M. Scott Professor of Law (emeritus) at Stanford University. From 1981 to 1983 he served as assistant attorney general in charge of the antitrust division of the United States Department of Justice. Baxter is the author of *People or Penguins: The Case for Optimal Pollution* (1974), from which this piece is excerpted. He is coauthor of *Retail Banking in the Electronic Age: The Law and Economics of Electronic Funds Transfer* (1977).

Baxter adopts an anthropocentric approach to environmental trade-offs. He states four general goals that, on his view, should serve as criteria for evaluating solutions to environmental problems. Baxter defends his anthropocentric approach and briefly discusses the kinds of trade-offs involved when interests in controlling pollution must be weighed against competing interests, including economic ones.

I start with the modest proposition that, in dealing with pollution, or indeed with any problem, it is helpful to know what one is attempting to accomplish. Agreement on how and whether to pursue a particular objective, such as pollution control, is not possible unless some more general objective has been identified and stated with reasonable precision. We talk loosely of having clean air and clean water, of preserving our wilderness areas, and so forth. But none of these is a sufficiently general objective: each is more accurately viewed as a means rather than as an end.

With regard to clean air, for example, one may ask, "how clean?" and "what does clean mean?" It is even reasonable to ask, "why have clean air?" Each of these questions is an implicit demand that a more general community goal be stated—a goal sufficiently general in its scope and enjoying sufficiently general assent among the community of actors that such "why" questions no longer seem admissible with respect to that goal.

If, for example, one states as a goal the proposition that "every person should be free to do whatever he wishes in contexts where his actions do not interfere with the interests of other human beings," the speaker is unlikely to be met with a response of "why." The goal may be criticized as uncertain in its implications or difficult to implement, but it is so basic a tenet of our civilization—it reflects a cultural value so broadly shared, at least in the abstract—that the question "why" is seen as impertinent or imponderable or both.

I do not mean to suggest that everyone would agree with the "spheres of freedom" objective just stated. Still less do I mean to suggest that a society could subscribe to four or five such general objectives that would be adequate in their coverage to serve as testing criteria by which all other disagreements might be measured. One difficulty in the attempt to construct such a list is that each new goal added will conflict, in certain applications, with each prior goal listed; and thus each goal serves as a limited qualification on prior goals.

Without any expectation of obtaining unanimous consent to them, let me set forth four goals that I generally use as ultimate testing criteria in attempting to frame solutions to problems of human organization. My position regarding pollution stems from these four criteria. If the criteria appeal to you and any part of what appears hereafter does not, our disagreement will have a helpful focus: which of us is correct, analytically, in supposing that his position on pollution would better serve these general goals. If the criteria do not seem acceptable to you, then it is to be expected that our more particular judgments will differ, and the task will then be yours to identify the basic set of criteria upon which your particular judgments rest.

My criteria are as follows:

1 The spheres of freedom criterion stated above.

2 Waste is a bad thing. The dominant feature of human existence is scarcity—our available resources, our aggregate labors, and our skill in employing both have always been, and will continue for some time to be, inadequate to yield to every man all the tangible and intangible satisfactions he would like to have. Hence, none of those resources, or labors, or skills, should be wasted—that is, employed so as to yield less than they might yield in human satisfactions.

3 Every human being should be regarded as an end rather than as a means to be used for the betterment of another. Each should be afforded dignity and regarded as having an absolute claim to an evenhanded application of such rules as the community may adopt for its governance.

4 Both the incentive and the opportunity to improve his share of satisfactions should be preserved to every individual. Preservation of incentive is dictated by the "no-waste" criterion and enjoins against the continuous, totally egalitarian redistribution of satisfactions, or wealth; but subject to that constraint, everyone should receive, by continuous redistribution if necessary, some minimal share of aggregate wealth so as to avoid a level of privation from which the opportunity to improve his situation becomes illusory.

The relationship of these highly general goals to the more specific environmental issues at hand may not be readily apparent, and I am not yet ready to demonstrate their pervasive implications. But let me give one indication of their implications. Recently scientists have informed us that use of DDT in food production is causing damage to the penguin population. For the present purposes let us accept that assertion as an indisputable scientific fact. The scientific fact is often asserted as if the correct implication—that we must stop agricultural use of DDT—followed from the mere statement of the fact of penguin damage. But plainly it does not follow if my criteria are employed.

My criteria are oriented to people, not penguins. Damage to penguins, or sugar pines, or geological marvels is, without more, simply irrelevant. One must go further, by my criteria, and say: Penguins are important because people enjoy seeing them walk about rocks; and furthermore, the well-being of people would be less impaired by halting use of DDT than by giving up penguins. In short, my observations about environmental problems will be people-oriented, as are my criteria. I have no interest in preserving penguins for their own sake.

It may be said by way of objection to this position, that it is very selfish of people to act as if each person represented one unit of importance and nothing else was of any importance. It is undeniably selfish. Nevertheless I think it is the only tenable starting place for analysis for several reasons. First, no other position corresponds to the way most people really think and act—i.e., corresponds to reality.

Second, this attitude does not portend any massive destruction of nonhuman flora and fauna, for people depend on them in many obvious ways, and they will be preserved because and to the degree that humans do depend on them.

Third, what is good for humans is, in many respects, good for penguins and pine trees—clean air for example. So that humans are, in these respects, surrogates for plant and animal life.

Fourth, I do not know how we could administer any other system. Our decisions are either private or collective. Insofar as Mr. Jones is free to act privately, he may give such preferences as he wishes to other forms of life: he may feed birds in winter and do with less himself, and he may even decline to resist an advancing polar bear on the ground that the bear's appetite is more important than those portions of himself that the bear may choose to eat. In short my basic premise does not rule out private altruism to competing life-forms. It does rule out, however, Mr. Jones' inclination to feed Mr. Smith to the bear, however hungry the bear, however despicable Mr. Smith.

Insofar as we act collectively on the other hand, only humans can be afforded an opportunity to participate in the collective decisions. Penguins cannot vote now and are unlikely subjects for the franchise—pine trees more unlikely still. Again each individual is free to cast his vote so as to benefit sugar pines if that is his inclination. But many of the more extreme assertions that one hears from some conservationists amount to tacit assertions that they are specially appointed representatives of sugar pines, and hence that their preferences should be weighted more heavily than the preferences of other humans who do not enjoy equal rapport with "nature." The simplistic assertion that agricultural use of DDT must stop at once because it is harmful to penguins is of that type.

Fifth, if polar bears or pine trees or penguins, like men, are to be regarded as ends rather than means, if they are to count in our calculus of social organization, someone must tell me how much each one counts, and someone must tell me how these life-forms are to be permitted to express their preferences, for I do not know either answer. If the answer is that certain people are to hold their proxies, then I want to know how those proxy-holders are to be selected: self-appointment does not seem workable to me.

Sixth, and by way of summary of all the foregoing, let me point out that the set of environmental issues under discussion—although they raise very complex technical questions of how to achieve any objective—ultimately raise a normative question: what *ought* we to do? Questions of *ought* are unique to the human mind and world—they are meaningless as applied to a nonhuman situation.

I reject the proposition that we *ought* to respect the "balance of nature" or to "preserve the environment" unless the reason for doing so, express or implied, is the benefit of man.

I reject the idea that there is a "right" or "morally correct" state of nature to which we should return. The word "nature" has no normative connotation. Was it "right" or "wrong" for the earth's crust to heave in contortion and create mountains and seas? Was it "right" for the first amphibian to crawl up out of the primordial ooze? Was it "wrong" for plants to reproduce themselves and alter the atmospheric composition in favor of oxygen? For animals to alter the atmosphere in favor of carbon dioxide both by breathing oxygen and eating plants? No answers can be given to these questions because they are meaningless questions.

All this may seem obvious to the point of being tedious, but much of the present controversy over environment and pollution rests on tacit normative assumptions about just such nonnormative phenomena: that it is "wrong" to impair penguins with DDT, but not to slaughter cattle for prime rib roasts. That it is wrong to kill stands of sugar pines with industrial fumes, but not to cut sugar pines and build housing for the poor. Every man is entitled to his own preferred definition of Walden Pond, but there is no definition that has any moral superiority over another, except by reference to the selfish needs of the human race.

From the fact that there is no normative definition of the natural state, it follows that there is no normative definition of clean air or pure water—hence no definition of polluted air—or of pollution—except by reference to the needs of man. The "right" composition of the atmosphere is one which has some dust in it and some lead in it and some hydrogen sulfide in it—just those amounts that attend a sensibly organized society thoughtfully and knowledgeably pursuing the greatest possible satisfaction for its human members.

The first and most fundamental step toward solution of our environmental problems is a clear recognition that our objective is not pure air or water but rather some optimal state of pollution. That step immediately suggests the question: How do we define and attain the level of pollution that will yield the maximum possible amount of human satisfaction?

Low levels of pollution contribute to human satisfaction but so do food and shelter and education and music. To attain ever lower levels of pollution, we must pay the cost of having less of these other things. I contrast that view of the cost of pollution control with the more popular statement that pollution control will "cost" very large numbers of dollars. The popular statement is true in some senses, false in others; sorting out the true and false senses is of some importance. The first step in that sorting process is to achieve a clear understanding of the difference between dollars and resources. Resources are the wealth of our nation; dollars are merely claim checks upon those resources. Resources are of vital importance; dollars are comparatively trivial.

Four categories of resources are sufficient for our purposes: At any given time a nation, or a planet if you prefer, has a stock of labor, of technological skill, of capital goods, and of natural resources (such as mineral deposits, timber, water, land, etc.). These resources can be used in various combinations to yield goods and services of all kinds—in some limited quantity. The quantity will be larger if they are combined efficiently, smaller if combined inefficiently. But in either event the resource stock is limited, the goods and services that they can be made to yield are limited; even the most efficient use of them will yield less than our population, in the aggregate, would like to have.

If one considers building a new dam, it is appropriate to say that it will be costly in the sense that it will require x hours of labor, y tons of steel and concrete, and z amount of capital goods. If these resources are devoted to the dam, then they cannot be used to build hospitals, fishing rods, schools, or electric can openers. That is the meaningful sense in which the dam is costly.

Quite apart from the very important question of how wisely we can combine our resources to produce goods and services, is the very different question of how they get distributed—who gets how many goods? Dollars constitute the claim checks which are distributed among people and which control their share of national output. Dollars are nearly valueless pieces of paper except to the extent that they do represent claim checks to some fraction of the output of goods and services. Viewed as claim checks, all the dollars outstanding during any period of time are worth, in the aggregate, the goods and services that are available to be claimed with them during that period—neither more nor less.

It is far easier to increase the supply of dollars than to increase the production of goods and services—printing dollars is easy. But printing more dollars doesn't help because each dollar then simply becomes a claim to fewer goods, i.e., becomes worth less.

The point is this: many people fall into error upon hearing the statement that the decision to build a dam, or to clean up a river, will cost $X million. It is regrettably easy to say: "It's only money. This is a wealthy country, and we have lots of money." But you cannot build a dam or clean a river with $X million—unless you also have a match, you can't even make a fire. One builds a dam or cleans a river by diverting labor and steel and trucks and factories from making one kind of goods to making another. The cost in dollars is merely a shorthand way of describing the extent of the diversion necessary. If we build a dam for $X million, then we must recognize that we will have $X million less housing and food and medical care and electric can openers as a result.

Similarly, the costs of controlling pollution are best expressed in terms of the other goods we will have to give up to do the job. This is not to say the job should not be done. Badly as we need more housing, more medical care, and more can openers, and more symphony orchestras, we could do with somewhat less of them, in my judgment at least, in exchange for somewhat cleaner air and rivers. But that is the nature of the trade-off, and analysis of the problem is advanced if that unpleasant reality is kept in mind. Once the trade-off relationship is clearly perceived, it is possible to state in a very general way what the optimal level of pollution is. I would state it as follows:

People enjoy watching penguins. They enjoy relatively clean air and smog-free vistas. Their health is improved by relatively clean water and air. Each of these benefits is a type of good or service. As a society we would be well advised to give up one washing machine if the resources that would have gone into that washing machine can yield greater human satisfaction when diverted into pollution control. We should give up one hospital if the resources thereby freed would yield more human satisfaction when devoted to elimination of noise in our cities. And so on, trade-off by trade-off, we should divert our productive capacities from the production of existing goods and services to the production of a cleaner, quieter, more pastoral nation up to—and no further than—the point at which we value more highly the next washing machine or hospital that we would have to do without than we value the next unit of environmental improvement that the diverted resources would create.

Now this proposition seems to me unassailable but so general and abstract as to be unhelpful—at least unadministerable in the form stated. It assumes we can measure in some way the incremental units of human satisfaction yielded by very different types of goods. . . . But I insist that the proposition stated describes the result for which we should be striving—and again, that it is always useful to know what your target is even if your weapons are too crude to score a bull's eye.

QUESTIONS

1 Does the life of a penguin have value only if humans value it?
2 Is human benefit the only morally relevant criterion in determining our obligations in regard to the rest of the natural world?

The Land Ethic

Aldo Leopold

Aldo Leopold (1887–1948), famous as an advocate of environmental conservation, was a professional forester in his early years and later became professor of game management at the University of Wisconsin. Often identified as the father of wildlife conservation in America, he is the author of the classic text *Game Management* (1933). He is also the author of *A Sand County Almanac* (1949), which contains the essay that is partially reprinted here.

Leopold articulates a biocentric point of view under the heading of a *land ethic.* His understanding of "land" is very broad, including "soils, waters, plants, and animals." He argues that we must stop thinking of land merely as property and start thinking of it as worthy of respect and moral consideration in its own right. In accordance with Leopold's land ethic, humankind is not the conqueror of the "land-community" but "plain member and citizen" of it; we must respect fellow members of the community and the community as a whole. Leopold explicitly argues against a system of environmental conservation based solely on economic considerations. He also illustrates some of the interconnected workings of the land-community by employing the image of a pyramid. Leopold's discussion culminates in his famous statement of a moral principle formulated in reference to the "integrity, stability, and beauty of the biotic community."

When god-like Odysseus returned from the wars in Troy, he hanged all on one rope a dozen slave-girls of his household whom he suspected of misbehavior during his absence.

This hanging involved no question of propriety. The girls were property. The disposal of property was then, as now, a matter of expediency, not of right and wrong.

Concepts of right and wrong were not lacking from Odysseus' Greece: witness the fidelity of his wife through the long years before at last his black-prowed galleys clove the wine-dark seas for home. The ethical structure of that day covered wives, but had not yet been extended to human chattels. During the three thousand years which have since elapsed, ethical criteria have been extended to many fields of conduct, with corresponding shrinkages in those judged by expediency only.

THE ETHICAL SEQUENCE

This extension of ethics, so far studied only by philosophers, is actually a process in ecological evolution. Its sequences may be described in ecological as well as in philosophical terms. An ethic, ecologically, is a limitation on freedom of action in the struggle for existence. An ethic, philosophically, is a differentiation of social from anti-social conduct. These are two definitions of one thing. The thing has its origin in the tendency of interdependent individuals or groups to evolve modes of co-operation. The ecologist calls these symbioses. Politics and economics are advanced symbioses in which the original free-for-all competition has been replaced, in part, by co-operative mechanisms with an ethical content.

The complexity of co-operative mechanisms has increased with population density, and with the efficiency of tools. It was simpler, for example, to define the anti-social uses of sticks and stones in the days of the mastodons than of bullets and billboards in the age of motors.

The first ethics dealt with the relation between individuals; the Mosaic Decalogue is an example. Later accretions dealt with the relation between the individual and society. The Golden Rule tries to integrate the individual to society; democracy to integrate social organization to the individual.

There is as yet no ethic dealing with man's relation to land and to the animals and plants which grow upon it. Land, like Odysseus' slave-girls, is still property. The land-relation is still strictly economic, entailing privileges but not obligations.

The extension of ethics to this third element in human environment is, if I read the evidence correctly, an evolutionary possibility and an ecological necessity. It is the third step in a sequence. The first two have already been taken. Individual thinkers since the days of Ezekiel and Isaiah have asserted that the despoliation of land is not only inexpedient but wrong. Society, however, has not yet affirmed their belief. I regard the present conservation movement as the embryo of such an affirmation.

An ethic may be regarded as a mode of guidance for meeting ecological situations so new or intricate, or involving such deferred reactions, that the path of social expediency is not discernible to the average individual. Animal instincts are modes of guidance for the individual in meeting such situations. Ethics are possibly a kind of community instinct in-the-making.

THE COMMUNITY CONCEPT

All ethics so far evolved rest upon a single premise: that the individual is a member of a community of interdependent parts. His instincts prompt him to compete for his place in that community, but his ethics prompt him also to co-operate (perhaps in order that there may be a place to compete for).

The land ethic simply enlarges the boundaries of the community to include soils, waters, plants, and animals, or collectively, the land.

This sounds simple: do we not already sing our love for and obligation to the land of the free and the home of the brave? Yes, but just what and whom do we love? Certainly not the soil, which we are sending helter-skelter downriver. Certainly not the waters, which we assume have no function except to turn turbines, float barges, and carry off sewage. Certainly not the plants, of which we exterminate whole communities without batting an eye. Certainly not the animals, of which we have already extirpated many of the largest and most beautiful species. A land ethic of course cannot prevent the alteration, management, and use of these 'resources,' but it does affirm their right to continued existence, and, at least in spots, their continued existence in a natural state.

In short, a land ethic changes the role of *Homo sapiens* from conqueror of the land-community to plain member and citizen of it. It implies respect for his fellow-members, and also respect for the community as such.

In human history, we have learned (I hope) that the conqueror role is eventually self-defeating. Why? Because it is implicit in such a role that the conqueror knows, *ex cathedra,* just what makes the community clock tick, and just what and who is valuable, and what and who is worthless, in community life. It always turns out that he knows neither, and this is why his conquests eventually defeat themselves.

In the biotic community, a parallel situation exists. Abraham knew exactly what the land was for: it was to drip milk and honey into Abraham's mouth. At the present moment, the assurance with which we regard this assumption is inverse to the degree of our education.

The ordinary citizen today assumes that science knows what makes the community clock tick; the scientist is equally sure that he does not. He knows that the biotic mechanism is so complex that its workings may never be fully understood. . . .

SUBSTITUTES FOR A LAND ETHIC

When the logic of history hungers for bread and we hand out a stone, we are at pains to explain how much the stone resembles bread. I now describe some of the stones which serve in lieu of a land ethic.

One basic weakness in a conservation system based wholly on economic motives is that most members of the land community have no economic value. Wildflowers and songbirds are examples. Of the 22,000 higher plants and animals native to Wisconsin, it is doubtful whether more than 5 per cent can be sold, fed, eaten, or otherwise put to economic use. Yet these creatures are members of the biotic community, and if (as I believe) its stability depends on its integrity, they are entitled to continuance.

When one of these non-economic categories is threatened, and if we happen to love it, we invent subterfuges to give it economic importance. At the beginning of the century songbirds were supposed to be disappearing. Ornithologists jumped to the rescue with some distinctly shaky evidence to the effect that insects would eat us up if birds failed to control them. The evidence had to be economic in order to be valid.

It is painful to read these circumlocutions today. We have no land ethic yet, but we have at least drawn nearer the point of admitting that birds should continue as a matter of biotic right, regardless of the presence or absence of economic advantage to us.

A parallel situation exists in respect of predatory mammals, raptorial birds, and fish-eating birds. Time was when biologists somewhat overworked the evidence that these creatures preserve the health of game by killing weaklings, or that they control rodents for the farmer, or that they prey only on 'worthless' species. Here again, the evidence had to be economic in order to be valid. It is only in recent years that we hear the more honest argument that predators are members of the community, and that no special interest has the right to exterminate them for the sake of a benefit, real or fancied, to itself. . . .

Some species of trees have been 'read out of the party' by economics-minded foresters because they grow too slowly, or have too low a sale value to pay as timber crops: white cedar, tamarack, cypress, beech, and hemlock are examples. In Europe, where forestry is ecologically more advanced, the non-commercial tree species are recognized as members of the native forest community, to be preserved as such, within reason. Moreover, some (like beech) have been found to have a valuable function in building up soil fertility. The interdependence of the forest and its constituent tree species, ground flora, and fauna is taken for granted.

Lack of economic value is sometimes a character not only of species or groups, but of entire biotic communities: marshes, bogs, dunes, and 'deserts' are examples. Our formula in such cases is to relegate their conservation to government as refuges, monuments, or parks. The difficulty is that these communities are usually interspersed with more valuable private lands; the government cannot possibly own or control such scattered parcels. The net effect is that we have relegated some of them to ultimate extinction over large areas. . . .

To sum up: a system of conservation based solely on economic self-interest is hopelessly lopsided. It tends to ignore, and thus eventually to eliminate, many elements in the land community that lack commercial value, but that are (as far as we know) essential to its healthy functioning. It assumes, falsely, I think, that the economic parts of the biotic clock will function without the uneconomic parts. . . .

THE LAND PYRAMID

An ethic to supplement and guide the economic relation to land presupposes the existence of some mental image of land as a biotic mechanism. We can be ethical only in relation to something we can see, feel, understand, love, or otherwise have faith in.

The image commonly employed in conservation education is 'the balance of nature.' For reasons too lengthy to detail here, this figure of speech fails to describe accurately what little we know about the land mechanism. A much truer image is the one employed in ecology: the biotic pyramid. I shall first sketch the pyramid as a symbol of land. . . .

Plants absorb energy from the sun. This energy flows through a circuit called the biota, which may be represented by a pyramid consisting of layers. The bottom layer is the soil. A plant layer rests on the soil, an insect layer on the plants, a bird and rodent layer on the insects, and so on up through various animal groups to the apex layer, which consists of the larger carnivores.

The species of a layer are alike not in where they came from, or in what they look like, but rather in what they eat. Each successive layer depends on those below it for food and often for other services, and each in turn furnishes food and services to those above. Proceeding upward, each successive layer decreases in numerical abundance. Thus, for every carnivore there are hundreds of his prey, thousands of their prey, millions of insects, uncountable plants. The pyramidal form of the system reflects this numerical progression from apex to base. Man shares an intermediate layer with the bears, raccoons, and squirrels which eat both meat and vegetables.

The lines of dependency for food and other services are called food chains. Thus soil-oak-deer-Indian is a chain that has now been largely converted to soil-corn-cow-farmer. Each species, including ourselves, is a link in many chains. The deer eats a hundred plants other than oak, and the cow a hundred plants other than corn. Both, then, are links in a hundred chains. The pyramid is a tangle of chains so complex as to seem disorderly, yet the stability of the system proves it to be a highly organized structure. Its functioning depends on the co-operation and competition of its diverse parts.

In the beginning, the pyramid of life was low and squat, the food chains short and simple. Evolution has added layer after layer, link after link. Man is one of thousands of accretions to the height and complexity of the pyramid. Science has given us many doubts, but it has given us at least one certainty: the trend of evolution is to elaborate and diversify the biota.

Land, then, is not merely soil; it is a fountain of energy flowing through a circuit of soils, plants, and animals. Food chains are the living channels which conduct energy upward; death and decay return it to the soil. The circuit is not closed; some energy is dissipated in decay, some is added by absorption from the air, some is stored in soils, peats, and long-lived forests; but it is a sustained circuit, like a slowly augmented revolving fund of life. There is always a net loss by downhill wash, but this is normally small and offset by the decay of rocks. It is deposited in the ocean and, in the course of geological time, raised to form new lands and new pyramids.

The velocity and character of the upward flow of energy depend on the complex structure of the plant and animal community, much as the upward flow of sap in a tree depends on its complex cellular organization. Without this complexity, normal circulation would presumably not occur. Structure means the characteristic numbers, as well as the characteristic kinds and functions, of the component species. This interdependence between the complex structure of the land and its smooth functioning as an energy unit is one of its basic attributes.

When a change occurs in one part of the circuit, many other parts must adjust themselves to it. Change does not necessarily obstruct or divert the flow of energy; evolution is a long series of self-induced changes, the net result of which has been to elaborate the flow mechanism and to lengthen the circuit. Evolutionary changes, however, are usually slow and local. Man's invention of tools has enabled him to make changes of unprecedented violence, rapidity, and scope. . . .

THE OUTLOOK

It is inconceivable to me that an ethical relation to land can exist without love, respect, and admiration for land, and a high regard for its value. By value, I of course mean something far broader than mere economic value; I mean value in the philosophical sense. . . .

The 'key-log' which must be moved to release the evolutionary process for an ethic is simply this: quit thinking about decent land-use as solely an economic problem. Examine each question in terms of what is ethically and esthetically right, as well as what is economically expedient. A thing is right when it tends to preserve the integrity, stability, and beauty of the biotic community. It is wrong when it tends otherwise.

It of course goes without saying that economic feasibility limits the tether of what can or cannot be done for land. It always has and it always will. The fallacy the economic determinists have tied around our collective neck, and which we now need to cast off, is the belief that economics determines *all* land-use. This is simply not true. An innumerable host of actions and attitudes, comprising perhaps the bulk of all land relations, is determined by the land-users' tastes and predilections, rather than by his purse. The bulk of all land relations hinges on investments of time, forethought, skill, and faith rather than on investments of cash. As a land-user thinketh, so is he.

I have purposely presented the land ethic as a product of social evolution because nothing so important as an ethic is ever 'written.' Only the most superficial student of history supposes that Moses 'wrote' the Decalogue; it evolved in the minds of a thinking community, and Moses wrote a tentative summary of it for a 'seminar.' I say tentative because evolution never stops.

The evolution of a land ethic is an intellectual as well as emotional process. Conservation is paved with good intentions which prove to be futile, or even dangerous, because they are devoid of critical understanding either of the land, or of economic land-use. I think it is a truism that as the ethical frontier advances from the individual to the community, its intellectual content increases.

The mechanism of operation is the same for any ethic: social approbation for right actions; social disapproval for wrong actions.

By and large, our present problem is one of attitudes and implements. We are remodeling the Alhambra with a steamshovel, and we are proud of our yardage. We shall hardly relinquish the shovel, which after all has many good points, but we are in need of gentler and more objective criteria for its successful use.

QUESTIONS

1 Do songbirds and wildflowers have a right to exist? Do cockroaches and weeds have a right to exist?
2 Leopold claims that "[a] thing is right when it tends to preserve the integrity, stability, and beauty of the biotic community" and "[i]t is wrong when it tends otherwise." What are the implications of this principle for our way of life?
3 To what extent would you endorse Leopold's land ethic?

Environmental Ethics

Bernard E. Rollin

Bernard E. Rollin is professor of philosophy at Colorado State University. He is the author of *Animal Rights and Human Morality* (1981), *The Unheeded Cry: Animal Consciousness, Animal Pain, and Science* (1989), and *The Frankenstein Syndrome: Ethical and Social Issues in the Genetic Engineering of Animals* (1995).

In contrast to Baxter's anthropocentric approach and Leopold's biocentric approach, Rollin adopts a sentientist approach to environmental issues. He contends that because humans and other animals are sentient beings who can be harmed, they have intrinsic value and moral rights. Rivers, forests, species, and ecosystems, in contrast, have only instrumental value since they are not sentient beings and thus cannot be harmed, except in a metaphorical sense. Nonetheless, Rollin maintains, once we recognize the intrinsic value of *all* sentient beings, we can develop a rich environmental ethic based on the interests of human beings and other animals.

The past two decades have witnessed a major revolutionary thrust in social moral awareness, one virtually unknown in mainstream Western ethical thinking, although not unrecognized in other cultural traditions; for example, the Navajo, whose descriptive language for nature and animals is suffused with ethical nuances; the Australian Aboriginal people; and the ancient Persians. This thrust is the recognition that nonhuman entities enjoy some moral status as objects of moral concern and deliberation. Although the investigation of the moral status of nonhuman entities has sometimes been subsumed under the global rubric of environmental ethics, such a blan-

Reprinted with permission from *Problems of International Justice* (Westview, 1988), edited by Steven Luper-Foy, pp. 125–131.

ket term does not do adequate justice to the substantial conceptual differences of its components.

THE MORAL STATUS OF NONHUMAN THINGS

As a bare minimum, environmental ethics comprises two fundamentally divergent concerns—namely, concern with individual nonhuman animals as direct objects of moral concern and concern with species, ecosystems, environments, wilderness areas, forests, the biosphere, and other nonsentient natural or even abstract objects as direct objects of moral concern. Usually, although with a number of major exceptions,[1] those who give primacy to animals have tended to deny the moral significance of environments and species as direct objects of moral concern, whereas those who give moral primacy to enviro-ecological concerns tend to deny or at least downplay the moral significance of individual animals.[2] Significant though these differences are, they should not cloud the dramatic nature of this common attempt to break out of a moral tradition that finds loci of value only in human beings and, derivatively, in human institutions.

Because of the revolutionary nature of these attempts, they also remain somewhat undeveloped and embryonic. . . .

The most plausible strategy in attempting to revise traditional moral theory and practice is to show that the seeds of the new moral notions or extensions of old moral notions are, in fact, already implicit in the old moral machinery developed to deal with other issues. Only when such avenues are exhausted will it make sense to recommend major rebuilding of the machinery, rather than putting it to new uses. The classic examples of such extensions are obviously found in the extension of the moral/legal machinery of Western democracies to cover traditionally disenfranchised groups such as women and minorities. The relatively smooth flow of such applications owes much of its smoothness to the plausibility of a simple argument of the form:

> Our extant moral principles ought to cover all humans.
> Women are humans.
> ∴Our extant moral principles ought to cover women.

On the other hand, conceptually radical departures from tradition do not lend themselves to such simple rational reconstruction. Thus, for example, the principle of *favoring* members of traditionally disenfranchised groups at the expense of innocent members of nondisenfranchised groups for the sake of rectifying historically based injustice is viewed as much more morally problematic and ambivalent than simply according rights to these groups. Thus, it would be difficult to construct a simple syllogism in defense of this practice that would garner universal acquiescence with the ease of the one indicated previously.

Thus, one needs to distinguish between moral revolutionary thrusts that are ostensibly paradoxical to common sense and practice because they have been ignored in a wholesale fashion, yet are in fact logical extensions of common morality, and those revolutionary thrusts that are genuinely paradoxical to previous moral think-ing and practice because they are not implicit therein. Being genuinely paradoxical does not invalidate a new moral thrust—it does, however, place upon its proponents a substantially greater burden of proof. Those philosophers, like myself, who have argued for a recognition of the moral status of individual animals and the rights and legal status that derive therefrom, have attempted to place ourselves in the first cat-egory. We recognize that a society that kills and eats billions of animals, kills mil-lions more in research, and disposes of millions more for relatively frivolous rea-sons and that relies economically on animal exploitation as a mainstay of social wealth, considers talk of elevating the moral status of animals as impossible and para-doxical. But this does not mean that such an elevation does not follow unrecognized from moral principles we all hold. Indeed, the abolition of slavery or the liberation of women appeared similarly paradoxical and economically impossible, yet gradu-ally both were perceived as morally necessary, in part because both were implicit, albeit unrecognized, in previously acknowledged assumptions.[3]

My own argument for elevating the status of animals has been a relatively straight-forward deduction of unnoticed implications of traditional morality. I have tried to show that no morally relevant grounds for excluding animals from the full applica-tion of our moral machinery will stand up to rational scrutiny. Traditional claims that rely on notions such as animals have no souls, are inferior to humans in power or in-telligence or evolutionary status, are not moral agents, are not rational, are not pos-sessed of free will, are not capable of language, are not bound by social contract to humans, and so forth, do not serve as justifiable reasons for excluding animals and their interests from the moral arena.

By the same token, morally relevant similarities exist between us and them in the case of the "higher" animals. Animals can suffer, as Jeremy Bentham said; they have interests; what we do to them matters to them; they can feel pain, fear, anxiety, lone-liness, pleasure, boredom, and so on. Indeed, the simplicity and power of the argu-ment calling attention to such morally relevant similarities has led Cartesians from Descartes to modern physiologists with a vested interest against attributing moral status to animals to declare that animals are machines with no morally relevant modes of awareness, a point often addressed today against moral claims such as mine. In fact, such claims have become a mainstay of what I have elsewhere called the "common sense of science." Thus, one who argues for an augmented moral status for animals finds it necessary to establish philosophically and scientifically what com-mon sense takes for granted—namely, that animals *are* conscious.[4] Most people whose common sense is intact are not Cartesians and can see that moral talk cannot be withheld from animals and our treatment of them.

In my own work, appealing again to common moral practice, I have stressed our society's quasi-moral, quasi-legal notion of rights as a reflection of our commitment to the moral primacy of the individual, rather than the state. Rights protect what are hypothesized as the fundamental interests of human beings from cavalier encroach-ment by the common good—such interests as speech, assembly, belief, property, pri-vacy, freedom from torture, and so forth. But those animals who are conscious also have fundamental interests arising out of *their* biologically given natures (or *teloi*), the infringement upon which matters greatly to them, and the fulfillment of which is central to their lives. Hence, I deduce the notion of animal rights from our common moral theory and practice and attempt to show that conceptually, at least, it is a deduction from the moral framework of the status quo rather than a major revision therein. Moral concern for individual animals follows from the hitherto ignored presence of morally relevant characteristics, primarily sentience, in animals. As a result, I am comfortable in attributing what Immanuel Kant called "intrinsic value," not merely use value, to animals if we attribute it to people.[5]

The task is far more formidable for those who attempt to make nonsentient natural objects, such as rivers and mountains, or, worse, quasi-abstract entities, such as species and ecosystems, into direct objects of moral concern. Interestingly enough, in direct opposition to the case of animals, such moves appear prima facie plausible to common morality, which has long expressed concern for the value and preservation of some natural objects, while condoning wholesale exploitation of others. In the same way, common practice often showed extreme concern for certain favored kinds of animals, while systematically exploiting others. Thus, many people in the United States strongly oppose scientific research on dogs and cats, but are totally unconcerned about such use of rodents or swine. What is superficially plausible, however, quite unlike the case of animals, turns out to be deeply paradoxical given the machinery of traditional morality.

Many leading environmental ethicists have attempted to do for nonsentient natural objects and abstract objects the same sort of thing I have tried to do for animals—namely, attempted to elevate their status to direct objects of intrinsic value, ends in themselves, which are morally valuable not only because of their relations and utility to sentient beings, but in and of themselves.[6] To my knowledge, none of these theorists has attempted to claim, as I do for animals, that the locus of such value lies in the fact that what we do to these entities matters to them. No one has argued that we can harm rivers, species, or ecosystems in ways that matter to them.

Wherein, then, do these theorists locate the intrinsic value of these entities? This is not at all clear in the writings, but seems to come down to one of the following doubtful moves:

1 Going from the fact that environmental factors are absolutely essential to the well-being or survival of beings that are loci of intrinsic value to the conclusion that environmental factors therefore enjoy a similar or even higher moral status. Such a move is clearly fallacious. Just because I cannot survive without insulin, and I am an object of intrinsic value, it does not follow that insulin is, too. In fact, the insulin is a paradigmatic example of instrumental value.

2 Going from the fact that the environment "creates" all sentient creatures to the fact that its welfare is more important than theirs. This is really a variation on (1) and succumbs to the same sort of criticism, namely, that this reasoning represents a genetic fallacy. The cause of something valuable need not itself be valuable and certainly not necessarily more valuable than its effect—its value must be established independently of its result. The Holocaust may have caused the state of Israel; that does not make the Holocaust more valuable than the state of Israel.

3 Confusing aesthetic or instrumental value for sentient creatures, notably humans, with intrinsic value and underestimating aesthetic value as a category. We shall return to this shortly, for I suspect it is the root confusion in those attempting to give nonsentient nature intrinsic value.

4 Substituting rhetoric for logic at crucial points in the discussions and using a poetic rhetoric (descriptions of natural objects in terms such as "grandeur," "majesty," "novelty," "variety") as an unexplained basis for according them "intrinsic value."

5 Going from the metaphor that infringement on natural objects "matters" to them in the sense that disturbance evokes an adjustment by their self-regulating properties, to the erroneous conclusion that such self-regulation, being analogous to conscious coping in animals, entitles them to direct moral status.

In short, traditional morality and its theory do not offer a viable way to raise the moral status of nonsentient natural objects and abstract objects so that they are direct objects of moral concern on a par with or even higher than sentient creatures. Ordinary morality and moral concern take as their focus the effects of actions on beings who can be helped and harmed, in ways that matter to them, either directly or by implication. If it is immoral to wreck someone's property, it is because it is someone's; if it is immoral to promote the extinction of species, it is because such extinction causes aesthetic or practical harm to humans or to animals or because a species is, in the final analysis, a group of harmable individuals.

There is nothing, of course, to stop environmental ethicists from making a recommendation for a substantial revision of common and traditional morality. But such recommendations are likely to be dismissed or whittled away by a moral version of Occam's razor: Why grant animals rights and acknowledge in animals intrinsic value? Because they are conscious and what we do to them matters to them? Why grant rocks, or trees, or species, or ecosystems rights? Because these objects have great aesthetic value, or are essential to us, or are basic for survival? But these are paradigmatic examples of *instrumental* value. A conceptual confusion for a noble purpose is still a conceptual confusion.

There is nothing to be gained by attempting to elevate the moral status of nonsentient natural objects to that of sentient ones. One can develop a rich environmental ethic by locating the value of nonsentient natural objects in their relation to sentient ones. One can argue for the preservation of habitats because their destruction harms animals; one can argue for preserving ecosystems on the grounds of unforeseen pernicious consequences resulting from their destruction, a claim for which much empirical evidence exists. One can argue for the preservation of animal species as the sum of a group of individuals who would be harmed by its extinction. One can argue for preserving mountains, snail darters, streams, and cockroaches on aesthetic grounds. Too many philosophers forget the moral power of aesthetic claims and tend to see aesthetic reasons as a weak basis for preserving natural objects. Yet the moral imperative not to destroy unique aesthetic objects and even nonunique ones is an onerous one that is well ingrained into common practice—witness the worldwide establishment of national parks, preserves, forests, and wildlife areas.

Rather than attempting to transcend all views of natural objects as instrumental by grafting onto nature a mystical intrinsic value that can be buttressed only by poetic rhetoric, it would be far better to nurture public appreciation of subtle instrumental value, especially aesthetic value. People can learn to appreciate the unique beauty of a desert, or of a fragile ecosystem, or even of a noxious creature like a tick, when they understand the complexity and history therein and can read the story each life form contains. I am reminded of a colleague in parasitology who is loath to destroy worms he has studied upon completing his research because he has aesthetically learned to value their complexity of structure, function, and evolutionary history and role.

It is important to note that the attribution of value to nonsentient natural objects as a relational property arising out of their significance (recognized or not) for sentient beings does not denigrate the value of natural objects. Indeed, this attribution does not even imply that the interests or desires of individual sentient beings always trump concern for nonsentient ones. Our legal system has, for example, valuable and irreplaceable property laws that forbid owners of aesthetic objects, say a collection of Vincent Van Gogh paintings, to destroy them at will, say by adding them to one's funeral pyre. To be sure, this restriction on people's right to dispose of their own property arises out of a recognition of the value of these objects to other humans, but this is surely quite sensible. How else would one justify such a restriction? Nor, as we said earlier, need one limit the value of natural objects to their relationship to humans. Philosophically, one could, for example, sensibly (and commonsensically) argue for preservation of acreage from the golf-course developer because failure to do so would mean the destruction of thousands of sentient creatures' habitats—a major infringement of their interests—while building the golf course would fulfill the rarefied and inessential interests of a few.

Thus, in my view, one would accord moral concern to natural objects in a variety of ways, depending on the sort of object being considered. Moral status for individual animals would arise from their sentience. Moral status of species and their protection from humans would arise from the fact that a species is a collection of morally relevant individuals; moral status also would arise from the fact that humans have an aesthetic concern in not letting a unique and irreplaceable aesthetic object (or group of objects) disappear forever from our *Umwelt* (environment). Concern for wilderness areas, mountains, deserts, and so on would arise from their survival value for sentient animals as well as from their aesthetic value for humans. (Some writers have suggested that this aesthetic value is so great as to be essential to human mental/physical health, a point perfectly compatible with my position.[7]

Nothing in what I have said as yet tells us how to weigh conflicting interests, whether between humans and other sentient creatures or between human desires and environmental protection. How does one weigh the aesthetic concern of those who oppose blasting away part of a cliff against the pragmatic concern of those who wish to build on a cliffside? But the problem of weighing is equally thorny in traditional ethics—witness lifeboat questions or questions concerning the allocation of scarce medical resources. Nor does the intrinsic value approach help in adjudicating such issues. How does one weigh the alleged intrinsic value of a cliffside against the interests of the (intrinsic-value-bearing) homebuilders?

Furthermore, the intrinsic value view can lead to results that are repugnant to common sense and ordinary moral consciousness. Thus, for example, it follows from what has been suggested by one intrinsic value theorist that if a migratory herd of plentiful elk were passing through an area containing an endangered species of moss, it would be not only permissible but obligatory to kill the elk in order to protect the moss because in one case we would lose a species, in another "merely" individuals.[8] In my view, such a case has a less paradoxical resolution. Destruction of the moss does not matter to the moss, whereas elk presumably care about living or being injured. Therefore, one would give prima facie priority to the elk. This might presumably be trumped if, for example, the moss were a substratum from which was extracted an ingredient necessary to stop a raging, lethal epidemic in humans or animals. But such cases—and indeed most cases of conflicting interests—must be decided on the actual occasion. These cases are decided by a careful examination of the facts of the situation. Thus, our suggestion of a basis for environmental ethics does not qualitatively change the situation from that of current ethical deliberation, whereas granting intrinsic value to natural objects would leave us with a "whole new ball game"—and one where we do not know the rules.

In sum, then, the question of environmental ethics . . . must be analyzed into two discrete components. First are those questions that pertain to direct objects of moral concern—nonhuman animals whose sentience we have good reason to suspect—and that require the application of traditional moral notions to a hitherto ignored domain of moral objects. Second are those questions pertaining to natural objects or abstract natural objects. Although it is nonsensical to attribute intrinsic or direct moral value to these objects, they nonetheless must become (and are indeed becoming) central to our social moral deliberations. This centrality derives from our increasing recognition of the far-reaching and sometimes subtle instrumental value these objects have for humans and animals. Knowing that contamination of remote desert areas by pollutants can destroy unique panoplies of fragile beauty, or that dumping wastes into the ocean can destroy a potential source of antibiotics, or that building a pipeline can have undreamed-of harmful effects goes a long way toward making us think twice about these activities—a far longer way than endowing them with quasi-mystical rhetorical status subject to (and begging for) positivistic torpedoing. . . .

NOTES

1 See the chapters in Tom Regan, *All That Dwell Therein* (Berkeley: University of California Press, 1982).

2 See Aldo Leopold, *A Sand County Almanac* (Oxford: Oxford University Press, 1949); J. Baird Callicott, "Animal Liberation: A Triangular Affair," *Environmental Ethics* 2 (1980):311–338; Holmes Rolston III, *Philosophy Gone Wild* (Buffalo, N.Y.: Prometheus Books, 1986).

3 See the discussions of this point in Peter Singer, *Animal Liberation* (New York: New York Review of Books, 1975); and B. Rollin, *Animal Rights and Human Morality* (Buffalo, N.Y.: Prometheus Books, 1981).

4 See my "Animal Pain," in M. Fox and L. Mickley (eds.), *Advances in Animal Welfare Science 1985* (The Hague; Martinus Nijhoff, 1985); and my "Animal Consciousness and Scientific Change," *New Ideas in Psychology* 4, no. 2 (1986):141–152, as well as the replies to the latter by P. K. Feyerabend, H. Rachlin, and T. Leahey in the same issue, p. 153. See

also my [*The Unheeded Cry: Animal Consciousness, Animal Pain, and Science* (Oxford: Oxford University Press, 1989)].

5 See my *Animal Rights,* Part I.

6 See the works mentioned in footnotes 1 and 2.

7 This point is made with great rhetorical force in Edward Abbey, *Desert Solitaire* (New York: Ballantine Books, 1971).

8 See Holmes Rolston, "Duties to Endangered Species," *Philosophy Gone Wild.*

QUESTIONS

1 Is Rollin correct in holding that only sentient beings have intrinsic value?

2 Do you agree that once we recognize the subtle instrumental value of ecosystems, forests, etc., we will have a very strong foundation for revising those human activities that damage or destroy nonsentient natural objects?

Deep Ecology

Bill Devall and George Sessions

Bill Devall is professor emeritus of sociology at Humboldt State University (California). He is the author of *Simple in Means, Rich in Ends: Practicing Deep Ecology* (1988). George Sessions is chair of the philosophy department at Sierra College (California). He is the editor of *Deep Ecology for the Twenty-First Century* (1995). Devall and Sessions are coauthors of *Deep Ecology: Living as if Nature Mattered* (1985).

Devall and Sessions present deep ecology as a systematic alternative to "the dominant worldview of technocratic-industrial societies." They identify *self-realization* and *biocentric equality* as the two basic norms or intuitions underlying deep ecology. The norm of self-realization challenges the ordinary (Western) understanding of the self and ultimately requires each of us to identify with the nonhuman world. The norm of biocentric equality attributes equal intrinsic worth to "all organisms and entities in the ecosphere." Devall and Sessions also identify a set of eight principles considered basic to deep ecology. A commentary is then provided to explain each of the eight principles.

The term *deep ecology* was coined by Arne Naess in his 1973 article, "The Shallow and the Deep, Long-Range Ecology Movements."[1] Naess was attempting to describe the deeper, more spiritual approach to Nature exemplified in the writings of Aldo Leopold and Rachel Carson. He thought that this deeper approach resulted from a more sensitive openness to ourselves and nonhuman life around us. The essence

Reprinted with permission of the publisher from Bill Devall and George Sessions, *Deep Ecology: Living as if Nature Mattered* (Salt Lake City: Gibbs M. Smith, Inc., Peregrine Smith Books, 1985), pp. 65–73.

of deep ecology is to keep asking more searching questions about human life, society, and Nature as in the Western philosophical tradition of Socrates. As examples of this deep questioning, Naess points out "that we ask why and how, where others do not. For instance, ecology as a science does not ask what kind of a society would be the best for maintaining a particular ecosystem—that is considered a question for value theory, for politics, for ethics." Thus deep ecology goes beyond the so-called factual scientific level to the level of self and Earth wisdom.

Deep ecology goes beyond a limited piecemeal shallow approach to environmental problems and attempts to articulate a comprehensive religious and philosophical worldview. The foundations of deep ecology are the basic intuitions and experiencing of ourselves and Nature which comprise ecological consciousness. Certain outlooks on politics and public policy flow naturally from this consciousness. And in the context of this book, we discuss the minority tradition as the type of community most conducive both to cultivating ecological consciousness and to asking the basic questions of values and ethics addressed in these pages.

Many of these questions are perennial philosophical and religious questions faced by humans in all cultures over the ages. What does it mean to be a unique human individual? How can the individual self maintain and increase its uniqueness while also being an inseparable aspect of the whole system wherein there are no sharp breaks between self and the *other?* An ecological perspective, in this deeper sense, results in what Theodore Roszak calls "an awakening of wholes greater than the sum of their parts. In spirit, the discipline is contemplative and therapeutic."[2]

Ecological consciousness and deep ecology are in sharp contrast with the dominant worldview of technocratic-industrial societies which regards humans as isolated and fundamentally separate from the rest of Nature, as superior to, and in charge of, the rest of creation. But the view of humans as separate and superior to the rest of Nature is only part of larger cultural patterns. For thousands of years, Western culture has become increasingly obsessed with the idea of *dominance:* with dominance of humans over nonhuman Nature, masculine over the feminine, wealthy and powerful over the poor, with the dominance of the West over non-Western cultures. Deep ecological consciousness allows us to see through these erroneous and dangerous illusions.

For deep ecology, the study of our place in the Earth household includes the study of ourselves as part of the organic whole. Going beyond a narrowly materialist scientific understanding of reality, the spiritual and the material aspects of reality fuse together. While the leading intellectuals of the dominant worldview have tended to view religion as "just superstition," and have looked upon ancient spiritual practice and enlightenment, such as found in Zen Buddhism, as essentially subjective, the search for deep ecological consciousness is the search for a more objective consciousness and state of being through an active deep questioning and meditative process and way of life.

Many people have asked these deeper questions and cultivated ecological consciousness within the context of different spiritual traditions—Christianity, Taoism, Buddhism, and Native American rituals, for example. While differing greatly in other regards, many in these traditions agree with the basic principles of deep ecology.

Warwick Fox, an Australian philosopher, has succinctly expressed the central intuition of deep ecology: "It is the idea that we can make no firm ontological divide in the field of existence: That there is no bifurcation in reality between the human and the non-human realms . . . to the extent that we perceive boundaries, we fall short of deep ecological consciousness."[3]

From this most basic insight or characteristic of deep ecological consciousness, Arne Naess has developed two *ultimate norms* or intuitions which are themselves not derivable from other principles or intuitions. They are arrived at by the deep questioning process and reveal the importance of moving to the philosophical and religious level of wisdom. They cannot be validated, of course, by the methodology of modern science based on its usual mechanistic assumptions and its very narrow definition of data. These ultimate norms are *self-realization* and *biocentric equality.*

I SELF-REALIZATION

In keeping with the spiritual traditions of many of the world's religions, the deep ecology norm of self-realization goes beyond the modern Western *self* which is defined as an isolated ego striving primarily for hedonistic gratification or for a narrow sense of individual salvation in this life or the next. This socially programmed sense of the narrow self or social self dislocates us, and leaves us prey to whatever fad or fashion is prevalent in our society or social reference group. We are thus robbed of beginning the search for our unique spiritual/biological personhood. Spiritual growth, or unfolding, begins when we cease to understand or see ourselves as isolated and narrow competing egos and begin to identify with other humans from our family and friends to, eventually, our species. But the deep ecology sense of self requires a further maturity and growth, an identification which goes beyond humanity to include the nonhuman world. We must see beyond our narrow contemporary cultural assumptions and values, and the conventional wisdom of our time and place, and this is best achieved by the meditative deep questioning process. Only in this way can we hope to attain full mature personhood and uniqueness.

A nurturing nondominating society can help in the "real work" of becoming a whole person. The "real work" can be summarized symbolically as the realization of "self-in-Self" where "Self" stands for organic wholeness. This process of the full unfolding of the self can also be summarized by the phrase, "No one is saved until we are all saved," where the phrase "one" includes not only me, an individual human, but all humans, whales, grizzly bears, whole rain forest ecosystems, mountains and rivers, the tiniest microbes in the soil, and so on.

II BIOCENTRIC EQUALITY

The intuition of biocentric equality is that all things in the biosphere have an equal right to live and blossom and to reach their own individual forms of unfolding and self-realization within the larger Self-realization. This basic intuition is that all organisms and entities in the ecosphere, as parts of the interrelated whole, are equal in intrinsic worth. Naess suggests that biocentric equality as an intuition is true in principle, although in the process of living, all species use each other as food, shelter, etc. Mutual predation is a biological fact of life, and many of the world's religions have struggled with the spiritual implications of this. Some animal liberationists who attempt to side-step this problem by advocating vegetarianism are forced to say that the entire plant kingdom including rain forests have no right to their own existence. This evasion flies in the face of the basic intuition of equality.[4] Aldo Leopold expressed this intuition when he said humans are "plain citizens" of the biotic community, not lord and master over all other species.

Biocentric equality is intimately related to the all-inclusive Self-realization in the sense that if we harm the rest of Nature then we are harming ourselves. There are no boundaries and everything is interrelated. But insofar as we perceive things as individual organisms or entities, the insight draws us to respect all human and nonhuman individuals in their own right as parts of the whole without feeling the need to set up hierarchies of species with humans at the top.

The practical implications of this intuition or norm suggest that we should live with minimum rather than maximum impact on other species and on the Earth in general. Thus we see another aspect of our guiding principle: "simple in means, rich in ends." . . .

A fuller discussion of the biocentric norm as it unfolds itself in practice begins with the realization that we, as individual humans, and as communities of humans, have vital needs which go beyond such basics as food, water, and shelter to include love, play, creative expression, intimate relationships with a particular landscape (or Nature taken in its entirety) as well as intimate relationships with other humans, and the vital need for spiritual growth, for becoming a mature human being.

Our vital material needs are probably more simple than many realize. In technocratic-industrial societies there is overwhelming propaganda and advertising which encourages false needs and destructive desires designed to foster increased production and consumption of goods. Most of this actually diverts us from facing reality in an objective way and from beginning the "real work" of spiritual growth and maturity.

Many people who do not see themselves as supporters of deep ecology nevertheless recognize an overriding vital human need for a healthy and high-quality natural environment for humans, if not for all life, with minimum intrusion of toxic waste, nuclear radiation from human enterprises, minimum acid rain and smog, and enough free flowing wilderness so humans can get in touch with their sources, the natural rhythms and the flow of time and place.

Drawing from the minority tradition and from the wisdom of many who have offered the insight of interconnectedness, we recognize that deep ecologists can offer suggestions for gaining maturity and encouraging the processes of harmony with Nature, but that there is no grand solution which is guaranteed to save us from ourselves.

The ultimate norms of deep ecology suggest a view of the nature of reality and our place as an individual (many in the one) in the larger scheme of things. They cannot be fully grasped intellectually but are ultimately experiential. . . .

As a brief summary of our position thus far, figure 1 summarizes the contrast between the dominant worldview and deep ecology.

Figure 1

Dominant Worldview	*Deep Ecology*
Dominance over Nature	Harmony with Nature
Natural environment as resource for humans	All nature has intrinsic worth/biospecies equality
Material/economic growth for growing human population	Elegantly simple material needs (material goals serving the larger goal of self-realization)
Belief in ample resource reserves	Earth "supplies" limited
High technological progress and solutions	Appropriate technology; nondominating science
Consumerism	Doing with enough/recycling
National/centralized community	Minority tradition/bioregion

III BASIC PRINCIPLES OF DEEP ECOLOGY

In April 1984, during the advent of spring and John Muir's birthday, George Sessions and Arne Naess summarized fifteen years of thinking on the principles of deep ecology while camping in Death Valley, California. In this great and special place, they articulated these principles in a literal, somewhat neutral way, hoping that they would be understood and accepted by persons coming from different philosophical and religious positions.

Readers are encouraged to elaborate their own versions of deep ecology, clarify key concepts and think through the consequences of acting from these principles.

Basic Principles

1 The well-being and flourishing of human and nonhuman Life on Earth have value in themselves (synonyms: intrinsic value, inherent value). These values are independent of the usefulness of the nonhuman world for human purposes.

2 Richness and diversity of life forms contribute to the realization of these values and are also values in themselves.

3 Humans have no right to reduce this richness and diversity except to satisfy *vital* needs.

4 The flourishing of human life and cultures is compatible with a substantial decrease of the human population. The flourishing of nonhuman life requires such a decrease.

5 Present human interference with the nonhuman world is excessive, and the situation is rapidly worsening.

6 Policies must therefore be changed. These policies affect basic economic, technological, and ideological structures. The resulting state of affairs will be deeply different from the present.

7 The ideological change is mainly that of appreciating *life quality* (dwelling in situations of inherent value) rather than adhering to an increasingly higher standard of living. There will be a profound awareness of the difference between big and great.

8 Those who subscribe to the foregoing points have an obligation directly or indirectly to try to implement the necessary changes.

Naess and Sessions Provide Comments on the Basic Principles

RE (1)   This formulation refers to the biosphere, or more accurately, to the ecosphere as a whole. This includes individuals, species, populations, habitat, as well as human and nonhuman cultures. From our current knowledge of all-pervasive intimate relationships, this implies a fundamental deep concern and respect. Ecological processes of the planet should, on the whole, remain intact. "The world environment should remain 'natural' " (Gary Snyder).

The term "life" is used here in a more comprehensive nontechnical way to refer also to what biologists classify as "nonliving"; rivers (watersheds), landscapes, ecosystems. For supporters of deep ecology, slogans such as "Let the river live" illustrate this broader usage so common in most cultures.

Inherent value as used in (1) is common in deep ecology literature ("The presence of inherent value in a natural object is independent of any awareness, interest, or appreciation of it by a conscious being.")[5]

RE (2)   More technically, this is a formulation concerning diversity and complexity. From an ecological standpoint, complexity and symbiosis are conditions for maximizing diversity. So-called simple, lower, or primitive species of plants and animals contribute essentially to the richness and diversity of life. They have value in themselves and are not merely steps toward the so-called higher or rational life forms. The second principle presupposes that life itself, as a process over evolutionary time, implies an increase of diversity and richness. The refusal to acknowledge that some life forms have greater or lesser intrinsic value than others (see points 1 and 2) runs counter to the formulations of some ecological philosophers and New Age writers.

Complexity, as referred to here, is different from complication. Urban life may be more complicated than life in a natural setting without being more complex in the sense of multifaceted quality.

RE (3)   The term "vital need" is left deliberately vague to allow for considerable latitude in judgment. Differences in climate and related factors, together with differences in the structures of societies as they now exist, need to be considered (for some Eskimos, snowmobiles are necessary today to satisfy vital needs).

People in the materially richest countries cannot be expected to reduce their excessive interference with the nonhuman world to a moderate level overnight. The stabilization and reduction of the human population will take time. Interim strategies need to be developed. But this in no way excuses the present complacency—the extreme seriousness of our current situation must first be realized. But the longer we wait the more drastic will be the measures needed. Until deep changes are made, substantial decreases in richness and diversity are liable to occur: the rate of extinction of species will be ten to one hundred times greater than any other period of earth history.

RE (4)   The United Nations Fund for Population Activities in their State of World Population Report (1984) said that high human population growth rates (over 2.0 percent annum) in many developing countries "were diminishing the quality of life for many millions of people." During the decade 1974–1984, the world population grew by nearly 800 million—more than the size of India. "And we will be adding about one Bangladesh (population 93 million) per annum between now and the year 2000."

The report noted that "The growth rate of the human population has declined for the first time in human history. But at the same time, the number of people being added to the human population is bigger than at any time in history because the population base is larger."

Most of the nations in the developing world (including India and China) have as their official government policy the goal of reducing the rate of human population increase, but there are debates over the types of measures to take (contraception, abortion, etc.) consistent with human rights and feasibility.

The report concludes that if all governments set specific population targets as public policy to help alleviate poverty and advance the quality of life, the current situation could be improved.

As many ecologists have pointed out, it is also absolutely crucial to curb population growth in the so-called developed (i.e., overdeveloped) industrial societies. Given the tremendous rate of consumption and waste production of individuals in these societies, they represent a much greater threat and impact on the biosphere per capita than individuals in Second and Third World countries.

RE (5)   This formulation is mild. For a realistic assessment of the situation, see the unabbreviated version of the I.U.C.N.'s *World Conservation Strategy*. There are other works to be highly recommended, such as Gerald Barney's *Global 2000 Report to the President of the United States.*

The slogan of "noninterference" does not imply that humans should not modify some ecosystems as do other species. Humans have modified the earth and will probably continue to do so. At issue is the nature and extent of such interference.

The fight to preserve and extend areas of wilderness or near-wilderness should continue and should focus on the general ecological functions of these areas (one such function: large wilderness areas are required in the biosphere to allow for continued evolutionary speciation of animals and plants). Most present designated wilderness areas and game preserves are not large enough to allow for such speciation.

RE (6)   Economic growth as conceived and implemented today by the industrial states is incompatible with (1)–(5). There is only a faint resemblance between ideal sustainable forms of economic growth and present policies of the industrial societies. And "sustainable" still means "sustainable in relation to humans."

Present ideology tends to value things because they are scarce and because they have a commodity value. There is prestige in vast consumption and waste (to mention only several relevant factors).

Whereas "self-determination," "local community," and "think globally, act locally," will remain key terms in the ecology of human societies, nevertheless the implementation of deep changes requires increasingly global action—action across borders.

Governments in Third World countries (with the exception of Costa Rica and a few others) are uninterested in deep ecological issues. When the governments of industrial societies try to promote ecological measures through Third World governments, practically nothing is accomplished (e.g., with problems of desertification). Given this situation, support for global action through nongovernmental international organizations becomes increasingly important. Many of these organizations are able to act globally "from grassroots to grassroots," thus avoiding negative governmental interference.

Cultural diversity today requires advanced technology, that is, techniques that advance the basic goals of each culture. So-called soft, intermediate, and alternative technologies are steps in this direction.

RE (7)   Some economists criticize the term "quality of life" because it is supposed to be vague. But on closer inspection, what they consider to be vague is actually the nonquantitative nature of the term. One cannot quantify adequately what is important for the quality of life as discussed here, and there is no need to do so.

RE (8)   There is ample room for different opinions about priorities: what should be done first, what next? What is most urgent? What is clearly necessary as opposed to what is highly desirable but not absolutely pressing?

NOTES

1 Arne Naess, "The Shallow and The Deep, Long-Range Ecology Movements: A Summary," *Inquiry* 16 (Oslo, 1973), pp. 95–100.
2 Theodore Roszak, *Where the Wasteland Ends* (New York: Anchor, 1972).
3 Warwick Fox, "Deep Ecology: A New Philosophy of Our Time?" *The Ecologist,* v. 14, 5–6, 1984, pp. 194–200. Arne Naess replies, "Intuition, Intrinsic Value and Deep Ecology," *The Ecologist,* v. 14, 5–6, 1984, pp. 201–204.
4 Tom Regan, *The Case for Animal Rights* (New York: Random House, 1983). For excellent critiques of the animal rights movement, see John Rodman, "The Liberation of Nature?" *Inquiry* 20 (Oslo, 1977). J. Baird Callicott, "Animal Liberation," *Environmental Ethics* 2, 4, (1980); see also John Rodman, "Four Forms of Ecological Consciousness Reconsidered" in T. Attig and D. Scherer, eds., *Ethics and the Environment* (Englewood Cliffs, N.J.: Prentice-Hall, 1983).
5 Tom Regan, "The Nature and Possibility of an Environmental Ethic," *Environmental Ethics* 3 (1981), pp. 19–34.

QUESTIONS

1 To what extent would you endorse the two basic norms of deep ecology?
2 To what extent would you endorse the eight basic principles of deep ecology?
3 Critics sometimes complain that deep ecology is an "anti-human" philosophy. Is there any substance to this charge?

Radical American Environmentalism and Wilderness Preservation: A Third World Critique

Ramachandra Guha

Ramachandra Guha is reader in sociology at the Institute of Economic Growth in Delhi, India. A sociologist and historian, he has written extensively on the historical roots of ecological conflict and on environmental ideas in East and West. He is the author of *The Unquiet Woods: Ecological Change and Peasant Resistance in the Himalaya* (1990) and the coauthor of *This Fissured Land: An Ecological History of India* (1993).

Guha advances a critique of the American deep ecology movement from a Third World perspective. He states and criticizes three of the central tenets he identifies with American deep ecology: (1) its distinction between anthropocentric and biocentric approaches to environmental issues, (2) its focus on wilderness preservation, and (3) its conviction that the American version of deep ecology represents the most radical trend in environmentalism. In respect to (1), Guha argues that this distinction is of little use in helping us to understand the dynamics of environmental degradation. In respect to (2), he maintains that the implementation of the wilderness agenda is causing serious deprivation in Third World countries. In respect to (3), Guha points out that American deep ecologists fail to seriously question the ecological and sociopolitical basis of the consumer society, even though its consumerism is responsible for so much environmental degradation. He gives examples from other cultures (Germany and India) to illustrate what he considers a far more radical environmentalism—one that emphasizes equity and the integration of ecological concerns with livelihood and work.

I INTRODUCTION

The respected radical journalist Kirkpatrick Sale recently celebrated "the passion of a new and growing movement that has become disenchanted with the environmental establishment and has in recent years mounted a serious and sweeping attack on it—style, substance, systems, sensibilities and all."[1] The vision of those whom Sale calls the "New Ecologists"—and what I refer to in this article as deep ecology—is a compelling one. Decrying the narrowly economic goals of mainstream environmentalism, this new movement aims at nothing less than a philosophical and cultural revolution in human attitudes toward nature. In contrast to the conventional lobbying efforts of environmental professionals based in Washington, it proposes a militant defence of "Mother Earth," an unflinching opposition to human attacks on undisturbed wilderness. With their goals ranging from the spiritual to the political, the adherents of deep ecology span a wide spectrum of the American environmen-

Reprinted with permission of the author and the publisher from *Environmental Ethics,* vol. 11 (Spring 1989), pp. 71–76, 78–83.

tal movement. As Sale correctly notes, this emerging strand has in a matter of a few years made its presence felt in a number of fields: from academic philosophy (as in the journal *Environmental Ethics*) to popular environmentalism (for example, the group Earth First!).

In this article I develop a critique of deep ecology from the perspective of a sympathetic outsider. . . . . I speak admittedly as a partisan, but of the environmental movement in India, a country with an ecological diversity comparable to the U.S., but with a radically dissimilar cultural and social history.

My treatment of deep ecology is primarily historical and sociological, rather than philosophical, in nature. Specifically, I examine the cultural rootedness of a philosophy that likes to present itself in universalistic terms. I make two main arguments: first, that deep ecology is uniquely American, and despite superficial similarities in rhetorical style, the social and political goals of radical environmentalism in other cultural contexts (e.g., West Germany and India) are quite different; second, that the social consequences of putting deep ecology into practice on a worldwide basis (what its practitioners are aiming for) are very grave indeed.

II THE TENETS OF DEEP ECOLOGY

While I am aware that the term *deep ecology* was coined by the Norwegian philosopher Arne Naess, this article refers specifically to the American variant.[2] Adherents of the deep ecological perspective in this country, while arguing intensely among themselves over its political and philosophical implications, share some fundamental premises about human-nature interactions. As I see it, [the following are three of] the defining characteristics of deep ecology:

First, deep ecology argues, that the environmental movement must shift from an "anthropocentric" to a "biocentric" perspective. In many respects, an acceptance of the primacy of this distinction constitutes the litmus test of deep ecology. A considerable effort is expended by deep ecologists in showing that the dominant motif in Western philosophy has been anthropocentric—i.e., the belief that man and his works are the center of the universe—and conversely, in identifying those lonely thinkers (Leopold, Thoreau, Muir, Aldous Huxley, Santayana, etc.) who, in assigning man a more humble place in the natural order, anticipated deep ecological thinking. In the political realm, meanwhile, establishment environmentalism (shallow ecology) is chided for casting its arguments in human-centered terms. Preserving nature, the deep ecologists say, has an intrinsic worth quite apart from any benefits preservation may convey to future human generations. The anthropocentric-biocentric distinction is accepted as axiomatic by deep ecologists, it structures their discourse, and much of the present discussion remains mired within it.

The second characteristic of deep ecology is its focus on the preservation of unspoilt wilderness—and the restoration of degraded areas to a more pristine condition—to the relative (and sometimes absolute) neglect of other issues on the environmental agenda. I later identify the cultural roots and portentous consequences of this obsession with wilderness. For the moment, let me indicate three distinct sources from which it springs. Historically, it represents a playing out of the preservationist (read *radical*) and utilitarian (read *reformist*) dichotomy that has plagued American environmentalism since the turn of the century. Morally, it is an imperative that follows from the biocentric perspective; other species of plants and animals, and nature itself, have an intrinsic right to exist. And finally, the preservation of wilderness also turns on a scientific argument—viz., the value of biological diversity in stabilizing ecological regimes and in retaining a gene pool for future generations. Truly radical policy proposals have been put forward by deep ecologists on the basis of these arguments. The influential poet Gary Snyder, for example, would like to see a 90 percent reduction in human populations to allow a restoration of pristine environments, while others have argued forcefully that a large portion of the globe must be immediately cordoned off from human beings.[3] . . .

Third, deep ecologists, whatever their internal differences, share the belief that they are the "leading edge" of the environmental movement. As the polarity of the shallow/deep and anthropocentric/biocentric distinctions makes clear, they see themselves as the spiritual, philosophical, and political vanguard of American and world environmentalism.

III TOWARD A CRITIQUE

Although I analyze each of these tenets independently, it is important to recognize, as deep ecologists are fond of remarking in reference to nature, the interconnectedness and unity of these individual themes.

1 Insofar as it has begun to act as a check on man's arrogance and ecological hubris, the transition from an anthropocentric (human-centered) to a biocentric (humans as only one element in the ecosystem) view in both religious and scientific traditions is only to be welcomed. What is unacceptable are the radical conclusions drawn by deep ecology, in particular, that intervention in nature should be guided primarily by the need to preserve biotic integrity rather than by the needs of humans. The latter for deep ecologists is anthropocentric, the former biocentric. This dichotomy is, however, of very little use in understanding the dynamics of environmental degradation. The two fundamental ecological problems facing the globe are (i) overconsumption by the industrialized world and by urban elites in the Third World and (ii) growing militarization, both in a short-term sense (i.e., ongoing regional wars) and in a long-term sense (i.e., the arms race and the prospect of nuclear annihilation). Neither of these problems has any tangible connection to the anthropocentric-biocentric distinction. Indeed, the agents of these processes would barely comprehend this philosophical dichotomy. The proximate causes of the ecologically wasteful characteristics of industrial society and of militarization are far more mundane: at an aggregate level, the dialectic of economic and political structures, and at a micro-level, the life style choices of individuals. These causes cannot be reduced, whatever the level of analysis, to a deeper anthropocentric attitude toward nature; on the contrary, by constituting a grave threat to human survival, the ecological degradation they cause does not even serve the best interests of human beings! If my identification of the major dangers to the integrity of the natural world is correct, invoking the bogy of anthropocentrism is at best irrelevant and at worst a dangerous obfuscation.

2 If the above dichotomy is irrelevant, the emphasis on wilderness is positively harmful when applied to the Third World. If in the U.S. the preservationist/utilitarian division is seen as mirroring the conflict between "people" and "interests," in countries such as India the situation is very nearly the reverse. Because India is a long settled and densely populated country in which agrarian populations have a finely balanced relationship with nature, the setting aside of wilderness areas has resulted in a direct transfer of resources from the poor to the rich. Thus, Project Tiger, a network of parks hailed by the international conservation community as an outstanding success, sharply posits the interests of the tiger against those of poor peasants living in and around the reserve. The designation of tiger reserves was made possible only by the physical displacement of existing villages and their inhabitants; their management requires the continuing exclusion of peasants and livestock. The initial impetus for setting up parks for the tiger and other large mammals such as the rhinoceros and elephant came from two social groups, first, a class of ex-hunters turned conservationists belonging mostly to the declining Indian feudal elite and second, representatives of international agencies, such as the World Wildlife Fund (WWF) and the International Union for the Conservation of Nature and Natural Resources (IUCN), seeking to transplant the American system of national parks onto Indian soil. In no case have the needs of the local population been taken into account, and as in many parts of Africa, the designated wildlands are managed primarily for the benefit of rich tourists. Until very recently, wildlands preservation has been identified with environmentalism by the state and the conservation elite; in consequence, environmental problems that impinge far more directly on the lives of the poor— e.g., fuel, fodder, water shortages, soil erosion, and air and water pollution—have not been adequately addressed.[4]

Deep ecology provides, perhaps unwittingly, a justification for the continuation of such narrow and inequitable conservation practices under a newly acquired radical guise. Increasingly, the international conservation elite is using the philosophical, moral, and scientific arguments used by deep ecologists in advancing their wilderness crusade. A striking but by no means atypical example is the recent plea by a prominent American biologist for the takeover of large portions of the globe by the author and his scientific colleagues. Writing in a prestigious scientific forum, the *Annual Review of Ecology and Systematics,* Daniel Janzen argues that only biologists have the competence to decide how the tropical landscape should be used. As "the representatives of the natural world," biologists are "in charge of the future of tropical ecology," and only they have the expertise and mandate to "determine whether the tropical agroscape is to be populated only by humans, their mutualists, commensals, and parasites, or whether it will also contain some islands of the greater nature—the nature that spawned humans, yet has been vanquished by them." Janzen exhorts his colleagues to advance their territorial claims on the tropical world more forcefully, warning that the very existence of these areas is at stake: "if biologists want a tropics in which to biologize, they are going to have to buy it with care, energy, effort, strategy, tactics, time, and cash."[5]

This frankly imperialist manifesto highlights the multiple dangers of the preoccupation with wilderness preservation that is characteristic of deep ecology. As I have suggested, it seriously compounds the neglect by the American movement of far more pressing environmental problems within the Third World. But perhaps more importantly, and in a more insidious fashion, it also provides an impetus to the imperialist yearning of Western biologists and their financial sponsors, organizations such as the WWF and IUCN. The wholesale transfer of a movement culturally rooted in American conservation history can only result in the social uprooting of human populations in other parts of the globe. . . .

3 How radical, finally, are the deep ecologists? Notwithstanding their self-image and strident rhetoric (in which the label "shallow ecology" has an opprobrium similar to that reserved for "social democratic" by Marxist-Leninists), even within the American context their radicalism is limited and it manifests itself quite differently elsewhere.

To my mind, deep ecology is best viewed as a radical trend within the wilderness preservation movement. Although advancing philosophical rather than aesthetic arguments and encouraging political militancy rather than negotiation, its practical emphasis—viz., preservation of unspoilt nature—is virtually identical. For the mainstream movement, the function of wilderness is to provide a temporary antidote to modern civilization. As a special institution within an industrialized society, the national park "provides an opportunity for respite, contrast, contemplation, and affirmation of values for those who live most of their lives in the workaday world."[6] Indeed, the rapid increase in visitations to the national parks in postwar America is a direct consequence of economic expansion. The emergence of a popular interest in wilderness sites, the historian Samuel Hays points out, was "not a throwback to the primitive, but an integral part of the modern standard of living as people sought to add new 'amenity' and 'aesthetic' goals and desires to their earlier preoccupation with necessities and conveniences."[7]

Here, the enjoyment of nature is an integral part of the consumer society. The private automobile (and the life style it has spawned) is in many respects the ultimate ecological villain, and an untouched wilderness the prototype of ecological harmony; yet, for most Americans it is perfectly consistent to drive a thousand miles to spend a holiday in a national park. They possess a vast, beautiful, and sparsely populated continent and are also able to draw upon the natural resources of large portions of the globe by virtue of their economic and political dominance. In consequence, America can simultaneously enjoy the material benefits of an expanding economy and the aesthetic benefits of unspoilt nature. The two poles of "wilderness" and "civilization" mutually coexist in an internally coherent whole, and philosophers of both poles are assigned a prominent place in this culture. Paradoxically as it may seem, it is no accident that Star Wars technology and deep ecology both find their fullest expression in that leading sector of Western civilization, California.

Deep ecology runs parallel to the consumer society without seriously questioning its ecological and socio-political basis. In its celebration of American wilderness, it also displays an uncomfortable convergence with the prevailing climate of nationalism in the American wilderness movement. For spokesmen such as the historian Roderick Nash, the national park system is America's distinctive cultural contribution to the world, reflective not merely of its economic but of its philosophical and ecological maturity as well. In what Walter Lippman called the American century, the "American invention of national parks" must be exported worldwide. Betraying an economic determinism that would make even a Marxist shudder, Nash believes that environmental preservation is a "full stomach" phenomenon that is confined to the rich, urban, and sophisticated. Nonetheless, he hopes that "the less developed nations may eventually evolve economically and intellectually to the point where nature preservation is more than a business."[8]

The error which Nash makes (and which deep ecology in some respects encourages) is to equate environmental protection with the protection of wilderness. This is a distinctively American notion, born out of a unique social and environmental history. The archetypal concerns of radical environmentalists in other cultural contexts are in fact quite different. The German Greens, for example, have elaborated a devastating critique of industrial society which turns on the acceptance of environmental limits to growth. Pointing to the intimate links between industrialization, militarization, and conquest, the Greens argue that economic growth in the West has historically rested on the economic and ecological exploitation of the Third World. Rudolf Bahro is characteristically blunt:

> The working class here [in the West] is the richest lower class in the world. And if I look at the problem from the point of view of the whole of humanity, not just from that of Europe, then I must say that the metropolitan working class is the worst exploiting class in history. . . . What made poverty bearable in eighteenth or nineteenth-century Europe was the prospect of escaping it through exploitation of the periphery. But this is no longer a possibility, and continued industrialism in the Third World will mean poverty for whole generations and hunger for millions.[9]

Here the roots of global ecological problems lie in the disproportionate share of resources consumed by the industrialized countries as a whole *and* the urban elite within the Third World. Since it is impossible to reproduce an industrial monoculture worldwide, the ecological movement in the West must begin by cleaning up its own act. The Greens advocate the creation of a "no growth" economy, to be achieved by scaling down current (and clearly unsustainable) consumption levels. This radical shift in consumption and production patterns requires the creation of alternate economic and political structures—smaller in scale and more amenable to social participation—but it rests equally on a shift in cultural values. The expansionist character of modern Western man will have to give way to an ethic of renunciation and self-limitation, in which spiritual and communal values play an increasing role in sustaining social life. This revolution in cultural values, however, has as its point of departure an understanding of environmental processes quite different from deep ecology.

Many elements of the Green program find a strong resonance in countries such as India, where a history of Western colonialism and industrial development has benefited only a tiny elite while exacting tremendous social and environmental costs. The ecological battles presently being fought in India have as their epicenter the conflict over nature between the subsistence and largely rural sector and the vastly more powerful commercial-industrial sector. Perhaps the most celebrated of these battles

concerns the Chipko (Hug the Tree) movement, a peasant movement against defor-
estation in the Himalayan foothills. Chipko is only one of several movements that
have sharply questioned the nonsustainable demand being placed on the land and
vegetative base by urban centers and industry. These include opposition to large dams
by displaced peasants, the conflict between small artisan fishing and large-scale
trawler fishing for export, the countrywide movements against commercial forest operations, and opposition to industrial pollution among downstream agricultural and
fishing communities.[10]

Two features distinguish these environmental movements from their Western
counterparts. First, for the sections of society most critically affected by environmental degradation—poor and landless peasants, women, and tribals—it is a question of sheer survival, not of enhancing the quality of life. Second, and as a consequence, the environmental solutions they articulate deeply involve questions of
equity as well as economic and political redistribution. Highlighting these differences,
a leading Indian environmentalist stresses that "environmental protection per se is
of least concern to most of these groups. Their main concern is about the use of the
environment and who should benefit from it."[11] They seek to wrest control of nature
away from the state and the industrial sector and place it in the hands of rural communities who live within that environment but are increasingly denied access to it.
These communities have far more basic needs, their demands on the environment
are far less intense, and they can draw upon a reservoir of cooperative social institutions and local ecological knowledge in managing the "commons"—forests, grass-
lands, and the waters—on a sustainable basis. If colonial and capitalist expansion
has both accentuated social inequalities and signaled a precipitous fall in ecological
wisdom, an alternate ecology must rest on an alternate society and polity as well.

This brief overview of German and Indian environmentalism has some major implications for deep ecology. Both German and Indian environmental traditions allow
for a greater integration of ecological concerns with livelihood and work. They also
place a greater emphasis on equity and social justice (both within individual countries and on a global scale) on the grounds that in the absence of social regeneration
environmental regeneration has very little chance of succeeding. Finally, and perhaps most significantly, they have escaped the preoccupation with wilderness preservation so characteristic of American cultural and environmental history.

IV A HOMILY

In 1958, the economist J. K. Galbraith referred to overconsumption as the unasked
question of the American conservation movement. There is a marked selectivity, he
wrote, "in the conservationist's approach to materials consumption. If we are concerned about our great appetite for materials, it is plausible to seek to increase the
supply, to decrease waste, to make better use of the stocks available, and to develop
substitutes. But what of the appetite itself? Surely this is the ultimate source of the
problem. If it continues its geometric course, will it not one day have to be restrained? Yet in the literature of the resource problem this is the forbidden question.
Over it hangs a nearly total silence."[12]

The consumer economy and society have expanded tremendously in the three decades since Galbraith penned these words; yet his criticisms are nearly as valid today. I have said "nearly," for there are some hopeful signs. Within the environmental movement several dispersed groups are working to develop ecologically benign technologies and to encourage less wasteful life styles. Moreover, outside the self-defined boundaries of American environmentalism, opposition to the permanent war economy is being carried on by a peace movement that has a distinguished history and impeccable moral and political credentials.

It is precisely these (to my mind, most hopeful) components of the American social scene that are missing from deep ecology. In their widely noticed book, Bill Devall and George Sessions make no mention of militarization or the movements for peace, while activists whose practical focus is on developing ecologically responsible life styles (e.g., Wendell Berry) are derided as "falling short of deep ecological awareness."[13] A truly radical ecology in the American context ought to work toward a synthesis of the appropriate technology, alternate life style, and peace movements. By making the (largely spurious) anthropocentric-biocentric distinction central to the debate, deep ecologists may have appropriated the moral high ground, but they are at the same time doing a serious disservice to American and global environmentalism.

NOTES

1 Kirkpatrick Sale, "The Forest for the Trees: Can Today's Environmentalists Tell the Difference," *Mother Jones* 11, no. 8 (November 1986): 26.
2 One of the major criticisms I make in this essay concerns deep ecology's lack of concern with inequalities *within* human society. In the article in which he coined the term *deep ecology,* Naess himself expresses concerns about inequalities between and within nations. However, his concern with social cleavages and their impact on resource utilization patterns and ecological destruction is not very visible in the later writings of deep ecologists. See Arne Naess, "The Shallow and the Deep, Long-Range Ecology Movement: A Summary," *Inquiry* 16 (1973): 96 (I am grateful to Tom Birch for this reference).
3 Gary Snyder, quoted in Sale, "The Forest for the Trees," p. 32. See also Dave Foreman, "A Modest Proposal for a Wilderness System," *Whole Earth Review,* no. 53 (Winter 1986–87): 42–45.
4 See Centre for Science and Environment, *India: The State of the Environment 1982: A Citizens Report* (New Delhi: Centre for Science and Environment, 1982); R. Sukumar, "Elephant-Man Conflict in Karnataka," in Cecil Saldanha, ed., *The State of Karnataka's Environment* (Bangalore: Centre for Taxonomic Studies, 1985). For Africa, see the brilliant analysis by Helge Kjekshus, *Ecology Control and Economic Development in East African History* (Berkeley: University of California Press, 1977).
5 Daniel Janzen, "The Future of Tropical Ecology," *Annual Review of Ecology and Systematics* 17 (1986): 305–06; emphasis added.
6 Joseph Sax, *Mountains Without Handrails: Reflections on the National Parks* (Ann Arbor: University of Michigan Press, 1980), p. 42. Cf. also Peter Schmitt, *Back to Nature: The Arcadian Myth in Urban America* (New York: Oxford University Press, 1969), and Alfred Runte, *National Parks: The American Experience* (Lincoln: University of Nebraska Press, 1979).

7 Samuel Hays, "From Conservation to Environment: Environmental Politics in the United States since World War Two," *Environmental Review* 6 (1982): 21. See also the same author's book entitled *Beauty, Health and Permanence: Environmental Politics in the United States, 1955–85* (New York: Cambridge University Press, 1987).
8 Roderick Nash, *Wilderness and the American Mind,* 3rd ed. (New Haven: Yale University Press, 1982).
9 Rudolf Bahro, *From Red to Green* (London: Verso Books, 1984).
10 For an excellent review, see Anil Agarwal and Sunita Narain, eds., *India: The State of the Environment 1984–85: A Citizens Report* (New Delhi: Centre for Science and Environment, 1985). Cf. also Ramachandra Guha, *The Unquiet Woods: Ecological Change and Peasant Resistance in the Indian Himalaya* (Berkeley: University of California Press, 1990).
11 Anil Agarwal, "Human-Nature Interactions in a Third World Country," *The Environmentalist* 6, no. 3 (1986): 167.
12 John Kenneth Galbraith, "How Much Should a Country Consume?" in Henry Jarrett, ed., *Perspectives on Conservation* (Baltimore: Johns Hopkins Press, 1958), pp. 91–92.
13 Devall and Sessions, *Deep Ecology,* p. 122. For Wendell Berry's own assessment of deep ecology, see his "Amplications: Preserving Wildness," *Wilderness* 50 (Spring 1987): 39–40, 50–54.

QUESTIONS

1 Is overconsumption by the industrialized world and by urban elites in the Third World one of the most serious ecological problems we face today? If yes, what changes would you be willing to make in your life to help solve the problem?
2 Should the overcoming of inequalities in a society have priority over concerns such as the preservation of wilderness areas?

The Power and the Promise of Ecological Feminism

Karen J. Warren

Karen J. Warren is associate professor of philosophy and chair of the department of philosophy at Macalester College. She is the author of many articles on ecofeminism, including "Feminism and Ecology: Making Connections." She is also coeditor of *Environmental Philosophy: From Animal Rights to Radical Ecology* (1993) and editor of *Ecological Feminism* (1994).

Warren writes from the perspective of ecological feminism—the view that there are important connections between the domination of women and the domination of nonhuman nature. In her account of the logic of domination, she brings out

Reprinted with permission of the author and the publisher from *Environmental Ethics,* vol. 12 (Summer 1990), pp. 125–132, 134–138, 143–144.

some of the conceptual connections between these two kinds of domination in order to support her claims that (1) traditional feminism must expand to include ecological feminism and (2) ecological feminism provides a framework for developing a distinctively feminist environmental ethic. As part of her attempt to show what ecological feminism can bring to environmental ethics, Warren explains the argumentative significance of first person narrative with its commitment to care, kinship, and appropriate reciprocity.

INTRODUCTION

Ecological feminism (ecofeminism) has begun to receive a fair amount of attention lately as an alternative feminism and environmental ethic. Since Francoise d'Eaubonne introduced the term *ecofeminisme* in 1974 to bring attention to women's potential for bringing about an ecological revolution,[1] the term has been used in a variety of ways. As I use the term in this paper, ecological feminism is the position that there are important connections—historical, experiential, symbolic, theoretical—between the domination of women and the domination of nature, an understanding of which is crucial to both feminism and environmental ethics. I argue that the promise and power of ecological feminism is that *it provides a distinctive framework both for reconceiving feminism and for developing an environmental ethic which takes seriously connections between the domination of women and the domination of nature.* I do so by discussing the nature of a feminist ethic and the ways in which ecofeminism provides a feminist and environmental ethic. I conclude that any feminist theory *and* any environmental ethic which fails to take seriously the twin and interconnected dominations of women and nature is at best incomplete and at worst simply inadequate.

FEMINISM, ECOLOGICAL FEMINISM, AND CONCEPTUAL FRAMEWORKS

. . . Feminist philosophers claim that some of the most important feminist issues are *conceptual* ones: these issues concern how one conceptualizes such mainstay philosophical notions as reason and rationality, ethics, and what it is to be human. Ecofeminists extend this feminist philosophical concern to nature. They argue that, ultimately, some of the most important connections between the domination of women and the domination of nature are conceptual. To see this, consider the nature of conceptual frameworks.

A *conceptual framework* is a set of *basic* beliefs, values, attitudes, and assumptions which shape and reflect how one views oneself and one's world. It is a socially constructed lens through which we perceive ourselves and others. It is affected by such factors as gender, race, class, age, affectional orientation, nationality, and religious background.

Some conceptual frameworks are oppressive. An *oppressive conceptual framework* is one that explains, justifies, and maintains relationships of domination and subordination. When an oppressive conceptual framework is *patriarchal,* it explains, justifies, and maintains the subordination of women by men.

I have argued elsewhere that there are three significant features of oppressive conceptual frameworks: (1) value-hierarchical thinking, i.e., "up-down" thinking which places higher value, status, or prestige on what is "up" rather than on what is "down"; (2) value dualisms, i.e., disjunctive pairs in which the disjuncts are seen as oppositional (rather than as complementary) and exclusive (rather than as inclusive), and which place higher value (status, prestige) on one disjunct rather than the other (e.g., dualisms which give higher value or status to that which has historically been identified as "mind," "reason," and "male" than to that which has historically been identified as "body," "emotion," and "female"); and (3) logic of domination, i.e., a structure of argumentation which leads to a justification of subordination.[2]

The third feature of oppressive conceptual frameworks is the most significant. A logic of domination is not *just* a logical structure. It also involves a substantive value system, since an ethical premise is needed to permit or sanction the "just" subordination of that which is subordinate. This justification typically is given on grounds of some alleged characteristic (e.g., rationality) which the dominant (e.g., men) have and the subordinate (e.g., women) lack.

Contrary to what many feminists and ecofeminists have said or suggested, there may be nothing *inherently* problematic about "hierarchical thinking" or even "value-hierarchical thinking" in contexts other than contexts of oppression. Hierarchical thinking is important in daily living for classifying data, comparing information, and organizing material. Taxonomies (e.g., plant taxonomies) and biological nomenclature seem to require *some* form of "hierarchical thinking." Even "value-hierarchical thinking" may be quite acceptable in certain contexts. (The same may be said of "value dualisms" in non-oppressive contexts.) For example, suppose it is true that what is unique about humans is our conscious capacity to radically reshape our social environments (or "societies"), as Murray Bookchin suggests.[3] Then one could truthfully say that humans are better equipped to radically reshape their environments than are rocks or plants—a "value-hierarchical" way of speaking.

The problem is not simply *that* value-hierarchical thinking and value dualisms are used, but *the way* in which each has been used *in oppressive conceptual frameworks* to establish inferiority and to justify subordination. It is the logic of domination, *coupled with* value-hierarchical thinking and value dualisms, which "justifies" subordination. What is explanatorily basic, then, about the nature of oppressive conceptual frameworks is the logic of domination.

For ecofeminism, that a logic of domination is explanatorily basic is important for at least three reasons. First, without a logic of domination, a description of similarities and differences would be just that—a description of similarities and differences. Consider the claim, "Humans are different from plants and rocks in that humans can (and plants and rocks cannot) consciously and radically reshape the communities in which they live; humans are similar to plants and rocks in that they are both members of an ecological community." Even if humans are "better" than plants and rocks with respect to the conscious ability of humans to radically transform communities, one does not *thereby* get any *morally* relevant distinction between humans and nonhumans, or an argument for the domination of plants and rocks by humans. To get *those* conclusions one needs to add at least two powerful assumptions, viz., (A2) and (A4) in argument A below:

(A1) Humans do, and plants and rocks do not, have the capacity to consciously and radically change the community in which they live.

(A2) Whatever has the capacity to consciously and radically change the community in which it lives is morally superior to whatever lacks this capacity.

(A3) Thus, humans are morally superior to plants and rocks.

(A4) For any X and Y, if X is morally superior to Y, then X is morally justified in subordinating Y.

(A5) Thus, humans are morally justified in subordinating plants and rocks.

Without the two assumptions that *humans are morally superior* to (at least some) nonhumans, (A2), and that *superiority justifies subordination,* (A4), all one has is some difference between humans and some nonhumans. This is true *even if* that difference is given in terms of superiority. Thus, it is the logic of domination, (A4), which is the bottom line in ecofeminist discussions of oppression.

Second, ecofeminists argue that, at least in Western societies, the oppressive conceptual framework which sanctions the twin dominations of women and nature is a patriarchal one characterized by all three features of an oppressive conceptual framework. Many ecofeminists claim that, historically, within at least the dominant Western culture, a patriarchal conceptual framework has sanctioned the following argument B:

(B1) Women are identified with nature and the realm of the physical; men are identified with the "human" and the realm of the mental.

(B2) Whatever is identified with nature and the realm of the physical is inferior to ("below") whatever is identified with the "human" and the realm of the mental; or, conversely, the latter is superior to ("above") the former.

(B3) Thus, women are inferior to ("below") men; or, conversely, men are superior to ("above") women.

(B4) For any X and Y, if X is superior to Y, then X is justified in subordinating Y.

(B5) Thus, men are justified in subordinating women.

If sound, argument B establishes *patriarchy,* i.e., the conclusion given at (B5) that the systematic domination of women by men is justified. But according to ecofeminists, (B5) is justified by just those three features of an oppressive conceptual framework identified earlier: value-hierarchical thinking, the assumption at (B2); value dualisms, the assumed dualism of the mental and the physical at (B1) and the assumed inferiority of the physical vis-à-vis the mental at (B2); and a logic of domination, the assumption at (B4), the same as the previous premise (A4). Hence, according to ecofeminists, insofar as an oppressive patriarchal conceptual framework has functioned historically (within at least dominant Western culture) to sanction the twin dominations of women and nature (argument B), both argument B and the patriarchal conceptual framework, from whence it comes, ought to be rejected.

Of course, the preceeding does not identify which premises of B are false. What is the status of premises (B1) and (B2)? Most, if not all, feminists claim that (B1), and many ecofeminists claim that (B2), have been assumed or asserted within the dominant Western philosophical and intellectual tradition. As such, these feminists assert, as a matter of historical fact, that the dominant Western philosophical tradition has assumed the truth of (B1) and (B2). Ecofeminists, however, either deny (B2) or do not affirm (B2). Furthermore, because some ecofeminists are anxious to deny any ahistorical identification of women with nature, some ecofeminists deny (B1) when (B1) is used to support anything other than a strictly historical claim about what has been asserted or assumed to be true within patriarchal culture—e.g., when (B1) is used to assert that women properly are identified with the realm of nature and the physical. Thus, from an ecofeminist perspective, (B1) and (B2) are properly viewed as problematic though historically sanctioned claims: they are problematic precisely because of the way they have functioned historically in a patriarchal conceptual framework and culture to sanction the dominations of women and nature.

What *all* ecofeminists agree about, then, is the way in which *the logic of domination* has functioned historically within patriarchy to sustain and justify the twin dominations of women and nature. Since *all* feminists (and not just ecofeminists) oppose patriarchy, the conclusion given at (B5), all feminists (including ecofeminists) must oppose at least the logic of domination, premise (B4), on which argument B rests—whatever the truth-value status of (B1) and (B2) *outside* of a patriarchal context.

That *all* feminists must oppose the logic of domination shows the breadth and depth of the ecofeminist critique of B: it is a critique not only of the three assumptions on which this argument for the domination of women and nature rests, viz., the assumptions at (B1), (B2), and (B4); it is also a critique of patriarchal conceptual frameworks generally, i.e., of those oppressive conceptual frameworks which put men "up" and women "down," allege some way in which women are morally inferior to men, and use that alleged difference to justify the subordination of women by men. Therefore, ecofeminism is necessary to *any* feminist critique of patriarchy, and, hence, necessary to feminism. . . .

Third, ecofeminism clarifies why the logic of domination, and any conceptual framework which gives rise to it, must be abolished in order both to make possible a meaningful notion of difference which does not breed domination and to prevent feminism from becoming a "support" movement based primarily on shared experiences. In contemporary society, there is no one "woman's voice," no *woman* (or *human*) *simpliciter:* every woman (or human) is a woman (or human) of some race, class, age, affectional orientation, marital status, regional or national background, and so forth. Because there are no "monolithic experiences" that all women share, feminism must be a "solidarity movement" based on shared beliefs and interests rather than a "unity in sameness" movement based on shared experiences and shared victimization. In the words of Maria Lugones, "Unity—not to be confused with solidarity—is understood as conceptually tied to domination."[4]

Ecofeminists insist that the sort of logic of domination used to justify the domination of humans by gender, racial or ethnic, or class status is also used to justify the domination of nature. Because eliminating a logic of domination is part of a feminist critique—whether a critique of patriarchy, white supremacist culture, or imperialism—ecofeminists insist that *naturism* is properly viewed as an integral part of any feminist solidarity movement to end sexist oppression and the logic of domination which conceptually grounds it. . . .

CLIMBING FROM ECOFEMINISM TO ENVIRONMENTAL ETHICS

Many feminists and some environmental ethicists have begun to explore the use of first-person narrative as a way of raising philosophically germane issues in ethics often lost or underplayed in mainstream philosophical ethics. Why is this so? What is it about narrative which makes it a significant resource for theory and practice in feminism and environmental ethics? Even if appeal to first-person narrative is a helpful literary device for describing ineffable experience or a legitimate social science methodology for documenting personal and social history, how is first-person narrative a valuable vehicle of argumentation for ethical decision making and theory building? One fruitful way to begin answering these questions is to ask them of a particular first-person narrative.

Consider the following first-person narrative about rock climbing:

> For my very first rock climbing experience, I chose a somewhat private spot, away from other climbers and on-lookers. After studying "the chimney," I focused all my energy on making it to the top. I climbed with intense determination, using whatever strength and skills I had to accomplish this challenging feat. By midway I was exhausted and anxious. I couldn't see what to do next—where to put my hands or feet. Growing increasingly more weary as I clung somewhat desperately to the rock, I made a move. It didn't work. I fell. There I was, dangling midair above the rocky ground below, frightened but terribly relieved that the belay rope had held me. I knew I was safe. I took a look up at the climb that remained. I was determined to make it to the top. With renewed confidence and concentration, I finished the climb to the top.
>
> On my second day of climbing, I rappelled down about 200 feet from the top of the Palisades at Lake Superior to just a few feet above the water level. I could see no one—not my belayer, not the other climbers, no one. I unhooked slowly from the rappel rope and took a deep cleansing breath. I looked all around me—really looked—and listened. I heard a cacophony of voices—birds, trickles of water on the rock before me, waves lapping against the rocks below. I closed my eyes and began to feel the rock with my hands—the cracks and crannies, the raised lichen and mosses, the almost imperceptible nubs that might provide a resting place for my fingers and toes when I began to climb. At that moment I was bathed in serenity. I began to talk to the rock in an almost inaudible, child-like way, as if the rock were my friend. I felt an overwhelming sense of gratitude for what it offered me—a chance to know myself and the rock differently, to appreciate unforeseen miracles like the tiny flowers growing in the even tinier cracks in the rock's surface, and to come to know a sense of *being in relationship* with the natural environment. It felt as if the rock and I were silent conversational partners in a longstanding friendship. I realized then that I had come to care about this cliff which was so different from me, so unmovable and invincible, independent and seemingly indifferent to my presence. I wanted to be with the rock as I climbed. Gone was the determination to conquer the rock, to forcefully impose my will on it; I wanted simply to work respectfully with the rock as I climbed. And as I climbed, that is what I felt. I felt myself *caring* for this rock and feeling thankful that climbing provided the opportunity for me to know it and myself in this new way.

There are at least four reasons why use of such a first-person narrative is important to feminism and environmental ethics. First, such a narrative gives voice to a felt sensitivity often lacking in traditional analytical ethical discourse, viz., a sensitivity to conceiving of oneself as fundamentally "in relationship with" others, including the nonhuman environment. It is a modality which *takes relationships themselves seriously*. It thereby stands in contrast to a strictly reductionist modality that takes relationships seriously only or primarily because of the nature of the *relators* or parties to those relationships (e.g., relators conceived as moral agents, right holders, interest carriers, or sentient beings). In the rock-climbing narrative above, it is the climber's relationship with the rock she climbs which takes on special significance—which is itself a locus of value—in addition to whatever moral status or moral considerability she or the rock or any other parties to the relationship may also have.

Second, such a first-person narrative gives expression to a variety of ethical attitudes and behaviors often overlooked or underplayed in mainstream Western ethics, e.g., the difference in attitudes and behaviors toward a rock when one is "making it to the top" and when one thinks of oneself as "friends with" or "caring about" the rock one climbs. These different attitudes and behaviors suggest an ethically germane contrast between two different types of relationship humans or climbers may have toward a rock: an imposed conqueror-type relationship, and an emergent caring-type relationship. This contrast grows out of, and is faithful to, felt, lived experience.

The difference between conquering and caring attitudes and behaviors in relation to the natural environment provides a third reason why the use of first-person narrative is important to feminism and environmental ethics: it provides a way of conceiving of ethics and ethical meaning as *emerging out of* particular situations moral agents find themselves in, rather than as being *imposed on* those situations (e.g., as a derivation or instantiation of some predetermined abstract principle or rule). This emergent feature of narrative centralizes the importance of *voice*. When a multiplicity of cross-cultural *voices* are centralized, narrative is able to give expression to a range of attitudes, values, beliefs, and behaviors which may be overlooked or silenced by imposed ethical meaning and theory. As a reflection of and on felt, lived experiences, the use of narrative in ethics provides a stance from which ethical discourse can be held accountable to the historical, material, and social realities in which moral subjects find themselves.

Lastly, and for our purposes perhaps most importantly, the use of narrative has argumentative significance. Jim Cheney calls attention to this feature of narrative when he claims, "To contextualize ethical deliberation is, in some sense, to provide a narrative or story, from which the solution to the ethical dilemma emerges as the fitting conclusion."[5] Narrative has argumentative force by suggesting *what counts* as an appropriate conclusion to an ethical situation. One ethical conclusion suggested by the climbing narrative is that what counts as a proper ethical attitude toward mountains and rocks is an attitude of respect and care (whatever that turns out to be or involve), not one of domination and conquest.

In an essay entitled "In and Out of Harm's Way: Arrogance and Love," feminist philosopher Marilyn Frye distinguishes between "arrogant" and "loving" perception as one way of getting at this difference in the ethical attitudes of care and conquest.[6] Frye writes:

> The loving eye is a contrary of the arrogant eye.
>
> The loving eye knows the independence of the other. It is the eye of a seer who knows that nature is indifferent. It is the eye of one who knows that to know the seen, one must consult something other than one's own will and interests and fears and imagination. One must look at the thing. One must look and listen and check and question.
>
> The loving eye is one that pays a certain sort of attention. This attention can require a discipline but *not* a self-denial. The discipline is one of self-knowledge, knowledge of the scope and boundary of the self. . . . In particular, it is a matter of being able to tell one's own interests from those of others and of knowing where one's self leaves off and another begins. . . .
>
> The loving eye does not make the object of perception into something edible, does not try to assimilate it, does not reduce it to the size of the seer's desire, fear and imagination, and hence does not have to simplify. It knows the complexity of the other as something which will forever present new things to be known. The science of the loving eye would favor The Complexity Theory of Truth [in contrast to The Simplicity Theory of Truth] and presuppose The Endless Interestingness of the Universe.[7]

According to Frye, the loving eye is not an invasive, coercive eye which annexes others to itself, but one which "knows the complexity of the other as something which will forever present new things to be known."

When one climbs a rock as a conqueror, one climbs with an arrogant eye. When one climbs with a loving eye, one constantly "must look and listen and check and question." One recognizes the rock as something very different, something perhaps totally indifferent to one's own presence, and finds in that difference joyous occasion for celebration. One knows "the boundary of the self," where the self—the "I," the climber—leaves off and the rock begins. There is no fusion of two into one, but a complement of two entities *acknowledged* as separate, different, independent, yet *in relationship;* they are in relationship *if only* because the loving eye is perceiving it, responding to it, noticing it, attending to it.

An ecofeminist perspective about both women and nature involves this shift in attitude from "arrogant perception" to "loving perception" of the nonhuman world. Arrogant perception of nonhumans by humans presupposes and maintains *sameness* in such a way that it expands the moral community to those beings who are thought to resemble (be like, similar to, or the same as) humans in some morally significant way. Any environmental movement or ethic based on arrogant perception builds a moral hierarchy of beings and assumes some common denominator of moral considerability in virtue of which like beings deserve similar treatment or moral consideration and unlike beings do not. Such environmental ethics are or generate a "unity in sameness." In contrast, "loving perception" presupposes and maintains *difference*—a distinction between the self and other, between human and at least some nonhumans—in such a way that perception of the other as other *is* an expression of love for one who/which is recognized at the outset as independent, dissimilar, different. As Maria Lugones says, in loving perception, "Love is seen not as fusion and erasure of difference but as incompatible with them."[8] "Unity in sameness" alone is an *erasure of difference.*

"Loving perception" of the nonhuman natural world is an attempt to understand what it means *for humans* to care about the nonhuman world, a world *acknowledged* as being independent, different, perhaps even indifferent to humans. Humans *are* different from rocks in important ways, even if they are also both members of some ecological community. A moral community based on loving perception of oneself *in relationship with* a rock, or with the natural environment as a whole, is one which acknowledges and respects difference, whatever "sameness" also exists. The limits of loving perception are determined only by the limits of one's (e.g., a person's, a community's) ability to respond lovingly (or with appropriate care, trust, or friendship)—whether it is to other humans or to the nonhuman world and elements of it.

If what I have said so far is correct, then there are very different ways to climb a mountain and *how* one climbs it and *how* one narrates the experience of climbing it matter ethically. If one climbs with "arrogant perception," with an attitude of "conquer and control," one keeps intact the very sorts of thinking that characterize a logic of domination and an oppressive conceptual framework. Since the oppressive conceptual framework which sanctions the domination of nature is a patriarchal one, one also thereby keeps intact, even if unwittingly, a patriarchal conceptual framework. Because the dismantling of patriarchal conceptual frameworks is a feminist issue, *how* one climbs a mountain and *how* one narrates—or tells the story—about the experience of climbing also are *feminist issues.* In this way, ecofeminism makes visible why, at a conceptual level, environmental ethics is a feminist issue. I turn now to a consideration of ecofeminism as a distinctively feminist and environmental ethic.

ECOFEMINISM AS A FEMINIST AND ENVIRONMENTAL ETHIC

. . . [A]n ecofeminist ethic involves a reconception of what it means to be human, and in what human ethical behavior consists. Ecofeminism denies abstract individualism. Humans are who we are in large part by virtue of the historical and social contexts and the relationships we are in, including our relationships with nonhuman nature. Relationships are not something extrinsic to who we are, not an "add on" feature of human nature; they play an essential role in shaping what it is to be human. Relationships of humans to the nonhuman environment are, in part, constitutive of what it is to be a human.

By making visible the interconnections among the dominations of women and nature, ecofeminism shows that both are feminist issues and that explicit acknowledgement of both is vital to any responsible environmental ethic. Feminism *must* embrace ecological feminism if it is to end the domination of women because the domination of women is tied conceptually and historically to the domination of nature.

A responsible environmental ethic also *must* embrace feminism. Otherwise, even the seemingly most revolutionary, liberational, and holistic ecological ethic will fail to take seriously the interconnected dominations of nature and women that are so much a part of the historical legacy and conceptual framework that sanctions the exploitation of nonhuman nature. Failure to make visible these interconnected, twin dominations results in an inaccurate account of how it is that nature has been and continues to be dominated and exploited and produces an environmental ethic that lacks the depth necessary to be truly *inclusive* of the realities of persons who at least in dominant Western culture have been intimately tied with that exploitation, viz., women. Whatever else can be said in favor of such holistic ethics, a failure to make visible ecofeminist insights into the common denominators of the twin oppressions of women and nature is to perpetuate, rather than overcome, the source of that oppression. . . .

NOTES

1 Francoise d'Eaubonne, *Le Feminisme ou la Mort* (Paris: Pierre Horay, 1974), pp. 213–52.
2 The account offered here is a revision of the account given earlier in my paper "Feminism and Ecology: Making Connections," *Environmental Ethics* 9 (1987): 3–21. I have changed the account to be about "oppressive" rather than strictly "patriarchal" conceptual frameworks in order to leave open the possibility that there may be some patriarchal conceptual frameworks (e.g., in non-Western cultures) which are *not* properly characterized as based on value dualisms.
3 Murray Bookchin, "Social Ecology versus 'Deep Ecology,' " in *Green Perspectives: Newsletter of the Green Program Project,* no. 4–5 (Summer 1987): 9.
4 Maria Lugones, "Playfulness, 'World-Traveling,' and Loving Perception," *Hypatia* 2, no. 2 (Summer 1987): 3.
5 Jim Cheney, "Eco-Feminism and Deep Ecology," *Environmental Ethics* 9 (1987): 144.
6 Marilyn Frye, "In and Out of Harm's Way: Arrogance and Love," in *The Politics of Reality* (Trumansburg, New York: The Crossing Press, 1983), pp. 66–72.
7 Ibid., pp. 75–76.
8 Maria Lugones, "Playfulness," p. 3.

QUESTIONS

1 Does ecofeminism offer a useful framework for environmental ethics?
2 Can you provide an example that illustrates a shift in attitude from "arrogant perception" to "loving perception" in the case of one human's perception of another human or a human's perception of something in the nonhuman world?

SUGGESTED ADDITIONAL READINGS FOR CHAPTER 11

ARMSTRONG, SUSAN J., and RICHARD G. BOTZLER, eds.: *Environmental Ethics: Divergence and Convergence.* New York: McGraw-Hill, 1993. The readings in this valuable anthology are arranged in eleven chapters. Chapters 6, 7, 8, and 9 include useful material under the following headings: anthropocentrism, individualism, ecocentrism, ecofeminism.
CALLICOTT, J. BAIRD: *In Defense of the Land Ethic: Essays in Environmental Philosophy.* Albany: State University of New York Press, 1989. In this collection of essays, originally published between 1979 and 1987, Callicott articulates, defends, and extends Aldo Leopold's seminal environmental philosophy.
Environmental Ethics. This journal, identifying itself as "An Interdisciplinary Journal Dedicated to the Philosophical Aspects of Environmental Problems," began publication in 1979.

It is an invaluable source of material relevant to the issues under discussion in this chapter.

Hypatia: A Journal of Feminist Philosophy, vol. 6, Spring 1991. Karen J. Warren was guest editor for this special issue, which provides a collection of philosophical articles on ecological feminism.

JOHNS, DAVID M.: "The Relevance of Deep Ecology to the Third World: Some Preliminary Comments." *Environmental Ethics,* vol. 12, Fall 1990, pp. 233–252. Johns discusses and criticizes some of Ramachandra Guha's major contentions regarding the American deep ecology movement.

LIST, PETER C., ed.: *Radical Environmentalism: Philosophy and Tactics.* Belmont, Calif.: Wadsworth, 1993. This collection of readings deals first with so-called radical environmental philosophies (e.g., deep ecology and ecofeminism) and then deals with the activism and tactics of radical environmentalists.

REGAN, TOM, ed.: *Earthbound: New Introductory Essays in Environmental Ethics.* New York: Random House, 1984. In this collection of original essays, a wide range of issues in environmental ethics is addressed.

SAGOFF, MARK: *The Economy of the Earth: Philosophy, Law, and the Environment.* Cambridge: Cambridge University Press, 1988. Sagoff criticizes and rejects the conceptual vocabulary of resource and welfare economics, with its emphasis on cost–benefit analysis, which is often used in justifications of environmental policies. He argues for an alternative, more morally sensitive approach to environmental policy.

SESSIONS, GEORGE, ed.: *Deep Ecology for the 21st Century.* Boston: Shambhala, 1995. This collection of thirty-nine articles provides a wide range of perspectives on deep ecology. The writings of Arne Naess are especially featured.

STONE, CHRISTOPHER D.: *Earth and Other Ethics: The Case for Moral Pluralism.* New York: Harper & Row, 1987. Arguing for a need to rethink some of the most basic assumptions of ethics, Stone says that no one ethical framework can provide answers to all our ethical dilemmas, including those centered on the environment.

VANDEVEER, DONALD, and CHRISTINE PIERCE, eds.: *The Environmental Ethics and Policy Book.* Belmont, Calif.: Wadsworth, 1994. Part IV of this extensive anthology presents a diverse collection of readings under the title, "Constructing an Environmental Ethic." In Part VI, the various readings deal with specific environmental problems (e.g., preserving biodiversity) and related policy matters.